Frommer's

New Mexico

Here's what the critics say about Frommer's:

"Amazingly easy to use. Very portable, very complete."
—Booklist

♦

"The only mainstream guide to list specific prices. The Walter Cronkite of guidebooks—with all that implies"
—Travel & Leisure

♦

"Complete, concise, and filled with useful information."
—New York Daily News

♦

"Hotel information is close to encyclopedic."
—Des Moines Sunday Register

Other Great Guides for Your Trip:

Frommer's Santa Fe, Taos & Albuquerque

Frommer's Irreverent Guide to Santa Fe

Frommer's USA

Frommer's®

5th Edition

New Mexico

by Lesley S. King

MACMILLAN • USA

ABOUT THE AUTHOR

Lesley S. King grew up on a ranch in northern New Mexico, where she still returns on weekends to help work cattle. A freelance writer and photographer, she's a contributor to *New Mexico Magazine* and an avid kayaker and skier. Formerly the managing editor of *The Santa Fean,* she has written about food and restaurants for *The New York Times,* the Anasazi culture for United Airlines' *Hemispheres* magazine, ranches for *American Cowboy,* and birds for *Audubon.* She is also the author of *Frommer's Santa Fe, Taos & Albuquerque.*

Julia Ward, Lesley's assistant, helped greatly with fact checking and bringing new ideas to the project.

MACMILLAN TRAVEL

A Simon & Schuster Macmillan Company
1633 Broadway
New York, NY 10019

Find us online at **www.frommers.com**

Copyright © 1999 by Simon & Schuster, Inc.
All maps copyright © by Simon & Schuster, Inc.

All rights reserved. No part of this book may be reproduced or transmitted in any form or by any means, electronic or mechanical, including photocopying, recording, or by any information storage and retrieval system, without permission in writing from the Publisher.

MACMILLAN is a registered trademark of Macmillan, Inc.
FROMMER'S is a registered trademark of Arthur Frommer. Used under license.

ISBN 0-02-862371-1
ISSN 1053-2455

Editors: Bill Goodwin and Neil Schlecht
Production Editors: Lori Cates and Mark Enochs
Design by Michele Laseau
Digital Cartography by Roberta Stockwell and Ortelius Design
Photo Editor: Richard Fox
Page Creation by John Bitter, Jerry Cole, and Heather Pope

SPECIAL SALES

Bulk purchases (10+ copies) of Frommer's and selected Macmillan travel guides are available to corporations, organizations, mail-order catalogs, institutions, and charities at special discounts, and can be customized to suit individual needs. For more information write to Special Sales, Macmillan General Reference, 1633 Broadway, New York, NY 10019.

Manufactured in the United States of America.

Contents

12   Southeastern New Mexico   370

Appendix: Useful Toll-Free Numbers & Web Sites   406

Index   409

List of Maps

AN INVITATION TO THE READER

In researching this book, we've discovered many wonderful places—hotels, inns, restaurants, shops, and more. We're sure you'll find others. Please tell us about them, so we can share the information with your fellow travelers in upcoming editions. If you were disappointed with a recommendation, we'd love to know that, too. Please write to:

Frommer's New Mexico
Macmillan Travel
1633 Broadway
New York, NY 10019

AN ADDITIONAL NOTE

Please be advised that travel information is subject to change at any time—and this is especially true of prices. We therefore suggest that you write or call ahead for confirmation when making your travel plans. The authors, editors, and publisher cannot be held responsible for the experience of readers while traveling. Your safety is important to us, however, so we encourage you to stay alert and be aware of your surroundings. Keep a close eye on cameras, purses, and wallets, all favorite targets of thieves and pickpockets.

WHAT THE SYMBOLS MEAN

✪ Frommer's Favorites

Hotels, restaurants, attractions, and entertainment you should not miss.

The following abbreviations are used for credit cards:

AE	American Express	EURO	Eurocard
CB	Carte Blanche	JCB	Japan Credit Bank
DC	Diners Club	MC	MasterCard
DISC	Discover	V	Visa
ER	EnRoute		

FIND FROMMER'S ONLINE

Arthur Frommer's Budget Travel Online (www.frommers.com) offers more than 6,000 pages of up-to-the-minute travel information—including the latest bargains and candid, personal articles updated daily by Arthur Frommer himself. No other Web site offers such comprehensive and timely coverage of the world of travel.

The Best of New Mexico

I will never forget when I was in second grade, standing on the dusty playground at Alvarado Elementary School in Albuquerque pointing west toward the volcanoes. "We went beyond those volcanoes," I bragged to my friend about what my family had done over the weekend. "No way," my friend replied. Actually, a number of times I'd been much farther than the 10 miles between us and the volcanoes, and I now know that the journey's distance had to do with culture rather than miles. In a half day's drive we had traveled to the Intertribal Indian Ceremonial in Gallup, where I had eaten food and seen people and clothing totally foreign to me. My sister had gotten lost in this strange land, and it had been a scary adventure finding her. To me, that experience back in the second grade speaks volumes about the otherworldliness of New Mexico.

The world has never let me take my strangely exotic home state for granted. When I was a kid we used to travel to Illinois to visit my grandfather, and when people there heard we were from New Mexico, they would often cock their heads and say things like, "Do you have sidewalks there?" and, "This bubble gum must be a real treat for you," as though such inventions hadn't yet arrived in my home state.

Our state magazine even dedicates a full page each month to the variety of ways in which New Mexico is forgotten. The most notable was when a resident called the Atlanta Olympic committee to reserve tickets and the salesperson insisted that the person contact their international sales office. So, it seems people either don't know our state exists at all, or they believe it's a foreign country south of the border.

Ironically, those naive impressions hold some truth. New Mexico is definitely lost in some kind of time warp. Our history dates back far before Columbus set foot on the continent. The whole attitude here is often slower than the rest of the world. Like our neighbors down in Mexico, we use the word *mañana*—which doesn't so much mean "tomorrow" as it does "not today."

When you set foot here, you may find yourself a bit lost within the otherworldliness. You may be shocked at the way people so readily stop and converse with you, or you may find yourself in a landscape where there isn't a single landmark from which to negotiate.

In the chapters that follow, I will give you some signposts to help you discover for yourself the many mysteries of our otherworldly state. But first, here are my most cherished New Mexico experiences.

1 The Best of Natural New Mexico

- **Capulin Volcano National Monument:** Last active 60,000 years ago, Capulin Volcano National Monument is located about 27 miles east of Raton. A hike around its rim offers views into neighboring Oklahoma and Colorado, and another walk down into its lush mouth allows you to see the point from which the lava spewed. See chapter 9.
- **Rio Grande Gorge:** A hike into this dramatic gorge is unforgettable. You'll first see it as you come over a rise heading toward Taos. It's a colossal slice in the earth formed during the late Cretaceous period 130 million years ago and the early Tertiary period, about 70 million years ago. Drive about 35 miles north of Taos, near the village of Cerro, to the Rio Grande Wild River Area. From the lip of the canyon you descend through millions of years of geologic history and land inhabited by Indians since 16,000 B.C. You're liable to encounter raccoons and other wildlife, and once you reach the river you'll see fishers, rafters, and kayakers. There you can dip your toes in the fabled *Rio*. If you're visiting during spring and early summer, and like an adrenaline rush, be sure to hook up with a professional guide and raft the Taos Box, a 17-mile stretch of Class IV white water. See chapter 8.
- **Blue Hole** (Santa Rosa): You'll find this odd natural wonder in Santa Rosa, "city of natural lakes." An 81-foot-deep artesian well, its waters are cool and completely clear. Often it appears like a fish bowl, full of scuba divers. See chapter 9.
- **El Malpais National Monument** (Grants): Near Grants, the incredible volcanic landscape known as El Malpais (The Badlands) features vast lava flows, lava tubes, ice caves, sandstone cliffs, and natural bridges. You'll also find Anasazi ruins and ancient Native American trails. See chapter 10.
- **White Sands National Monument:** Located 15 miles southwest of Alamogordo, White Sands National Monument preserves the best part of the world's largest gypsum dune field. For a truly unforgettable experience, camp overnight so you can watch the sun rise on the smooth, endless dunes. See chapter 12.
- **Carlsbad Caverns National Park:** One of the world's largest and most complex cave systems is located in the extreme southeastern region of the state. The 80 known caves have spectacular stalagmite and stalactite formations. Explore the Big Room in a 1-mile self-guided tour, and then catch the massive bat flight from the cave entrance at sunset. See chapter 12.

2 The Most Interesting Native American Sights

- **Petroglyph National Monument** (Albuquerque): In the past few years this monument has made national news, and for good reason; a struggle has raged in U.S. Congress over whether or not to allow a road through these lava flows that were once a hunting and gathering area for prehistoric Native Americans, who left a chronicle of their beliefs etched on the dark basalt boulders. History in the making aside, the site has 15,000 petroglyphs and provides a variety of hiking trails in differing levels of difficulty right on the outskirts of Albuquerque. See chapter 6.
- **Indian Pueblo Cultural Center** (Albuquerque): Owned and operated as a nonprofit organization by the 19 pueblos of New Mexico, this is a fine place to begin an exploration of Native American culture. The museum is modeled after

Pueblo Bonito, a spectacular 9th-century ruin in Chaco Culture National Historic Park, and contains art and artifacts old and new. See chapter 6.

- **Coronado State Monument** (Bernalillo): Excavated ruins reveal hundreds of rooms and unique murals, examples of which are displayed in the monument's small archeological museum. See chapter 6.
- **Pecos National Historical Park:** It's hard to rank New Mexico's many ruins, but this one, sprawled on a plain about 25 miles east of Santa Fe, is one of the most impressive, resonating with the history of the Pueblo Revolt of 1680, the only successful revolt of indigenous people in the New World. You'll see evidence of where the Pecos people burned the mission church before joining in the attack on Santa Fe. You'll also see where the Spanish conquistadors later compromised, allowing sacred kivas to be built next to the reconstructed mission. See chapter 7.
- **Puye Cliff Dwellings:** These ruins offer a view of centuries of culture so well preserved you can almost hear ancient life clamoring around you. You'll encounter dwellings believed to have been inhabited from 1200 to the late 1500s, many on a 200-foot volcanic tuff cliff face. The settlement typifies Pajaritan culture in the placement of its houses and its symbolic decorations, and visitors can access the rooms and caves by sturdy ladders and steps. Petroglyphs are evident in many of the rocky cliff walls. See chapter 7.
- **Bandelier National Monument:** Along with Puye Cliff Dwellings, these ruins provide a spectacular peek into the lives of the Anasazi Pueblo culture, which flourished in the area between A.D. 1100 and 1550, a period later than the time Chaco Canyon flourished. (Recent findings suggest that some Chaco residents ended up at Bandelier.) Less than 15 miles south of Los Alamos, the ruins spread across a peaceful canyon. You'll probably see deer and rabbits as you hike through the canyon to the most dramatic site, a kiva and dwelling in a cave 140 feet above the canyon floor—reached by a climb up long pueblo-style ladders. There's also a visitor center and museum with self-guided or ranger-led tours. See chapter 7.
- **Taos Pueblo:** A rich place to stroll and eat Indian fry bread while glimpsing the lifestyles of some 200 Taos Pueblo residents who still live much as their ancestors did 1,000 years ago, in sculpted mud homes without electricity and running water. When you enter the pueblo you'll see where they dwell, in two large buildings, each with rooms piled on top of each other, forming structures that echo the shape of Taos Mountain to the northeast. The remaining 2,000 residents of Taos Pueblo live in conventional homes on the Pueblo's 95,000 acres. See chapter 8.
- **Acoma Pueblo:** This spectacular adobe village is perched high atop a sheer rock mesa. Known as "sky city," its 65 or so inhabitants still live without electricity and running water. The sculpted mission church and the cemetery seem to be perched on the very edge of the world. Visitors can hike down through a rock cut, once the main entrance to the pueblo. See chapter 10.
- **Chaco Culture National Historical Park:** A combination of a stunning setting and well-preserved ruins makes the long drive to Chaco Canyon an incredible adventure into Anasazi culture. What's most interesting here is how changes in architecture—beginning in the mid-800s when the Anasazi started building on a larger scale than they had previously—chart the area's cultural progress. This progress led to Chaco becoming the economic center of the San Juan Basin by A.D. 1000. As many as 5,000 people may have lived in some 400 settlements in and around Chaco. As masonry techniques advanced through the years, walls

rose more than 4 stories in height. Some of these are still visible today. There are many good hikes and bike rides in the area, as well as a campground. See chapter 10.

- **Aztec Ruins National Monument:** These ruins of a 500-room Native American pueblo abandoned by the Anasazi more than 200 years ago features a completely reconstructed kiva that is 50 feet in diameter. See chapter 10.

3 The Best Outdoor Activities

- **River Rafting and Kayaking:** I spend from April through October in my kayak, so I know both the thrill and the pristine scenery you'll encounter rafting or kayaking in New Mexico. Half- or full-day white-water rafting trips down the Rio Grande and Rio Chama originate in Taos and can be booked through a variety of outfitters in the area. The wild **Taos Box,** a steep-sided canyon south of the Wild Rivers Recreation Area, offers a series of Class IV rapids that rarely lets up for some 17 miles. The water drops up to 90 feet per mile, providing one of the most exciting 1-day white-water tours in the West. See chapter 8.
- **Hiking:** What's unique about hiking in New Mexico is the variety of terrain, from the pure desert of White Sands in the south to the alpine forest of Valle Vidal in the north. In between, there's everything from the lava flow badlands of El Malpais to the hauntingly sculpted rock formations at Abiquiu that artist Georgia O'Keeffe made famous in her paintings. For details about White Sands hikes see chapter 12, for northern New Mexico hikes, see especially chapters 7 and 8, and for El Malpais and Georgia O'Keeffe country see chapter 10.
- **Skiing:** I've skied in the East and widely in Colorado, Utah, and Wyoming, and my favorite mountain is still Taos Ski Valley (see chapter 8). With its rustic Bavarian feel and its steep mogul runs, it's an awesome playland. Santa Fe (see chapter 7) and Apache (see chapter 12) also provide some challenge, plus plenty of terrain for beginners and intermediates, as do some of the smaller areas in the state. If you're looking for a few pointers, the ski school at Taos Ski Valley is one of the best in the country. If you're into cross- or backcountry adventure, you'll find plenty here too, especially in the Taos, Red River (see chapter 8), and Chama (see chapter 10) areas.
- **Horseback Riding:** New Mexico's history is stamped with the hoof, originating when the Spanish Conquistadors brought horses to the New World years after the indigenous breeds had disappeared during the Ice Age. Riding in New Mexico for me still has that Old West feel, with trails that wind through wilderness, traversing passes and broad meadows. You can go out in groups or alone, depending on your skill level and needs, and you can choose a day trip or a weeklong camping trip. Some of the best rides are in the Pecos Wilderness (see chapter 7) and on Taos Pueblo land (see chapter 8).
- **Ballooning:** Back in the 1960s, my parents were part owners in the first hot-air balloon in New Mexico. We'd spend weekends riding the air over Albuquerque (though us kids spent most of our time chasing the balloon). Today, with the Kodak International Balloon Fiesta in Albuquerque bringing more than 850 balloons to the area, it's become the sport's world capital. Fortunately, visitors can let loose the tethers and float free too. You'll be amazed at how odd it feels to scoot over the ground in complete silence. On a clear day you can take a short balloon ride or opt for a longer one that involves brunch or lunch somewhere along the way. Most of the operators are located in Albuquerque (see chapter 6 for recommendations).

- **Llama Trekking:** Careful, they might spit at you, but that's the only drawback of these docile, wide-eyed creatures that gladly carry all your stuff while you dance freely along the trail. Most outfitters are into gourmet food, so whether you choose a half-day trek or a weeklong one, you'll eat well and have plenty of energy left to enjoy nature. Some of the best Llama trekking is in the Taos area, where there are two excellent operators (see chapter 8).

- **Fishing:** Ask any avid fisher in the nation if he's fished the San Juan (see chapter 10), and if he hasn't been there, he'll still know what you're talking about. A world-class catch-and-release fishing spot in northwestern New Mexico, it's ideal for the competent caster, since many of the fish have been caught so many times they'll swim around your ankles and dare you to figure out exactly what they want to eat. Other rivers in New Mexico provide a less frustrating, but equally beautiful challenge, and the lakes offer plenty of angling too. Bass, trout, cutthroat, walleye, and perch are among the varieties of fish that may nibble at your hook.

- **Biking:** Come the warmer months, when I'm not in my kayak, I'm on my bike exploring. And actually, at times I'll head south and can then bike year-round. Almost anywhere you go within the state you'll find trails. I've hooked onto some fun old mining roads in the Black Range down south, and explored sage forest on the rim of the Taos Gorge in the north. See "Biking" in the city and regional chapters, especially Taos (chapter 8).

4 The Best Scenic & Historic Drives

- **The Enchanted Circle:** If you're in the mood to explore, take this 90-mile loop north of Taos through old Hispanic villages, the Wild West mining town of Red River and the expansive Moreno Valley, and along the base of some of New Mexico's tallest peaks. Then you'll skim the shores of a high mountain lake at Eagle Nest, pass through the resort village of Angel Fire, and head back to Taos along the meandering Rio Fernando de Taos. See chapter 8.

- **The Turquoise Trail:** This state-designated scenic and historic route begins on NM 14 not far from Albuquerque and winds some 46 miles to Santa Fe along the eastern side of the Sandia Mountains. It will take you through the old mining towns of Madrid, Golden, and Cerrillos, where gold, silver, and turquoise were once mined. Now these are quaint villages with some shops and restaurants. See chapter 6.

- **The High Road to Taos:** This spectacular 80-mile route into the mountains between Santa Fe and Taos takes you through red painted desert, villages bordered by apple and peach orchards, and the foothills of 13,000-foot peaks. You can stop in Cordova, known for its wood-carvers, or Chimayo, famous for its weavers. At the fabled Santuario de Chimayo, you can rub healing dust between your fingers. You'll also pass through Truchas, a village stronghold on a mountain mesa 1½ miles above sea level. See chapter 7.

- **The Jemez Mountain Trail:** This meandering road not far from Albuquerque takes you along narrow corn fields and through apple orchards, past Jemez Pueblo, where villagers create pottery and jewelry, and into the mountains to the ancient Anasazi ruins at Bandelier National Monument. See chapter 6.

- **The Camino Real:** If you want to trace a bit of New Mexico's trade history, drive the Camino Real, which once served as the major trade route between Mexico and New Mexico, stretching 1,800 miles from Santa Fe to Mexico City. It was

originally known as the Camino Real de Tierra Adentro, or Royal Highway of
the Interior Land, and can still be found paralleling major highways, including
I-25 from Santa Fe to Las Cruces. For more information contact the Director,
New Mexico State Monuments, Museum of New Mexico, P.O. Box 2087, Santa
Fe, NM 87504 (☎ **800/495-1279**).

- **The Santa Fe Trail:** Another important trade route, the Santa Fe Trail once
served as a highway to businessmen from the eastern United States who were able
to supply New Mexico with less expensive commercial goods than those that
were imported from Mexico. The Santa Fe Trail became extremely important to
New Mexico and great efforts were made to protect it after war was declared on
Mexico in 1846. The war didn't eradicate the trail, but the Santa Fe Railway did
take its place and effectively rendered it extinct until a few years ago when the
Santa Fe Trail Association began to bring it back into the consciousness of the
state. In parts of northeastern New Mexico, the old ruts are very visible, especially around the ruins at Fort Union National Monument. For more information on the Santa Fe Trail, contact the New Mexico Department of Tourism,
Room 751, Lamy Building, 491 Old Santa Fe Trail, Santa Fe, NM 87503
(☎ **800/545-2040**). See chapter 9.

5 The Best Wacky Sightseeing

- **American International Rattlesnake Museum** (Albuquerque): Not for the
squeamish, this little museum at the back of a curios store in Albuquerque is a
snake-lover's paradise, with rattlers of many shapes and colors coiled for striking,
or at least appearing to be. Though I found it a little sad to see these creatures in
captivity, the owners invest a lot of energy into educating visitors on the importance of these fearsome reptiles to the ecosystem. Kids love it. See chapter 6.
- **Toy Train Depot** (Alamogordo): John Koval (who you're likely to meet at the
door), started this Alamogordo nonprofit museum housed in a genuine 1898
railroad depot 10 years ago as a means to celebrate the railroad's important
presence in the area. The museum meanders through three rooms, each filled
with tracks laid along colorful miniature city- and landscapes, 1,200 feet of
track altogether. The highlight is the last room, a re-creation of Alamogordo,
Carrizozo, and Cloudcroft where six trains swirl over bridges, through tunnels,
and along flats, while train whistles blow and switch lights blink. See chapter 12.
- **Cumbres and Toltec Scenic Railroad** (Chama): This old-style rail trip takes you
through some of the West's most spectacular country—broad meadows and
mountain peaks, all on the country's longest and highest narrow-gauge steam
railroad, built in 1880. The trip starts in Chama and takes a 64-mile journey to
Antonito, Colorado. See chapter 10.
- **Very Large Array (VLA)** (Socorro): If you have the least bit of curiosity about
the heavens, be sure to stop in at this site on the plains west of Socorro where
27 dish-shaped antennae, each 82 feet in diameter, are spread out forming a
single gigantic radio telescope. You'll recognize it from its appearance in the
movie "Contact." All types of celestial objects are photographed by the telescope,
including the sun and its planets, stars, quasars, galaxies, and even the faint
remains of the "big bang" that scientists say occurred some 10 billion years ago.
The visitor center contains displays on the VLA and radio astronomy in general,
and a self-guided walking tour gives visitors a closer view of the antennae, which
resemble giant TV satellite dishes. See chapter 11.

- **Rock Hound State Park** (Deming): If you're into rocks, maybe you won't find it odd that there's an entire park devoted to the pursuit of your hobby. This is probably one of the few places in New Mexico where you're not only allowed, but encouraged, to take whatever you find. See chapter 11.
- **Dexter National Fish Hatchery** (Dexter): It sounds like a strange place to visit on your vacation, but the Dexter National Fish Hatchery is actually quite fascinating. It is dedicated to the preservation, study, and raising of endangered fish species. Self-guided tours are available. See chapter 12.
- **Eagle Ranch Pistachio Groves** (White Sands): My father, an apple farmer, raves about this site not far from Truth or Consequences. Set out on the open plains north of White Sands, they're believed to be New Mexico's first and largest pistachio groves. Eagle Ranch offers tours on weekdays as well as a visitor center, art gallery, and gift shop. See chapter 12.

6 The Best Museums

- **Albuquerque Museum** (Albuquerque): Take a journey down into the caverns of New Mexico's past in this museum, which owns the largest U.S. collection of Spanish colonial artifacts. Displays include Don Quixote–style helmets, swords, even horse armor. You can wander through an 18th-century house compound with adobe floor and walls, and see gear used by *vaqueros,* the original cowboys who came to the area in the 16th century. See chapter 6.
- **Museum of Fine Arts** (Santa Fe): This museum's permanent collection of more than 8,000 works emphasizes regional art and includes landscapes and portraits by all the Taos masters and the contemporary artists R. C. Gorman, Amado Peña Jr., and Georgia O'Keeffe, among others. The museum also has a collection of photographic works by such masters as Ansel Adams, Edward Weston, and Elliot Porter. See chapter 7.
- **Museum of International Folk Art** (Santa Fe): Whenever I want to escape routine of the everyday life, I stroll through this museum and witness the magic created by cultures all over the planet. Its perpetually expanding collection of folk art is the largest in the world, with 130,000 objects from more than 100 countries. You'll find an amazing array of imaginative works, ranging from Hispanic folk art *santos* (carved saints) to Indonesian textiles and African sculptures. See chapter 7.
- **Millicent Rogers Museum** (Taos): This museum is small enough to give a glimpse of some of the finest Southwestern arts and crafts you'll see without being overwhelming. It was founded in 1953 by family members after the death of Millicent Rogers. Rogers was a wealthy Taos émigré who in 1947 began acquiring a magnificent collection of beautiful Native American arts and crafts. Included are Navajo and Pueblo jewelry, Navajo textiles, Pueblo pottery, Hopi and Zuni kachina dolls, paintings from the Rio Grande Pueblo people, and basketry from a wide variety of Southwestern tribes. See chapter 8.
- **Van Vechten Lineberry Taos Art Museum** (Taos): Taos's newest museum offers visitors a look at works by the Taos Society of Artists, which give a sense of what Taos was like in the late 19th and early 20th centuries, capturing the panoramas as well as the personalities of the Native American and Hispanic villages. A variety of other works are displayed within the 20,000-square-foot state-of-the-art museum, including impressive paintings by Duane Van Vechten, the former wife of the museum's founder. See chapter 8.

- **Kit Carson Historic Museums** (Taos): What's nice about Taos is that you can see historic homes inside and out. You can wander through **Kit Carson's old home;** built in 1825, it's an excellent example of a hacienda and is filled with a fine collection of 19th-century Western Americana. Taos Society artist **Ernest Blumenschein's home** is also a museum. Built in 1797 and restored by Blumenschein in 1919, it represents another New Mexico architectural phenomenon: homes that were added onto year after year. Doorways are typically low, and floors rise and fall at the whim of the earth beneath them. The **Martinez Hacienda** is an example of a hacienda stronghold. Built without windows facing outward, it originally had 20 small rooms, many with doors opening out to the courtyard. One of the few refurbished examples of colonial New Mexico architecture and life, the hacienda has been developed into a living museum featuring weavers, blacksmiths, and woodcarvers. See chapter 8.
- **Museum of the Horse** (Ruidoso): This museum holds a collection of more than 10,000 horse-related items, including saddles, sleighs, a horse-drawn fire engine, a stagecoach, and paintings by artists such as Frederic Remington, Charles Russell, and Frank Tenney Johnson. See chapter 12.

7 The Best Places to Discover New Mexico's History

- **Old Town** (Albuquerque): Once the center of Albuquerque commerce, Old Town thrived until the early 1880s when businesses relocated nearer to the railroad tracks. It has been a center of tourism since being rediscovered in the 1930s. Today you can visit shops, galleries, and restaurants in Old Town, as well as the Church of San Felipe de Neri, the first structure built when colonists established Albuquerque in 1706. See chapter 6.
- **Palace of the Governors** (Santa Fe): In order to fully appreciate this structure at the heart of Santa Fe, it's important to know that this is where in 1680 the only successful Native American uprising took place. Before the uprising, this was the seat of power in the area, and after De Vargas reconquered the natives it resumed that position. Built in 1610 as the original capitol of New Mexico, the palace has been in continuous public use longer than any other structure in the United States. A watchful eye can find remnants of the history this building has seen through the years, such as a fireplace and chimney chiseled into the adobe wall, and storage pits where the Pueblo Indians kept corn, wheat, barley, and other goods during their reign at the palace. After the reconquest, the pits were used to dispose of trash. Most notable is the front of the Palace where Native Americans sell jewelry, pottery, and some weavings in the sun under the protection of the portal. See chapter 7.
- **St. Francis Cathedral** (Santa Fe): Santa Fe's grandest religious structure is an architectural anomaly here because its design is French. Just a block east of the Plaza, it was built between 1869 and 1886 by Archbishop Jean-Baptiste Lamy in the style of the great cathedrals of Europe. Inside the small adobe Our Lady of the Rosary chapel is full of the romance of Spanish Catholicism. Built in 1807, it's the only portion that remains from Our Lady of the Assumption Church, founded along with Santa Fe in 1610. See chapter 7.
- **Loretto Chapel** (Santa Fe): Take time to stroll through this ornate structure patterned after the famous Sainte-Chapelle church in Paris. This chapel for the Sisters of Loretto, who had established a school for young women in Santa Fe in 1852, was constructed in 1873 by the same French architects and Italian masons

who built Archbishop Lamy's cathedral. Most notable is the spiral staircase said to be magically built by a mysterious carpenter who disappeared without bothering to collect his fee. See chapter 7.

- **Georgia O'Keeffe's Home** (Abiquiu): Hand-smoothed adobe walls, elk antlers, and a blue door—you'll encounter these images and many more that inspired the famous artist's work. When you view the landscape surrounding her residence in Abiquiu, you'll understand why she was so inspired. Be sure to reserve long in advance. See chapter 7.

- **San Francisco de Asis Church** (Taos): I think this is the most beautiful church in the world. Though some might not see how it could compete with Chartres or Notre Dame de Paris, for me it's like a Picasso sculpture: simple and direct, it has massive hand-smoothed adobe walls and a rising sense that nearly lifts the heavy structure off the ground. Maybe that's why such notables as Ansel Adams and Georgia O'Keeffe have recorded its presence in art. See chapter 8.

- **Fechin Institute** (Taos): At one point in my writing career, the magazine I was editing did a story on this home of Russian artist Nicolai Fechin. I fell so in love with a photograph of the living room, with thick vigas and posts hand carved by the artist, that I pinned the photograph above my desk and (jokingly) told visitors that it was *my* living room. It's rich with the artist's paintings, drawings, woodcarvings, and built of adobe, much of which was sculpted by his hands. The Fechin Institute was his home and canvas between 1927 and 1933. See chapter 8.

8 The Best Festivals & Events

See "New Mexico Calendar of Events," in chapter 3, for more information about the following special events.

- **New Mexico Arts and Crafts Fair** (Albuquerque): Every year in June Albuquerque hosts the second-largest arts and crafts fair in the country. More than 300 New Mexico artisans are represented.

- **Kodak Albuquerque International Balloon Fiesta** (Albuquerque): Wake up at dawn on an October morning and head out onto a grand field where torches and fans blow, filling colorful envelopes with hot air. As the sun rises and you munch on a thick waffle or breakfast burrito, watch the balloons take flight, more than 850 of them, in shapes ranging from a cow to a liquor bottle. The world's largest balloon rally will enliven that childhood love of balloons with events such as a sunrise mass ascension and the special shapes rodeo, as well as a glowing night flight.

- **Indian Market** (Santa Fe): Most of the Southwest's Native American artists spend the year preparing for this event, the largest all–Native American market in the country. Plan far ahead because people from all over the world come to Santa Fe Plaza in August to view the works and to buy. It's a rich celebration of baskets, blankets, pottery, wood carvings, rugs, paintings, and sculptures shown and sold (quickly!) in rows of booths surrounding the Plaza. Most notable in the past few years is the Native American fashion show, where stunning contemporary and traditional designs are shown.

- **Spanish Market** (Santa Fe): More than 300 Hispanic artists from New Mexico and southern Colorado exhibit and sell their work in this lively community event on the Santa Fe Plaza in July. Artists are featured in special demonstrations, while an entertaining mix of traditional Hispanic music, dance, foods, and pageantry creates the ambience of a village celebration. Artwork for sale includes *santos* (painted and carved saints), textiles, tin work, furniture, straw appliqué, and metalwork.

- **Fiesta de Santa Fe** (Santa Fe): The city parties wildly over the first weekend after Labor Day. First celebrated in 1712, to commemorate the Spanish reconquest of Santa Fe in 1692, it is the oldest community celebration in the United States. Events include masses, parades, mariachi concerts, and dances. Best of all is the burning of Zozobra (Old Man Gloom) a giant marionette who each year dies screaming while crowds cheer.

- **Intertribal Indian Ceremonial** (Gallup): Fifty tribes from throughout the United States gather in Gallup for parades, rodeos, dances, athletic competitions, and an arts and crafts show during the second week of August.

- **Chile Festival** (Hatch): New Mexicans love their chiles, and every year they celebrate their favorite fiery food item with a festival in Hatch, New Mexico (chile capital of the world), on Labor Day weekend. Events include a queen contest, skeet shoot, and chile *ristra* (strung chile), wreath, and arrangement contest. See chapter 11.

- **Great American Duck Race** (Deming): This quacky event draws upwards of 25,000 spectators. More than 400 waddling entrants race down a 16-foot long, eight-lane course at Deming Duck Downs competing for the top prize, now over $2,000. The event takes place in late August. See chapter 3.

9 The Best Family Experiences

- **Sandia Peak Tramway** (Albuquerque): The world's longest tramway ferries passengers 2.7 miles from Albuquerque's city limits to the summit of the 10,378-foot Sandia Peak. On the way you'll likely see rare Rocky Mountain bighorn sheep and birds of prey. In the summer, you may see hang gliders taking off from the giant precipice to soar in the drafts that sweep up the mountain. Go in the evening to watch the sun burn its way out of the western sky; then enjoy the glimmering city lights on your way down. See chapter 6.

- **Albuquerque Bio Park: Aquarium and Botanic Garden** (Albuquerque): For those of us born and raised in the desert, this attraction quenches years of soul thirst. Exhibits focus on sea areas fed by the Rio Grande River. You'll pass by many large tanks and within an eels' den, through which you get to walk since it's an arched aquarium over your path. The culminating show is a 285,000-gallon shark tank, where many species of fish and 15 to 20 sand tiger, brown, and nurse sharks swim around looking ominous.

  Within a state-of-the art 10,000-square-foot conservatory, you'll find a desert collection which features plants from the lower Chihuahuan and Sonoran deserts, and a Mediterranean collection that includes many exotic species native to the Mediterranean climates of Southern California, South Africa, Australia, and the Mediterranean Basin. See chapter 6.

- **Rio Grande Zoo** (Albuquerque): More than 1,200 animals of 300 species live on 60 acres of riverside bosque among ancient cottonwoods. Open-moat exhibits with animals in naturalized habitats are a treat for zoo-goers. Major exhibits include the polar bears, giraffes, sea lions (with underwater viewing), the cat walk, the bird show, and ape country with its gorilla and orangutans. The zoo has an especially fine collection of elephants, mountain lions, koalas, reptiles, and native Southwestern species. A children's petting zoo is open during the summer, and the New Mexico Symphony Orchestra performs. See chapter 6.

- **El Rancho de las Golondrinas** (Santa Fe): A living museum, El Rancho de las Golondrinas re-creates an 18th- and 19th-century Spanish village. Kids like to visit the working molasses mill, the blacksmith shop, shearing and weaving rooms, and water mills. There are animals here as well. See chapter 7.
- **Santa Fe Children's Museum** (Santa Fe): Designed for whole families to experience, this museum offers interactive exhibits and hands-on activities in the arts, humanities, science, and technology. Most notable is a 16-foot climbing wall that kids can scale, outfitted with helmets and harnesses. Special performances and hands-on sessions with artists and scientists are regularly scheduled. Recently *Family Life* magazine named this as one of the "10 hottest children's museums in the nation." See chapter 7.
- **The New Mexico Museum of Mining** (Grants): This museum takes you down into a spooky, low-lit replica mine. You begin in the station where uranium was loaded and unloaded and travel back into the earth through places defined on wall plaques with such interesting names as "track drift" (where ore comes up in cars from the mine) and "stope" (a room stripped of all ore and off-limits in an actual mine) and you learn the functions of equipment such as a "mucker" (a machine that digs the tunnel for tracks) and a "loaded round" (which blasts holes in rock).

  Most of all you get to sense the dark and dirty work that mining can be, and when the elevator pauses a moment before taking you to the surface, you may hold your breath fearful that you won't get to return from this strange underworld. See chapter 10.
- **White Sands National Monument:** Like a strange, lost land of white, this place is a dream for kids. They can roll around in the fine sand or sled across it, all the while discovering the mysterious creatures that inhabit this truest of deserts. Bring extra clothing and lots of sunscreen (the reflection off the sand can cause some pretty nasty sunburns). See chapter 12.
- **Carlsbad Caverns National Park:** Truly one of the world's natural wonders, these caverns swallow visitors into what feels like a journey to the center of the earth, where nocturnal creatures thrive and water drips onto your body. Stalactites and stalagmites create another universe of seemingly alien life forms. Kids won't like the fact that they can't go climbing on the formations, but they'll be too fascinated to complain much. See chapter 12.
- **Living Desert Zoo and Gardens State Park:** Spread across a vast plateau, this park offers visitors an hour or so long trek through desert lands full of odd plants that survive on who knows what, into zoo exhibits of hawks, cats, and bears. What's best about this zoo is the animals aren't just captive, they're rehabilitating. See chapter 12.

10 The Best Bed & Breakfast Inns

- **Hacienda Antigua** (Albuquerque; ☎ **800/201-2986**): This 200-year-old adobe inn was once the first stagecoach stop out of Old Town in Albuquerque and now offers a glimpse of those old days with refreshing modern touches. The guest rooms surround a quiet courtyard, and there's a pool and hot tub tucked away. The place sings of old New Mexico, with history evident in places such a La Capilla, the home's former chapel, which is now a guest room. Each room also has a fireplace, and modern touches such as hair dryers, coffeemakers, and unstocked minirefrigerators. See chapter 6.

- **Adobe and Pines Inn** (Taos; ☎ 800/723-8267): With this inn, the owners wanted to create a magical escape. They succeeded. Much of it is located in a 150-year-old adobe that's set around a courtyard marked by an 80-foot-long grand portal. It's surrounded by pine and fruit trees on what's believed to be sacred land. Each room has a private entrance, fireplace (three even have a fireplace in the bathroom), and each is uniquely decorated, some with jet tubs. The theme here is the use of colors, which are richly displayed on the walls and in the furnishings. For breakfast, you can expect such delights as baked soufflé-like pancakes or apple caramel bread pudding. See chapter 8.
- **Alma del Monte—Spirit of the Mountain** (Taos; ☎ 800/273-7203): This bed-and-breakfast recently built on sage-covered lands bordered by fast-rising mountains offers a luxury Taos experience. The house is a new horseshoe-shaped, Pueblo-style adobe; each room opens onto the courtyard outfitted with a fountain and hammocks hanging in the warm months. Luxury bedding, soaps, jet tubs, and kiva fireplaces in each room make this a romantic dream. Above all, the rooms are quiet, since no roads border the property. See chapter 8.
- **Casa de las Chimeneas** (Taos; ☎ 505/758-4777): This 80-year-old adobe home has, since its opening in 1988, been a model of Southwestern elegance. Now, with a new addition, it has become a full-service luxury inn as well. The addition includes a spa with a small fitness room and sauna, as well as complete massage and facial treatments given by Mountain Massage and Spa Treatments, for an additional charge. The newest rooms have heated Saltillo tile floors, gas kiva fireplaces, and jetted tubs. If you prefer a more antique-feeling room, the older section is delightful, each room with original works of art and elegant bedding, a private entrance, and minirefrigerators stocked with complimentary soft drinks, juices, and mineral water. All rooms have kiva fireplaces and most look out on flower and herb gardens. See chapter 8.
- **Dos Casas Viejas** (Santa Fe; ☎ 505/983-1636): These two old houses (*dos casas viejas*), located not far from the Plaza, offer the kind of luxury accommodations you'd expect from a fine hotel. Behind an old wooden security gate is a meandering brick lane along which are the elegant guest rooms. The rooms, each with a patio and private entrance, are finely renovated and richly decorated, all with Mexican-tile floors and kiva fireplaces; most have diamond-finished stucco walls and embedded vigas. Breakfast can be enjoyed on the patio alongside the elegant lap pool or (after you collect it in a basket) on your private patio. If you'd like a spa experience Dos Casas now has in-room treatments, from massage to facials to salt glows. See chapter 7.
- **Kokopelli's Cave** (Farmington; ☎ 505/325-7855): This is an actual cave, but it's like none you've ever seen. Carved deep into the side of a cliff, it's a three-room luxury apartment complete with carpet, VCR, and kitchen. There's space enough for a family here. Best of all is the bathroom where water pours off rocks, creating a waterfall. Golden eagles nest in the area, and ringtail cats tend to wander across the balcony. See chapter 10.

11 The Best Historic Hotels

- **La Posada de Albuquerque** (Albuquerque; ☎ 800/777-5732): Built in 1939 by Conrad Hilton as the famed hotelier's first inn in his home state of New Mexico, this hostelry on the National Register of Historic Places feels like old Spain. Though it was remodeled in 1996, the owners have kept the finer qualities. An elaborate Moorish brass-and-mosaic fountain stands in the center of the tiled lobby floor and old-fashioned tin chandeliers hang from the 2-story ceiling. All guest room furniture is handcrafted, covered with cushions of Southwestern design. There are spacious rooms with big windows looking out across the city and toward the mountains. See chapter 6.

• **The Lodge at Cloudcroft** (Cloudcroft; ☎ 800/395-6343 or 505/682-2566): The only hotel in New Mexico listed in the "Top 100 Hotels in the United States," the Lodge is an antique jewel, a well-preserved survivor of another era. From the grand fireplace in the lobby to the homey Victorian decor in the guest rooms, this mansion exudes gentility and class. Its nine-hole golf course, one of the nation's highest, challenges golfers across rolling hills between 8,600 and 9,200 feet elevation and is the site of numerous regional tournaments. Rooms in the lodge are filled with antiques, from sideboards and lamps to mirrors and steam radiators. See chapter 12.

• **The Bishop's Lodge** (Santa Fe; ☎ 505/983-6377): This resort holds special significance for me, as my parents met in the lodge and were later married in the chapel. It's a place rich with history. More than a century ago, when Bishop Jean-Baptiste Lamy was the spiritual leader of northern New Mexico's Roman Catholic population, he often escaped clerical politics by hiking into this valley called Little Tesuque. He built a retreat and the humble chapel (now on the National Register of Historic Places) with high-vaulted ceilings and a hand-built altar. Today Lamy's 1,000-acre getaway has become The Bishop's Lodge.

Recently purchased by an Australian real estate company, it's currently undergoing an $11 million renovation. The guest rooms, spread through 10 buildings, all feature handcrafted furniture and regional artwork. The Lodge is an active resort with activities such as horseback riding, hiking, tennis, and swimming filling guests' time. See chapter 7.

• **The Historic Taos Inn** (☎ 800/TAOS-INN): It's rare to see a hotel that has withstood the years with grace. The Historic Taos Inn has. Never do you forget that you're within the thick walls of a number of 19th-century Southwestern homes; and yet you're surrounded by 20th-century luxury. Dr. Thomas Paul Martin, the town's first (and for many years only) physician, purchased the complex in 1895. In 1936, a year after the doctor's death, his widow, Helen, enclosed the plaza—now the inn's darling 2-story lobby—and turned it into a hotel. In 1981–82, the inn was restored; it's now listed on both the State and National Registers of Historic Places.

All the rooms are unique and comfortable, decorated with Spanish colonial art, Taos-style furniture, and interesting touches such as hand-woven Oaxacan bedspreads and little *nichos* often adorned with Mexican pottery. See chapter 8.

• **St. James Hotel** (Cimarron; ☎ 800/748-2694): This landmark hotel offers travelers a romantically historic stay in this Old West town. It looks much the same today as it did in 1873, when it was built by Henri Lambert, previously a chef for Napoléon, Abraham Lincoln, and Gen. Ulysses S. Grant. In its early years, as a rare luxury on the Santa Fe Trail, it had a dining room, a saloon, gambling rooms, and lavish guest rooms outfitted with Victorian furniture. Today, you will find lace and cherry wood in the bedrooms, though the feel is frontier elegance rather than lavishness. Rooms don't have televisions or phones—the better to evoke the days when famous guests such as Zane Grey, who wrote *Fighting Caravans* at the hotel, were residents. Annie Oakley's bed is here, and a glass case holds a register with the signatures of Buffalo Bill Cody and the notorious Jesse James. See chapter 9.

- **Casa de Patrón Bed and Breakfast** (Lincoln; ☎ 505/653-4676): The main building of Casa de Patrón, an adobe, was built around 1860 and housed Juan Patrón's old store (the home is on the National Register of Historic Places). In addition, Billy the Kid used part of the house as a hideout at some point during his time in the Lincoln area. Jeremy and Cleis Jordan have capitalized on the presence of that notorious punk by collecting portraits and photographs and hanging them throughout the cozy sitting and dining areas of the inn. In the old part of the house the rooms are friendly with a homey feel created by quilts and a major collection of washboards adorning the walls. More sophisticated are the Old Trail House rooms, one with a Jacuzzi tub. See chapter 12.
- **Ellis Store and Co. Country Inn** (Lincoln; ☎ 800/653-6460): With part of this house dating from 1850, this is believed to be the oldest existing residence in Lincoln County. Billy the Kid spent several weeks here, although somewhat unwillingly, according to court records that show payment of $64 for 2 weeks' food and lodging for the Kid and a companion held under house arrest. The guest rooms in the main house are a step back into the 1800s, with wood-burning fireplaces or stoves providing heat, antique furnishings, and handmade quilts. With prior notice, the innkeepers will prepare a six-course meal with such specialties as exotic game (African antelope or venison). See chapter 12.
- **Bear Mountain Guest Ranch** (Silver City; ☎ 800/880-2538 or 505/538-2538): Rustic and austere, this may just be the very first bed-and-breakfast—ever. At least that's the story innkeeper Myra McCormic tells and the theory is supported by strong evidence. The inn itself was built in 1928, but the grounds show evidence of hunter and gatherer visitors dating from 6000 B.C. This is a nature-lover's delight—McCormick hosts birding, wild plant, and archaeological workshops throughout the year. Rooms are large with maple floors, high ceilings, and French windows. They have good but basic furnishings. What's best here is you can count on complete quiet. The food is modest ranch fare, well prepared and tasty. See chapter 11.

12 The Best Restaurants

- **Range Cafe** (Bernalillo; ☎ 505/867-1700): This cafe, about 15 minutes north of Albuquerque, has sophisticated food in an old diner-style atmosphere. There's a soda fountain in the center of the large space, and all the tables and chairs are hand-painted with whimsical stars and clouds. The proprietors here have come from such notable restaurants as Scalo in Albuquerque and Prairie Star on Santa Ana Pueblo, and the chef was quickly nabbed from the Double A in Santa Fe after it closed, so you can count on exquisite food. The food ranges from Tom's meat loaf to Range scallops, with a grilled tomato and cilantro cream sauce with pine nuts over red chile linguine. See chapter 6.
- **Kanome: An Asian Diner** (Albuquerque; ☎ 505/265-7773): This new restaurant has a contemporary airy atmosphere with burnished orange walls and delightfully imaginative Pacific Rim food. My favorite dish is the Balinese skewered pork and cashews. The Chinese duck with Tsing Tao peanut sauce is also tasty. The chef uses free-range chicken and organic vegetables. Save room for the homemade ice cream. See chapter 6.
- **Coyote Cafe** (Santa Fe; ☎ 505/983-1615): World-renowned chef and cookbook author Mark Miller has been "charged with single-handedly elevating the chile to haute status." That statement from the *New York Times Magazine* sums

up for me the experience of eating at this trendy nouveau Southwest restaurant a block from the Plaza. The atmosphere is urban Southwest, with calfskin-covered chairs and a zoo of carved animals watching from a balcony. Feast on delicacies such as pork carnitas tamales or Maine scallops with ancho–wild mushroom serape and pumpkin-cascabel sauce. See chapter 7.

- **Santacafé** (Santa Fe; ☎ **505/984-1788**): The food is Southwestern with an Asian flair, surrounded by a minimalist decor that accentuates the beautiful architecture of the 18th-century Padre Gallegos House, 2 blocks from the Plaza. The dishes change to take advantage of seasonal specialties, each served with precision. A simple starter such as miso soup is enriched with a lobster-mushroom roulade. One of my favorites is the seared chile-garlic prawns served with fresh pea (or lima) and mushroom risotto. Some have criticized chef Ming Tsai for overdoing his recipes; others claim the prices are too steep. I just find the experience inventively delicious in all respects. See chapter 7.
- **Anasazi Restaurant** (Santa Fe; ☎ **505/988-3236**): You'll dine on delectable nouveau-Southwestern cuisine while surrounded by diamond-finished walls decorated with petroglyph symbols creating the feel of the home of the ancient people who once inhabited the area. A must here is the grilled corn tortilla soup with ginger-pork pot stickers. For dinner, try the cinnamon chile–rubbed beef tenderloin with white-cheddar chipotle, chile mashed potatoes, and mango salsa. See chapter 7.
- **The Shed** and **La Choza** (Santa Fe; ☎ **505/982-9030** or 505/982-0909, respectively): A Santa Fe luncheon institution since 1954, The Shed occupies several rooms in part of a rambling hacienda that was built in 1692. Its sister restaurant La Choza also has whimsically painted walls. The sauces have been refined over years, creating amazing flavors in basic dishes like enchiladas and burritos. The mocha cake is renowned. See chapter 7.
- **Trading Post Café** (Taos; ☎ **505/758-5089**): One of my tastiest writing assignments was profiling chef/owner René Mettler's excellent restaurant for *The New York Times*. Notables such as R. C. Gorman, Dennis Hopper, and Gene Hackman are drawn to the gallery atmosphere here, with rough plastered walls washed with an orange hue set off by sculptures, paintings, and photographs from the Lumina Gallery. The meals are also artistically served. "You eat with your eyes," says Mettler. You'll find such creations as angel-hair pasta with chicken, wild mushrooms, and Gorgonzola and creole pepper shrimp, with saffron rice and fried leeks. See chapter 8.
- **Joseph's Table** (Taos; ☎ **505/751-4512**): Taos funk meets European flair at this intimate restaurant recently featured in *Travel and Leisure*. Between faux-painted walls, chef/owners Joseph and Gina Wrede serve up such dishes as steak au poivre and grilled Chilean sea bass presented in structural layers with delicious sides such as mashed potatoes and mushroom salads. See chapter 8.
- **Blackjack's Grill** (Las Vegas; ☎ **888/448-8438** or 505/425-6791): Las Vegas has needed a sophisticated restaurant, and now finally has one. Though at press time Blackjack's is only serving during the summer months, the owner hopes to be open year-round by our publication date. The atmosphere is festive, especially on the patio. The artfully presented food includes such dishes as halibut with a sesame seed crust built on top of risotto and crisply cooked zucchini and carrots. See chapter 9.
- **Something Special Bakery and Tea Room** (Farmington; ☎ **505/325-8183**): In a quaint Victorian home, the little restaurant has wooden floors and tables and an open, friendly feel. Best of all is the vine-draped arbor-shaded patio in back.

Breakfast is decadent—pastries, such as a blueberry cream cheese or a spinach and feta croissant, all made with wholesome ingredients. You'll find such delights as spicy Thai chicken served over veggies and rice. Every day there are 10 desserts, such unthinkable delicacies as blueberry/raspberry chocolate cake or a strawberry Napoleon. See chapter 10.

- **Way Out West Restaurant and Brewing Company** (Las Cruces; ☎ **505/ 541-1969**): This nouveau-Southwest restaurant serves tasty beer and inventive food. Big windows offer a fantastic view of the Organ Mountains and a broad veranda is an excellent place to sit in the spring and fall. Every day there's a special "catch of the day." A good selection of wines, a product of this brewery as well, are served. See chapter 11.
- **Double Eagle** (Las Cruces; ☎ **505/523-6700**): Continental cuisine is alive and well behind the walls of this historic hacienda (it's more than 150 years old) located in Las Cruces. The decor is lush and dramatic—chandeliers hung with Baccarat crystals—and the food is richly traditional—steaks are the way to go. See chapter 11.
- **La Lorraine** (Ruidoso; ☎ **505/257-2954**): This little piece of France offers specialties like pâté, duck a l'orange, and chateâubriand in an elegant French provincial decor, with lace curtains and candlelight. See chapter 12.

Getting to Know New Mexico 2

When I was a child in New Mexico, we'd sing a song while driving the dusty roads en route to such ruins as Chaco Canyon or Puye Cliff Dwellings. Sung to the tune of "Oh Christmas Tree" it went like this:

> New Mexico, New Mexico
> Don't know why we love you so.
> It never rains
> It never snows
> The winds and sand
> They always blow.
> And how we live
> God only knows.
> New Mexico, we love you so.

Although this song exaggerates the conditions here, the truth remains that in many ways New Mexico has an inhospitable environment. So why are so many people drawn here, and why do so many of us stay?

Ironically, the very extremes that this song presents are the reason. From the moment you set foot in this 121,666-square-mile state, you are met with wildly varied terrain, temperature, and temperament. On a single day you might experience temperatures from 25°F (–4°C) to 75°F (22°C). From the vast heat and dryness of White Sands in summer to the 13,161-foot subzero, snow-encrusted Wheeler Peak in the winter, New Mexico's beauty is carved by extremes.

Culturally, this is also the case. Few places have such distinct cultures living side by side. Pueblo, Navajo, and Apache tribes occupy much of the state's lands. Many of them still live within the traditions of their people, practicing native religious rituals, speaking their native languages, some even living without running water and electricity. Meanwhile, the Hispanic culture here remains deeply linked to its Spanish roots, practicing a devout Catholicism, speaking a Spanish that some say sounds like it did in the 15th century, some still living by subsistence farming in tiny mountain villages. The people you meet on the street may surprise you with their extreme temperaments. Some are so friendly they'll talk your ear off on the sidewalk on some small-town plaza, while others, such as the Native Americans, are much more stoic and guarded.

But the reasons people are drawn here are more complex still. New Mexico has its very own sense of time and its own social mores. The

New Mexico

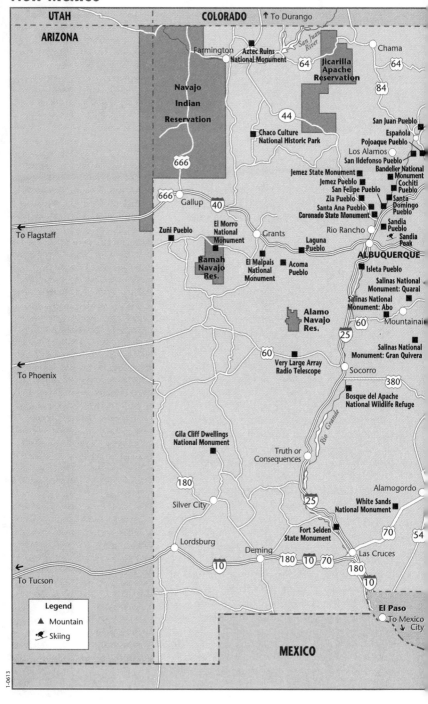

Legend
▲ Mountain
⛷ Skiing

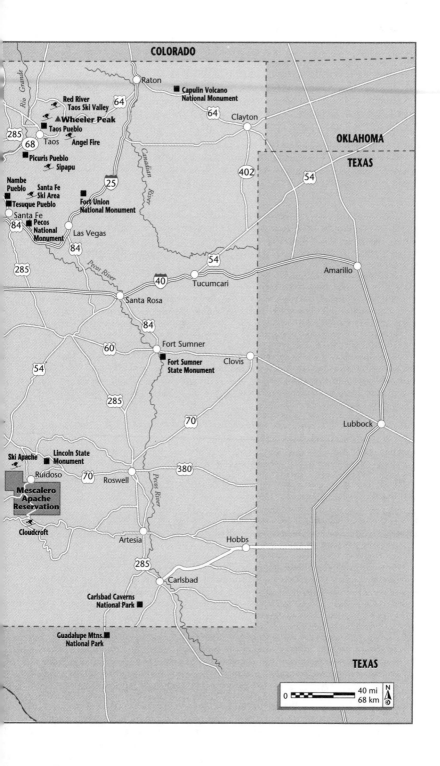

COLORADO

Raton

Capulin Volcano
National Monument

Red River
Taos Ski Valley
64
▲Wheeler Peak
Taos Pueblo
285
68
Taos
Angel Fire

64
Clayton

OKLAHOMA

TEXAS

Picuris Pueblo
Sipapu

Nambe
Pueblo
Santa Fe
Ski Area
Tesuque Pueblo
Santa Fe
84
Pecos
National
Monument

25

Fort Union
National Monument

402

54

Las Vegas

84

Pecos River

54

Amarillo

285

40
Tucumcari

Santa Rosa

84

60
Fort Sumner

54

Fort Sumner
State Monument
Clovis

285

70

Lubbock

Ski Apache
Lincoln State
Monument

380

70
Ruidoso
Roswell

Mescalero
Apache
Reservation

Pecos River

Cloudcroft

Artesia
Hobbs

285

Carlsbad

Carlsbad Caverns
National Park

Guadalupe Mtns.
National Park

TEXAS

0   40 mi   N
     68 km

19

pace is slower here, the objectives of life less defined. People rarely arrive on time for appointments here, and at times businesses won't hold to the hours their calendars say. In towns like Taos, some businesses shut down completely when there's good powder at Taos Ski Valley. You may meet a Hispanic farmer whose goal is not to make money, but instead to spend time with his family, and to do it today, not tomorrow. In most cases people wear the clothes they want here. You'll see men dressed for formal occasions wearing a buttoned collar with a bolo tie and women wearing cowboy boots with skirts. The other day I saw a man wearing a broad-brimmed bull-riders hat and lemon yellow cowboy boots—go tell.

All of this leads to a certain lost-and-not-caring-to-be-found spell the place casts on visitors that's akin to some kind of voodoo magic. Wildly foreign images cross your vision and stay there: pilgrims walking for days to a church where magical dirt might heal them and loved ones; Native Americans dancing for hours in summer heat while curtains of rain pound their way toward them; cowboys herding Herefords across uninterrupted prairie while giant thunderheads build above their heads. These images play their magic on us and leave us less certain of what's important.

So then we find ourselves, standing amid the dust or sparkling light, within the extreme heat or cold, not sure whether to speak Spanish or English. That's when the release comes, the time when we let go completely of society's common goals, its pace, and social mores. We settle in, slip into a kayak, and let the river take us down, or hike a peak and look at it all from high above. Or simply climb into a car and drive past ancient ruins along the roadside being excavated at that instant, past ghost mining towns, and under hot-air balloons, by chile fields and around hand-smoothed *santuarios*, all on the road to nowhere, New Mexico's best destination. At some point in your travels you'll likely find yourself on this road and you'll realize that there's no destination so fine.

And after that surrender, you may find yourself looking about with a new clarity. Having experienced the slower pace, you may question your own life's speediness. Having tasted New Mexico's relaxed style, you may look askance at those nylon stockings and heels or that suit and tie. And next time you climb in the car in your own state or country, you might just head down a road you've never been on and hope that it goes nowhere.

1 The Natural Environment

LAY OF THE LAND

It would be easy, and accurate, to call New Mexico "high and dry" and leave it at that. The lowest point in the state, in the southeastern corner, is still over 2,800 feet in elevation, higher than the highest point in at least a dozen other states. The southern Rocky Mountains, whose beginnings came during the Cenozoic era more than 70 million years ago, extend well into New Mexico, rising above 13,000 feet in the Sangre de Cristo range and sending a final afterthought above 10,000 feet, just east of Alamogordo. Volcanic activity created the mountain range, and its aftereffects can be seen throughout the state—from Shiprock (the remaining core of a long-eroded volcano) to Capulin Volcano National Monument. Two fault lines, which created the Rio Grande Rift Valley, home to the Rio Grande, run through the center of the state and seismic activity continues to change the face of New Mexico even today.

While archaeologists have discovered fossils indicating that most of New Mexico was once covered by ancient seas, the surface area of the state is now quite dry. The greater portion of New Mexico receives fewer than 20 inches of precipitation annually, the bulk of that coming either as summer afternoon thunderstorms or winter snowfall. In an area of 121,666 square miles—the fifth-largest American state—there are only 221 square miles of water. Rivers and lakes occupy less than 0.2% of the landscape. The most obvious and most important source of water is the Rio Grande, the "Big River" of Hispanic lore. It nourishes hundreds of small farms from the Pueblo country of the north to the bone-dry Chihuahuan Desert of the far south.

There is, however, more water than meets the eye in New Mexico. Systems circulating beneath the earth's surface have created all sorts of beautiful and fascinating geologic formations, including the natural wonder known as Carlsbad Caverns, one of the greatest cave systems in the world. Other caves have formed throughout the state, many of which have collapsed over the centuries creating large sinkholes. These sinkholes have since filled with water and formed beautiful lakes. Bottomless Lakes State Park, located near the town of Roswell, is a good example of this type of geological activity.

Other natural wonders you'll encounter during a visit to New Mexico include red-, yellow-, and orange-hued high, flat mesas and the 275-square-mile White Sands National Monument that contains more than 8 billion tons of pure white gypsum and is the largest field of sand dunes of this kind in the entire world. Here mountains meet desert and the sky is arguably bigger, bluer, and more fascinating than any other place in the country. Words can't do justice to the spectacular colors of the landscape: colors that have drawn contemporary artists from around the world for nearly a century, colors that have made Taos and Santa Fe synonymous with artists' communities. The blues, browns, greens, reds, oranges, and yellows in every imaginable variation make this land a living canvas. This is truly big sky country, where it seems you can see forever.

THE FLORA & FAUNA OF NEW MEXICO

Six of the earth's seven "life zones" are represented in New Mexico, from subtropical desert to alpine tundra. As a result, the state is home to an unusually diverse variety of plant and animal life. You'll see sage-speckled plains and dense stands of pine trees, as well as cactus and tender perennials (typically found in much cooler climates). Living among the trees and out on the desert plains are deer, bear, scorpions, and rattlesnakes.

At the highest elevations (those above 12,000 feet) is the alpine zone, which offers very little in the way of a home for plants and animals. Areas in New Mexico that fall into the alpine zone include Wheeler Peak and several other mountains in the Enchanted Circle area near Taos. These peaks are above the timberline and conditions are harsh. Only a few animals, such as pikas and marmots, are able to survive at this elevation, and the only trees you'll see are bristlecone pines. In the "summer" only a few hardy wildflowers have the strength to bloom in the alpine zone.

Heading down the mountain to about 12,000 to 9,500 feet is the Hudsonian zone. At this altitude, there is typically a great deal of snowfall in the late fall to late spring. There isn't much of a growing season in the Hudsonian zone, but there are more plants in this area than in the Alpine zone, creating more habitats for a greater number of animals. Rodents, birds, bighorn sheep, elk, mountain goats, and marmots live in New Mexico's Hudsonian zone among the bristlecone pine, blue spruce, and sub-alpine firs.

A very small percentage of New Mexico is in the Canadian zone, which includes certain areas of the White, Mogollons, Jemez, San Juan, and Sangre de Cristo Mountains. There you will find deer and elk (which migrate to warmer areas during the winter) as well as a variety of spruce, fir, and aspen trees.

With elevations between 8,500 and 6,500 feet, most of north-central New Mexico (primarily Santa Fe, Taos, and portions of Albuquerque) is well within the transition zone. This is where you'll find ponderosa pines standing alongside oak trees and juniper bushes. North-central New Mexico gets quite a bit more rain than other areas of the state and as a result you'll find a large number of wildflowers in bloom here in the spring and summer (columbine, pennyroyal, and New Mexico groundsel, to name a few), as well as a greater variety of wildlife. Keep your eyes open for black bears, mountain lions, deer, elk, quail, and wild turkey, especially if you're hiking in less-populated areas.

The northern portion of the state, from 6,500 to 4,500 feet, is in the upper Sonoran life zone. Here you'll find a combination of plants and animals found in the lower Sonoran life zone and the transition zone. Cacti are as prevalent as juniper, oak, and piñon; and rattlesnakes, scorpions, centipedes, and tarantulas make their home here along with mountain lions, javelinas, and pronghorns.

The southern portion of the state, where the heat rises off dusty flatlands and the elevation is below 4,500 feet, falls within the lower Sonoran life zone. Traveling through Las Cruces, Alamogordo, and Carlsbad you'll see all sorts of cacti, including prickly pear and cholla. Don't expect, however, to see the giant saguaro cactus most commonly associated with the desert landscape. The arid environment in the lower Sonoran zone is home to animals that thrive in the heat and don't need as much water as those found at higher altitudes. It's the perfect climate for rattlesnakes, centipedes, tarantulas, and scorpions.

Following are some of the more unusual flora and fauna you're apt to encounter during your travels through the state.

FLORA

CHOLLA   The types of cholla, a variety of cactus, most commonly found in New Mexico are tree, plateau, cane, stanly club, and dagger club. Tree cholla, with tuberculate "branches," can grow up to 10 feet in height and has ¾- to 1¼-inch-long spines. It grows primarily at elevations between 4,000 and 6,000 feet and produces magenta flowers. Plateau cholla is a short, shrublike plant that grows at elevations of 4,000 to 8,000 feet among other plants like piñon and juniper. If not surrounded by other bushes, grasses, and trees, plateau cholla can grow up to 7 feet in height if the water supply is sufficient. In drier areas, plateau cholla forms a short, wide mat along the ground. Spines are ¾ inch in length, and its flowers, which bloom in May, are pale to dark yellow. The fruit of this cactus is yellow when ripe. Cane cholla is similar to tree cholla in height and shape; however, it produces pink, purple, yellow, or white flowers. Stanly club and Dagger club cholla are short plants that form mats along the ground. Stanly club likes to grow on the mesas and plains of New Mexico, while Dagger club prefers rocky conditions. Both are extremely spiny and both produce small (1¼- to 2-inch) yellow flowers.

COLUMBINE   Generally speaking, columbine is any perennial plant in the buttercup family. In New Mexico these delicate wildflowers can be seen growing at roadsides around Santa Fe and Taos. Hummingbirds love columbine, and Native Americans once used the seeds of this flower to cure headaches and fever.

GROUNDSEL   Groundsel is a name that encompasses any plant in the aster family. Groundsel might be found growing as a vine, shrub, or tree. However, the variety found in New Mexico simply resembles a small, yellow daisy. Native Americans have been known to use groundsel to heal open wounds as well as to stimulate menses.

JUNIPER   An aromatic evergreen in the cypress family, juniper grows best in the temperate zone and is prevalent in New Mexico. Like other evergreens, juniper produces cones; however juniper cones look more like berries and are best known as juniper berries, which are used in cooking as well as in flavoring gin. Plains Indians used juniper as incense in religious gatherings.

PENNYROYAL   The American pennyroyal is an annual plant with small blue to purplish flowers. Admirers of the pennyroyal have discovered that the plant has more than aesthetic value. In fact, an oil found in pennyroyal is said to be excellent insect repellent, and a tea made from pennyroyal was once thought to be a cure for a variety of illnesses.

PRICKLY PEAR   Like the cholla cactus, there is also a wide variety of prickly pear cacti in New Mexico. There are simply too many to discuss here; however, most varieties can be identified by large, flat, spiny, teardrop-shaped branches and oblong purple or reddish fruit. Among the varieties seen in New Mexico are Fragile, Loose, Porcupine, Cliff, Starvation, Juniper, Red-Spined, Hair-Spined, Potts, Purple Fruited, Major, and Desert.

YUCCA   The state flower of New Mexico, yucca is a treelike succulent of the lily family. When they flower, yucca plants produce a long stalk of white or light purple flowers. It is interesting to note that the yucca plant is pollinated by the aptly named yucca moth, which depends on the plant as a "feeding ground" for its larvae. Without the yucca moth, the yucca plant usually doesn't produce flowers or fruit.

FAUNA

JAVELINA   Also known as the collared peccary, the javelina is a small, wild pig with curved tusks. It is the only pig that is native to North and South America. The javelina can live in a variety of environments, but will most likely be found in the dry scrublands of New Mexico. Charcoal gray in color, the javelina has a white stripe around its neck and weighs up to 50 pounds. It travels in small groups feeding on insects, reptiles, worms, fruits, and roots.

MARMOT   A ground-living rodent with its roots in the squirrel family, the most common varieties of marmot are the chipmunk, prairie dog, and woodchuck. They live in burrows either in the plains or mountainous regions of North America and Eurasia and are active during daylight hours. Green plants are their food of choice. Their stout bodies are covered with brown, white-tipped fur. The yellow-bellied marmot makes its home in New Mexico.

PIKA   A relative of hare and rabbits, the pika is also known as the rock rabbit or mouse hare. They make their homes in rocky environments above the timberline in western North America and northern Asia, and they live in communities. Though they resemble the rabbit, they have shorter ears and their hind and forelegs are of equal length. Because they live in such cold environments, their entire bodies, including the bottoms of their feet, are fur covered. Coloration varies from red to gray. Pika live on a diet of green plants, which are in short supply during the cold winter months. Pika circumvent this problem by cutting and drying vegetation in the sun for winter storage.

PRONGHORN   Very distantly related to the antelope of Asia and Africa, the pronghorn is sometimes called the American antelope, and is in fact native to the western United States—New Mexico, in particular. It is approximately 3 feet in height and has a light brown coat with distinctive white markings on its throat (two strips), rump, and underside. Both the male and female pronghorns have horns. These animals live on open plains and eat shrubs, such as sagebrush, and some grasses. Pronghorns are the fastest North American mammal. In spite of their speed, they are prey to wolves and coyotes. Unchecked hunting nearly caused the extinction of the pronghorn in the early part of this century; however, they are now a protected species and are making a strong comeback.

ROADRUNNER   I would be remiss if I didn't mention the roadrunner, New Mexico's state bird. It is a member of the family of birds more commonly known as cuckoos. With its long tail, erect body, and heavy bill, the roadrunner is quite distinctive looking. Though it is a bird, it doesn't fly very well and prefers to run along the ground (hence its name) at high speeds. In fact, the roadrunner can run at a speed of up to 15 miles an hour. You'll see roadrunners all over the place during your travels around the state.

2 The Regions in Brief

North-Central New Mexixo   The most highly populated and well traveled area of the state, north-central New Mexico roughly includes the cities of Albuquerque, Santa Fe, and Taos. It is also the economic center of New Mexico. In this portion of the state lush mountains, incredibly, seem to rise directly out of the parched plateaus that have made New Mexico's landscape famous. Temperatures are generally lower in this area than they are in the rest of the state, and skiing is one of the most popular winter activities in both Santa Fe and Taos.

Northeastern New Mexico   Covering the area north of Interstate 40 and east of the Sangre de Cristo Mountains, northeastern New Mexico is prairie land once inhabited and/or visited by some of the West's most legendary gunslingers. Towns to visit for a bit of Wild West history are Cimarron and Las Vegas. The northeastern portion of the state also includes attractions such as Fort Union National Monument, a portion of the Santa Fe Trail, Kiowa National Grasslands, and Capulin Volcano National Monument. Due to its abundance of state parks and wildlife reserves, as well as the fact that it borders the ski resort towns of Angel Fire, Taos, Red River, and Santa Fe, this region is an excellent area for sports enthusiasts.

Northwestern New Mexico   This region, which covers the upper left corner of the state, is the place to go if you're interested in Native American culture. Sandstone bluffs here mark the homes of Pueblo, Navajo, and Apache Indians in an area once inhabited by the Anasazi Indians of the past. My favorite places to visit in this section of the state are Acoma Pueblo, Chaco Culture National Historical Park, and Aztec Ruins National Monument. A major portion of the northwest region is part of a Navajo reservation, the largest in the country. This is also the gateway to the famous Four Corners region. The town of Grants, near Acoma, will give you a glimpse into uranium mining. Railroad fanatics, hikers, hunters, and fishers should make the trip up to Chama, home of the Cumbres and Toltec Railroad and a popular starting point for outdoor adventures.

Southwestern New Mexico   This region, like northeastern New Mexico, is another great place to visit if you're interested in the history of the Wild West and Native American culture, for it was once home to Billy the Kid and Geronimo. The Rio Grande, lifeline to this part of the state, acts as a border between the southwest and southeast portions of the state. Attractions west of the river include Gila National Forest, once home to the Mogollon Indians, whose past is preserved in the Gila Cliff Dwellings National Monument. The Chiricahua Apaches, a tribe once led by the famous Geronimo, also lived in this area. The town of Silver City, which survives today as an economic center of this area, was once a booming mine town. Surrounding ghost towns weren't as lucky. Las Cruces, located at the foot of the Organ Mountains, is the state's second largest city, and Truth or Consequences, named for a television and radio game show, is located north of Las Cruces off I-25. Socorro is a center of Hispanic culture, and Deming and Lordsburg are working ranch towns.

Southeastern New Mexico   Bounded on the west by the Rio Grande River, to the north by Interstate 40, and to the east by Texas, southeastern New Mexico is home to two of the most interesting natural wonders in this part of the country: Carlsbad Caverns and White Sands National Monument. The underground caverns filled with stalactites and stalagmites are infinitely interesting and hauntingly beautiful. Snow-white dunes at White Sands National Monument, which rise out of the desert landscape, are an extraordinary sight as you make the drive to Alamogordo. White Sands is a great place to camp out and watch the sunrise. This portion of the state is yet another former home of Billy the Kid. It is also where he died. Southeastern New Mexico has something of a dubious past as well: The world's first atomic bomb was detonated here.

3 New Mexico Today

On rock faces throughout New Mexico, you'll find circular symbols carved in sandstone, the wavy mark of Avanu the river serpent, or the ubiquitous Kokopelli playing his magic flute. These petroglyphs are constant reminders of the enigmatic history of the Anasazi, the Indians that inhabited this area from A.D. 1100 until as late as 1550. Part of my fascination with this land is the mysterious presence of these ancient people and others such as the Mogollon in the south, even today. Excavations continue in the area; the other day, right on a highway shoulder between Santa Fe and Española, I saw archaeologists excavating two sites, brushing away dirt to expose kivas and ancient walls.

The Spanish conquistadors, in their inimitable fashion, imposed a new, foreign order upon the resident Native Americans and their land. They brought their own rich culture bolstered by a fervent belief in spreading Catholicism. As an inevitable component of conquest, they changed most Native American names—today you'll find a number of Native Americans with Hispanic names—and renamed the villages "pueblos." The Spaniards' most far-reaching legacy, however, was the forceful conversion of Indian populations to Catholicism, a religion that many Indians still practice today. In each of the pueblos you'll see a large, often beautiful Catholic church, usually made with sculpted adobe. The churches, set against the ancient adobe dwellings, are symbolic of the melding of two cultures. During the holiday seasons here you'll see Pueblo people perform their ritual dances outside their local Catholic church.

The mix of cultures is today very much apparent in New Mexican cuisine. When the Spaniards came to the New World, they brought cows and sheep. They quickly learned to appreciate the indigenous foods here, most notably corn, beans, squash, and chiles. Look also for such Pueblo dishes as the thin-layered blue piki bread, or *chauquehue,* a thick corn pudding similar to polenta. See "New Mexican Cuisine," near the end of this chapter.

GROWING PAINS   New Mexico is experiencing a reconquest of sorts, as the Anglo population soars, and outside money and values again make their way in. The process continues to transform New Mexico's three distinct cultures and their unique ways of life, albeit in a less violent manner than during the Spanish conquest.

Certainly, the Anglos who have moved here in recent years—many of them from large cities—have added a cosmopolitan flavor to life here. The variety of restaurants has greatly improved, as have entertainment options. For their small size, towns such as Taos, Santa Fe, Albuquerque, and Las Cruces offer a broad variety of restaurants and cultural events. Santa Fe has developed a strong dance and drama scene, with treats such as flamenco and opera that you'd expect to find in New York or Los Angeles. And Albuquerque has an exciting nightlife scene downtown; you can walk from club to club and hear a wealth of jazz, rock, country, and alternative music.

Yet many newcomers, attracted by the adobe houses and exotic feel of the place, often bring only a loose appreciation for the area. Some tend to romanticize the lifestyle of the other cultures and trivialize their beliefs. Native American symbology, for example, is employed in ever-popular Southwestern decorative motifs; New Age groups appropriate valued rituals, such as sweats (in which believers sit encamped in a very hot, enclosed space to cleanse their spirits). The effects of cultural and economic change are even apparent throughout the countryside, where land is being developed at an alarming rate, often as lots for new million-dollar homes.

Transformation of the local way of life and landscape is also apparent in the stores continually springing up in the area. For some of us, these are a welcome relief from Western clothing stores and provincial dress shops. The downside is that city plazas, which once contained pharmacies and grocery stores frequented by residents, are now crowded with T-shirt shops and galleries appealing to tourists. Many locals in these cities now rarely visit their plazas except during special events such as fiestas.

Environmental threats are another regional reality. Nuclear waste issues form part of an ongoing conflict affecting the entire Southwest, and a section of southern New Mexico near Carlsbad has been designated a nuclear waste site. Much of the waste would pass through Santa Fe; the problem necessitated construction of a bypass that will, when completed, direct a great deal of transit traffic around the west side of the city.

Still, new ways of thinking have also brought positive changes to the life here, and many locals have directly benefited from New Mexico's expansion, influx of wealthy newcomers, and popularity as a tourist destination. Businesses and industries, large and small, have come to the area. In Albuquerque, Intel Corporation now employs more than 5,000 workers, and *Outside* magazine recently relocated from Chicago to Santa Fe. Local artists and artisans also benefit from growth. Many craftspeople—furniture makers, tin workers, and weavers—have expanded their businesses. The influx of people has broadened the sensibility of a fairly provincial state. Pockets of the state have become refuges for many gays and lesbians, as well as for political exiles, such as Tibetans. With them has developed a level of creativity and tolerance you would generally find in very large cities but not in smaller communities such as these.

CULTURAL QUESTIONS   Faced with new challenges to their ways of life, both Native Americans and Hispanics are marshaling forces to protect their cultural identities. A prime concern is language. Through the years, many native people have begun to speak more and more English, with their children getting little exposure to their native tongue. Today, elders are working with schoolchildren in language classes. Some of the pueblos, such as Santa Clara, have even developed written dictionaries, the first time their languages have been presented in this form.

Many pueblos have introduced programs to conserve the environment, preserve ancient seed strains, and protect religious rites. Since their religion is tied closely to nature, a loss of their natural resources would threaten the entire culture. Certain rituals have been closed off to outsiders, the most notable being the Shalako at Zuni, a popular and elaborate series of year-end ceremonies.

Hispanics, through art and observance of cultural traditions, are also embracing their roots. Throughout New Mexico you'll see, adorning many walls, murals that depict important historical events, such as the Treaty of Guadalupe Hidalgo of 1848. The **Spanish Market** in Santa Fe has expanded into a grand celebration of traditional arts—from tin working to santo carving. Public schools in the area have bilingual education programs in place, allowing young people to embrace their Spanish-speaking roots.

Hispanics are also making their voices heard, insisting on more conscientious development of their neighborhoods and rising to positions of power in government. When she was in office, former Santa Fe mayor Debbie Jaramillo made national news as an advocate of the Hispanic people, and Congressman Bill Richardson, Hispanic despite his Anglo surname, was appointed U.S. ambassador to the United Nations, and later was appointed U.S. energy secretary.

GAMBLING WINS & LOSSES Gambling, a fact of life and source of much-needed revenues for Native American populations across the country, has been a center of controversy in New Mexico for a number of years. In 1994, Gov. Gary Johnson signed a compact with the state's tribes, ratified by the U.S. Department of the Interior, to allow full-scale gambling. Tesuque Pueblo was one of the first to begin a massive expansion, and many other pueblos followed suit.

In early 1996, however, the State Supreme Court ruled that without legislative action on the matter, the casinos were operating illegally. Native Americans remained resolute in their determination to forge ahead with the casinos. Demonstrations of community strength, by the Pojoaque Pueblo and others, ultimately made an impact on legislators. In 1997, lawmakers agreed to allow gaming by Indian as well as fraternal and veteran organizations.

Many New Mexicans are concerned about the tone gambling sets in the state. The casinos are for the most part large and unsightly, neon-bedecked buildings that stand out sorely on some of New Mexico's most picturesque land. Though most residents appreciate the boost that gambling can ultimately bring to the Native American economies, many critics wonder where gambling profits actually go—and if the casinos can possibly be a good thing for the pueblos and tribes. Some detractors suspect that profits go directly into the pockets of outside backers.

A number of pueblos and tribes, however, are showing signs of prosperity, and they are using newfound revenues to buy fire-fighting and medical equipment and to invest in local schools. According to the Indian Gaming Association, casinos directly employ more than 4,000 workers and pump more than $260 million in revenues into the state's economy. Isleta Pueblo has built a $3.6 million youth center, money which their lieutenant governor says came from gambling revenues. Sandia Pueblo has built a $2 million medical and dental clinic and expanded its police department. Gov. Alex Lujan calls these projects "totally funded by gaming revenues."

SANTA FE The splendor of diverse cultures really shines in Santa Fe, and it does so in a setting that's unsurpassed. There's a magic in Santa Fe that's difficult to explain, but you'll sense it when you glimpse an old adobe building set against blue mountains and giant billowing thunderheads or when you hear a ranchero song come from a low-rider's radio and you smell chicken and chile grilling at a roadside vending booth. Although it's quickening, the pace of life here is still a few steps slower than the rest of the country. There's also a level of creativity here that you'll find in few other places in the world. Artists who have fled big-city jobs are here to follow their passions, as are locals who grew up making crafts and continue to do so. Conversations often center around how to structure one's day so as to take advantage of the incredible outdoors while still making enough money to survive.

Meanwhile, Santa Fe's precipitous growth and enduring popularity with tourists have been the source of conflict and squabbling. Outsiders have bought up land in the hills around the city, building housing developments and sprawling single-family homes. The hills that local populations claimed for centuries as their own are being overrun, while property taxes for all skyrocket. On the positive side, however, local outcry has prompted the city to implement zoning restrictions on where and how development can proceed. Some of the restrictions include banning building on ridge tops and on steep slopes and limiting the size of homes built.

Santa Fe's last mayor, Debbie Jaramillo, was one of the first local politicians to take a strong stand against growth. A fiery native of Santa Fe, she came into office as a representative of *la gente* (the people), and set about discouraging tourism and rapid development. She took a lot of heat for her positions, which to some seemed xenophobic and antibusiness. The mayor initially failed to offer tax breaks or incentive money to some businesses interested in settling in the area, but by the time she left office had softened her position on development. Our newly elected mayor, Larry Delgado, has taken a middle-road approach to the issue; Santa Feans are waiting to see how this affects the local economy and the future of the city's development.

TAOS   A funky town in the middle of a beautiful, sage-covered valley, Taos is full of narrow streets dotted with galleries and artisan shops. You might find an artist's studio tucked into a century-old church or a small furniture maker working at the back of his own shop.

More than any other major northern New Mexico community, Taos has successfully opposed much of the heavy development slated for the area. In 1987, locals vociferously protested plans to expand the airport; plans have been stalled indefinitely pending environmental impact statements. In 1991, a $40 million golf course and housing development slated for the area was met with such community dissension that its developers eventually desisted. It's hard to say where Taos gets its rebellious strength; the roots may lie in the hippie community that settled here in the '60s, or possibly the Pueblo community around which the city formed. After all, Taos Pueblo was at the center of the 17th-century Pueblo Revolt.

Still, changes are upon Taoseños. The "blinking light" that for years residents used as a reference point has given way to a real traffic light. You'll also see the main route through town becoming more and more like Cerrillos Road in Santa Fe, as fast-food restaurants and service businesses set up shop. Though the town is working to streamline alternate routes to channel through-traffic around downtown, there's no feasible way of widening the main drag because the street, which started out as a wagon trail, is bordered closely by historic buildings.

ALBUQUERQUE   The largest city in New Mexico, Albuquerque has borne the brunt of the state's most massive growth. Currently, the city sprawls over 16 miles, from the lava-crested mesas on the west side of the Rio Grande to the steep alluvial slopes of the Sandia Mountains on the east, and north and south through the Rio Grande Valley. New subdivisions sprout up constantly.

Despite the growth, this town is most prized by New Mexicans for its genuineness. You'll find none of the self-conscious artsy atmosphere of Santa Fe here. Instead, there's a traditional New Mexico feel that's evident when you spend some time in the heart of the city. It centers around downtown, a place of shiny skyscrapers built around the original Route 66, which still maintains some of its 1950s charm.

The most emblematic growth problem concerns the **Petroglyph National Monument** on the west side. The area is characterized by five extinct volcanoes. Adjacent lava flows became a hunting and gathering place for prehistoric Native Americans who left a chronicle of their beliefs etched in the dark basalt boulders. Some 15,000 petroglyphs have been found in this archaeological preserve. Now there's a push to carve out a highway corridor right through the center of the monument. Opponents have fought the extension for nearly a decade. Some Native American groups, likening the highway to building a road through a church, oppose the extension on grounds that the petroglyphs are sacred to their culture. U.S. Interior Secretary Bruce Babbitt has refused to give permission for the road to go through. Sen. Pete Domenici, however, has introduced a bill into the Senate that would allow the road to be built. The bill must be approved by Congress before construction can begin.

SOUTHERN NEW MEXICO   When I travel around southern New Mexico I'm always struck by what a small farm-town feel the cities have. The majority of people seem to be friendly and unassuming. Unlike the northern part of the state where the concept of "growth" has been tested and found wanting, southern New Mexico still welcomes the concept. That's partially why the Waste Isolation Pilot Project so easily gained the support of people in the Carlsbad area. This deep-geologic repository for permanent disposal of radioactive waste has been controversial for almost 20 years since its inception. At this writing, plans for the first shipments of waste to the site have been made.

While this takes place in southeastern New Mexico, in the southwest part of the state, exciting and ground-breaking nature conservation efforts are moving forward. This is nothing new. Since 1924 when forester Aldo Leopold finally succeeded in having the Gila area designated as the United States' first wilderness area, there has been a strong consciousness toward maintaining the resources here. In this area are two of the state's last free-flowing rivers of any size, the Gila and Mimbres. The Nature Conservancy has since the late 1970s purchased property in order to protect habitats of animals such as the Gila woodpecker, Gila trout, and Southwest willow flycatcher. Often seen as a threat to the ranching industry, the Conservancy has initiated a number of community-based efforts to preserve habitat, while encouraging the grazing that is necessary to rancher's lifestyles.

Meanwhile, New Mexico has received national attention as others purchase property and set out to save the environment here. Most notable in this effort is media mogul Ted Turner. "If I'm going to save the West, I'll have to buy it," he once said. He's amassed a total of 1.3 million acres of Montana, Nebraska, and New Mexico ranch land, a space the size of Delaware. He owns three New Mexico ranches, the Armendaris and the Ladder in the south-central part of the state and the Vermejo Park in the north. On his southern ranches he immediately cleared off all cattle and began raising bison, animals believed to be easier on grasslands than their bovine cousins. He's reintroduced desert big-horn sheep onto the Armendaris, and rebuilt the antelope populations on the Ladder. New Mexicans are waiting to see what he will do with the Vermejo Park.

If you look at a map you'll no doubt come to realize that the outer regions of the state are primarily home to the national parks and monuments that make New Mexico unique. Fortunately natural wonders like Capulin Volcano, White Sands National Monument, Carlsbad Caverns, and El Malpais National Monument are well preserved. Surrounding towns maintain a slow pace, and major growth is unlikely.

Most important for travelers, New Mexico's extreme popularity as a tourist destination—it was the "in" place to be through much of the '80s—has dropped off. Though many artists and other businesspeople lament the loss of the crowds, most people are glad that the wave has subsided. It's good news for travelers too, who no longer have to compete so heavily for restaurant seats or space when hiking through ruins. Though parts of New Mexico have lost some of the unique charm that attracted so many to the area, the overall feeling is still one of mystery and a cultural depth unmatched in the world. People here recognize the need to preserve the land and what New Mexicans have traditionally valued as integral to their unique lifestyle.

4 A Look at the Past

Dateline

- **3,000 B.C.** First evidence of stable farming settlements in region.
- **A.D. 700** Earliest evidence of Anasazi presence.
- **1540** Francisco Vásquez de Coronado marches to Cíbola in search of a Native American "city of gold."
- **1542** Coronado returns to New Spain, declaring his mission a failure.
- **1610** Immigration to New Mexico increases; Don Pedro de Peralta establishes Santa Fe as capital.
- **1680** Pueblo Indians revolt against Spanish.
- **1692** Spanish recapture Santa Fe.
- **1706** Albuquerque established.
- **1739** First French traders enter Santa Fe.
- **1779** Cuerno Verde, leader of rebellious Comanche tribes, falls to Spanish forces.
- **1786** Comanches and Utes sign treaty with Spanish.
- **1821** Mexico gains independence from Spain.
- **1828** Kit Carson, the legendary frontiersman, arrives in Taos.
- **1846** Mexican War breaks out; Gen. Stephen Kearny takes possession of New Mexico for United States.
- **1847** Revolt in Taos against U.S. control; newly appointed governor Charles Bent killed.
- **1848** Under provisions of Treaty of Guadalupe Hidalgo, Mexico officially cedes New Mexico to United States.
- **1861** Victorious Confederate general proclaims all of New Mexico south of the 34th parallel the new,

continues

IN THE BEGINNING   Archaeologists say that humans first migrated to the Southwest, moving southward from the Bering Land Bridge, about 12,000 B.C. Sites such as Sandia Cave and Folsom—where weapon points were discovered that for the first time clearly established that our prehistoric ancestors hunted now-extinct mammals such as woolly mammoths—are internationally known. When these large animals died off during the late Ice Age (about 8,000 B.C.), people turned to hunting smaller game and gathering wild food.

Stable farming settlements, as evidenced by the remains of domestically grown maize, date from about 3,000 B.C. As the nomadic peoples became more sedentary, they built permanent residences, pit houses, and made pottery. Cultural differences began to emerge in their choice of architecture and decoration: The Mogollon people, in the southwestern part of modern New Mexico, created brown and red pottery and built large community lodges; the Anasazi, in the north, made gray pottery and smaller lodges for extended families.

The Mogollon, whose pottery dates from about 100 B.C., were the first of the sophisticated village cultures. They lived primarily in modern-day Catron and Grant counties. The most important Mogollon ruins extant today are in the Gila River Valley, including Gila Cliff Dwellings National Monument north of Silver City.

By about A.D. 700, and perhaps a couple of centuries earlier, the Anasazi of the northwest had absorbed village life and expanded through what is now known as the Four Corners Region (where New Mexico, Arizona, Utah, and Colorado come together). Around A.D. 1000, their culture eclipsed that of the Mogollon. Chaco Canyon National Historic Park, Aztec Ruins National Monument, and Salmon Ruins all exhibit an architectural excellence and skill, and a scientific sensitivity to nature, that marks this as one of America's classic pre-Columbian civilizations.

Condominium-style communities of stone and mud adobe bricks, three and four stories high, were focused around central plazas. The villages incorporated circular spiritual chambers called kivas. The Anasazi also developed means to irrigate their fields of corn, beans, and squash by controlling the flow of water from the San Juan River and its tributaries.

From Chaco Canyon, they built a complex system of well-engineered roads leading in four directions to other towns or ceremonial centers. Artifacts found during excavation, such as seashells and macaw feathers, indicate they had a far-reaching trade network. The incorporation of solar alignments into some of their architecture has caused modern archeoastronomers to speculate on the importance of the equinoxes to their religion.

The disappearance of the Anasazi culture, and the emergence of the Pueblo culture in its place, is something of a mystery today. Those who study such things are in disagreement as to why the Anasazi left their villages around the 13th century. Some suggest drought or soil exhaustion; others, invasion, epidemic, or social unrest. But by the time the first Spanish arrived in the 1500s, the Anasazi were long gone and the Pueblo culture was well established throughout northern and western New Mexico, from Taos to Zuni, near Gallup. Most of the people lived on the east side of the Continental Divide, in the Rio Grande valley.

Certain elements of the Anasazi civilization had clearly been absorbed by the Pueblos, including the apartment-like adobe architecture, the creation of rather elaborate pottery, and the use of irrigation or flood farming in their fields. Agriculture, and especially corn, was the economic mainstay.

Each pueblo, as the scattered villages and surrounding farmlands were known, fiercely guarded its independence. When the Spanish arrived, there were no alliances between villages, even among those that shared a common language or dialect. No more than a few hundred people lived in any one pueblo, an indication that the natives had learned to keep their population (which totaled 40,000 to 50,000) down in order to preserve their soil and other natural resources. But not all was peaceful: They alternately fought and traded with each other, as well as with nomadic Apaches. Even before the Spanish arrived, a pattern had been established.

THE ARRIVAL OF THE SPANISH   The Spanish controlled New Mexico for 300 years, from the mid-16th to the mid-19th century—twice as long as the United States has. The Hispanic legacy in language and culture is stronger today in New Mexico than anywhere else in the Southwest, no doubt a result of the prominence of the Rio Grande valley as the oldest and most populous fringe province of the viceroyalty of New Spain.

Confederate territory of Arizona.

- **1862** Confederates routed from New Mexico.
- **1864** Navajos relocated to Bosque Redondo Reservation.
- **1868** Navajos return to their homeland.
- **1878–81** Lincoln County War erupts; comes to epitomize the lawlessness and violence of the Wild West.
- **1879** Atchison, Topeka, and Santa Fe Railroad routes main line through Las Vegas, Albuquerque, El Paso, and Deming, where connection is made with California's Southern Pacific line.
- **1881** Legendary outlaw Billy the Kid killed by Pat Garrett.
- **1886** Apache chief Geronimo captured; signals end of New Mexico's Indian wars.
- **1898** Painters Ernest Blumenschein and Bert Phillips settle in Taos.
- **1912** New Mexico becomes the 47th state.
- **1914** Blumenschein and Phillips form Taos Society of Artists; Taos becomes a major center of influence in midcentury American art and letters.
- **1916** Construction of Elephant Butte Dam brings irrigation to southern New Mexican farms.
- **1924** Native Americans granted full U.S. citizenship.
- **1943** Los Alamos National Laboratory built; "Manhattan Project" scientists spend two years in complete seclusion developing nuclear weapons.
- **1945** First atomic bomb exploded at Trinity Site.
- **1947** Reports of a flying saucer crash near Roswell

continues

make national headlines, despite U.S. Air Force's denials that it has occurred.

- **1972** Pioneer balloonist Sid Cutter establishes Albuquerque International Balloon Fiesta.
- **1981** The Very Large Array, the world's most powerful radio telescope, begins observations of distant galaxies from the desert west of Socorro.
- **1982** U.S. space shuttle *Columbia* lands at Holloman Air Force Base, near White Sands National Monument.
- **1984** New Mexico's last remaining section of famed Route 66, near San Jon, is abandoned.
- **1990** New Mexico's last uranium mine, near Grants, closes.
- **1992** The 70th anniversary of the Inter-Tribal Indian Ceremonial is held at Gallup.
- **1994** Under pressure from Congress, U.S. Air Force reopens investigation of the 1947 flying saucer crash reports, concluding that the debris found was likely from tests of a secret Cold War spy balloon; UFO believers allege a cover-up.
- **1998** The Waste Isolation Pilot Project, the nation's first deep-geologic repository for permanent disposal of radioactive waste receives the go-ahead to begin storage operations.

The spark that sent the first European explorers into what is now New Mexico was a fabulous medieval myth that seven Spanish bishops had fled the Moorish invasion of the 8th century, sailed westward to the legendary isle of Antilia, and built themselves seven cities of gold. Hernán Cortés's 1519 discovery and conquest of the Aztecs' treasure-laden capital of Tenochtitlán, now Mexico City, fueled belief in the myth. When a Franciscan friar 20 years later claimed to have sighted, from a distance, "a very beautiful city" in a region known as Cíbola while on a reconnaissance mission for the viceroyalty, the gates were open.

Francisco Vásquez de Coronado, the ambitious young governor of New Spain's western province of Nueva Galicia, was commissioned to lead an expedition to the "seven cities." Several hundred soldiers, accompanied by servants and missionaries, marched overland to Cíbola with him in 1540, along with a support fleet of three ships in the Gulf of California. What they discovered, after 6 hard months on the trail, was a bitter disappointment: Instead of a city of gold, they found a rock-and-mud pueblo at Hawikuh, the westernmost of the Zuni towns. The expedition wintered at Tiguex, on the Rio Grande near modern Santa Fe, before proceeding to the Great Plains seeking more treasure at Quivira, in what is now Kansas. The grass houses of the Wichita Indians were all they found.

Coronado returned to New Spain in 1542, admitting failure. Historically, though, his expedition was a great success, contributing the first widespread knowledge of the Southwest and Great Plains, and discovering en route the Grand Canyon.

By the 1580s, after important silver discoveries in the mountains of Mexico, the Spanish began to wonder if the wealth of the Pueblo country might lie in its land rather than its cities. They were convinced that they had been divinely appointed to convert the natives of the New World to Christianity. And so a northward migration began, orchestrated and directed by the royal government. It was a mere trickle in the late 16th century. Juan de Onate established a capital in 1598 at San Gabriel, near San Juan Pueblo, but a variety of factors led to its failure. Then in 1610, under Don Pedro de Peralta, the migration began in earnest.

It was not dissimilar to America's schoolbook stereotype. Bands of armored conquistadors did troop through the desert, humble robed friars striding by their sides. But most of the pioneers came up the valley of the Rio Grande with oxcarts and mule trains rather than armor, intent on transplanting their Hispanic traditions of government, religion, and material culture to this new world.

Regional Historical Interest

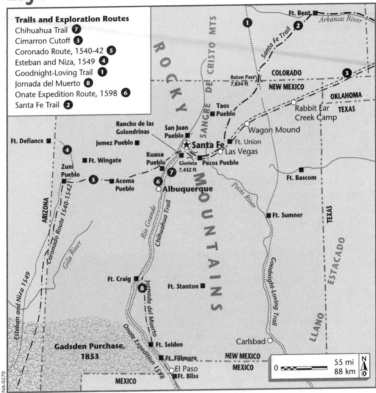

Trails and Exploration Routes
Chihuahua Trail ❼
Cimarron Cutoff ❸
Coronado Route, 1540-42 ❺
Esteban and Niza, 1549 ❹
Goodnight-Loving Trail ❶
Jornada del Muerto ❽
Onate Expedition Route, 1598 ❻
Santa Fe Trail ❷

Peralta built his new capital at Santa Fe and named it La Villa Real de la Santa Fe de San Francisco de Asis, the Royal City of the Holy Faith of St. Francis of Assisi. His capitol building, the Palace of the Governors, has been continuously occupied as a public building ever since by Spanish, Mexicans, Americans, and for 12 years (1680–92) by the Pueblo Indians. Today it is a museum.

RELIGION & REVOLT The 17th century in New Mexico was essentially a missionary era, as Franciscan priests attempted to turn the Indians into model Hispanic peasants. Their churches became the focal point of every pueblo, with Catholic schools a mandatory adjunct. By 1625 there were an estimated 50 churches in the Rio Grande valley. But the Native Americans weren't enthused about doing "God's work"—building new adobe missions, tilling fields for the Spanish, and weaving garments for export to Mexico—so soldiers backed the padres in extracting labor, a system known as *repartimiento*. Simultaneously, the *encomienda* system provided that a yearly tribute in corn and blankets be levied upon each Indian. The Pueblos were pleased to take part in Catholic religious ceremonies and proclaim themselves converts. To them, spiritual forces were actively involved in the material world. If establishing harmony with the cosmos meant absorbing Jesus Christ and various saints into their hierarchy of *kachinas* and other spiritual beings, so much the better. But the Spanish friars demanded they do away with their traditional singing and masked dancing, and with other "pagan practices." When the Pueblo religion was violently crushed and driven literally underground, resentment toward the Spanish grew and

Impressions

For a greatness of beauty I have never experienced anything like New Mexico. . . Just a day itself is tremendous there.

—D. H. Lawrence, "New Mexico," *Survey Graphic,* 1931

On the license plates in New Mexico it reads: "the Land of Enchantment." And that it is, by God! . . . Everything is hypnagogic, chthonian, and super-celestial. Here Nature has gone Gaga and Dada.

—Henry Miller, *The Air-Conditioned Nightmare,* 1945

festered. Rebellions at Taos and Jemez in the 1630s left village priests dead, but the Pueblos were savagely repressed.

A power struggle between church and state in Nuevo Mexico weakened the hand of the Spanish colonists, and a long drought in the 1660s and 1670s gave the warlike Apaches reason to scourge the Spanish and Pueblo settlements for food. The Pueblos blamed the friars, and their ban on traditional rain dances, for the drought. The hanging of four medicine men as "sorcerers," and the imprisonment of 43 others, was the last straw for the Rio Grande natives. In 1680, the Pueblo Revolt erupted.

Popé, a San Juan shaman, catalyzed the revolt. Assisted by other Pueblo leaders, he unified the far-flung Native Americans, who never before had confederated. They pillaged and burned the province's outlying settlements, then turned their attention upon Santa Fe, besieging the citizens who had fled to the Palace of the Governors. After 9 days, having reconquered Spain's northernmost American province, they let the refugees retreat south to Mexico.

Popé ordered that the Pueblos should return to the lifestyle they had had before the arrival of the Spanish. All Hispanic items, from tools to livestock to fruit trees, were to be destroyed, and the blemish of baptism was to be washed away in the river. But the shaman misjudged the influence of the Spanish upon the Pueblo people. They were not the people they had been a century earlier, and they *liked* much of the material culture they had absorbed from the Europeans. What's more, they had no intention of remaining confederated; their independent streaks were too strong.

In 1692, led by newly appointed Gov. Don Diego de Vargas, the Spanish recaptured Santa Fe without bloodshed. Popé had died, and without a leader to reunify them, the Pueblos were no match for the Spanish. Vargas pledged not to punish them, but to pardon and convert. Still, when he returned the following year with 70 families to recolonize the city, he had to use force. And for the next several years, bloody battles persisted throughout the Pueblo country.

By the turn of the 18th century, Nuevo Mexico was firmly in Spanish hands. This time, however, the colonists seemed to have learned from some of their past errors. They were more tolerant in their religion, less ruthless in their demands and punishments.

ARRIVAL OF THE ANGLOS   By the 1700s, there were signals that new interlopers were about to arrive in New Mexico. The French had laid plans to begin colonizing the Mississippi River, and hostile Native American tribes were on the warpath. The Spanish viceroyalty fortified its position in Santa Fe as a defensive bastion and established a new villa at Albuquerque in 1706.

In 1739, the first French trade mission entered Santa Fe, welcomed by the citizenry but not by the government. For 24 years, until 1763, a black-market trade thrived between Louisiana and New Mexico. It ended only when France lost its toehold on its North American claims during the French and Indian War against Great Britain.

The Native Americans were more fearsome foes. Apache, Comanche, Ute, and Navajo launched repeated raids against each other and the Rio Grande settlements for most of the 18th century, which led the Spanish and Pueblos to pull closer together for mutual protection. Pueblo and Hispanic militias fought side by side in campaigns against the invaders. But by the 1770s, the attacks had become so savage and destructive that the viceroy in Mexico City created a military jurisdiction in the province, and Gov. Juan Bautista de Anza led a force north to Colorado to defeat the most feared of the Comanche chiefs, Cuerno Verde ("Green Horn"), in 1779. Seven years later, the Comanches and Utes signed a lasting treaty with the Spanish and thereafter helped keep the Apaches in check.

France sold the Louisiana Territory to the young United States in 1803, and the Spanish suddenly had a new intruder to fear. The Lewis and Clark expedition of 1803 went unchallenged, much as the Spanish would have liked to challenge it; but in 1807, when Lt. Zebulon Pike built a stockade on a Rio Grande tributary in Colorado, he and his troops were taken prisoner by troops from Santa Fe. Pike was taken to the New Mexican capital, where he was interrogated extensively, and then to Chihuahua, Mexico. The report he wrote upon his return was United States' first inside look at Spain's frontier province.

At first, pioneering American merchants—excited by Pike's observations of New Mexico's economy—were summarily expelled from Santa Fe or jailed, their goods confiscated. But after Mexico gained independence from Spain in 1821, traders were welcomed. The wagon ruts of the Santa Fe Trail soon extended from Missouri to New Mexico, and from there to Chihuahua. (Later, it became the primary southern highway to California.)

As the merchants hastened to Santa Fe, Anglo American and French Canadian fur trappers headed into the wilderness. Their commercial hub became Taos, a tiny village near a large pueblo a few days' ride north of Santa Fe. Many married into native or Hispanic families. Perhaps the best known was Kit Carson, a sometime federal agent, sometime scout, whose legend is inextricably interwoven with that of early Taos. He spent 40 years in Taos, until his death in 1868.

In 1846, the Mexican War broke out and New Mexico became a territory of the United States. There were several causes of the war, including the U.S. annexation of Texas in 1845, disagreement over the international boundary, and unpaid claims owed to American citizens by the Mexican government. But foremost was the prevailing U.S. sentiment of "manifest destiny," the belief that the Union should extend "from sea to shining sea." Gen. Stephen Kearny marched south from Colorado; in the Las Vegas plaza, he announced that he had come to take possession of New Mexico for the United States. His arrival in Santa Fe on August 18, 1846, went unopposed.

An 1847 revolt in Taos resulted in the slaying of the new governor of New Mexico, Charles Bent, but U.S. troops defeated the rebels and executed their leaders. That was the last threat to American sovereignty in the territory. In 1848, the Treaty of Guadalupe Hidalgo officially transferred title of New Mexico, along with Texas, Arizona, and California, to the United States.

Kearny promised New Mexicans that the United States would respect their religion and property rights and would safeguard their homes and possessions from hostile Indians. His troops behaved with a rigid decorum. The United States upheld Spanish policy toward the Pueblos, assuring the survival of their ancestral lands, their traditional culture, and their old religion—which even 3 centuries of Hispanic Catholicism could not do away with.

THE CIVIL WAR As conflict between the North and South flared east of the Mississippi, New Mexico found itself caught in the debate over slavery. Southerners wanted to expand slavery to the western territories, but abolitionists fought a bitter campaign to prevent that from happening. New Mexicans themselves voted against slavery twice, while their delegate to Congress engineered the adoption of a slavery code. In 1861, the Confederacy, after its secession from the Union, laid plans to make New Mexico theirs as a first step toward capturing the West.

In fact, southern New Mexicans, including those in Tucson (Arizona was then a part of the New Mexico Territory), were disenchanted with the attention paid them by Santa Fe and already were threatening to form their own state. So when Confederate Lt. Col. John Baylor captured Fort Fillmore, near Mesilla, and on August 1, 1861, proclaimed all of New Mexico south of the 34th parallel to be the new territory of Arizona, there were few complaints.

The following year, Confederate Gen. Henry Sibley assembled three regiments of 2,600 Texans and moved up the Rio Grande. They defeated Union loyalists in a bloody battle at Valverde, near Socorro; easily took Albuquerque and Santa Fe, which were protected only by small garrisons; and proceeded toward the federal arsenal at Fort Union, 90 miles east of Santa Fe. Sibley planned to replenish his supplies there before continuing north to Colorado, then west to California.

On March 27–28, 1862, the Confederates were met head-on in Glorieta Pass, about 16 miles outside of Santa Fe, by regular troops from Fort Union supported by a regiment of Colorado Volunteers. By the second day, the rebels were in control, until a detachment of Coloradans circled behind the Confederate troops and destroyed their poorly defended supply train. Sibley was forced into a rapid retreat back down the Rio Grande. A few months later, Mesilla was reclaimed for the Union, and the Confederate presence in New Mexico was ended.

THE LAND WARS The various tribes had not missed the fact that whites were fighting among themselves, and they took advantage of this weakness to step up their raids upon border settlements. In 1864, the Navajos, in what is known in tribal history as "The Long Walk," were relocated to the new Bosque Redondo Reservation on the Pecos River at Fort Sumner, in east-central New Mexico. Militia Col. Kit Carson led New Mexico troops in this venture, a position to which he acceded as a moderating influence between the Navajos and those who called for their uncondi-tional surrender or extermination.

It was an ill-advised decision: The land could not support 9,000 people; the government failed to supply adequate provisions; and the Navajo were unable to live peacefully with the Mescalero. By late 1868, the tribes retraced their routes to their homelands, where the Navajos gave up their warlike past. The Mescalero's raids were squashed in the 1870s and they were confined to their own reservation in the Sacramento Mountains of southern New Mexico.

Corralling the rogue Apaches of southwestern New Mexico presented the territory with its biggest challenge. Led by chiefs Victorio, Nana, and Geronimo, these bands wreaked havoc upon the mining region around Silver City. Eventually, however, they succumbed, and the capture of Geronimo in 1886 was the final chapter in New Mexico's long history of Indian wars.

As the Native American threat decreased, more and more livestock and sheep ranchers established themselves on the vast plains east of the Rio Grande, in the San Juan basin of the northwest, and in other equally inviting parts of the territory. Cattle drives up the Pecos Valley, on the Goodnight-Loving Trail, are the stuff of legend; so, too, was Roswell cattle baron John Chisum, whose 80,000 head of beef probably represented the largest herd in America in the late 1870s.

Mining grew as well. Albuquerque blossomed in the wake of a series of major gold strikes in the Madrid Valley, close to ancient turquoise mines; other gold and silver discoveries through the 1870s gave birth to boomtowns—now mostly ghost towns—like Hillsboro, Chloride, Mogollon, Pinos Altos, and White Oak. The copper mines of Santa Rita del Cobre, near Silver City, are still thriving.

In 1879, the Atchison, Topeka, and Santa Fe Railroad sent its main line through Las Vegas, Albuquerque, El Paso, and Deming, where it joined with the Southern Pacific line coming eastward from California. (The Santa Fe station was, and is, at Lamy, 17 miles southeast of the capital.) Now linked by rail to the great markets of America, New Mexico's economic boom period was assured.

But ranching invites cattle rustling and range wars, mining beckons feuds and land fraud, and the construction of railroads has often been tied to political corruption and swindles. New Mexico had all of them, especially during the latter part of the 19th century. Best known of a great many conflicts was the Lincoln County War (1878–81), which began as a feud between rival factions of ranchers and merchants. It led to such utter lawlessness that Pres. Rutherford B. Hayes ordered a federal investigation of the territorial government and the installation as governor of Gen. Lew Wallace (whose novel *Ben-Hur* was published in 1880).

One of the central figures of the Lincoln County conflict was William "Billy the Kid" Bonney, a headstrong youth (b. 1858) who became probably the best-known outlaw of the American West. He blazed a trail of bloodshed from Silver City to Mesilla, Santa Fe to Lincoln, and Artesia to Fort Sumner, where he was finally killed by Sheriff Pat Garrett in July 1881.

By the turn of the century, most of the violence had been checked. The mineral lodes were drying up, and ranching was taking on increased importance. Economic and social stability were coming to New Mexico.

STATEHOOD, ART & ATOMS   Early in the 20th century, its Hispanic citizens having proved their loyalty to the United States by serving gallantly with Theodore Roosevelt's Rough Riders during the Spanish-American War, New Mexico's long-awaited dream of becoming an integral part of the Union was finally recognized. On January 6, 1912, Pres. William Howard Taft signed a bill making New Mexico the 47th state.

Within a few years, Taos began gaining fame as an artists' community. Two painters from the East Coast, Ernest Blumenschein and Bert Phillips, settled in Taos in 1898, lured others to join them, and in 1914 formed the Taos Society of Artists, one of the most influential schools of art in America. Writers and other intellectuals soon followed, including Mabel Dodge Luhan, novelists D. H. Lawrence and Willa Cather, and poet-activist John Collier. Other artists settled in Santa Fe and elsewhere in northern New Mexico; the best known was Georgia O'Keeffe, who lived miles from anywhere in tiny Abiquiu. Today, Santa Fe and Taos are world renowned for their contributions to art and culture.

The construction in 1916 of the Elephant Butte Dam near Hot Springs (now Truth or Consequences) brought irrigated farming back to a drought-ravaged southern New Mexico. Potash mining boomed in the southeast in the 1930s. Native Americans fared well, gaining full citizenship in 1924, two years after the All Pueblo Council was formed to fight passage in Congress of a bill that would have given white squatters rights to Indian lands. And in 1934, with ex-Taos intellectual John Collier as commissioner of Indian Affairs, tribes were accorded partial self-government. The Hispanics, meanwhile, became the most powerful force in state politics, and remain so today.

But the most dramatic development in 20th-century New Mexico was induced by the Second World War. In 1943, the U.S. government sealed off a tract of land on the

Pajarito Plateau, west of Santa Fe, that previously had been an exclusive boys' school. On the site, in utter secrecy, it built the Los Alamos National Laboratory, otherwise known as Project Y of the Manhattan Engineer District—the "Manhattan Project." Its goal: to split the atom and develop the world's first nuclear weapons.

Under the direction of J. Robert Oppenheimer, later succeeded by Norris E. Bradbury, a team of 30 to 100 scientists lived and worked in almost complete seclusion for 2 years. Their work resulted in the atomic bomb, tested for the first time at the Trinity Site, north of White Sands, on July 16, 1945. The bombings of Hiroshima and Nagasaki, Japan, 3 weeks later, signaled to the world that the nuclear age had arrived.

Even before that time, New Mexico was climbing the ladder of stature in America's scientific community. Robert H. Goddard, considered the founder of modern rocketry, conducted many of his experiments near Roswell in the 1930s, during which time he became the first person to shoot a liquid-fuel rocket faster than the speed of sound. Clyde Tombaugh, the discoverer of the planet Pluto in 1930, helped establish the department of astronomy at New Mexico State University in Las Cruces. And former Sen. Harrison (Jack) Schmitt, an exogeologist and the first civilian to walk on the moon in 1972, is a native of the Silver City area.

Today the White Sands Missile Range is one of America's most important astrophysics sites, and the International Space Hall of Fame in nearby Alamogordo honors men and women from around the world who have devoted their lives to space exploration. Aerospace research and defense contracts are economic mainstays in Albuquerque, and Kirtland Air Force Base is the home of the Air Force Special Weapons Center. Los Alamos, of course, continues to be a national leader in nuclear technology.

Despite the rapid approach of the 21st century in many parts of the state, there are other areas still struggling to be a part of the 20th. Many Native Americans, be they Pueblo, Navajo, or Apache, and Hispanic farmers, who till small plots in isolated rural regions, hearken to a time when life was slower paced. But life in New Mexico was never simple, for anyone.

5 Art & Architecture

A LAND OF ART

It's all in the light—or at least that's what many artists claim drew them to northern New Mexico. In truth, the light is only part of the attraction: Nature in this part of the country, with its awe-inspiring thunderheads, endless expanse of blue skies, and rugged desert, is itself a canvas. To record the wonders of earth and sky, the early natives of the area, the Anasazi and Mogollon, imprinted images (in the form of petroglyphs and pictographs) on the sides of caves and on stones, as well as on the sides of pots they shaped from clay dug in the hills.

Today's Native American tribes carry on that legacy, as do the other cultures that have settled here. Life in northern New Mexico is shaped by the arts. Everywhere you turn you'll see pottery, paintings, jewelry, and weavings. You're liable to meet an artist whether you're having coffee in a Taos cafe or walking along Canyon Road in Santa Fe.

The area is full of little villages that maintain their own artistic specialties. Each Indian pueblo has a trademark design, such as **Santa Clara's** and **San Ildefonso's** black pottery and **Zuni's** needlepoint silver work. Navajos are renowned for their silver jewelry, often with turquoise, and for their weaving and sand painting; Apaches are master basket makers. Bear in mind that the images used often have deep symbolic significance. When purchasing art or an artifact, you may want to talk to its maker about what the symbols mean.

Hispanic villages are also distinguished by their artistic identities. **Chimayo** has become a center for Hispanic weaving, while the village of **Cordova** is known for its *santo* (icon) carving. Santos, *retablos* (paintings), and *bultos* (sculptures), as well as works in tin, are traditional devotional arts tied to the Roman Catholic faith. Often these works are sold out of artists' homes in these villages, allowing you to glimpse the lives of the artists and the surroundings that inspire them.

Villagers, whether Hispanic or Native American, take their goods to the cities, where for centuries people have bought and traded. Under the portals along the plazas of Santa Fe, Taos, and Albuquerque, you'll find a variety of works in silver, stone, and pottery for sale. In the cities you'll find streets lined with galleries, some very slick, some more modest. At major markets, such as the **Spanish Market** and **Indian Market** in Santa Fe, some of the top artists from the area sell their works. Smaller shows at the pueblos also attract artists and artisans. The **Northern Pueblo Artists and Craftsman show** at Santa Clara Pueblo in July continues to grow each year.

Drawn by the beauty of the local landscape and respect for indigenous art, artists from all over have flocked here, particularly during the 20th century. And they have established locally important art societies; one of the most notable is the **Taos Society of Artists.** An oft-repeated tale explains the roots of this society. The artists Bert Phillips and Ernest L. Blumenschein were traveling through the area from Colorado on a mission to sketch the Southwest when their wagon broke down north of Taos. The scenery so overwhelmed them that they abandoned their journey and stayed. Joseph Sharp joined them, and still later came Oscar Berninghaus, Walter Ufner, Herbert Dunton, and others. You can see a brilliant collection of some of their romantically lit portraits and landscapes at the Van Vechten Lineberry Museum in Taos. The 100th anniversary marking the artists' "broken wheel" was celebrated in 1998.

A major player in the development of Taos as an artists' community was the arts patron Mabel Dodge Luhan. Herself a writer, she financed the work of many an artist, and in the 1920s she held court for many notables, including Georgia O'Keeffe, Willa Cather, and D. H. Lawrence. This illustrious history goes a long way to explaining how it is that Taos, a town of less than 5,000, has more than 90 arts and crafts galleries and more than 100 resident painters.

Santa Fe has its own art society, begun in the 1920s by a nucleus of five painters who became known as **Los Cinco Pintores.** Jozef Bakos, Fremont Ellis, Walter Mruk, Willard Nash, and Will Shuster lived in the area of dusty Canyon Road (now the arts center of Santa Fe, with more than 1,000 artists, countless galleries, and many museums). Despite its small size, Santa Fe is, remarkably, considered the third largest art market in the United States.

Perhaps the most celebrated artist associated with Northern New Mexico was **Georgia O'Keeffe** (1887–1986), a painter who worked and lived most of her later years in the region. O'Keeffe's first sojourn to New Mexico in 1929 inspired her sensuous paintings of the area's desert landscape and bleached animal skulls. The house where she lived in Abiquiu (42 miles northwest of Santa Fe on U.S. 84) is now open for limited public tours (see chapter 7 for details). The **Georgia O'Keeffe Museum** in Santa Fe, the only museum in the United States entirely dedicated to a woman artist, opened in Santa Fe in 1997.

Santa Fe is also home to the **Institute of American Indian Arts** and the **School of Indian Art,** where many of today's leading Native American artists have studied, including the Apache sculptor Allan Houser (whose works you can see near the State Capitol building and in other public areas in Santa Fe). The best-known Native American painter is R. C. Gorman, an Arizona Navajo who has made his home in Taos for more than 2 decades. Now in his late 50s, Gorman is internationally acclaimed for his bright, somewhat surrealistic depictions of Navajo women. A relative newcomer to national fame is Dan Namingha, a Hopi artist who weaves native symbology into contemporary concerns.

If you look closely, you'll find notable works from a number of local artists. There's Tammy Garcia, a young Taos potter who year after year continues to sweep the awards at Indian Market with her intricately shaped and carved pots. Cippy Crazyhorse, a Cochiti, has acquired a steady following of patrons of his silver jewelry. All around the area you'll see the frescoes of Frederico Vigil, a noted muralist and Santa Fe native. From the village of Santa Cruz comes a new rising star named Andres Martinez, noted for his Picasso-esque portraits of Hispanic village life.

For the visitor interested in art, however, some caution should be exercised: There's a lot of schlock out there targeting the tourist trade. Yet if you persist, you're likely to find much inspiring work as well. The museums and many of the galleries are excellent repositories of local art. Their offerings range from small-town folk art to works by major artists who show internationally.

A RICH ARCHITECTURAL MELTING POT

Nowhere else in the United States are you likely to see such extremes of architectural style as in New Mexico. The state's distinctive architecture reflects the diversity of cultures that have left their imprint on the region. The first people in the area were the Mogollon and Anasazi, who built stone and mud homes at the bottom of canyons and inside caves (which look rather like condominiums to the modern urban eye). **Pueblo-style adobe architecture** evolved and became the basis for traditional New Mexican homes: sun-dried clay bricks mixed with grass for strength, mud-mortared, and covered with additional protective layers of mud. Roofs are supported by a network of *vigas*—long beams whose ends protrude through the outer facades—and *latillas*, smaller stripped branches layered between the *vigas*. Other adapted Pueblo architectural elements include plastered adobe-brick kiva fireplaces, *bancos* (adobe benches that protrude from walls), and *nichos* (small indentations within a wall in which religious icons are placed). These adobe homes are characterized by flat roofs and soft, rounded contours.

To Pueblo style the Spaniards wedded many elements, such as portals (porches held up with posts, often running the length of a home) and enclosed patios, as well as the simple, dramatic sculptural shapes of Spanish mission arches and bell towers. They also brought elements from the Moorish architecture found in southern Spain: heavy wooden doors and elaborate corbels—carved wooden supports for the vertical posts.

With the opening of the Santa Fe Trail in 1821 and later the 1860s gold boom, both of which brought more Anglo settlers, came the next wave of building. New arrivals contributed architectural elements such as neo-Grecian and Victorian influences popular in the middle part of the United States at the time. Distinguishing features of what came to be known as **Territorial-style** architecture can be seen today; they include brick facades and cornices as well as porches, often placed on the second story. You'll also note millwork on doors and wood trim around windows and doorways, double-hung windows, as well as Victorian bric-a-brac.

Santa Fe Plaza is an excellent example of the convergence of these early architectural styles. On the west side is a Territorial-style balcony, while the Palace of Governors is marked by Pueblo-style vigas and oversized Spanish/Moorish doors.

In Santa Fe you'll see the Romanesque architecture of the **St. Francis Cathedral** and **Loretto chapel,** brought by Archbishop Lamy from France, as well as the railroad station built in the **Spanish Mission style**—popular in the early part of this century.

Since 1957, strict state building codes in Santa Fe have required that all new structures within the city's immediate circumference conform to one of two revival styles: Pueblo or Territorial. The regulation also limits the height of the buildings and restricts the types of signs permitted. It also requires buildings to be topped by flat roofs. In 1988 additional citywide standards were established in an effort to impose some degree of architectural taste on new developments.

Albuquerque also has a broad array of styles, most evident in a visit to Old Town. There you'll find the large Italianate brick house known as the **Herman Blueher home** built in 1898; throughout Old Town, you'll find little *placitas*, homes and haciendas built around a courtyard, a strategy developed not only for defense purposes but also as a way to accommodate several generations of the same family in different wings of a single dwelling. **The Church of San Felipe de Neri** at the center of Old Town is centered between two "folk Gothic" towers. This building was begun in a cruciform plan in 1793; subsequent architectural changes resulted in an interesting mixture of styles.

Most notable architecturally in Taos is the **Taos Pueblo,** the site of two structures emulated in homes and business buildings throughout the Southwest. Built to resemble Taos Mountain, which stands behind it, the two structures are pyramidal in form, with the different levels reached by ladders. Also quite prevalent is architecture echoing colonial hacienda style. What's nice about Taos is that you can see historic homes inside and out. You can wander **through Kit Carson's old home;** built in 1825, it's an excellent example of a hacienda and is filled with a fine collection of 19th-century Western Americana. Taos Society artist **Ernest Blumenschein's home** is also a museum. Built in 1797 and restored by Blumenschein in 1919, it represents another New Mexico architectural phenomenon: homes that were added onto year after year. Doorways are typically low, and floors rise and fall at the whim of the earth beneath them. The **Martinez Hacienda** is an example of a hacienda stronghold. Built without windows facing outward, it originally had 20 small rooms, many with doors opening out to the courtyard. One of the few refurbished examples of colonial New Mexico architecture and life, the hacienda is on the National Historic Registry.

As you head into villages in the north, you'll see steep pitched roofs on most homes. This is because the common flat-roof style doesn't shed snow; the water builds up and causes roof problems. In just about any town in New Mexico, you may detect the strong smell of tar, a sure sign that another resident is laying out thousands to fix his enchanting but frustratingly flat roof.

Today very few new homes are built of adobe. Instead, most are constructed with wood frames and plasterboard, and then stuccoed over. Several local architects are currently employing innovative architecture to create a Pueblo-style feel. They incorporate straw bails, pumice-crete, rammed earth, old tires, even aluminum cans in the construction of homes. Most of these elements are used in the same way bricks are used, stacked and layered, then covered over with plaster and made to look like adobe. Often it's difficult to distinguish homes built with these materials from those built with wood-frame construction. West of Taos a number of "earthships" have been built. Many of these homes are constructed with alternative materials, some bermed into the sides of hills, using the earth as insulation and the sun as an energy source.

A visitor could spend an entire trip to New Mexico focusing on the architecture. As well as relishing the wealth of architectural styles, you'll find more subtle elements everywhere. You may encounter an oxblood floor, for example. An old Spanish tradition, oxblood is spread in layers and left to dry, hardening into a glossy finish that's known to last for centuries. You're also likely to see coyote fences—narrow cedar posts lined up side by side—a system early settlers devised to ensure safety of their animals. Winding around homes and buildings you'll see *acequias,* ancient irrigation canals still maintained by locals for watering crops and trees. Throughout the area you'll notice that old walls are whimsically bowed and windows and floors are often crooked, constant reminders of the effects time has had upon even these stalwart structures.

6 Religion & Ritual

Religion has always been a central, defining element in the life of the Native American people. Within the cosmos, which they view as a single whole, all living creatures are mutually dependent. Thus every relationship a human being may have, whether with a person, animal, or even plant, has spiritual significance. A hunter prays before killing a deer, asking the creature to sacrifice itself to the tribe. A slain deer is treated as a guest of honor, and the hunter performs a ritual in which he sends the animal's soul back to its community, so that it may be reborn. Even the harvesting of plants requires prayer, thanks, and ritual.

The Pueblo people believe that their ancestors originally lived underground—which, as the place from which plants spring, is the source of all life. According to their beliefs, the original Pueblos, encouraged by burrowing animals, entered the world of humans—the so-called "fifth" world—through a hole, a sipapu. The ways in which this came about and the deities that the Pueblo people revere vary from tribe to tribe. Most, however, believe this world is bounded by four sacred mountains, where four sacred colors—coral, black, turquoise, and yellow or white—predominate.

There is no single great spirit ruling over this world; instead it is watched over by a number of spiritual elements. Most common are Mother Earth and Father Sun. In this desert land, the sun is an element of both life and death. The tribes watch the skies closely, tracking solstices and planetary movements, to determine the optimal time for crop planting.

Ritualistic dances are occasions of great symbolic importance. Usually held in conjunction with the feast days of Catholic saints (including Christmas Eve), Pueblo ceremonies demonstrate the parallel absorption of Christian elements without the surrendering of traditional beliefs. To this day, communities enact medicine dances, fertility rites, and prayers for rain and for good harvests. The spring and summer corn, or tablita, dances are among the most impressive. Ceremonies begin with an early morning mass and procession to the Plaza; the image of the saint is honored at the forefront. The rest of the day is devoted to song, dance, and feasting, with performers masked and clad as deer, buffalo, eagles, or other creatures.

The all-night Shalako festival at Zuni Pueblo in late November or early December is the most spectacular of the Pueblo ceremonies. Colorfully costumed *kachinas,* or spirit dancers, act out the Zuni story of creation and evolution. Everyone awaits the arrival of the *shalakos,* 12-foot-tall kachinas who bless new and renovated homes in the village.

Visitors are usually welcome to attend Pueblo dances, but they should respect the tribe's requests not to be photographed or recorded. It was exactly this lack of respect that led the Zunis to ban outsiders from attending many of their famous Shalako ceremonies.

Navajos believe in a hierarchy of supernatural beings, the Holy Ones, who can travel on a sunbeam, a thunderbolt, or the wind. At their head is Changing Woman,

Indian Pueblos & Ancient Cultures

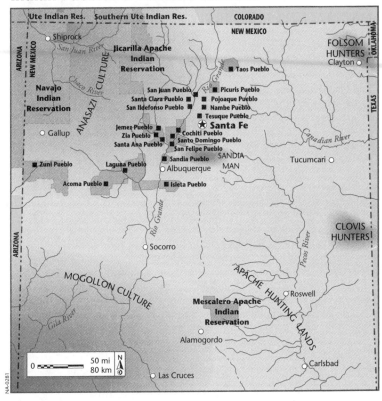

the earth mother, who vigilantly assures humans' well-being by teaching them to live in harmony with nature. Her children, the Hero Twins, ward off our enemies—all but Old Age and Death. Religious symbolism, which pervades art and music, underscores the Navajo belief that their homeland was created by the Holy Ones for them to live in. Typical of Navajo dancing are the *yeibichai* rituals, curative ceremonies marked by circular social dances with long song cycles.

The Apaches have a similar creation belief. They were created by Father Sun and Mother Earth ("the White Painted Lady") to live in the Southwest region, and the Holy Ones' twin sons helped them ward off wicked creatures by teaching them how to ride horses and use a bow and arrow. The most important ceremony among the Apaches today, including the Mescaleros, is the 4-day puberty ritual for young girls. The colorful masked *gahans,* or mountain spirits, perform to celebrate the subject's womanhood, when the White Painted Lady resides within her body.

Catholicism, imposed by the Spaniards, has infused northern New Mexico with an elaborate set of beliefs. This is a Catholicism heavy with iconography, expressed in carved santos (statues) and beautiful retablos (paintings) that adorn the altars of many cathedrals. Catholic churches are the focal point of most New Mexico villages. When you take the high road to Taos, be sure to note the church in **Las Trampas,** as well as the one in **Ranchos de Taos;** both have 3- to 4-foot-thick walls sculpted from adobe and inside have an old-world charm, with beautiful retablos decorating the walls and vigas (roof beams) holding up the roofs.

Hispanics in northern New Mexico, in particular, maintain strong family and Catholic ties, and they continue to honor traditions associated with both. Communities plan elaborate celebrations such as the *quinciniera* for young girls reaching womanhood; and weddings with big feasts and dances in which well-wishers pin money to the bride's elaborately laced gown.

If you happen to be in the area during a holiday, you may even get to see a religious procession or pilgrimage. Most notable is the **pilgrimage to the Santuario de Chimayo,** an hour's drive north of the state capital. Constructed in 1816, the sanctuary has long been a pilgrimage site for Catholics who attribute miraculous healing powers to the earth found in the chapel's anteroom. Several days before Easter, fervent believers begin walking the highway headed north or south to Chimayo, some carrying large crosses, others carrying nothing but a small bottle of water, most praying for a miracle.

In recent years, New Mexico has become known (and in some circles, ridiculed) for **New Age** pilgrims and celebrations. The roots of the local movement are hard to trace. It may have something to do with New Mexico's centuries-old reputation as a place where rebel thinkers come to enjoy the freedom to believe what they want. Native spirituality and deeply felt connection to the land are also factors that have drawn New Agers. At any rate, the liberated atmosphere here has given rise to a thriving New Age network, one that now includes alternative churches, healing centers, and healing schools. You'll find all sorts of alternative medicine and fringe practices here, from aromatherapy to Rolfing—a form of massage that realigns the muscles and bones in the body—and chelation therapy, in which an IV drips ethylene diamine tetra-acetic acid into your blood to remove heavy metals. If those sound too invasive, you can always try psychic surgery.

New Age practices and beliefs have given rise to a great deal of local humor targeting their supposed psychobabble. One pointed joke asks: "How many Santa Feans does it take to change a lightbulb?" Answer: "None. They just form a support group and learn to live in the dark." For many, however, there's much good to be found in the movement. The Dalai Lama visited Santa Fe because the city is seen as a healing center and has become a refuge for Tibetans; notable speakers such as Ram Das and John Bradshaw frequently talk in the area. Many practitioners find the alternatives—healing resources and spiritual paths—they are looking for in the receptive New Mexico desert and mountains.

7 New Mexican Cuisine

New Mexicans are serious about eating, and the area's cuisine reflects the amalgam of cultural influences found here. Locals have given their unique blend of Hispanic and Pueblo recipes a rather prosaic, but direct, label: "New Mexico Cuisine."

Food here isn't the same as Mexican cuisine or even those American variations of "Tex-Mex" and "Cal-Mex." New Mexican cooking is a product of Southwestern history: Native Americans taught the Spanish conquerors about corn—how to roast it and how to make corn pudding, stewed corn, cornbread, cornmeal, and *posole* (hominy)—and they also taught the Spanish how to use chile peppers, a crop indigenous to the New World, having been first harvested in the Andean highlands as early as 4000 B.C. The Spaniards brought the practice of eating beef to the area.

Waves of newcomers have introduced other elements to the food here. From Mexico came the interest in seafood. You'll find fish tacos on many menus as well as shrimp enchiladas and ceviche. New Southwestern cuisine combines elements from various parts of Mexico, such as sauces from the Yucatán Peninsula, and fried bananas

You Say Chili, We Say Chile

It's never "chili" in New Mexico. New Mexicans are adamant that *chile*, the Spanish spelling of the word, is the only way to spell it—no matter what your dictionary might say.

Go ahead, look up *chile*. It's not in there. I guarantee it. Well, maybe it is, but only as a secondary spelling for the word *chili*. Personally, I think that's only been put there to appease the population of New Mexico.

The peppers that New Mexicans will identify only as chiles are grown throughout the state. The climate is perfect for cultivating and drying the small but powerful red and green New Mexican varieties. The state's residents have such a personal attachment to their most famous agricultural product that in 1983 they directed their senior U.S. senator, Pete Domenici, to enter New Mexico's official stand on the spelling of *chile* into the Congressional Record.

The town of Hatch, New Mexico, bills itself as the chile capital of the world. But wherever you travel, chiles make an appearance on every menu in the state. Just about everything you'll order during your stay in New Mexico will be covered with a sauce made from chiles. As a general rule, green chile sauce is hotter than the red chile sauce, but be sure to ask. No matter which you order, your eyes will start watering, your sinuses will drain, and your palate will be on fire after one heaping forkful. Be warned: No amount of water or beer will take the sting away. (Drink milk. A sopaipilla drizzled with honey also might help, too.)

Don't let my words of caution scare you away from genuine New Mexico chiles. The pleasure of eating them outweighs the pain. Start slow, with salsas and chile sauces first, maybe *rellenos* (stuffed peppers) next, then *rajas* (roasted peeled chiles cut into strips). Before you know it, you'll be buying *chile ristras* (dried chiles strung together for cooking as well as decorative use). You might even buy bags of chile powder and maybe a chile plant to bring home. By then you will have realized that you've never had a chili that tasted quite like this—and you'll know why it's a chile.

served with bean dishes, typical of Costa Rica and other Central American locales. You'll also find Asian elements mixed in, such as pot stickers in a tortilla soup.

The basic ingredients of northern New Mexico cooking are three indispensable, locally grown vegetables: **chile, beans,** and **corn.** Of these, perhaps the most crucial is the chile, whether brilliant red or green and with various levels of spicy bite. Red chile is green chile at its ripest stage. Chile forms the base for the red and green sauces that top most northern New Mexico dishes such as enchiladas and burritos. One is not necessarily hotter than the other; spiciness depends on where and during what kind of season (dry or wet) the chiles were grown. You'll also find salsas, generally made with jalapeños, tomatoes, onions, and garlic, used for chip dipping and as a spice on tacos.

Beans—spotted or painted pinto beans with a nutty taste—are simmered with garlic, onion, cumin, and red chile powder and served as a side dish. When mashed and refried in oil, they become *frijoles refritos*. **Corn** supplies the vital dough for tortillas called *masa*. New Mexican corn comes in six colors, of which yellow, white, and blue are the most common.

Even if you are familiar with Mexican cooking, the dishes you know and love are likely to be prepared differently here. The following is a rundown of some regional dishes, a number of which are not widely known outside the Southwest:

Biscochito   A cookie made with anise.

Carne adovada   Tender pork marinated in red chile sauce, herbs, and spices, and then baked.

Chiles relleños   Peppers stuffed with cheese, deep-fried, then covered with green chile sauce.

Chorizo burrito (also called a "breakfast burrito")   Mexican sausage, scrambled eggs, potatoes, and scallions wrapped in a flour tortilla with red or green chile sauce and melted Jack cheese.

Empañada   A fried pie with nuts and currants.

Enchiladas   Tortillas filled with peppers or other foods.

Fajitas   Strips of beef or chicken sautéed with onions, green peppers, and other vegetables and served on a sizzling platter.

Green chile stew   Locally grown chiles cooked in a stew with chunks of meat, beans, and potatoes.

Huevos rancheros   Fried eggs on corn tortillas, topped with cheese and red or green chiles, served with pinto beans.

Pan dulce   A Native American sweetbread.

Posole   A corn soup or stew (called hominy in other parts of the South), sometimes prepared with pork and chile.

Sopaipillas   A lightly fried puff pastry served with honey as a dessert or stuffed with meat and vegetables as a main dish. Sopaipillas with honey have a cooling effect on your palate after you've eaten a spicy dish.

Tamales   Made from cornmeal mush, wrapped in husks and steamed.

Vegetables and nuts   Despite the prosaic name, unusual local ingredients, such as piñon nuts, jicama, and prickly pear cactus, will often be a part of your meals.

Planning a Trip to New Mexico

As with any trip, a little preparation is essential before you start your journey to New Mexico. This chapter will provide you with a variety of planning tools, including information on when to go, how to get there, how to get around once you're there, and some suggested itineraries.

1 Visitor Information

The best place to obtain detailed information is the **New Mexico Department of Tourism,** Lamy Building, 491 Old Santa Fe Trail, Room 751, Santa Fe, NM 87503 (☎ **800/545-2040;** www. newmexico.org). You can also look up other state tourism information at www.swcp.com/nm/.

The various cities and regions of the state are represented by convention and visitors bureaus and/or chambers of commerce. Their addresses, telephone numbers, and Internet addresses are listed in the appropriate chapters in this book.

2 When to Go

THE CLIMATE Summers are hot throughout most of the state, though distinctly cooler at higher elevations. Winters are relatively mild in the south, harsher in the north and in the mountains. Spring and fall are pleasant all over. Rainfall is sparse except in the higher mountains; summer afternoon thunderstorms and winter snows account for most precipitation.

Santa Fe and Taos, at 7,000 feet, have midsummer highs in the 80s Fahrenheit (about 30°C), overnight midwinter lows in the teens (about –11°C). Temperatures in Albuquerque, at 5,000 feet, often run about 10°F (about 2°C) warmer. Snowfall is common from November through March, and sometimes as late as May, though it seldom lasts long. Santa Fe averages 32 inches total annual snowfall. At the high-mountain ski resorts, as much as 300 inches (25 feet) may fall in a season—and stay. The plains and deserts of the southeast and south commonly have summer temperatures in excess of 100°F (38°C).

New Mexico Temperatures & Precipitation

	Jan	Apr	July	Oct	Annual Rainfall
	High–Low (in °F)	High–Low (in °F)	High–Low (in °F)	High–Low (in °F)	(inches)
Alamogordo	57–28	78–40	95–65	79–42	7.5
Albuquerque	47–28	70–41	91–66	72–45	8.9
Carlsbad	60–28	81–46	96–67	79–47	13.5
Chama	33–3	54–22	73–37	52–18	9.3
Cloudcroft	41–19	56–33	73–48	59–36	25.8
Farmington	44–16	70–36	92–58	70–37	7.5
Las Cruces	56–26	79–45	95–66	82–47	8.6
Roswell	56–24	78–42	91–65	75–45	12.7
Ruidoso	50–17	65–28	82–48	67–31	21.4
Santa Fe	40–18	59–35	80–57	62–38	14.0
Taos	40–10	62–30	87–50	64–32	12.1
Truth or Consequences	54–27	75–44	92–66	75–47	8.5

NEW MEXICO CALENDAR OF EVENTS

January

- **New Year's Day.** Transfer of canes to new officials and various dances at most pueblos. Turtle Dance at Taos Pueblo (no photography allowed). January 1. Call ☎ 800/793-4955 or 505/852-4265 for more information.
- **Three Kings' Day.** Pueblos honor their new tribal officers with ceremonies. Various dances are held at all eight northern pueblos. January 6. Call ☎ 800/793-4955 or 505/852-4265 for more information.
- **Winter Wine Festival,** Taos Ski Valley. A variety of wine offerings and food tastings prepared by local chefs. Mid-January. Call ☎ 505/776-2291 for details.

February

- **Candelaria Day Celebration,** Picuris Pueblo. Traditional dances. February 2. Call ☎ 505/587-2519 for more information.
- ✪ **Winter Fiesta,** Santa Fe. Annual retreat from the midwinter doldrums appeals to skiers and nonskiers alike. Highlights include the Great Santa Fe Chile Cookoff; ski races, both serious and frivolous; snow-sculpture contests; snowshoe races; and hot-air balloon rides.

  Where: Santa Fe Ski Area. **When:** The first weekend in February. **How:** Most events are free. Call ☎ 800/777-2489 or 505/984-6760 for information.
- **Mt. Taylor Winter Quadrathlon.** Hundreds of athletes come from all over the West to bicycle, run, cross-country ski and snowshoe up and down this mountain. Mid-February. For information call ☎ 800/748-2142.

March

- **Fiery Food Show,** Albuquerque. Annual trade show features chiles and an array of products that can be made from them. Early March. Call ☎ 505/298-3835.
- **Rio Grande Arts and Crafts Festival,** Albuquerque. Juried show at the State Fairgrounds features 200 artists and craftspeople from around the country. Second week of March. Call ☎ 505/292-7457 for more information.
- **Rockhound Roundup,** Deming. Gems, jewelry, tools, and crafted items are displayed and sold at the Southwest New Mexico State Fairgrounds. Mid-March. Call ☎ 505/546-9281.

• **Easter Weekend Celebration,** Nambé, San Juan, and San Ildefonso Pueblos. Celebrations include masses, parades, Corn Dances, and other dances, such as the Bow and Arrow Dance at Nambé. There's a street party in the historic district of Silver City, and a balloon rally at Truth or Consequences. Late March or early April. Call ☎ **800/793-4955** or 505/852-4265 for information about Pueblo celebrations.

April

• **Albuquerque Founders' Day.** Part of the weekend-long Fiestas de Albuquerque, which include a parade, auction, and street entertainment in Old Town. Third weekend in April. Call ☎ **505/768-3483** for more information.
• **Gathering of Nations Powwow,** University Arena, Albuquerque. Dance competitions, arts-and-crafts exhibitions, and Miss Indian World contest. Mid- to late April. Call ☎ **505/836-2810.**
• **American Indian Week,** Indian Pueblo Cultural Center, Albuquerque. A celebration of Native American traditions and culture. Begins late in the second week of April. Call ☎ **505/843-7270.**
• **Gila Bird & Nature Festival,** Silver City. Guided field trips show the vast array of local birds, reptiles, native plants, land forms, and prehistoric Mimbres culture of the region. Three days in late April. Call ☎ **800/548-9378.**

May

• **Cinco de Mayo Fiestas,** statewide. The restoration of the Mexican republic (from French occupation 1863–67) is celebrated in, among other places, Hobbs (☎ **800/658-6291** or 505/397-3202); Las Cruces at Old Mesilla Plaza (☎ **800/FIESTAS** or 505/524-8521); and Truth or Consequences (☎ **800/ 831-9487** or 505/894-3536). First weekend in May.
• **¡Magnifico! Albuquerque Festival of the Arts.** This celebration features various visual and performing art events held throughout the year. In mid-May the performing arts are honored in several locations. For a schedule of all events, call ☎ **800/733-9918** or 505/842-9918, ext. 3353.
✪ **Taos Spring Arts Festival.** Contemporary visual, performing, and literary arts are highlighted during two weeks of gallery openings, studio tours, performances by visiting theatrical and dance troupes, live musical events, traditional ethnic entertainment, a film festival, literary readings, and more.
   Where: Venues throughout Taos and Taos County. **When:** The first 2 weeks in May. **How:** Tickets are available from many galleries and from the Taos County Chamber of Commerce, P.O. Drawer I, Taos, NM 87571 (☎ **800/ 732-TAOS** or 505/758-3873).

June

✪ **New Mexico Arts and Crafts Fair.** This is the second-largest event of its type in the United States. More than 200 New Mexico artisans exhibit and sell their crafts, and there is nonstop entertainment for the whole family. Hispanic arts and crafts are also on display.
   Where: State Fairgrounds, Albuquerque. **When:** The last weekend in June (on Friday and Saturday from 10am to 10pm and on Sunday from 10am to 6pm). **How:** Admission cost varies. For information, call ☎ **505/ 884-9043.**

July

✪ **Santa Fe Opera.** World-class Santa Fe Opera season runs from the beginning of July to the end of August. Call ☎ **505/986-5955** for more information.

- **Fourth of July Celebrations.** Parades, fireworks, and various other events at Albuquerque, Capitan, Carlsbad, Clayton, Farmington, Gallup, Grants, Las Vegas, Lordsburg, Moriarty, Red River, Roswell, and Socorro. July 4. Call the chambers of commerce in each city or town for more information.

- **Apache Maidens' Puberty Rites,** Mescalero. A 4-day ceremonial concludes on July 4, with a rodeo and the Dance of the Mountain Spirits. Call ☎ 505/671-4495 for more information.

- **Nambé Waterfall Ceremonial.** Several rarely seen traditional dances are presented at Nambé Falls, Nambé Pueblo, on July 4. For more information, call ☎ 505/455-2036.

- **Rodeo de Santa Fe.** Parade, dance, and four rodeo performances take place in Santa Fe the weekend after July 4. Call ☎ 505/471-4300 for details.

- **Taos Pueblo Powwow.** Intertribal competitions in traditional and contemporary dances, Taos Pueblo, the second weekend in July. For more information, call ☎ 505/758-9593.

- **Eight Northern Pueblos Artist and Craftsman Show.** More than 600 Indian artists exhibit their work at one of the eight northern pueblos. Traditional dances, food booths, and more. Third weekend in July. Call ☎ 505/852-4265 for location and exact dates.

- ✪ **Spanish Market.** Santa Fe Plaza. More than 300 Hispanic artists from New Mexico and southern Colorado exhibit and sell their work. Event also features special demonstrations and Hispanic music, food, and pageantry. Last full weekend in July. For more information, call ☎ 505/983-4038.

August

- **Bat Flight Breakfast.** Carlsbad Caverns National Park. An early morning buffet breakfast is served while participants watch the bats return to the cave. Early August. Call ☎ 505/785-2232 for details and exact date.

- **Old Lincoln Days and Billy the Kid Pageant,** Lincoln. First weekend in August. Call ☎ 505/653-4025 for more information.

- ✪ **Intertribal Indian Ceremonial.** Fifty tribes from the United States and Mexico participate in rodeos, parades, dances, athletic competitions, and an arts and crafts show, at Red Rock State Park, east of Gallup. Second week in August. For more information, call ☎ 800/233-4528 or 505/863-3896.

- **Connie Mack World Series Baseball Tournament.** The very best high school players from throughout the United States and Puerto Rico compete in a 7-day, 17-game series, which is closely watched by scouts from college and professional teams. Ricketts Park, Farmington. Second week in August. Call ☎ 505/327-9673 for details.

- ✪ **Annual Indian Market.** Juried Native American art competition, musical entertainment, dances, food booths. Santa Fe Plaza. Third weekend in August. For more information, call ☎ 505/983-5220.

- **Great American Duck Race,** Deming. Devised in a bar in 1979, this event has grown to include a parade, tortilla toss, outhouse race, ballooning, dances, and, of course, the duck race. Takes place on the courthouse lawn ("Duck Downs"). Fourth weekend in August. Call ☎ 888/345-1125 for details.

September

- **The All American Futurity,** Ruidoso. With a purse of $2 million, this is the world's richest quarter horse race. Labor Day at Ruidoso Downs. Call ☎ 505/378-4431.

○ **Chile Festival,** Hatch. New Mexicans celebrate their favorite fiery food item with a festival in the "Chile Capital of the World." Labor Day weekend. Call ☎ 505/267-5050.

• **New Mexico State Fair,** Albuquerque State Fairgrounds. One of America's top 10 state fairs, it features 17 days of Spanish and Indian villages, midway, livestock exhibits, arts and crafts, country-and-western entertainment, and rodeo. Begins Friday after Labor Day. Call ☎ 505/265-1791 for more information.

○ **Fiesta de Santa Fe,** Santa Fe Plaza and surrounding areas. First celebrated in 1712, to commemorate the Spanish reconquest of Santa Fe in 1692, it is the oldest community celebration in the United States. Events include masses, parades, mariachi concerts, and dances. First Friday after Labor Day. Call ☎ 505/988-7575 for more information.

• **Stone Lake Fiesta,** Jicarilla Reservation, 19 miles south of Dulce. Apache festival with rodeo, ceremonial dances, and footrace. September 14 to 15. Call ☎ 505/759-3242, ext. 275 or 277, for more information.

• **Mexican Independence Day.** Parade and dances in Las Cruces at Old Mesilla Plaza (☎ 800/FIESTAS or 505/524-8521) and Carlsbad at San Jose Plaza (☎ 800/221-1224 or 505/887-6516), with a rodeo in Carlsbad. On the weekend closest to September 16.

• **Old Taos Trade Fair.** Reenactment of Spanish colonial living in the 1820s, with craft demonstrations, food, and entertainment. Martinez Hacienda, Taos. Last full weekend in September. For more information, call ☎ 505/758-0505.

• **Taos Fall Arts Festival.** Gallery openings, concerts, and crafts fair in Taos. Third weekend in September to first weekend of October. Call ☎ 800/732-8267 for more information.

• **Shiprock Navajo Fair,** Shiprock. The oldest and most traditional Navajo fair, it features a rodeo, dancing and singing, parade, arts and crafts exhibits. Late September or early October. Call ☎ 800/448-1240 for details.

October

• **The Whole Enchilada Fiesta,** Las Cruces. The world's biggest enchilada (sometimes over 7 feet wide) is created and eaten. Early October. Call ☎ 800/ FIESTAS.

• **Rio Grande Arts and Crafts Festival,** Albuquerque. Features artists and craftspeople from around the country. First and second weekend in October. For more information, call ☎ 505/292-7457.

○ **Kodak Albuquerque International Balloon Fiesta,** Albuquerque. World's largest balloon rally, with races, contests, and special events, including weekend mass ascensions. First to second weekend in October. For more information, call ☎ 800/733-9918.

• **Lincoln County Cowboy Symposium,** Ruidoso. Cowboy poets, musicians, storytellers, chuck-wagon cooks, and artisans gather. Early to mid-October. Call ☎ 800/263-5929.

November

• **Southwest Arts Festival,** Albuquerque. New Mexico's only juried national art event, held at the fairgrounds. Early to mid-November. Call ☎ 505/262-2448 for details.

• **Festival of the Cranes,** Bosque del Apache National Wildlife Refuge, near Socorro. Celebrates the return of 17,000 sandhill cranes (and a few extremely rare whooping cranes) from their summer breeding grounds in Idaho, with four days of guided hikes, lectures, and birding workshops. Third weekend of November. For more information, call ☎ 505/835-0424.

December

- **Yuletide in Taos.** *Farolito* (candle lantern) tours, candlelight dinners, dance performances, art events, ski-area activities. Taos. Throughout December. For more information, call ☎ **800/732-8267.**
- **Our Lady of Guadalupe Fiesta,** Tortugas, near Las Cruces. Pilgrimage to Tortugas Mountain and torchlight descent, followed by mass and traditional Hispanic dances. December 10 to 12. Call ☎ **505/526-8171** for more information.
- **Christmas on the Pecos,** Carlsbad. Pontoon boat rides take place each evening past a fascinating display of Christmas lights on riverside homes and businesses. Thanksgiving to New Year's Eve (except Christmas Eve). Call ☎ **800/221-1224.**
- **Sundown Torchlight Procession of the Virgin.** Vespers at San Juan, Picuris, Tesuque, Nambé, and Taos Pueblos; Matachine Dances at Taos Pueblo; and Buffalo Dances at Nambé Pueblo. December 24. For more information, call ☎ **800/793-4955** or 505/852-4265.
- **Farolito Walks.** On Christmas Eve, streets and rooftops are lined with farolitos, or candles placed inside paper bags to form lanterns. In Santa Fe, take the traditional walk up Canyon Road (call ☎ **505/983-7317** for more information); in Albuquerque, call the Convention and Visitors Bureau (☎ **800/733-9918**) for directions to displays.

3 Staying Healthy

One thing that sets New Mexico apart from most other states is its altitude. Most of the state is above 4,000 feet in elevation, and many heavily traveled areas, including Santa Fe, are at 7,000 feet or above. Getting plenty of rest, avoiding large meals, and drinking lots of nonalcoholic fluids (especially water) can help make the adjustment easier for flatlanders.

The reduced oxygen and humidity at these altitudes can bring on some unique problems, not the least of which is acute **mountain sickness.** Characterized in its early stages by headaches, shortness of breath, appetite loss and/or nausea, tingling in the fingers or toes, lethargy, and insomnia, it ordinarily can be treated with aspirin and a slower pace. If it persists or worsens, you must descend to a lower altitude.

Dehydration is always a concern in the desert. Visitors from humid climates may find New Mexico's dryness pleasant—dry heat is not as oppressive, and sweat evaporates almost immediately, cooling the skin. This is a mixed blessing, however, because many people don't feel thirsty here until they're already significantly dehydrated. Early symptoms of dehydration include headache and lethargy, and these may progress to impaired concentration and irregular heartbeat. If you feel any of these symptoms, immediately find a cool place to rest and drink plenty of water.

Better yet, prevent dehydration by carrying some bottled water with you and sipping it throughout the day, whether or not you feel thirsty. Backpackers and day-hikers should carry a gallon of water per person per day in the summertime. This may seem like an excessive amount (1 gallon of water weighs about 8 lbs.), but my experience has shown that it's necessary if I want to enjoy myself—and it's a bare minimum if you plan to use water for cooking or bathing.

If you're heading into the outdoors, see "Tips for Staying Healthy Outdoors" in chapter 5.

Other things to be wary of are **arroyos,** or dry creek beds that can be quickly filled by flash floods. These may occur without warning in the desert, when the sky above you is clear but it's raining upstream. If water is flowing across a road, *do not* try to drive through it because chances are the water is deeper and is flowing faster than you think. Just wait it out. Flash floods don't last long.

Most people are surprised to learn that water (flash floods) and exposure to cold cause more injuries and deaths in the desert than its heat and dryness do. The same clear skies that bake the desert in sunlight all day allow heat to escape rapidly at night. Evening breezes add to this effect. Hikers, in particular, must be prepared for both heat and cold, especially in the northern mountains where snow can occur at the highest elevations in June and even July. Be especially careful when the weather is both cold and damp. Wool and synthetic fiber fabrics like polypropylene will keep you warm and protect against hypothermia (subnormal body temperature) far better than cotton will.

Another danger of high elevations is **sunburn.** You can burn much faster here than at sea level, because the thinner atmosphere offers less protection from the sun. It's wise to wear sunscreen even when riding in a car on a sunny day.

Finally, if you're in the outdoors, be on the lookout for **snakes**—particularly rattlers. Respect their right to be here, but avoid them. Don't even get close enough to take a picture (unless you have a good zoom lens).

4 Tips for Travelers with Special Needs

FOR TRAVELERS WITH DISABILITIES Throughout New Mexico, steps have been taken to provide access for people with disabilities. Most hotels and even some bed-and-breakfasts have wheelchair-accessible rooms. The **Developmental Disabilities Planning Council** (☎ **800/552-8195**) will provide free information about traveling with disabilities in New Mexico. The brochure *Art of Accessibility* lists hotels, restaurants, and attractions in Albuquerque that are accessible to travelers with disabilities. *The Directory of Recreational Activities for Children with Disabilities* is a list of accessible camps, national forest campgrounds, amusement parks, and individual city services throughout New Mexico. *Access Santa Fe* lists accessible hotels, attractions, and restaurants in the state capital. No matter what, it is advisable to call hotels, restaurants, and attractions in advance to be sure that they are fully accessible, and to specifically reserve rooms equipped for the disabled.

The National Park Service offers the Golden Access Passport, which provides free admittance to any national park, monument, historical site, recreation area, or wildlife refuge in the country. It can usually be obtained, for no charge, from the ranger at the entrance booth in one of these areas. For more information, call the National Park Service Office of Communications at ☎ **505/988-6011.**

FOR SENIORS Travelers over the age of 65—in many cases 60, sometimes even 50—may qualify for special discounts. Some hotels offer seniors rates 10% to 20% lower than the published rates. Many attractions give seniors discounts of up to half off the regular adult admission price. Get in the habit of asking about discounts. Seniors who plan to visit national parks and monuments in New Mexico should consider getting a Golden Age Passport, which gives anyone over 62 lifetime access to any national park, monument, historic site, recreational area, or wildlife refuge that charges an entrance fee. Golden Age Passports can be obtained at any area managed by the National Park Service, typically from the ranger in the entrance booth. There is a one-time $10 processing fee. In New Mexico, contact the **National Park Service Office of Communications** at ☎ **505/988-6011** for more information.

Persons 50 and over can join the **American Association of Retired Persons (AARP),** 601 E St., NW, Washington, DC 20049 (☎ **202/434-AARP**), which arranges many travel discounts for its members. The AARP card is valuable throughout North America.

In addition, there are 24 active Elderhostel locations throughout the state. For information, call **New Mexico Elderhostel** at ☎ **505/473-6267.**

A note about health: Senior travelers are more often susceptible to changes in altitude and may experience heart or respiratory problems. Speak with your physician before your trip.

5 Getting There

If you live overseas, see "Getting to & Around the U.S.," in chapter 4.

BY PLANE

The recently expanded and renovated **Albuquerque International Sunport** (☎ **505/842-4366** for the administrative offices; call the individual airlines for flight information) is the hub for travel to most parts of New Mexico. A secondary hub for southern New Mexico is **El Paso International Airport** (☎ **915/772-4271**) in western Texas. Both airports are served by **American** (☎ 800/433-7300), **America West** (☎ 800/235-9292), **Continental** (☎ 800/523-3273), **Delta** (☎ 800/221-1212), **Frontier** (☎ 800/432-1359), and **Southwest** (☎ 800/435-9792). Additional airlines serving Albuquerque include **Mesa** (☎ 800/637-2247), **Northwest** (☎ 800/225-2525), **TWA** (☎ 800/221-2000), **United** (☎ 800/241-6522), and **US Airways** (☎ 800/428-4322).

There's no shortage of **discounted and promotional fares** that can result in savings of 50% or more. Watch for advertisements in your local newspaper and on TV, or call the airlines. And when you call the airlines, ask for their lowest fares, and ask if it's cheaper to book in advance, fly in midweek, or stay over a Saturday night. Don't stop at the 7-day advance purchase; ask how much the 14- and 30-day plans cost. Decide when you want to go before you call, since many of the best deals are nonrefundable.

BY CAR

Three interstate highways cross New Mexico. The north-south I-25 bisects the state, passing through Albuquerque and Las Cruces. The east-west I-40 follows the path of the old Route 66 through Gallup, Albuquerque, and Tucumcari in the north; while I-10 from San Diego crosses southwestern New Mexico until intersecting I-25 at Las Cruces.

Here are the approximate mileages to Albuquerque from various cities around the United States:

From	Distance (miles)	From	Distance (miles)
Atlanta	1,404	New Orleans	1,157
Boston	2,220	New York	1,997
Chicago	1,312	Oklahoma City	542
Dallas	644	Phoenix	458
Denver	437	St. Louis	1,042
Houston	853	Salt Lake City	604
Los Angeles	811	San Francisco	1,109
Miami	1,970	Seattle	1,453
Minneapolis	1,219	Washington, D.C.	1,883

If you're a member, your local branch of the **American Automobile Association (AAA)** will provide a free trip-routing plan. AAA also has nationwide emergency road service (☎ **800/AAA-HELP**).

See "Getting Around," below, for information about driving within New Mexico.

BY TRAIN

Amtrak has two routes through the state. The *Southwest Chief,* which runs between Chicago and Los Angeles, passes through New Mexico once daily in each direction, with stops in Gallup, Grants, Albuquerque, Lamy (for Santa Fe), Las Vegas, and Raton. A second train, the *Sunset Unlimited,* skims through the southwest corner of the state three times weekly in each direction—between Los Angeles and New Orleans—with stops in Lordsburg, Deming, and El Paso, Texas. Greyhound/Trailways bus lines provide through-ticketing for Amtrak between Albuquerque and El Paso.

You can get a copy of Amtrak's National Timetable from any Amtrak station, from travel agents, or by contacting Amtrak (☎ **800/USA-RAIL;** www.amtrak.com).

PACKAGE TOURS

Of course, you don't really need to take a package tour when traveling to New Mexico, but they are available and may be less expensive than if you booked the trip yourself because group tour operators often secure better rates than individual travelers. You pay one price for a package that varies from one tour operator to the next. Airfare, transfers, and accommodations are always covered, and sometimes meals and specific activities are thrown in. The specifics vary a great deal, so consult your travel agent to find out the best deals at the time you want to travel.

There are some drawbacks: The least expensive tours may put you up at a bottom-end hotel. And since the lower costs depend on volume, some more expensive tours could send you to a large, impersonal property. And since the tour prices are based on double occupancy, the single traveler is almost invariably penalized.

Ask your travel agent to find the best package tours to New Mexico. Many are offered by subsidiaries of the major airlines, including American, Continental, Delta, Northwest, and TWA. **American Express** (☎ **800/241-1700**) also has several tours available.

Tours within the state of New Mexico are offered by the following inbound operators:

Destination Southwest, 20 First Plaza Galeria, Suite 603, Albuquerque, NM 87102 (☎ **800/999-3109** or 505/766-9068; fax 505/766-9065).

Gray Line Tours, 800 Rio Grande NW, Suite 22, Albuquerque, NM 87104 (☎ **800/256-8991** or 505/242-3880; fax 505/243-0692).

Rojotours & Services, P.O. Box 15744, Santa Fe, NM 87506-5744 (☎ **505/474-8333;** fax 505/474-2992).

Sun Tours, 4300 San Mateo Blvd. NE, Suite B-155, Albuquerque, NM 87110 (☎ **505/889-8888;** fax 505/881-4119).

Travel New Mexico, 6101 Candelaria NE, Albuquerque, NM 87110 (☎ **800/333-7159** or 505/883-9718).

6 Getting Around

BY PLANE

Mesa Airlines (☎ **800/MESA-AIR**) flies from Albuquerque to Alamogordo, Carlsbad, Clovis, Farmington, Hobbs, Las Cruces, Roswell, and Silver City.

Cyberdeals for Net Surfers

It's possible to get some great deals on airfare, hotels, and car rentals via the Internet. So go grab your mouse and start surfing—you could save a bundle on your trip. The Web sites highlighted below are worth checking out, especially since all services are free.

Microsoft Expedia (**www.expedia.com**)   The best part of this multipurpose travel site is the "Fare Tracker": You fill out a form on the screen indicating that you're interested in cheap flights to Albuquerque, Santa Fe, or El Paso from your hometown, and, once a week, they'll e-mail you the best airfare deals. The site's "Travel Agent" will steer you to bargains on hotels and car rentals, and you can book everything, including flights, right on line. This site is even useful once you're booked: Before you go, log on to Expedia for oodles of up-to-date travel information, including weather reports and foreign exchange rates.

Travelocity (**www.travelocity.com**)   This is one of the best travel sites out there. In addition to its "Personal Fare Watcher," which notifies you via e-mail of the lowest airfares for up to five different destinations, Travelocity will track the three lowest fares for any routes on any dates in minutes. You can book a flight right then and there, and if you need a rental car or hotel, Travelocity will find you the best deal via the SABRE computer reservations system (a huge database used by travel agents worldwide). Click on "Last Minute Deals" for the latest travel bargains, including a link to "H.O.T. Coupons" (**www.hotcoupons.com**), where you can print out electronic coupons for travel in the United States and Canada.

Trip.Com (**www.thetrip.com**): This site is really geared toward the business traveler, but vacationers can also use Trip.Com's valuable fare-finding engine, which will e-mail you every week with the best city-to-city airfare deals on your selected route or routes.

BY CAR

If you plan to drive your own vehicle to and around New Mexico, give it a thorough road check before starting out. There are lots of wide-open desert and wilderness spaces here, and it is not fun to be stranded in the heat or cold with a vehicle that doesn't run. Check your lights, windshield wipers, horn, tires, battery, drive belts, fluid levels, alignment, and other possible trouble spots. Make sure your driver's license, vehicle registration, safety-inspection sticker, and auto-club membership (if you have one) are valid. Check with your auto insurance company to make sure you're covered when out of state, and/or when driving a rental car.

Gasoline is readily available at service stations throughout the state. Prices are cheapest in Albuquerque and 10% to 15% more expensive in more isolated communities. All prices are subject to the same fluctuations as elsewhere in the United States.

A word of warning: U.S. 666 between Gallup and Shiprock has been labeled America's "most dangerous highway" by *USA Today.* In addition, according to the 1997 edition of *Accident Facts,* New Mexico has the third highest per capita rate of traffic deaths in the nation. Drive carefully!

CAR RENTALS   **Car rentals** are available in every sizable town and city in the state, always at the local airport, and usually also downtown. Widely represented agencies include: **Alamo** (☎ 800/327-9633), **Avis** (☎ 800/831-2847), **Budget** (☎ 800/

Discount Tickets (**www.discount-tickets.com**)   Operated by the ETN (European Travel Network), this site offers discounts on airfares, accommodations, car rentals, and tours. It deals in flights between the United States and other countries, not domestic U.S. flights, so it's most useful for travelers coming from abroad.

E-Savers Programs   Several major airlines offer a free e-mail service known as **E-Savers,** via which they'll send you their best bargain airfares on a weekly basis. Here's how it works: Once a week (usually Wednesday), subscribers receive a list of discounted flights to and from various destinations, both international and domestic. Now here's the catch: These fares are only available if you leave the very next Saturday (or sometimes Friday night) and return on the following Monday or Tuesday. It's really a service for the spontaneously inclined and travelers looking for a quick getaway. But the fares are cheap, so it's worth taking a look. If you have a preference for certain airlines (in other words, the ones you fly most frequently), sign up with them first. Another caveat: You'll get frequent-flier miles if you purchase one of these fares, but you can't use miles to buy the ticket.

Here's a list of airlines and their Web sites, where you can not only get on the e-mailing lists, but also book flights directly:

- **American Airlines:** www.americanair.com
- **Continental Airlines:** www.flycontinental.com
- **TWA:** www.twa.com
- **Northwest Airlines:** www.nwa.com
- **US Airways:** www.usairways.com

Epicurious Travel (**travel.epicurious.com**), another good travel site, allows you to sign up for all of these airline e-mail lists at once.

—Jeanette Foster

527-0700), **Dollar** (☎ 800/369-4226), **Enterprise** (☎ 800/325-8007), **Hertz** (☎ 800/654-3131), and **Thrifty** (☎ 800/367-2277).

Drivers who need wheelchair-accessible transportation should call **Wheelchair Getaways of New Mexico,** 1015 Tramway Lane NE, Albuquerque (☎ **800/408-2626** or 505/247-2626); they rent vans by the day, week, or month.

DRIVING RULES   Unless otherwise posted, the **speed limits** on open roads are 75 miles per hour (120kmph) on interstate highways, 65 miles per hour (105kmph) on U.S. highways, and 55 miles per hour (90kmph) on state highways. Minimum age for drivers is 16. Safety belts are required for drivers and all passengers age 5 and over; children under 5 riding in the front must be in an approved child seat secured by the seat belt; and children 1 year or younger must ride in a child restraint seat in the back seat of the vehicle.

Indian reservations are considered sovereign nations, and they enforce their own laws. For instance, on the Navajo reservation (New Mexico's largest), it is prohibited to transport alcoholic beverages, to leave established roadways, or to travel without a seat belt. Motorcyclists must wear helmets.

EMERGENCIES   The State Highway and Transportation Department has a toll-free hot line (☎ 800/432-4269) providing up-to-the-hour information on road closures and conditions.

New Mexico Driving Times & Distances

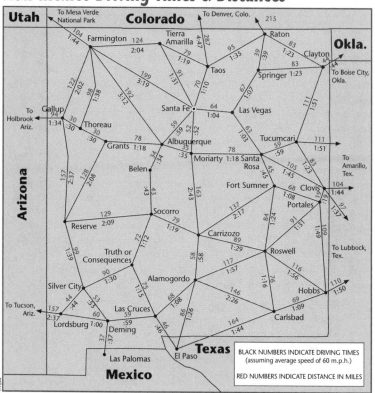

In case of an accident or road emergency, contact the **New Mexico State Police.** District offices are in **Alamogordo** (☎ 505/437-1313), **Albuquerque** (☎ 505/ 841-9256), **Clovis** (☎ 505/763-3426), **Española** (☎ 505/753-2277), **Farmington** (☎ 505/325-7547), **Gallup** (☎ 505/287-4141), **Hobbs** (☎ 505/392-5588), **Las Cruces** (☎ 505/524-6111), **Las Vegas** (☎ 505/425-6771), **Raton** (☎ 505/ 445-5571), **Roswell** (☎ 505/622-7200), **Santa Fe** (☎ 505/827-9300), **Socorro** (☎ 505/835-0741), and **Taos** (☎ 505/758-8878).

Members of the **American Automobile Association** can get free emergency road service by calling AAA's emergency number (☎ 800/222-4357).

MAPS   An excellent state highway map can be obtained from the **New Mexico Department of Tourism** (see "Visitor Information," above). More specific county and city maps are available from the **State Highway and Transportation Department,** 1120 Cerrillos Rd., Santa Fe, NM 87501 (☎ **505/827-5100**). The American Automobile Association (AAA) supplies detailed state and city maps free to members (see "Emergencies," above).

BY TRAIN

Amtrak's northern New Mexico line, the *Southwest Chief,* runs west-east and east-west once daily, with stops in Gallup, Grants, Albuquerque, Lamy (for Santa Fe), Las Vegas, and Raton. The *Sunset Unlimited* connects Lordsburg and Deming with El Paso, Texas, three times weekly each direction. Greyhound/Trailways bus lines provide through-ticketing for Amtrak passengers between Albuquerque and El Paso. For information, call ☎ **800/USA-RAIL.**

FAST FACTS: New Mexico

American Express   The American Express office in Albuquerque is at 5031 Indian School Road NE, Building C, Ste. 200 (☎ **800/219-1023;** fax 505/ 332-5911). To report a lost card, call ☎ **800/528-2122.**

Banks & ATMs   Major statewide banks are the Bank of America, Bank of New Mexico, and NationsBank. They're typically open Monday to Thursday 10am to 3pm and Friday 10am to 6pm. Drive-up windows may be open later. Some may also open Saturday morning. Most branches have cash machines available 24 hours.

Business Hours   In general, business hours are Monday to Friday 9am to 5pm, with many stores also open Friday night and Saturday. Some cities may have different hours; in Las Cruces, for instance, many merchants close their doors on Monday but are open all day Saturday.

Car Rentals   See "Getting Around," earlier in this chapter.

Climate   See "When to Go," earlier in this chapter.

Driving Rules   See "Getting Around," earlier in this chapter.

Drugstores   Twenty-four-hour prescription services are available at selected Walgreen's Drug Stores around the state. Prices at Thrifty and Wal-Mart outlets might be somewhat less. If you're having trouble getting a prescription filled, call the nearest hospital pharmacy.

Emergencies   For emergency medical help or information, call the New Mexico Medical Crisis Center at ☎ **800/432-6866.** The center is open 24 hours a day. In most cities, for police, sheriff, fire department, or ambulance, dial ☎ **911** at any time; otherwise, dial **0** and ask the operator to connect you.

Information   See "Visitor Information," earlier in this chapter.

Language   Spanish is almost as frequently spoken as English. You'll also hear Native American languages—Navajo (the most widely spoken surviving North American Indian dialect), Apache, Tewa, Tiwa, Zuni, Tanoan, and Keresan.

Liquor Laws   Drinking age is 21. Bars close at 2am; on Sunday they are open noon to midnight. Wine, beer, and spirits are sold at licensed supermarkets and liquor stores. A special allowance must be granted for liquor to be dispensed in proximity to any church. It is illegal to transport liquor through most Indian reservations.

Newspapers & Magazines   The *Albuquerque Journal,* published evenings, and the *Albuquerque Tribune,* published mornings, are widely available around the state. The *El Paso Times* is favored in southern New Mexico. National newspapers like *USA Today* and the *Wall Street Journal* can be purchased in cities and major hotels. The state's favorite magazine is *New Mexico,* a high-quality monthly published by the State Tourism and Travel Division since 1923.

Pets   Dogs, cats, and other small pets are accepted at some motels in most parts of the state, though not as universally in Albuquerque and Santa Fe as elsewhere. Some properties require owners to pay a damage deposit in advance. If you bring your pet, keep it well dusted with flea powder: *Plague bacilli,* a disease borne by fleas, is endemic to New Mexico.

Police   In the event of any emergency, contact the New Mexico State Police. Call ☎ **911** or **0** for an operator. Regional telephone numbers are listed in "Getting Around," earlier in this chapter.

Taxes The amount of gross receipts tax varies from town to town, currently ranging from 5.125% to 6.9375%, and is applied to purchases including hotel bills. On top of this amount, local governments add their own lodging tax, which also varies throughout the state (Santa Fe's rate of 4% is fairly average).

Telephone & Fax The area code for the entire state of New Mexico is **505.** No matter where you are in the state, if you're placing a call outside city limits it's usually considered long distance, and you must use the **505** area code.

Time New Mexico is on mountain standard time, 1 hour ahead of the West Coast and 2 hours behind the East Coast. Daylight saving time is in effect from April to October.

For Foreign Visitors   4

Although American fads and fashions have spread across Europe and other parts of the world so much that the United States may seem like familiar territory before your arrival, there are still many peculiarities and uniquely American situations that any foreign visitor will encounter.

1 Preparing for Your Trip

ENTRY REQUIREMENTS

Immigration laws are a hot political issue in the United States these days, and the following requirements may have changed by the time you plan your trip. Check at any U.S. embassy or consulate for current information and requirements.

DOCUMENT REQUIREMENTS Citizens of Canada and Bermuda may enter the United States without passports or visas; they need only proof of nationality, the most common and hassle-free form of which is a passport.

The U.S. State Department has a Visa Waiver Pilot Program allowing citizens of certain countries to enter the United States without a visa for stays of fewer than 90 days of holiday travel. At press time these included Andorra, Argentina, Australia, Austria, Belgium, Brunei, Denmark, Finland, France, Germany, Iceland, Ireland, Italy, Japan, Liechtenstein, Luxembourg, Monaco, the Netherlands, New Zealand, Norway, San Marino, Spain, Sweden, Switzerland, and the United Kingdom. (The program as applied to the United Kingdom refers to British citizens who have the "unrestricted right of permanent abode in the United Kingdom," that is, citizens from England, Scotland, Wales, Northern Ireland, the Channel Islands, and the Isle of Man; and not, for example, citizens of the British Commonwealth of Pakistan.)

Citizens from these countries need only a valid passport and a round-trip air or cruise ticket in their possession upon arrival. If they first enter the United States, they may then visit Mexico, Canada, Bermuda, and/or the Caribbean islands and return to the United States without needing a visa. Further information is available from any U.S. embassy or consulate.

Citizens of countries other than those specified above, or those traveling to the United Sates for reasons or length of time outside the restrictions of the Visa Waiver Program, or those who require waivers of inadmissibility must have two documents: a valid passport, with an expiration date at least 6 months later than the scheduled end of the visit to the United States (some countries are exceptions to the 6-month validity rule—contact any U.S. embassy or consulate for complete information); and a tourist visa, available from the nearest U.S. consulate.

To obtain a visa, the traveler must submit a completed application form (either in person or by mail) with a 1½-inch square photo and the required application fee. There may also be an issuance fee, depending on the type of visa and other factors. Usually you can obtain a visa right away or within 24 hours, but it may take longer during the summer rush period (June to August). If you cannot go in person, contact the nearest U.S. embassy or consulate for directions on applying by mail. Your travel agent or airline office may also be able to provide you with visa applications and instructions. The U.S. consulate or embassy that issues your visa will determine whether you will be issued a multiple- or single-entry visa. The Immigration and Naturalization Service officers at the port of entry in the United States will make an admission decision and determine your length of stay.

MEDICAL REQUIREMENTS   No inoculations are needed to enter the United States unless you're coming from, or have stopped over in, areas known to be suffering from epidemics, particularly cholera or yellow fever.

If you have a disease that needs treatment with medications containing narcotics or drugs requiring a syringe, carry a valid signed prescription from your physician to allay any suspicions that you are smuggling drugs.

CUSTOMS REQUIREMENTS   Every adult visitor may bring in free of duty: 1 liter of wine or hard liquor; 200 cigarettes or 100 cigars (although no Cuban cigars) or 3 pounds of smoking tobacco; and $100 worth of gifts. These exemptions are offered to travelers who spend at least 72 hours in the United States and who have not claimed them within the preceding 6 months. It's strictly forbidden to bring into the country foodstuff (particularly cheese, fruit, cooked meats, and canned goods) and plants (vegetables, seeds, tropical plants, and so on). Foreign tourists may bring in or take out up to $10,000 in U.S. or foreign currency with no formalities; larger sums must be declared to Customs on entering or leaving the country.

INSURANCE

Unlike Canada and Europe, there is no national health-care system in the United States, and the cost of medical care is extremely high. For this reason, we strongly advise every traveler to secure health insurance coverage before setting out. You may want to take out a comprehensive travel policy that covers sickness or injury costs (medical, surgical, and hospital); loss or theft of your baggage; trip-cancellation costs; guarantee of bail in case you are arrested; and costs of accidents, repatriation, or death.

Worldwide Assistance Services is the North American agent for Europ Assistance. They offer travel packages such as Travel Assistance U.S.A., for foreign visitors who will be staying in the United States between 15 days and 6 months. You can reach them at ☎ 800/777-8710 or within the United States at ☎ 800/821-2828.

Canadians should check with their provincial health scheme offices or call **Health-Canada** (☎ 613/957-8739) to find out the extent of their coverage and what documentation and receipts they must take home in case they are treated in the United States.

MONEY

The foreign-exchange bureaus so common in Europe are rare even at airports in the United States and nonexistent outside major cities. Try to avoid having to change foreign money (or traveler's checks denominated in a currency other than U.S. dollars) at a small-town bank or even a branch bank in a big city. In fact, leave any currency other than U.S. dollars at home—it may prove a greater nuisance to you than it's worth. For Albuquerque, Santa Fe, and Taos banks that handle foreign-currency exchange, see the "Fast Facts" sections in chapters 6, 7, and 8, respectively.

CURRENCY The U.S. monetary system has a decimal base: one American **dollar ($1)** = **100 cents (100¢)**.

Dollar bills commonly come in $1 ("a buck"), $5, $10, $20, $50, and $100 denominations (the last two are not welcome when paying for small purchases and are not accepted in taxis). There are also $2 bills (seldom encountered).

There are six denominations of coins: 1¢ (one cent or "penny"), 5¢ (five cents or "nickel"), 10¢ (ten cents or "dime"), 25¢ (twenty-five cents or "quarter"), 50¢ (fifty cents or "half dollar"), and the rare $1 piece.

TRAVELER'S CHECKS Traveler's checks *denominated in U.S. dollars* are readily accepted at most hotels, motels, restaurants, and large stores. But the best place to change traveler's checks is at a bank. Do not bring traveler's checks denominated in other currencies.

CREDIT CARDS A method of payment used quite often is the credit card. Cards commonly used in the United States include Visa (BarclayCard in Britain), Master-Card (Eurocard in Europe, Access in Britain, Chargex in Canada), American Express, Diners Club, Discover, and Carte Blanche. You can save yourself trouble by using "plastic money" rather than cash or traveler's checks in most hotels, motels, restaurants, and retail stores. A growing number of food and liquor stores also accept credit cards. You must have a credit card to rent a car. They can also be used for proof of identity or as "cash cards," enabling you to draw money from banks and automated-teller machines (ATMs) that accept them.

SAFETY

GENERAL Tourist areas are generally safe, but, despite recent reports of decreases in violent crime in many cities, it would be wise to contact the local tourist information offices in New Mexico before you arrive. They can provide you with safety brochures and local information if you're unsure about which neighborhoods to avoid. (See "Visitor Information," in specific city or regional chapters.)

Remember that hotels are open to the public, and in a large hotel, security may not be able to screen everyone who enters. Always lock your room door; don't assume that once inside your hotel you are automatically safe and no longer need to be aware of your surroundings.

New Mexico, and Santa Fe in particular, has one of the highest incidences of rape in the country. Women should not walk alone in isolated places, particularly at night.

DRIVING Question your rental agency about personal safety, or ask for a brochure of traveler safety tips when you pick up your car. Obtain written directions, or a map with the route clearly marked, from the agency to show you how to get to your destination. And, if possible, arrive and depart during daylight hours.

In recent years, "car-jacking," a crime that targets both cars and drivers, has been on the rise in all U.S. cities. Incidents involving German and other international tourists in Miami made news around the world. Rental cars are especially targeted. If you exit a highway into a questionable neighborhood, leave the area as quickly as possible. If you have an accident, even on the highway, stay in your car with the doors locked until you are able to assess the situation or until the police arrive. If you are bumped from behind by another car on the street or are involved in a minor accident with no injuries and the situation appears to be suspicious, motion to the other driver to follow you to the nearest police precinct, a well-lit service station, or an all-night store. Never get out of your car in such situations.

If you see someone on the road who indicates a need for help, do not stop. Take note of the location, drive to a well-lighted area, and telephone the police by dialing ☎ **911.**

Also, make sure that you have enough gasoline in your tank to reach your intended destination, so that you're not forced to look for a service station in an unfamiliar and possibly unsafe neighborhood—especially at night.

2 Getting to & Around the U.S.

GETTING THERE

British travelers should check out **British Airways** (☎ **0345/222-111** in the United Kingdom, or 800/247-9297 in the U.S.), which offers direct flights from London to Phoenix with a connection to Albuquerque, or to Houston and Dallas, where a connection to Albuquerque can be made on another airline. **Continental** (☎ **0800/776-464** in the United Kingdom, or 800/525-0280 in the U.S.) also has direct service from London to Houston with connections to Albuquerque, while **American Airlines** (☎ **0181/572-5555** in London, 0345/789-789 in other parts of the United Kingdom, or 800/433-7300 in the U.S.) has service from London to Dallas with connections to Albuquerque.

For Canadian travelers, both **American** (☎ **800/433-7300** in Canada and the U.S.) and **Canadian Airlines** (☎ **800/665-1177** in Canada, or 800/426-7000 in the U.S.) have nonstop service from Toronto and Montreal to Chicago, where connections can be made to Albuquerque on other airlines. **Delta** (☎ **800/221-1212** in Canada and the U.S.) has service from Montreal to Albuquerque via a direct flight to Cincinnati.

From Australia, **American Airlines** (☎ **800/433-7300** in the U.S.), **Quantas** (☎ **1800/062-123** in Australia, or 800/227-4500 in the U.S.), and United (☎ **800/241-6522** in the U.S.) all offer nonstop service from Sydney to Los Angeles. **Air New Zealand** (☎ **0800/737-000** in New Zealand, or 800/926-7255 in the U.S.) also flies to Los Angeles.

Some large American airlines offer travelers on their transatlantic or transpacific flights special discount tickets under the name **Visit USA,** allowing travel between any U.S. destinations at minimum rates. These tickets are not sold in the United States, and must therefore be purchased before you leave your foreign point of departure. This system is the best, easiest, and fastest way to see the United States at low cost. You should obtain information well in advance from your travel agent or the office of the airline concerned, since the conditions attached to these discount tickets can be changed without advance notice.

The visitor arriving by air, no matter what the point of entry, should cultivate patience before setting foot on U.S. soil. Getting through Immigration control may take as long as 2 hours on some days, especially summer weekends. Add the time it takes to clear Customs and you'll see that you should make very generous allowances for delays when coordinating connections between international and domestic flights—an average of 2 to 3 hours at least.

In contrast, travelers arriving by car or by rail from Canada will find that the border-crossing formalities have been streamlined practically to the vanishing point.

And air travelers from Canada, Bermuda, and some places in the Caribbean can sometimes go through Customs and Immigration at the point of departure, which is much quicker and less painful.

For further information about transportation to New Mexico, see chapter 3, "Planning a Trip to New Mexico."

GETTING AROUND THE U.S.

BY CAR   Car culture reigns supreme in America, and driving will give you the freedom to make, and alter, your own itinerary. And it offers the possibility of visiting some of the off-the-beaten-path locations, places that cannot be reached easily by public transportation. For information on renting cars in the United States, see "Getting Around" in chapter 3, and "Automobile Organizations" and "Automobile Rentals" in "Fast Facts: For the Foreign Traveler," below.

Please note that in the United States we drive on the **right side of the road** as in Europe, not on the left side as in the United Kingdom, Australia, and New Zealand.

BY TRAIN   Long-distance trains in the United States are operated by **Amtrak** (☎ 800/872-7245; www.amtrak.com), the national rail passenger corporation. International visitors can buy a **USA Railpass,** good for 15 or 30 days of unlimited travel on Amtrak. Prices in 1998 for a 15-day pass were $285 off-peak, $425 peak; a 30-day pass costs $375 off-peak, $535 peak. (June 1 through September 7 is considered peak season.) With a foreign passport, you can also buy passes at some Amtrak offices in the United States, including locations in Boston, Chicago, Los Angeles, Miami, New York, San Francisco, and Washington, D.C. Reservations are generally required and should be made for each part of your trip as early as possible. Even cheaper than the above are **regional USA Railpasses,** allowing unlimited travel through a specific section of the United States. Reservations are generally required and should be made for each part of your trip as early as possible.

Visitors should be aware of the limitations of long-distance rail travel in the United States. With a few notable exceptions, service is rarely up to European standards: Delays are common, routes are limited and often infrequently served, and fares are rarely much lower than discount airfares. Thus, cross-country train travel should be approached with caution.

BY BUS   Although ticket prices for short bus trips between cities are often the most economical form of public transit, at this writing bus passes are priced slightly higher than similar off-peak train passes, and the 60-day version costs more than a comparable peak season rail pass. Greyhound (☎ 800/231-2222; www.greyhound.com), the sole nationwide bus line, offers an **Ameripass** for unlimited travel anywhere on its system. In 1998, prices were $199 for 7 days, $299 for 15 days, $409 for 30 days, and $599 for 60 days. Senior citizen discounts are available for those 62 and over. Bus travel in the United States can be both slow and uncomfortable, so this option is not for everyone. Furthermore, bus stations are often situated in undesirable neighborhoods.

FAST FACTS: For the Foreign Traveler

Automobile Organizations   Auto clubs will supply maps, suggested routes, guidebooks, accident and bail-bond insurance, and emergency road service. The major auto club in the United States, with 955 offices nationwide, is the **American Automobile Association (AAA).** Members of some foreign auto clubs have reciprocal arrangements with the AAA and enjoy its services at no charge. If you belong to an auto club in your home country, inquire about AAA reciprocity before you leave. You may be able to join the AAA even if you're not a member of a reciprocal club; to inquire, call the AAA at ☎ **800/881-7585.** The AAA can provide you with an **International Driving Permit,** validating your foreign license. In addition, some automobile-rental agencies now provide many of these same services.

Automobile Rentals   To rent a car you will need a major credit or charge card and a valid driver's license. In addition, you usually need to be at least 25 years old; **Budget** (☎ **800/527-0700**), however, has a minimum age of 21. Be sure to return your car with the same amount of gas you started out with, since rental companies charge excessive prices for gasoline. See "Getting Around by Car," in individual city and regional chapters.

Climate   See "When to Go," in chapter 3.

Currency   See "Preparing for Your Trip," earlier in this chapter.

Electricity   The United States uses 110 to 120 volts AC (60 cycles), compared with 220 to 240 volts AC (50 cycles), as in most of Europe. In addition to a 100-volt transformer, small appliances of non-American manufacture, such as hair dryers or shavers, will require a plug adapter with two flat, parallel pins.

Embassies & Consulates   There is one consulate in New Mexico, the **Mexican Consulate,** at 400 Gold Ave. SW, Suite 100, Albuquerque, NM 87102 (☎ **505/ 247-2147**). All embassies are located in Washington, D.C.; some consulates are located in major U.S. cities, and most countries maintain a mission to the United Nations in New York City. The embassies and consulates of the major English-speaking countries—Australia, Canada, the Republic of Ireland, New Zealand, and the United Kingdom—are listed below. If you are from another country, you can get the telephone number of your embassy by calling "Information" in Washington, D.C. (☎ **202/555-1212**).

The embassy of **Australia** is at 1601 Massachusetts Ave. NW, Washington, DC 20036 (☎ **202/797-3000**). There is an Australian consulate at Century Plaza Towers, 19th Floor, 2049 Century Park East, Los Angeles, CA 90067 (☎ **310/229-4800**). The consulate in New York is located temporarily at 1 Liberty Plaza, 37th Floor, New York, NY 10006 (☎ **212/408-8400**).

The embassy of **Canada** is at 501 Pennsylvania Ave. NW, Washington, DC 20001 (☎ **202/682-1740**). There's a Canadian consulate in Los Angeles at 550 S. Hope St., 9th Floor, Los Angeles, CA 90071 (☎ **213/346-2700**). The one in New York is located at 1251 Ave. of the Americas, New York, NY 10020 (☎ **212/596-1600**).

The embassy of the **Republic of Ireland** is at 2234 Massachusetts Ave. NW, Washington, DC 20008 (☎ **202/462-3939**). The consulate in San Francisco is located at 44 Montgomery St., Suite 3830, San Francisco, CA 94104 (☎ **415/ 392-4214**). The consulate in New York is at 345 Park Ave., 17th Floor, New York, NY 10022 (☎ **212/319-2555**).

The embassy of **New Zealand** is at 37 Observatory Circle NW, Washington, DC 20008 (☎ **202/328-4800**). The consulate in Los Angeles is located at 12400 Wilshire Blvd., Suite 1150, Los Angeles, CA 90025 (☎ **310/207-1605**). The consulate in New York is at 780 Third Ave., Suite 1904, New York, NY 10017-2024 (☎ **212/832-4038**).

The embassy of the **United Kingdom** is at 3100 Massachusetts Ave. NW, Washington, DC 20008 (☎ **202/462-1340**). The consulate in Los Angeles is located at 11766 Wilshire Blvd., Suite 400, Los Angeles, CA 90025 (☎ **310/ 477-3322**). The consulate in New York is at 845 Third Ave., New York, NY 10022 (☎ **212/745-0200**).

Emergencies   Call ☎ **911** to report a fire, call the police, or get an ambulance. This is a toll-free call (no coins are required at a public telephone). Another useful way of reporting an emergency is to call the telephone company operator by dialing ☎ **0.**

Gasoline (Petrol)   One U.S. gallon equals 3.8 liters or .83 Imperial gallon. There are usually several grades (and price levels) of gasoline available at most gas stations, and their names change from company to company. Unleaded gas with the highest octane rating is the most expensive; however, most rental cars take the least expensive "regular" unleaded gas. Additionally, the price is often lower if you pay in cash instead of by credit or charge card. Most gas stations now offer lower-priced self-service gas pumps—in fact, some gas stations, particularly at night, are all self-service.

Holidays   On the following legal national holidays, banks, government offices, post offices, and many stores, restaurants, and museums are closed: January 1 (New Year's Day); the third Monday in January (Dr. Martin Luther King Jr.'s birthday observed); the third Monday in February (Presidents' Day, George Washington's birthday observed); the last Monday in May (Memorial Day); July 4 (Independence Day); the first Monday in September (Labor Day); the second Monday in October (Columbus Day); November 11 (Veterans' Day/ Armistice Day); fourth Thursday in November (Thanksgiving); and December 25 (Christmas). Also, the Tuesday following the first Monday in November is Election Day and is a legal holiday in presidential-election years (next in 2000).

Legal Aid   If you are charged with a minor infraction (for example, speeding on the highway), never attempt to pay the fine directly to a police officer; you may wind up arrested on the much more serious charge of attempted bribery. Pay fines by mail or directly to the clerk of the court. If you're accused of a more serious offense, it's wise to say and do nothing before consulting a lawyer. Under U.S. law, an arrested person is allowed one telephone call to a party of his or her choice. Call your embassy or consulate.

Mail   Domestic **postage rates** are 20¢ for a postcard and 32¢ for a letter. Check with any local post office for current international postage rates to your home country.

Generally found at intersections, **mailboxes** are blue with a red-and-white stripe and carry the designation **U.S. MAIL.** If your mail is addressed to a U.S. destination, don't forget to add the five-digit **postal code,** or ZIP (zone improvement plan) code, after the two-letter abbreviation of the state to which the mail is addressed (CA for California, NM for New Mexico, NY for New York, and so on).

Medical Emergencies   For emergency medical help or information, call the New Mexico Medical Crisis Center at ☎ **800/432-6866.** The center is open 24 hours a day.

Newspapers & Magazines   The airmail editions of foreign newspapers and magazines are on sale only belatedly, and usually only at airports and international bookstores in the largest cities.

Taxes   In the United States there is no VAT (value-added tax) or other indirect tax at a national level. Every state, and each county and city in it, has the right to levy its own local tax on purchases, including hotel and restaurant checks, airline tickets, and so on. Taxes are already included in the price of certain services, such as public transportation, cab fares, telephone calls, and gasoline. The amount of gross receipts tax varies from town to town, currently ranging from 5.125% to 6.9375%, and is applied to purchases including hotel bills. On top of this amount, local governments add their own lodging tax, which also varies throughout the state (Santa Fe's rate of 4% is fairly average).

Telephone   The telephone system in the United States is run by private corporations, so rates, especially for long-distance service and operator-assisted calls, can vary widely—even on calls made from public telephones. Local calls in the United States usually cost 35¢, as is the case throughout New Mexico.

Generally, hotel surcharges on long-distance and local calls are astronomical. It's typically cheaper to call collect, use a telephone charge card, or use a **public pay telephone,** which you'll find clearly marked in most public buildings and private establishments as well as on the street. Outside metropolitan areas, public telephones are more difficult to find. Gas stations and fast-food restaurants are your best bet. Many convenience groceries and packaging services sell **prepaid calling cards** in denominations up to $50; these can be the least expensive way to call home. Many public phones at airports now accept American Express, MasterCard, and Visa credit cards.

Most **long-distance and international calls** can be dialed directly from any phone (stock up on quarters if you're calling from a pay phone or use a telephone charge card). For calls to Canada and other parts of the United States, dial **1** followed by the area code and the seven-digit number. For international calls, dial **011** followed by the country code (Australia, 61; Republic of Ireland, 353; New Zealand, 64; United Kingdom, 44), then the city code (for example, 171 or 181 for London, 121 for Birmingham) and the telephone number of the person you wish to call.

For reverse-charge (collect) calls, and for person-to-person calls, dial 0 (zero, not the letter "O") followed by the area code and number you want; an operator will then come on the line, and you should specify that you are calling collect, or person-to-person, or both. If your operator-assisted call is international, ask for the overseas operator.

For local **directory assistance** ("information"), dial **411;** for long-distance information, dial **1,** then the appropriate area code and **555-1212.**

Time   The United States is divided into six **time zones:** From east to west, eastern standard time (EST), central standard time (CST), mountain standard time (MST), Pacific standard time (PST), Alaska standard time (AST), and Hawaii standard time (HST). Always keep the changing time zones in mind if you are traveling (or even telephoning) across long distances in the United States. For example, noon in New York City (EST) is 11am in Chicago (CST), 10am in Santa Fe (MST), 9am in Los Angeles (PST), 8am in Anchorage (AST), and 7am in Honolulu (HST).

New Mexico is on mountain standard time (MST), 7 hours behind Greenwich mean time.

Daylight saving time is in effect from the first Sunday in April through the last Saturday in October (actually, the change is made at 2am on Sunday), except in Arizona (excluding the large Navajo Indian Reservation, which does observe the change), Hawaii, part of Indiana, and Puerto Rico. Daylight saving time moves the clock 1 hour ahead of standard time. (Americans use the adage "spring ahead, fall back" to remember which way to change their clocks and watches.)

Tipping   This is part of the American way of life, based on the principle that one should pay for any special service received. Often service personnel receive little direct salary and must depend on tips for their income. Here are some rules of thumb:

Bartenders: 10% to 15% of the bill

Bellhops: $1 per piece of luggage; $3 to $5 for a lot of baggage

Cab drivers: 15% of the fare

Cafeterias, fast-food restaurants: no tip

Chambermaids: $1 a day

Checkroom attendants (restaurants, theaters): $1 per garment

Cinemas, movies, theaters: no tip

Doormen (hotels or restaurants): not obligatory

Gas-station attendants: no tip

Hairdressers: 15% to 20% of the bill

Redcaps (airport and railroad stations): $1 per piece of luggage; $3 to $5 for a lot of baggage

Restaurants, nightclubs: 15% to 20% of the check

Valet parking attendants: $1 per vehicle

Toilets   Foreign visitors often complain that public toilets are hard to find in most U.S. cities. True, there are none on the streets, but the visitor can usually find one in a bar, restaurant, hotel, museum, department store, gas station, or train or bus station. Some public places are equipped with pay toilets, which require you to insert one or more coins into a slot on the door before it will open.

5

The Active Vacation Planner

If outdoor activities are what you're looking for, I can't think of a better place to visit than New Mexico. From the dry flatlands of the southern regions of the state to the mountains and forests of north-central New Mexico, there is something available for everyone in every corner of the state. Whether you're interested in a short day hike or overnight horse trips, groomed ski trails or backcountry adventures, you won't be disappointed.

For more in-depth coverage of the activities that follow, contact some of the local outfitters or organizations that appear under "Outdoor Activities" and "Getting Outside" in regional chapters later in this book.

1 Ballooning, Hang Gliding & Soaring

You can't hear about New Mexico without hearing about **hot-air ballooning**—the two seem to go hand in hand. In fact, one of the state's greatest attractions is the annual Kodak Albuquerque International Balloon Fiesta in early October (see "New Mexico Calendar of Events" in chapter 3). Thousands of people travel from all over the world to see hundreds of huge, colorful balloons take flight simultaneously, and every year, hundreds more experience a flight on their own. It is possible to charter hot-air balloon rides in all regions of the state. Most companies offer a variety of packages from the standard flight to a more elaborate all-day affair that includes meals. For more information, you should contact individual chambers of commerce.

Hang gliding and **soaring** have reached new levels of popularity in New Mexico in the past few years. Favorite spots for hang gliding include the Sandia Mountains near Albuquerque and the area around Hobbs. Soaring in gliders is popular in Santa Fe, Taos, and Albuquerque. It's a wonderful experience—you'll feel like you're just floating in midair surrounded by absolute silence. See individual city or regional chapters for more information, or contact local chambers of commerce.

2 Bird Watching

Bird watchers know that New Mexico is located directly on the Central Flyway, which makes it a great spot for this activity all year long. Each different region of the state offers refuge to a wide variety of birds, including everything from doves, finches, bluebirds, and roadrunners (the state bird) to the rare and wonderful whooping crane. The bald eagle is also frequently spotted during winter and spring migrations. There are several wildlife refuge centers in New Mexico, most notably the **Bosque del Apache National Wildlife Refuge** (93 miles south of Albuquerque; ☎ **505/835-1828**). Others include the **Rio Grande Nature Center** (Albuquerque; ☎ **505/ 344-7240**), the **Las Vegas National Wildlife Refuge** (5 miles southeast of Las Vegas; ☎ **505/425-3581**), and **Bitter Lake National Wildlife Refuge** (13 miles northeast of Roswell; ☎ **505/622-6755**). Some common sightings at these areas might include sandhill cranes, snow geese, a wide variety of ducks, and falcons. New Mexico is also home to an amazing variety of hummingbirds. In fact, in early 1996, New Mexico was able to add the Cinnamon Hummingbird to its list of birds. Its sighting in Santa Teresa marked the occasion of only its second sighting in the United States. Four other birds were also added to New Mexico's list in 1996—the Acadian Flycatcher, the Berylline Hummingbird, the Black Skimmer, and the Ruff. This is simply astonishing, considering the fact that most states are removing species from their lists. The number of verified species in New Mexico is now 481. New Mexico ranks fourth (behind Texas, California, and Arizona) in the number of birds that live in or have passed through the state.

If you're interested in bird watching during your trip to New Mexico, contact the state office of the **National Audubon Society,** P.O. Box 9314, Santa Fe, NM 87504 (☎ **505/983-4609**). They'll be able to tell you who to contact in individual towns and cities for more information.

3 Hiking

Everywhere you go in New Mexico you'll find opportunities for hiking adventures. The terrain and climate are as varied as you might find during a trip to three or four different states. There's the heat and flatness of the desert plains, and the cold, forested alpine areas of the northern region of the state. You can visit both (going from 3,000 to 13,000 feet in elevation) and anything in between in the same day without much trouble. As you read in chapter 2, the plant and animal life you'll see along the way is as varied and interesting as the terrain. You can go hiking virtually anywhere you please (except on private land or Native American land without permission); however, most maintained and developed trails are in the northern region of the state. You can hike on your own or with a guide, or even with a llama to carry your gear for you.

I mention some of the best hiking trails in each region of the state below. See later chapters for details about outfitters, guides, llama trekking services, and who to contact for maps and other information. For general information, contact the **U.S. Forest Service,** 517 Gold Ave. SW, Albuquerque, NM 87102 (☎ **505/ 842-3292**); or specific forests: **Carson National Forest,** 208 Cruz Alta Rd., Taos, NM 87571 (☎ **505/758-6201**); **Cíbola National Forest,** 2113 Osuna Rd. NE, Albuquerque, NM 87113 (☎ **505/761-4650**); **Gila National Forest,** 3005 E. Camino del Bosque, Silver City, NM 88061 (☎ **505/388-8201**); **Lincoln National Forest,** 1101 New York Ave., Alamogordo, NM 88310 (☎**505/434-7200**); or **Santa Fe National Forest,** P.O. Box 1689 (NM 475), Santa Fe, NM 87504 (☎ **505/ 438-7840**).

An excellent book for avid hikers is *The Hiker's Guide to New Mexico* by Laurence Parent (Falcon Press Publishing Co., 1995). It includes a large number of hikes for a wide range of ability levels.

BEST HIKES   If you're around **Santa Fe,** I'd recommend hiking Santa Fe Baldy. It's a hike you can do in a day if you start out early, or if you'd like a less strenuous walk, plan to spend 1 night camping. This is a good first hike for those who came from lower altitudes but who are in good shape. Once you get to the top you'll have great views of the Sangre de Cristo and Jemez mountains, as well as the Rio Grande Valley. See chapter 7 for details.

If you're looking for something more challenging in the **north-central region** of the state, head up to Taos and give Wheeler Peak your best shot. The hike up New Mexico's highest peak is about 15 miles round-trip. If you're incredibly well conditioned you might be able to do the hike in a day. Otherwise, plan on hiking and camping for several days. The pain of getting to the top is well worth it—at the top you'll find some of New Mexico's most spectacular views. See chapter 8 for details.

If you want a much less difficult hike in the Taos area, try hiking down into Rio Grande Gorge. It's beautiful and can be hiked year-round. See chapter 8 for details.

In the **northeastern region** of New Mexico I'd recommend taking the 1-mile loop around Capulin Volcano. The crater rim offers great views and you can look down into the extinct caldera. It's a nice, easy walk for those who'd rather not overexert themselves. Any time is good for this hike except winter. See chapter 9 for details.

If you're heading to the **northwestern region** of the state, try hiking the Bisti/ De-Na-Zin Wilderness, 37 miles south of Farmington. Though there are no marked trails, the hiking is easy in this area of low, eroded hills and fanciful rock formations. You may see petrified wood or fossils from the dinosaurs that lived here millions of years ago. A walk to one of the more interesting areas is about 4 miles round-trip, and is best taken in spring or fall. See chapter 10 for details.

This region is also home to El Malpais National Monument, where you can hike into great lava tubes. The hiking is easy, but it's also easy to get lost in this area, so be sure to carry a compass and a topographical map. Also in El Malpais National Monument is the Zuni-Acoma Trail, which used to connect the Pueblo villages of Zuni and Acoma. It is a trail thought to be close to 1,000 years old. If you're up for this moderate to difficult 15-mile (round-trip) hike, you'll be trekking across three lava flows, and you won't have to fight for trail space with other hikers. This hike is an especially good one to take in spring or fall. See chapter 10 for details.

In the **southwestern region** is the Gila National Forest, which has more than 1,400 miles of trails ranging in length and difficulty. Your best bet is to purchase a guidebook devoted entirely to hiking the Gila Forest, but popular areas include the Crest Trail, West Fork Trail, and the Aldo Leopold Wilderness. One favorite day hike in the forest is The Catwalk, a moderately strenuous hike along a series of steel bridges and walkways suspended over Whitewater Canyon. See chapter 11 for details.

In the **southeastern region,** you'll find one of my favorite places in all of New Mexico: White Sands National Monument. Hiking the white sand dunes is easy, if sometimes awkward, and the magnificence of the view is unsurpassed. Be sure to take sunscreen, plenty of water, and a compass on this hike; there's no shade, and it's difficult to tell one dune from another here. See chapter 12 for more information.

Of course, there are hundreds of other hikes from which to choose. You should consider purchasing a hiking book, or contacting the National Park Service, National Forest Service, Bureau of Land Management, or other appropriate agency directly.

4 Fishing

There are scores of **fishing** opportunities in New Mexico. Warm-water lakes and streams are home to large- and small-mouth bass, walleye, stripers, catfish, crappie, and bluegill. In cold water lakes and streams, look for the state fish, the Rio Grande cutthroat, as well as kokanee salmon and rainbow, brown, lake, and brook trout.

Two of the best places for fishing are the San Juan River near Farmington, and Elephant Butte Lake, not far from Truth or Consequences. The San Juan River offers excellent trout fishing and is extremely popular with fly fishers. Elephant Butte is great for bass fishing; in fact, it is considered one of the top 10 bass fishing locations in the United States.

There are all sorts of other possibilities, such as the Rio Grande River, the Chama, Jemez, and Gila watershed areas, and the Pecos River. It would be impossible to describe them all in any detail here, so I recommend Ti Piper's *Fishing in New Mexico* (University of New Mexico Press, 1994). It's an excellent and wonderfully comprehensive book that describes every waterway in New Mexico in great detail. It includes information about regulations and descriptions of the types and varieties of fish you're likely to catch in New Mexico.

Fishing licenses, required of anyone 12 or older, cost nonresidents $39 a year, which runs April 1 to March 31. A 1-day license costs $8, and a 5-day license is $16. In addition, vendors who sell the licenses typically charge a $1 fee for their services. A Wildlife Habitat Improvement stamp ($5) must also be purchased for fishing in national forests or Bureau of Land Management–controlled waters. For recorded information regarding licensing and everything else you might need to know, call ☎ 800/ASK-FISH.

It's important to note that while it is not necessary to have a fishing license in order to fish on Indian reservation land, you must still receive written permission and an official tribal document before setting out on any fishing trips. Phone numbers for individual tribes and pueblos are listed separately in the regional and city chapters later in this book.

5 Mountain Biking

It's awesome to pedal out into the dry New Mexico air and see not only incredible terrain but ancient history as well. Just about the entire state is conducive to the sport, making it one of the most popular places in the United States for avid mountain bikers.

Albuquerque has some excellent and very challenging trails in the Sandia Mountains, as well as less strenuous routes west of town through Petroglyphs National Monument. See chapter 6. In **Santa Fe** you'll find some very rugged and steep mountain trails, most accessed off the road to Santa Fe Ski Area. See chapter 7. Despite its name, the La Tierra Torture Trail system west of the city is a less extreme area. **Taos** is a rider's paradise, with lots of extreme mountain trails, as well as some that are purely scenic, such as the west rim of the Rio Grande Gorge. See chapter 8.

In northwestern New Mexico, you can even ride around El Malpais National Monument, the **Grants** area, in the middle of winter. It's one of the best riding areas, in terms of scenic variety, in the state. You can also take your bike with you to Chaco Culture National Historical Park and ride from Anasazi ruin to ruin. The **Farmington** area and its Lions Wilderness Park and Road Apple Trail, both on the north end of town, are rideable even through the winter. See chapter 10.

In the southwestern region, bikes are not allowed in the Gila Wilderness, but they are permitted in other parts of Gila National Forest; you'll find terrific trails that originate in **Silver City**. In the southeast region, the **Cloudcroft** area has some excellent trails, a few that explore history as well as natural terrain.

Two books to check out are *Mountain Biking in Northern New Mexico* (University of New Mexico, 1994), which lists the 25 best rides in the area, and Sarah Bennett's *Mountain Biker's Guide to New Mexico* (Falcon Press, 1994).

If you don't want to strike out on your own, **New Mexico Mountain Bike Adventures,** 49 Main St., Cerrillos, NM 87010 (☎ **505/474-0074**) sponsors day and half-day trips as well as 3- to 6-day camping trips for all levels of ability. Multiday trips include the Jemez Mountains, a Continental Divide ride, and the Apache and Gila National Forests. **Sun Mountain Bike Company,** 121 Sandoval St., Santa Fe, NM 87501 (☎ **505/820-2902**), runs bike tours from April through October to some of the most spectacular spots in Northern New Mexico. Trips range from an easy Glorieta Mesa to the technical Glorieta Baldy.

6 Rockhounding

New Mexico abounds in rockhounding opportunities. Of course, you can't just go around picking up and taking rocks whenever it strikes your fancy—in many places it's illegal to take rocks—but there are a few places that not only allow rockhounding, but encourage it. **Rock Hound State Park** (☎ **505/546-6182**), located about 14 miles from Deming, is one such place (see chapter 11 for more information). Rock hounds from all over the country descend on this part of the state specifically for the purpose of finding great rocks like agate, jasper, and opal. At Rock Hound State Park, you're allowed to camp and take a handful or two of rocks home with you. For information on other popular rockhounding sites, contact the **New Mexico Bureau of Mines and Mineral Resources** (☎ **505/835-5410**).

7 Skiing & Snowboarding

New Mexico has some of the best snow skiing in the United States. With most downhill areas above 10,000 feet and many above 12,000 feet, there are several ski areas with vertical drops over 2,000 feet. Average annual snowfall at the 10 major areas ranges from 100 to 300 inches annually. Many areas, aided by vigorous snow-making efforts, are able to open around Thanksgiving, and most open by mid-December, making New Mexico a popular vacation spot around the holidays. As a result, you'll see a definite rise in hotel room rates in or around ski areas during the holiday season. Ski season runs through March and often into the first week in April.

Some of the best skiing in the state is at Taos and the surrounding resort towns of Angel Fire and Red River (see chapter 8). Additionally, Taos Ski Valley is home to one of the best ski schools in the country. All ski areas in New Mexico offer runs for a variety of skill levels (20% to 35% beginner, 35% to 50% intermediate, and 10% to 50% expert), and lift tickets range from about $30 to $45 for an adult all-day ticket.

Snowboarding is permitted at all New Mexico ski areas with the exception of Taos Ski Valley, and some of the best **cross-country skiing** in the region can be found at the Enchanted Forest near Taos Ski Valley and in Chama.

Equipment for downhill and cross-country skiing, as well as for snowboarding, can be rented at ski areas and nearby towns. Lessons are widely available.

For more information about individual ski areas, see regional and city chapters later in this book.

8 Water Sports

Water sports in New Mexico? Absolutely! Here you'll find a variety of water-sports activities, ranging from pleasure boating to white-water rafting and windsurfing.

There are fantastic opportunities in New Mexico for **white-water rafting** and **kayaking.** The waters in the Chama River and the Rio Grande are generally at their best during the spring and summer (late May to late July); however, some areas of the Rio Grande are negotiable year-round, especially those that fall at lower elevations where temperatures are warmer. If you opt not to schlep your own rafting gear with you to New Mexico, there are many companies that will supply you with everything you need. I'd recommend contacting some of the outfitters listed in later chapters no matter what you've brought with you or what your level of experience is because whitewater rafting and kayaking in certain areas of New Mexico (like Taos Box) can be quite dangerous. You should get tips from the professionals before you set out on your own. In addition to calling outfitters, you can also contact the **Bureau of Land Management,** 226 Cruz Alta Rd., Taos, NM 87571 (☎ 505/758-8851), for information.

Opportunities for **pleasure boating** are available on many of New Mexico's lakes and reservoirs. There are boat ramps at more than 45 state parks, dams, and lakes. Elephant Butte Lake is one of the best and most beautiful spots for boating (see chapter 11). Unfortunately, the rules and regulations vary greatly from one body of water to another, so you'll have to contact the governing agencies for each place in which you intend to go boating.

The **U.S. Army Corps of Engineers** (P.O. Box 1580, Albuquerque, NM 87103; ☎ 505/766-2719) oversees the following lakes: Abiquiu, Cochiti, Conchas, Galisteo, Jemez, Santa Rosa, and Two Rivers. Most other boating areas are regulated by the **State Parks Division,** P.O. Box 1147, Santa Fe, NM 87504 (☎ **888/NM-PARKS** or 505/827-7173), or by the **New Mexico Department of Game and Fish,** P.O. Box 25112, Santa Fe, NM 87504 (☎ **505/827-7911**). Some are, of course, overseen by tribes and pueblos, and in those cases you'll have to contact them directly.

Another popular pastime, particularly at Cochiti and Storrie Lakes in summer, is **windsurfing.** Elephant Butte is good for windsurfing all year.

9 Other Outdoor Activities

In addition to the activities listed above, there are many other recreational opportunities available in New Mexico. **Hot springs,** for example, are quite popular with both locals and visitors alike. They take many different forms and offer a wide variety of facilities and amenities; some, which aren't owned and operated by anyone but Mother Nature, offer no amenities. You'll find hot springs in the Santa Fe, Taos, and Las Vegas areas as well as in the southwestern regions of New Mexico. Many of them are listed later in this book. You might also try calling local chambers of commerce to see if they have any information on area hot springs.

GOLF

New Mexico provides the clear air and oft-cool climates that draw many golfers. Fees range broadly from inexpensive public courses in less populated areas ($11 to $25) to more exclusive courses in places where demand is greater ($25 to $50). The most challenging course in the state is the **Championship Course at the University of New Mexico,** 3601 University Blvd. SE, Albuquerque, NM (☎ 505/277-4546), and one of the most scenic is the **Pueblo de Cochiti Course,** 5200 Cochiti Highway, Cochiti Lake, NM (☎ 505/465-2230). If you're in the Farmington area, check out **Piñon Hills Golf Course,** 2101 Sunrise Parkway (☎ 505/326-6066), rated in 1995 by *Golf Digest* as the "best public golf course" in the United States. In the south, you can enjoy views, a challenging course, and cool climes even in summer at **The Links at Sierra Blanca** in Ruidoso, 105 Sierra Blanca Dr. (☎ 800/854-6571 or 505/258-5330).

HORSEBACK RIDING

What's unique about much of New Mexico's horseback riding is its variety. You'll find a broad range of riding terrain, from open plains to high mountain wilderness. In the Santa Fe area you can ride across the plains of the spectacular Galisteo basin with **Santa Fe Detours,** 54½ East San Francisco St. (☎ **800/338-6877** or 505/983-6565). In Taos, you can explore secluded Taos Pueblo land with The **Taos Indian Horse Ranch,** on Pueblo land off Ski Valley Road, just before Arroyo Seco (☎ **505/ 758-3212**). In Albuquerque, **Sandia Trails Horse Rentals,** 10601 N. 4th St. (☎ **505/898-6970**), offers the opportunity to ride on Sandia Indian Reservation land along the Rio Grande. In the Northwest try **5M Outfitters,** P.O. Box 361, Chama (☎ **505/588-7003**). In the southeast, try **Inn of the Mountain Gods,** Carrizo Canyon Rd. (☎ **505/257-5141**). If you're looking for a resort horseback riding experience try **Rancho Encantado,** Route 4, Box 57C, Santa Fe (☎ **800/722-9339** or 505/982-3537); or **Bishop's Lodge,** Bishop's Lodge Rd., Santa Fe (☎ **505/ 983-6377**).

TENNIS

Though New Mexico's high and dry climate is ideal for tennis much of the year, the sport is somewhat underdeveloped in the state. Certainly each of the major cities has municipal courts, information about which you'll find in the city and regional sections. If you're looking for a tennis resort experience, try **Rancho Encantado,** Route 4, Box 57C, Santa Fe, NM 87501 (☎ **800/722-9339** or 505/982-3537); **Bishop's Lodge,** Bishop's Lodge Rd. (P.O. Box 2367), Santa Fe, NM 87504 (☎ **505/ 983-6377**); or **Salsa del Salto in Taos,** P.O. Box 1468, El Prado, NM 87529 (☎ **800/530-3097** or 505/776-2422).

10 Tips for Staying Healthy Outdoors

New Mexico is unique for many reasons, not the least of which is the altitude. Visitors should be aware of New Mexico's high elevation for two reasons. The first is clothing: Don't come at any time of year, even in the middle of summer, without at least a warm sweater and rain gear. The second is health: Don't push yourself too hard during your first few days here. The air is thinner, the sun more direct. If you haven't engaged in physical activity on a regular basis, see your doctor before your trip just to be sure you're in good condition. Under the best of circumstances at these altitudes, you should expect to sunburn more easily and stop to catch your breath more frequently.

For more information on mountain sickness, dehydration, and other health and safety issues, see "Health & Insurance," in chapter 3.

Rain and thunderstorms are common in New Mexico on late-summer afternoons. If you get caught in a fast-developing thunderstorm, seek lower ground immediately. Rain in New Mexico can also cause serious problems. If it begins to rain while you're out hiking, stay out of ditches and narrow canyons; flash floods are not uncommon, especially in late summer, and they're very dangerous. If while driving you suddenly find that water is covering part of the roadway, don't try to drive across. It's best to wait it out, since the bulk of the water may be just around the corner upstream. The rain will stop and the water will recede—more quickly than you might imagine.

It is unfortunate that I have to warn you about **drinking stream water** while partaking in outdoor activities, but I'd be remiss if I didn't. There are still places where it's safe to drink water directly from its source; however, it's easier and more prudent to simply filter all water before you drink it if you're out hiking. You can buy

Hantavirus Pulmonary Syndrome: What You Should Know

Recent news reports regarding the rare but often fatal respiratory disease known as Hantavirus have frightened some potential visitors to New Mexico. First recognized in 1993, the disease has afflicted just over 100 people, and half of those cases were reported in the Four Corners states of Utah, Colorado, New Mexico, and Arizona. It is believed that the disease is spread through urine and droppings of deer mice and other rodents, so outdoor enthusiasts are in one of the highest categories of risk. While there is cause for concern, there are ways (recommended by the Centers for Disease Control) of protecting yourself and your family against Hantavirus:

- Avoid camping or sleeping in areas with signs of rodent droppings.
- Before using cabins that have been closed up for the winter or for an extended period of time, open them up and air them out for a while before spending any length of time inside. Check for rodent infestation as well.
- If you see a rodent burrow or den, do not disturb it or try to chase the animals out of the area—just set up camp somewhere else.
- Don't sleep on the bare ground. Use a mat or an elevated cot if possible.
- Don't set up camp near a woodpile.
- Keep foods in airtight, rodent-proof containers, and dispose of garbage promptly and efficiently.

If you have some exposure to rodents and begin to exhibit symptoms of the disease (difficulty breathing; headache; flulike fever; abdominal, joint, and lower back pain; and sometimes nausea), see a doctor immediately, and be sure to tell him or her where and when you were in contact with rodents. The sooner you seek medical attention the better your chances for survival.

mechanical filtration units at outdoors shops, or you can use chemical treatment such as iodine drops or chlorination. If you're going to drink from natural sources, try to get your water from springs located upstream from campgrounds. If you're going hiking or biking only for the day or have a place in mind to stop for the night where you can pick up provisions, it's much better to carry your own drinking water.

The only other thing you might be concerned about during outdoor activities is **wildlife.** Basically, you should keep your eyes and ears open, but most wildlife will be more afraid of you than you are of it. You should, however, watch out for snakes, especially rattlers, and keep a respectful distance if you see one. Like snakes, scorpions and poisonous spiders are much rarer than their reputations would suggest, but they do live here, too. They're most commonly found in woodpiles, in abandoned and decaying buildings, or under rocks. Don't reach into these places without first inspecting them carefully.

6 Albuquerque

During my earliest years in Albuquerque, the city was a dusty stop at the intersection of I-25 and I-40, two of the Southwest's major thoroughfares. We used to walk dirt roads to school and ride horses in the alfalfa fields that surrounded our house. Thirty years later there are only small pockets of that kind of rural life left within this city of 700,000, New Mexico's largest.

From the rocky crest of Sandia Peak at sunset, one can see the lights of the city spread out across 16 miles of high desert grassland. As the sun drops beyond the western horizon, it reflects off the Rio Grande, flowing through Albuquerque more than a mile below.

This waterway is the bloodline for the area, what allowed a city to spring up in this vast desert, and it continues to be at the center of the area's growth. Farming villages that line its banks are being stampeded by expansion. As the west side of the city sprawls, more means for transporting traffic across the river have had to be built, breaking up the pastoral valley area.

The railroad, which set up a major stop here in 1880, prompted much of Albuquerque's initial growth, but that economic explosion was nothing compared with what has happened since World War II. Designated a major national center for military research and production, Albuquerque became a trading center for this state, whose populace is spread widely across the land. That's why the city may strike visitors as nothing more than one big strip mall. Look closely and you'll see ranchers, Native Americans, and Hispanic villagers stocking up on goods to take back to the New Mexico boot heel or the Texas panhandle.

Climbing out of the valley is the legendary Route 66 (U.S. 66), a major route from the East to California before the interstates were built. It's well worth a drive, if only to see the rust that time has left. Old court hotels still line the street, many with their funky '50s signage. One enclave on this route is the University of New Mexico district, with a number of hippie-ish cafes and shops.

Farther downhill you'll come to downtown Albuquerque. During the day, this area is all suits and heels, but at night it becomes a hip nightlife scene. People from all over the state come to Albuquerque to check out the live music and dancing clubs, most within walking distance from each other.

The section called Old Town also is worth a visit. Though it's the most touristy part of town, it's also a unique Southwestern village with

Greater Albuquerque

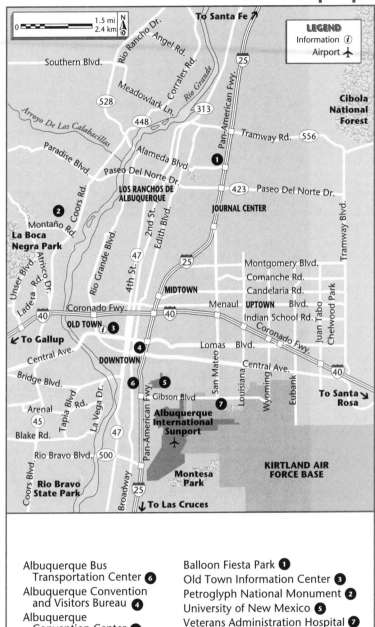

LEGEND
Information *i*
Airport ✈

Albuquerque Bus
  Transportation Center **6**
Albuquerque Convention
  and Visitors Bureau **4**
Albuquerque
  Convention Center **4**

Balloon Fiesta Park **1**
Old Town Information Center **3**
Petroglyph National Monument **2**
University of New Mexico **5**
Veterans Administration Hospital **7**

1-0327

a beautiful and intact plaza. Also in this area are Albuquerque's new aquarium and botanical gardens, as well as its continually upgrading zoo.

The city's warm, sunny climate and healthful altitude—varying from 4,200 to 6,000 feet—also bring in many vacationers and retirement residents. The fairgrounds is the site for the annual state fair and for a colorful and locally renowned annual arts-and-crafts show. Indian pueblos in the area welcome tourists, and along with other pueblos throughout New Mexico have worked together to create the Pueblo Cultural Center, a showplace of Indian crafts of both past and present. The country's longest aerial tramway takes visitors to the top of Sandia Peak, which protects the city's eastern flank. To the east run a series of volcanoes; the Petroglyph National Monument there is an amazing tribute to the areas ancient Native American past.

1 Orientation

ARRIVING

Since Albuquerque is the transportation hub for New Mexico, getting in and out of town is easy. For more detailed information, see "Getting There," in chapter 3.

BY PLANE   The **Albuquerque International Airport** is in the south-central part of the city, between I-25 on the west and Kirtland Air Force Base on the east, just south of Gibson Boulevard. Sleek and efficient, the airport is served by nine national airlines and two local ones.

Most hotels have courtesy vans to meet their guests and take them to their respective destinations. In addition, **Shuttlejack** (☎ 505/243-3244) and **Checker Airport Express** (☎ 505/765-1234) run services to and from city hotels. **Sun Tran** (☎ 505/843-9200), Albuquerque's public bus system, also makes airport stops. There is efficient taxi service to and from the airport, plus numerous car-rental agencies.

BY CAR   If you're driving, you'll probably arrive via either the east-west Interstate 40 or the north-south Interstate 25. Exits are well marked. For information and advice on driving in New Mexico, see "Getting There," in chapter 3.

BY TRAIN   Amtrak's "Southwest Chief" arrives and departs daily to and from Los Angeles and Chicago. The station is at 214 First St. SW, 2 blocks south of Central Avenue (☎ 800/USA-RAIL or 505/842-9650; www.amtrak.com). *Note:* A new train station was in the planning stage at press time, so call ahead to make sure the address listed here is still current.

BY BUS   Greyhound/Trailways (☎ 800/231-2222 for schedules, fares, and information; www.greyhound.com) and **TNM&O Coaches** (☎ 505/243-4435) arrive and depart from the Albuquerque Bus Transportation Center, 300 Second St. SW (at the corner of Lead and Second, near the train station).

VISITOR INFORMATION

The main office of the **Albuquerque Convention and Visitors Bureau** is at 20 First Plaza NW (☎ 800/284-2282 or 505/842-9918; www.abqcvb.org). It's open Monday through Friday from 8am to 5pm. There are information centers at the airport, on the lower level at the bottom of the escalator, open daily from 9:30am to 8pm; and in Old Town at 303 Romero St. NW, Suite 107, open daily from 9am to 5pm. Tape-recorded information about current local events is available from the bureau's toll-free phone number after 5pm weekdays and all day Saturday and Sunday.

CITY LAYOUT

The city's sprawl takes a while to get used to. A visitor's first impression is of a grid of arteries lined with shopping malls and fast-food eateries, with residences tucked behind on side streets.

If you look at a map of Albuquerque, the first thing you'll notice is that it lies at the crossroads of Interstate 25 north-south and Interstate 40 east-west. Refocus your attention on the southwest quadrant: Here you'll find both downtown Albuquerque and Old Town, site of many tourist attractions. Lomas Boulevard and Central Avenue, the old Route 66 (U.S. 66), flank downtown on the north and south. They come together 2 miles west of downtown near the Old Town Plaza, the historical and spiritual heart of the city. Lomas and Central continue east across I-25, staying about half a mile apart as they pass by the University of New Mexico (UNM) and the New Mexico State Fairgrounds. The airport is directly south of the UNM campus, about 3 miles via Yale Boulevard. Kirtland Air Force Base—site of Sandia National Laboratories and the National Atomic Museum—is an equal distance south of the fairgrounds on Louisiana Boulevard.

Roughly paralleling I-40 to the north is Menaul Boulevard, the focus of midtown and uptown shopping as well as the hotel districts. As Albuquerque expands northward, the Journal Center business park area, about 4½ miles north of the freeway interchange, is getting more attention. East of Eubank Boulevard are the Sandia Foothills, where the alluvial plain slants a bit more steeply toward the mountains.

When looking for an address, it is helpful to know that Central Avenue divides the city into north and south, and the railroad tracks, which run just east of First Street downtown, comprise the dividing line between east and west. Street names are followed by a directional: NE, NW, SE, or SW.

MAPS   The most comprehensive Albuquerque street map is distributed by the Convention and Visitors Bureau.

2 Getting Around

Albuquerque is easy to get around, thanks to its wide thoroughfares and grid layout, combined with its efficient transportation systems.

BY PUBLIC TRANSPORTATION   Sun Tran of Albuquerque (☎ 505/ **843-9200**) cloaks the arterials with its city bus network. Call for information on routes and fares.

BY TAXI   Yellow-Checker Cab (☎ 505/765-1234) serves the city and surrounding area 24 hours a day.

BY CAR   The Yellow Pages list more than 30 car-rental agencies in Albuquerque. Among them are the following well-known national firms: **Alamo,** 2601 Yale Blvd. SE (☎ **505/842-4057**); **Avis,** at the airport (☎ **505/842-4080**); **Budget,** at the airport (☎ **505/768-5900**); **Dollar,** at the airport (☎ **505/842-4304**); **Hertz,** at the airport (☎ **505/842-4235**); **Rent-A-Wreck,** 500 Yale Blvd. SE (☎ **505/232-7552**); and **Thrifty,** 2039 Yale Blvd. SE (☎ **505/842-8733**). Those not located at the airport itself are close by and can provide rapid airport pickup and delivery service.

Parking is generally not difficult in Albuquerque. Meters operate weekdays from 8am to 6pm and are not monitored at other times. Only the large downtown hotels charge for parking. Traffic is a problem only at certain hours. Avoid I-25 and I-40 at the center of town around 5pm.

FAST FACTS: Albuquerque

Airport   See "Orientation," above.

American Express   The American Express office is at 5031 Indian School Road NE, Building C, Ste. 200 (☎ **800/219-1023;** fax 505/332-5911). To report lost credit cards, call ☎ 800/528-2122.

Area Code   The telephone area code for all of New Mexico is **505.**

Car Rentals   See "Getting Around," in chapter 3, or "Getting Around," above.

Climate   See "When to Go," in chapter 3.

Currency Exchange   Foreign currency can be exchanged between 9am and 2pm at NationsBank, 303 Roma St. NW, ☎ 505/765-2211); or at any of the branches of First Security Bank (its main office is at Forty-First Plaza NW, ☎ **505/765-4000**).

Dentists   Call the Albuquerque District Dental Society at ☎ **505/260-7333** for emergency service.

Doctors   Call the University of New Mexico Medical Center Physician Referral Service at ☎ **505/843-0124** for a recommendation.

Embassies & Consulates   See "Fast Facts: For the Foreign Traveler," in chapter 4.

Emergencies   For police, fire, or ambulance, dial ☎ **911.**

Hospitals   The major facilities are Presbyterian Hospital, 1100 Central Ave. SE (☎ **505/841-1234,** 505/841-1111 for emergency services); and University of New Mexico Hospital, 2211 Lomas Blvd. NE (☎ **505/272-2111,** 505/843-2411 for emergency services).

Liquor Laws   The legal drinking age is 21 throughout New Mexico. Bars may remain open until 2am Monday through Saturday and until midnight on Sunday. Wine, beer, and spirits are sold at licensed supermarkets and liquor stores, but there are no package sales on election days until after 7pm. It is illegal to transport liquor through most Native American reservations.

Newspapers & Magazines   The two daily newspapers are the *Albuquerque Tribune,* published mornings, and the *Albuquerque Journal,* published evenings.

Police   For emergencies, call ☎ **911.** For other business, contact the Albuquerque City Police (☎ **505/768-1986**) or the New Mexico State Police (☎ **505/841-9256**).

Post Offices   The Main Post Office, 1135 Broadway NE (☎ **505/245-9561**), is open daily from 7:30am to 6pm. There are 25 branch offices, with about another dozen in surrounding communities.

Radio & TV   Albuquerque has some 30 local radio stations catering to all musical tastes. Albuquerque television stations include KOB, Channel 4 (NBC affiliate); KOAT, Channel 7 (ABC affiliate); KGGM, Channel 13 (CBS affiliate); KNME, Channel 5 (PBS affiliate); and KGSW, Channel 14 (Fox and independent). There are, of course, numerous local cable channels as well.

Taxes   In Albuquerque, the hotel tax is 10.5625%; it will be added to your bill. The sales tax is 5.8125%.

Time Zone   Albuquerque is on mountain time, 1 hour ahead of the West Coast and 2 hours behind the East Coast.

Useful Telephone Numbers   For time and temperature, call ☎ **505/ 247-1611;** for road information, call ☎ **800/432-4269;** and for emergency road service (AAA), call ☎ **505/291-6600.**

3   Where to Stay

Albuquerque's hotel glut is good news to travelers looking for quality rooms at a reasonable cost. Except during peak periods—specifically, the New Mexico Arts and Crafts Fair (late June), the New Mexico State Fair (September), and the Kodak Albuquerque International Balloon Fiesta (early October)—most of the city's hotels have vacant rooms, so guests can frequently request and get a lower room rate than the one posted.

In addition to the accommodations listed below, Albuquerque also has its share of budget hotel chains, including **Motel 6,** which has three locations in the city: 1701 University Blvd. NE at I-40, Albuquerque, NM 87102 (☎ **505/843-9228** or 505/891-6161); 13141 Central Ave. NE, I-40 at Tramway Boulevard Exit 167 (☎ **505/294-4600**); and at 6015 Iliff Rd. NW, I-40 at Coors Road Exit 155 (☎ **505/831-3400**).

A tax of 10.5625% is added to every hotel bill. All hotels listed offer rooms for nonsmokers and travelers with disabilities; all the bed-and-breakfasts do as well.

DOWNTOWN/OLD TOWN

This area is the best location to stay if you want to be close to many of the major sights and attractions. All of the following accommodations are between I-25 and the Rio Grande, and between I-40 and Route 66 (Central Avenue).

Casas de Sueños. 310 Rio Grande Blvd. SW, Albuquerque, NM 87104. ☎ **800/ CHAT-W/US** or 505/247-4560. 21 units. TV TEL. $95–$250 double. Rates include full breakfast and afternoon snacks. AE, CB, DC, DISC, MC, V. No children under 12.

The principal attraction of this B&B is its location. It's within walking distance from the Plaza, the aquarium, and botanical garden—even the zoo, though it's farther. You'll recognize Casas de Sueños by the bright sign and the snail-shaped front of the main building, which was designed by famed renegade architect Bart Prince. The buildings that comprise the Casas were once private homes—a compound that was part of a gathering place for artists and their admirers. Most of them face a garden courtyard filled with roses and exotic sculptures.

Each of the rooms has an individual theme; one room is designed to follow the color schemes of Monet's paintings, while another has an Asian motif, with a shadow puppet from Bali and a two-person Jacuzzi. The rooms are interesting though not pristine, better described as artsy in their design and upkeep. Some are equipped with kitchens, a few have their own hot tubs (some indoor, some out), and a number have fireplaces. Outside the garden area are two newer rooms that I found spacious and efficient, though lacking in charm. Every accommodation has its own entrance.

A delicious full breakfast buffet is served in the main building every morning. You'll find specialties such as asparagus soufflé and apple or pear cobbler. Massage therapy is available. No smoking is permitted indoors.

✪ **Hyatt Regency Albuquerque.** 330 Tijeras Ave. NW, Albuquerque, NM 87102. ☎ **800/233-1234** or 505/842-1234. Fax 505/766-6710. 409 units. A/C TV TEL. Weekdays $150–$175 double; weekends $89 double; $310–$725 suite. AE, CB, DC, DISC, MC, V. Self-parking $8, valet $11.

If you like luxury and want to be right downtown, this is the place to stay. This $60 million hotel, which opened in 1990, is pure shiny gloss and art deco. The lobby features a palm-shaded fountain beneath a pyramidal skylight, and throughout the hotel's public areas is an extensive art collection, including original Frederic Remington sculptures. The spacious guest rooms enhance the feeling of richness with mahogany furnishings, full-length mirrors, and big views of the mountains. Each room has Spectravision movie channels, a coffeemaker, and hair dryer. This is a nice location if you want to sample Albuquerque's nightlife as well as seasonal events on the recently renovated Civic Plaza. The hotel has a number of shops and is located right next door to the Galeria, a shopping area.

Dining/Diversions: McGrath's serves three meals daily in a setting of forest-green upholstery and black-cherry furniture. **Bolo Saloon** is noted for its whimsical oils of "where the deer and the antelope play" (at the bar).

Amenities: Concierge, room service, dry cleaning, laundry service, newspaper delivery, baby-sitting, secretarial services, express checkout, valet parking. You'll also find an outdoor swimming pool, small health club, sauna, business center, conference rooms, car-rental desk, beauty salon, boutiques.

○ **La Posada de Albuquerque.** 125 Second St. NW (at Copper Ave.), Albuquerque, NM 87102. ☎ **800/777-5732** or 505/242-9090. Fax 505/242-8664. 114 units. AC TV TEL. $89–$115 double; $195–$275 suite. AE, DISC, MC, V. Valet parking $5.

Built in 1939 by Conrad Hilton as the famed hotelier's first inn in his home state of New Mexico, this hostelry on the National Register of Historic Places feels like old Spain. Though remodeled in 1996, the owners have kept the finer qualities. An elaborate Moorish brass-and-mosaic fountain stands in the center of the tiled lobby floor while new carpet, drapes, and furniture in 1997 set off touches such as old-fashioned tin chandeliers hanging from the two-story ceiling. The lobby is surrounded on all sides by high archways, creating the feel of a 19th-century hacienda courtyard.

As in the lobby, all guest room furniture is handcrafted, but here it's covered with cushions of Southwestern design. There are spacious rooms with big windows looking out across the city and toward the mountains. If you want a feel for downtown Albuquerque as well as easy access to the Civic Plaza, nightclubs, and Old Town, this hotel will suit you well.

Conrad's Downtown, La Posada's elegantly redesigned restaurant, features Southwestern cuisine from Jane Butel, who has a cooking school on the premises. The **Lobby Bar** is a favorite gathering place and has entertainment Thursday through Saturday evenings.

The hotel offers room service, dry cleaning, laundry service, express checkout, valet parking, and access to a nearby health club.

Sheraton Old Town. 800 Rio Grande Blvd. NW, Albuquerque, NM 87104. ☎ **800/325-3535** or 505/843-6300. Fax 505/842-9863. 208 units. A/C TV TEL. $120–$130 double; $150 suite. Children stay free in parents' room. AE, CB, DC, DISC, MC, V. Free parking.

No Albuquerque hotel is closer to top tourist attractions than the Sheraton. It's only a 5-minute walk from the Old Town Plaza and two important museums. Constructed in 1975 and remodeled in 1993, with more updating in 1998, the building has mezzanine-level windows lighting the adobe-toned lobby, an airiness that carries into the rooms. They have unique handmade furniture such as *trasteros* (freestanding closets, like armoires) accented with willow shoots. Request a south-side room and you'll get a balcony overlooking Old Town and the pool, which is heated year-round. All rooms now offer coffeemakers, hair dryers, and irons and ironing boards.

Central Albuquerque Accommodations

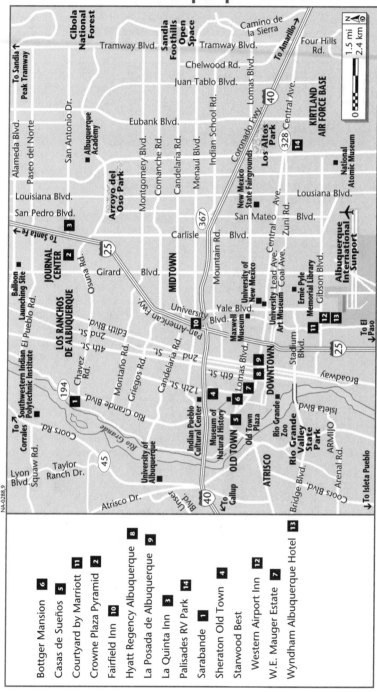

Bottger Mansion 6
Casas de Sueños 5
Courtyard by Marriott 11
Crowne Plaza Pyramid 2
Fairfield Inn 10
Hyatt Regency Albuquerque 8
La Posada de Albuquerque 9
La Quinta Inn 3
Palisades RV Park 14
Sarabande 1
Sheraton Old Town 4
Starwood Best
Western Airport Inn 12
W.E. Mauger Estate 7
Wyndham Albuquerque Hotel 13

Dining: The **Customs House Restaurant,** specializing in seafood and regional cuisine, serves weekday lunches and nightly dinners. The **Café del Sol** is the Sheraton's coffee shop.

Amenities: Concierge, room service, valet laundry, secretarial and baby-sitting services. There's also the Old Town Place, an attached shopping center, which has arts-and-crafts dealers, a bookstore, beauty salon, and Explora Science Center for children.

MIDTOWN/UPTOWN

This area, which extends from I-25 to Eubank Boulevard, and between Central Avenue and Montgomery Boulevard, is a popular resting place for business travelers, shoppers, and other visitors seeking a central location. It includes Freeway Loop, which surrounds the interchange of I-25 and I-40; several major hotels are on Menaul and University boulevards nearby.

Fairfield Inn. 1760 Menaul Rd. NE, Albuquerque, NM 87102. ☎ **800/228-2800** or 505/889-4000. Fax 505/872-3094. 188 units. A/C TV TEL. $62.95 double. Extra person $6. Children 18 and under stay free in parents' room. Continental breakfast included in the price of the room. AE, CB, DC, DISC, MC, V.

Owned by Marriott, this hotel has exceptionally clean rooms and a location with easy access to freeways that can quickly get you to Old Town, downtown, or the heights. Ask for an east-facing room to avoid the noise and a view of the highway. Rooms are medium-sized and have new bedspreads, lamp shades, carpet, and bathroom tile. Each has a balcony or terrace.

Local phone calls are free and valet laundry service is available. There's an indoor/outdoor swimming pool with saunas and a Jacuzzi as well as a medium-sized health club. You probably couldn't get more for your money (in a chain hotel) anywhere else.

NEAR THE AIRPORT

This district lies south of Central Avenue (Route 66) and primarily east of I-25, and includes Kirtland Air Force Base and Albuquerque International Airport. Most accommodations here are along Yale or Gibson boulevards near the airport entrance.

✪ **Courtyard by Marriott.** 1920 Yale Blvd. SE, Albuquerque, NM 87106. ☎ **800/321-2211** or 505/843-6600. Fax 505/843-8740. 164 units. A/C TV TEL. $94 single, $104 double; $99–$130 suite; weekend rates available. AE, DC, DISC, MC, V.

If you don't like high-rises such as the Wyndham Albuquerque Hotel, this is the best selection for airport area hotels. Opened in 1990, this four-story member of the Marriott family is built around an attractively landscaped courtyard reminiscent of a village green. Families appreciate the security system—access is only by key card between 11pm and 6am—though most of the hotel's clients are business travelers. The units are roomy and comfortable, with walnut furniture and firm beds. Ask for a balcony room on the courtyard. Among the nicer touches are coffee and tea service from a 190° faucet, on-command movie channel, full-size writing desks, irons and ironing boards, hair dryers, voice mail, clock radios, and massage showerheads.

The coffee shop is open daily for breakfast and dinner. There is an adjacent lounge. The hotel provides valet laundry and a courtesy van. Don't miss a trip to the lovely indoor pool and spacious whirlpool. There's also a laundry room and a small exercise room.

Starwood Best Western Airport Inn. 2400 Yale Blvd. SE, Albuquerque, NM 87106. ☎ **800/528-1234** or 505/242-7022. Fax 505/243-0620. 122 units. A/C TV TEL. $63–$69 double. Rates include continental breakfast. AE, CB, DC, DISC, MC, V.

Struggling to keep pace with the newer Comfort Inns and La Quintas springing up in the area, this hotel is receiving a remodel from the lobby to the rooms. At press time the lobby was getting a new a balcony area where breakfast was to be served. The rooms have new dark wood furniture, bedspreads, carpet and TVs. Units are still average-sized, except for the newer east wing where they are a little larger. Each is equipped with a hair dryer, iron, and ironing board; some have balconies and patios. All offer free local phone calls. Deluxe units are equipped with refrigerators. A courtesy van is available from 5am to midnight (hotel will pay for a taxi during odd hours), and the hotel also offers valet laundry service. Guests can enjoy an outdoor swimming pool and Jacuzzi, surrounded by grass.

Wyndham Albuquerque Hotel. 2910 Yale Blvd. SE, Albuquerque, NM 87106. ☎ **800/ 227-1117** or 505/843-7000. Fax 505/843-6307. 276 units. A/C TV TEL. $69–$149 double. AE, CB, DC, DISC, EURO, JCB, MC, V. Free parking. Small pets welcome with prior approval.

This recently remodeled hotel right at the airport now has an elegant feel. The lobby, grill, and lounge areas employ a lot of sandstone, wood, copper, and tile to lend an Anasazi feel. The hotel caters to air travelers with a 24-hour desk, shuttle service, and same day valet laundry. But it could also be a wise choice for a few days of browsing around Albuquerque, as it has good access to freeways and excellent views. Of course, you will hear some jet noise. The hotel recently came under the Wyndham name and with it came a multimillion-dollar remodel.

The Anasazi feel carries into the rooms of the 15-story hotel. Each room has a balcony, data ports, Nintendo on the television, a hair dryer, coffeemaker, iron, ironing board, and receives *USA Today.* Deluxe club rooms on the 15th floor offer oversized towels and bottled water, as well as a concierge lounge with complimentary hors d'oeuvres. Room service is also available. Facilities include an outdoor swimming pool, self-service laundry, two all-weather tennis courts, business center, and gift shop. The Rojo Grill serves a variety of American and Southwestern dishes, from tostadas to Ostrich medallions.

JOURNAL CENTER/NORTH CITY

North of Montgomery Boulevard, the focal point is the I-25 interchange with Osuna Road and San Mateo Boulevard. On the west side of the freeway, the Journal Center business park is dominated by the giant pyramid of the Holiday Inn. East of the freeway, at San Mateo and Academy boulevards, numerous hotels, restaurants, and shopping complexes dominate. This is the closest area to the Balloon Fiesta launch site.

Crowne Plaza Pyramid. 5151 San Francisco Rd. NE, Albuquerque, NM 87109. ☎ **800/ 544-0623** or 505/821-3333. Fax 505/822-8115. 365 units. A/C TV TEL. $119–$164 single; $139–$184 double; $140–$275 suite. Ask about special weekend and package rates. AE, CB, DC, MC, V. Free parking.

About a 15-minute drive from Old Town and downtown is this Aztec pyramid–shaped structure reached via the Paseo del Norte exit (exit 232) from I-25. Previously the Holiday Inn Pyramid, this structure, built in 1986, has recently come under the Crowne Plaza name and with it received a $4.5 million renovation. The 10 guest floors are grouped around a hollow skylit atrium. Vines drape from planter boxes on the balconies, and water falls five stories to a pool between the two glass elevators.

The rooms are spacious, though not extraordinary, all with picture windows and ample views. The renovation has added Spectravision movie channels, coffeemakers, hair dryers, makeup mirrors, irons, and ironing boards. The morning newspaper is delivered to your door. Rooms on the 10th-floor executive level offer more space and a few more amenities.

With lots of convention space at the hotel, you're likely to encounter name-tagged conventioneers here, though the service seems to be good enough to handle the crowds without inconvenience to you. However, the two elevators can't quite accommodate the crowds and the stairs are locked on the ground floor, so guests often must wait.

Dining/Diversions: The Terrace Restaurant offers American cuisine with a Southwestern flair. There are also two lounges on the premises.

Amenities: Concierge, room service, valet laundry, newspaper delivery, express checkout, indoor/outdoor pool, medium-sized health club, Jacuzzi, sauna, jogging track, business center, conference rooms, sundeck.

La Quinta Inn. 5241 San Antonio Dr., NE, Albuquerque, NM 87109. ☎ **800/531-5900** or 505/821-9000. Fax 505/821-2399. 130 units. A/C TV TEL. $70–$75 double (higher during Balloon Fiesta). Kids 18 and under stay free in parents' room. AE, CB, DC, DISC, MC, V. Pets welcome.

With its "new rooms" campaign, La Quinta is charging ahead in the inexpensive room category, and after my visit to this hotel I can see why. Though the bed was a little hard, the rest of the accommodation was ergonomically right; these fairly spacious rooms have a table and chairs where you need them, and a bathroom you can move around in. They are decorated tastefully in greens with art deco tile in the bathroom. If you're headed to the Balloon Fiesta, this is a good choice, since it's not far from the launch site, though you'll have to reserve as much as a year in advance. The lobby breakfast room is comfortable, with pillars that lend a dignified air. A kidney-shaped heated pool open May through October offers respite from Albuquerque's hot summers. King rooms have a recliner, and two-room suites are available.

If you like these inns, and want to stay at one near the airport, you can make reservations at the above 800 number for **La Quinta Airport Inn,** No. 816 at 2116 Yale Blvd., SE.

BED & BREAKFASTS
DOWNTOWN/OLD TOWN

Bottger Mansion. 110 San Felipe NW, Albuquerque, NM 87104. ☎ **800/758-3639** or 505/243-3639. 7 units. $79–$139 double. Rates include full breakfast. AE, DC, MC, V. Children are welcome, pets are not.

This fun B&B has the corner on the market of Spanish/Victorian style in Albuquerque. Clearly proprietor Patsy Garcia grew up around the Spanish New Mexico tradition and has awakened the Victorian in this historic 1912 mansion right in Old Town. There's lots of white lace about, and enough floral prints on synthetic fabrics so that some might find the place gaudy; I found it refreshing. My favorite room is Mercedes, with a pink tile floor, a queen bed, and Jacuzzi tub. The room called Julia has a king-size bed and is spacious, as are all the rooms except Marcelina. All rooms have nice-sized bathrooms with ceramic tile, and the larger ones have TV and VCR. Those facing south are sunnier but pick up a bit of street noise from nearby Central Avenue. Breakfast is another reason to come here. Patsy goes all out. In one sitting I was served, and ate, French toast, bacon, eggs with a tasty salsa, yogurt, juice and fruit, all deliciously prepared. It's served in a sunny indoor patio.

The W. E. Mauger Estate. 701 Roma Ave. NW, Albuquerque, NM 87102. ☎ **800/719-9189** or 505/242-8755. Fax 505/842-8835. www.thuntek.net/tc_arts/mauger. 9 units. AC TV TEL. $89–$179 double. Rates include full breakfast. AE, DC, DISC, MC, V. Children welcome ($15), as are small pets by prior arrangement ($30).

A restored Queen Anne–style home constructed in 1897, this former residence of wool baron William Mauger is listed on the National Register of Historic Places.

Today it is a wonderfully atmospheric Old West/Victorian–style bed-and-breakfast, with high ceilings and rich brass appointments. It's located close to downtown and Old Town, just 5 blocks from the convention center and only 5 miles from the airport. All rooms feature period furnishings, private bathrooms with showers, and one has a balcony. Each also has a coffeemaker, unstocked refrigerator, and hair dryer. A full breakfast is served each morning, in indoor and outdoor dining rooms.

ON THE OUTSKIRTS

Casa del Granjero. 414 C de Baca Lane NW, Albuquerque, NM 87114. ☎ **800/701-4144** or 505/897-4144. Fax 505/897-4144. 7 units. $89–$159 double. Extra person $20. Rates include full breakfast. DISC, MC, V.

From the pygmy goats to the old restored wagon out front, Casa del Granjero ("The Farmer's House") is true to its name. Located north of town—about a 15-minute drive from Old Town—it is quiet and has a rich, homey feeling. Butch and Victoria Farmer have transformed this residence—the original part of which is 120 years old—into a fine bed-and-breakfast. The great room has an enormous sculptured adobe fireplace, comfortable *bancos* (adobe benches) for lounging, a library, and is almost cluttered with Southwestern artifacts. There's a 52-inch television in the den.

The guest rooms, with Spanish nicknames, are beautifully furnished and decorated. Most have fireplaces. Cuarto del Rey features Mexican furnishings and handmade quilts and comforters. Cuarto de Flores has French doors that open onto a portal, and Cuarto Alegre has a king-size canopy bed done up in lace and satin. The newer Guest House has comfortable rooms and access to a kitchen, but a less luxurious and Southwestern feel. In the morning, a full breakfast is served at long tables decorated with colorful Mexican cloths or on the portal. Specialties include chiliquilles (an enchilada-like recipe from Yucatán), served with Cuban rice custard, coffee cake, and fruit. Catered lunches and dinners are also available by arrangement. There's an organic garden and raspberry patch, as well as a new Jacuzzi and sauna, conference room, and office center equipped with fax and computer. Smoking is permitted outdoors only, and no pets except horses are permitted. There are accommodations for travelers with disabilities. *A warning to women:* These are country folk, and the men will tend to call you "hon" and "darlin'."

✪ **Hacienda Antigua.** 6708 Tierra Dr., NW, Albuquerque, NM 87107. ☎ **800/201-2986** or 505/345-5399. Fax 505/345-3855. www.haciendaantigua.com/bnb/. E-mail: antigua@swcp.com. 5 units. A/C TEL. $85–$159 double. Extra person $25. Rates include breakfast. AE, DISC, MC, V.

Located on the north side of Albuquerque, just off Osuna Road, is Hacienda Antigua, a 200-year-old adobe home that was once the first stagecoach stop out of Old Town in Albuquerque. When Ann Dunlap and Melinda Moffit bought it, they were careful to preserve the building's historic charm while transforming it into an elegant bed-and-breakfast. The artistically landscaped courtyard, with its large cottonwood tree and abundance of greenery (including a large raspberry patch), offers a welcome respite for today's tired travelers.

The rooms are gracefully and comfortably furnished with antiques. There's the Don Pablo Suite with a king-size bed (covered with a stunning blue quilt), a sitting room with a kiva fireplace, and a bathroom with a wonderful old pedestal bathtub/shower; and La Capilla, the home's former chapel, which is furnished with a queen-size bed, a fireplace, and a beautiful carving of San Ysidro (the patron saint of farmers). All the rooms have such regional touches. They are also equipped with fireplaces, Caswell Massey soaps, hair dryers, coffeemakers, and unstocked mini-refrigerators. A gourmet breakfast is served in the garden during warm weather and by the fire in winter. Guests also have use of the pool and hot tub. Just a 20-minute drive from the airport, Hacienda Antigua is a welcome change from the anonymity of the downtown Albuquerque high-rise hotels, and Ann and Melinda are terrific hosts.

Hacienda Vargas. El Camino Real (P.O. Box 307), Algodones/Santa Fe, NM 87001. ☎ **800/ 261-0006** or 505/867-9115. Fax 505/867-1902. www.swcp.com.hacvar//. E-mail: hacvar@swcp.com. 7 units. A/C. $79–$149 double. Extra person $15. MC, V.

Unassuming in its elegance, Hacienda Vargas is located right on old Route 66. Owned and operated by the DeVargas family, the inn is situated in the small town of Algodones (about 20 miles from Albuquerque) and is a good place to stay if you're planning to visit both Santa Fe and Albuquerque but don't want to stay in one of the downtown hotels in either city. There's a real Mexican feel to the decor, with brightly woven place mats in the breakfast room and Spanish suits of armor hanging in the common area. Each guest room has a private entrance, many opening onto a court-yard. All rooms are furnished with New Mexico antiques, are individually decorated, and have handmade kiva fireplaces. Many have Jacuzzi tubs. Each of the four suites has a Jacuzzi tub, fireplace, and private patio. Hosts Jule and Paul DeVargas are extremely gracious and helpful—they'll make you feel right at home. A full breakfast is served every morning in the dining room. The only drawback here is the train tracks near the back of the house, and during my stay the last train went by around midnight. At all other times the inn is quiet and restful.

La Hacienda Grande. 21 Baros Lane, Bernalillo, NM 87004. ☎ **505/867-1887.** Fax 505/ 867-4621. 6 units (all with bath). A/C. $99–$129 double. Extra person $15. Rates include breakfast. AE, DISC, MC, V. Free parking.

Twenty minutes from Albuquerque, this is the place to stay if you want to experience the feel of historic adobe architecture at its finest. The 250-year-old structure built around a courtyard was once a stage coach stop on El Camino Real, the route north from Mexico. Three years ago it was purchased by Shoshana Zimmerman, who did a complete interior renovation, adding bathrooms to each unit, yet preserving the spirit of the old place. Two-foot-thick walls and brick or flagstone floors, as well as elegant vigas distinguish the architecture. A real attention to soul comfort distinguishes the decorating. Shoshana has implemented some feng shui principles in her choice of music in the main room (often Native American flute), scents, and textures. All the rooms offer views out toward country meadows. My favorite room is the San Felipe, with a queen bed, Jacuzzi tub, and a freestanding ceramic fireplace (five of the rooms have wood-burning kiva fireplaces). If you love morning sun, request the Santa Clara. Most of the bathrooms are small and have showers rather than baths. Early each morning coffee and tea are left in thermoses outside your door. Breakfast is served in a sunny room that was once a chapel. My favorite is the huevos motuleños, a mixture of tortillas, eggs, green chile, and goat cheese. Other favorites are Amaretto French toast and pumpkin pancakes. There are phone jacks in each room, and phones are available at the front desk. In addition, televisions and VCRs are available upon request. Smoking is prohibited except on the patio.

Sarabande. 5637 Rio Grande Blvd. NW, Albuquerque, NM 87107. ☎ **888/506-4923** or 505/345-4923. Fax 505/345-9130. www.sarabandebb.com. E-mail: Janie@sarabandebb.com. 3 units. A/C TV TEL. $85–$125 double. Rates include breakfast. AE, DISC, MC, V. Free parking.

A bit of grandmotherly comfort describes this place situated in the North Valley, a lovely 10-minute drive from Old Town. Once you pass through the front gate and into the well tended courtyard gardens with fountains, you'll forget that you're staying on the fringes of a big city. With cut-glass windows, lots of pastels, traditional antiques, and thick carpet (in all but the poolside room), you'll be well pampered here. Innkeepers Betty Vickers and Margaret Magnussen have filled the home with fine art as well as comfortable modern furniture. The Rose Room has a Japanese soaking tub and kiva fireplace. The Iris Room, with its stained-glass window depicting irises, has a king-size bed. Both rooms open onto a wisteria-shaded patio where breakfast can be taken in the morning. Out back are a 50-foot heated lap pool and a hot tub (which can be used through the winter). There is a library stocked with magazines, books by local authors, and books about New Mexico (including local sports and recreation). Betty and Margaret are avid hikers and will be happy to recommend hiking options for you. All-terrain bikes are available for guest use free of charge. Breakfast (fresh fruit, fresh-squeezed juice, coffee, and homemade breads) may be served in the courtyard or the dining room. Don't miss the chocolate-chip cookies offered in the afternoon.

RV PARKS

Albuquerque Central KOA. 12400 Skyline Rd. NE, Albuquerque, NM 87123. ☎ **800/ 562-7781** or 505/296-2729. $22 tent site; $30–$32 RV site, depending on the hookup; $38 one-room cabin; $48 two-room cabin. All prices are valid for up to two people; each additional adult is $5 extra. AE, DISC, MC, V.

This RV park sits in the foothills east of Albuquerque. It features a bathhouse, Laundromat, hot tub, outdoor swimming pool (open summers only), miniature golf course and playground, a convenience store, and bicycles to rent during summer. Cabins are available.

Albuquerque North KOA. 555 Hill Rd., Bernalillo, NM 87004. ☎ **505/867-5227.** $20 tent site; $25–$30 RV site, depending on the hookup; $32 one-bedroom cabin; and $40.95 two-bedroom cabin. All prices include a pancake breakfast and are valid for up to two people; additional adults are each $3 extra. DISC, MC, V.

More than 1,000 cottonwood and pine trees shade this park, and in the warm months there are many flowers. Located at the foot of the mountains 14 miles from Albuquerque, this campground has a Laundromat, outdoor swimming pool (open May to October), playground, convenience store, cafe, and free outdoor movies. There's a free pancake breakfast daily. Reservations are recommended. There are also 6 camping cabins available.

Palisades RV Park. 9201 Central Ave. NW, Albuquerque, NM 87121. ☎ **505/831-5000.** Fax 505/352-2983. 110 sites. $20 per day; $100 per week; $220 plus electricity per month. MC, V.

Sitting out on the barren west mesa, this RV park does have nice views of the Sandia Mountains and is the closest RV park to Old Town and the new Biopark (10-minute drive); however, it is also in a fairly desolate setting, with only a few trees about. In midsummer it will be hot. The owner is on-site and there's a bathhouse, Laundromat, reception room, small convenience store, and propane is available.

4 Where to Dine

IN OR NEAR OLD TOWN

Chef du Jour. 119 San Pasquale SW. ☎ **505/247-8998.** Menu items lunch $2.50–$7.50; dinner $4–$14. MC, V. Mon–Fri 11am–2pm; Fri–Sat 5:30–8:30pm. ECLECTIC.

This small, quiet and informal one-room cafe serves elegantly prepared food at very reasonable prices. When I was here recently, I ran into an old friend, who said that when the place first opened, she ate lunch here every day and took home dinner from here at night. She claims that she didn't cook for a year. The chef confirmed that she was barely exaggerating. The restaurant is a little difficult to find; travel south from the Plaza, cross Lomas and find San Pasquale. Inside, there's an open kitchen along one side and oddly matched tables. Original floral paintings and a red floor make it very bright. Once you get a taste of what's on the menu (which changes every week), you'll be coming back for more. Take special note of the condiments, all of which are home-made, from the ketchup to the salsa. Recent menu offerings included spicy garlic soup, a great garden burger, green-corn tamales (served with Southwest mango salsa), and marinated fish on a French roll. There is also a salad du jour. Chef du Jour has some outdoor tables. If you call in advance, the restaurant will fax you a copy of its current menu. They're now serving microbrew beers and hard ciders.

Duran Central Pharmacy. 1815 Central NW. ☎ **505/247-4141.** Menu items $4.20–$7.50. No credit cards. Mon–Fri 9am–6:30pm, Sat 9am–2pm. NEW MEXICAN.

Sounds like an odd place to eat, I know. Although you could go to one of the touristy New Mexican restaurants in the middle of Old Town and have lots of atmosphere and mediocre food, you can also come here, where locals eat, and feast. It's a few blocks up Central, east of Old Town. On your way through the pharmacy, you may want to stock up on specialty soaps; there's a pretty good variety here.

The restaurant itself is plain, with a red tile floor and small tables, as well as a counter. For years I used to come here for a bowl of green chile and a homemade tortilla, which is still an excellent choice. Now I go for the full meals, such as the blue-corn enchilada plate or the huevos rancheros (eggs over corn tortillas, smothered with chile). The menu is short, but you can count on authentic northern New Mexican food. No smoking is permitted.

✪ **La Crêpe Michel.** 400 San Felipe C2. ☎ **505/242-1251.** Reservations accepted. Main courses $3.50–$17.50. MC, V. Tues–Sun 11:30am–2pm; Thurs–Sat 6–9pm. FRENCH.

This small find is tucked away in a secluded walkway not far from the Plaza. Run by chef Claudie Zamet-Wilcox from France, it has a cozy, informal European feel, with checked table coverings and simple furnishings. Service is friendly and calm, which makes this a good place for a romantic meal. You can't miss with any of the crepes. I found the *crêpe aux fruits de mer* (blend of sea scallops, bay scallops, and shrimp in a velouté sauce with mushrooms) especially nice, as is the *crêpe à la volaille* (chunks of chicken in a cream sauce with mushrooms and Madeira wine). For a heartier meal, try one of the specials listed on a board on the wall. My mahimahi Basquaise came in a light vegetable sauce, and my companion's *filet de boeuf* had a delicious béarnaise. Both were served with vegetables cooked just enough to leave them crisp and tasty. For dessert, don't leave without having a *crêpe aux fraises* (strawberry crepe). Because of its proximity to a church, no alcoholic beverages are served.

✪ **Maria Teresa.** 618 Rio Grande Blvd. NW. ☎ **505/242-3900.** Reservations recom-mended. Lunch $7–$10.95; dinner $12.95–$23. AE, DC, MC, V. Daily 11am–2:30pm and 5–9pm. NEW MEXICAN/CONTINENTAL.

If you're looking for excellent food in a Victorian Old West atmosphere, walk a block north of the Plaza and eat here. In summer, there's a small enclosed patio that's enchanting. This 1840s Salvador Armijo House, a National Historic property, has 32-inch-thick adobe walls and is furnished with Victorian antiques and paintings. Tables are well spaced through seven rooms, a great place for an intimate meal. Service is formal and professional, though on a busy day, it may be slow. Lunches include a variety of pasta and salad dishes. I enjoyed the crispy crab cake served with

Central Albuquerque Dining

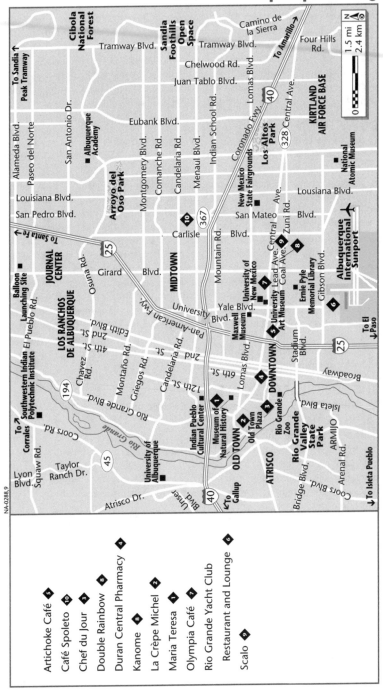

Artichoke Café 5
Café Spoleto 10
Chef du Jour 3
Double Rainbow 8
Duran Central Pharmacy 4
Kanome 8
La Crèpe Michel 2
Maria Teresa 1
Olympia Café 7
Rio Grande Yacht Club
Restaurant and Lounge 6
Scalo 9

thick asparagus spears, though you may prefer it with Southwestern pasta salad. Or try the Old Town tortilla roll filled with cheese, veggies, and your choice of meat or fish, served with guacamole. Dinner entrees include soup or salad, and range from fish to meats. My favorite is the sautéed jumbo prawns, but others prefer the seared fillet of beef tenderloin, topped with bérnaise sauce. For dessert you may want to choose from a variety of specialty drinks such as a Chocolate Cream Fizz (Godiva chocolate liqueur topped with cream and spritzed with club soda.) There's a full bar.

DOWNTOWN

✪ **Artichoke Cafe.** 424 Central Ave. SE. ☎ **505/243-0200.** Reservations recommended. Main courses $9.95–$19.95. AE, DISC, MC, V. Mon–Fri 11am–2:30pm; Mon–Sat 5:30–10pm. CONTINENTAL.

An art gallery as well as a restaurant, this popular spot near downtown has startling paintings and sculptures set against azure walls, a hint at the innovative dining experience offered here. Set in three rooms, with dim lighting, this is a nice romantic place. The waitstaff is friendly and efficient, though a little slow on a busy night. I was impressed by the list of special drinks available, a variety of interesting waters that included my favorite Ame, as well as ginger beer, Jamaican ice coffee, microbrews, and an excellent list of California and French wines. Of course, you'll want to start with an artichoke; you can have one steamed with three dipping sauces or roasted and stuffed with forest mushrooms and rock shrimp. For lunch, there are a number of salads and gourmet sandwiches, as well as entrees such as flash-fried sea scallops with ginger and lime sauce. Check out the dinner specials. My favorite was a wahoo on glass noodles with a miso broth. From the menu, try the pumpkin ravioli with butternut squash, spinach, and ricotta filling with a hazelnut and sage butter sauce with Madeira wine.

THE NORTHEAST HEIGHTS

✪ **Cafe Spoleto.** 2813 San Mateo NE. ☎ **505/880-0897.** Reservations recommended. Main courses $12–$18. Tues–Sat 5:30–9:30pm. AE, DISC, MC, V. MEDITERRANEAN.

Bathed in candlelight, this quiet contemporary restaurant offers one of the best dining experiences in Albuquerque. It's set with simple pine tables accented by subdued modern art, a nice place for a romantic dinner or a night out before theater. Service is friendly and efficient. The menu changes every 2 weeks, so be prepared for some innovation. You might start with bruschetta with grilled pears, caramelized onions, and gorgonzola or wild mushroom and leek soup. My favorite entree here is the unconventional paella, made with risotto, chicken, Italian sausage, mussels, cranberry beans, and red and gold peppers. The grilled mahimahi is also nice, served with baby beets, rösti potatoes, and green beans.

The County Line. 9600 Tramway Blvd. NE. ☎ **505/856-7477.** Reservations not accepted. Main courses $8.95–$14.95. AE, CB, DC, DISC, MC, V. Mon–Thurs 5–9pm, Fri–Sat 5–10pm, Sun 4–9pm. BARBECUE AND STEAKS.

My brother and his wife like to take their kids to this restaurant after visiting the nearby ice-skating rink. The place is popular and doesn't take reservations, but if you call before you leave your hotel they'll put your name on the waiting list; by the time you get there you'll probably be next in line. If not, you can always wait at the ever-crowded bar. The restaurant is loud and always busy, but it has a spectacular view of the city lights. It's decor is Old Route 66, with wagon-wheel furniture, aged license plates, and cowboy-boot lamps.

When you finally get a table, you'll be given a Big Chief Writing Tablet menu offering great Southwestern barbecue at very reasonable prices. The service is so good it borders on pushy, but it's friendly too. We all like the garlic mashed potatoes, and most of us order the baby back ribs, but there's also a mixed platter that has a spicy sausage. They've also added grilled fish to the menu. A kid's menu, paper and markers, and take-home cups make it a treat for the little ones. If you're not very hungry you should probably consider going somewhere else.

High Finance Restaurant and Tavern. 40 Tramway Rd., on top of Sandia Peak. ☎ **505/ 243-9742.** Reservations requested. Main courses $13.95–$35. Tramway $10 with dinner reservations ($13 without). AE, DC, DISC, MC, V. Daily in winter 4:30–8pm; summer and 4:30–10pm. CONTINENTAL.

People don't rave about the food at this restaurant, but they do rave about the experience of eating here. Set high above Albuquerque, at the top of the Sandia Peak Tramway, it offers a fun and romantic adventure. The decor follows the name's theme, with lots of shiny brass and comfortable furniture, and the service is decent. You might start with the sesame fried calamari, served with greens and a Thai dipping sauce. There are a number of pasta dishes, which are nice, or you can try skillet-roasted ahi tuna served with a curry glaze, udon noodles, and stir-fried vegetables. For the meat lovers, there's prime rib or a nice fillet. Drinks from a full bar, as well as from a good wine and beer list, are available.

UNIVERSITY & NOB HILL

Double Rainbow. 3416 Central Ave. SE. ☎ **505/255-6633.** Reservations not accepted. All menu items under $9. AE, DISC, MC, V. Daily 6:30–midnight. CAFE/BAKERY.

Albuquerque's literati hang out at this cafe, as do university professors and hippies. They come for the many coffee drinks such as chocolate cappuccino or iced java (made with cream and chocolate), as well as for salads and sandwiches, and to read from a decent selection of magazines and newspapers. In the warm months people eat at small tables on the sidewalk. Any time of year, the three rooms inside (set around a mural of cirrus clouds) are often bustling. You'll find soups such as New Mexico chicken and rice or broccoli cheddar, various kinds of quiche, and an incredible huevos rancheros (flour tortilla, black beans, cheese, and home fries). There's a pot roast for the hungry and a Szechuan chicken salad for the lighter appetite. For dessert, try one of the elaborate baked goods such as a tricolor mousse with white, milk, and dark chocolate, or sample from a variety of ice-cream flavors. Double Rainbow has another branch at 4501 Juan Tabo NE (☎ 505/275-8311), which features a large outdoor patio and a slightly more extensive menu.

✪ Kanome: An Asian Diner. 3128 Central Ave. SE. ☎ **505/265-7773.** Reservations recommended. Main courses $4.50–$12.50. Sun–Thurs 5–10pm.

I heard friends talk of this new restaurant long before I tried it. The comments on the food were all good, though some joked about the restaurant's theme: "inspired by Asian communal meals" and the way the waiter comes and explains the concept of sharing dishes, as though this were new to an Asian dining experience. But this place is *not* typical. It has a contemporary airy atmosphere with burnished orange walls and wonderful collaged tables: pumpkin seeds, Chinese noodles, and vintage post cards embedded in clear plastic. It's not a cozy place, but the service is very friendly and efficient. The food is served with a flair and you eat with fine wooden chopsticks. My favorite is the Balinese skewered pork and cashews. The Chinese duck with Tsing Tao peanut sauce is also tasty. The chef uses free range chicken and organic vegetables.

Save room for the homemade ice cream. I tried three flavors and my favorite was the java, but each was excellent.

Olympia Cafe. 2210 Central Ave. SE. ☎ **505/266-5222.** Menu items $1.50–$10.25. AE, DC, DISC, MC, V. Mon–Fri 11am–10pm, Sat noon–10pm. GREEK.

In northern New Mexico, the hands-down favorite for Greek food is the Olympia. It's very informal (you order at a counter and wait for your number to pick up food), right across from the university, and diners eat there at all times of day. It has a lively atmosphere, with the enthusiastic Greek emanating from the kitchen. With a full carry-out menu, it's also a great place to grab a meal on the run. In the summer months I like to get the Greek salad, served with fresh pita bread, and white bean soup. A standard is the falafel sandwich with tahini. The restaurant is well known for its gyros (slices of beef and lamb broiled on a vertical spit wrapped in pita), and I hear the moussaka is excellent. For dessert, try the baklava.

✪ **Scalo.** 3500 Central Ave. SE (Nob Hill). ☎ **505/255-8782.** Reservations recommended. Main courses $7.95–$16.95; lunch $5.75–$9. AE, CB, DC, DISC, MC, V. Mon–Sat 11:30am–2:30pm and 5:30–11:30pm, Sun 5–9pm. Bar, Mon–Sat 11am–1am. NORTHERN ITALIAN.

This is a favored Italian restaurant for locals. And with a new chef, in the past year the food has become even better. The place has a simple bistro-style elegance, with white linen-clothed tables indoors, plus outdoor tables in a covered, temperature-controlled patio. The kitchen, which makes its own pasta and breads, specializes in contemporary adaptations of classical northern Italian cuisine.

Seasonal menus focus on New Mexico produce. Featured appetizers include *calamaretti fritti* (fried baby squid served with a spicy marinara and lemon aioli) and *caprini con pumante* (local goat cheese with fresh focaccia, capers, tapenade, and a roasted garlic spread). There's a selection of pastas (excellent ravioli) for lunch and dinner, as well as meat, chicken, and fish dishes. The *filetto con salsa balsamica* (grilled fillet of beef with rosemary, green peppercorns, garlic, and a balsamic demiglace sauce) is one of my favorites, and the fish specials are worth trying. Dessert selections change daily.

SOUTHEAST NEAR THE AIRPORT

Rio Grande Yacht Club Restaurant & Lounge. 2500 Yale Blvd. SE. ☎ **505/243-6111.** Reservations recommended at dinner. Main courses $5.25–$9.95 at lunch, $9.95–$32.95 at dinner. AE, CB, DC, DISC, MC, V. Mon–Fri 11am–2pm, daily 5:30–10:30pm. SEAFOOD.

This is a festive restaurant with decent seafood and steaks. Red, white, and blue sails are draped beneath the skylight of a large room dominated by a tropical garden. The walls, hung with yachting prints and photos, are made of wood strips, like those of a ship's deck. The lunch menu features burgers, sandwiches, salads, and a few New Mexican specialties. At dinner, however, fresh fish is the main attraction. Swordfish, sea scallops, ahi tuna, fresh oysters, and other denizens of the deep are prepared broiled, poached, blackened, teriyaki, Veracruz, au gratin, Mornay, stuffed, and more. If you'd rather have something else, the chef here also prepares certified Angus beef, shrimp, Alaskan king crab, several chicken dishes, and even barbecued baby back pork ribs. If you find it difficult to choose one of these, you might want to try a steak and seafood combination. The bar here is a good place for evening drinks. You'll hobnob with flight crews and sample such delicacies as smoked trout and lahvosh (Armenian cracker bread covered with Havarti and Parmesan, baked until bubbly.) Don't leave without sharing an Aspen snowball (vanilla ice cream rolled in walnuts and covered in hot fudge).

OUT OF TOWN

Prairie Star. 1000 Jemez Canyon Dam Rd., Bernalillo. ☎ **505/867-3327.** Reservations recommended. Main courses $14–$26. AE, CB, DC, DISC, MC, V. Sun–Thurs 5–9pm Fri and Sat 5–10pm (lounge opens at 4pm). CONTEMPORARY REGIONAL.

A new chef has gotten people talking about the food at this elegant restaurant by adding a Native American touch to the cuisine. Located on the Santa Ana Pueblo about 30 minutes north of Albuquerque, the restaurant is set in a 6,000-square-foot sprawling adobe home, with a marvelous view across the high plains and a golf course. It was built in the 1940s in Mission architectural style. Exposed vigas and full latilla ceilings, as well as hand-carved fireplaces and bancos, complement the thick adobe walls in the dining room. There is a lounge at the top of the circular stairway.

Diners can start with blue corn crab cakes, with a chile tartar or a variety of salads. For an entree try the salmon paillard, topped with prickly pear sauce and served with new potatoes. There is a variety of grilled items such as a filet mignon and even a grilled ostrich fillet, as well as some New Mexican dishes. Desserts vary nightly.

✪ **Range Cafe.** 925 Camino del Pueblo, Bernalillo. ☎ **505/867-1700.** www.rangecafe.com. No reservations. Breakfast/lunch $2.95–$8.95; dinner $6.50–$19.95. AE, DISC, MC, V. Daily 7:30 until closing (at least 9pm). NEW MEXICAN/AMERICAN.

This cafe on the main drag of Bernalillo, about 15 minutes north of Albuquerque, is a perfect place to stop on your way out of town. However, the food's so good you may just want to make a special trip here. Housed in what was once an old drugstore, the restaurant has tin molding on the ceiling and is decorated with Western touches, such as cowboy boots and period photos. There's a soda fountain in the center of the large space, and all the tables and chairs are hand painted with whimsical stars and clouds.

The food ranges from New Mexican enchiladas and burritos to chicken-fried steak to sandwiches and elegantly prepared meals. The proprietors here have come from such notable restaurants as Scalo in Albuquerque and Prairie Star on Santa Ana Pueblo, and the chef was quickly nabbed from the Double A in Santa Fe after it closed, so you can count on exquisite food. For breakfast, try the pancakes or the breakfast burrito. For lunch or dinner, I recommend Tom's meat loaf, served with roasted garlic mashed potatoes, mushroom gravy, and sautéed vegetables. For dinner, you might try Range scallops, with a grilled tomato and cilantro cream sauce with pine nuts over red chile linguine. Taos Cow ice cream is the order for dessert, served in cones or malts, shakes, or sundaes, or try the baked goods and specialty coffees. No smoking is permitted. Next door the Range has opened a retail space selling local arts and crafts.

5 What to See & Do

Albuquerque's original town site, known today as Old Town, is the central point of interest for visitors. Here, grouped around the Plaza, are the venerable Church of San Felipe de Neri and numerous restaurants, art galleries, and crafts shops. Several important museums are situated close by. Within a few blocks are the recently completed Albuquerque Aquarium and the Rio Grande Botanic Garden (near Central Avenue and Tingley Drive NW). The project includes a 25,000-square-foot aquarium and a 50-acre botanical garden, both well worth the visit.

But don't get stuck in Old Town. Elsewhere you will find the Sandia Peak Tramway, Kirtland Air Force Base and the National Atomic Museum, the University of New Mexico with its museums, and a number of natural attractions. Within day-trip range are several pueblos and a trio of significant monuments (see "Touring the Pueblos Around Albuquerque," in section 10 below).

THE TOP ATTRACTIONS

Old Town
Northeast of Central Ave. & Rio Grande Blvd. NW

A maze of cobbled courtyard walkways leads to hidden patios and gardens, where many of Old Town's 150 galleries and shops are located. Adobe buildings, many refurbished in the Pueblo Revival style in the 1950s, are grouped around the tree-shaded **Plaza,** created in 1780. Pueblo and Navajo artisans often display their pottery, blankets, and silver jewelry on the sidewalks lining the Plaza.

The buildings of Old Town once served as mercantile shops, grocery stores, and government offices, but the importance of Old Town as Albuquerque's commercial center declined after 1880, when the railroad came through 1¼ miles east of the Plaza and businesses relocated to be closer to the trains. Old Town clung to its historical and sentimental roots, but the quarter fell into disrepair until the 1930s and 1940s, when it was rediscovered by artisans and other shop owners, and the tourism industry burgeoned.

When Albuquerque was established in 1706, the first building erected by the settlers was the **Church of San Felipe de Neri,** which faces the Plaza on its north side. It's a cozy church with wonderful stained-glass windows and vivid retablos. This house of worship has been in almost continuous use for about 290 years.

When the original building collapsed about 1790, it was reconstructed and subsequently expanded several times, all the while remaining the spiritual heart of the city. The windows are some 20 feet from the ground and its walls are 4 feet thick—to make the church also serviceable as a fortress against Indian attack. A spiral stairway leading to the choir loft is built around the trunk of an ancient spruce. Confessionals, altars, and images are hand carved; Gothic spires, added in the late 19th century, give the church a European air from the outside. The church's annual parish fiesta, held the first weekend in June, brings food and traditional dancing to the plaza.

Next door to the church is the **Rectory,** built about 1793. Also on the north plaza is **Loyola Hall,** the Sister Blandina Convent, built originally of adobe in 1881 as a residence for Sisters of Charity teachers who worked in the region. When the Jesuit fathers built **Our Lady of the Angels School,** 320 Romero St., in 1877, it was the only public school in Albuquerque.

The **Antonio Vigil House,** 413 Romero St., is an adobe-style residence with traditional viga ends sticking out over the entrance door. The **Florencio Zamora Store,** 301 Romero St., was built in the 1890s of "pugmill" adobe for a butcher and grocer. The **Jesus Romero House,** 205 Romero St., was constructed by another grocer in 1915 in "Prairie-Mediterranean" style. Just down the street, the **Jesus Romero Store,** built in 1893, has Territorial and Queen Anne structural features. On the south plaza, the **Manuel Springer House** had a hipped roof and bay windows, still visible under its commercial facade of today. The adjacent **Cristobal Armijo House,** a banker's two-story adobe, was completed in 1886 in combined Italianate and Queen Anne architectural styles.

Casa Armijo, in the 200 block of San Felipe Street, dates from before 1840; it was a headquarters for both Union and Confederate troops during the Civil War days. The nearby **Ambrosio Armijo House and Store,** also on San Felipe, an 1882 adobe structure, once had the high false front of wooden boards so typical of Old West towns in movies. The **Herman Blueher House,** at 302 San Felipe St., built by a businessman in 1898, is a three-story Italianate mansion with fancy porches on two levels, now obscured by storefronts.

Central Albuquerque Attractions

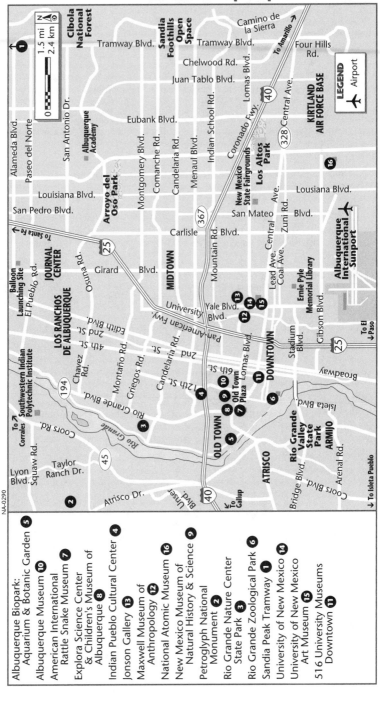

N
1.5 mi
2.4 km
0

Cibola National Forest

Camino de la Sierra
To Amarillo →

Tramway Blvd.
Sandia Foothills Open Space
Tramway Blvd.
Four Hills Rd.

Chelwood Rd.

Juan Tablo Blvd.

LEGEND
✈ Airport

Eubank Blvd.

KIRTLAND AIR FORCE BASE

Alameda Blvd.
Paseo del Norte
San Antonio Dr.
Albuquerque Academy

Montgomery Blvd.
Comanche Rd.
Candelaria Rd.
Menaul Blvd.
Indian School Rd.
Coronado Fwy.
Lomas Blvd.
Central Ave.
328
Central Ave.

40

Los Altos Park

New Mexico State Fairgrounds

16

Louisiana Blvd.
San Pedro Blvd.

Arroyo del Oso Park

Louisiana Blvd.

367

San Mateo

Blvd.
Zuni Rd.

Albuquerque International Sunport
✈

To Santa Fe ←

25
JOURNAL CENTER

El Pueblo Rd.

Balloon Launching Site

Osuna Rd.

Carlisle
Blvd.

Mountain Rd.

Lead Ave.
Coal Ave.
Central Ave.

Ernie Pyle Memorial Library

Gibson Blvd.

25

To El Paso ↓

LOS RANCHOS DE ALBUQUERQUE

Girard

Blvd.

MIDTOWN

Edith Blvd.
2nd St.
4th St.

University Blvd.
Pan-American Fwy.

Yale Blvd.
13
14
15
12

Stadium Blvd.

Southwestern Indian Polytechnic Institute

194

Chavez Rd.

Montaño Rd.
Griegos Rd.
Candelaria Rd.
2nd St.
12th St.
6th St.

DOWNTOWN

To Corrales

Coors Rd.

Rio Grande Blvd.

3

4
8 9 10
7
Old Town Plaza
11
6

Lomas Blvd.

Broadway

Rio Grande

45

OLD TOWN

5

Rio Grande Valley State Park

Isleta Blvd.

ARMIJO

Lyon Blvd.
Squaw Rd.
Taylor Ranch Dr.

2

Atrisco Dr.

Unser Blvd.

40

To Gallup ↓

ATRISCO

Bridge Blvd.
Coors Blvd.
Arenal Rd.

→ To Isleta Pueblo

NA-0290

Albuquerque Biopark: Aquarium & Botanic Garden **5**
Albuquerque Museum **10**
American International Rattle Snake Museum **7**
Explora Science Center & Children's Museum of Albuquerque **8**
Indian Pueblo Cultural Center **4**
Jonson Gallery **13**
Maxwell Museum of Anthropology **12**
National Atomic Museum **16**
New Mexico Museum of Natural History & Science **9**
Petroglyph National Monument **2**
Rio Grande Nature Center State Park **3**
Rio Grande Zoological Park **6**
Sandia Peak Tramway **1**
University of New Mexico **14**
University of New Mexico Art Museum **15**
516 University Museums Downtown **11**

99

It's sad to see the changes the past 10 years or so have wrought on Old Town shopping. When I was growing up in the area, this was the place to go to buy gifts. Now, many of the interesting shops (such as the basket shop right on the Plaza, which used to be packed with thousands of dusty baskets) have become trinket stores. However, you can still find good buys from the Native Americans selling jewelry on the Plaza. Look especially for silver bracelets and strung turquoise. If you want to take something fun home and spend very little, buy a dyed corn necklace. Your best bet when wandering around Old Town is to just peek into shops, but there are a few places you'll definitely want to spend time in. See "Shopping," below, for recommendations.

An excellent Old Town historic **walking tour** originates at the Albuquerque Museum (see below) at 11am Tuesday through Sunday during spring, summer and fall. If this time isn't convenient, the museum publishes a brochure for a self-guided walking tour of Old Town.

The **Old Town Easter Parade,** held annually on the Saturday preceding Easter, brings the Easter Bunny to the streets of the quarter, along with a variety of floats and marching bands. On Christmas Eve, thousands of *luminarias* or *farolitos*—brown paper bags filled with sand and lighted candles—line the narrow streets and flat-roofed buildings surrounding the plaza.

✪ Indian Pueblo Cultural Center. 2401 12th St. NW. ☎ **800/766-4405** or 505/843-7270. Admission $4 adults, $3 seniors, $1 students; free for children 4 and under. Daily 9am–5:30pm; restaurant 7:30am–4pm. Closed New Year's Day, Thanksgiving Day, and Christmas.

Owned and operated as a nonprofit organization by the 19 pueblos of New Mexico, this is a fine place to begin an exploration of Native American culture. Located about a mile northeast of Old Town, this museum—modeled after Pueblo Bonito, a spectacular 9th-century ruin in Chaco Culture National Historic Park—consists of several parts.

Begin your exploration in the basement, where a permanent exhibit depicts the evolution from prehistory to present of the various pueblos, including displays of the distinctive handcrafts of each community. Note especially how pottery differs in concept and design from pueblo to pueblo. You'll also find a small screening room where you can see films of some of New Mexico's most noted Native American artists making their wares, including San Ildefonso potter María Martínez firing her pottery with open flames.

The Pueblo House Children's Museum, located in a separate building, is a hands-on experience that gives children the opportunity to learn about and understand the evolution of Pueblo culture. There they can touch pot shards, play with heishi (shell) drills, even don fox tails and dance.

Upstairs is an enormous (10,000-square-foot) gift shop featuring fine pottery, rugs, sandpaintings, kachinas, drums, and jewelry, among other things. Southwestern clothing and souvenirs are also available. Prices here are quite reasonable.

Every weekend throughout the year, Native American dancers perform at 11am and 2pm in an outdoor arena surrounded by original murals. Often artisans demonstrate their crafts expertise there as well. During certain weeks of the year, such as the Balloon Fiesta, dances are performed daily.

A restaurant serves traditional Native American foods. I wouldn't eat a full meal here, but you might want to stop in for some Indian fry bread and a bowl of *posole*.

✪ Albuquerque Museum. 2000 Mountain Rd. NW. ☎ **505/243-7255.** Free admission, but donations are appreciated. Tues–Sun 9am–5pm. Closed major holidays.

Take an interesting journey down into the caverns of New Mexico's past in this museum on the outskirts of Old Town. Drawing on the largest U.S. collection of

Spanish colonial artifacts, displays here include Don Quixote–style helmets, swords, and even horse armor. You can wander through an 18th-century house compound with adobe floor and walls, and see gear used by *vaqueros,* the original cowboys who came to the area in the 16th century. A weaving exhibition allows kids to try spinning wool, and a trapping section provides them with pelts to touch. In an old-style theater, two films on Albuquerque history are shown. In the History Hopscotch area, kids can explore an old trunk or play with antique blocks and other toys. An Old Town walking tour originates here at 11am Tuesday through Sunday during spring, summer, and fall. In the upper floors there are permanent art collections, and best of all, a huge exhibit space where you'll find some extraordinary shows. The 1999 schedule includes *Imagenes de Oro: Colonial & Modern Images from Guatemala and New Mexico; WPA Photographs; Intermountain Weavers;* and *Impressionism.* A gift shop sells books and jewelry and has a nice selection of Navajo dolls.

Rio Grande Nature Center State Park. 2901 Candelaria Rd. NW. ☎ **505/344-7240.** www.unm.edu/natrcent. E-mail: natrcent@unm.edu. Admission $1 adults, 50¢ children 6 and older, free for children under 6. Daily 10am–5pm. Closed Jan 1, Thanksgiving, Dec 25.

Whenever I'm in Albuquerque and want to get away from it all, I come here. The center, located just a few miles north of Old Town, spans 270 acres of riverside forest and meadows that include stands of 100-year-old cottonwoods and a 3-acre pond. Located on the Rio Grande Flyway, an important migratory route for many birds, it's an excellent place to see sandhill cranes, Canada geese, and quail. More than 260 species have made this their temporary or permanent home. In a protected area where dogs aren't allowed (you can bring dogs on most of the 2 miles of trails), you'll find exhibits of native grasses, wildflowers, and herbs. Inside a building built half above and half below ground, you can sit next to the pond in a glassed-in viewing area and comfortably watch ducks and other birds in their avian antics. There are 21 self-guided interpretive exhibits as well as photo exhibits, a library, a small nature store, and children's resource room. On Saturday mornings you can join in a guided nature walk. Other weekend programs are available for adults and children including nature photography and bird and wildflower identification classes. Call for a schedule.

See "Especially for Kids," in section 6 below, for more museums and attractions in the Old Town area.

✪ **Sandia Peak Tramway.** 10 Tramway Loop NE. ☎ **505/856-7325.** www. sandiapeak.com. Admission $14 adults, $10 seniors and children 5–12, free for children under 5. Memorial Day to Labor Day, daily 9am–10pm; spring and fall, Thurs–Tues 9am–8pm, Wed 5–8pm; ski season, Mon–Tues and Thurs–Fri 9am–8pm, Wed noon–8pm, Sat–Sun 8:30am–8pm. To reach the base of the tram, take I-25 north to Tramway Rd. (Exit 234), then proceed east about 5 miles on Tramway Rd. (NM 556); or take Tramway Blvd., Exit 167 (NM 556), north of I-40 approximately 8½ miles. Turn east the last half mile on Tramway Rd.

This is a fun and exciting half-day or evening outing, allowing incredible views of the Albuquerque landscape and wildlife. The Sandia Peak tram is a "jigback"; in other words, as one car approaches the top, the other nears the bottom. The two pass halfway through the trip, in the midst of a 1½-mile "clear span" of unsupported cable between the second tower and the upper terminal.

Several hiking trails are available on Sandia Peak and one of them—La Luz Trail—is partly flat and quite easy. The views in all directions are extraordinary. *Note:* The trails on Sandia may not be suitable for children.

There is a popular and expensive restaurant, High Finance Restaurant and Tavern, at Sandia's summit, (see "Where to Dine," earlier in this chapter). Special tram rates apply with dinner reservations.

MORE SIGHTS TO SEE & PLACES TO BE

✪ **National Atomic Museum.** Wyoming Blvd. and K St. (P.O. Box 5800), Kirtland Air Force Base. ☎ **505/284-3243.** www.sandia.gov/AtomMus/AtomMus.htm. Adults $2, ages 7–18 and seniors $1, children 6 and under free. Visitors must obtain passes (and a map) at the Wyoming or Gibson Gate of the base. Children under 12 not admitted without parent or adult guardian. Daily 9am–5pm. Closed Jan 1, Easter, Thanksgiving, Dec 25.

Shortly after the successful detonation of the first atomic bomb, Robert Oppenheimer, who headed the Manhattan Project, quoted from ancient Hindu texts: "I am become death, the shatterer of worlds." This and other valuable information highlight the 51-minute film *Ten Seconds That Shook the World,* which is shown daily at 10:30 and 11:30am, and 2 and 3pm at this museum, an experience worth fitting into a busy schedule. The museum itself offers the next-best introduction to the nuclear age after the Bradbury Science Museum in Los Alamos. The film has lots of actual footage from the days of the race to build the first nuclear weapon, and though it does present a quite positive view of the bombing of Japan, viewers really get a sense of the historical context within which the decision was made.

The museum itself makes for an interesting 1- or 2-hour visit. It traces the history of nuclear weapons development beginning with the top-secret Manhattan Project of the 1940s, including a copy of the letter Albert Einstein wrote to Pres. Franklin D. Roosevelt suggesting the possible need to beat the Germans at creating an atomic bomb—a letter that surprisingly went ignored for nearly 2 years.

You'll find a permanent Marie Curie exhibit in the lobby and full-scale models of the "Fat Man" and "Little Boy" bombs, as well as displays and films on the peaceful application of nuclear technology and other alternative energy sources. Fusion is explained in a manner that laypeople can understand; other exhibits deal with the use and development of robotics, with plenty of strange R-2, D-2 types moving around for kids to enjoy. Outdoor exhibits include a B-52 "Stratofortress," an F-1015D "Thunderchief," and a 280mm atomic cannon. The museum is directly across the street from the Interservice Nuclear Weapons School—do you think they offer summer courses?—adjacent to Sandia National Laboratory.

Petroglyph National Monument. 6001 Unser Blvd. NW (west of Coors Rd.). ☎ **505/899-0205.** Admission $1 per vehicle weekdays, $2 weekends. Summer, daily 9am–6pm; winter, daily 8am–5pm. Visitor Center 8am–5pm. Closed Jan 1, Dec 25.

In the past few years this monument has made national news, and for good reason; a struggle has raged in Congress over whether or not to allow a road through these lava flows that were once a hunting and gathering area for prehistoric Native Americans, who left a chronicle of their beliefs etched on the dark basalt boulders. The issue is heated not only because such a road would disturb the 15,000 petroglyphs, but also because it would set a precedent that might allow roads through other national monuments around the country. One ranger said he sees Albuquerque expanding so fast that the monument is "like a speed bump in the development of the West Mesa." It's a sad, but true analogy. History in progress aside, this place is worth visiting, a nice outdoor adventure after a morning in a museum. You'll want to stop at the Visitor's Center to get a map, check out the new interactive computer, and, in summer, hook up with a ranger-led tour. From there drive north to the Boca Negra area where you'll have a choice of three trails. Take the Mesa Point Trail (30 minutes) that climbs quickly up the side of a hill offering many petroglyph sightings as well as an outstanding view of the Sandia Mountains. If you're traveling with your dog, you can bring it along on the Rinconada Trail. It's fun because hikers have to search the rocks more for the petroglyphs, and there are many to be found. This trail (located a few miles south of the Visitor's Center) runs for miles around a huge *rincon* (corner) at the base of the lava flow. Camping is not permitted in the park; it's strictly for day use, with picnic areas, drinking water, and rest rooms provided.

University of New Mexico. Yale Blvd. NE (north of Central Ave.). ☎ **505/277-0111.**

The state's largest institution of higher learning stretches across an attractive 70-acre campus about 2 miles east of downtown Albuquerque, north of Central Avenue and east of University Boulevard. The five campus museums, none of which charges admission, are constructed (like other UNM buildings) in a modified Pueblo style. Popejoy Hall, in the south-central part of the campus, hosts many performing-arts presentations, including those of the New Mexico Symphony Orchestra; other public events are held in nearby Keller Hall and Woodward Hall.

I've found the best way to see the museums and parts of the campus is on a walking tour, which can make for a nice 2- to 3-hour morning or afternoon outing. Begin on the west side of campus at the Maxwell. You'll find parking meters there, as well as Maxwell Museum parking for which you can get a permit inside.

The **Maxwell Museum of Anthropology,** situated on the west side of the campus on Redondo Drive at Ash Street NE (☎ **505/277-4404**), is an internationally acclaimed repository of Southwestern anthropological finds. What's really intriguing here is not just the ancient pottery, tools, and yucca weavings, but the anthropological context within which these items are set. You'll see a reconstruction of an archaeological site complete with string markers, brushes, and field notes, as well as microscope lenses you can examine to see how archaeologists perform temper analysis to find out where pots were made, and pollen analysis to help reconstruct past environments. It's open Tuesday to Friday from 9am to 4pm, Saturday from 10am to 4pm, and Sunday from noon to 4pm; closed holidays. From the Maxwell, walk east into the campus until you come to the Duck Pond and pass Mitchell Hall; then turn south (right) and walk down a lane until you reach Northrup Hall.

In Northrup Hall (☎ **505/277-4204**), about halfway between the Maxwell Museum and Popejoy Hall in the southern part of the campus, the adjacent **Geology Museum** (☎ **505/277-4204**) and **Meteorite Museum** (☎ **505/277-1644**) cover the gamut of recorded time from dinosaur bones to moon rocks. Within the Geology Museum, you'll see stones that create spectacular works of art, from little black on white orbs of orbicular granite to the brilliant blue of dioptase. In the Meteorite Museum, 550 meteorite specimens comprise the sixth-largest collection in the United States. You'll see and touch a sink-sized piece of a meteorite that weights as much as a car, as well as samples of the many variations of stones that fall from the sky. The Geology Museum is open Monday to Friday from 7:30am to noon and 1 to 4:30pm; the Meteorite Museum, Monday to Friday from 9am to noon and 1 to 4pm.

Right next door and to the south, in the basement of the Biology Department at Castetter Hall, the **Museum of Southwestern Biology** (☎ **505/277-4392**), is a working research museum. In order to see it, you need a reservation. It has extensive research holdings of global flora and fauna, especially representative of Southwestern North America, Central America, South America, and parts of Asia.

From here you walk east straight through a mall that will take you by the art building to the Fine Arts Center.

The **University of New Mexico Art Museum** (☎ **505/277-4001**) is located here, just north of Central Avenue and Cornell Street. The museum features changing exhibitions of 19th- and 20th-century art. Its permanent collection includes Old Masters paintings and sculpture, significant New Mexico artists, Spanish colonial artwork, the Tamarind Lithography Archives, and one of the largest university-owned photography collections in the country. This is my favorite part. You'll see modern and contemporary works, images that will remain in your psyche for years. It's open Tuesday to Friday from 9am to 4pm; Tuesday evening from 5 to 8pm; and Sunday from 1 to 4pm; closed holidays. A gift shop offers a variety of gifts and posters. Admission is free.

By now you'll probably want a break. Across the mall to the north is the Student Union Building (SUB), where you can get anything from muffins to pizza. Campus maps can be obtained here, along with directions. Once you're refreshed, head out the north door of the SUB and walk west through Smith Plaza, then turn north by the bus stop to Las Lomas Road, where you'll turn right and walk a half block to the intimate **Jonson Gallery** at 1909 Las Lomas Blvd. NE (☎ **505/277-4967**), on the north side of the central campus. This museum displays more than 2,000 works by the late Raymond Jonson, a leading modernist painter in early 20th-century New Mexico, as well as works by contemporary artists. This is my least favorite of the campus museums, so if you're going to miss one, make it this one. The gallery is open Tuesday to Friday from 9am to 4pm and Tuesday evening from 5 to 8pm.

From the Johnson you can walk west on Las Lomas to Redondo Rd, where you'll turn south and arrive back at the Maxwell where your car is parked. If you have the time, drive straight down Central to a branch of the University of New Mexico's Art Museum, **516 University Museums Downtown** (☎ **505/242-8244**), at 516 Central Ave. SW. Its two floors of exhibition space feature changing exhibitions drawn from art and anthropological collections of the University Art Museum and Maxwell Museum of Anthropology, as well as works by significant New Mexico and regional artists. Gallery talks, lectures, and demonstrations are featured regularly. It's open Tuesday to Saturday from 11am to 4pm (closed holidays). There is a gift shop offering cards, posters, jewelry, and art gift items. Admission is free.

Once you leave there, step next door to **Skip Maisel's** (see "Shopping," in section 9) where, adorning the outside of the store, there are murals painted in 1933 by notable Navajo painter Harrison Begay and Pueblo painter Pablita Velarde.

COOKING SCHOOLS

If you've fallen in love with New Mexican and Southwestern cooking during your stay (or even before you arrived), you might like to sign up for cooking classes with Jane Butel, a leading Southwest cooking authority and author of 14 cookbooks. At **Jane Butel's Cooking School,** 125 Second St. NW (La Posada de Albuquerque; ☎ **800/ 472-8229** or 505/243-2622; fax 505/243-8297), you'll learn the history and techniques of Southwestern cuisine and have ample opportunity for hands-on preparation. If you choose the weeklong session, you'll start by learning about chiles. The second and third days you'll try your hand at native breads and dishes, the fourth focuses on more innovative dishes, and the fifth and last day covers appetizers, beverages, and desserts. Weekend sessions are also available. Call or fax for current schedules and fees.

6 Especially for Kids

If you're traveling with children, you'll be happy to know that there are a number of Albuquerque attractions that are guaranteed to keep the kids interested. One of the city's best child-oriented activities takes place on Sunday year-round except during the Christmas season and Easter. On Romero Street in the Old Town, costumed actors re-create **Wild West shoot-outs.** There are four shows: 1:30, 2:30, 3:30, and 4:30pm.

You'll know they're about to begin when you hear the warning shots 5 minutes before show time. Call **New Mexico Gunfighters** at ☎ 505/266-9011 for more information. On weekends, there are also regular puppet plays at the **Old Town Puppet Theatre** (☎ 505/243-0208).

○ **Albuquerque Bio Park: Aquarium and Botanic Garden.** 2601 Central Ave. NW. ☎ 505/764-6200. Admission $2.50 ages 3–5 and over 65; $4.50 ages 16–64. Daily 9am–4:30pm, Sat–Sun June, July, and Aug 9am–6pm. Ticket sales stop at 4:30pm to allow time to view the facilities. Closed Jan 1, Thanksgiving, Dec 25.

For those of us born and raised in the desert, this attraction quenches years of soul thirst. The self-guided aquarium tour begins with a beautifully produced 9-minute film that describes the course of the Rio Grande River from its origin to the Gulf Coast. Then you'll move on to the touch pool, where at certain times of day children can gently touch hermit crabs and starfish. You'll pass by a replica of a salt marsh, where a gentle tidal wave moves in and out, and you'll explore the eel tank, through which you get to walk since it's an arched aquarium over your path. There's a colorful coral reef exhibit, as well as the culminating show, in a 285,000-gallon shark tank, where many species of fish and 15 to 20 sand tiger, brown, and nurse sharks swim around looking ominous.

Within a state-of-the art 10,000-square-foot conservatory, you'll find the botanical garden split into two sections. The smaller one houses the desert collection and features plants from the lower Chihuahuan and Sonoran deserts, including unique species from Baja California. The larger pavilion exhibits the Mediterranean collection and includes many exotic species native to the Mediterranean climates of southern California, South Africa, Australia, and the Mediterranean Basin. Allow at least 2 hours to see both parks. There is a restaurant on the premises.

American International Rattlesnake Museum. 202 San Felipe St. NW. ☎ 505/242-6569. Admission $2 adults, $1 children. Daily 10am–6:30pm.

This unique museum, located just off Old Town Plaza, has living specimens of common, uncommon, and very rare rattlesnakes of North, Central, and South America in naturally landscaped habitats. Oddities such as albino and patternless rattlesnakes are included, as is a display popular with youngsters—baby rattlesnakes. More than 30 species can be seen, followed by a 7-minute film on this contributor to the ecological balance of our hemisphere. Throughout the museum are rattlesnake artifacts from early American history, Native American culture, medicine, the arts, and advertising.

You'll also find a gift shop that specializes in Native American jewelry, T-shirts, and other memorabilia related to the natural world and the Southwest, all with an emphasis on rattlesnakes.

Explora Science Center and Children's Museum of Albuquerque. 800 Rio Grande Blvd. NW, Suite 10. ☎ 505/842-1537. Admission $4 ages 13–64, $2 ages 3–12 and 65 or over, and free for children 2 and under. Tues–Sat 9am–4pm, Sun noon–5pm.

At this exploration center there's something for everyone: bubbles, whisper disks, a puppet theater, a giant loom, a dress-up area, zoetropes, a capture-your-shadow wall, art activities, science demonstrations, and a giant pinhole camera. The museum also sponsors entertaining educational workshops. "The Me I Don't Always See" was a health exhibit designed to teach children about the mysteries of the human body, and a Great Artists Series featured live performances about artists' lives and work followed by a related art activity. You'll also find hands-on science and technology exhibits. Kids will learn about air pressure by flying a model plane and floating a ball on a stream of air. A new facility is planned to open in 2000 at 18th Street and Mountain.

○ **New Mexico Museum of Natural History and Science.** 1801 Mountain Rd. NW. ☎ **505/841-2800.** Admission $5.25 adults, $4.20 seniors, $2.10 children 3–11. Museum and Dynamax, $8.40 adults, $6.30 seniors, $3.15 children 3–11. Children under 12 must be accompanied by an adult. Daily 9am–5pm. Closed nonholiday Mondays Jan and Sept, and Dec 25.

A trip through this museum will take you through 12 billion years of natural history, from the formation of the universe to the present day. Begin looking at a display of stones and gems, then stroll through the "Age of Giants" display, where you'll find dinosaur skeletons cast from the real bones. As you walk beneath an allosaurus, stegosaurus, and others, you can examine real teeth and even feel the weight and texture of a real bone. Moving along, you come into the Cretaceous period and learn of the progression of flooding in the Southwestern United States beginning 100 million ago and continuing until 66 million years ago, when New Mexico became dry. This exhibit takes you through a tropical oasis, with aquariums of alligator gars, fish that were here 100 million years ago and still exist today. Next, step into the Evolator (kids love this!), a simulated time-travel ride that moves and rumbles taking you 2,000 meters up (or down) and through 38 million years of history. Then, you'll feel the air grow hot as you walk into a cave and see the inner workings of a volcano including simulated magma flow. Soon you'll find yourself in the age of the mammoths, and moving through the ice age. Other stops along the way include a Naturalist Center, where kids can peek through microscopes and make their own bear or raccoon footprints in sand, and Fossilworks, where real archaeologists work behind glass excavating bones of a seismosaurus. Don't miss the computer-generated sound of a parasaurolophus nearby. For an additional charge, the Dynamax theater surrounds you with images and sound. And look for the large new space accommodating traveling exhibitions. A gift shop on the ground floor sells imaginative nature games and other curios. This museum has good access for people with disabilities, including scripts for people who have hearing impairment, and exhibit text written in braille.

Rio Grande Zoo. 903 10th St. SW. ☎ **505/764-6200.** Admission $4.25 adults, $2.25 children and seniors, free for children 2 and under. Children under 12 must be accompanied by an adult. Daily 9am–4:30pm, and on summer weekends until 6pm. Closed Jan 1, Thanksgiving, Dec. 25.

More than 1,200 animals from 300 species live on 60 acres of riverside bosk among ancient cottonwoods. Open-moat exhibits with animals in naturalized habitats are a treat for zoo-goers. Major exhibits include the polar bears, giraffes, sea lions (with underwater viewing), the cat walk, the bird show, and ape country with its gorilla and orangutans. The zoo has an especially fine collection of elephants, mountain lions, koalas, reptiles, and native Southwestern species. A children's petting zoo is open during the summer. There are numerous snack bars on the zoo grounds, and La Ventana Gift Shop carries film and souvenirs.

7 Ballooning, Biking & Other Outdoor Pursuits

BALLOONING   Visitors not content to just watch the colorful craft rise into the clear-blue skies have a choice of several hot-air balloon operators; rates start at about $130 per person per hour: **Braden's Balloons Aloft,** 3900 Second St. NW (☎ **505/ 345-6199**); **Rainbow Ryders,** 10305 Nita Pl. NE (☎ **505/293-0000**); **World Balloon Corporation,** 4800 Eubank Blvd. NE (☎ **505/293-6800**).

The annual **Kodak Albuquerque International Balloon Fiesta** is held the first through second weekends of October (see "The Best Festivals & Events," in chapter 1, and "New Mexico Calendar of Events," in chapter 3, for details).

BIKING   Albuquerque is a major bicycling hub in the summer, for both road racers and mountain bikers. Bikes can be rented from **Rio Mountain Sport,** 1210 Rio Grande NW (☎ **505/766-9970**), and they come with helmets, maps, and locks. A great place to bike is Sandia Peak in Cíbola National Forest. You can't take your bike on the tram, but chair lift no. 1 is available for up- or downhill transportation with a bike. If you'd rather not rent a bike from the above-mentioned sports store, bike rentals are available at the top and bottom of the chair lift. The lift ride one way with a bike is $7; all day with a bike will cost you $12. Helmets are mandatory. Bike maps are available; the clearly marked trails range from easy to very difficult. Mountain Bike Challenge Events are held on Sandia Peak in May, July, August, and September.

Down in the valley, there's a bosk trail that runs along the Rio Grande and is easily accessible to Old Town and the Biopark. To the east, the Foothills Trail runs along the base of the mountains. Across the Rio Grande, on the west mesa, Petroglyph National Park is a nice place to ride. If you're looking for more technical mountain biking, head up through Tijeras Canyon to Cedro Peak. For information about other mountain-bike areas, contact the Albuquerque Convention and Visitors Bureau.

BIRD WATCHING   ✪ **Bosque del Apache National Wildlife Refuge** (☎ **505/ 835-1828**) is a haven for migratory waterfowl such as snow geese and cranes. It's located 90 miles south of Albuquerque on I-25, and is well worth the drive. You'll find 7,000 acres of carefully managed riparian habitat, which include marshlands, meadows, agricultural fields, and old-growth cottonwood forests lining the Rio Grande River. Particularly if you're here from November through March, the experience is thrilling, not only for the variety of birds—more than 300 species— but for the sheer numbers of them. Huge clouds of snow geese and sandhill cranes take flight at dawn and dusk, the air filling with the sounds of their calls and wing flaps. In early December, the refuge may harbor as many as 45,000 snow geese, 57,000 ducks of many different species, and 18,000 sandhill cranes. You may even be fortunate enough, as I was on my last visit, to see a whooping crane or two. There are also plenty of raptors about including numerous red-tailed hawks and northern harriers (sometimes called marsh hawks), Cooper's hawks and kestrels, and even bald and golden eagles. The refuge has a 15-mile auto tour loop, which you should drive very slowly. The southern half of the loop travels past numerous water impoundments, where the majority of the ducks and geese are, and the northern half has the meadows and farmland, where you'll see roadrunners and other land birds, and where the cranes and geese feed from midmorning through the afternoon.

FISHING   There are no real fishing opportunities in Albuquerque as such, but there is a nearby fishing area known as **Shady Lakes.** Nestled among cottonwood trees, it's located near I-25 on Albuquerque's north side. The most common catches are rainbow trout, black bass, bluegill, and channel catfish. To reach Shady Lakes, take I-25 north to the Tramway exit. Follow Tramway Road west for a mile and then go right on NM 313 for a half mile. Call ☎ **505/898-2568** for information. **Sandia Lakes Recreational Area** (☎ **505/897-3971**), also located on NM 313, is another popular fishing spot. There is a bait and tackle shop there.

GOLF   There are quite a few public courses in the Albuquerque area. The **Championship Golf Course at the University of New Mexico,** 3601 University Blvd. SE (☎ **505/277-4546**), is one of the best in the Southwest and was rated one of the country's top 25 public links by *Golf Digest.* **Paradise Hills Golf Course,** 10035 Country Club Lane NW (☎ **505/898-7001**), is a popular 18-hole golf course that has recently been completely renovated.

Other Albuquerque courses to check with for tee times are **Ladera,** located at 3401 Ladera Dr. NW (☎ **505/836-4449**); **Los Altos** at 9717 Copper Ave. NE (☎ **505/ 298-1897**); **Puerto del Sol,** 1800 Girard Blvd. SE (☎ **505/265-5636**); and **Arroyo del Oso,** 6401 Osuna Rd. NE (☎ **505/888-8115**).

If you're willing to drive a short distance just outside Albuquerque, you can play at the **Santa Ana Golf Club at Santa Ana Pueblo,** 288 Prairie Star Rd. (P.O. Box 1736), Bernalillo, NM 87004 (☎ **505/867-9464**), which was rated by *The New York Times* as one of the best public golf courses in the country. Rentals are available (call for information), and greens fees range from $29 to $35.

In addition, **Isleta Pueblo,** 4001 Hwy. 47, has recently completed building an 18-hole golf course (☎ **505/869-0950**).

HIKING   The 1.6-million-acre **Cíbola National Forest** offers ample hiking opportunities. In the Sandia Ranger District alone there are 16 recreation sites, including Sandia Crest, though only Cedro Peak allows overnight camping. For details, contact **Sandia Ranger Station,** NM 337 south toward Tijeras (☎ **505/ 281-3304**).

Elena Gallegos/Albert G. Simms Park, near the base of the Sandia Peak Tramway at 1700 Tramway Blvd. NE (☎**505/768-5300**), is a 640-acre mountain picnic area with hiking-trail access to the Sandia Mountain Wilderness.

HORSEBACK RIDING   There are a couple of places in Albuquerque that offer guided or unguided horseback rides. At **Sandia Trails Horse Rentals,** 10601 N. 4th St. (☎ **505/898-6970**), you'll have the opportunity to ride on Sandia Indian Reservation land along the Rio Grande. The horses are friendly and are accustomed to children. In addition, **Turkey Track Stables,** 1306 U.S. 66 E. Tijeras (☎ **505/281-1772**), located about 15 miles east of Albuquerque, offers rides on trails in the Manzano foothills.

RIVER RAFTING   This sport is generally practiced farther north, in the area surrounding Santa Fe and Taos.

In mid-May each year, the **Great Race** takes place on a 7.5-mile stretch of the Rio Grande through Albuquerque. Many categories of craft, including rafts, kayaks, canoes, and homemade craft, race down the river. Call ☎ **505/768-3483** for details.

SKIING   The **Sandia Peak Ski Area** is a good place for family skiing. There are plenty of beginner and intermediate runs. However, if you're looking for more challenge or more variety, you'd better head north to Santa Fe or Taos. The ski area has twin base-to-summit chair lifts to its upper slopes at 10,360 feet and a 1,700-foot vertical drop. There are 30 runs (35% beginner, 55% intermediate, 10% advanced) above the day lodge and ski-rental shop. Four chairs and two pomas (small surface lifts) accommodate 3,400 skiers an hour. All-day lift tickets are $34 for adults, $25 for children and seniors (age 62 and over), and free for those age 72 and over; rental pack-ages are $15 for adults, $12 for kids. The season runs from mid-December to mid-March. Contact **10 Tramway Loop NE** (☎ **505/242-9133**) for more information, or call the hot line for ski conditions (☎ **505/857-8977**).

Cross-country skiers can enjoy the trails of the Sandia Wilderness from the ski area, or they can go an hour north to the remote Jemez Wilderness and its hot springs.

TENNIS   There are 29 public parks in Albuquerque with tennis courts. You can use the courts for free on a first-come, first-served basis. Because of the city's size, your best bet is to call the Albuquerque Convention and Visitors Bureau to find out which park is closest to your hotel.

8 Spectator Sports

BASEBALL   The **Albuquerque Dukes,** 1994 champions of the Class AAA Pacific Coast League, are a farm team of the Los Angeles Dodgers. They play 72 home games from mid-April to early September in the city-owned 10,500-seat Albuquerque Sports Stadium, 1601 Stadium Blvd. SE (at University Boulevard; ☎ 505/243-1791).

BASKETBALL   The **University of New Mexico** (UNM) team, nicknamed "The Lobos," plays an average of 16 home games from late November to early March. Capacity crowds cheer the team at the 17,121-seat University Arena (fondly called "The Pit") at University and Stadium boulevards. The arena was the site of the National Collegiate Athletic Association championship tournament in 1983.

FOOTBALL   The **UNM Lobos** football team plays a September to November season, usually with five home games, at the 30,000-seat University of New Mexico Stadium, opposite both Albuquerque Sports Stadium and University Arena at University and Stadium boulevards.

HORSE RACING   The **Downs at Albuquerque,** New Mexico State Fairgrounds (☎ 505/266-5555 for post times), is near Lomas and Louisiana boulevards NE. Racing and betting, on thoroughbreds and quarter horses, take place on weekends from October to December and during the state fair in September.

The Downs has a glass-enclosed grandstand, exclusive club seating, valet parking, and complimentary racing programs and tip sheets. General admission is free; reserved second-floor seating is $2.

9 Shopping

Visitors seeking regional specialties will find many local artists and galleries of interest in Albuquerque, although neither group is as concentrated as in Santa Fe and Taos. The galleries and regional fashion designers around the Plaza in Old Town comprise a kind of a shopping center for tourists, with more than 40 merchants represented. The Sandia Pueblo runs its own crafts market at the reservation off I-25 at Tramway Road, just beyond Albuquerque's northern city limits.

Albuquerque has the three largest shopping malls in New Mexico, two within 2 blocks of each other on Louisiana Boulevard just north of I-40: **Coronado Center** and **Winrock Center.** The other is on the west mesa at 10,000 Coors Blvd. NW (☎ 505/899-SHOP).

Business hours vary, but shops are generally open Monday to Saturday from 10am to 6pm; many have extended hours; some have reduced hours; and a few, especially in shopping malls or during the high tourist season, are open on Sunday.

The Albuquerque sales tax is 5.5625%.

BEST BUYS

The best buys in Albuquerque are Southwestern regional items, including **arts and crafts** of all kinds—traditional Native American and Hispanic as well as contemporary works. In local Native American art, look for silver and turquoise jewelry, pottery, weavings, baskets, sand paintings, and Hopi *kachina* dolls. Hispanic folk art—handcrafted furniture, tinwork and *retablos,* and religious paintings—is worth seeking out. The best contemporary art is in paintings, sculpture, jewelry, ceramics, and fiber art, including weaving.

Other items of potential interest are fashions in Southwestern print designs; gourmet foods and ingredients, including blue-corn flour and chile ristras; and unique regional souvenirs, especially local Native American and Hispanic creations.

By far the greatest concentration of **galleries** is in Old Town; others are spread around the city, with smaller groupings in the university district and the northeast heights. Consult the brochure published by the Albuquerque Gallery Association, *A Select Guide to Albuquerque Galleries,* or Wingspread Communications' annual *The Collector's Guide to Albuquerque,* widely distributed at shops. Once a month, usually from 5 to 9pm on the third Friday, the Albuquerque Art Business Association (☎ 505/842-9918 for information) sponsors an **ArtsCrawl** to dozens of galleries and studios. If you're in town, it's a great way to meet the artists.

You'll also find some interesting shops in the **Nob Hill** area, which is just west of the University of New Mexico. This whole area has an art deco feel.

SHOPPING OLD TOWN
ARTS & CRAFTS
Amapola Gallery. 2045 S. Plaza St. NW (Old Town). ☎ **505/242-4311.**

Fifty artists and craftspeople show their talents at this lovely cooperative gallery off a cobbled courtyard. You'll find pottery, paintings, textiles, carvings, baskets, jewelry, and other items.

La Piñata. No. 2 Patio Market (Old Town). ☎ **505/242-2400.**

This shop features (what else?) piñatas, in shapes from dinosaurs to parrots to pigs, as well as paper flowers, puppets, toys, and crushable bolero hats decorated with ribbons.

Mariposa Gallery. 113 Romero St. NW (Old Town). ☎ **505/842-9097.**

Fine contemporary crafts, including fiber arts, jewelry, clay works, sculptural glass, and other media, are sold here.

Mineral and Fossil Gallery. 2011 Mountain Rd. NW, Suite E-1 (San Felipe Plaza, Old Town). ☎ **800/354-6213** or 505/843-8297.

A great place to find natural art, from fossils to geodes to cave bear skeletons.

R. C. Gorman Nizhoni Gallery Old Town. 323 Romero St. NW, Suite 1 (Old Town). ☎ **505/843-7666.**

The painting and sculpture of famed Navajo artist Gorman, a resident of Taos, are shown here. Most works are available in limited-edition lithographs.

Tanner Chaney Galleries. 410 Romero NW (Old Town). ☎ **800/444-2242** or 505/ 247-2242.

In business since 1875, this gallery has fine jewelry, pottery, and rugs.

FOOD
The Candy Lady. 524 Romero NW (Old Town). ☎ **800/214-7731** or 505/243-6239. www.thecandylady.com.

Making chocolate for more than 18 years, The Candy Lady is especially known for 21 varieties of fudge, including jalapeño flavor.

SOUTHWESTERN APPAREL
Jeanette's Originals. 205-B San Felipe NW (Old Town). ☎ **505/842-1093.**

Stop by here for those all-important, matching mother-daughter fashions, as well as men's Navajo and ribbon shirts. You'll also find velvet broomstick skirts and denim skirts and tops.

ELSEWHERE IN TOWN
ART

Dartmouth Street Gallery. 3011 Monte Vista NE. ☎ **800/474-7751** or 505/266-7751.

This gallery features vapor mirage works of Larry Bell, paintings by Angus Macpherson, tapestries, sculpture, and works on paper by contemporary New Mexico artists.

✪ **Skip Maisel's.** 510 Central Ave. SW. ☎ **505/242-6526.**

If you want a real bargain in Native American arts and crafts this is the place to shop. You'll find a broad range of quality and price here in goods such as pottery, weavings, and kachinas. Take note! Adorning the outside of the store are murals painted in 1933 by notable Navajo painter Harrison Begay and Pueblo painter Pablita Velarde.

Weyrich Gallery (Rare Vision Art Galerie). 2935-D Louisiana Blvd. at Candelaria Rd. ☎ **505/883-7410.**

Contemporary paintings, sculpture, textiles, jewelry, and ceramics by regional and nonregional artists are exhibited at this spacious midtown gallery.

BOOKS

Bookworks. 4022 Rio Grande Blvd. NW. ☎ **505/344-8139.**

This store, selling both new and used books, has one of the most complete Southwestern nonfiction and fiction sections. Recently enlarged, Bookworks carries major offerings in children's books, gift books, travel, art, literature, gardening, cooking, and architecture. Recently expanded, there's now a coffee bar and stage area for readings. The shop also carries CDs, cassettes, and books on tape.

✪ **Page One.** 11018 Montgomery Blvd. (at Juan Tabo). NE. ☎ **505/294-2026.**

New Mexico's largest bookstore has more than 135,000 titles in stock, close to 5,000 foreign and domestic magazines, and more than 150 out-of-state and foreign newspapers. It also carries road maps, computer books, and software. There's a cafe, serving coffee, snacks, and sandwiches.

CRAFTS

Bien Mur Indian Market Center. I-25 at Tramway Rd. NE. ☎ **800/365-5400** or 505/821-5400.

The Sandia Pueblo's crafts market is on its reservation, just beyond Albuquerque's northern city limits. The market sells turquoise and silver jewelry, pottery, baskets, kachina dolls, handwoven rugs, sand paintings, and other arts and crafts. The market is open Monday through Saturday from 9am to 5:30pm and Sunday from 11am to 5pm.

Gallery One. In the Nob Hill Shopping Center, 3500 Central SE. ☎ **505/268-7449.**

This gallery features folk art, jewelry, contemporary crafts, cards and paper, and natural fiber clothing.

✪ **Ortega's Indian Arts and Crafts.** 6600 Menaul Blvd. NE, 53. ☎ **505/881-1231.**

An institution in Gallup, adjacent to the Navajo Reservation, Ortega's now has this Albuquerque store. They do sales, repairs, engravings, and appraisals of silver and turquoise jewelry.

The Pueblo Loft. In the Nob Hill Shopping Center, 3500 Central SE. ☎ **505/268-8764.**

Owner Kitty Trask takes pride in the fact that all items featured at The Pueblo Loft are crafted by Native Americans. For 9 years, her slogan has been, "Every purchase is an American Indian work of art."

A Taste of the Grape

In addition to everything else New Mexico has to offer, wineries seem to be springing up all over the state. Wineries in Albuquerque or within short driving distance of the city include **Anderson Valley Vineyards** at 4920 Rio Grande Blvd. NW, Albuquerque, NM 87107 (☎ **505/344-7266**); **Sandia Shadows Vineyard and Winery,** 11704 Coronado NE, Albuquerque, NM 87122 (☎ **505/856-1006**); and **Gruet Winery,** 8400 Pan-American Fwy. NE, Albuquerque, NM 87113 (☎ **505/821-0055**).

✪ **Wright's Collection of Indian Art.** Park Square, 6600 Indian School Rd. NE. ☎ **505/883-6122.**

This gallery, first opened in 1907, features a free private museum and carries fine handmade Native American arts and crafts, both contemporary and traditional.

FASHIONS

Albuquerque Pendleton. 1100 San Mateo NE, Suite 4. ☎ **505/255-6444.**

Cuddle up within a large selection of blankets and shawls, and haul them away in a handbag.

The Courtyard. San Mateo and Lomas blvds. NE. ☎ **505/883-3200.**

Albuquerque Pendleton, TLC Intimate Apparel, and D'Elegance Jewelry are among the upscale boutiques at this award-winning midtown shopping area. The various shops also feature retail fashions, gift items, home furnishings, and luggage. There's also a florist, a beauty salon, and a restaurant. Most shops are open Monday through Saturday from noon to 5pm. Extended holiday hours are in effect Thanksgiving through Christmas.

Western Warehouse. 6210 San Mateo Blvd. NE. ☎ **505/883-7161.**

Family Western wear, including an enormous collection of boots, is retailed here. This store claims the largest selection of work wear and work boots in New Mexico (8,000 pairs of boots altogether).

FOOD

La Mexicana. 1523 4th St. SW. ☎ **505/243-0391.**

This is a great place to go shopping if you're a diehard fan of Mexican food. Many items at La Mexicana are imported directly from Mexico, and others, like tortillas, tamales, and Mexican pastries, are made fresh daily.

Rocky Mountain Chocolate Factory. 380 Coronado Center. ☎ **800/658-6151** or 505/888-3399.

Old-fashioned candy made right before your eyes. All chocolates are handmade.

FURNITURE

Ernest Thompson Furniture. 4531 Osuna NE, at the corner of I-25 and Osuna. ☎ **800/568-2344** or 505/344-1994.

Original-design, handcrafted furniture is exhibited in the factory showroom. Thompson is a fifth-generation furniture maker who still uses traditional production techniques.

Strictly Southwestern. 1321 Eubank Blvd. NE. ☎ **505/292-7337.**

You'll find nice solid pine and oak Southwestern-style furniture here. Lighting, art, pottery, and other interior items are also available.

GIFTS/SOUVENIRS

Jackalope International. 834 Highway 44, Bernalillo, NM, 87004. ☎ **505/867-9813.**

Wandering through this vast shopping area is like an adventure to another land, to many lands, really. You'll find Mexican *trasteros* (armoires) next to Balinese puppets. The store sells sculpture, pottery, and Christmas ornaments as well.

MARKETS

Flea Market. New Mexico State Fairgrounds.

Every Saturday and Sunday, year-round, the fairgrounds host this market from 8am to 5pm. It's a great place to browse for turquoise and silver jewelry and locally made crafts, as well as newly manufactured inexpensive goods like socks and T-shirts. The place takes on a fair atmosphere, the smell of cotton candy filling the air. There's no admission charge.

10 Albuquerque After Dark

Albuquerque has an active performing-arts and nightlife scene, as befits a city of half a million people. As also befits this area, the performing arts are multicultural, with Hispanic and (to a lesser extent) Native American productions sharing stage space with Anglo works, including theater, opera, symphony, and dance. Albuquerque also attracts many national touring companies. Country music predominates in nightclubs, though aficionados of rock, jazz, and other forms of music can find them here as well.

Complete information on all major cultural events can be obtained from the **Albuquerque Convention and Visitors Bureau** (☎ **800/284-2282** for recorded information after 5pm). Current listings appear in the two daily newspapers; detailed weekend arts calendars can be found in the Thursday evening *Tribune* and the Friday morning *Journal.* The monthly *On the Scene* also carries entertainment listings.

Tickets for nearly all major entertainment and sporting events can be obtained from Ticketmaster, 4004 Carlisle Blvd. NE (☎ **505/884-0999**). Discount tickets are often available for midweek and matinee performances. Check with specific theaters or concert halls.

THE PERFORMING ARTS
CLASSICAL MUSIC

Chamber Orchestra of Albuquerque. 2730 San Pedro Dr. NE, Suite H-23. ☎ **505/ 881-0844.** www.aosys.com/coa. Tickets $14–$25, depending on seating and performance.

This 32-member professional orchestra performs from September to June, primarily at St. John's United Methodist Church, 2626 Arizona St. NE. There is a subscription series of seven classical concerts. The orchestra regularly features guest artists of national and international renown.

New Mexico Ballet Company. 4200 Wyoming Blvd. NE, Suite B (P.O. Box 21518). ☎ **505/292-4245.** www.mandala.net/nmballet. Tickets $15–$25 adults, half price for children under 12 and students.

Founded in 1972, the state's oldest ballet company performs two or three times a year at Popejoy Hall. Typically there is a fall production such as *The Legend of Sleepy Hollow,* a December performance of *The Nutcracker* or *A Christmas Carol,* and a contemporary spring production.

New Mexico Symphony Orchestra (NMSO). 3301 Menaul Blvd. NE, Suite 4. ☎ **800/ 251-6676** for tickets and information, or 505/881-9590. Ticket prices vary with concert; call for details.

My first introduction to symphony was with the NMSO. Though I didn't quite understand the novelty of hearing live symphony, I loved picking out the distinct sounds and following them as they melded together. The NMSO first played in 1932 (long before I attended, thank you), and has continued as a strong cultural force throughout the state. The symphony performs classics and pops, family, and neighborhood concerts. It plays for more than 20,000 grade school students and visits communities through the state in its annual tour program. Concert venues are generally Popejoy Hall on the University of New Mexico campus, the Albuquerque Convention Center and the Rio Grande Zoo, all of which are accessible to people with disabilities. Each season a few notable artists visit; in 1998 such guests included Burt Bacharach and Vikki Carr. I recommend going to one of the outdoor concerts under the bandshell at the Rio Grande Zoo.

THEATER

Albuquerque Civic Light Opera Association. 4804 Central Ave. SE. ☎ **505/262-9301.** Tickets $10–$19.50 adults; students and seniors receive a $2 discount.

During a March-to-December season, five major Broadway musicals are presented each year at either Popejoy Hall or the ACLOA's own new 890-seat theater. Most productions are staged for three consecutive weekends, including some Sunday matinees.

Albuquerque Little Theatre. 224 San Pasquale Ave. SW. ☎ **505/242-4750.** Tickets $9–$13, 12–6pm Mon–Fri.

The Albuquerque Little Theatre has been offering a variety of productions ranging from comedies to dramas to musicals since 1930. Six plays are presented here annually during a September-to-May season. Located across from Old Town, Albuquerque Little Theatre offers plenty of free parking.

La Compañía de Teatro de Albuquerque. P.O. Box 884, Albuquerque, 87103-0884. ☎ **505/242-7929.** Tickets, $9 adults; $7 students age 18 and above and seniors; $6 children under 18.

Productions given by the company can provide a focused view into New Mexico culture. One of the few major professional Hispanic companies in the United States and Puerto Rico, La Compañía stages a series of bilingual productions (most original New Mexican works) every year from late September through May. Comedies, dramas, and musicals are offered, along with an occasional Spanish-language play. Performances take place in the KiMo Theater, South Broadway Cultural Center (1025 Broadway SE), and in other venues regionally. A recent production titled *The Merchant of Santa Fe* was a spin off *The Merchant of Venice,* and involved the crypto-Jews of northern New Mexico. (Crypto-Jews are residents of the state who have centuries-old and hidden ties to Judaism, ties that have been concealed since their ancestors fled the Spanish Inquisition.)

Vortex Theatre. Buena Vista (just South of Central Ave.). ☎ **505/247-8600.** Tickets $8 adults, $7 students and seniors, $6 for everyone on Sun.

A 20-year-old community theater known for its innovative productions, the Vortex is Albuquerque's "Off-Broadway" theater, presenting a range of plays from classic to original. An original short play festival is scheduled for 4 weeks every year. *Antony and Cleopatra* played in 1998. Performances take place on Friday and Saturday at 8pm and on Sunday at 6pm. The black-box theater seats 90.

THE CLUB & MUSIC SCENE
COMEDY CLUBS/DINNER THEATER
Laffs Comedy Caffé. 3100-D Juan Tabo Blvd. (at Candelaria Rd. NE). ☎ **505/296-5653.**

Top acts from each coast, including comedians who have appeared on *The Late Show with David Letterman* and HBO, are booked at Albuquerque's top comedy club. Shows Wednesday, Thursday, and Sunday begin at 8:30pm ($5 per person with a two-item minimum purchase); on Friday and Saturday, shows start at 8:30 and 10:30pm ($7 per person with a two-item minimum purchase). Wednesday is nonsmoking night. The club serves a full dinner menu with all items under $10. You must be 21 or older to attend.

Mystery Cafe. 2601 Wyoming Blvd. NE, Suite 115-E, Albuquerque, 87112. ☎ **505/237-1385.** Performances at Sheraton Uptown (at Menaul and Louisiana). Performances Fri–Sat 7pm. Approximately $33.

If you're in the mood for a little interactive dinner theater, the Mystery Cafe might be just the ticket. You'll help the characters in this ever-popular, delightfully funny show solve the mystery as they serve you a four-course meal. Reservations are a must.

COUNTRY MUSIC
Midnight Rodeo. 4901 McLeod Rd. NE (near San Mateo Blvd.). ☎ **505/888-0100.** No cover Sun–Thurs, $3 Fri–Sat.

The Southwest's largest nightclub of any kind, this place has bars in all corners; it even has its own shopping arcade, including a boutique and gift shop. A deejay spins records nightly until closing; the hardwood dance floor is so big (5,500 square feet) that it resembles an indoor horse track. Free dance lessons are offered on Sunday from 5:30 to 7pm and Thursday from 7 to 8pm.

A busy kitchen serves simple but hearty meals to dancers who work up appetites. Now there's even a rock-and-roll dance bar within Midnight Rodeo.

ROCK/JAZZ
In recent years an interesting club scene has opened up downtown. Almost any night of the week, but particularly Thursday through Saturday nights, the place is hopping, as people wander from one club to another. The 20-something crowd should try **The Zone and The Z-Pub** (that's one joint) at 120 Central SW (☎ **505/343-7933**).

Brewsters Pub. 312 Central Ave. SW (Downtown). ☎ **505/247-2533.**

Tuesday through Sunday, Brewsters Pub offers live blues or light rock entertainment in a sports bar–type setting. There are 29 beers on tap, as well as a wide variety of bottled beer. Sports fans can enjoy the game on a big-screen TV. Barbecue is served at lunch and dinner.

The Cooperage. 7220 Lomas Blvd. NE. ☎ **505/255-1657.** Cover $3–$5.

Salsa on Thursday and Saturday night and rhythm and blues on Friday night keeps dancers hopping inside this gigantic wooden barrel.

Dingo Bar. 313 Gold Ave. SW (Downtown). ☎ **505/243-0663.** Cover charge varies with performance, but can run up to $20 per person.

The Dingo Bar is one of Albuquerque's premier rock clubs. Nightly live entertainment runs from punk rock to classic rock 'n' roll to blues and jazz. The atmosphere is earthy, with patrons ranging from hippies to suits.

MORE ENTERTAINMENT

Albuquerque's best nighttime attraction is the **Sandia Peak Tramway** (see "What to See & Do," in section 5) and the High Finance Restaurant and Tavern at the summit (see "Where to Dine," in section 4). Here you can enjoy a view nonpareil of the Rio Grande Valley and the city lights.

The best place to catch foreign films, art films, and limited-release productions is the **Guild Cinema,** 3405 Central Ave. NE (☎ **505/255-1848**). For film classics, check out the **Southwest Film Center,** on the University of New Mexico (UNM) campus (☎ **505/277-5608**), with double features Wednesday through Sunday, changing nightly (when classes are in session). There are a number of major Albuquerque first-run theaters, which can easily be located in the phone book.

The **Isleta Gaming Palace,** 11,000 Broadway SE (☎ **800/460-5686** or 505/869-2614), is a luxurious, air-conditioned casino (blackjack, poker, slots, bingo, and keno) with a full-service restaurant, no-smoking section, and free bus transportation on request. Hours are Monday through Thursday 9am to 5am; Friday through Sunday 24 hours a day.

11 Touring the Pueblos Around Albuquerque

Ten Native American pueblos are located within an hour's drive of central Albuquerque. Two of them, Acoma and Laguna, are discussed in chapter 10, "Northwestern New Mexico." The others, from south to north, are discussed here, followed by Coronado and Jemez state monuments, which preserve ancient pueblo ruins. If you'd like to combine a tour of the archaeological sites and inhabited pueblos, consider driving the Jemez Mountain Trail. Head north on Interstate 25 to Bernalillo, where you can visit the Coronado State Monument. Continue west on NM 44 to Zia Pueblo. Six miles farther on NM 44 takes you to NM 4, where you'll turn north and drive through orchards and along narrow corn fields to Jemez Pueblo. Farther north on NM 4, you'll find another archaeological site, the Jemez State Monument. You'll also find Jemez Springs, where you can stop for a hot soak. The road continues to the Los Alamos area, where you can see the spectacular ruins at Bandelier National Monument. From there you have the option of returning the way you came, or via Santa Fe.

AREA PUEBLOS
ISLETA PUEBLO

Located just 14 miles south of Albuquerque, off I-25 or U.S. 85, Isleta Pueblo (P.O. Box 1270, Isleta, NM 87022; ☎ **505/869-3111**) is the largest of the Tiwa-speaking pueblos, comprising several settlements on the west side of the Rio Grande. The largest village, Shiaw-iba, contains the Mission of San Agustin de Isleta, one of the few mission churches not destroyed in the 17th-century Pueblo rebellion. Grasslands and wooded bosks along the river are gradually becoming part of Albuquerque's growing urban sprawl; already, some governmental agencies and commercial interests are leasing property from the Isleta. Most of the pueblo's 4,000-plus residents work in Albuquerque; others are employed in farming and ranching, private business, or in the pueblo's operations.

Isleta women potters make red wares distinctive for their red-and-black designs on white backgrounds. The tribe operates a casino (see "Albuquerque After Dark," above) and fishing and camping areas at Isleta Lakes. Permits ($2 to $7 daily) can be purchased at the recreation area.

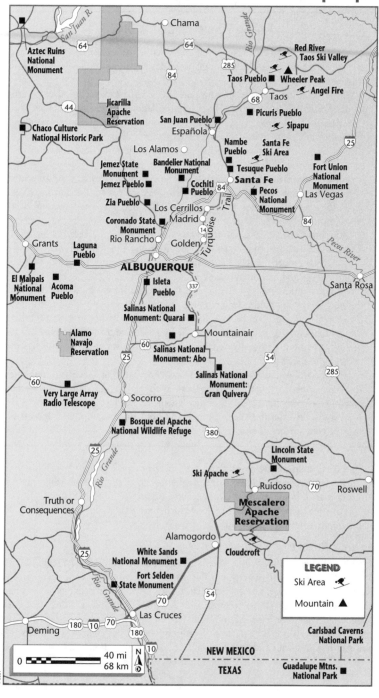

Chama

Aztec Ruins
National
Monument

64

San Juan R.

Rio Grande

Red River
Taos Ski Valley

285

Taos Pueblo ■ Wheeler Peak ▲

44

Jicarilla
Apache
Reservation

84

68 Taos

Angel Fire

San Juan Pueblo ■

Picuris Pueblo ■

Chaco Culture
National Historic Park

Española

Sipapu

25

Los Alamos

Nambe
Pueblo

Santa Fe
Ski Area

Jemez State
Monument

Bandelier National
Monument

Fort Union
National
Monument

Jemez Pueblo

Cochiti
Pueblo

Tesuque Pueblo ■

Santa Fe

Las Vegas

Zia Pueblo

84

Pecos
National
Monument

Coronado State
Monument

Los Cerrillos

Madrid

84

Rio Rancho

Golden

14

Pecos River

Grants

Laguna
Pueblo

Turquoise Trail

ALBUQUERQUE

Santa Rosa

El Malpais
National
Monument

Acoma
Pueblo

Isleta
Pueblo

337

Salinas National
Monument: Quarai

Alamo
Navajo
Reservation

60

25

Mountainair

Salinas National
Monument: Abo

54

60

Very Large Array
Radio Telescope

Socorro

Salinas National
Monument:
Gran Quivera

285

Bosque del Apache
National Wildlife Refuge

380

Lincoln State
Monument

25

Rio Grande

Ski Apache

Ruidoso

70

Roswell

Truth or
Consequences

Mescalero
Apache
Reservation

Alamogordo

White Sands
National Monument ■

Cloudcroft

25

Fort Selden
State Monument

54

Rio Grande

70

Las Cruces

Deming

180 10 70

180

10

0 ⌗ 40 mi
68 km

N

NEW MEXICO

TEXAS

Carlsbad Caverns
National Park

Guadalupe Mtns.
National Park

LEGEND

Ski Area 🎿

Mountain ▲

1-0331

117

Pueblo Etiquette: Do's & Don'ts

Those who are not Native American are welcome to visit Indian pueblos and reservations; however, there are some guidelines you should follow as a guest on tribal land.

Native American reservations and pueblos have their own systems of government and, therefore, their own laws and regulations. If you don't follow their laws, you will be subject to punishment as outlined by the Indian government. The best thing that could happen is that you'd simply be asked to leave (which I've seen on a number of occasions because visitors were not behaving in a respectful manner).

Stay out of cemeteries and ceremonial rooms, such as kivas, as these are sacred grounds. Remember, these are not museums or tourist attractions in their own right; they are people's homes. Don't peek into doors and windows, and don't climb on top of buildings.

Most pueblos require a permit to carry a camera or to sketch or paint on location, and many prohibit picture taking at any time. If you want to take pictures, make video, or sketch anything on pueblo or reservation land, find out about permits and fees in advance.

Do not wander around on your own if the Indians have asked that you visit the pueblo only by guided tour. If, on a guided tour, you are asked not to take pictures of something, or are asked to stay out of a certain area, please follow the guidelines. If you don't have to visit by guided tour, don't go into private buildings without being escorted by someone who lives there or who has the authority to take you inside.

Be respectful of ceremonial dances. Do not speak during dances or ceremonies (silence is mandatory) and don't applaud at the end of the dance—they aren't dancing for your amusement, they are dancing as part of their ceremony.

In short, be respectful and courteous and don't do anything you wouldn't do in your own mother's house.

The Isleta hold an evergreen dance in late February. The big day of the year is the feast day honoring St. Augustine, September 4, when a midmorning mass and procession are followed by an afternoon harvest dance.

The pueblo is open to visitors daily during daylight hours. Admission is free. Photography is limited to the church.

SANDIA PUEBLO

Established about 1300, Sandia Pueblo (Box 6008, Bernalillo, NM 87004; ☎ **505/ 867-3317**) was one of the few pueblos visited by Coronado's contingent in 1540. Remains of that village, known as Nafiat, or "sandy," are still visible near the present church. The Sandia people temporarily fled to Hopi country after the Pueblo rebellion of 1680, but returned to the Rio Grande in 1742. Many of today's 300 Tiwa-speaking (Tanoan) inhabitants work in Albuquerque or at Pueblo Enterprises. They also run the Bien Mur Indian Market Center on Tramway Road (☎ **800/365-5400** or 505/821-5400). It's about 10 miles north of Albuquerque off I-25.

The pueblo celebrates its St. Anthony feast day on June 13 with a midmorning mass, procession, and afternoon corn dance. Another dance honors newly elected governors in January.

The pueblo is open to visitors during daylight hours, and admission is free. No photographing, recording, or sketching are allowed.

SANTA ANA PUEBLO

Though partially abandoned and closed to visitors except for ceremonial events, the Santa Ana Pueblo (Star Route, Box 37, Bernalillo, NM 87004; ☎ 505/867-3301) on the lower Jemez River claims a population of about 550. Many "residents" who maintain family homes at the pueblo actually live nearer the stream's confluence with the Rio Grande, in a settlement known as Ranchos de Santa Ana near Bernalillo, where farming is more productive.

Pottery, wood carvings, ceremonial bands, red cloth belts, and unique wooden crosses with straw inlay are produced in the old village by a handful of craftspeople. Marketing is handled by the Ta-Ma-Myia Cooperative Association.

Guests are normally welcomed only on ceremonial days. Pueblo members perform the turtle and corn dances on New Year's Day; the eagle, elk, buffalo, and deer dances on January 6, Three Kings Day; the spring corn basket dance at Easter; various dances for St. Anthony's Day on June 29 and St. Anne's Day on July 26; and several days of dances at Christmastime.

The pueblo is about 30 miles north of Albuquerque, reached via I-25 to Bernalillo, then 8 miles northwest on NM 44. Admission is free; photography is prohibited.

ZIA PUEBLO

This pueblo (135 Capitol Square Dr., Zia Pueblo, NM, 87053; ☎ 505/867-3304) of 720 inhabitants blends in so perfectly with the soft tans of the stone and sand of the desertlike land around it that it's very hard to see—it's like a chameleon on a tree trunk. The pueblo is best known for its famous sun symbol—now the official symbol of the state of New Mexico—adapted from a pottery design showing three rays going in each of the four directions from a sun, or circle. It is hailed in the pledge to the state flag as "a symbol of perfect friendship among united cultures."

Zia has a reputation for excellence in pottery making. Its pottery is identified by its unglazed terra-cotta coloring and traditional geometric designs and plant and animal motifs painted on a white slip. Paintings, weaving, and sculptures are also prized products of the artists of the Zia community. Their work can be viewed and purchased at the **Zia Cultural Center** located at the pueblo. Our Lady of the Assumption, the patron saint, is given a celebratory corn dance on her day, August 15.

The pueblo is about 8 miles northwest of the Santa Ana Pueblo, just off NM 44. It's open to visitors during daylight hours, and admission is free. Photography is not permitted.

JEMEZ PUEBLO

The more than 3,000 Jemez natives—including descendants of the Pecos Pueblo, east of Santa Fe, abandoned in 1838—are the only remaining people to speak the Towa dialect of the Tanoan group. The Jemez are famous for their excellent dancing and feast-making; their feast days attract residents from other pueblos, turning the celebrations into multi-tribal fairs. Two rectangular kivas are central points for groups of dancers. Try to attend the Feast of Our Lady of Angels on August 12; the Feast of San Diego on November 12, when the Pecos bull dance is performed; or the Feast of Our Lady of Guadalupe on December 12 for the Matachines dance, based on a Spanish morality play.

Woven belts, plaited yucca-fiber baskets, and cloth for garments are the primary crafts. Jemez pottery is also beautifully crafted.

There is fishing and picnicking along the Jemez River on government forest lands, and camping at the Dragonfly Recreation Area. Pueblo stores sell fishing permits at $2 to $5 daily, and permits for game hunting may be bought from the pueblo governor's office.

The pueblo (P.O. Box 100, Jemez, NM 87024; ☎ **505/834-7235**) is 42 miles northwest of Albuquerque via I-25 to Bernalillo, NM 44 to San Ysidro, and NM 4 for 43 final miles. It's open to visitors daily during daylight hours, although it may be closed certain ceremonial days. Admission is free; no photography is permitted.

SAN FELIPE PUEBLO

This conservative pueblo of 2,400 people, located on a mesa on the west bank of the Rio Grande, is known for its beautiful ritual ceremonies. The plaza has been worn into the shape of a bowl by the feet of San Felipe's dancers over the centuries. In the grandest of these dances, hundreds of men, women, and children move through their rhythmic steps all day long in the spring corn dance on May 1, performed in honor of the pueblo's patron, St. Philip (San Felipe). The dancing is done to a great chorus of male singers intoning music that reaches back into prehistory and evokes strong emotions in participants and in visitors, too. Other ceremonial events here are a January 6 corn dance, a February 2 buffalo dance for Candelaria Day, and many dances over several days around Christmastime.

San Felipe (P.O. Box 4339, San Felipe, NM 87001; ☎ **505/867-3381**) is 30 miles northeast of Albuquerque via I-25 and an access road. Admission is free. Photography is not permitted. The pueblo is open to visitors during daylight hours.

SANTO DOMINGO PUEBLO

One of New Mexico's largest pueblos, with 3,450 residents, this farming community on the east bank of the Rio Grande is also one of the state's most traditional. Craftspeople are known for their beautiful silver jewelry, unique necklaces of heishi (shell fragments), innovative pottery, and fine weaving.

At the dramatic Santo Domingo Pueblo feast day, August 4, the corn dance is performed as it is done nowhere else. It is a lavish production involving clowns, scores of singers and drummers, and 500 tireless and skilled dancers in imaginative traditional costumes. Other festive occasions during the year include Three Kings Day, January 6, when dances may or may not be performed; Candelaria Day, February 2, when some dances are performed, though the type of dance is not scheduled; the Easter spring corn dance and basket dance; the San Pedro's Day corn dance, June 29; and many traditional dances in the Christmas season, including the New Year's corn dance.

Santo Domingo (P.O. Box 99, Santo Domingo, NM 87052; ☎ **505/465-2214**) is 50 miles northeast of Albuquerque via I-25 north to NM 22. The pueblo is open daily to visitors during daylight hours. Admission is free, but no photography or sketching is permitted.

COCHITI PUEBLO

Occupied continuously since the 14th century, Cochiti Pueblo (P.O. Box 70, Cochiti Pueblo, NM 87072; ☎ **505/465-2244**), the northernmost of the Keresan-speaking pueblos stretches along the Rio Grande. Its Church of San Buenaventura, though rebuilt and remodeled since, still contains sections of its original 1628 structure.

Cochiti (pop. 920) is well known for its pottery, especially the famous "storyteller" figures created by Helen Cordero. Beadwork and soft leather moccasins are other craft specialties. The pueblo's double-headed dance drums, made from hollowed-out cottonwood logs and covered with leather, are used in ceremonies throughout the Rio Grande area.

San Buenaventura Feast Day is July 14, when the corn and rain dances are performed. Other events include a New Year's Day corn dance; eagle, elk, buffalo, or deer dances on January 6, Three Kings Day; the spring corn dance for Easter; more such dances on May 3, Santa Cruz Day, but this is closed to the public; and ceremonies for several days around Christmas.

The pueblo is about 40 miles north of Albuquerque, via U.S. 85, then north on NM 22 and NM 16. It is open to visitors daily during daylight hours; admission is free. No photography, sketching, or tape recording is permitted. Fishing and bird hunting on pueblo grounds requires purchase of a permit from the pueblo governor. Cochiti Lake, though fairly silty, is popular for water sports, especially windsurfing.

TWO STATE MONUMENTS IN THE AREA

Coronado State Monument. NM 44 (P.O. Box 95), Bernalillo, NM 87004. ☎ **505/ 867-5351.** Admission $3 adults, free for children 16 and under. Daily 8am–5pm. Closed major holidays. To get to the site (20 miles north of Albuquerque), take I-25 to Bernalillo and NM 44 west for 1 mile.

When the Spanish explorer Coronado traveled through this region in 1540–41 while searching for the Seven Cities of Cíbola, he wintered at a village on the west bank of the Rio Grande—probably one located on the ruins of the ancient Anasazi Pueblo known as Kuaua. Those excavated ruins have been preserved in this state monument.

Hundreds of rooms can be seen, and a kiva has been restored so that visitors can descend a ladder into the enclosed space, once the site of sacred rites. Unique multicolored murals, depicting human and animal forms, were found on successive layers of wall plaster in this and other kivas here; some examples are displayed in the monument's small archaeological museum.

Jemez State Monument. NM 4 (P.O. Box 143), Jemez Springs, NM 87025. ☎ **505/ 829-3530.** Admission $3 adults, free for children 16 and under. Daily 8:30am–5pm. Closed Jan 1, Easter Sunday, Thanksgiving, Dec 25. From Albuquerque, take NM 44 to NM 4, and then continue on NM 4 for about 18 miles.

All that's left of the Mission of San José de los Jemez, founded by Franciscan missionaries in 1621, is preserved at this site. Visitors will find massive walls standing alone; sparse small door and window openings underscore the need for security and permanence in those times. The mission was excavated between 1921 and 1937, along with portions of a prehistoric Jemez Pueblo. The pueblo, near the Jemez Hot Springs, was called Giusewa—"place of the boiling waters."

A small **museum** at the site displays artifacts found during the excavation, describes traditional crafts and foods, and weaves the thread of history of the Jemez peoples to the 21st century in a series of exhibits. An instructional trail winds through the ruins.

12 Also Worth a Look: Salinas Pueblo Missions National Monument

Salinas Pueblo Missions National Monument. P.O. Box 517, Mountainair, NM 87036. ☎ **505/847-2585.** Free admission. Sites daily 9am–6pm in summer, 9am–5pm the rest of the year. Visitor center in Mountainair daily 8am–5pm. Closed Jan 1 and Dec 25. Abo is 9 miles west of Mountainair on U.S. 60. Quarai is 8 miles north of Mountainair on NM 55. Gran Quivira is 25 miles south of Mountainair on NM 55. All roads are paved.

The Spanish conquistadors' Salinas Jurisdiction, on the east side of the Manzano Mountains (southeast of Albuquerque), was an important 17th-century trade center because of the salt extracted by the Native Americans from the salt lakes. Franciscan priests, using native labor, constructed missions of Abo red sandstone and blue-gray limestone for the native converts. The ruins of some of the most durable missions— along with evidence of preexisting Anasazi and Mogollon cultures—are the highlights of a visit to Salinas Pueblo Missions National Monument. The monument consists of three separate units: the ruins of Abo, Quarai, and Gran Quivira. They are situated around the quiet town of **Mountainair,** 75 miles southeast of Albuquerque at the junction of U.S. 60 and NM 55.

Abo (☎ 505/847-2400) boasts the 40-foot-high ruins of the **Mission of San Gregorio de Abo,** a rare example of medieval architecture in the United States. Quarai (☎ 505/847-2290) preserves the largely intact remains of the **Mission of La Purísima Concepción de Cuarac** (1630). Its vast size, 100 feet long and 40 feet high, contrasts with the modest size of the pueblo mounds. A small museum in the visitor center has a scale model of the original church, along with a selection of artifacts found at the site. **Gran Quivira** (☎ 505/847-2770) once had a population of 1,500. Las Humanes has 300 rooms and seven kivas. Rooms dating from 1300 can be seen. There are indications that an older village, dating from 800, may have previously stood here. Ruins of two churches (one almost 140 feet long) and a Convento have been preserved. A museum with many artifacts from the site, a 40-minute movie showing the excavation of some 200 rooms, plus a short history video of Las Humanes can be seen at the visitor center.

All three pueblos and the churches that were constructed above them are believed to have been abandoned in the 1670s. Self-guided tour pamphlets can be obtained at the units' respective visitor centers and at the **Salinas Pueblo Missions National Monument Visitor Center** in Mountainair, on U.S. 60 one block west of the intersection of U.S. 60 and NM 55. The visitor center offers an audiovisual presentation on the region's history, a bookstore, and an art exhibit.

13 En Route to Santa Fe Along the Turquoise Trail

New Mexico Highway 14 begins 16 miles east of downtown Albuquerque, at I-40's Cedar Crest exit, and winds 46 miles to Santa Fe along the east side of the Sandia Mountains. Best known as the Turquoise Trail, this state-designated scenic and historic route traverses the revived "ghost towns" of Golden, Madrid, and Cerrillos, where gold, silver, coal, and turquoise were once mined in great quantities. Modern-day settlers, mostly artists and craftspeople, have brought a renewed frontier spirit to these old mining towns. The drive is well worth the extra hour or so it will take you to get to Santa Fe.

SCANDIA PARK   Before reaching the first of the ghost towns, however, travelers can make a turn at **Sandia Park,** 6 miles north of the I-40 junction, to begin climbing 10,678-foot **Sandia Crest** on NM 536. The road is paved, well maintained, and wide enough to accommodate tour buses, with no severe hairpin turns; there is parking at the summit overlook. Sandia Crest is the high point of the Sandia Mountains and, like Sandia Peak, offers a spectacular panoramic view in all directions. Many miles of **Cíbola National Forest** trails, including the popular north-south Sandia Crest Trail, run through here.

En route to the summit, on NM 536 in Sandia Park, is the **Tinkertown Museum** (☎ 505/281-5233), a miniature wood-carved Western village with more than 10,000 objects on display, including 500 animations—among them a turn-of-the-century circus. There are also antique dolls and old-time music machines. In 1994 a

45-foot antique wooden sailing ship (built in England in 1936) was added to the museum collection. Tinkertown is open April 1 to October 31 daily from 9am to 6pm. Admission is $2.50 for adults, $2 for seniors, and $1 for children under 16, free for kids under 4.

If you turn north off NM 536 onto the unpaved NM 165 and proceed about 5 tortuous miles on the rough, narrow byway, you'll come to **Sandia Cave,** a short walk from the road. Artifacts identified as those of "Sandia Man," dating from 23,000 B.C., were found in this cave. They are believed to be some of the oldest evidence of humankind ever discovered in the United States, although some doubt has recently been cast on the authenticity of the find.

GOLDEN   The ghost town of **Golden** is 10 miles north of the Sandia Park junction on NM 14. Its sagging houses, with their missing boards and the wind whistling through their broken eaves, make it a purist's ghost town. There is a general store open, though, as well as a bottle seller's "glass garden." Nearby are ruins of an Indian pueblo called Paako, abandoned around 1670. Such communities of mud huts were all the Spaniards ever found on their avid quests for the gold of Cíbola.

MADRID   Pronounced with the accent on the first syllable (*Ma*-drid), **Madrid** is 12 miles north of Golden. Madrid and neighboring Cerrillos were in a fabled turquoise-mining area dating from prehistory. This semiprecious stone, known in the Old World since 4000 B.C., got its name from the French for "Turkish." In Mexico it was sacred to the Aztec royal house and was forbidden to commoners; it was believed to have an affinity to its owner, to grow pale in prophecy of a coming misfortune, or to glow richly with its wearer's good health. A visitor might still find a bit of raw turquoise in the tailings of an ancient pit mine. The Spanish worked these mines, using local Native American slave labor, until 1680, when a rockfall killed 30 of the miners. Their lack of concern was one of the final sparks contributing to the Pueblo revolt of that year.

Gold and silver mines followed, and when they faltered, there was still coal. The Turquoise Trail towns supplied fuel to locomotives of the Santa Fe Railroad until the 1950s, when the railroad converted to diesel fuel. Madrid used to produce 100,000 tons of coal a year.

In 1919, an idealistic mine owner named Huber transformed a gloomy scene into a showcase village with a new recreation center, hotel, hospital, school, church, post office, department store, drugstore, auto showroom, beauty shop, fire station, dental office, tennis and basketball courts, golf course, shooting range, a brass band, and a Christmas light show; early transcontinental planes used to detour over the town for a look. But the town emptied when the mine closed in 1956.

Twenty years later, the owner's son sold everything at auction: tipple, breaker, tavern, church, store, houses, roads—the lot. A handful of diehards, many of them artists and craftspeople, bought property and stayed on. Today the village seems stuck in the 1960s: Its funky, ramshackle houses have many counterculture residents, the "hippies" of yore, who operate several crafts stores and import shops. During Christmastime, the town still presents a light show well worth catching.

Madrid's **Old Coal Mine Museum** (☎ 505/473-0743) is an on-site museum that features mining and railroad relics, including antique cars, tools, workshops, and a fully restored 1900 Baldwin Steam Locomotive—you can even climb aboard and ring the bell! The museum is open daily, weather permitting; admission is $3 for adults and seniors, and $1 for children 6 to 12; children under 6 are free.

Next door, the **Mine Shaft Tavern** continues its lively and colorful career by offering a variety of burgers on the menu and presenting live music Saturday and Sunday afternoon and some Friday and Saturday nights; it's open for dinner Wednesday and Friday through Sunday, and attracts folks from Santa Fe and Albuquerque. It's adjacent to the **Madrid Opera House,** claimed to be the only such establishment on earth with a built-in steam locomotive on its stage. (The structure was an engine repair shed; the balcony is made of railroad track.)

CERRILOS   Cerrillos once had eight daily newspapers, several hotels, and two dozen saloons, serving miners from 30 mines. Today the main street includes the Cerrillos Bar—part of the original Tiffany Saloon, founded by the New York jewelry family, a dilapidated hotel, a "What Not Shop" within another storefront, and a few shops, including, on a back street, the Casa Grande Trading Post (☎ **505/474-5348**), which houses a turquoise mining museum, rock and gift shop, and petting zoo. To find the best Cerrillos activity, take main street north out of town where you'll come to the hitching post of the Broken Saddle Riding Company (☎ **505/470-0074**), an outfit that takes riders on horseback through this spectacular countryside.

Santa Fe 7

Ever since I was a child and my family would come to visit friends in this city at the base of the mountains, Santa Fe has appeared to me as an exotic and sophisticated place. I always felt ordinary and provincial coming in from the eastern plains to wander the strange crooked streets here or to attend parties with notable Native American artists dressed in finely tailored traditional clothing. Even then I knew that when I grew up, I would live in Santa Fe. But in order to be sure, I left New Mexico altogether and wandered the world from Nairobi to La Paz. I lived in Madrid and Seoul, but I never found anywhere I liked as much as our state capital, an odd city of 70,000 people living 7,000 feet above sea level.

Though the city has changed considerably since I was a young girl, it has retained its exotic nature while becoming even more sophisticated. The Native Americans light the area with viewpoints and lifestyles deeply tied to nature and completely contrary to the American norm. Many of the Hispanics here still live within extended families and practice a devout Catholicism; they bring a slower pace to the city and an appreciation for deep-rooted ties. Meanwhile, a strong cosmopolitan element contributes cutting-edge cuisine, world-class opera, first-run art films, and some of the finest artwork in the world, seen easily while wandering on foot from gallery to gallery, museum to museum.

And while you wander, you'll get to journey back into a history fraught with dramatic conflict. Santa Fe is the longest continuously occupied capital city in the United States. It has been under the rule of five governments: Spain (1610–80 and 1692–1821), the Pueblos (1680–92), Mexico (1821–46), the United States (since 1846 except for a short Confederate occupancy in 1862).

The city's history is told through its architecture. For its first 2 centuries and longer, it was constructed mainly of adobe bricks. When the United States took over the territory from Mexico in 1846 and trade began flowing from the eastern states, new tools and materials began to change the face of the city. The old adobe took on brick facades and roof decoration in what became known as the Territorial style. But the flat roofs were retained so that the city never lost its unique, low profile, creating a sense of serenity to be found in no other American city.

Bishop Jean-Baptiste Lamy, the inspiration for the character of Bishop Latour in Willa Cather's *Death Comes for the Archbishop,* built the French Romanesque St. Francis Cathedral shortly after he was appointed to head the diocese in 1851. Other structures still standing include what is claimed to be the oldest house in the United States, built of adobe by Native Americans purportedly 800 years ago. The San Miguel Mission is the oldest mission church in the country, while the state capitol, built in the circular form of a ceremonial Indian *kiva,* is among the newest in the United States.

The city was originally named La Villa Real de la Santa Fe de San Francisco de Asis (The Royal City of the Holy Faith of St. Francis of Assisi) by its founder, Spanish governor Don Pedro de Peralta. He built the Palace of the Governors as his capitol on the north side of the central Plaza, where it stands today as an excellent museum of the city's 4 centuries of history. It is one of the major attractions in the Southwest, and under its portico, Native Americans sit cross-legged, selling their crafts to eager tourists, as they have done for decades.

The Plaza is the focus of numerous bustling art markets and Santa Fe's early September fiesta, celebrated annually since 1770. The fiesta commemorates the time following the years of the Pueblo revolt, when the city was reconquered by Spanish governor Don Diego de Vargas in 1692. The elm-tree shaded Plaza was also the terminus of the Santa Fe Trail from Missouri, and of the earlier Camino Real (Royal Road) up from Mexico, when the city thrived on the wool and fur of the Chihuahua trade.

What most captures me now, though, is the city's setting, backed by rolling hills and the blue peaks of the Sangre de Cristo Mountains. In the summer, thunderheads build into giant swirling structures above those peaks and move over the city, dropping cool rain. In the winter, snow will often cover the many flat-roofed adobe homes, creating a poetic abstraction that at every glance convinces you that the place itself is exotic art.

1 Orientation

Part of the charm of Santa Fe is that it's so easy to get around. Like most cities of Hispanic origin, it was built around a parklike central plaza. Centuries-old adobe buildings and churches still line the narrow streets. Many of them house shops, restaurants, art galleries, and museums.

Santa Fe sits high and dry at the foot of the Sangre de Cristo Range. Santa Fe Baldy rises to more than 12,600 feet a mere 12 miles northeast of the Plaza. The city's downtown straddles the Santa Fe River, a tiny tributary of the Rio Grande that is little more than a trickle for much of the year. North is the Española Valley (a beautiful view of which is afforded from the Santa Fe Opera grounds) and beyond that, the village of Taos, 66 miles distant (see chapter 8). South are ancient Indian turquoise mines in the Cerrillos Hills; southwest is metropolitan Albuquerque, 58 miles away (see chapter 6). To the west, across the Caja del Rio Plateau, is the Rio Grande, and beyond that, the 11,000-foot Jemez Mountains and Valle Grande, an ancient and massive volcanic caldera. Native American pueblos dot the entire Rio Grande valley an hour's drive in any direction.

ARRIVING

BY PLANE   The **Santa Fe Municipal Airport** (☎ 505/473-7243), just outside the southwestern city limits on Airport Road off Cerrillos Road, has three paved runways, used primarily by private planes. In conjunction with United Airlines, commuter flights are offered by United Express, which is operated by **Great Lakes Aviation** (☎ 800/241-6522). There are four daily departures from Denver during the week and three on weekends. When departing from Santa Fe, passengers can connect to other United Airlines flights in Denver. **Aspen Mountain Air,** affiliated with American Airlines (☎ **800/433-7300**), offers flights to Dallas/Ft. Worth. Call for schedules and fares.

    Getting to and from the airport: Virtually all air travelers to Santa Fe arrive in Albuquerque, where they either rent a car or take one of the bus services. See "Getting There," in chapter 3, for details.

BY TRAIN & BUS   For detailed information about train and bus service to Santa Fe, see "Getting There," in chapter 3.

BY CAR   I-25 skims past Santa Fe's southern city limits, connecting it along one continuous highway from Billings, Montana, to El Paso, Texas. I-40, the state's major east–west thoroughfare, which bisects Albuquerque, affords coast-to-coast access to "The City Different." (From the west, motorists leave I-40 in Albuquerque and take I-25 north; from the east, travelers exit I-40 at Clines Corners and continue 52 miles to Santa Fe on US 285.) For those coming from the northwest, the most direct route is via Durango, Colorado, on US 160, entering Santa Fe on US 84.

    For information on car rentals in Albuquerque, see "Getting There," in chapter 3; and for agencies in Santa Fe, see "Getting Around," later in this chapter.

VISITOR INFORMATION

The **Santa Fe Convention and Visitors Bureau** is located at 201 W. Marcy St., in Sweeney Center at the corner of Grant Street downtown (P.O. Box 909), Santa Fe, NM 87504-0909 (☎ **800/777-CITY** or 505/984-6760). If you would like information before you leave home but don't want to wait for it to arrive by mail, try this Web site address: **www.santafe.org**. It will take you directly to the Santa Fe Convention and Visitors Bureau's home page.

CITY LAYOUT

MAIN ARTERIES & STREETS   The limits of downtown Santa Fe are demarcated on three sides by the horseshoe-shaped Paseo de Peralta and on the west by St. Francis Drive, otherwise known as U.S. 84/285. Alameda Street follows the north side of the Santa Fe River through downtown, with the State Capitol and other federal buildings on the south side of the river, and most buildings of historic and tourist interest on the north, east of Guadalupe Street.

    The Plaza is Santa Fe's universally accepted point of orientation. Its four diagonal walkways meet at a central fountain, around which a strange and wonderful assortment of people of all ages, nationalities, and lifestyles can be found at nearly any hour of the day or night.

    If you stand in the center of the Plaza looking north, you'll be gazing directly at the Palace of the Governors. In front of you is Palace Avenue; behind you, San Francisco Street. To your left is Lincoln Avenue and to your right is Washington Avenue, which divides the downtown avenues into "east" and "west." St. Francis Cathedral is the massive Romanesque structure a block east, down San Francisco Street. Alameda Street is 2 full blocks behind you.

    Near the intersection of Alameda Street and Paseo de Peralta, you'll find Canyon Road running east toward the mountains. Much of this street is one way. The best way to see it is to walk up or down, taking time to explore shops and galleries and even have lunch or dinner.

    Running to the southwest from the downtown area, beginning opposite the state office buildings on Galisteo Avenue, is Cerrillos Road. Once the main north–south highway connecting New Mexico's state capital with its largest city, it is now a

6-mile-long motel and fast-food strip. St. Francis Drive, which crosses Cerrillos Road 3 blocks south of Guadalupe Street, is a far less tawdry byway, linking Santa Fe with I-25, located 4 miles southeast of downtown. The Old Pecos Trail, on the east side of the city, also joins downtown and the freeway. St. Michael's Drive connects the three arteries.

FINDING AN ADDRESS   Because of the city's layout, it's often difficult to know exactly where to look for a particular street address. It's best to call ahead for directions.

MAPS   Free city and state maps can be obtained at tourist information offices. An excellent state highway map is published by the **New Mexico Department of Tourism,** 491 Old Santa Fe Trail (P.O. Box 20002), Santa Fe, NM 87504 (☎ **800/ 733-6396** or 505/827-7336). There's also a Santa Fe Visitors Center in the same building. More specific county and city maps are available from the **State Highway and Transportation Department,** 1120 Cerrillos Rd., Santa Fe, NM 87504 (☎ **505/827-5100**). Members of the **American Automobile Association,** 1644 St. Michael's Dr. (☎ **505/471-6620**), can obtain free maps from the AAA office. Other good regional maps can be purchased at area bookstores. Gousha publishes a laminated "FastMap" of Santa Fe and Taos that has proved indispensable during my travels.

2 Getting Around

BY BUS   The public bus system, **Santa Fe Trails** (☎ **505/438-1464**), has seven routes. You can pick up a map from the Convention and Visitors Bureau. Buses operate Monday through Friday from 6:30am to 10:30pm and Saturday from 8am to 8pm. There is no service on Sunday or holidays. Call for a current schedule and fare information.

BY CAR   Cars can be rented from any of the following firms in Santa Fe: **Avis,** Garrett's Desert Inn, 311 Old Santa Fe Trail (☎ **800/831-2847** or 505/982-4361); **Budget,** 1946 Cerrillos Rd. (☎ **800/527-0700** or 505/984-8028); **Enterprise,** 2641A Cerrillos Rd. and 4450 Cerrillos Rd. (☎ **800/325-8007** or 505/473-3600); and **Hertz,** Santa Fe Hilton, 100 Sandoval St. (☎ **800/654-3131** or 505/982-1844).

If Santa Fe is your base for an extended driving exploration of New Mexico, remember there are a lot of wide-open desert and wilderness spaces in New Mexico, and if your car were to break down you could be stranded for hours in extreme heat or cold before someone might pass by. See "Getting Around," in chapter 3, for more information, advice, and driving regulations.

Street **parking** is difficult to find during summer months. There's a parking lot near the federal courthouse, 2 blocks north of the Plaza; another one behind Santa Fe Village, a block south of the Plaza; and a third at Water and Sandoval Streets. If you stop by the Santa Fe Convention and Visitors Bureau, at the corner of Grant and Marcy streets, you can pick up a wallet-size guide to Santa Fe parking areas. The map shows both street and lot parking.

BY TAXI   It's best to telephone for a cab, because they are difficult to flag from the street. Expect to pay a standard fee of $1.85 for the service and an average of about $1.50 per mile. **Capital City Cab** (☎ **505/438-0000**) is the main company in Santa Fe.

BY BICYCLE/ON FOOT   A bicycle is an excellent way to get around town. Check with **Palace Bike Rentals,** 409 E. Palace Ave. (☎ **505/986-0455**), or **Sun Mountain Bike Company,** 121 Sandoval St. (☎ **505/820-2902**), for rentals.

The best way to see downtown Santa Fe is on foot. Free walking-tour maps are available at the tourist information center in Sweeney Center, 201 W. Marcy St. (☎ **800/777-CITY** or 505/984-6760), and several walking tours are included later in this chapter.

FAST FACTS: Santa Fe

Airport   See "Orientation," above.

American Express   There is no office in Santa Fe; the nearest one is in Albuquerque (see "Fast Facts: Albuquerque," in chapter 6).

Baby-Sitters   Most hotels can arrange for sitters on request. Alternatively, call the **Santa Fe Kid Connection** at ☎ **505/471-3100.**

Business Hours   **Offices** and **stores** are generally open Monday through Friday from 9am to 5pm, with many stores also open Friday night, Saturday, and Sunday in the summer season. Most **banks** are open Monday through Thursday from 10am to 3pm and Friday from 10am to 6pm; drive-up windows may be open later. Some may also be open Saturday morning. Most branches have cash machines available 24 hours. See also "Fast Facts: New Mexico," in chapter 3.

Car Rentals   See "Getting Around," above.

Climate   Santa Fe is consistently 10°F (about 6°C) cooler than the nearby desert but has the same sunny skies, averaging more than 300 days of sunshine out of 365. Midsummer (July and August) days are dry and sunny (around 80°F), often with brief afternoon thunderstorms; evenings are typically in the upper 50s. Winters are mild and fair, with occasional and short-lived snow (average annual snowfall is 32 inches, although the ski basin gets an average of 225 inches). The average annual rainfall is 14 inches, most of it in summer; the relative humidity is 45%. (See also "When to Go," in chapter 3.)

Currency Exchange   You can exchange foreign currency at two banks in Santa Fe: NationsBank, 1234 St. Michael's Dr. (☎ **505/471-1234**), and First Security Bank, 121 Sandoval St. (☎ **800/677-2962**).

Dentists   Located in the geographic center of the city is Dr. Leslie E. La Kind, 400 Botulph Lane (☎ **505/988-3500**). Dr. La Kind offers emergency service.

Doctors   The Lovelace Alameda Clinic, 901 W. Alameda St. (☎ **505/995-2900**), is in the Solano Center near St. Francis Drive. It's open daily from 8am to 8pm. For Physicians and Surgeons Referral and Information Services, call the American Board of Medical Specialties at ☎ **800/776-2378.**

Embassies & Consulates   See "Fast Facts: For the Foreign Traveler," in chapter 4.

Emergencies   For police, fire, or ambulance emergency, dial ☎ **911.**

Eyeglass Repair   The **Quintana Optical Dispensary,** 109 E. Marcy St. (☎ **505/988-4234**), provides 2-hour prescription service Monday through Friday from 9am to 5pm and Saturday from 9am to noon. They will also repair your glasses.

Hospitals   St. Vincent Hospital, 455 St. Michael's Dr. (☎ **505/983-3361,** or 505/820-5250 for emergency services), is a 268-bed regional health center. Patient services include urgent and emergency-room care and ambulatory surgery. Other health services include the Women's Health Services Family Care and Counseling Center (☎ **505/988-8869**). Lovelace Health Systems has a walk-in office at 901 W. Alameda St. (☎ **505/995-9773**).

Hot Lines   The following hot lines are available in Santa Fe: battered families (☎ **505/473-5200**), poison control (☎ **800/432-6866**), psychiatric emergencies (☎ **505/820-5242** or 505/982-2255), and sexual assault (☎ **505/ 986-9111**).

Information   See "Visitor Information," above.

Libraries   The Santa Fe Public Library is half a block from the Plaza at 145 Washington Ave. (☎ **505/984-6780**). There are branch libraries at Villa Linda Mall and at 1730 Llano St., just off St. Michael's Drive. The New Mexico State Library is at 325 Don Gaspar Ave. (☎ **505/827-3800**). Specialty libraries include the Archives of New Mexico, 1205 Camino Carlos Rey, and the New Mexico History Library, 120 Washington Ave.

Liquor Laws   See "Fast Facts: New Mexico" in chapter 3.

Lost Property   Contact the city police at ☎ 505/473-5000.

Newspapers & Magazines   *The New Mexican,* Santa Fe's daily paper, is the oldest newspaper in the West. Its offices are at 202 E. Marcy St. (☎ **505/ 983-3303**). The weekly *Santa Fe Reporter,* published on Wednesday, is often more willing to be controversial, and its entertainment listings are excellent. Regional magazines published locally are *New Mexico Magazine* (monthly, statewide interest) and the *Santa Fean Magazine* (monthly, Southwestern lifestyles).

Pharmacies   The **R&R Professional Pharmacy,** at 1691 Galisteo St. (☎ **505/ 988-9797**), is open Monday through Friday from 9am to 6pm (8:30am to 5:30pm in summer) and Saturday from 9am to noon. Emergency and delivery service is available.

Photographic Needs   Everything from film purchases to minor camera repairs to 1-hour processing can be handled by the **Camera Shop,** 109 E. San Francisco St. (☎ **505/983-6591**). Twenty-four-hour processing is available at **Camera & Darkroom,** 216 Galisteo St. (☎ **505/983-2948**).

Police   In case of emergency, dial ☎ **911.**

Post Offices   The **Main Post Office** is at 120 S. Federal Place (☎ **505/ 988-6351**), 2 blocks north and 1 block west of the Plaza. It's open from 7:30am to 5:45pm. The Coronado Station branch is at 2071 S. Pacheco St. (☎ **505/ 438-8452**), and is open from 7:30am to 5pm. Some of the major hotels have stamp machines and mailboxes with twice-daily pickup. The ZIP code for central Santa Fe is 87501.

Radio & Television   Santa Fe's radio stations include KSFR-FM 90.7 (classical and jazz), KNYN-FM 95.5 (country), KBAC-FM 98.1 (adult contemporary), KBOM-FM 106.7 (oldies), and KVSF 1260 AM (news and talk). Albuquerque stations are easily received in Santa Fe. There are three Albuquerque network TV affiliates: KOB-TV (Channel 4, NBC), KOAT-TV (Channel 7, ABC), and KQRE-TV (Channel 13, CBS). The latter has an office at the State Capitol.

Safety   Though the tourist district appears very safe, Santa Fe is not on the whole a safe city; theft is common (see "New Mexico Today," in chapter 2), and the number of reported rapes has risen. The good news is that Santa Fe's overall crime statistics do appear to be falling. Still, when walking the city streets, guard your purse carefully, because there are many bag-grab thefts, particularly during the summer tourist months. Also, be as aware of your surroundings as you would in any other major city.

Taxes   A tax of 10.25% is added to all lodging bills. A tax of 6.25% is added to all sales.

Taxis   See "Getting Around," above.

Telephone Numbers   Information on **road conditions** in the Santa Fe area can be obtained by calling the State Highway and Transportation Department (☎ **800/432-4269**). For **time and temperature,** call ☎ **505/473-2211.**

Time Zone   See "Fast Facts: New Mexico" in chapter 3.

Weather   For weather forecasts, call ☎ **505/988-5151.**

3 Where to Stay

There may not be a bad place to stay in Santa Fe. From downtown hotels to Cerrillos Road motels, ranch-style resorts to quaint bed-and-breakfasts, the standard of accommodation is universally high.

You should be aware of the seasonal nature of the tourist industry in Santa Fe. Accommodations are often booked solid through the summer months, and most places raise their prices accordingly. High periods actually fluctuate from one establishment to another, with some charging higher rates from May all the way to November. Usually it can pay to shop around during the "in-between" or "shoulder" seasons of May through June and September through October. Some hotels raise their rates again over the Christmas holidays, and most charge their highest prices during Indian Market, the third weekend of August. During these periods, it's essential to make reservations well in advance.

No matter the season, discounts are often available to seniors, affiliated groups, corporate employees, and others. Be sure to ask if you're eligible for these lower rates.

A combined city-state **tax** of 10.25% is added to every hotel bill in Santa Fe. And, unless otherwise indicated, all recommended accommodations come with private bathroom. All hotels listed offer rooms for nonsmokers and for travelers with disabilities. For the B&Bs, I've indicated in the text whether they do or don't.

In this chapter, hotels/motels are listed first by geographical area (downtown, Northside, or Southside) and then by price range, based on midsummer rates for doubles: **very expensive** refers to rooms that average $150 or more per night; **expensive** rooms are those that go for $110 to $150; **moderate** encompasses rooms that range from $75 to $110; and **inexpensive,** those that cost up to $75.

DOWNTOWN

Everything within the horseshoe-shaped Paseo de Peralta and east a few blocks on either side of the Santa Fe River, is considered downtown Santa Fe. All of these accommodations are within walking distance of the Plaza.

VERY EXPENSIVE

Eldorado Hotel. 309 W. San Francisco St., Santa Fe, NM 87501. ☎ **800/955-4455** or 505/988-4455. Fax 505/995-4544. 245 units. A/C MINIBAR TV TEL. Rates from $129–$279 double in low season and $249–$359 double in high season. Year-round $249–$975 suite. Ski and other package rates are available. AE, CB, DC, DISC, MC, V. Valet parking $9. Pets are accepted.

Since its opening in 1986, the Eldorado has stood like a monolith at the center of town. Locals wonder how the five-story structure bypassed the two-story zoning restrictions. Still, the architects did manage to meld Pueblo Revival style with an

Reservations Services

Although Santa Fe has more than 4,500 rooms in more than 100 hotels, motels, bed-and-breakfast establishments, and other accommodations, it can still be difficult to find available rooms at the peak of the tourist season. Year-round assistance is available from **Santa Fe Central Reservations,** 320 Artist Rd., Suite 10 (☎ **800/ 776-7669** or 505/983-8200; fax 505/984-8682). This service will also book tickets for the Santa Fe Opera, Chamber Music Festival, María Benitez Teatro Flamenco, and the Desert Chorale, as well as Jeep trips into the high country, white-water rafting, horseback riding, mountain-bike tours, and golf packages. **Emergency Lodging Assistance,** especially during busy seasons, is available free after 4pm daily (☎ **505/986-0043**).

interesting cathedral feel, inside and out. The lobby is grand, with a high ceiling that continues into the court area and the cafe.

Take your time while wandering through, since the place is adorned with well over a million dollars' worth of art, most of it from northern New Mexico. Most notable in the entry to the court is an *olla*, or pot, made in the early 1920s by a Zia potter, and decorated with a parrot, a bird sacred to the Anasazi as well as the Pueblo people.

The rooms continue the artistic Southwestern motif. There's a warmth here, created in particular by the kiva fireplaces in many of the rooms as well as the tapestries supplied by Seret and Sons, a local antique dealer. This hotel and the Inn of the Anasazi are the establishments in town for those who desire consistency and fine service. The suites here come with a butler who will do "anything legal" for you, including walking your dog.

You'll find small families and businesspeople staying here, as well as conference-goers. Most of the rooms have views of downtown Santa Fe, many from balconies (request an east-facing room to be sure). The hotel rightfully prides itself on the spaciousness and quiet of its rooms, each with a hair dryer and Spectravision movie channels.

If you're really indulging, join the ranks of Mick Jagger, Geena Davis, and King Juan Carlos of Spain and try the penthouse five-room presidential suite. Just down the street from the main hotel is Zona Rosa, which houses two-, three-, and four-bedroom condo suites with full kitchens.

Dining/Diversions: The innovative and elegant Old House restaurant was built on the preserved foundation of an early 1800s Santa Fe house. The viga-latilla (pine beam and cedar branch) ceiling, polished wood floor, pottery and *kachinas* (Pueblo Indian carved dolls) in niches give it a distinct regional touch, found also in its creative Southwestern cuisine. More casual meals are served in the spacious Eldorado Court. The lobby lounge offers low-key entertainment.

Amenities: Concierge, room service, butlers, dry cleaning and laundry service, nightly turndown, twice-daily maid service, safe-deposit boxes. There's also a heated rooftop swimming pool and Jacuzzi, medium-sized health club (with a view), his-and-her saunas, professional massage therapist, business center, beauty salon, and boutiques.

Hilton of Santa Fe. 100 Sandoval St. (P.O. Box 25104), Santa Fe, NM 87504-2387. ☎ **800/336-3676,** 800/HILTONS, or 505/988-2811. Fax 505/986-6439. 157 units. A/C TV TEL. $119–$299 double, $219–$549 suite, $299–$599 casita, depending on time of year. Call for rates. Extra person $20. AE, CB, DC, DISC, MC, V. Parking $5.

With its landmark bell tower, the Hilton encompasses a full city block (a few-minutes' walk from the Plaza) and incorporates most of the historic landholdings of the

Downtown Santa Fe Accommodations

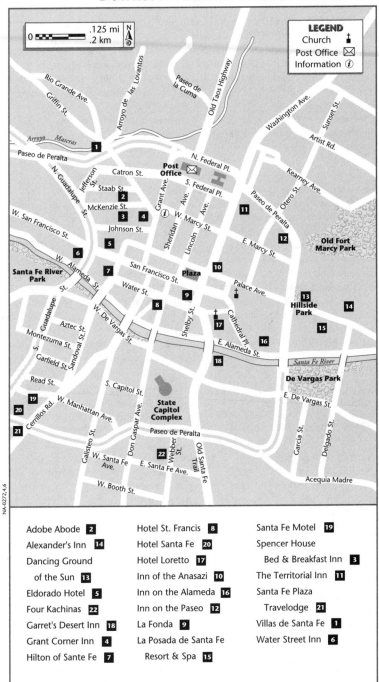

Adobe Abode **2**

Alexander's Inn **14**

Dancing Ground
   of the Sun **13**

Eldorado Hotel **5**

Four Kachinas **22**

Garret's Desert Inn **18**

Grant Corner Inn **4**

Hilton of Sante Fe **7**

Hotel St. Francis **8**

Hotel Santa Fe **20**

Hotel Loretto **17**

Inn of the Anasazi **10**

Inn on the Alameda **16**

Inn on the Paseo **12**

La Fonda **9**

La Posada de Santa Fe
   Resort & Spa **15**

Santa Fe Motel **19**

Spencer House
   Bed & Breakfast Inn **3**

The Territorial Inn **11**

Santa Fe Plaza
   Travelodge **21**

Villas de Santa Fe **1**

Water Street Inn **6**

350-year-old Ortiz family estate. It's built around a central pool and patio area and is a fine blend of ancient and modern styles.

Rooms are fairly standard, not nearly as refined as those in the Eldorado, but many visitors like this hotel because it offers all the amenities of a fine hotel at a fairly reasonable price. It also has an intimacy that some of the other large downtown hotels lack. The lobby is cozy, with huge vigas and a big fireplace; it's decorated in a refined Southwestern style.

Remodeled in 1997 in a warm Aztec-Southwestern style, the guest rooms are large, most with a small patio or balcony. All rooms now have hair dryers, irons and ironing boards, robes, safes, VCRs, Spectravision movie channels, and coffeemakers.

In June 1994 the Hilton opened Casa Ortiz de Santa Fe, a small building adjacent to the main hotel, which houses three casitas. The building was once the coach house (ca. 1625) of Nicholas Ortiz III. Today the thick adobe walls encompass elegant Southwestern-style suites. Each has a living room with kiva fireplace, fully stocked kitchenette (with microwave, stove, and minirefrigerator), and bathroom with whirlpool tub. All three have fireplaces.

Dining: Two restaurants occupy the premises of the early 18th-century Casa Ortiz. The Piñon Grill serves a variety of wood-fire grilled items in a casual atmosphere. The Chamisa Courtyard, which serves breakfast, features casual garden-style tables amid lush greenery under a large skylight; it's built on the home's enclosed patio. El Cañon Wine and Coffee Bar specializes in fine wines by the glass and gourmet coffees. El Cañon also serves breakfast, lunch, and dinner. Specialties include freshly baked breads and pastries as well as sandwiches.

Amenities: Concierge, room service, courtesy van, dry cleaning, laundry service, outdoor swimming pool, Jacuzzi, small health club, car-rental agency, travel agency, gift shop.

Hotel Loretto. 211 Old Santa Fe Trail (P.O. Box 1417), Santa Fe, NM 87501. ☎ **800/ 727-5531** or 505/988-5531. Fax 505/984-7988. 145 units. A/C TV TEL. Jan–Apr $189–$259 double; May–Oct $239–$379 double; Nov–Dec 20 $189–$259 double; Dec 21–Dec 31, $239–$379 double. Extra person $15. Children 17 and under stay free in parents' room. AE, CB, DC, DISC, MC, V. Free parking.

This much-photographed hotel, just 2 blocks from the Plaza, was built in 1975 to resemble the Taos Pueblo. Light and shadow dance upon the five-level structure as the sun crosses the sky. Two years ago it came under new ownership and is now undergoing a multimillion-dollar makeover. The outdated decor has been replaced by a Southwest/Montana ranch style put into place by the decorator of Ted Turner and Jane Fonda. The new owners, Noble House Hotels and Resorts (owners of the Adolphus Hotel in Dallas and Little Palm in Key West), are determined to compete with other large hotels such as the Eldorado. With faux painted walls and an interesting and cozy new lobby lounge, they may just manage to catch up. Still, the hotel's rooms are pretty standard, a bit small, and the bathrooms are basic. With the renovation, the hotel hopes to attract more groups. Overall it is fairly quiet and has nice views—especially on the northeast side, where you'll see both the historic St. Francis Cathedral and the Loretto Chapel (with its "miraculous" spiral staircase; see "What to See & Do," later in this chapter). Each room has a coffeemaker, bottled water, and hair dryers.

Dining: Named for a carved wooden serpent above the bar, Nellie's serves fine nouveau Southwestern cuisine in a hip-folk-artsy environment. A coffee shop serves sandwiches, stews, muffins, and Starbucks coffee.

Amenities: Concierge, room service, valet laundry, business center, and audiovisual conferencing equipment. There's also an outdoor heated swimming pool (mid-May to mid-October), shopping arcade (with a fine-art gallery, boutiques, gift shops, sundries shop, and hair salon). Tennis and golf privileges nearby can be arranged.

✪ Inn of the Anasazi. 113 Washington Ave., Santa Fe, NM 87501. ☎ **800/688-8100** or 505/988-3030. Fax 505/988-3277. 59 units. A/C MINIBAR TV TEL. Nov–Mar $199–$345 double; Apr–Oct $235–$395 double. Holiday and festival rates may be higher. AE, CB, DC, DISC, MC, V. Valet parking $10.

In an incredible feat, the designers of this fine luxury hotel have managed to create a feeling of grandness in a very limited space. Flagstone floors, vigas, and latillas are enhanced by oversized cacti that evoke the feeling of an Anasazi cliff dwelling and lend a warm and welcoming ambience. Accents are appropriately Navajo, in a nod to the fact that the Navajo live in the area the Anasazi once inhabited. A half block off the Plaza, this hotel was built in 1991 to cater to travelers who know their hotels. Amenities include stereos and VCRs in all rooms, as well as private safes, coffeemakers with custom blended coffee beans, bathroom telephones, hair dryers, 100% cotton linens, and organic bath oils and shampoos, as well as organic food in the restaurant. On the ground floor are a living room and library with oversized furniture and replicas of Anasazi pottery and Navajo rugs.

Even the smallest rooms are spacious, with pearl-finished walls and decor in cream tones accented by novelties such as iron candle sconces, original art, four-poster beds, gaslit kiva fireplaces, and humidifiers. All the rooms are quiet and comfortable, though none have dramatic views.

Dining: See the Anasazi Restaurant listing under "Where to Dine," below, for a full description.

Amenities: Concierge, room service (6am to 11pm), laundry service, newspaper delivery, in-room massage, twice-daily maid service, tours of galleries and museums, stationary bicycles available for use in guest rooms, free coffee or refreshments in lobby. You'll also find video rentals, library/boardroom, and audiovisual and communication equipment. Access to a nearby health club can be arranged.

✪ Inn on the Alameda. 303 E. Alameda St., Santa Fe, NM 87501. ☎ **800/289-2122** or 505/984-2121. Fax 505/986-8325. 68 units. A/C TV TEL. Jan–Mar $144–$204 double, $219–$289 suite; Mar–June $159–$219 double, $234–$304 suite; July–Oct $174–$234 double, $249–$319 suite; Nov–Dec $144–$202 double, $219–$289 suite. Holidays and special events may be higher; rates subject to change. Rates include breakfast. AE, DC, DISC, MC, V. Free parking. Pets are welcome (the hotel offers a pet program that features pet amenities and a pet-walking map).

Just across the street from the bosk-shaded Santa Fe River and 3 blocks from the Plaza sits the Inn on the Alameda, a cozy stop for those who like the services of a hotel with the intimacy of an inn. Begun 10 years ago as a bed-and-breakfast, it now sprawls into four buildings. There are casita suites to the west, two three-story buildings at the center, and another one-story that contains suites. All are Pueblo-style adobe, ranging in age, but most were built in the late 1980s.

The owner, Joe Schepps, appreciates traditional Southwestern style; he's used red brick in the dining area and Mexican equipal furniture (leather and willow) in the lobby. He went all out here in the construction, using thick vigas and shiny latillas set around a grand fireplace.

The rooms follow a similar good taste, though the decor is more standard Santa Fe style (boxy with pastel upholstery) than the lobby might lead you to expect. All rooms have VCRs and hair dryers. The newer deluxe rooms and suites in the easternmost building are in the best shape. The traditional rooms are quaint, some with interesting angled bed configurations. Beware of the casitas on the western corner of the property. After some recent tree trimming, they've tended to pick up traffic noise. Still, take note of the trees surrounding the inn—cottonwoods and aspens, which, when you step out on some balconies, make you feel as though you're in a tree house. If you're an art shopper this is an ideal spot because it's a quick walk to Canyon Road. Amenities include robes in all rooms and refrigerators and kiva fireplaces in some rooms.

Dining/Diversions: An elaborate continental "Breakfast of Enchantment" is served each morning in the Agoyo Room, outdoor courtyard, or your own room. A full-service bar is open nightly.

Amenities: Concierge, limited room service, dry cleaning and self-serve laundry, newspaper delivery, baby-sitting can be arranged. There's also a medium-sized fitness facility, massage and two open-air Jacuzzis.

✪ **La Fonda.** 100 E. San Francisco St. (P.O. Box 1209), Santa Fe, NM 87501. ☎ **800/ 523-5002** or 505/982-5511. Fax 505/988-2952. 191 units. A/C TV TEL. $195 standard double, $205 deluxe double; $225–$550 suite. Extra person $15. Children under 12 stay free in parents' room. AE, CB, DC, DISC, MC, V. Parking $6 in a covered garage.

Whether you stay in this hotel on the southeast corner of the Plaza or elsewhere, it's worth strolling through, just to get a sense of how Santa Fe once was, and still in some ways is. This was the inn at the end of the Santa Fe Trail; it saw trappers, traders, and merchants, as well as notables such as Pres. Rutherford B. Hayes and Gen. Ulysses S. Grant. The original inn was dying of old age in 1920 when it was razed and replaced by the current La Fonda. Its architecture is Pueblo Revival: imitation adobe with wooden balconies and beam ends protruding over the tops of windows. Inside the lobby is rich and slightly dark with people bustling about, drinking in the cafe and buying jewelry from Native Americans.

As you head farther into this four-story building you may come across Ernesto Martinez, who wanders around finding things to paint. You'll see his colorful, playful designs throughout the hallways and in the rooms decorating tin mirror frames and carved wooden headboards.

The hotel has seen some renovation through the years, as well as a whole new wing recently completed to the east where you'll find deluxe suites and new meeting spaces. Overall, however, this hotel isn't the model of refinement. For that, you'd best go to the Hotel Santa Fe or other newer places. No room is the same here, and while each has its own funky touch, some are more kitsch than quaint. All rooms have hair dryers, Spectravision movie channels, irons, and ironing boards. Some have minirefrigerators, fireplaces, and private balconies. If you want a feel of the real Santa Fe, this is the place to stay.

Dining/Diversions: The French Pastry Shop is the place to get cappuccino and crepes; La Fiesta Lounge draws many locals to their economical New Mexican food lunch buffet; and La Plazuela offers what some believe to be the best chile rellenos in town, in a skylit garden patio. The Bell Tower Bar, at the southwest corner of the hotel, is the highest point in downtown Santa Fe—a great place for a cocktail and a view of the city.

Amenities: Concierge, room service, dry cleaning and laundry service, tour desk, in-room massage, baby-sitting, express check-out, free coffee and refreshments in lobby. There's also an outdoor swimming pool, two indoor Jacuzzis, sundeck, cold plunge, massage room, ballroom, and shopping arcade.

La Posada de Santa Fe Resort and Spa. 330 E. Palace Ave., Santa Fe, NM 87501. ☎ **800/727-5276** or 505/986-0000. Fax 505/982-6850. 159 units. A/C MINIBAR TV TEL. May–Oct plus Thanksgiving and Christmas seasons $189–$397 double; $289–$497 suite. Nov–Apr (except holidays) $159–$315 double; $225–$385 suite. Various packages available. AE, CB, DC, DISC, MC, V. Free parking.

If you're in the mood to stay in a little New Mexico adobe village, you'll enjoy this hotel just 3 blocks from the Plaza. The main building is an odd mix of architecture. The original part was a Victorian mansion built in 1882 by Abraham Staab, a German immigrant, for his bride, Julia. Later it was adobeized—an adobe structure was literally built around it—so that now the Victorian presence is only within the charming bar and a half-dozen rooms, which still maintain the original brick, mahogany, and marble, as well as Italian paintings, French furniture, and tapestries. It is said that Julia Staab, who died in 1896, continues to haunt the place. Mischievous but good-natured, she is Santa Fe's best-known and most frequently witnessed ghost.

The rest of the hotel follows in the Pueblo-style construction and is quaint, especially in the summer when surrounded by acres of green grass. Here you get to experience squeaky maple floors, vigas and latillas, and, in many rooms, kiva fireplaces. Fortunately, the hotel has recently come under new ownership and major renovations are taking place in the common and guest rooms. At press time, these changes were just beginning with plans for completion in April 1999. The hotel attracts travelers and a fair number of families. Most rooms don't have views but have outdoor patios, and most are tucked back into the quiet compound. All have coffeemakers and hair dryers.

Dining/Diversions: The hotel has a restaurant, open for three meals daily, serving "food of the Americas." From spring to early fall meals are also served outside on a big patio. The lounge has seasonal happy-hour entertainment (usually local musicians).

Amenities: Concierge, limited room service, dry cleaning and laundry service, in-room massage, twice-daily maid service, free coffee and refreshments in lobby. The hotel also has a heated outdoor swimming pool and boutiques. After March 1999, the hotel plans to have a Jacuzzi, sauna, sundeck, business center, and beauty salon.

EXPENSIVE

✪ **Hotel St. Francis.** 210 Don Gaspar Ave., Santa Fe, NM 87501. ☎ **800/529-5700** or 505/983-5700. Fax 505/989-7690. 84 units. A/C TV TEL. May 1–Oct 31 plus the weeks of Dec 25 and Jan 1, $118–$208 double; $228–$353 suite. Nov–Feb $88–$158 double; $178–$278 suite. Mar–Apr $98–$173 double; $178–$278 suite. Children under 12 stay free in parents' room. AE, CB, DC, DISC, MC, V. Free parking.

If you long for the rich fabrics, fine antiques, and slow pace of a European Hotel, this is your place. One block from the Plaza, the building was first constructed in the 1880s and has seen a fire, countless government officials come to dine and drink, and finally dilapidation. It was renovated in 1986. The now elegantly redecorated lobby is crowned by a Victorian fireplace with hovering cherubs, a theme repeated throughout the hotel.

The rooms follow the European decor, each with its own unique bent. You'll find a fishing room, golf room, garden room, and music room, the motif evoked by the furnishings: a vintage set of golf clubs here, a sheet of music in a dry flower arrangement there. The hotel attracts individual travelers as well as families and many Europeans, well cared for by a concierge who speaks six languages. Request a room facing east and you'll wake each day to a view of the mountains, seen through lovely lace. All rooms have refrigerators and closet safes.

Dining/Diversions: A recent renovation has given the restaurant and bar a European gentlemen's club ambience. Breakfast, lunch, and dinner specials are served daily with prices worth checking out. The lobby and veranda are favorite spots for locals to take their afternoon tea. You'll eat scones, pastries, and tea sandwiches—all baked in-house—and drink tea, sherry, port, or champagne.

Amenities: Concierge, room service, dry cleaning and laundry service, free coffee or refreshments in lobby. You'll also find Spectravision movie channels and a guest membership at a nearby health club.

ⓘ Family-Friendly Hotels

Bishop's Lodge *(see page 140)*   A children's pony ring, riding lessons, tennis courts with instruction, a pool with lifeguard, stocked trout pond just for kids, a summer daytime program, horseback trail trips, and more make this a veritable day camp for all ages.

El Rey Inn *(see page 143)*   Kids will enjoy the play area, table games, and pool; parents will appreciate the kitchenettes and laundry facilities.

Rancho Encantado *(see page 141)*   Horseback riding (on trails or pony ring), pool, tennis courts, and many indoor and outdoor games will keep kids happily busy here.

Villas de Santa Fe. 400 Griffin St., Santa Fe, NM 87501. ☎ **800/869-6790** or 505/988-3000. Fax 505/988-4700. 90 suites. A/C TV TEL. $104–$155 1-bedroom suite with 1 or 2 beds; $124–$175 1-bedroom suite with gas fireplace; $185–$310 2-bedroom, 2-bathroom suite with gas fireplace. Rates include continental breakfast. AE, DC, DISC, MC, V. Free parking.

Formerly the Homewood Suites, this hotel is upscale practicality. Tucked within a residential neighborhood within walking distance from the Plaza, Villas is the place you go when you want a bit of luxury and the ability to cook and eat as you do at home. Built in 1994, its guest rooms on three stories are decorated in Southwestern style with an efficiency that marks the place. The rooms are consistently comfortable, with full kitchens that include microwaves, stoves, refrigerators, and dishwashers, as well as amenities such as pay movies and Nintendo, ironing boards and irons, recliners, and sleeper sofas. Some have balconies and patios and some have gas fireplaces. There is a homey feel in the main room where an extended continental breakfast is served around a kitchen environment.

Amenities: Complimentary grocery shopping, local shuttle service, valet laundry service, year-round heated outdoor pool, two outdoor Jacuzzis, well-equipped health club, Laundromat, Suite Shop (with vending and beverages), and picnic area with gas grill.

MODERATE

Garrett's Desert Inn. 311 Old Santa Fe Trail, Santa Fe, NM 87501. ☎ **800/888-2145** or 505/982-1851. Fax 505/989-1647. 82 units. A/C TV TEL. $69–$114 depending on season and type of room. AE, DC, DISC, MC, V. Free parking.

Completion of this hotel in 1957 prompted the Historic Design Review Board to implement zoning restrictions throughout downtown. Apparently, residents were appalled by the huge air conditioners adorning the roof. Though they're still unsightly, the hotel makes up for them in other ways. First, with all the focus today on retro fashions, this hotel 3 blocks from the Plaza is totally in. It's a clean, two-story, concrete block building around a broad parking lot. The hotel underwent a complete remodeling in 1994; it managed to maintain some '50s touches, such as art deco colored tile in the bathrooms and plenty of space in the rooms, while enlarging the windows and putting in sturdy doors and wood accents. Rooms are equipped with tile vanities and hair dryers. Above all, it's centrally located, within walking distance from the Plaza and Canyon Road, but also far enough from busy streets to provide needed quiet. There is a concierge, limited room service, baby-sitting and express check-out. Locals frequent the hotel's Le Cafe on the Trail for crepes and pancakes. There's a year-round heated pool.

Hotel Santa Fe. 1501 Paseo de Peralta, Santa Fe, NM 87501. ☎ **800/825-9876** or 505/982-1200. Fax 505/984-2211. 220 units. A/C MINIBAR TV TEL. Jan 4–Feb 11, $99 double; $129 suite. Feb 12–April 30, $119 double; $139 suite. May 1–June 24, $129 double; $159 suite. June 25–Aug 28, $149 double; $179 suite. Aug 29–Oct 31, $139 double; $169 suite. Nov 1–Dec 23, $109 double; $129 suite. Dec 24–Jan 3, $149 double; $179 suite. Extra person $10. Children 17 and under stay free in parents' room. AE, CB, DC, DISC, MC, V. Free parking.

About a 10-minute walk south of the Plaza you'll find this newer three-story establishment, the only Native American–owned hotel in Santa Fe. The Picuris Pueblo is the majority stockholder here, and part of the pleasure of staying is the culture they bring to your visit. This is not to say that you'll get any sense of the rusticity of a pueblo in your accommodations—this sophisticated 6-year-old hotel is decorated in Southwestern style with a few novel aspects such as an Allan Houser bronze buffalo dancer watching over the front desk and an *horno*-shaped (Pueblo bread oven) fireplace surrounded by comfortable furniture in the lobby.

The rooms are medium-sized with clean lines and comfortable beds, the decor accented with pine Taos-style furniture. You will get a strong sense of the Native American presence on the patio during the summer, when Picuris dancers come to perform and bread bakers uncover the *horno* and prepare loaves for sale.

Rooms on the north side get less street noise from Cerrillos Road and have better views of the mountains, but you won't have the sun shining onto your balcony.

The restaurant is another place where the hotel's origins are recognizable. The famed Corn Dance Cafe serves a standard breakfast, but for lunch and dinner you can dine on Native American food from all over the Americas. Expect buffalo and turkey instead of beef and chicken. Many of the dishes are accompanied by what chef Loretta Oden calls the three sisters: corn, beans, and squash.

Amenities here include concierge, limited room service, dry cleaning and laundry service, in-room massage, twice-daily maid service, baby-sitting, secretarial services, courtesy shuttle to the Plaza and Canyon Road. There's also a lovely outdoor heated pool, a Jacuzzi, conference rooms, Laundromat, car-rental desk, and Picuris Pueblo gift shop. Access to a nearby health club can be arranged.

Santa Fe Budget Inn. 725 Cerrillos Rd., Santa Fe, NM 87501. ☎ **800/288-7600** or 505/982-5952. Fax 505/984-8879. 160 units. A/C TV TEL. July 4–Oct 25 and Dec 25–Jan 2, $75–$86 double ($10–$20 higher during Indian Market). Rest of the year $50–$58 double. Sun–Thurs supersaver rate may apply in the off-season. AAA and AARP members receive $3 discounts. AE, CB, DC, MC, V. Free parking.

If you're looking for a convenient almost-downtown location at a reasonable price, this is one of your best bets. This two-story stucco adobe motel with portals is spread through three buildings and is about a 10-minute walk from the Plaza. Built in 1985, it was remodeled in 1994. The rooms are plain, basic, and fairly small. Santa Fe Opera and Fiesta posters add a splash of color. The bathrooms and furniture could use some updating, but if you're a traveler who spends a lot of time out of the room this shouldn't matter because the place is clean and functional with comfortable (on the soft side) beds and good reading lights. Outside there's a small park in back and an outdoor pool (open in summer) tucked away. To avoid street noise ask for a room at the back of the property. An adjacent restaurant serves American and New Mexican food.

INEXPENSIVE

Santa Fe Motel. 510 Cerrillos Rd., Santa Fe, NM 87501. ☎ **800/745-9910** or 505/982-1039. Fax 505/986-1275. 21 units. A/C TV TEL. $54–$89 double; $69–$121 kitchenette; $89–$149 casita. Extra person $10. Continental breakfast included with the price of the room. AE, DC, MC, V. Free parking.

If you like walking to the Plaza and restaurants but don't want to pay big bucks, this little compound is a good choice. Rooms here are larger than at the nearby Budget and have more personality than those at the Travelodge. Ask for one of the casitas in back—you'll pay more but get a little turn-of-the-century charm (when they were built), plus more quiet and privacy. Some have vigas, others skylights, fireplaces, and patios. The main part of the motel, built in 1955, is two-story Territorial style, with upstairs rooms that open onto a portal with a bit of a view. Under new ownership in 1998, the hotel's rooms are, at press time, being renovated. They're decorated in a Southwest motif and have very basic furnishings, but nice firm beds. The bathrooms are supposed to be receiving much-needed updating. In the main building kitchenettes are available and include refrigerator, microwave, stove, coffeemaker, and toaster. Fresh-brewed coffee is served each morning in the office, where a bulletin board lists Santa Fe activities.

Santa Fe Plaza Travelodge. 646 Cerrillos Rd., Santa Fe, NM 87501. ☎ **800/578-7878** or 505/982-3551. Fax 505/983-8624. 48 units. A/C TV TEL. Nov–Apr $39–$75 double; May–Oct $65–$88 double. These rates subject to change. AE, CB, DC, DISC, MC, V. Free parking.

You can count on the motel next door to Hotel Santa Fe (6 blocks to the Plaza) on busy Cerrillos Road for comfort, convenience, and a no-frills stay. The rooms are very clean, nicely lit, and despite the busy location, relatively quiet. New mattresses and a pretty Southwestern ceiling border added to the decor make the rooms comfortable. Each room has a minirefrigerator, table and chairs, and a coffeemaker. The curbside pool, though basic, will definitely provide relief on hot summer days. A newspaper is delivered each morning.

NORTHSIDE

Within easy reach of the Plaza, Northside encompasses the area that lies north of the loop of the Paseo de Peralta.

VERY EXPENSIVE

✪ Bishop's Lodge. Bishop's Lodge Rd. (P.O. Box 2367), Santa Fe, NM 87504. ☎ **505/983-6377.** Fax 505/989-8739. 88 units. A/C TV TEL. European Plan (meals not included), low season (midwinter) $105–$215 double; midseason rates (fall and spring and winter break) $155–$305 double; high summer season $179–$389 double. Additional person $15. Children 3 and under stay free in parents' room. The summer American Plan package offers breakfast and choice of lunch or dinner as well as children's programs: late May to late June $271–$441 double; early July to late Aug $311–$481 double. Extra person $61. AE, DC, DISC, MC, V. Free parking.

This resort holds special significance for me, as my parents met in the lodge and were later married in the chapel. Years later, the whole family used to come here from Albuquerque so my parents could relax and we children could ride horses. It's a place rich with history. More than a century ago, when Bishop Jean-Baptiste Lamy was the spiritual leader of northern New Mexico's Roman Catholic population, he often escaped clerical politics by hiking into this valley called Little Tesuque. He built a retreat and a humble chapel (now on the National Register of Historic Places) with high-vaulted ceilings and a hand-built altar. Today Lamy's 1,000-acre getaway has become Bishop's Lodge.

Purchased in 1918 from the Pulitzer family (of publishing fame) by Denver mining executive James R. Thorpe, it remained in his family's hands until 1998, when the Australian real estate company ERE Yarmouth purchased it. The company plans an $11 million renovation over the next 3 years, including the addition of 56 guest rooms, a spa, and 10,000 square feet of meeting space as well as replacement of bedding and other furnishings. The lobby, lounge, and restaurant will also be renovated.

The guest rooms, spread through 10 buildings, all feature handcrafted furniture and regional artwork. Guests receive a complimentary fruit basket upon arrival. Standard rooms are spacious and many have balconies, while deluxe rooms feature traditional kiva fireplaces, a combination bedroom/sitting room, and private decks or patios; some older units have flagstone floors and viga ceilings. All rooms have coffeemakers, robes, and in-room safes, and receive a morning newspaper. Deluxe suites are extremely spacious, with living rooms, separate bedrooms, private patios and decks, and artwork of near-museum quality. All deluxe units come with fireplaces, refrigerators, and in-room safes. The Lodge is an active resort three seasons of the year; in the winter, it takes on the character of a romantic country retreat.

Dining/Diversions: Bishop's Lodge dining room features regional Southwestern cuisine. Attire is casual at breakfast and lunch, slightly more formal at dinner. There's a full vintage wine list, and El Rincon Bar serves before- and after-dinner drinks.

Amenities: Concierge, room service, laundry service, newspaper delivery, in-room massage, twice-daily maid service, baby-sitting, express checkout, courtesy shuttle three times daily, free coffee or refreshments in the lobby in the mornings, seasonal cookouts, and breakfast rides. There's an outdoor pool with a seasonal lifeguard, small health club, aerobics classes, four tennis courts, pro shop and instruction, Jacuzzi, sauna, hiking and self-guided nature walk (the Lodge is a member of the Audubon Cooperative Sanctuary System), daily guided horseback rides, introductory riding lessons, a children's pony ring, supervised skeet and trap shooting, a stocked trout pond for children, Ping-Pong, summer daytime program with counselors for children.

Rancho Encantado. Rte. 4, Box 57C, Santa Fe, NM 87501. ☎ **800/722-9339** or 505/982-3537. Fax 505/983-8269. 45 units. A/C TV TEL. Guest rooms $125–$275 double. Villas $130–$205 pueblo room, $210–$350 one bedroom, $250–$420 two bedroom, depending on the season. AE, DISC, DC, MC, V. Free parking.

Located 8 miles north of Santa Fe in the foothills of the Sangre de Cristo Mountains, Rancho Encantado, with its sweeping panoramic views, offers travelers luxury accommodations and plenty of wild Southwest activities. The resort was begun by Betty Egan, a former World War II captain in the Women's Army Corps, who purchased the property in the mid-1960s. Mrs. Egan, then recently widowed, was determined to begin a new and prosperous life with her family, and so in 1968 the 168-acre ranch became Rancho Encantado. The property came under new ownership in 1995, and with it came long-needed upgrades to sleeping rooms, the main lodge, and grounds.

The handsome main lodge is comfortable and unassuming, decorated in traditional Southwestern style with hand-painted tiles, ceiling vigas, tile floors, antique furnishings, Pueblo rugs, and Hispanic art objects hanging on stuccoed walls. The large fireplace in the living room/lounge is a focal point, especially on cold winter afternoons. In the main lodge and adjoining area the rooms are quite cozy with a hint of Victorian bed-and-breakfast feel. All rooms provide coffeemakers and minirefrigerators; most have fireplaces.

Surrounding the lodge are clusters of cottages and casitas. These are comfortable units with a homey feel, though they've needed a decorator's touch, and are, at press time, receiving it: new fabrics and soft goods, carpet, draperies, bedspreads, and some furnishings. Across the street from the main building are two-bedroom/two-bathroom villas. These newer split-level adobe units are equipped with fireplaces in the living room and master bedroom plus a full kitchen. Currently the owners are breaking ground on 25 new Pueblo-style junior parlor suites, each with a kiva fireplace and private patio. Expected completion date is spring 1999. Whichever you choose, you're sure to find the accommodations here more than adequate; satisfied guests have included Princess Anne, Robert Redford, Jimmy Stewart, Whoopi Goldberg, and John Wayne.

The new owners have expanded special programs at the resort. Watch for summer sunset margarita horseback rides, barbecues and chuck-wagon breakfast cookouts, barn dances, and Native American and Hispanic storytelling and dancing, as well as a children's summer camp which includes music, art projects, hiking, basketball, swimming, and horseback riding. In winter you can take a sleigh ride through the countryside.

Dining/Diversions: Rancho Encantado's restaurant is a favorite dinner spot for opera-goers. The food is good and the atmosphere relaxing. The west wall of the dining room has picture windows that overlook the Jemez Mountains, offering diners a first-rate view of the spectacular New Mexico sunset. Some of the traditional dishes remain, with an addition of some contemporary Western cuisine. You may enjoy tenderloin of beef, served with a Jack Daniel's sauce, or a smoked salmon burrito. You can also get a good egg salad sandwich. The Cantina, with its big-screen TV, is a popular gathering spot; there is also a snack bar on the premises.

Amenities: Laundry service, limited room service, baby-sitting, and courtesy limo to Plaza. There's also an outdoor pool, small health club, Jacuzzi, tennis courts (tennis pro in summer), hiking trails, horseback riding, sand volleyball, basketball, horseshoes, pool table, bocce court (Italian lawn bowling), and library.

EXPENSIVE

Radisson Deluxe Hotel Santa Fe. 750 N. St. Francis Dr., Santa Fe, NM 87501. ☎ **800/ 333-3333** or 505/982-5591. Fax 505/988-2821. 128 units, 32 condos. A/C TV TEL. $89–$149 double, $218–$436 suite, $119–$209 condo, depending on time of year. AE, CB, DC, DISC, MC, V. Free parking.

Set on a hill as you head north toward the Santa Fe Opera, this three-story hotel provides a decent stay. The lobby is unremarkable, with tile floors and aged wood trim. Previously remodeled in 1994, the hotel recently came under new ownership; more renovation is ongoing. In some ways it needs it: The rooms' door frames need repairs, and many hallways need repainting. I'd reserve a stay here for summer months when the elegant pool is open. The rooms are decorated in blond furniture with a Southwestern motif, some with views of the mountains, others overlooking the pool. All are equipped with hair dryers, irons, and ironing boards. There's free drop-off and pickup to the opera, Plaza, and elsewhere in town. Premium rooms are more spacious, some with large living rooms and private balconies. Each parlor suite has a Murphy bed and kiva fireplace in the living room, a big dining area, a wet bar and refrigerator, and a jetted bathtub. Cielo Grande condo units nearby come with fully equipped kitchens, fireplaces, and private decks.

Dining/Diversions: The Santa Fe Salsa Company Restaurant and Bar serves three meals a day. Dinner main courses are international with a Southwestern flair. A jazz combo plays nightly in the bar, and the nightclub features the quick Spanish steps of New Mexico's best-known flamenco dancer, María Benitez, and her Estampa Flamenca troupe.

Amenities: Outdoor swimming pool, Jacuzzi, access to health club next door, Laundromat, room service, shuttle service, dry cleaning and laundry service. Complimentary *USA Today* provided each morning. Child care can be arranged.

SOUTHSIDE

Santa Fe's major strip, Cerrillos Road, is U.S. 85, the main route to and from Albuquerque and the I-25 freeway. It's about 5¼ miles from the Plaza to the

Villa Linda Mall, which marks the southern boundary of the city. Most motels are on this strip, although several of them are east, closer to St. Francis Drive (U.S. 84) or the Las Vegas Highway.

MODERATE

Best Western Santa Fe. 3650 Cerrillos Rd., Santa Fe, NM 87505. ☎ **800/528-1234** or 505/438-3822. Fax 505/438-3795. 116 units. A/C TV TEL. Jan 1–May 15 and Oct 16–Dec 31, $50–$75 double, $75–$95 suite; May 16–Oct 15, $60–$100 double, $85–$145 suite. Children 12 and under stay free in parents' room. Rates include continental breakfast. AE, CB, DC, DISC, MC, V. Free parking.

Previously the Days Inn, this three-story pink hotel 15 minutes' drive from the Plaza offers clean cookie-cutter–type rooms at a reasonable price. It's a security-conscious hostelry; rooms can be entered only from interior corridors and there are private safes in each room. Built in 1990, its renovation is ongoing with new bedspreads and drapes in 1997. The lobby is decorated in light pastels, with little tables where guests can eat a continental breakfast. The indoor hot tub and pool are very clean and sprightly decorated, a good family spot to relax between outings. Rooms are a bit narrow, with Aztec motif bedspreads and blonde furniture. Some doubles are more spacious, with a couch. All bathrooms are small but functional. Suites are larger, some with a Jacuzzi in the room itself; others have two rooms, a sleeper sofa in one. Amenities include a 24-hour desk, guest laundry, and, in the lobby, coffee and tea throughout the day.

✪ **El Rey Inn.** 1862 Cerrillos Rd. (P.O. Box 4759), Santa Fe, NM 87502. ☎ **800/521-1349** or 505/982-1931. Fax 505/989-9249. 94 units. A/C TV TEL. $60–$145 double; $95–$185 suite. Rates include continental breakfast. AE, CB, DC, DISC, MC, V. Free parking.

Staying at "The King" makes you feel like you're traveling the old Route 66 through the Southwest. The white stucco buildings of this court motel are decorated with bright trim around the doors and hand-painted Mexican tiles on the walls. Opened in the 1930s, it received additions in the 1950s and remodeling is ongoing. The lobby has vigas and tile floors decorated with Oriental rugs and dark Spanish furniture. No two rooms are alike. The oldest section, nearest the lobby, feels a bit cramped, though the rooms have style, with art-deco tile in the bathrooms and vigas on the ceilings. Some have little patios. Be sure to request to be as far back as possible from Cerrillos Road.

The two stories of suites around the Spanish colonial courtyard are the sweetest deal I've seen in all of Santa Fe. These feel like a Spanish inn, with carved furniture and cozy couches. Some rooms have kitchenettes. The owners recently purchased the motel next door and have now added 10 deluxe units around the courtyard. The new rooms offer more upscale amenities and gas log fireplaces, as well as distinctive furnishings and artwork. Complimentary continental breakfast is served in a sunny room or on a terrace in the warmer months. There's also a sitting room with a library and games tables, outdoor swimming pool, Jacuzzi, sauna, picnic area, children's play area, and Laundromat. For its cheaper rooms, El Rey is Santa Fe's best moderately (and even inexpensively) priced accommodation.

INEXPENSIVE

✪ **La Quinta Inn.** 4298 Cerrillos Rd., Santa Fe, NM 87505. ☎ **800/531-5900** or 505/471-1142. Fax 505/438-7219. 130 units. A/C TV TEL. June–mid-Oct $80–$88 double; late Oct–May $60–$66 double. Children 18 and under stay free in parents' room. Large discount for AAA members. Rates include continental breakfast. AE, CB, DC, DISC, MC, V. Free parking. Pets stay free.

Though it's a good 15-minute drive from the Plaza, this is my choice of economical Cerrillos Road chain hotels. Built in 1986, it was just fully remodeled in a very comfortable and tasteful way. The rooms within the three-story white brick buildings have an unexpectedly elegant feel, with lots of deep colors and art deco tile in the bathrooms. There's plenty of space in these rooms, and they're lit for mood as well as for reading. Each has a coffeemaker. A continental breakfast is served in the intimate lobby. The kidney-shaped pool has a nice lounging area, heated April to October. If you're a shopper or movie-goer, this hotel is just across a parking lot from the Villa Linda Mall. The Kettle, a 24-hour coffee shop, is adjacent. La Quinta also has a 24-hour desk, Laundromat (as well as valet laundry), and complimentary coffee at all times in the lobby. Continental breakfast includes fresh fruit, Danish, cereal, bagels, coffee, tea, and juice.

BED & BREAKFASTS

If you prefer a homey, intimate setting to the sometimes impersonal ambience of a large hotel, one of Santa Fe's bed-and-breakfast inns may be right for you. All those listed here are located in or close to the downtown area and offer comfortable accommodations at expensive to moderate prices. All have rooms for nonsmokers and for people with disabilities.

✪ **Adobe Abode.** 202 Chapelle St., Santa Fe, NM 87501. ☎ **505/983-3133.** Fax 505/986-0972. E-mail: adobebnb@sprynet.com. 6 units. TV TEL. $115–$155 double. Rates include breakfast. DISC, MC, V. Free parking.

A short walk from the Plaza, in the same quiet residential neighborhood where the new Georgia O'Keeffe Museum resides, Adobe Abode is one of Santa Fe's most imaginative B&Bs. The living room is filled with everything from Mexican folk art and pottery to Buddhas and ethnic masks. The open kitchen features a country pine table as well as Balinese puppets. The creativity of the owner/innkeeper, Pat Harbour, shines in each of the guest rooms as well. The Out of Africa Room, in the main house, has elegant fabrics and tribal art. The Texas Hill Country Room features antiques and designer denim and plaid bedding. Both are in the main house, which was built in 1907 and renovated in 1989. In back are casitas occupying newer buildings, designed with flair. The Bronco Room is filled with cowboy paraphernalia: hats, Pendleton blankets, pioneer chests, and my favorite, an entire shelf lined with children's cowboy boots. Finally, Pat has added a new two-room suite, the Provence Suite, which she decorated in sunny yellow and bright blue. Two rooms have fireplaces, while several have private patios. All rooms have coffeemakers and terry-cloth robes. Complimentary sherry, fruit, and Santa Fe cookies are served daily in the living room. Every morning a healthful breakfast of fresh-squeezed orange juice, fresh fruit, homemade muffins, scones or pastries, and a hot dish is served in the kitchen.

✪ **Alexander's Inn.** 529 East Palace Ave., Santa Fe, NM 87501. ☎ **888/321-5123** or 505/986-1431. Fax 505/982-8572. 12 units (10 with bathroom), 4 cottages. A/C TV TEL. $75–$160 double. Rates include continental breakfast. MC, V. Free parking. Children and pets are accepted.

I'd fear my long-standing friendship with innkeeper Carolyn Lee biases my opinion about her inn, except that it receives outstanding recommendations from such publications as *Glamour* magazine ("one of the most romantic inns in the Southwest") and *Southwest Art* ("101 reasons to visit Santa Fe"). Eleven years ago Carolyn had a dream of starting an inn and she put her whole self into this 1903 Victorian/New England–style house in a quiet residential area 6 blocks from the Plaza. Naming it after her son, she filled it with delicious antiques, bedding, and draperies. The rooms here have stenciling on the walls, hook and Oriental rugs, muted colors such as apricot and lilac, and white iron or four-poster queen-size beds (there are some king-size beds as well). Recently though, she's expanded into a new property even closer to the Plaza.

The Hacienda offers guests a delightful Southwest stay in rooms gathered around a sunny patio and is an excellent deal. My favorite room here is the bright Cottonwood, with decor in muted tones, and the Sunflower, with French doors, maple floors, a kiva fireplace, and luxurious king bed. All have spacious bathrooms with Mexican tile. Separate from both properties are cottages complete with kitchens (equipped with stove, oven, and refrigerator, some with microwave) and living rooms with kiva fireplaces. Some of these don't have quite the charm of rooms in the main house and Hacienda; others have plenty of Southwestern charm, so discuss your desires when making reservations. Fresh flowers adorn all the rooms throughout the year, and all have robes, hair dryers, and makeup mirrors. Guests can enjoy privileges at El Gancho Tennis Club as well as the hot tub in the back garden at the main inn. An extended continental breakfast of homemade baked goods is served on the veranda every morning, as well as afternoon tea and cookies.

Dancing Ground of the Sun. 711 Paseo de Peralta, Santa Fe, NM 87501. ☎ **800/645-5673** or 505/986-9797. Fax 505/986-8082. www.dancingground.com. E-mail: innkeeper@ dancingground.com. 7 units. A/C TV TEL. Nov–Apr $75–$210 double; May–Oct and all holidays $95–$255 double. Rates include continental breakfast. MC, V. Free parking.

A great deal of thought and energy went into decorating these units, and it shows. Each of the eight rooms, five of which are casitas, has been outfitted with handcrafted Santa Fe–style furnishings made by local artisans, and the decor of each room focuses on a mythological Native American figure, whose likeness has been hand-painted on the walls of that unit. There's Corn Dancer, who represents the anticipation of an abundant harvest; Kokopelli, a flute player believed to bring good fortune and abundance to the Native American people; and other themes. Many have ceiling vigas and all have nice touches, such as *nichos* (little niches) that come with an older adobe building such as this, constructed in the 1930s. Each of the five casitas has a fireplace and a fully equipped kitchen with microwave, refrigerator, stove, and coffeemaker. Two are equipped with washer and dryer. Spirit Dancer and Deer Dancer, completed in 1996, are the inn's newest rooms and both have kitchenettes. Each evening, the next day's breakfast of healthful, fresh-baked food is delivered to your door for you to enjoy at any hour. The two casitas closest to the street may have some street noise, but it should die down by bedtime.

۞ Dos Casas Viejas. 610 Agua Fría St., Santa Fe, NM 87501. ☎ **505/983-1636.** Fax 505/ 983-1749. 8 units. TV TEL. $165–$245 single or double. Free off-street parking.

These two old houses (*dos casas viejas*), located not far from the Plaza in what some call the barrio on Agua Fría Street, offer the kind of luxury accommodations you'd expect from a fine hotel. Behind an old wooden security gate is a meandering brick lane along which are the elegant guest rooms. The innkeepers, Susan and Michael Strijek, maintain the place impeccably. The grounds are manicured, and the rooms, each with a patio and private entrance, are finely renovated and richly decorated. All rooms have Mexican-tile floors and kiva fireplaces; most have diamond-finished stucco walls and embedded vigas. They're furnished with Southwestern antiques and original art. Some have canopy beds and one has an imaginative sleigh bed; all are covered with fine linens and down comforters. Each room is supplied with robes, a hair dryer, and complimentary gourmet treats and refreshments. Valet laundry, newspaper delivery, and free coffee or refreshments in the lobby are available. Guests can use the library and dining area (where a European breakfast is served each morning) in the main building. Breakfast can also be enjoyed on the patio alongside the elegant lap pool or (after you collect it in a basket) on your private patio. If you'd like a spa experience, Dos Casas now has in-room treatments, from massage to facials to salt glows.

Four Kachinas Inn. 512 Webber St., Santa Fe, NM 87501. ☎ **800/397-2564** or 505/ 982-2550. Fax 505/989-1323. www.southwestern.com. E-mail: 4kachina@swcp.com. 6 units. TV TEL. $68–$132 double. Rates include continental breakfast and afternoon snacks. DISC, MC, V. Free parking.

Wild Kachinas and Navajo rugs stand out against clean and simple architectural lines at this quiet inn on a residential street within walking distance of downtown. The rooms are consistent, comfortable, and medium-sized. Each is named for a Hopi kachina: The Koyemsi Room is named for the "fun-loving, mudhead clown kachina"; the Poko Room, for the dog kachina that "represents the spirits of domestic animals"; the Hon Room, for the "powerful healing bear kachina"; and the Tawa Room, for the sun god kachina. Three of the rooms are on the ground floor. The upstairs room offers a view of the Sangre de Cristo Mountains. All have private patios. In a separate building, constructed of adobe bricks that were made on the property, is a lounge where guests can gather at any time of day to enjoy art and travel books and complimentary beverages and snacks. Be sure to try the coconut pound cake, a treat for which innkeeper John Daw consistently wins a blue ribbon at the county fair. An extended continental breakfast of juice, coffee or tea, pastries, yogurt, and fresh fruit is brought to guests' rooms each morning. One of the rooms here is completely accessible for travelers with disabilities.

✪ **Grant Corner Inn.** 122 Grant Ave., Santa Fe, NM 87501. ☎ **800/964-9003** or 505/ 983-6678 for reservations, or 505/984-9001 for guest rooms. Fax 505/983-1526. 12 units (10 with bathroom), 1 hacienda. A/C TV TEL. $80–$120 double without bathroom; $100–$155 double with bathroom. Hacienda guest rooms, rented separately, $110–$130; $215–$255 for entire house. Rates include full gourmet breakfast. MC, V. Free parking. Certain rooms appropriate for children.

This early 20th-century manor just 2 blocks west of the Plaza and next door to the new Georgia O'Keeffe Museum offers a quiet stay in a fanciful Victorian ambience. Each room is furnished with antiques, from brass or four-poster beds to armoires and quilts, and monogrammed terry-cloth robes are available for those staying in rooms with shared bathrooms. All rooms have ceiling fans, and some are equipped with small refrigerators. Each room has its own character. For example, no. 3 has a hand-painted German wardrobe closet dating from 1772 and a washbasin with brass fittings in the shape of a fish; no. 8 has a private outdoor deck that catches the morning sun; and no. 11 has an antique collection of dolls and stuffed animals. Two rooms have kitchenettes, and two also have laundry facilities. The inn's office doubles as a library and gift shop. In addition to the rooms mentioned above, Grant Corner Inn now offers accommodations in its Hacienda, located at 604 Griffin St. It's a Southwestern-style condominium with two bedrooms, living and dining rooms, and a kitchen. It can be rented in its entirety or the rooms can be rented separately, depending on your needs.

Breakfast, for both the inn and the Hacienda, is served each morning in front of the living-room fireplace or on the front veranda in summer. The meals are so good that an enthusiastic public arrives for brunch here every Sunday (the inn is also open to the public for weekday breakfasts).

Inn on the Paseo. 630 Paseo de Peralta, Santa Fe, NM 87501. ☎ **800/457-9045** or 505/984-8200. Fax 505/989-3979. 20 units. A/C TV TEL. $85–$165 double. Rates include extended continental breakfast. AE, DC, MC, V. Free parking.

Located just a few blocks from the Plaza, this is a good choice for travelers who want to be able to walk to the shops, galleries, and restaurants but would rather not stay at a larger hotel. As you enter the inn you'll be welcomed by the warmth of the large fireplace in the foyer. Southwestern furnishings dot the spacious public areas and the work of local artists adorns the walls. The guest rooms are medium-sized, meticulously clean, and very comfortable with a hotel feel. The arrangements are fairly consistent from room to room, but the bathrooms are a bit stark (each with a hair dryer). Still, one room boasts a fireplace and many feature four-poster beds and private entrances. The focal point of each room is an original handmade patchwork quilt. The owner is a third-generation quilter, and she made all the quilts you'll see hanging throughout the inn (more than 25 of them). A breakfast buffet is served on the sundeck in warmer weather and indoors by the fire on cooler days. It consists of muffins, breads, granola, fresh fruit, and coffee or tea. Complimentary refreshments are served every afternoon.

✪ Spencer House Bed & Breakfast Inn. 222 McKenzie St., Santa Fe, NM 87501. ☎ **800/647-0530** (7am–6pm) or 505/988-3024. Fax 505/984-9862. 4 units, 1 cottage. A/C. $95–$175 double. Rates include breakfast. AE, MC, V. Free parking.

The Spencer House is unique among Santa Fe bed-and-breakfasts. Instead of Southwestern-style furnishings, you'll find beautiful antiques from England, Ireland, and colonial America. One guest room features an antique brass bed, another a pencil-post bed, yet another an English panel bed, and all rooms use Ralph Lauren fabrics and linens. Each room is outfitted with a fluffy down comforter and a hair dryer. All bathrooms are completely new, modern, and very spacious. Owner Jan McConnell takes great pride in the Spencer House and keeps it spotlessly clean. From the old Bissell carpet sweeper and drop-front desk in the reading nook to antique trunks in the bedrooms, no detail has been overlooked. In summer, a full breakfast—coffee, tea, yogurt, cereal, fresh fruit, and main course—is served on the outdoor patio. In winter, guests dine indoors by the wood-burning stove. Afternoon tea is served in the breakfast room. In 1995, two new rooms were added. One has a fireplace and private patio. The second is an 800-square-foot cottage with a living room, dining area, full kitchen and bathroom, private patio, and screened-in porch. Take note of the careful renovation of this 1920s adobe, as it received an award from the Santa Fe Historical Board.

Territorial Inn. 215 Washington Ave., Santa Fe, NM 87501. ☎ **800/745-9910** or 505/989-7737. Fax 505/986-9212. 10 units (8 with bathroom). A/C TV TEL. $80–$165 double. Higher rates during special events. Extra person $20. Rates include continental breakfast. AE, DC, MC, V. Free parking.

This two-story, Territorial-style building, which dates from the 1890s and is situated 1½ blocks from the Plaza, has a delightful Victorian feel with plenty of amenities. Constructed of stone and adobe with a pitched roof, it has two stories connected by a curving tiled stairway. Eight of its rooms, typically furnished with Early American antiques, offer private bathrooms; the remaining two share a bathroom. All rooms are equipped with ceiling fans and sitting areas, and two have fireplaces. Each room also has robes, hair dryers, and Spectravision movie channels. Free coffee and refreshments are available in the lobby, and an in-room massage as well as access to a nearby health club can be arranged. An extended continental breakfast is served in a sophisticated common area or in warm months in the back garden, which is shaded by large cottonwoods. There is also a rose garden and a gazebo-enclosed hot tub.

✪ Water Street Inn. 427 Water St., Santa Fe, NM 87501. ☎ **800/646-6752** or 505/984-1193. Fax 505/984-6235. 11 units. A/C TV TEL. $95–$200 double. Rates include continental breakfast and afternoon hors d'oeuvres and refreshments. AE, DISC, MC, V. Free parking. Children and pets are welcome with prior approval.

An award-winning adobe restoration to the west of the Hilton hotel and 4 blocks from the Plaza, this friendly inn features beautiful Mexican-tile bathrooms, several kiva fireplaces or wood stoves, and antique furnishings. Each room is packed with Southwestern art and books. A happy hour, with quesadillas and margaritas, is offered in the living room or on the upstairs portal in the afternoon, where an extended continental breakfast is also served. All rooms are decorated in a Moroccan/Southwestern style. Room 3 features a queen-size hideaway sofa to accommodate families. Room 4 provides special regional touches in its decor and boasts a chaise lounge, fur rug, built-in seating, and corner fireplace. Four new suites have elegant contemporary Southwestern furnishings and outdoor private patios with fountains. Now there's also an outdoor Jacuzzi. All rooms have balconies or terraces, VCRs, and offer newspaper delivery and twice-daily maid service.

RV PARKS & CAMPGROUNDS
RV PARKS
At least four private camping areas, mainly for recreational vehicles, are located within a few minutes' drive of downtown Santa Fe. Typical rates are $23 for full RV hookups, $18 for tents. Be sure to book ahead at busy times.

Babbitt's RV Resort. 3574 Cerrillos Rd., Santa Fe, NM 87505. ☎ **505/473-1949.** Fax 505/471-9220. MC, V.

The resort has 95 spaces with full hookups, picnic tables, showers, rest rooms, laundry, and a soda and candy concession. It's just 5 miles south of the Plaza, so it's plenty convenient, but keep in mind that it is surrounded by the city.

Rancheros de Santa Fe Campground. 736 Old Las Vegas Hwy. (exit 290 off I-25), Santa Fe, NM 87505. ☎ **800/426-9259** or 505/466-3482. www.rancheros.com. DISC, MC, V.

Tents, motor homes, and trailers requiring full hookups are welcome here. The park's 130 sites are situated on 22 acres of piñon and juniper forest. Facilities include tables, grills and fireplaces, hot showers, rest rooms, Laundromat, grocery store, nature trails, outdoor swimming pool, playground, games room, free nightly movies, public telephones, and propane. Cabins are also available. It's located about 6 miles southeast of Santa Fe and is open from March 15 to November 1.

Santa Fe KOA. 934 Old Las Vegas Hwy. (exit 290 or 294 off I-25), Santa Fe, NM 87505. ☎ **505/466-1419** or 505/KOA-1514 for reservations. DISC, MC, V.

This campground about 11 miles northeast of Santa Fe sits among the foothills of the Sangre de Cristo Mountains. It offers full hookups, pull-through sites, tent sites, picnic tables, showers, rest rooms, laundry, store, Santa Fe–style gift shop, playground, recreation room, propane, and dumping station. A tent site is $18.95; RV hookup $23.95.

CAMPGROUNDS
There are three forested sites along NM 475 going toward the Santa Fe Ski Basin. All are open from May to October. Overnight rates start at about $6, depending on the particular site.

Hyde Memorial State Park. 740 Hyde Park Rd., Santa Fe, NM 87501. ☎ **505/983-7175.**

About 8 miles from the city, this pine-surrounded park offers a quiet retreat. Its campground includes shelters, water, tables, and pit toilets. Seven RV pads with electrical pedestals and an RV dump station are available. There are nature and hiking trails as well as a small winter skating pond.

Santa Fe National Forest. P.O. Box 1689 (NM 475), Santa Fe, NM 87504. ☎ **505/ 982-8674** (this number only works seasonally; if you don't reach anyone, call ☎ 505/ 753-7331, and be patient; this is the number for the Española Ranger Station and they're not as helpful as they could be).

Black Canyon campground, with 44 sites, is located just before you reach Hyde State Park. The sites sit within thick forest, with hiking trails nearby. It has potable water and sites for trailers up to 32 feet long. Big Tesuque, a first-come, first-served campground, with 10 newly rehabilitated sites, is about 12 miles from town. The sites here are closer to the road and sit at the edge of aspen forests. Both Black Canyon and Big Tesuque campgrounds, located along the Santa Fe Scenic Byway, NM 475, are equipped with vault toilets.

4 Where to Dine

Santa Fe may not be a major city, but it abounds in dining options with hundreds of restaurants of all categories. Competition among them is steep, and spots are continually opening and closing. Locals watch closely to see which ones will survive. Some chefs create dishes that incorporate traditional Southwestern foods with ingredients not indigenous to the region; their restaurants are referred to in the listings as "creative Southwestern." There is also standard regional New Mexican cuisine, and beyond that diners can opt for excellent steak and seafood, as well as continental, European, Asian, and, of course, Mexican menus.

Especially during peak tourist seasons, dinner reservations may be essential. Reservations are always recommended at better restaurants.

In the listings below, **very expensive** refers to restaurants where most dinner main courses are priced above $25; **expensive** includes those where the main courses generally cost between $18 and $25; **moderate** means those in the $12 to $18 range; and **inexpensive** refers to those charging $12 and under.

DOWNTOWN

This area includes the circle defined by the Paseo de Peralta and St. Francis Drive, as well as Canyon Road.

EXPENSIVE

✪ **Anasazi Restaurant.** 113 Washington Ave. ☎ **505/988-3236.** Reservations recommended. Breakfast $5.25–$9.50; lunch $8–$11.75; dinner $17.50–$29. AE, CB, DC, DISC, MC, V. Daily 7–10:30am, 11:30am–2:30pm, and 5:30–10pm. CREATIVE SOUTHWESTERN/ NATIVE AMERICAN.

This ranks right up there with Santacafé as one of Santa Fe's richest dining experiences. And though it's part of the Inn of the Anasazi (see "Where to Stay," above), it's a fine restaurant in its own right. You'll dine surrounded by diamond-finished walls decorated with petroglyph symbols. Stacked flagstone furthers the Anasazi feel of this restaurant named for the ancient people who once inhabited the area. There's no pretension here; the wait staff is friendly but not overbearing, and tables are spaced nicely, making it a good place for a romantic dinner. All the food is inventive, and organic meats and vegetables are used whenever available.

For breakfast try the breakfast burrito with homemade chorizo, green chile potatoes, and refried Anasazi beans. A must with lunch or dinner is the grilled corn tortilla soup with ginger-pork pot stickers. It's thick, served with tortilla strips and thinly sliced scallions, and a chile-spiced bread stick like a snake in the grass. For an entree, I enjoyed grilled swordfish with a roasted corn puree, light enough to enhance the fish flavor rather than diminish it. For dinner I recommend the cinnamon chile–rubbed beef tenderloin with white-cheddar chipotle, chile mashed potatoes, and mango salsa. Desserts are thrilling; try the sour-cream chocolate cake, rich and moist. There are daily specials, as well as a nice list of wines by the glass and special wines of the day.

Bistro 315. 315 Old Santa Fe Trail. ☎ **505/986-9190.** Reservations recommended. Main courses $17–$29 at dinner. AE, MC, V. Summer daily 11:30am–2pm and 5:30–9:30pm. Winter Mon–Sat 11:30am–2pm and 5:30–9pm. FRENCH.

Bistro 315 has enjoyed instant success since it opened in 1995, and no wonder—heading it up are Matt Yohalem, a graduate of Johnson and Wales, and Chef Poissonier, formerly with Le Cirque under Chef Daniel Boulud. The restaurant has recently expanded and still fills up. The food is simply excellent. The menu changes seasonally; on my last visit there I started with croquettes of goat cheese and bell pepper coulis and moved on to a cassoulet, with lamb, sausage, chicken, and vegetables in a rich sauce. The grilled tomato soup was also excellent, and I was fortunate to be there on a night when grilled smoked chicken was on the menu. My favorite dessert here is the warm tarte Tatin served with crème fraîche. Because the restaurant is so popular, reservations are an absolute must.

Cafe Pasqual's. 121 Don Gaspar Ave. ☎ **505/983-9340.** Reservations recommended for dinner. Breakfast $4.75–$10.75; lunch $4.95–$10.75; dinner $17.95–$26.75. AE, MC, V. Mon–Sat 7am–3pm; Mon–Sun 6–10pm (until 10:30pm in summer). Brunch Sun 8am–3pm. INNOVATIVE MEXICAN WITH ASIAN INFLUENCES.

"You have to become the food, erase the line between it as an object and you. You have to really examine its structure, its size, its color, its strength, its weakness, know who grew it, how long it's been out of the field," says Pasqual's owner Katharine Kagel. This attitude is completely apparent in this restaurant where the walls are lined with murals depicting voluptuous villagers playing guitars, drinking, and even flying. Needless to say it's a festive place, though it's also excellent for a romantic dinner. Service is jovial and professional. My favorite dish for breakfast or lunch is the *huevos motuleños* (two eggs over easy on blue-corn tortillas and black beans topped with sautéed bananas, feta cheese, salsa, and green chile). Soups and salads are also served for lunch, and there's a delectable grilled-salmon burrito with herbed goat cheese and cucumber salsa. The frequently changing dinner menu offers grilled meats and seafoods, plus vegetarian specials. Start with the vegetable pot stickers and move on to the chicken mole Puebla (chicken with a dark sauce made from chocolate), served with a Oaxacan tamale. Avoid the pollo pibil, since it isn't as interesting as most of the other dishes. There's a communal table for those who would like to meet new people over a meal. Pasqual's offers imported beers and wine by the bottle or glass. Try to go at an odd hour—late morning or afternoon, or make a reservation for dinner; otherwise you'll have to wait. The restaurant also sells colorful calendars, T-shirts, and Kagel's cookbook.

✪ **Coyote Cafe.** 132 Water St. ☎ **505/983-1615.** Reservations recommended. Main courses $6.50–$15.95 (Rooftop Cantina); fixed-price dinner $39.50 (Coyote Cafe). AE, DC, DISC, MC, V. Cafe Oct–Apr, daily 11:30am–2:30pm and 6–9pm; Apr–Oct, daily 6–9pm. Rooftop Cantina daily 11:30am–9pm. CREATIVE SOUTHWESTERN.

World-renowned chef and cookbook author Mark Miller has been "charged with single-handedly elevating the chili to haute status." That statement from *New York Times Magazine* sums up for me the experience of eating at this trendy nouveau Southwest restaurant a block from the Plaza. The atmosphere is urban Southwest, with calfskin-covered chairs and a zoo of carved animals watching from a balcony. The exhibition kitchen shows lots of brass and tile, and the wait staff is well mannered, efficient, and friendly. It's the place to go for a fun night out, or you can sample the

Downtown Santa Fe Dining

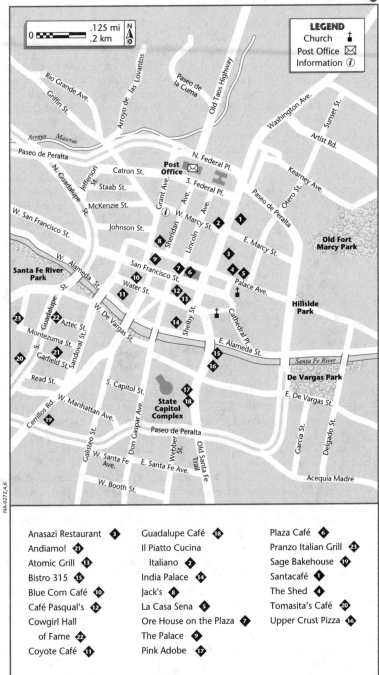

LEGEND
Church ✝
Post Office ✉
Information ⓘ

Anasazi Restaurant 3
Andiamo! 21
Atomic Grill 13
Bistro 315 15
Blue Corn Café 10
Café Pasqual's 12
Cowgirl Hall
of Fame 22
Coyote Café 11

Guadalupe Café 18
Il Piatto Cucina
Italiano 2
India Palace 14
Jack's 8
La Casa Sena 5
Ore House on the Plaza 7
The Palace 9
Pink Adobe 17

Plaza Café 6
Pranzo Italian Grill 23
Sage Bakehouse 19
Santacafé 1
The Shed 4
Tomasita's Café 20
Upper Crust Pizza 16

great food for lunch at a fraction of the price. Some complain that on a busy night the space is noisy, and I'm especially careful not to sit on the *banco* (stone bench) toward the northeastern corner where a fan rumbles.

The menu changes seasonally, so if the food I mention isn't available, look for variations. An incredible lunch is the pork carnitas tamale appetizer ordered as an entree. It comes with chipotle-orange barbecue sauce and black bean–avocado relish. My mother loves the chicken enchilada, especially nice if you like to go light on the cheese—the red chile sauce is amazing. Dinners are three-course affairs, though diners can order à la carte at the counter and watch the chefs in action. The affair starts with Coyote cocktails that might include a Brazilian daiquiri or margarita del Maguey. For an appetizer you have a number of choices, including a chile cured salmon gravlax salad with mango-habañero sauce or a Mexican garlic and scallop soup. You can't go wrong with the new rotisserie chicken recently added to the menu, served with sweet potato mash, though I like to go with something that allows the chef's talents to shine more, such as the seared Maine scallops with ancho–wild-mushroom serape and pumpkin-cascabel sauce. You can order drinks from the full bar or wine by the glass. Smoking is not allowed.

The Coyote Cafe has two adjunct establishments. In summer, the place to be seen is the Rooftop Cantina, where light Mexican fare and cocktails are served on a festively painted terrace (try the Yucatán taquitos). On the ground floor is the Coyote Cafe General Store, a retail gourmet Southwestern food market featuring the Coyote Cafe's own food line called Coyote Cocina (try the salsa), as well as hot sauces and salsas from all over the world.

Geronimo. 724 Canyon Rd. ☎ **505/982-1500.** Reservations recommended. Lunch $8–$13; dinner $18–$30. AE, MC, V. Tues–Sun 11:30am–2:15pm; daily 6–10pm. CREATIVE CONTINENTAL.

When Geronimo opened in 1991, no one was sure if it would succeed since so many previous restaurants at this site had failed. But this elegant eatery has done more than just survive—it has flourished, and now, with a new chef, the food is better than ever. It occupies an old adobe structure known as the Borrego House, built by Geronimo Lopez in 1756 and now completely restored. Numerous small dining rooms help it retain the comfortable feel of an old Santa Fe home.

I especially recommend lunch here, because you can get a taste of this often complex food for a fraction of the dinner price. Reserve a spot on the porch and watch the action on Canyon Road. My favorite at lunch is the house smoked ruby trout salad, with crimson beluga lentils and organic grains with a sweet sesame dressing. The open-faced smoked salmon sandwich with herbed aioli and homemade potato chips is also nice. And if you've never tried one, go for the buffalo burger—it's more flavorful than beef. For a dinner appetizer try the charcoal-grilled cold-water lobster tail on herb-spun angel hair pasta. For an entree, the grilled black pepper elk tenderloin with scallion risotto is a bit exotic, while the grilled ahi tuna on braised shiitakes with wilted watercress is just delicious. For dessert, you won't be disappointed by the trio of brûlées—espresso chocolate, Chambord, and orange—or the Belgian chocolate Grand Marnier cake. The menu changes seasonally, and there is an excellent wine list.

La Casa Sena. 125 E. Palace Ave. ☎ **505/988-9232.** Reservations recommended. Lunch $7.75–$10; dinner $18–$27. Five-course chef's tasting menu $42, with wine $57. La Cantina main courses $12.50–$23. AE, CB, DC, DISC, MC, V. Mon–Sat 11:30am–3pm; daily 5:30–10pm. Brunch Sat–Sun 11am–3pm. CREATIVE SOUTHWESTERN.

Though this restaurant suffered a fire in 1996, it's been restored and reopened, and many believe the food is even better now. It sits within the Sena compound, a prime example of a Spanish hacienda, a Territorial-style adobe house built in 1867 by Civil War hero Maj. José Sena for his wife and 23 children. The house, which surrounds a garden courtyard, is today a veritable art gallery, with museum-quality landscapes on the walls and Taos-style handcrafted furniture. The cuisine in the main dining room might be described as northern New Mexican with a continental flair. Lunches include Caribbean pork soft tacos and almond-encrusted salmon with gazpacho salsa. In the evening, diners might start with a salad of mixed organic greens, goat cheese, and a fresh herb vinaigrette, then move to American corn-fed lamb chops with habañero-papaya sauce, tropical fruit *ensalada,* and crispy root vegetables.

In the adjacent **La Cantina,** servers sing Broadway show tunes as they carry platters from the kitchen to the table. The more moderately priced Cantina menu offers the likes of blue-corn crusted salmon or honey-glazed Mexican pork loin. Both restaurants have exquisite desserts. Try the black and white bittersweet chocolate terrine with raspberry sauce. The award-winning wine list features more than 850 wines. There's patio dining in summer.

Pink Adobe. 406 Old Santa Fe Trail. ☎ **505/983-7712.** Reservations recommended. Lunch $4.75–$8.75; dinner $10.75–$23.25. AE, CB, DC, DISC, MC, V. Mon–Fri 11:30am–2pm; daily 5:30–10pm. CONTINENTAL/SOUTHWESTERN.

More show than flavor? Probably. This restaurant a few blocks off the Plaza offers a swirl of local old-timer gaiety, and food that is more imaginative than flavorful, but has remained popular since the restaurant opened in 1946. I remember eating my first lamb curry here, and my mother ate her first blue-corn enchilada, back in the '50s, and was taken aback by the odd colors. The restaurant occupies an adobe home believed to be at least 350 years old. Guests enter through a narrow side door into a series of quaint, informal dining rooms with tile or hardwood floors. Stuccoed walls display original modern art or Priscilla Hoback pottery on built-in shelves.

For lunch I'll always have a chicken enchilada topped with an egg. The gypsy stew (chicken, green chile, tomatoes, and onions in sherry broth) sounds great but is on the bland side. At the dinner hour the Pink Adobe offers the likes of escargot and shrimp rémoulade as appetizers. I recommend the lamb curry or the poulet marengo (chicken baked with brandy wine and mushrooms). You can't leave without trying the hot French apple pie.

Smoking is allowed only in the **Dragon Room,** the lounge across the alleyway from the restaurant. Under the same ownership, the charming bar (a real local scene) has its own menu offering traditional New Mexican food. Locals go there especially to eat hearty green chile stew. The full bar is open Monday through Friday from 11:30am to 2am, Saturday 5pm to 2am, and Sunday 5pm to midnight. There's live entertainment Tuesday, Thursday, and Saturday.

✪ **Santacafé.** 231 Washington Ave. ☎ **505/984-1788.** Reservations recommended. Lunch $5–$10; dinner $17–$27. AE, MC, V. Mon–Sat 11:30am–2pm; nightly 6–10pm. NEW AMERICAN.

When you eat at this fine restaurant, be prepared for spectacular bursts of flavor. The food is Southwestern with an Asian flair, surrounded by a minimalist decor that accentuates the beautiful architecture of the 18th-century Padre Gallegos House, 2 blocks from the Plaza. The white walls are decorated only with deer antlers, and each room contains a fireplace. In warm months you can sit under elm trees in the charming courtyard. Beware that on busy nights the rooms are noisy.

The dishes change to take advantage of seasonal specialties, each served with precision. A simple starter such as miso soup is enriched with a lobster-mushroom roulade. One of my favorites is the seared chile-garlic prawns served with fresh pea

ⓘ Family-Friendly Restaurants

Bobcat Bite *(see page 161)*   The name and the ranch-style atmosphere will appeal to families that are looking for great steaks and huge hamburgers at low prices.

Cowgirl Hall of Fame *(see page 157)*   Kids love the Kid's Corral where, among other things, they can play a game of horseshoes.

Upper Crust Pizza *(see page 160)*   Many people think they have the best pizza in town, and they'll deliver it to tired tots and their families at downtown hotels.

(or lima) and mushroom risotto. A more adventurous eater might try the pan-seared achiote duck breast with raisin couscous, spiced pecans, and pineapple pasilla puree. There's an extensive wine list, with wine by the glass as well. Desserts are made in-house and are artistically presented. Some have criticized chef Ming Tsai for overdoing his recipes; others claim the prices are too steep. I just find the experience inventively delicious in all respects.

MODERATE

Andiamo! 322 Garfield St. ☎ **505/995-9595.** Reservations recommended. Main courses $7.50–$17.50. AE, DISC, MC, V. Wed–Mon 5:30–9pm, until 9:30pm Fri–Sat. ITALIAN.

Quite a few new restaurants have sprung up in Santa Fe over the past few years, several of which were created by defectors of some of the city's most popular eateries. Andiamo! is one of those making a successful go of it. Chris Galvin, once the sous chef at Cafe Escalera, has joined forces with business partner Joan Gillcrist at this fine restaurant. They have created an authentically Tuscan atmosphere in which a daily changing menu features antipasto, pasta, and excellent desserts. Still, as with many of these little spin-offs, you tend to feel a bit cramped into the space, and noise levels can get out of hand. I enjoyed the Caesar salad and the penne with merguez, with a bit of musky flavor from the lamb sausage. For dessert I'd recommend the polenta pound cake with lemon crème Anglaise. Beer and wine are served at this nonsmoking restaurant.

El Farol. 808 Canyon Rd. ☎ **505/983-9912.** Reservations recommended. Tapas $3.95–$8.95; main courses $10.95–$22.50. DC, DISC, MC, V. Daily 11:30am–4pm and 6–10pm. SPANISH.

This is the place to head for local ambience and old-fashioned flavor. El Farol (The Lantern) is the Canyon Road artists' quarter's original neighborhood bar. Recently it has become a center of controversy; some of the neighborhood folks resent the amplified music played into the night, and a recent arson incident burned part of the restaurant. At press time the owner was busy repairing the damage, and he was excited to say the fire led to a brightening of the rooms and upgrading of the front porch. The restaurant has cozy low ceilings and hand-smoothed adobe walls. Thirty-five varieties of tapas are offered, including such delicacies as *gambas al ajillo* (shrimp with a sherry-garlic sauce) and grilled cactus with romesco sauce. I like to order two or three tapas and have my companion do the same so that we can share. However, if you prefer a full dinner, try the paella or the marinated lamb chops with huckleberry, cranberry, or rosemary sauce. Jazz, folk, and ethnic musicians play almost every night beginning at 9:30pm. In summer, an outdoor patio seating 50 is open to diners.

Il Piatto Cucina Italiano. 96 West Marcy St. ☎ **505/984-1091.** Reservations recommended. Main courses $8–$15. AE, MC, V. Lunch Mon–Fri 11:30am–2pm; dinner Mon–Sat 5:30–9pm. TRADITIONAL NORTHERN ITALIAN.

This is a spin-off from a more expensive restaurant. A child of Bistro 315, Il Piatto brings executive chef Matt Yohalem's expertise to thinner wallets. It's an Italian cafe, simple and elegant, with contemporary art on the walls—nice for a romantic evening. Service is efficient, though on a busy night, overworked. The menu changes seasonally, complemented by a few perennial standards. For a starter, try the fresh arugula with pine nuts, raisins, shaved onions, and Parmesan. Among entrees, my favorite is the fettuccine carbonara (rich cream-and-egg sauce and prosciutto), though you can't go wrong with the Italian sausage served over polenta. A full wine and beer menu is available.

India Palace. 227 Don Gaspar Ave. (at the back of the Water St. parking compound). ☎ **505/986-5859.** Reservations accepted. Main courses $7.95–$19.95; luncheon buffet $6.95. AE, DC, DISC, MC, V. Daily 11:30am–2:30pm and 5–10pm, 364 days a year, except Super Bowl Sunday. EAST INDIAN.

Once every few weeks I get a craving for the lamb *vindaloo* served at this restaurant in the center of downtown. A festive ambience, with pink walls painted with mosque shadows, makes this a nice place for a romantic meal. The service is efficient and most of the waiters are from India, as is chef Amarjit Behal. The tandoori chicken, fish, lamb, and shrimp are rich and flavorful, as is the *baingan bhartha* (eggplant in a delicious sauce). A luncheon buffet provides an excellent selection of vegetarian and nonvegetarian dishes at a reasonable price. Beer and wine are available, or you might want some *chai* tea.

Jack's. 135 W. Palace. ☎ **505/983-7220.** Reservations recommended. Main courses $9–$12 at lunch; $12–$19 at dinner. AE, MC, V. Tues–Sun 11:30am–3pm and 5:30–9pm; same hours daily June–Sept. NEW AMERICAN.

Within 1 week, two friends told me their favorite new restaurant in Santa Fe was Jack's. My opinion? It's well worth a visit. Jack Shaab, the proprietor who was previously a partner in Bistro 315 and Il Piatto, both successful Santa Fe eateries, has covered major ground in a short while. He already has a strong following, so expect a crowd during high season. You won't find the stunning Southwestern decor of Santacafé here; this is an edgier, more citified ambience. It's decorated in black and brown, with butcher paper on the tables and crayons you can use for coloring while waiting to be served. The service is unpredictable—sometimes efficient, sometimes negligent.

If you don't feel like trying out this upstart for an expensive dinner, come for lunch. For an appetizer, I suggest the sautéed salmon cakes with wasabi aioli, found on both the lunch and the dinner menus. For lunch, I enjoyed the vegetable tart with goat cheese and roasted tomato sauce. If you like hearty flavors, order the cornmeal-crusted chicken breast, stuffed with feta, ricotta, and sun-dried tomatoes and served with a mushroom cream sauce. For dinner you might try the sautéed Chilean sea bass with roasted sweet-pepper rice. You'll also find duck breast, pork tenderloin, and a mixed grill of lamb. The chocolate mousse I ordered for dessert at first seemed too frozen, but was in fact just extremely rich, almost chewy. It had its own identity, much like the entire dining experience here. There's a full bar, as well as a nice wine menu.

Ore House on the Plaza. 50 Lincoln Ave. ☎ **505/983-8687.** Reservations recommended. Main courses $12–$23. AE, MC, V. Mon–Sat 11:30am–2:30pm, Sun noon–2:30pm; daily 5:30–10pm. STEAKS/SEAFOOD AND NEW MEXICAN.

The Ore House's second-story balcony, at the southwest corner of the Plaza, is an ideal spot from which to watch the passing scene while you enjoy cocktails and hors d'oeuvres. In fact, it is *the* place to be between 4 and 6pm every afternoon. The decor is Southwestern, with plants and lanterns hanging amid white walls and booths. The menu, now presided over by chef Eduardo Rios, has fresh seafood and steaks, as well as some interesting Nueva Latina dishes that incorporate some interesting sauces. Daily fresh fish specials include salmon and swordfish (poached, blackened, teriyaki, or lemon), rainbow trout, lobster, and shellfish. Steak Ore House (wrapped in bacon and topped with crabmeat and béarnaise sauce) and chicken Ore House (a grilled breast stuffed with ham, Swiss cheese, green chile, and béarnaise) are local favorites. The Ore House also caters to noncarnivores with vegetable platters.

The bar, with solo music Wednesday through Saturday nights, is proud of its 66 different custom margaritas. It offers a selection of domestic and imported beers and an excellent wine list. An appetizer menu is served from 2:30 to 5pm daily, and the bar stays open until midnight or later (on Sunday it closes at midnight).

The Palace. 142 W. Palace Ave. ☎ **505/982-9891.** Reservations recommended. Lunch $5.25–$10.50; dinner $12.50–$23.95 AE, DISC, MC, V. Mon–Sat 11:30am–4pm; daily 5:45–10pm. ITALIAN/CONTINENTAL.

When the Burro Alley site of Doña Tules's 19th-century gambling hall was excavated in 1959, an unusual artifact was discovered: a brass door knocker, half shaped like a horseshoe, and the other half like a saloon girl's stockinged leg. That knocker has become the logo of The Palace, which maintains a Victorian flavor as well as a bit of a bordello flair with lots of plush red upholstery. The brothers Lino, Pietro, and Bruno Pertusini brought a long family tradition into the restaurant business: Their father was chef at the Villa d'Este on Lake Como, Italy. You'll find an older crowd here and fairly small portions.

The Caesar salad, prepared tableside, is always good, as are the meat dishes such as the grilled Black Angus New York strip. Fish dishes are inventive and tasty. Try crab cakes with a sauce aurore for lunch or grilled cornmeal-dusted trout with crab filling for dinner. For a light meal, my father likes to order the spaghetti pomodoro; the cannelloni is also nice but much richer. They serve a variety of vegetarian dishes, and there are usually daily specials. The wine list is long and well considered. There is outdoor dining, and the bar is open Monday through Saturday from 11:30am to 2am and Sunday from 5:45pm to midnight, with nightly entertainment including dancing on Saturday after 9pm.

✪ **Pranzo Italian Grill.** 540 Montezuma St., Sanbusco Center. ☎ **505/984-2645.** Reservations recommended. Lunch $5.95–9.95 at lunch; dinner $5.95–$17.50. AE, DC, DISC, MC, V. Mon–Sat 11:30am–3pm; nightly 5–11pm. REGIONAL ITALIAN.

Housed in a renovated warehouse and freshly redecorated in warm Tuscan colors, this sister of Albuquerque's redoubtable Scalo restaurant caters to local Santa Feans with a contemporary atmosphere of modern abstract art and food prepared on an open grill. Homemade soups, salads, creative thin-crust pizzas, and fresh pastas are among the less expensive menu items. *Bianchi e nere al capesante* (black-and-white linguine with bay scallops in a light seafood sauce) and *pizza pollo affumicato* (with smoked chicken, pesto, and roasted peppers) are consistent favorites. Steak, chicken, veal, and fresh seafood grills—heavy on the garlic—dominate the dinner menu. The bar offers the Southwest's largest collection of grappas, as well as a wide selection of wine and champagne by the glass. The upstairs rooftop terrace is lovely for seasonal moon-watching over a glass of wine. **Portare Via Cafe,** adjacent to the restaurant, is a great place for a light breakfast or lunch. The cinnamon rolls and scones are particularly good, and cappuccino and pastries are served throughout the day. Sandwiches are available at lunch.

INEXPENSIVE

Atomic Grill. 103 E. Water St. ☎ **505/820-2866.** Most items under $8.50. Summer daily 7am–3am. Rest of year Mon–Fri 11am–3am, Sat 7am–3am, Sun 7am–1am. AE, DISC, MC, V. CREATIVE MEXICAN/AMERICAN.

A block south of the Plaza, this cafe offers decent patio dining at reasonable prices. Of course, there's indoor dining as well. The whole place has a hip and comfortable feel, and the food is prepared imaginatively. This isn't my choice for downtown restaurants but it's great if you're dining at an odd hour, particularly late at night. For breakfast try the raspberry French toast made with home-baked challah bread, served with apricot butter and maple syrup. For lunch, the green chile stew is tasty, although made with not quite enough chicken habañero sausage. The fish tacos are also nice, if a little bland (ask for extra salsa), and the burgers are good. They've recently added wood-fired pizzas; try the grilled chicken pesto. For dessert, the carrot cake is big enough to share and quite tasty. Wine by the glass and 100 different beers are available. They also deliver to the downtown area from 11am to midnight.

Blue Corn Cafe. 133 W. Water. ☎ **505/984-1800.** Reservations accepted for parties of 6 or more. Main courses $6.25–$9.75. AE, DC, DISC, MC, V. Daily 11am–11pm. NEW MEXICAN.

If you're ready for a fun and inexpensive night out eating decent New Mexican food, this is your place. The decor is clean and breezy, with white walls, wooden tables (imprinted with chiles), and abstract art. The atmosphere is fun, though not quiet, so it's a good place for kids. The wait staff is overworked, thus a bit slow, but friendly and well intentioned. I recommend sampling dishes from the combination menu. You can get two to five items served with your choice of rice, beans, or posole (one of the best I've tasted). I had the chicken enchilada, which I recommend, and the chalupa, which I don't because it was soggy. You can have tacos, tamales, and rellenos too. Every night there are specialties worth trying. The shrimp fajitas were tasty, served with a nice guacamole and the usual toppings. Recently, the Blue Corn opened a brewery and so you might also want to sample the High Altitude Pale Ale or the Plaza Porter. My choice is the prickly pear iced tea (black tea with enough cactus juice to give it a zing). The Spanish flan is tasty and large enough to share. The **Blue Corn Cafe & Brewery** (4056 Cerrillos Rd., Suite G; ☎ **505/438-1800**), at the corner of Cerrillos and Rodeo roads, has similar fare and atmosphere and a southside location.

✪ Cowgirl Hall of Fame. 319 S. Guadalupe St. ☎ **505/982-2565.** Reservations recommended. Lunch $2.95–$9.95; dinner $4.50–$14.95. AE, DC, DISC, MC, V. Mon–Thurs 11am–11pm, Fri 11am–midnight, Sat 8am–midnight, Sun 8am–10:30pm. The bar is open Mon–Sat until 2am, Sun until midnight. REGIONAL AMERICAN/BARBECUE/CAJUN.

Whenever I want to have lots of fun eating, I go to the Cowgirl. The main room is a bar—a hip hangout spot, and a good place to eat as well if you don't mind the smoke. The back room is more quiet, with wood floors and tables and plenty of cowgirl memorabilia. Best of all is the warm season when you sit out on a brick patio lit with strings of white lights. The service here is fast and friendly and the food is always excellent. In wintertime, my favorite is a big bowl of gumbo or crawfish étoufée, and the rest of the time I order Jamaican jerk chicken or pork tenderloin when it's a special. Careful, both can be *hot.* The bunkhouse smoked brisket with potato salad, barbecue beans, and coleslaw is excellent, as is the cracker-fried catfish with jalapeño-tartar sauce. Recent specialties of the house included butternut squash casserole and grilled-salmon soft tacos (to die for). The daily blue plate special is a real buy, especially on Tuesday night when they serve chile rellenos for $4.95. There's even a special "kid's corral" that has horseshoes, a rocking horse, a horse-shaped rubber tire swing, hay bales, and a beanbag toss. Happy hour is from 3 to 6pm. There is live music almost every night.

A new restaurant at the same site caters to more refined tastes, with a Rocky Mountain lodge atmosphere. The **Mustang Grill** has natural beef, veal, lamb, fish, and vegetarian dishes at prices ranging from $15 to $22. You might start with an appetizer of mesquite-smoked duck breast and move on to pan-seared venison medallions with wild mushroom ragout. Dishes are served with such delicacies as corn pancakes, blackened nopales, or risotto. Hours are Friday, Saturday, and Sunday from 5:30 to 10pm. Reservations are recommended.

✪ **Guadalupe Cafe.** 422 Old Santa Fe Trail. ☎ 505/982-9762. Breakfast $4.50–$8.75; lunch $6–$12; dinner $6.95–$15.95. DISC, MC, V. Mon–Fri 7am–2pm, Sat–Sun 8am–2pm; Mon–Sat 5:30–9pm. NEW MEXICAN.

When I want New Mexican food, I go to this restaurant, and like many Santa Feans, I go there often. This casually elegant cafe, recently featured in *Bon Appétit* magazine, is in a white stucco building that's warm and friendly and has a nice-sized patio for dining in warmer months. Service is generally friendly and conscientious. For breakfast try the spinach-mushroom burritos or huevos rancheros, and for lunch the chalupas or stuffed sopaipillas. Any other time, I'd start with fresh roasted ancho chiles (filled with a combination of Montrachet and Monterey Jack cheese, piñon nuts, and topped with your choice of chile) and move on to the sour-cream chicken enchilada or any of their other Southwestern dishes. Order both red and green chile ("Christmas") so that you can sample some of the best sauces in town. They've recently added some delicious salads to the menu, such as a Caesar with chicken. For those who don't enjoy Mexican food, there are also *hamburguesas* (hamburgers) and a selection of traditional favorites such as chicken-fried steak, turkey piñon meat loaf, and chicken salad. Daily specials are available and don't miss the famous chocolate-amaretto adobe pie for dessert. Beer, wine, and margaritas are served.

✪ **La Choza.** 905 Alarid St. ☎ 505/982-0909. Lunch or dinner $6.75–$8.75. DISC, MC, V. Winter Mon–Thurs 11am–8pm, Fri–Sat 11am–9pm. Summer Mon–Sat 11am–9pm. NEW MEXICAN.

The sister restaurant of The Shed (see below) offers some of the best New Mexican food in town at a convenient location near the intersection of Cerrillos Road and St. Francis Drive. At peak times, you may have to wait a little while here, although often you'll be seated quickly. It's a warm, casual eatery, the walls vividly painted with magical images, especially popular on cold days when diners gather around the wood-burning stove and fireplace. Service is friendly and efficient, starting with complimentary chips and salsa. The menu offers enchiladas, tacos, and burritos on blue-corn tortillas, as well as green chile stew, chile con carne, and carne adovada. The portions are medium-sized, so if you're hungry start with guacamole or nachos. For years I've ordered the cheese or chicken enchilada, two dishes I will always recommend. My new favorite, though, is the blue corn burritos (tortillas stuffed with beans and cheese) served with posole; the dish can be made vegetarian if you'd like. For dessert, you can't leave without trying the mocha cake (chocolate cake with a mocha pudding filling, served with whipped cream). This may be the best dessert you'll ever eat. Vegetarians and children have their own menus. Beer and wine are available.

Plaza Cafe. 54 Lincoln Ave. (on the Plaza). ☎ 505/982-1664. No reservations. Main courses $2.50–$10.25. AE, DISC, MC, V. Daily 10am–7pm. AMERICAN/NEW MEXICAN/GREEK.

Santa Fe's lone holdout to diner-style eating, this cafe has excellent food in a bright and friendly atmosphere. I like to meet friends here, sit in a booth, eat and laugh about life. A restaurant since the turn of the century, it's been owned by the Razatos family since 1947. The decor has changed only enough to stay comfortable and clean, with red upholstered banquettes, art deco tile, and a soda fountain–style service counter. Service is always quick and conscientious, and only during the heavy tourist seasons will you have to wait long for a table. The hamburgers and sandwiches are good. I also like their soups and New Mexican dishes such as the green chile stew, or, if you're more adventurous, the pumpkin posole. The Greek dishes are also worth trying. Monday, Wednesday, and Friday there are Greek specials such as vegetable moussaka; beef and lamb gyros are offered every day. My assistant, Julia, loves their Italian sodas, which come in many flavors, from vanilla to Amaretto. Or you can have a shake, a piece of coconut cream pie, or their signature dessert, cajeta (apple and pecan pie with Mexican caramel). Beer and wine are available.

Sage Bakehouse. 535-C, Cerrillos Rd. ☎ **505/820-SAGE.** All menu items under $6. Mon–Fri 7am–5pm, Sat 8am–3pm. DISC, MC, V. GOURMET CAFE.

Restaurants all over Santa Fe use elegantly sharp sourdough bread from this bakery on Cerrillos Road across from the Hotel Santa Fe. And whenever I'm going visiting I'll stop and pick up a peasant loaf or some rich olive bread. If you're a bread lover, you might want to stop in for breakfast or lunch. The atmosphere is quiet and hip, with lots of marble and metal, a rounded counter, and a few small tables, as well as sidewalk seating during the warm months. Breakfasts include good espressos and mochas, and a bread basket that allows you to sample some of the splendid treats. There are also large blueberry muffins. Lunches are simple, only a few sandwiches from which to choose, but you can bet they're good. Try the black forest ham and Gruyère on rye, or the roasted red bell pepper and goat cheese on olive. People all over town are talking about the chocolate chip cookies. Rumor has it there's more chocolate than cookie in them.

✪ The Shed. 113½ E. Palace Ave. ☎ **505/982-9030.** Reservations accepted at dinner. Lunch $4.75–$8; dinner $6.75–$13.95. DISC, MC, V. Mon–Sat 11am–2:30pm; Wed–Sat 5:30–9pm. NEW MEXICAN.

During lunchtime lines often form outside The Shed, half a block east of the Palace of the Governors. A luncheon institution since 1953, it occupies several rooms and the patio of a rambling hacienda that was built in 1692. Festive folk art adorns the doorways and walls. The food is delicious, some of the best in the state, and a complement to traditional Hispanic and Pueblo cooking. The chicken or cheese enchilada is renowned in Santa Fe. Tacos and burritos are good, too, all served on blue-corn tortillas with pinto beans and posole. The green chile soup is a local favorite. The Shed's Joshua Carswell has added vegetarian and low-fat Mexican foods to the menu, as well as a wider variety of soups and salads and grilled chicken and steak. Don't leave without trying the mocha cake, possibly the best dessert you'll ever eat. Beer and wine are available.

Tomasita's Cafe. 500 S. Guadalupe St. ☎ **505/983-5721.** No reservations. Lunch $4.25–$9.50; dinner $4.75–$9.95. MC, V. Mon–Sat 11am–10pm. NEW MEXICAN.

When I was in high school, I used to eat at Tomasita's, a little dive on a back street. I always ordered a burrito, and I think people used to bring liquor in bags. Recently, President Clinton ate here during a brief visit to Los Alamos. It's now in a new building near the train station, and of course its food has become renowned. The atmosphere is simple—hanging plants and wood accents—with lots of families sitting at booths or tables and a festive spillover from the bar, where many come to drink margaritas. Service is quick, if not a little rushed, which is my biggest gripe about the new Tomasita's. Sure the food is still tasty, but unless you go at some totally odd hour you'll wait for a table, and once you're seated, you may eat and be out again in less than an hour. The burritos are still excellent, though you may want to try the chile rellenos, a house specialty. Vegetarian dishes, burgers, steaks, and daily specials are also offered. There's full bar service.

Upper Crust Pizza. 329 Old Santa Fe Trail. ☎ **505/982-0000.** No reservations. Pizzas $4.95–$16.05. DISC, MC, V. Summer daily 11am–11pm. Winter Mon–Thurs and Sun 11am–10pm, Fri–Sat 11am–11pm. PIZZA.

Santa Fe's best pizzas are found here, in an adobe house near the old San Miguel mission. Meals-in-a-dish include the Grecian gourmet pizza (feta and olives) and the whole-wheat vegetarian pizza (topped with sesame seeds). You can either eat here (inside or in a street-side patio) or request free delivery (it takes about 30 minutes) to your downtown hotel. Beer and wine are available, as are salads, calzones, and stromboli.

NORTHSIDE
EXPENSIVE

El Nido. NM 22, Tesuque. ☎ **505/988-4340.** Reservations recommended. Main courses $13.95–$23.95. AE, MC, V. Tues–Thurs and Sun 5:30–9:30pm, Fri–Sat 5:30–10pm. STEAK/SEAFOOD.

This is my favorite place to eat when I'm with my friend Carla. Her family is old Santa Fe, as is this restaurant. In the warm atmosphere, decorated with bird cages and smooth adobe partitions and bancos, we always encounter interesting characters, and since Carla eats here weekly, she knows what to order. In fact, during our last visit she pointed to a corner of the front room (where two fires blaze in winter) and jokingly said she was born there. In the 1950s and 1960s her parents used to party and dance at El Nido into the wee hours of the morning. Indeed, El Nido (the Nest) has been a landmark for many years. Built as a residence in the 1920s, it was a dance hall and Ma Nelson's brothel before it became a restaurant in 1939. The food here is fresh and well prepared with just a touch of fusion (European and Cajun influences) added to the specials. I'd suggest coming here if you're a bit overloaded by the seasonings at restaurants such as Santacafé, Coyote Cafe, and the Anasazi. The place is roomy, and the service is friendly and informal. Carla insists on oysters Rockefeller for an appetizer, though you can also start with a lighter ceviche. For entrees, she always has the salmon, which comes broiled with a light dill sauce on the side. I enjoy the broiled lamb chops, served with a light and tasty spinach mint sauce. All meals come with salad and baked potato, rice, or french fries. For dessert, try the crème brûlée, or, if you're a chocolate lover, try the chocolate piñon torte. There's a full bar, including a good selection of wines and local microbrew beers.

INEXPENSIVE

Tesuque Village Market. NM 22 (P.O. Box 231) Tesuque, 87574. ☎ **505/988-8848.** Main courses $4.95–$12. MC, V. Summer 6am–10pm; winter 7am–9pm. AMERICAN/ SOUTHWESTERN.

Parked in front of this charming market and restaurant you'll see Range Rovers and beat-up ranch trucks, an indication that the food here has broad appeal. Located under a canopy of cottonwoods at the center of this quaint village, the restaurant is so good it's worth the trip 15 minutes north of Santa Fe. During warmer months you can sit on the porch; in other seasons the interior is comfortable, with plain wooden tables next to a deli counter and upscale market. For me this is a breakfast place, where blue-corn pancakes rule. Friends of mine like the breakfast burritos and huevos rancheros. Lunch and dinner are also popular, and there's always a crowd (though, if you have to wait for a table, the wait is usually brief). For lunch, I recommend the burgers, and for dinner, one of the hearty specials such as lasagna, or my favorite, pork chops verde (boneless pork chops with a green chile sauce). For dessert, there's a variety of house-made pastries and cakes at the deli counter, as well as fancy granola bars and oversized cookies in the market. A kids menu is available.

SOUTHSIDE

Santa Fe's motel strip and other streets south of the Paseo de Peralta have their share of good, reasonably priced restaurants.

MODERATE

✪ Old Mexico Grill. 2434 Cerrillos Rd., College Plaza South. ☎ **505/473-0338.** Reservations recommended for large parties. Lunch $5.95–$9.95; dinner $8.75–$17.50. DISC, MC, V. Tues–Fri 11:30am–2:30pm; Sun–Thurs 5:30–9pm, Fri–Sat 5:30–9:30pm. MEXICAN.

Rethink Mexican food at this festive restaurant off Cerrillos Road at St. Michael's. Certainly you'll find tacos here, served the Mexican way on soft corn tortillas, with excellent salsas. But you'll also find tasty moles and pipians, with sauces of ground pumpkin seeds and the highest quality chiles. On weekends this is a very busy place, with chefs in the exhibition cooking area working feverishly on the open mesquite grill, but other times you can find a cozy corner for a romantic meal. Service is usually cordial and efficient. I like to start with *ceviche de camarones y conchas* (shrimp and scallops cooked in lime juice with onions peppers and cilantro), then move onto a plate of *arrancheras de pollo* (chicken fajitas) or *de camarones* (shrimp fajitas). Or, if I'm feeling more daring, I might try the *carne asada a la tampiqueña* (beef tenderloin with a toasted pepita/avocado sauce, garnished with sun-dried tomatoes and roasted poblano peppers) served with a cheese enchilada, beans, and guacamole. There is a nice selection of soups and salads at lunch and dinner and a variety of homemade desserts. A full bar serves Mexican beers (10 in all) and margaritas.

INEXPENSIVE

Bobcat Bite. Old Las Vegas Hwy. ☎ **505/983-5319.** No reservations. Menu items $3.50–$11.95. No credit cards. Wed–Sat 11am–7:50pm. STEAKS/BURGERS.

This local classic (in business for more than 40 years), located about 5 miles southeast of Santa Fe, is famed for its high-quality steaks—such as the 13-ounce rib eye—and huge hamburgers, including a remarkable green chile cheeseburger. The ranch-style atmosphere and friendly service appeal to families.

Green Onion. 1851 St. Michael's Dr. ☎ **505/983-5198.** Lunch $5–$8; dinner $5–$9.50. AE, DISC, MC, V. Mon–Sat 11am–2am, Sun 11am–midnight. NEW MEXICAN, BURGERS, SANDWICHES, PIZZA.

This isn't my choice for food, but on that odd occasion when I get a desire to down some beer and scream at a TV screen, this is where I go. Roast-beef burritos and chicken enchiladas highlight an established menu at this sports bar, which also features a choice of sandwiches and pizza. You can view sports on a big-screen TV, or play darts, foosball, and video games.

Guadalajara Grill. 3877 Cerrillos Rd. ☎505/424-3544. Main courses $2.50–$9.95. AE, DISC, MC, V. Sun–Thurs 10:30am–9pm; Friday and Sat 10:30am–10pm; closed Tues in winter. MEXICAN.

A brother restaurant to the Guadalajara Grill in Taos, this is a good casual place to sample authentic Mexican, rather than *New* Mexican food. Seven brothers from the restaurant's namesake town own and run these restaurants and offer dishes with flavors a little more distinct, less melded than our own here. Next to a liquor store, the restaurant is set in a small strip mall just north of the Cerrillos/Rodeo Road intersection. The room is square with bright plastic-covered tables and a funky purple neon light on the ceiling. It's a festive atmosphere, the service friendly and efficient. To start, you can sample a frozen margarita or your choice of 12 Mexican beers. My favorite dish here is the tacos, served with soft, hand-made corn tortillas— well-seasoned meat and an excellent salsa. At lunch the menu is à la carte; at dinner all entrees come with rice and beans. Other favorites for lunch are a variety of types of burritos, and for dinner *camaron al mojo de ajo* (shrimp sautéed with garlic and lime juice). If you're really daring you can sample the *barbacoa lengua* (cow tongue), or *cachete* (cow cheek), cooked until tender.

Mu du noodles. 1494 Cerrillos Rd. ☎ **505/983-1411.** Accepts reservations for parties of 5 or larger only. Main courses lunch $6.75–$8.75; dinner $8.50–$11. Mon–Fri 11:30am–2:30pm; Mon–Sat 5:30–9pm (sometimes 10pm in summer); after 8:30pm always call to be sure. AE, DC, DISC, MC, V. PACIFIC RIM CUISINE.

If you're ready for a light, healthful meal with lots of flavor, head to this small restaurant about an 8-minute drive from downtown. There are two rooms, with plain pine tables and chairs and sparse Asian prints on the walls. The back room with carpet is cozier, and a woodsy-feeling patio is definitely worth requesting during the warmer months. The wait staff is friendly and unimposing. Appetizers include duck pockets and turkey pot stickers, as well as specials daily. I almost always order the Malaysian laksa, thick rice noodles in a blend of coconut milk, hazel nuts, onions, red curry, stir-fried with chicken or tofu and julienned vegetables and sprouts. You may want to each order a different dish and share. The Pad Thai is lighter and spicier than most, served with a chile/vinegar sauce. Beer, wine, and sake is available, termed "imported and hand crafted," which means they're tailored to meet the standards of menu. I'm especially fond of the ginseng ginger ale and Way 2 Cool root beer they serve.

5 What to See & Do

One of the oldest cities in the United States, Santa Fe has long been a center for the creative and performing arts, so it's not surprising that most of the city's major sights are related to local history and the arts. The city's Museum of New Mexico, art galleries and studios, historic churches, and cultural sights associated with local Native American and Hispanic communities all merit a visit. It would be easy to spend a full week sightseeing in the city without ever heading out to any nearby attractions. Of special note is the Georgia O'Keeffe museum opened just last summer.

SUGGESTED ITINERARIES

If You Have 2 Days

For an overview, start your first day at the Palace of the Governors; as you leave you might want to pick up a souvenir from the Native Americans selling crafts and jewelry beneath the portal facing the plaza. After lunch, take a self-guided walking tour of old Santa Fe, starting at the Plaza.

On Day 2, spend the morning at the Museum of Fine Arts and the afternoon browsing in the galleries on Canyon Road.

If You Have 3 Days

On the third day, visit the cluster of museums on Camino Lejo—the Museum of International Folk Art, the Museum of Indian Arts and Crafts, and the Wheelwright Museum of the American Indian. Then wander through the historic Barrio de Analco and spend the rest of the afternoon shopping.

If You Have 4 Days or More

Devote your fourth day to exploring the pueblos, including San Juan Pueblo, headquarters of the Eight Northern Indian Pueblos Council, and Santa Clara Pueblo, with its Puye Cliff Dwellings.

On Day 5, go out along the High Road to Taos (see "Taking the High Road to Taos," below), with a stop at El Santuario de Chimayo, returning down the Rio Grande Valley. If you have more time, take a trip to Los Alamos, birthplace of the atomic bomb and home of the Bradbury Science Museum, and Bandelier National Monument.

If You're an Outdoors Lover

Start with the first-day recommendation, just to get a feel for the culture of Santa Fe. Then, in spring or early summer, you might plan a raft trip down the Taos Box Canyon (a full-day event). During spring, summer, or fall, you could also contact one of the bicycle rental or touring companies and have them show you the way or take you to the Caja del Rio area or the West Rim of the Taos Box Canyon (see "Ballooning, Biking & Other Outdoor Activities," below). If you go to one of these Taos destinations, plan to return via the High Road.

On the following day, head up to the Windsor Trail for a hike in the Pecos Wilderness. A rigorous daylong trip will take you to the top of Santa Fe Baldy, where you'll have a 360° view of northern New Mexico. Or perhaps you'd prefer to spend the day hiking and visiting ruins around Bandelier National Monument near Los Alamos. During winter, plan at least a day of skiing at the world-acclaimed Taos Ski Valley; however, you also might want to take cross-country skis up to the Norski Trail near the Santa Fe Ski area, a pretty trek that meanders through an aspen forest. You can also snowshoe or backcountry ski on the Windsor Trail.

THE TOP ATTRACTIONS

✪ **Palace of the Governors.** North Plaza. ☎ **505/827-6483.** Admission $5 adults, free for children under 16. Four-day passes good at all 4 branches of the Museum of New Mexico (and the Georgia O'Keeffe Museum) cost $10 for adults. Tues–Sun 10am–5pm. Closed Jan 1, Thanksgiving, Dec 25.

In order to fully appreciate this structure, it's important to know that this is where the only successful Native American uprising took place in 1680. Before the uprising, this was the local seat of power, and after De Vargas reconquered the natives it resumed that position. Built in 1610 as the original capitol of New Mexico, the Palace has been in continuous public use longer than any other structure in the United States. A watchful eye can find remnants of the conflicts this building has seen through the years. You'll want to begin out front, where Native Americans sell jewelry, pottery, and some weavings in the sun under the protection of the portal. This is a good place to buy, and it's an especially fun place to shop, especially if you take the time to visit with the artisans about their work. When you buy a piece you may learn its history, a treasure as valuable as the piece itself.

After entering the building, begin to the right, where a map illustrates 400 years of New Mexico history. Continue west and get a sense of that history, from the

Greater Santa Fe

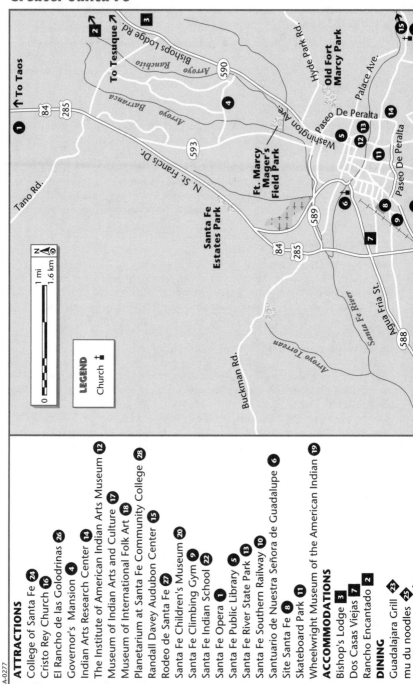

LEGEND
Church †

0   1 mi
  1.6 km

To Taos →

To Tesuque ↗

To Tesuque ↗

Bishops Lodge Rd.

Hyde Park Rd.

Old Fort Marcy Park

Palace Ave.

Paseo De Peralta

Washington Ave.

Ft. Marcy Mager's Field Park

Santa Fe Estates Park

Tano Rd.

N. St. Francis Dr.

Arroyo Rancbito

Arroyo Barranca

Buckman Rd.

Arroyo Torreon

Santa Fe River

Agua Fria St.

Paseo De Peralta

ATTRACTIONS
College of Santa Fe **24**
Cristo Rey Church **16**
El Rancho de las Golodrinas **26**
Governor's Mansion **4**
Indian Arts Research Center **14**
The Institute of American Indian Arts Museum **12**
Museum of Indian Arts and Culture **17**
Museum of International Folk Art **18**
Planetarium at Santa Fe Community College **28**
Randall Davey Audubon Center **15**
Rodeo de Santa Fe **27**
Santa Fe Children's Museum **20**
Santa Fe Climbing Gym **9**
Santa Fe Indian School **22**
Santa Fe Opera **1**
Santa Fe Public Library **5**
Santa Fe River State Park **13**
Santa Fe Southern Railway **10**
Santuario de Nuestra Señora de Guadalupe **6**
Site Santa Fe **8**
Skateboard Park **11**
Wheelwright Museum of the American Indian **19**

ACCOMMODATIONS
Bishop's Lodge **3**
Dos Casas Viejas **7**
Rancho Encantado **2**

DINING
Guadalajara Grill **23**
mu du noodles **25**

NA-0277

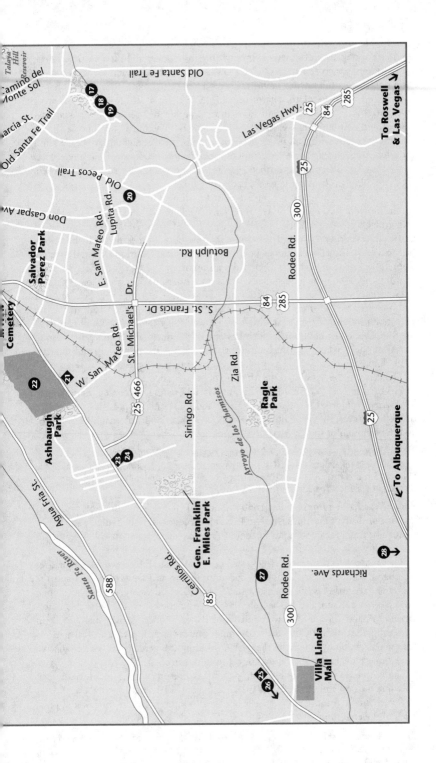

16th-century Spanish explorations through the frontier era and modern times. Peek into a rickety stagecoach and examine tools used by early Hispanic residents such as farm implements and kitchen utensils. There's a replica of a mid–19th-century chapel, with a simple, bright-colored altarpiece made in 1830 for a Taos church by folk artist José Rafael Aragón. What I find most interesting are the period photos scattered throughout. The building's exterior seems elaborate now, but it was once a simple flat-topped adobe with thin posts. You can see a fireplace and chimney chiseled into the adobe wall, and, in the west section of the museum, a cutaway of the adobe floor. Farther in this direction, unearthed in a recent excavation, are storage pits where the Pueblo Indians kept corn, wheat, barley, and other goods during their reign at the palace. After the reconquest the pits were used to dispose of trash.

The museum focuses little on regional Native American culture (most Native American artifacts previously housed here have been moved to the Museum of Indian Arts and Culture). However, recently a world-class collection of pre-Columbian art objects has been added. You'll see ceramics, gold, and stone work of South and Central America from 1500 B.C. to A.D. 1500. There's also an impressive 18th-century Segesser Hide painting collection, which documents events from America's Spanish Colonial past.

Governors' offices from the Mexican and 19th-century U.S. eras have been restored and preserved. My favorite display is a set of spurs ranging from the 16th to the late 19th centuries, including a spur with 5-inch rowels. There are two shops of particular interest. One is the bookstore, which has one of the finest selections of art, history, and anthropology books in the Southwest. The other is the print shop and bindery, where limited-edition works are produced on hand-operated presses.

The Palace is the flagship of the Museum of New Mexico system; the main office is at 113 Lincoln Ave. (☎ **505/827-6451,** or 505/827-6463 for recorded information). The system comprises five state monuments and four Santa Fe museums: the Palace of the Governors, the Museum of Fine Arts, the Museum of International Folk Art, and the Museum of Indian Arts and Culture.

✪ **Museum of Fine Arts.** 107 W. Palace (at Lincoln Ave.). ☎ **505/827-4455.** Admission $5 adults, free for seniors on Wed, free for children under 17. Four-day passes are available ($10 for 5 museums). Tues–Sun 10am–5pm; Fri evening the museum is open 5–8pm, free. Closed Jan 1, Easter, Thanksgiving, Dec 25.

Located catercorner from the Plaza and just opposite the Palace of the Governors, this was one of the first Pueblo Revival–style buildings constructed in Santa Fe (in 1917). As such, it was a major stimulus in Santa Fe's development as an art colony earlier in this century.

The museum's permanent collection of more than 8,000 works emphasizes regional art and includes landscapes and portraits by all the Taos masters and the contemporary artists R. C. Gorman, Amado Peña Jr., and Georgia O'Keeffe, among others. The museum also has a collection of photographic works by such masters as Ansel Adams, Edward Weston, and Elliot Porter. Modern artists, many of them far from the mainstream of traditional Southwestern art, are featured in temporary exhibits throughout the year. Two sculpture gardens present a range of three-dimensional art from the traditional to the abstract.

Graceful St. Francis Auditorium, patterned after the interiors of traditional Hispanic mission churches, adjoins the art museum (see "Santa Fe After Dark," later in this chapter). A museum shop sells books on Southwestern art, prints, and postcards of the collection.

✪ **St. Francis Cathedral.** Cathedral Place at San Francisco St. ☎ **505/982-5619.** Donations appreciated. Open daily. Visitors may attend mass Mon–Sat at 7am and 5:15pm; Sun at 8 and 10am, noon, and 7pm.

Downtown Santa Fe Attractions

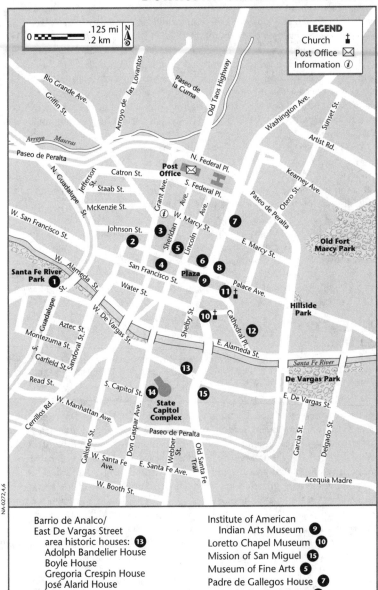

LEGEND
Church †
Post Office ✉
Information ⓘ

0 .125 mi
.2 km
N

Rio Grande Ave.
Griffin St.
Arroyo de las Lovantos
Paseo de la Cuma
Old Taos Highway
Washington Ave.
Sunset St.
Artist Rd.
Arroyo Mascras
Paseo de Peralta
N. Guadalupe St.
Jefferson St.
Catron St.
Post Office ✉
N. Federal Pl.
S. Federal Pl.
Kearney Ave.
Otero St.
Staab St.
McKenzie St.
Grant Ave.
Marcy Ave.
W. Marcy St.
Paseo de Peralta
ⓘ
W. San Francisco St.
Johnson St.
❸
❷
Sheridan St.
❺
Lincoln Ave.
E. Marcy St.
❼
Old Fort Marcy Park
Santa Fe River Park
❶
W. Alameda St.
San Francisco St.
❹
Plaza
❻
❽
❾
Palace Ave.
❶❶ †
Hillside Park
Water St.
Guadalupe St.
Aztec St.
W. De Vargas St.
Shelby St.
❶⓿ †
Cathedral Pl.
❶❷
Montezuma St.
Sandoval St.
Garfield St.
Read St.
E. Alameda St.
Santa Fe River
De Vargas Park
❶❸
S. Capitol St.
❶❹
State Capitol Complex
❶❺
E. De Vargas St.
Cerrillos Rd.
W. Manhattan Ave.
Don Gaspar Ave.
Paseo de Peralta
Webber St.
Old Santa Fe Trail
Garcia St.
Delgado St.
Galisteo St.
W. Santa Fe Ave.
E. Santa Fe Ave.
W. Booth St.
Acequia Madre

NA-0272,4,6

Barrio de Analco/
East De Vargas Street
area historic houses: ❶❸
Adolph Bandelier House
Boyle House
Gregoria Crespin House
José Alarid House
Oldest House
Tudesqui House
Bergere House ❸
Catholic Museum & Lamy Garden ❶❷
Delgado House ❹
Georgia O'Keefe Museum ❷

Institute of American
Indian Arts Museum ❾
Loretto Chapel Museum ❶⓿
Mission of San Miguel ❶❺
Museum of Fine Arts ❺
Padre de Gallegos House ❼
Palace of the Governors ❻
Prince Plaza ❽
Roundhouse (State Capitol) ❶❹
Santuario de Nuestra Señora
de Guadalupe ❶
St. Francis Cathedral ❶❶

167

Santa Fe's grandest religious structure is an architectural anomaly in Santa Fe because its design is French. Just a block east of the Plaza, it was built between 1869 and 1886 by Archbishop Jean-Baptiste Lamy in the style of the great cathedrals of Europe. French architects designed the Romanesque building—named after Santa Fe's patron saint—and Italian masons assisted with its construction. The small adobe Our Lady of the Rosary chapel on the northeast side of the cathedral has a Spanish look. Built in 1807, it's the only portion that remains from Our Lady of the Assumption Church, founded along with Santa Fe in 1610. The new cathedral was built over and around the old church.

A wooden icon set in a niche in the wall of the north chapel, Our Lady of Peace, is the oldest representation of the Madonna in the United States. Rescued from the old church during the 1680 Pueblo Rebellion, it was brought back by Don Diego de Vargas on his (mostly peaceful) reconquest 12 years later; thus the name. Today Our Lady of Peace plays an important part in the annual Feast of Corpus Christi in June and July.

During a $600,000 renovation in 1986, an early 18th-century wooden statue of St. Francis of Assisi was moved to the center of the altar screen. The cathedral's front doors feature 16 carved panels of historic note and a plaque memorializing the 38 Franciscan friars who were martyred during New Mexico's early years. There's also a large bronze statue of Bishop Lamy himself; his grave is under the main altar of the cathedral.

MORE ATTRACTIONS
MUSEUMS

Catholic Museum and the Archbishop Lamy Commemorative Garden. 223 Cathedral Place. ☎ **505/983-3811.** Donations appreciated. Mon–Fri 8:30am–4:30pm; Sat by appointment.

This museum will be especially interesting if you've read Willa Cather's *Death Comes for the Archbishop,* a fictional account of Archbishop Lamy's experience in northern New Mexico. If you haven't read it, as you visit the St. Francis Cathedral, Bishop's Lodge, and other areas around Santa Fe, take special note of tales of the Archbishop, since he is central to the area's history. Though the exhibition changes every few years (and a new one should arrive right around press time), you are still likely to see a portrait of the determined, thin-lipped Frenchman who resolutely battled what he felt was apostasy on the part of the Spanish clergy in New Mexico. You'll also see Lamy's boar hair trunk and the golden chalice given to him by Pope Pius IX in 1854. The next exhibit planned is called "400 Years of Faith" and will contain historic documents and artifacts from 400 years of Catholicism in New Mexico. The adjacent Lamy garden isn't much to see, but the gift shop in the museum has a nice collection of religious articles made locally.

✪ **Georgia O'Keeffe Museum.** 217 Johnson St. ☎ **505/995-0785.** Admission $5 (4-day, 5-museum passes to the Museum of New Mexico available). Tues–Sun 10am–5pm (Fri until 8pm).

For years, anxious visitors to Santa Fe asked, "Where are the O'Keeffes?" Locals flushed and were forced to answer: "The Metropolitan Museum of Art in New York and the National Gallery of Art in Washington, D.C." Although this East Coast artist is known the world over for her haunting depictions of the shapes and colors of northern New Mexico, particularly the Abiquiu area, until now little of her work hung in the state. The local Museum of Fine Arts owns just 15 of her works.

The new museum, inaugurated in July 1997, contains the largest collection of O'Keeffes in the world: more than 80 oil paintings, drawings, watercolors, pastels, and sculptures. It is the only museum in the United States dedicated solely to one woman's work. You can see such "Killer O'Keeffes" as *Jimson Weed,* painted in 1932, and *Evening Star No. VII,* from 1917. The rich and varied collection adorns the walls of this former Baptist church with adobe walls—a cathedral-like, 10,000-square-foot space downtown.

O'Keeffe's images and fame are, of course, tied inextricably to local desert landscapes. She first visited New Mexico in 1917 and returned for extended periods from the '20s through the '40s. The idea of bringing O'Keeffe's works together came from the private collector Anne Windfohr Marion. The Texas heiress heads the Burnett Foundation, which, along with the Georgia O'Keeffe Foundation, donated the initial 33 works. Ms. Marion and her husband, John L. Marion, a former chairman of Sotheby's North America, chose the designer of the Andy Warhol Museum in Pittsburgh, Richard Gluckman, to create the space for the O'Keeffe Museum.

Indian Arts Research Center. School of American Research (SAR), 660 Garcia St. (off Canyon Rd.). ☎ **505/954-7205.** E-mail: iarc@sarsf.org. Free admission for Native Americans and SAR members; $15 suggested donation for others. Public tours are given most Fridays at 2pm (call for reservations). Group tours can also be arranged.

Having grown up in New Mexico surrounded by Native American arts, I had but a hodgepodge of knowledge of whose work looked like what, and when it had been created. Then I visited the vault here and was able to put my knowledge into an understandable framework. The School of American Research, of which this is a division, was established in 1907 as a center for advanced studies in anthropology and related fields. It sponsors scholarship, academic research, publications, and educational programs, all in the name of keeping traditional arts alive.

The school has collected more than 10,000 objects, in the process compiling one of the world's finest collections of Southwest Indian pottery, jewelry, weavings, Kachinas, paintings, baskets, and other arts that span from the prehistoric era (around A.D. 300 to 500) to the present. You'll be led through temperature- and humidity-controlled rooms filled with work separated by tribe. Here you can see the unique styles of each pueblo's pottery, from the Zia's swirling rainbow patterns full of birds and animal life to the San Ildefonso black-on-black that María Martínez made world famous. You'll also see the transformation of Navajo weavings from the muted Phase I, when they used all natural dyes, through the bold Phase III, when German dyes predominated creating near-neon intensity. Above all, you'll get a sense of the importance of preserving ancient art, a fount from which contemporary Native Americans can always draw and the rest of us can learn.

Admission, however, is restricted; see above for details.

Institute of American Indian Arts Museum. 108 Cathedral Place. ☎ **505/988-6211.** Admission (2-day pass) $4 adults, $2 seniors and students, free for children 16 and under. Mon–Sat 10am–5pm, Sun noon–5pm.

A visit to this museum (the most comprehensive collection of contemporary Native American art in the world), offers a profound look into the lives of a people trapped between two worlds: traditional and contemporary. Here you'll see cutting-edge art that pushes the limits of many media, from creative writing to textile manufacturing to painting. One young artist says in a video, "I feel like if I see one more warrior riding off into the sunset, I'm going to throw up." Rather than clichéd images, you are more likely to see a series of clay canteens demonstrating the evolution of an art form from traditional and utilitarian (spherical shape) to a creative concept (tubular). Much of the work originates from artists from The Institute of American Indian Arts (IAIA), the nation's only congressionally chartered institute of higher education devoted solely to the study and practice of the artistic and cultural traditions of all American Indian and Alaska native peoples.

Exhibits change periodically. Two upcoming shows include "Native American Quilts" and "Savage Truths," work from some young artists bent on attacking the status quo. The museum store has a broad collection of contemporary jewelry, pottery, and other crafts as well as books and cards.

✪ **Museum of Indian Arts and Culture.** 710 Camino Lejo. ☎ **505/827-6344.** Admission $5 adults, free for children under 17. Tues–Sun 10am–5pm.

A new interactive permanent exhibit here has made this one of the most exciting Native American museum experiences in the Southwest. "Here, Now and Always" takes visitors through thousands of years of Native American history. More than 70,000 pieces of basketry, pottery, clothing, carpets, and jewelry—much of it quite old—are on continual rotating display. You begin in the new exhibit by entering through a tunnel that symbolizes the *sipapu,* the Anasazi entrance into the upper worlds; you are greeted by the sounds of trickling water, drums, and Native American music. Videos show Native Americans telling creation stories. The rest of the exhibit is just as innovatively presented. The exhibit allows visitors to reflect on the lives of modern-day Native Americans by juxtaposing a traditional Pueblo kitchen with a modern kitchen. You can step into a Navajo Hogan and stroll through a trading post. The rest of the museum houses a lovely pottery collection as well as changing exhibits. There's always a contemporary show.

Look for demonstrations of traditional skills by tribal artisans and regular programs in a 70-seat multimedia theater. Call for information on year-round lectures and classes on native traditions and arts, as well as regular performances of Native American music and dancing by tribal groups. In February, look for an annual fiber show, and in June a presentation on oral traditions.

The laboratory, founded in 1931 by John D. Rockefeller Jr., is itself a point of interest. Designed by the well-known Santa Fe architect John Gaw Meem, it is an exquisite example of Pueblo Revival architecture.

✪ **Museum of International Folk Art.** 706 Camino Lejo. ☎ **505/827-6350.** Admission $5 adults, free for children under 17. Wed, free for seniors ($10 for 5 museums pass available). Tues–Sun 10am–5pm. The museum is located about 2 miles south of the Plaza, in the Sangre de Cristo foothills. Drive southeast on Old Santa Fe Trail, which becomes Old Pecos Trail, and look for signs pointing left onto Camino Lejo.

This branch of the Museum of New Mexico may not seem quite as typically South-western as other Santa Fe museums, but it's the largest of its kind in the world. With a collection of some 130,000 objects from more than 100 countries, it's my favorite city museum. It was founded in 1953 by the Chicago collector Florence Dibell Bartlett, who said: "If peoples of different countries could have the opportunity to study each other's cultures, it would be one avenue for a closer understanding between men." That's the basis on which the museum operates today.

The special collections include Spanish colonial silver, traditional and contemporary New Mexican religious art, Mexican tribal costumes, Mexican majolica ceramics, Brazilian folk art, European glass, African sculptures, East Indian textiles, and the marvelous Morris Miniature Circus. Particularly delightful are numerous dioramas, all done with colorful miniatures, of people around the world at work and play in typical town, village, and home settings.

Recent acquisitions include American weather vanes and quilts, Palestinian costume jewelry and amulets, and Bhutanese and Indonesian textiles.

Fetishes: Gifts of Power

According to Zuni lore, in the early years of man's existence, the Sun sent down his two children to assist humans, who were under siege from earthly predators. The Sun's sons, as it were, shot lightning bolts from their shields and destroyed the predators. For generations, Zunis, traveling across their lands in western New Mexico, have found stones shaped like particular animals. The Zuni believe the stones to be the remains of those long-lost predators, still containing their soul or last breath.

Today in many shops in Santa Fe you too can pick up a carved animal figure, called a fetish. According to belief, the owner of the fetish is able to absorb the power of that creature, whatever it may be. Many fetishes were long ago used for protection and might in the hunt. Today people own fetishes for many reasons. One might carry a bear for health and strength, or an eagle for keen perspective. A mole might be placed in a home's foundation for protection from elements underground, a frog buried with crops for fertility and rain, a ram carried in the purse for prosperity. For love, some locals recommend pairs of fetishes—often foxes or coyotes carved from a single piece of stone.

Many fetishes, arranged with bundles on top and attached with sinew, serve as an offering to the animal spirit that resides within the stone. Fetishes are still carved in many of the pueblos. Shop around for a little while until you begin to appreciate the difference between clumsily carved ones and more gracefully executed ones. A good fetish is not necessarily one that is meticulously carved. Some fetishes are barely carved at all, since the original shape of the stone already contains the form of the animal. Once you have a sense of the quality and elegance available, decide which animal (and power) suits you best. Native Americans caution, however, that the fetish cannot be expected to impart an attribute you don't already possess. Instead it will help elicit the power that already resides within you. Good sources for fetishes are **Dewey Galleries Limited,** 53 Old Santa Fe Tr. 2nd Floor (on the Plaza; ☎ **505/982-8632**); **Keshi,** 227 Don Gaspar (☎ **505/989-8728**); and **Morning Star Gallery,** 513 Canyon Rd. (☎ **505/982-8187**).

Children love to look at the hundreds of toys on display throughout the museum. Many of them are housed in a wing built especially to hold part of a collection donated in 1982 by Alexander and Susan Girard. Alexander Girard, a notable architect and interior designer, and his wife, Susan, spent their lives traveling the world collecting dolls, animals, fabrics, masks, and dioramas. They had a home in Santa Fe, where they spent many years before they died. Their donation included more than 100,000 pieces, 10,000 of which are exhibited at the museum.

The Hispanic Heritage Wing houses the country's finest collection of Spanish colonial and Hispanic folk art. Folk-art demonstrations, performances, and workshops are often presented here. The 80,000-square-foot museum also has a lecture room, a research library, and a gift shop where a variety of folk art is available for purchase.

Wheelwright Museum of the American Indian. 704 Camino Lejo. ☎ **800/607-4636** or 505/982-4636. Donations appreciated. Mon–Sat 10am–5pm, Sun 1–5pm. Closed Jan 1, Thanksgiving, Dec 25.

Next door to the Folk Art, this museum offers an esoteric collection of living arts of all Native American cultures. The building resembles a Navajo hogan, with its doorway facing east (toward the rising sun) and its ceiling formed in the interlocking "whirling log" style. It was founded in 1937 by Boston scholar Mary Cabot Wheelwright in collaboration with a Navajo medicine man, Hastiin Klah, to preserve and document Navajo ritual beliefs and practices. Klah took the designs of sand paintings used in healing ceremonies and adapted them into the woven pictographs that are a major part of the museum's treasure. In 1976 the museum's focus was altered to include the living arts of all Native American cultures. The museum offers three to four exhibits per year. You may see a basketry exhibit or mixed media Navajo toys, or amazing contemporary Navajo rugs. An added treat here is the Case Trading Post, an arts-and-crafts shop built to resemble the typical turn-of-the-century trading post found on the Navajo reservation, with vigas and a squeaky wood floor. Whole cases are devoted to a particular artist's work, so you get a sense of the scope of a silversmith's work or whimsical nature of a wood carver's. Many pieces are reasonably priced. Storyteller Joe Hayes holds the attention of listeners outside a tepee at dusk on certain days in July and August. The museum has excellent access for people with disabilities.

CHURCHES

Cristo Rey. Upper Canyon Rd. at Camino Cabra. ☎ **505/983-8528.** Free admission. Open most days, but call for hours.

This Catholic church ("Christ the King" in Spanish), a huge adobe structure, was built in 1940 to commemorate the 400th anniversary of Coronado's exploration of the Southwest. Parishioners did most of the construction work, even making adobe bricks from the earth where the church stands. The local architect John Gaw Meem designed the building, in missionary style, as a place to keep some magnificent stone *reredos* (altar screens) created by the Spanish during the colonial era and recovered and restored in the 20th century.

✪ **Loretto Chapel Museum.** 207 Old Santa Fe Trail (between Alameda and Water sts.). ☎ **505/984-7971.** Admission $2 adults, $1 children 7–13, free for children 6 and under. Mon–Sat 9:30am–4:30pm, Sun 10:30am–4:30pm.

Though no longer consecrated for worship, the Loretto Chapel is an important site in Santa Fe. Patterned after the famous Sainte-Chapelle church in Paris, it was constructed in 1873—by the same French architects and Italian masons who were building Archbishop Lamy's cathedral—as a chapel for the Sisters of Loretto, who had established a school for young women in Santa Fe in 1852.

The chapel is especially notable for its remarkable spiral staircase: It makes two complete 360° turns with no central or other visible support! (A railing was added later.) The structure is steeped in legend. The building was nearly finished in 1878 when workers realized the stairs to the choir loft wouldn't fit. Hoping for a solution more attractive than a ladder, the sisters made a novena to St. Joseph, and were rewarded when a mysterious carpenter appeared astride a donkey and offered to build a staircase. Armed with only a saw, a hammer, and a T-square, the master constructed this work of genius by soaking slats of wood in tubs of water to curve them and holding them together with wooden pegs. Then he disappeared without bothering to collect his fee.

Mission of San Miguel. 401 Old Santa Fe Trail (at E. De Vargas St.). ☎ **505/983-3974.** Admission $1 for adults, free for children 6 and under. Mon–Sat 10am–4pm, Sun 2:30–4:30pm. Summer hours start earlier. Mass daily at 5pm.

If you really want to get the feel of colonial Catholicism, visit this church. Better yet, attend Mass here. You won't be disappointed. Built in 1610, the church has massive adobe walls, high windows, an elegant altar screen (erected in 1798), and a 780-pound San José Bell (now found inside), which was cast in Spain in 1356. If that doesn't impress you, perhaps the buffalo hide and deerskin Bible paintings used in 1630 by Franciscan missionaries to teach the Native Americans will. Anthropologists have excavated near the altar, down to the original floor—ground said by some to be part of a 12th-century pueblo. A small store just off the sanctuary sells religious articles.

Santuario de Nuestra Señora de Guadalupe. 100 S. Guadalupe St. ☎ **505/988-2027.** Donations appreciated. Mon–Sat 9am–4pm. Closed weekends Nov–Apr.

At press time, this church with poetic lines and a chimerical history is embroiled in controversy. The Archdiocese of Santa Fe has asked the Guadalupe Historic Foundation—which renovated the *santuario* and now leases it from the archdiocese as a community building—to voluntarily terminate its lease so that the sanctuary may be used as a place of perpetual adoration. At least one priest and a few parishioners didn't approve of the space being used for chamber music concerts, flamenco dance programs, dramas, lectures, and art shows. After some conflict, during which the priest was fired from his post, the Foundation complied.

Built between 1795 and 1800 at the end of El Camino Real by Franciscan missionaries, this is believed to be the oldest shrine in the United States honoring the Virgin of Guadalupe, the patron saint of Mexico. Better known as Santuario de Guadalupe, the shrine's adobe walls are almost three feet thick, and the deep-red plaster wall behind the altar was dyed with oxblood in traditional fashion when the church was restored earlier in this century.

It's well worth a visit to see photographs of the transformation of the building over time; its styles have ranged from flat-topped Pueblo to New England town meeting and today's northern New Mexico style. On one wall is a famous oil painting, *Our Lady of Guadalupe,* created in 1783 by the renowned Mexican artist José de Alzibar. Painted expressly for this church, it was brought from Mexico City by mule caravan.

OTHER ATTRACTIONS

✪ **El Rancho de las Golondrinas.** 334 Los Pinos Rd. ☎ **505/471-2261.** Admission $4 adults, $3 seniors and teens, $1.50 children 5–12, free for children under 5. Festival weekends $6 adults, $4 seniors and teens, $2.50 children 5–12. June–Sept Wed–Sun 10am–4pm; Apr–May and Oct open by advance arrangement. Closed Nov–Mar.

This 200-acre ranch, about 15 miles south of the Santa Fe Plaza via I-25 (take Exit 276), was once the last stopping place on the 1,000-mile El Camino Real from Mexico City to Santa Fe. Today it's a living 18th- and 19th-century Spanish village, comprising a hacienda, a village store, a schoolhouse, and several chapels and kitchens. There's also a working molasses mill, wheelwright and blacksmith shops, shearing and weaving rooms, a threshing ground, a winery and vineyard, and four water mills, as well as dozens of farm animals. A walk around the entire property is 1¾ miles in length.

The Spring Festival (the first weekend of June) and the Harvest Festival (the first weekend of October) are the year's highlights at Las Golondrinas ("The Swallows"). On these festival Sundays the museum opens with a procession and mass dedicated to San Ysidro, patron saint of farmers. Other festivals and theme weekends are held throughout the year. Volunteers in authentic costume demonstrate shearing, spinning, weaving, embroidery, wood carving, grain milling, blacksmithing, tinsmithing, soap making, and other activities. There's an exciting atmosphere of Spanish folk dancing, music, theater, and food. When driving from Albuquerque via I-25, take Exit 276B.

Roundhouse (State Capitol). Paseo de Peralta and Old Santa Fe Trail. ☎ **505/986-4589.**

Some are surprised to learn that this is the only round capitol building in America. Built in 1966, it's designed in the shape of a Zia Pueblo emblem (or sun sign, which is also the state symbol). It symbolizes the Circle of Life: four winds, four seasons, four directions, and four sacred obligations. Surrounding the capitol is a lush 6½ -acre garden boasting more than 100 varieties of plants, including roses, plums, almonds, nectarines, Russian olive trees, and sequoias. Benches and sculptures (by notable artists) have been placed around the grounds for the enjoyment of visitors. Inside you'll find standard functional offices. The walls are hung with New Mexican art. Call the number above for tour information.

Santa Fe Southern Railway. 410 S. Guadalupe St. ☎ **888/929-8600** or 505/989-8600. Fax 505/983-7620. Tickets range from $5 for children to $21 for adults; $45 for Fri sunset ride includes dinner (May–Oct). Depending on the season, trains depart the Santa Fe Depot on various days (call to check) at 10:30am and return by 3pm. The sunset ride departs a half hour before sunset and returns 4 hours later.

"Riding the old Santa Fe" always referred to riding the Atchison, Topeka & Santa Fe Railroad. Ironically, the main route of the AT&SF bypassed Santa Fe, which probably forestalled some development for the capital city. Still, a spur was run off the main line to Santa Fe in 1880, and today an 18-mile ride along that spur offers views of some of New Mexico's most spectacular scenery and a glimpse of railroad history.

The Santa Fe Depot is a well-preserved tribute to the Mission architecture that the railroad brought to the West in the early 1900s. Characterized by light-colored stuccoed walls, arched openings, and tile roofs, this style was part of an architectural revolution in Santa Fe at a time that builders snubbed the traditional Pueblo style. Standing on the brick platform, you'll hear a bell ring and a whistle blow; the train is ready to roll.

Inside the restored coach, passengers are surrounded by aged mahogany and faded velvet seats. The train snakes through crowded Santa Fe intersections onto the New Mexico plains, broad landscapes spotted with piñon and chamisa, with views of the Sandia and Ortiz mountains. Arriving in the small track town of Lamy, you get another glimpse of a Mission-style station, this one surrounded by spacious lawns where passengers picnic. Others choose to eat new American food at the historic Legal Tender Restaurant. Friday night, May through October, passengers can take an evening train and watch bold New Mexico sunsets while eating a buffet prepared by a local caterer. There's live music at a campfire during the layover where coffee and dessert are served. There's also a cash bar selling beer, wine, and margaritas. Recently they've added specialty trains at various times during the year, including a Santa Train, Halloween Mystery Train, Romantic Valentines Day Train, and Rodeo Train.

GETTING CLOSE TO NATURE

Arroyo de los Chamisos Trail. Begin at Santa Fe High School on Yucca St. or on Rodeo Rd. near Sam's Club. ☎ **505/473-7228.**

This trail, which meanders through the southwestern part of town, is of special interest to those staying in hotels along Cerrillos Rd. The new 2.5-mile paved path follows a chamisa-lined *arroyo* (stream) and has mountain views. Great for walking or bicycling; dogs must be kept on a leash.

Old Fort Marcy Park. 617 Paseo de Peralta (also access it by traveling 3 blocks up Artist Road and turning right). ☎ **505/473-7228.**

Marking the 1846 site of the first U.S. military reservation in the Southwest, this park overlooks the northeast corner of downtown. Only a few mounds remain from the fort, but the Cross of the Martyrs, at the top of a winding brick walkway from Paseo de Peralta near Otero Street, is a popular spot for bird's-eye photographs. The cross was erected in 1920 by the Knights of Columbus and the Historical Society of New Mexico to commemorate the Franciscans killed during the Pueblo Rebellion of 1680. It has since played a role in numerous religious processions. It's open daily 24 hours.

Randall Davey Audubon Center. Upper Canyon Rd. ☎ **505/983-4609.** Admission $1 for trail. Daily 9am–5pm. House tours conducted sporadically during the summer for $3 per person; call for hours.

Named for the late Santa Fe artist who willed his home to the National Audubon Society, this wildlife refuge occupies 135 acres at the mouth of Santa Fe Canyon. Just a few minutes' drive from the Plaza, it's an excellent escape. More than 100 species of birds and 120 types of plants live here, and varied mammals have been spotted, including black bears, mule deer, mountain lions, bobcats, raccoons, and coyotes. Trails winding through more than 100 acres of the nature sanctuary are open to day hikers, but not to dogs. There's also a natural history bookstore on site.

Santa Fe River Park. Alameda St. ☎ **505/473-7236.**

This is a lovely spot for an early morning jog, a midday walk beneath the trees, or perhaps a sack lunch at a picnic table. The green strip, which does not close, follows the midtown stream for about 4 miles as it meanders along the Alameda from St. Francis Drive upstream beyond Camino Cabra, near its source.

COOKING, ART & PHOTOGRAPHY CLASSES

If you are looking for something to do that's a little off the beaten tourist path, you might consider taking a class.

You can master the flavors of Santa Fe with an entertaining 3-hour demonstration cooking class at the ✪ **Santa Fe School of Cooking and Market,** on the upper level of the Plaza Mercado, 116 W. San Francisco St. (☎ **505/983-4511;** fax 505/ 983-7540). The class teaches about the flavors and history of traditional New Mexican and contemporary Southwestern cuisines. "Cooking Light" classes are offered for those who prefer to cook with less fat. Prices range from $35 to $60 and include a meal; call for a class schedule. The adjoining market offers a variety of regional foods and cookbooks, with gift baskets available.

If Southwestern art has you hooked, you can take a drawing and painting class led by Santa Fe artist Jane Shoenfeld. Students sketch such outdoor subjects as the Santa Fe landscape and adobe architecture. In case of inclement weather, classes are held in the studio. Each class lasts for 3 hours, and art materials are included in the fee, which ranges from $68 to $95. All levels of experience are welcome. Children's classes can be arranged. Contact Jane at **Sketching Santa Fe,** P.O. Box 5912, Santa Fe, NM 87502 (☎ **505/986-1108;** fax 505/986-3845; www.Sfol.com.shoenfeld). Shoenfeld also holds 5-day workshops in Abiquiu at the Ghost Ranch. Call or refer to her Web page for dates.

Some of the world's most outstanding photographers convene in Santa Fe at various times during the year for the **Santa Fe Photography & Digital Workshops,** P.O. Box 9916, Santa Fe, 87504-5916 (☎ **505/983-1400;** www.sfworkshop.com. E-mail: sfworkkshop@aol.com), at a delightful campus in the hills on the east side of town. Most courses are full time, lasting a week; however others are shorter. I took one from *National Geographic* photographer Michael "Nick" Nichols and greatly advanced my work. Courses range from Nevada Wier's Travel Photography class to Sam Abell's Project Workshop, in which photographers with ongoing projects work to find cohesion. Best of all, the teachers hold free slide lectures each Wednesday night at 8pm. Call for specific dates and prices. These courses aren't cheap, but they're worth it. Most include food and lodging packages.

WINE TASTINGS

If you enjoy sampling regional wines, consider visiting the wineries within easy driving distance of Santa Fe: **Balagna Winery/Il Santo Cellars,** 223 Rio Bravo Dr., in Los Alamos (☎ **505/672-3678**), north on U.S. 84/285 and then west on NM 502; **Santa Fe Vineyards** (Route 1, Box 216A), about 20 miles north of Santa Fe on U.S. 84/285 (☎ **505/753-8100**); **Madison Vineyards & Winery,** in Ribera (☎ **505/ 421-8028**), about 45 miles east of Santa Fe on I-25 North; and the **Black Mesa Winery,** 1502 NM 68, in Velarde (☎ **800/852-6372**), north on U.S. 84/285 to NM 68.

Be sure to call in advance to find out when the wineries are open for tastings and to get specific directions.

ESPECIALLY FOR KIDS

Don't miss taking the kids to the **Museum of International Folk Art,** where they'll love the international dioramas and the toys (discussed earlier in this chapter). Also visit the tepee at the **Wheelwright Museum of the American Indian** (discussed earlier in this chapter), where storyteller Joe Hayes spins traditional Spanish *cuentos,* Native American folk tales, and Wild West tall tales on weekend evenings. **Bishop's Lodge** and **Rancho Encantado** both have extensive children's programs during the summer. These include horseback riding, swimming, arts and crafts programs, as well as special activities such as archery and tennis. Kids are sure to enjoy ✪ **El Rancho de las Golondrinas** (discussed above), a 200-acre ranch 15 miles south of Santa Fe, today a living 18th- and 19th-century Spanish village comprising a hacienda, a village store, a schoolhouse, and several chapels and kitchens.

Aerial's Gym. 720 St. Michael's Dr. (near St. Francis) ☎ **505/424-6741.**

This gym provides kids with a fun adventure while allowing parents time to explore Santa Fe. In a huge air-conditioned space, kids can play on tumbling mats, balance beams, and bars. They can swirl their hands on a sand table and slide on a zip line. The "Parent's Night Out" program is on Friday and Saturday night from 6 to 10pm; it costs $6 per hour. The gym has a summer program every afternoon from noon to 4pm, Monday to Friday. Kids ages 4 and up can do gymnastics, art projects, play games, and eat a snack for $20 per day, or $85 per week. Weekday mornings from 8:30am to noon there's a similar program for youngsters 2 to 4 at the same price. Be sure to make advance reservations. Regular gymnastics classes are also available; call for times.

Planetarium at Santa Fe Community College. 6401 Richards Ave. (south of Rodeo Rd.). ☎ **505/428-1677,** or 505/428-1777 for the information line. Admission $3.50 adults, $2 seniors and children 12 and under. Wed, adult and family show 7–8pm; Sat, children's show 10:30–11:30am; Celestial Highlights, a live program mapping the night sky for that particular month, is on the first Thurs of the month from 7–8pm.

The Planetarium offers imaginative programs, combining star shows with storytelling and other interactive techniques. Some of the titles reveal the inventiveness of the programs: Rusty Rocket's Last Blast, in which kids launch a model rocket; Planet Patrol; and the Solar System Stakeout, in which kids build a solar system. There's also a 10-minute segment on the current night sky. Programs vary, from those designed for preschoolers to ones for high school kids.

Rodeo de Santa Fe. 2801 Rodeo Rd. ☎ **505/471-4300.**

The rodeo is held annually the weekend following the Fourth of July. It's a colorful and fun Southwestern event for kids, teens, and adults. (See "New Mexico Calendar of Events" in chapter 3 for details.)

✪ **Santa Fe Children's Museum.** 1050 Old Pecos Trail. ☎ **505/989-8359.** www.sfchildmuseum.org. Admission $3 adults, $2 children under 12. Thurs and Sat 10am–5pm, Fri 9am–5pm, Sun noon–5pm. In June–Aug, also open Wed 10am–5pm.

Designed for the whole family to experience, this museum offers interactive exhibits and hands-on activities in the arts, humanities, science, and technology. Most notable is a 16-foot climbing wall that kids can scale, outfitted with helmets and harnesses. Special performances and hands-on sessions with artists and scientists are regularly scheduled. Recently *Family Life* magazine named this as one of the "10 hottest children's museums in the nation."

Santa Fe Climbing Gym. 825 Early St. ☎ **505/986-8944.**

The walls and ceiling of this two-story, cavernous gym are covered with foot and hand holds. A number of programs appeal to kids. Year-round you'll find "Kid's Climb," supervised indoor climbing for ages 7 to 14. It takes place Friday afternoon and Saturday morning from September through May and on Saturday morning during the summer. The cost of $15 to $20 includes instruction, activities, and equipment. No experience is needed, but reservations are a must. In summer, there's also "Kids' Rock," a fully supervised outdoor climbing experience in which transportation and equipment are included in the price of $65 to $75. Kids ages 7 and up can attend. In summer, group instruction is also available on Tuesday evening. These are small classes, good for beginners and younger kids.

Santa Fe Public Library. 145 Washington Ave. ☎ **505/984-6780.** Mon–Thurs 10am–9pm, Fri–Sat 10am–6pm, Sun 1–5pm. Call for additional information.

Special programs, such as storytelling and magic shows, can be found here weekly. The library is located in the center of town, 1 block from the Plaza. Call for additional information.

Skateboard Park. De Vargas St. ☎ **505/473-7236** or 505/438-1485. Open 24 hours. Admission free.

Split-level ramps for daredevils, park benches for onlookers, and climbing structures for youngsters are located at this park near downtown.

6 Organized Tours

BUS, CAR & TRAM TOURS

Gray Line Tours. 1330 Hickox St. ☎ **505/983-9491.**

The trolleylike Roadrunner departs several times daily in summer (less often in winter) from the La Fonda Hotel on the Plaza, beginning at 10am, for 1½-hour city tours. Buy tickets as you board. Daily tours to Taos, Chimayo, and Bandelier National Monument are also offered.

LorettoLine. At the Inn at Loretto, 211 Old Santa Fe Trail. ☎ **505/983-3701.**

For an open-air tour of the city, contact LorettoLine. Tours last 1½ hours and are offered daily from April to October. Tour times are every hour on the hour during the day from 10am to 3pm. Tickets are $9 for adults, $4 for children.

WALKING TOURS

As with the above independent strolls, these are the best way to get an appreciable feel for Santa Fe's history and culture.

Afoot in Santa Fe. At the Inn at Loretto, 211 Old Santa Fe Trail. ☎ **505/983-3701.**

Personalized 2½-hour tours are offered twice daily (9:30am and 1:30pm) from the Inn at Loretto at a cost of $10. Reservations are not required.

Storytellers and the Southwest: A Literary Walking Tour. 985 Agua Fria, No. 110. ☎ **505/989-4561.** $10 per person; two-person minimum.

Barbara Harrelson, a former Smithsonian museum docent and avid reader, takes you on a 2-hour literary walking tour of downtown, exploring the history, legends, characters, and authors of the region through its landmarks and historic sites. It's a great way to absorb the unique character of Santa Fe. Tours take place by appointment.

Walking Tour of Santa Fe. 54½ E. San Francisco St. (tour meets at 107 Washington Ave.) ☎ **800/338-6877** or 505/983-6565.

One of Santa Fe's best walking tours begins under the T-shirt tree at Tees & Skis, 107 Washington Ave., near the northeast corner of the Plaza (at 9:30am and 1:30pm) and lasts about 2½ hours. The tour costs $10 for adults. Children under 12 are free.

MISCELLANEOUS TOURS

Pathways Customized Tours. 161-F Calle Ojo Feliz. ☎ **505/982-5382.** Tours $50–$200 per couple.

Don Dietz offers several planned tours, including a downtown Santa Fe walking tour, a full city tour, a trip to the cliff dwellings and native pueblos, a "Taos adventure," and a trip to Georgia O'Keeffe country (with a focus on the landscape that inspired the art now possible to view in the new O'Keeffe Museum). He will try to accommodate any special requests you might have. These tours last anywhere from 1½ to 9 hours, depending on the one you choose. Don has extensive knowledge of the area's culture, history, geology, and flora and fauna and will help you make the most of your precious vacation time.

Rain Parrish. 704 Kathryn St. ☎ **505/984-8236.** Prices average approximately $125 per couple.

A Navajo (Diné) anthropologist, artist, and curator, offers custom guide services focusing on cultural anthropology, Native American arts, and the history of the Native Americans of the Southwest. Some of these are true adventures, to insider locations. Ms. Parrish includes visits to local Pueblo villages.

Rojo Tours & Services. P.O. Box 15744, Santa Fe, NM. 87506-5744 ☎ **505/474-8333.** Fax 505/474-2992.

Customized private tours are arranged to pueblos, cliff dwellings, and ruins, as well as art tours with studio visits.

Santa Fe Detours. 54½ East San Francisco St. ☎ **800/338-6877** or 505/983-6565.

Santa Fe's most extensive tour-booking agency accommodates almost all travelers' tastes, from bus and rail tours to river rafting, backpacking, and cross-country skiing.

✪ **Southwest Safaris.** P.O. Box 945, Santa Fe, NM 87504. ☎ **800/842-4246** or 505/988-4246.

This tour is one of the most interesting Southwest experiences I've had. We flew in a small plane at 500 feet off the ground from Santa Fe to the Grand Canyon while experienced pilot Bruce Adams explained 300 million years of geologic history. We passed over the ancient ruins of Chaco Canyon and the vivid colors of the Painted Desert, as well as over many land formations on Navajo Nation land so remote they remain nameless. Then, of course, there was the spectacular Grand Canyon, where we landed for a Jeep tour and lunch on a canyon-side bench. Trips to many Southwest destinations are available, including Monument Valley, Mesa Verde, Canyon de Chelly, Arches/Canyonlands, as well as the ruins at Aztec, New Mexico. Recently Adams has added local 1- and 2-hour scenic flights to places such as the Valle Grande, Acoma Pueblo, or following the canyons of the Rio Grande north. Prices range from $99 to $449.

7 Ballooning, Biking & Other Outdoor Pursuits

In addition to all the activities and recreation centers listed below, there will be a new full-service family recreation center on the southside of Santa Fe by early to mid-1999. The complex will include a 50-meter pool, an ice-skating rink, three gyms, a workout room, racquetball courts, and an indoor running track. Contact the **Santa Fe Convention and Visitors Bureau** for more information.

BALLOONING   New Mexico is renowned for its spectacular Balloon Fiesta, which takes place annually in Albuquerque. If you want to take a ride, you'll probably have to go to Albuquerque or Taos, but you can book your trip in Santa Fe through **Santa Fe Detours,** 54½ East San Francisco St. (☎ **800/338-6877** or 505/983-6565). Flights take place early in the day. Rates begin at around $135 a flight. If you've got your heart set on a balloon flight, I would suggest that you make your reservations early because flights are sometimes canceled due to bad weather. That way, if you have to reschedule, you'll have enough time to do so.

BIKING   You can cycle along main roadways and paved country roads year-round in Santa Fe, but be aware that traffic is particularly heavy around the Plaza, and all over town motorists are not especially attentive to bicyclists, so you need to be especially alert. Mountain biking has exploded here and is especially popular in the spring, summer, and fall; the high-desert terrain is rugged and challenging, but mountain bikers of all levels can find exhilarating rides. The Santa Fe Convention and Visitors Bureau can supply you with bike maps.

I recommend the following trails: West of Santa Fe, the **Caja del Rio** area has nice dirt roads and some light technical biking; **Bland Canyon** in the Jemez Mountains to the south near Cochiti Pueblo is an exciting ride with views and stream crossings; the **railroad tracks south of Santa Fe** provide wide-open biking on beginner to intermediate technical trails; and the **Borrego Trail** up toward the Santa Fe Ski Area is a very challenging technical ride.

In Santa Fe bookstores, look for *Mountain Biking in Northern New Mexico: Historical and Natural History Rides* by Craig Martin and *The New Mexican Mountain Bike Guide* by Brant Hayengand and Chris Shaw. Both are excellent guides to trails in Santa Fe, Taos, and Albuquerque. The books outline tours for beginner, intermediate, and advanced riders. **Palace Bike Rentals,** 409 E. Palace Ave. (☎ **505/986-0455**), rents high-quality regular mountain bikes for $15 for a half day and $20 for a full day (until sunset) or front-suspension bikes for $20 per half day and $25 per full day (until sunset). They also have multiple-day rates. Children's bikes are available, as are child seats and child trailers. **Sun Mountain Bike Company,** 121 Sandoval St. (☎ **505/820-2902**), rents quality front-suspension and full-suspension mountain bikes for $20 to $27 for a half day and $30 to $40 for a full day. Add $10 and they'll deliver to and pick up from your hotel. Weekly rentals can be arranged. Both shops supply accessories such as helmets, locks, water, maps, and trail information. My buddy Louie Gonzales, a native New Mexican, owns **Sun Mountain Bike Company,** listed above, and he recently began running bike tours from April through October to some of the most spectacular spots in Northern New Mexico. Trips range from an easy Glorieta Mesa tour to my favorite, the West Rim Trail, which snakes along the Taos Gorge, to the technical Glorieta Baldy, with prices from $60 to $109. All tours include bikes, transportation, and a New Mexican meal or snack.

FISHING   In the lakes and waterways around Santa Fe, anglers typically catch trout (there are five varieties in the area). Other local fish include bass, perch, and kokanee salmon. The most popular fishing holes are Cochiti and Abiquiu lakes as well as the Rio Chama, Pecos River, and the Rio Grande. A world-renowned fly-fishing destination, the **San Juan River,** near Farmington, is worth a visit and can make for an exciting 2-day trip in combination with a tour around **Chaco Culture National Historical Park** (see chapter 10). Check with the **New Mexico Game and Fish Department** (☎ 505/827-7911) for information (including maps of area waters), licenses, and fishing proclamations. **High Desert Angler,** 435 S. Guadalupe St. (☎ 505/988-7688), specializes in fly-fishing gear and guide services.

GOLF   There are three courses in the Santa Fe area: the 18-hole **Santa Fe Country Club,** on Airport Road (☎ 505/471-2626); and the often-praised, 18-hole **Cochiti Lake Golf Course,** 5200 Cochiti Hwy., Cochiti Lake, about 35 miles southwest of Santa Fe via I-25 and NM 16 and 22 (☎ 505/465-2239). A new 18-hole municipal course on the south side of Santa Fe will open sometime in 1998. For information, call the **City Recreation Department** (☎ 505/438-1485). **Santa Fe Golf and Driving Range,** 4680 Wagon Rd. (☎ 505/474-4680), is also open to the public throughout the year. They have 42 practice tees, golf merchandise, and rental clubs, and will provide instruction.

HIKING   It's hard to decide which of the 1,000 miles of nearby national forest trails to challenge. Four wilderness areas are especially attractive: **Pecos Wilderness,** with 223,000 acres east of Santa Fe; **Chama River Canyon Wilderness,** 50,300 acres west of Ghost Ranch Museum; **Dome Wilderness,** 5,200 acres of rugged canyon land adjacent to Bandelier National Monument; and **San Pedro Parks Wilderness,** 41,000 acres west of Los Alamos. Also visit the 58,000-acre **Jemez Mountain National Recreation Area.** Information on these and other wilderness areas is available from the **Santa Fe National Forest,** P.O. Box 1689 (NM 475), Santa Fe, NM 87504 (☎ 505/438-7840). If you're looking for company on your trek, contact the Santa Fe branch of the **Sierra Club,** 621 Old Santa Fe Trail, Suite 10 (☎ 505/983-2703). You can pick up a hiking schedule in the local newsletter outside the office.

Some people enjoy taking a chairlift ride to the summit of the **Santa Fe Ski Area** (☎ 505/ 982-4429) and hiking around up there in the spring and summer months. You might also consider purchasing *The Hiker's Guide to New Mexico* (Falcon Press Publishing Co.) by Laurence Parent; it outlines 70 hikes throughout the state. Another title, *75 Hikes in New Mexico* by Craig Martin (The Mountaineers) is also fun and useful.

HORSEBACK RIDING   Trips ranging in length from a few hours to overnight can be arranged by **Santa Fe Detours,** 54½ East San Francisco St. (☎ 800/338-6877 or 505/983-6565). You'll ride with "experienced wranglers" and can even arrange a trip that includes a cookout or brunch. Rides are also major activities at two local guest ranches: **The Bishop's Lodge** and **Rancho Encantado** (see "Where to Stay," above).

HUNTING   Mule deer and elk are taken by hunters in the Pecos Wilderness and Jemez Mountains, as are occasional black bears and bighorn sheep. Wild turkeys and grouse are frequently bagged in the uplands, geese and ducks at lower elevations. Check with the **New Mexico Game and Fish Department** (☎ **505/827-7911**) for information and licenses.

RIVER RAFTING & KAYAKING   Although Taos is the real rafting center of New Mexico, several companies serve Santa Fe during the April to October white-water season. They include **Southwest Wilderness Adventures,** P.O. Box 9380, Santa Fe, NM 87501 (☎ **800/869-7238** or 505/983-7262); **New Wave Rafting,** 103 E. Water St. (☎ **800/984-1444** or 505/984-1444); and **Santa Fe Rafting Co.,** 1000 Cerrillos Rd. (☎ **800/467-RAFT** or 505/988-4914). You can expect the cost of a full-day trip to range from about $70 to $90 before tax and the 3% federal land use fee. The day of the week (weekdays are less expensive) and group size may also affect the price. The companies listed above each offer 2- and 3-day trips as well. If you're a kayaker or would like to become one, the center for the sport is **Wild River Sports,** 1303 Cerrillos Rd. (☎ **505/982-7040**). Owners Brian and Heather Dudney can set you up with rental equipment and an ACA-certified instructor, or sell you any gear you may need, as well as give you directions to the best boating spots in the area. Beginner lessons cost $45 for a 2-hour pool class, $185 for a pool/river class, and $245 for a more extensive pool/lake/river class. All prices include equipment and boat rental. Canoes, inflatable kayaks, paddles, life vests, flotation, helmets, and wet suits are all rentable here. First-timer classes take place each Tuesday night, except for a few months midwinter. Call for location and times.

RUNNING   Despite its elevation, Santa Fe is popular with runners and hosts numerous competitions, including the annual **Old Santa Fe Trail Run** on Labor Day. Each Wednesday, Santa Fe runners gather at 6pm at the Plaza and set out on foot for runs in the surrounding area. This is a great opportunity for travelers to find their way and to meet some locals. **Santa Fe Striders** (☎ **505/983-2144**), sponsors various runs during the year. Call for information.

ROCK CLIMBING   During long winter evenings, while some go to the gym and pump metal, I like to go to **Santa Fe Climbing Gym,** 825 Early St. (☎ **505/986-8944**) and pump my own weight. Throughout the year there's open climbing nightly, though you do need to know how to climb and belay yourself (use a support rope), you can easily learn by taking an introductory class offered every week. Call for the particular day. On Sunday afternoon, the gym provides belays, a good way for a first-timer to check out the sport. There are also ongoing classes and clinics focusing on a variety of skills, from lead climbing to outdoor climbing. You can also hire a private outdoor guide. Rates for adults are $12 to $15 day; introductory class $40; outdoor private $75 to $175. (See "Especially for Kids," above, for kids' programs and prices.)

SKIING   There's something available for every ability level at Ski Santa Fe, about 16 miles northeast of Santa Fe via Hyde Park (Ski Basin) Road. Lots of locals ski here, particularly on weekends; if you can, go on weekdays. It's a good family area and fairly small, so it's easy to split off from and later reconnect with your party. Built on the upper reaches of 12,000-foot Tesuque Peak, the area has an average annual snowfall of 225 inches and a vertical drop of 1,650 feet. Seven lifts, including a 5,000-foot triple chair and a new quad chair, serve 39 runs and 590 acres of terrain, with a total capacity of 7,800 riders an hour. Base facilities, at 10,350 feet, center around **La Casa Mall,** with a cafeteria, lounge, ski shop, and boutique. Another restaurant, Totemoff's, has a midmountain patio.

The ski area is open daily from 9am to 4pm; the season often runs from Thanksgiving to early April, depending on snow conditions. Rates for all lifts are $40 for adults, $27 for children and seniors, free for kids less than 46 inches tall (in their ski boots), and free for seniors 72 and older. For more information, contact **Ski Santa Fe,** 1210 Luisa St., Suite 5, Santa Fe, NM 87505 (☎ **505/982-4429**). For 24-hour reports on snow conditions, call ☎ **505/983-9155.** The **New Mexico Snow Phone** (☎ **505/984-0606**) gives statewide reports. Ski packages are available through **Santa Fe Central Reservations** (☎ **800/776-7669** outside New Mexico, or 505/983-8200 within New Mexico).

Cross-country skiers find seemingly endless miles of snow to track in the **Santa Fe National Forest** (☎ **505/438-7840**). A favorite place to start is at the Black Canyon campground, about 9 miles from downtown en route to the Santa Fe Ski Area. In the same area are the **Borrego Trail** (high intermediate) and the **Norski Trail,** 7 miles up from Black Canyon.

Other popular activities at the ski area in winter include snowshoeing, snow-boarding, sledding, and inner tubing. Snowshoe and snowboard rentals are available at a number of downtown shops and the ski area.

SOARING   Soaring is available for those who don't believe the sky is the limit. There are two types of soaring. In one, you and the pilot are in a propless and motorless plane that generally seats only two people. A powered plane tows you up and you glide about catching updrafts to stay afloat for hours. In the other, the plane is equipped with a retractable prop. This allows you to take off without use of a tow plane. Once at altitude, the prop retracts, leaving you to glide. Either type allows for plenty of scenic viewing and the thrill of free birdlike flight. For information and rates, call **Santa Fe Soaring** (☎ **505/424-1928**).

SPAS   If traveling, skiing, or other activities have left you weary, a great place to treat your body and mind is **Ten Thousand Waves,** a Japanese-style health spa about 3 miles northeast of Santa Fe on Hyde Park Road (☎ **505/982-9304**). This serene retreat, nestled in a grove of piñon, offers hot tubs, saunas, and cold plunges, plus a variety of massage and other body work techniques. Bathing suits are optional in the 10-foot communal hot tub, where you can stay as long as you want for $13. Nine private hot tubs cost $18 to $25 an hour, with discounts for seniors and children. You can also arrange therapeutic massage, hot-oil massage, in-water watsu massage, herbal wraps, salt glows, and facials. New in 1996 were four treatment rooms that feature dry brush aromatherapy treatments and Ayurvedic treatments; a women's communal tub; and lodging at the **Houses of the Moon,** a six-room Japanese-style inn. The spa is open on Sunday, Monday, Wednesday, and Thursday from 10am to 9:30pm; Tuesday from 4:30 to 9:30pm; and Friday and Saturday from 10am to midnight (winter hours are shorter, so be sure to call). Reservations are recommended, especially on weekends.

Another option is a stay at a spa. **Vista Clara Ranch Resort and Spa** is still finding its way after recently opening 25 minutes south of Santa Fe, just outside Galisteo (☎ **888/663-9772** or 505/466-4772; www.vistaclara.com). This spa/resort has a stunning setting and some fine amenities. In 1998, the new owner Kaye Sandford and her crew were busy rescuing the buildings from nature. Now the two-story structure, built in 1987, shows the gloss of a major renovation. Rooms are tastefully austere with wood floors, viga ceilings, and hand-carved furniture. The bathrooms are ample, all with tub/shower and pretty Mexican tile. The pool is large and ozone-cleaned as is the hot tub (with an amazing sunset view); the whole experience is odorless.

Facilities include a large underground *kiva* where fitness classes take place, and a charming therapy center where guests can have a steam bath, sauna, massage, and body treatments such as masks and salt glows, as well as beauty treatments—even astrological readings. Guided nature hikes up to a stone dike covered with petroglyphs, art classes, and horseback riding occupy visitors' days. Best of all is the food. Three meals daily are prepared by Steven and Kirstin Jarret, light healthful food, what Kirstin calls "rustic and sophisticated flavors of the Southwest and beyond." Spa packages are available for $1,380 for 5 nights, and $1,950 for 7 nights,. Overnight lodging, spa treatments, and activities are also available on an à la carte basis.

SWIMMING The City of Santa Fe operates four indoor pools and one outdoor pool. The pool closest to downtown is found at the **Fort Marcy Complex** (☎ **505/ 984-6725**) on Camino Santiago, off Bishop's Lodge Road. Admission to the pool is $1.25 for adults, $1 for students, and 50¢ for children 8 to 13. Call the Santa Fe Convention and Visitors Bureau (☎ **800/777-CITY** or 505/984-6760) for information about the other area pools.

TENNIS Santa Fe has 44 public tennis courts and 4 major private facilities. The **City Recreation Department** (☎ **505/438-1485**) can help you locate indoor, outdoor, and lighted public courts.

SPECTATOR SPORTS

The ponies generally run from Memorial Day through September at **The Downs at Santa Fe** (☎ **505/471-3311**), about 11 miles south of Santa Fe off U.S. 85, near La Cienega. However, in 1997 San Ildefonso Pueblo purchased the track, and, at press time, there's rumor it will not open this year. Call to be sure. General admission, if there are horses, is free. A closed-circuit TV system shows instant replays of each race's final-stretch run and transmits out-of-state races for legal betting.

The **Rodeo de Santa Fe,** 2801 Rodeo Rd. (☎ **505/471-4300**), is held annually the weekend following the Fourth of July. (See "New Mexico Calendar of Events," in chapter 3, for details.)

8 Shopping

Each time I head out to shop in northern New Mexico I'm amazed by the treasures in the forms of handcrafts, art, and artifacts that I find. There's a broad range of work, from very traditional Native American crafts and Hispanic folk art to extremely innovative contemporary work. The cultures here are so alive and changing, the work transforms constantly, with traditional themes always at the heart of it.

Some call Santa Fe one of the top art markets in the world, and it's no wonder. Galleries speckle the downtown area, and as an artists' thoroughfare Canyon Road is preeminent. Still, the greatest concentration of Native American crafts is displayed beneath the portal of the Palace of the Governors. Any serious arts aficionado should try to attend one or more of the city's great arts festivals—the Spring Festival of the Arts in May, the Spanish Market in July, the Indian Market in August, or the Fall Festival of the Arts in October.

THE SHOPPING SCENE

Few visitors to Santa Fe leave the city without acquiring at least one item from the Native American artisans at the Palace of the Governors. When you are thinking of making such a purchase, keep the following pointers in mind:

Silver jewelry should have a harmony of design, clean lines, and neatly executed soldering. Navajo jewelry typically features large stones, with designs shaped around the stone. Zuni jewelry usually has patterns of small or inlaid stones. Hopi jewelry rarely uses stones; it usually has a motif incised into the top layer of silver and darkened.

Turquoise of a deeper color is usually higher quality, as long as it hasn't been color treated (undesirable because the process adds false color to the stone). Often turquoise is "stabilized," which means it is soaked in resin, and then the resin is baked into the stone. This makes the stone less fragile, and also prevents it from changing color with age and contact with body oils. Many people find the aging effect desirable. Beware of "reconstituted turquoise." In this process the stone is disassembled and reassembled; it usually has a uniformly blue color that looks very unnatural.

Pottery is traditionally hand-coiled and of natural clay, not thrown on a potter's wheel using commercial clay. It is hand-polished with a stone, hand-painted, and fired in an outdoor oven (usually an open fire pit) rather than an electric kiln. Look for an even shape; clean, accurate painting; a high polish (if it is a polished piece); and an artist's signature.

Navajo rugs are appraised according to tightness and evenness of weave, symmetry of design, and whether natural (preferred) or commercial dyes have been used.

Kachina dolls are more highly valued according to the detail of their carving: fingers, toes, muscles, rib cages, feathers, and so on. Elaborate costumes are also desirable. Oil staining is preferred to the use of bright acrylic paints.

Sand paintings should display clean, narrow lines, even colors, balance, an intricacy of design, and smooth craftsmanship.

Local museums, particularly the Wheelwright Museum and the Institute of American Indian Art, can provide a good orientation to contemporary craftsmanship.

Contemporary artists are mainly painters, sculptors, ceramists, and fiber artists, including weavers. Peruse one of the outstanding **gallery catalogs** for an introduction to local dealers—*The Collector's Guide to Santa Fe and Taos* by Wingspread Incorporated (P.O. Box 13566-L, Albuquerque, NM 87192), *The Santa Fe Catalogue* by Modell Associates (P.O. Box 1007, Aspen, CO 81612), or *Performance de Santa Fe* by Cynthia Stearns (P.O. Box 8932, Santa Fe, NM 87504-8932). They're widely available at shops or can be ordered directly from the publishers. For a current listing of gallery openings, with recommendations on which ones to attend, purchase a copy of the monthly magazine the *Santa Fean* by Santa Fean, LLC (444 Galisteo, Santa Fe, NM 87501).

Business hours vary quite a bit among establishments, but most are open at least Monday through Friday from 10am to 5pm, with mall stores open until 8 or 9pm. Most shops are open similar hours on Saturday, and many also open on Sunday afternoon during the summer. Winter hours tend to be more limited.

After the high-rolling 1980s, during which art markets around the country soared, came the penny-pinching 1990s. Many galleries in Santa Fe were forced to shut their doors. Those that remain tend to specialize in particular types of art, a refinement process that has improved the gallery scene here. Still, some worry that the lack of serious art buyers in the area leads to fewer good galleries and more T-shirt and trinket stores. The Plaza has its share of those, but still has a good number of serious galleries, appealing to those buyers whose interests run to accessible art—Southwestern landscapes and the like. On Canyon Road, the art is often more experimental and more diverse, from contemporary sculpture to eastern European portraiture.

THE TOP GALLERIES
CONTEMPORARY ART

Adieb Khadoure Fine Art. 610 Canyon Rd. ☎ **505/820-2666.**

This is a working artists' studio featuring contemporary artists Jeff Uffelman and Hal Larsen and Santa Fe artist Phyllis Kapp. Their works are shown in the gallery daily from 10am to 6pm, and Adieb Khadoure also sells elegant rugs, furniture, and pottery from around the world.

Canyon Road Contemporary Art. 403 Canyon Rd. ☎ **505/983-0433.**

This gallery represents some of the finest emerging U.S. contemporary artists as well as internationally known artists. You'll find figurative, landscape, and abstract paintings, as well as raku pottery.

✪ **LewAllen Contemporary.** 129 W. Palace Ave. ☎ **505/988-8997.**

This is one of my favorite galleries. You'll find bizarre and beautiful contemporary works in a range of mediums from granite to clay to twigs. There are always exciting works on canvas as well.

Hahn Ross Gallery. 409 Canyon Rd. ☎ **505/984-8434.**

Owner Tom Ross, a children's book illustrator, specializes in representing artists who create colorful, fantasy-oriented works. I'm especially fond of the wild party scenes by Susan Contreras. Check out the new sculpture garden here.

La Mesa of Santa Fe. 225 Canyon Rd. ☎ **505/984-1688.**

Step into this gallery and let your senses dance. Dramatically colored ceramic plates, bowls and other kitchen items fill one room. Contemporary Kachinas by Gregory Lomayesva—a real buy—line the walls, accented by steel lamps and rag rugs. An adventure.

Leslie Muth Gallery. 131 W. Palace Ave. ☎ **505/989-4620.**

Here you'll find "Outsider Art," wild works made by untrained artists in a bizarre variety of media, from sculptures fashioned from pop bottle lids to portraits painted on flattened beer cans. Much of it is extraordinary and affordable.

✪ **Shidoni Foundry, Gallery, and Sculpture Gardens.** Bishop's Lodge Rd. Tesuque. ☎ **505/988-8001.**

Shidoni Foundry is one of the area's most exciting spots for sculptors and sculpture enthusiasts. At the foundry visitors may take a tour through the facilities to view casting processes. In addition, there is a 5,000-square-foot contemporary gallery, a bronze gallery, and a wonderful sculpture garden.

NATIVE AMERICAN & OTHER INDIGENOUS ART

Frank Howell Gallery. 103 Washington Ave. ☎ **505/984-1074.**

If you've never seen the wonderful illustrative hand of (sadly, the late) Frank Howell, you'll want to visit this gallery. You'll find a variety of contemporary American and American Indian art. There's sculpture by award-winner Tim Nicola, as well as fine art, jewelry, and graphics.

Glenn Green Galleries. 50 E. San Francisco St. ☎ **505/988-4168.**

This gallery, which maintains exclusive representation for Allan Houser's bronze and stone sculptures, also exhibits paintings, prints, photographs, and jewelry by other important artists.

✪ **Joshua Baer & Company.** 116½ E. Palace Ave. ☎ **505/988-8944.**

This is a great place to explore. You'll find 19th-century Navajo blankets, pottery, jewelry, and primitive art from around the world.

Maslak-Mcleod. 225 E. De Vargas. ☎ **505/820-6389.**

Enter a world of strange creatures from the north in this gallery that specializes in Inuit and other native Canadian art. Here you'll find seals carved from bone and native myths emerging from stone.

✪ **Morning Star Gallery.** 513 Canyon Rd. ☎ **505/982-8187.**

This is one of my favorite places to browse. Throughout the rambling gallery are American Indian art masterpieces elegantly displayed. You'll see a broad range of works, from late 19th-century Navajo blankets to 1920s Zuni needlepoint jewelry.

✪ **Ortega's On the Plaza.** 101 W. San Francisco St. ☎ **800/874-9297** or 505/988-1866.

A hearty shopper could spend hours here, perusing inventive turquoise and silver jewelry and especially fine strung beadwork, as well as rugs and pottery. In an adjacent room is a wide array of clothing, all with a hip Southwestern flair.

PHOTOGRAPHY

Andrew Smith Gallery. 203 W. San Francisco St. ☎ **505/984-1234.**

I'm always amazed when I enter this gallery and see works I've seen reprinted in major magazines for years. There they are, photographic prints, large and beautiful, hanging on the wall. Here you'll see famous works by Edward Curtis, Eliot Porter, Ansel Adams, Annie Leibovitz, and others.

Photo-eye Gallery. 370 Garcia St. ☎ **505/988-5152.**

You're bound to be surprised each time you step into this new gallery a few blocks off Canyon Road. Dealing in contemporary photography, the gallery represents 40 renowned, as well as emerging, artists. The company has also taken on the Platinum Gallery collection, from the notable Santa Fe gallery that closed in 1996.

SPANISH & HISPANIC ART

Montez Gallery. Sena Plaza Courtyard, 125 E. Palace Ave., Ste. 33. ☎ **505/982-1828.**

This shop is rich with Hispanic art, decorations, and furnishings such as *santos* (saints), *retablos* (paintings), *bultos* (sculptures), and *trasteros* (armoires).

Santos of New Mexico. 2712 Paseo de Tularosa. ☎ **505/473-7941.**

Here you'll find the work of award-winning *Santero* Charles M. Carillo: traditional New Mexican *santos* crafted out of cottonwood root and decorated with homemade pigments, as well as hand-adzed panels. By appointment only.

Traditional Art. Altermann & Morris Galleries, 225 Canyon Rd. ☎ **505/983-1590.**

This is a well of interesting traditional art, mostly 19th- and 20th-century American paintings and sculpture. The gallery represents Remington and Russell, in addition to Taos founders, Santa Fe artists, and members of the Cowboy Artists of America and National Academy of Western Art. Stroll through the sculpture garden and meet whimsical bronzes of children and dogs.

✪ **Gerald Peters Gallery.** 1011 Paseo de Peralta (P.O. Box 908). ☎ **505/988-8961.**

By fall 1998, Gerald Peters plans to be moved into a new two-story Pueblo-style building. The works displayed here are so fine you'll feel as though you're in a

museum. You'll find 19th- and 20th-century American painting and sculpture, featuring art of Georgia O'Keeffe, William Wegman, and the founders of the Santa Fe
and Taos artist colonies.

The Mayans Gallery Ltd. 601 Canyon Rd. ☎ **505/983-8068.** www.artnet.com/
mayans.html. E-mail: arte2@aol.com.

Established in 1977, this is one of the oldest galleries in Santa Fe; you'll find 20th-
century American and Latin American paintings, photography, prints, and sculpture.

✪ **Nedra Matteucci Galleries.** 1075 Paseo de Peralta. ☎ **505/982-4631.**

As you approach this gallery, note the elaborately crafted stone and adobe wall that
surrounds it, merely a taste of what's to come. The gallery specializes in 19th- and
20th-century American art. Inside you'll find a lot of high-ticket works such as
those of early Taos and Santa Fe painters, as well as classic American impressionism,
historical Western modernism, and contemporary Southwestern landscapes and
sculpture, including monumental pieces displayed in the sculpture garden.

✪ **Owings-Dewey Fine Art.** 76 E. San Francisco St., upstairs. ☎ **505/982-6244.**

These are treasure-filled rooms. You'll find 19th- and 20th-century American painting
and sculpture including works by Georgia O'Keeffe, Robert Henri, Maynard Dixon,
Fremont Ellis, and Andrew Dasburg, as well as antique works such as Spanish colonial
retablos, bultos, and tinwork. Don't miss the Day of the Dead exhibition around
Halloween.

MORE SHOPPING A TO Z
ANTIQUES
El Paso Import Company. 418 Sandoval St. ☎ **505/982-5698.**

Whenever I'm in the vicinity of this shop, I always browse through. It's packed, and
I mean packed, with colorful, weathered colonial and ranchero furniture. The home
furnishings and folk art here are imported from Mexico and have a primitive feel.

Jackalope. 2820 Cerrillos Rd. ☎ **505/471-8539.**

Spread over 7 acres of land, this is a wild place to spend a morning browsing through
exotic furnishings from India and Mexico, as well as imported textiles, pottery,
jewelry, and clothing. A great place to find gifts.

BELTS
Caballo. 727 Canyon Rd. ☎ **505/984-0971.**

The craftspeople at Caballo fashion "one of a kind, one at a time" custom-made belts.
Everything is hand-tooled, hand-carved, and hand-stamped. The remarkable buckles
are themselves worthy of special attention. This shop merits a stop.

BOOKS
Collected Works Bookstore. 208-B W. San Francisco St. ☎ **505/988-4226.**

This is a good downtown book source, with a carefully chosen selection of books up
front, in case you're not sure what you want, and shelves of Southwest, travel, nature,
and other books.

Horizons—The Discovery Store. 328 S. Guadalupe St. ☎ **505/983-1554.**

Here you'll find adult and children's books, science-oriented games and toys,
telescopes, binoculars, and a variety of unusual educational items. I always find
interesting gifts for my little nieces in this store.

Nicholas Potter, Bookseller. 211 E. Palace Ave. ☎ **505/983-5434.**

This store handles rare and used hardcover books, and sells tickets to local events.

CRAFTS

Davis Mather Folk Art Gallery. 141 Lincoln Ave. ☎ **505/983-1660.**

This small shop is a wild animal adventure. You'll find New Mexican animal wood carvings in shapes of lions, tigers, bears, and even chickens, as well as other folk and Hispanic arts.

Gallery 10. 225 Canyon Rd. ☎ **505/983-9707.**

"Important art by native peoples" is how this gallery dubs its offerings, And they're right. This is definitely museum-quality Native American pottery, weavings, basketry, and contemporary paintings and photography. My favorite potter, Tammy Garcia, has work here when she's not sold out of it.

✪ **Nambe Foundry Outlets.** 924 Paseo de Peralta (at Canyon Rd.). ☎ **505/988-5528.**

Here you'll find cooking, serving, and decorating pieces, fashioned from an exquisite sand-cast and handcrafted alloy. Also available at their stores at 104 W. San Francisco St. (☎ **505/988-3574**), and 216A Paseo del Pueblo Norte (Yucca Plaza), Taos (☎ **505/758-8221**).

FASHIONS

Dewey Trading Company. 53 Old Santa Fe Trail. ☎ **505/983-5855.**

Look for Native American trade blankets and men's and women's apparel here.

Jane Smith Ltd. 550 Canyon Rd. ☎ **505/988-4775.**

This is the place for flashy Western-style clothing. You'll find boots with more colors on them than there are Crayolas and jackets made by Elvis's very own designer. There are also flamboyant takes on household goods such as bedding and furniture.

Judy's Unique Apparel. 714 Canyon Rd. ☎ **505/988-5746.**

Judy's has eclectic separates made locally or imported from around the globe. You'll find a wide variety of items here, many at surprisingly reasonable prices.

Origins. 135 W. San Francisco St. ☎ **505/988-2323.**

A little like a Guatemalan or Turkish marketplace, this store is packed with wearable art, folk art, and work of local designers. Look for good buys on ethnic jewelry. Throughout the summer there are trunk shows, with a chance to meet the artists.

Overland Sheepskin Company. 217 Galisteo St. ☎ **505/983-4727.**

The rich smell of leather will draw you in the door, and possibly hold onto you until you purchase a coat, blazer, hat, or other finely made leather item.

FOOD

The Chile Shop. 109 E. Water St. ☎ **505/983-6080.**

This store has too many cheap trinket items for me. But many find novelty items to take back home. You'll find everything from salsa to cornmeal and tortilla chips. The shop also stocks cookbooks and pottery items.

Cookworks. 322 S. Guadalupe St. ☎ **505/988-7676.**

For the chef or merely the wannabe, this is a fun place for browsing. You'll find inventive food products and cooking items spread across three shops. There's also gourmet food and cooking classes.

Coyote Cafe General Store. 132 W. Water St. ☎ **505/982-2454.**

This store is an adjunct to one of Santa Fe's most popular restaurants. The big thing here is the enormous selection of hot sauces; however, you can also get a wide variety of Southwestern food items, T-shirts, and aprons.

Señor Murphy Candy Maker. 100 E. San Francisco St. (La Fonda Hotel). ☎ **505/982-0461.**

This candy store is unlike any you'll find in other parts of the country—everything here is made with local ingredients. The chile piñon nut brittle is a taste sensation! Señor Murphy has another shop at 223 Canyon Rd. (☎ **505/983-9243**).

FURNITURE

Southwest Spanish Craftsmen. 328 S. Guadalupe St. ☎ **505/982-1767.**

The Spanish colonial and Spanish provincial furniture, doors, and home accessories in this store are a bit too elaborate for my tastes, but if you find yourself dreaming of carved wood, this is your place.

Taos Furniture. 1807 Second St. (P.O. Box 5555). ☎ **505/988-1229.**

Prices are a little better away from downtown at this shop where you'll find classic Southwestern furnishings handcrafted in solid Ponderosa pine, both contemporary and traditional.

GIFTS & SOUVENIRS

El Nicho. 227 Don Gaspar Ave. ☎ **505/984-2830.**

For the thrifty art shopper this is the place to be. Inside the funky Santa Fe village, you'll find handcrafted Navajo and Oaxacan folk art as well as carvings, jewelry, and other items by local artisans.

Thea. 612A Agua Fría St. ☎ **505/995-9618.**

This new shop is so rich and enticing that you won't want to leave. Owned by Svetlana Britt, an exotic Russian woman, it features candles, scents, and aromatherapy. These are excellent gift items, colorfully and elaborately packaged. Named for the goddess of light, the whole store has a luminous quality.

JEWELRY

Packards. 61 Old Santa Fe Trail. ☎ **505/983-9241.**

Opened by a notable trader, Al Packard, and later sold to new owners, this store on the Plaza is worth checking out to see some of the best jewelry available. You'll also find exquisite rugs and pottery.

Tresa Vorenberg Goldsmiths. 656 Canyon Rd. ☎ **505/988-7215.**

You'll find some wildly imaginative designs in this jewelry store where more than 30 artisans are represented. All items are handcrafted and custom commissions are welcomed.

NATURAL ART

Mineral & Fossil Gallery of Santa Fe. 127 W. San Francisco St. ☎ **800/762-9777** or 505/984-1682.

You'll find ancient artwork here, from fossils to geodes in all sizes and shapes. There's also natural mineral jewelry and decorative items for the home, including lamps, wall clocks, furniture, art glass, and carvings. Mineral & Fossil also has galleries in Scottsdale, Sedona, and Denver.

✪ **Stone Forest.** 213 S. St. Francis Dr. ☎ **888/682-2987** or 505/986-8883.

A stroll through this gallery's sculpture garden is a centering and enlivening experience. Each year proprietor Michael Zimber travels to Asia and brings back innovative designs that he reshapes using his own artistic sense, creating amazing hand-crafted granite fountains, benches, bird baths, Japanese lanterns, and interior accents.

POTTERY & TILES

Artesanos Imports Company. 222 Galisteo St. ☎ **505/983-1743** or 505/982-0860.

This is like a trip south of the border, with all the scents and colors you'd expect on such a journey. You'll find a wide selection of Talavera tile and pottery, as well as light fixtures and many other accessories for the home. There's even an outdoor market where you can buy fountains and chile ristras.

Santa Fe Pottery. 323 S. Guadalupe St. ☎ **505/989-3363.**

The work of more than 50 master potters from New Mexico and the Southwest is on display here. You'll find everything from mugs to lamps.

RUGS

Seret & Sons Rugs, Furnishings, and Architectural Pieces. 149 E. Alameda St. (☎ **505/988-9151**) and 232 Galisteo St. (☎ **505/983-5008**).

If you're like me and find Middle Eastern decor irresistible, you need to wander through either of these shops. You'll find kilims and Persian and Turkish rugs, as well as some of the Moorish-style ancient doors and furnishings that you see around Santa Fe.

WINE & BEER

Kokoman Circus. 301 Garfield St. ☎ **505/983-7770.**

Specialty wine, beer, and gourmet food abounds at this new shop/cafe not far from some of the close-to-town hotels. Beware: The deli has delicious, but *expensive* food.

MALLS & MARKETS

De Vargas Center Mall. N. Guadalupe St. and Paseo de Peralta. ☎ **505/982-2655.**

There are more than 55 merchants and restaurants in this mall just northwest of downtown. This is Santa Fe's small, struggling mall. Though there are fewer shops than Villa Linda, this is where I shop because I don't tend to get the mall phobia I get in the more massive places. Hours are Monday through Thursday from 10am to 7pm, Friday from 10am to 9pm (may change to earlier), Saturday from 10am to 6pm, and Sunday from noon to 5pm.

Farmers' Market. 500 Montezuma St, in the rail yard adjacent to Sanbusco Market Center. ☎ **505/983-4098.**

Every Saturday and Tuesday from 7am to noon, you'll find a farmers' market with everything from fruit, vegetables, and flowers to cheese, cider, and salsa. Great local treats!

Sanbusco Market Center. 500 Montezuma St. ☎ **505/989-9390.**

Unique shops and restaurants occupy this remodeled warehouse near the old Santa Fe Railroad Yard. Though most of the shops in this little mall are overpriced, it's a fun place to window-shop. There's a farmers' market in the adjacent rail yard next to the Santa Fe Clay building, open from 7am to noon on Tuesday and Saturday in the summer.

Trader Jack's Flea Market. U.S. 84/285 (about 8 miles north of Santa Fe). No phone.

If you're a flea-market hound, you'll be happy to find Trader Jack's. More than 500 vendors here sell everything from used cowboy boots (you might find some real beauties) to clothing, jewelry, books, and furniture, all against a big northern New Mexico view. The flea market is open from mid-April to late November on Friday, Saturday, and Sunday.

Villa Linda Mall. 4250 Cerrillos Rd. (at Rodeo Rd.). ☎ **505/473-4253.**

Santa Fe's largest mall (including department stores) is near the southwestern city limits, not far from the I-25 on-ramp. If you're from a major city, you'll probably find shopping here very provincial. Anchors include JCPenney, Sears, Dillard's, and Mervyn's. Hours are Monday through Saturday from 10am to 9pm, Sunday from noon to 6pm.

9 Santa Fe After Dark

Santa Fe is a city committed to the arts. Its night scene is dominated by highbrow cultural events, beginning with the world-famous Santa Fe Opera; the club and popular music scene run a distant second.

Complete information on all major cultural events can be obtained from the **Santa Fe Convention and Visitors Bureau** (☎ **800/777-CITY** or 505/984-6760) or from the **City of Santa Fe Arts Commission** (☎ **505/984-6707**). Current listings are published each Friday in the "Pasatiempo" section of *The New Mexican,* the city's daily newspaper, and in the *Santa Fe Reporter,* published every Wednesday.

Nicholas Potter, Bookseller, 211 E. Palace Ave. (☎ **505/983-5434**), carries tickets to select events. You can also order by phone from Ticketmaster (☎ **505/ 842-5387** for information, or 505/884-0999 to order). Discount tickets may be available on the night of a performance; the opera, for example, offers standing-room tickets on the day of the performance. Sales start at 10am.

A variety of free concerts, lectures, and other events are presented in the summer, cosponsored by the City of Santa Fe and the Chamber of Commerce. The **El Corazón de Santa Fe** ("the heart of Santa Fe") program has featured Saturday night musical and cultural events on the Plaza, and the city hopes to continue the program, though with a new mayoral administration there was no confirmation of plans for 1999.

The **Santa Fe Summer Concert Series** (☎ **505/256-1777**), at the Paolo Soleri Outdoor Amphitheatre on the campus of the Santa Fe Indian School (Cerrillos Road), has brought such name performers as B. B. King, Frank Zappa, and Kenny Loggins to the city. More than two dozen concerts and special events are scheduled each summer.

Note: Many companies noted here perform at locations other than their listed addresses, so check the site of the performance you plan to attend.

THE PERFORMING ARTS

No fewer than 24 performing-arts groups flourish in this city of 60,000. Many of them perform year-round, but others are seasonal. The acclaimed Santa Fe Opera, for instance, has just a 2-month summer season, in July and August.

OPERA & CLASSICAL MUSIC

✪ **Santa Fe Opera.** P.O. Box 2408, Santa Fe, NM 87504-2408. ☎ **800/280-4654,** or 505/986-5900 for tickets. Tickets $20–$110 Mon–Thurs; $28–$118 Fri–Sat. Wheelchair seating. $14 Mon–Thurs; $20 Fri–Sat. Standing room (sold on day of performance beginning at 10am) $6 Mon–Thurs; $8 Fri–Sat; $15 Opening Night Gala. Backstage tours: First Mon in July to last Fri in Aug, Mon–Sat at 1pm; $6 adults, free for children 15 and under.

Opera fans are talking about this new theater just completed for the 1998 season. Like the old one it's located on a wooded hilltop 7 miles north of the city off U.S. 84/285, and is still partially open-air, now with open sides only (the original theater had a partially open ceiling). A controversial structure, this new one replaced the original built in 1968, known for its sweeping curves attuned to the contour of the surrounding terrain. At night, the lights of Los Alamos could be seen in the distance under clear skies. Planners assure that such novelties are found in the new structure as well.

Many rank the Santa Fe Opera second only to the Metropolitan Opera of New York as the finest company in the United States today. Established in 1957 by John Crosby, still the opera's artistic director, it consistently attracts famed conductors, directors, and singers (the list has included Igor Stravinsky). At the height of the season the company is 500 strong, including the skilled craftspeople and designers who work on the sets. The opera company is noted for its performances of the classics, little-known works by classical European composers, and American premieres of 20th-century works.

The 9-week, 40-performance opera season runs from early June through late August. In 1999, you can see such classics as *Carmen* by Bizet and *Idomeneo* by Mozart. Usually there is a Strauss opera; in 1999 it will be *Ariadne Auf Naxos*. And for the less traditional-minded, there's *Countess Maritza* by Kalman and *Dialogues of the Carmelites* by Poulenc. All performances begin at 9pm, until the last 2 weeks of the season when performances begin at 8:30pm.

A gift shop has been added, as well as additional parking. The entire theater is now wheelchair accessible.

ORCHESTRAL & CHAMBER MUSIC

Santa Fe Pro Musica Chamber Orchestra & Ensemble. 320 Galisteo, Ste. 502 (P.O. Box 2091), Santa Fe, NM 87504-2091. ☎ **505/988-4640.** Tickets $15–$35.

This chamber ensemble performs everything from Bach to Vivaldi to contemporary masters. During Holy Week the Santa Fe Pro Musica presents its annual Baroque Festival Concert. Christmas brings candlelight chamber ensemble concerts. Pro Musica's season runs October through April.

✪ **Santa Fe Symphony Orchestra and Chorus.** P.O. Box 9692, Santa Fe, NM 87504. ☎ **800/480-1319** or 505/983-1414. Tickets $8–$35 (six seating categories).

This 60-piece professional symphony orchestra has grown rapidly in stature since its founding in 1984. Matinee and evening performances of classical and popular works are presented in a subscription series at Sweeney Center (Grant Avenue at Marcy Street) from August to May. There's a preconcert lecture before each performance. During the spring there are music festivals (call for details).

Serenata of Santa Fe. P.O. Box 8410, Santa Fe, NM 87504. ☎ **505/989-7988.** Tickets $12 general admission, $15 reserved seats.

This professional chamber-music group specializes in bringing lesser-known works of the masters to the concert stage. Concerts are presented from September to May. Call the number above for location, dates, and details.

CHORAL GROUPS

Desert Chorale. 219 Shelby St. (P.O. Box 2813), Santa Fe, NM 87504. ☎ **800/905-3315** (ProTix) or 505/988-7505. Tickets $22–$35 adults, half price for students.

This 24- to 30-member vocal ensemble, New Mexico's only professional choral group, recruits members from all over the country. It's nationally recognized for its eclectic blend of both Renaissance melodies and modern avant-garde compositions. During summer months the chorale performs classic concerts at various locations, including the Loretto Chapel, as well as smaller cameo concerts at more intimate settings throughout Santa Fe and Albuquerque. The chorale also performs a popular series of Christmas concerts during December. Most concerts begin at 8pm (3 or 6pm on Sunday).

Sangre de Cristo Chorale. P.O. Box 4462, Santa Fe, NM 87502. ☎ **505/662-9717.** Tickets $10–$40 depending on the season.

This 34-member ensemble has a repertoire ranging from classical, baroque, and Renaissance works to more recent folk music and spirituals, much of it presented a cappella. The group gives concerts in Santa Fe, Los Alamos, and Albuquerque. The Christmas dinner concerts are extremely popular.

Santa Fe Women's Ensemble. 424 Kathryn Place, Santa Fe, NM 87501. ☎ **505/983-2137.** Tickets $13 and $16, students $8 and $12.

This choral group of 12 semiprofessional singers offers classical works sung a cappella as well as with varied instrumental accompaniment during April and December. Both the "Spring Offering" (in mid-April) and the "Christmas Offering" concerts (in mid-December) are held in the Loretto Chapel (Old Santa Fe Trail at Water Street). Call for tickets.

MUSIC FESTIVALS & CONCERT SERIES

Santa Fe Chamber Music Festival. 239 Johnson St., Ste. B (P.O. Box 853), Santa Fe, NM 87504. ☎ **505/983-2075,** or 505/982-1890 for the box office (after June 22). Tickets $15–$40.

This festival brings an extraordinary group of international artists to Santa Fe every summer. Its 6-week season of some 50 concerts runs from mid-July through mid-August and is held in the beautiful St. Francis Auditorium. Each festival season features chamber-music masterpieces, new music by a composer in residence, jazz, free youth concerts, preconcert lectures, and open rehearsals. Performances are Monday, Tuesday, Thursday, and Friday at 8pm; Saturday at various evening times; and Sunday at 6pm. Open rehearsals, youth concerts, and preconcert lectures are free to the public.

Santa Fe Concert Association. P.O. Box 4626, Santa Fe, NM 87502. ☎ **800/905-3315** (ProTix), or 505/984-8759 for tickets. Tickets $15–$65.

Founded in 1938, the oldest musical organization in northern New Mexico has a September-to-May season that includes approximately 15 annual events. Among them are a distinguished artists' series featuring renowned instrumental and vocal soloists and chamber ensembles, special Christmas Eve and New Year's Eve concerts, and sponsored performances by local artists. All performances are held at the St. Francis Auditorium.

THEATER COMPANIES

Greer Garson Theater Center. College of Santa Fe, 1600 St. Michael's Dr. ☎ **505/473-6511.** Tickets $8–$17 adults and $5 students ($22–$35 for summer season Santa Fe Stages performances; see below for details).

In this graceful, intimate theater, the college's Performing Arts Department produces four plays annually, with five presentations of each, given between October and May. Usually the season consists of a comedy, a drama, a musical, and a classic. The college also sponsors studio productions and 10 contemporary music concerts.

✪ **Santa Fe Playhouse.** 142 E. De Vargas St., Santa Fe, NM 87501. ☎ **505/988-4262.** Tickets $10 adults, $8 students and seniors; on Sun people are asked to "pay what you wish."

Founded in the 1920s, this is the oldest extant theater group in New Mexico. Still performing in a historic adobe theater in the Barrio de Analco, it attracts thousands for its dramas, avant-garde theater, and musical comedy. Its popular one-act melodramas call on the public to boo the sneering villain and swoon for the damsel in distress.

✪ **Santa Fe Stages.** 105 E. Marcy St., Ste. 107. ☎ **505/982-6683.** Tickets $25–$40.

Most locals couldn't imagine international theater and dance troupes coming to Santa Fe, but it happened beginning in 1994 when artistic director Martin Platt founded this theater. He recently left Santa Fe for London to expand a theater business of which he is part owner, and locals hope the offerings will continue to be outstanding here. Staged at two theaters on the College of Santa Fe campus, and at times at the St. Francis Auditorium downtown, the gatherings are small and intimate, adding to the audience's enjoyment.

Shakespeare In Santa Fe. 355 E. Palace Ave. (box office only), Santa Fe, NM 87501. ☎ **505/982-2910.** Reserved seating is available for various prices; lawn and surrounding area is available with a suggested donation of $5.

Every Friday, Saturday, and Sunday during July and August, in the library courtyard of St. John's College (southeast of downtown, off Camino del Monte Sol), Shakespeare in Santa Fe presents Shakespeare in the Park. Sunset picnic suppers are sold by Wild Oats Market, or you can bring your own.

DANCE COMPANIES

✪ **María Benitez Teatro Flamenco.** Institute for Spanish Arts, P.O. Box 8418, Santa Fe, NM 87501. ☎ **800/905-3315,** or 505/982-1237 for tickets. Tickets $18–$29.50 (subject to change).

This is a performance you won't want to miss. True flamenco is one of the most thrilling of dance forms, displaying the inner spirit and verve of the Gypsies of Spanish Andalusia, and María Benitez, trained in Spain, is a fabulous performer. The Benitez Company's "Estampa Flamenca" summer series is performed nightly except Tuesday from July through early September. With a recent remodel, the María Benitez Theater at the Radisson Hotel is modern and showy.

MAJOR CONCERT HALLS & ALL-PURPOSE AUDITORIUMS

Paolo Soleri Amphitheatre. At the Santa Fe Indian School, 1501 Cerrillos Rd. ☎ **505/989-6318.** Call for tickets or contact Ticketmaster at 505/884-0999.

I'm not much of a rock concert-goer because they're always too loud, smoky, and crowded for me. That's why this is practically the only place I'll go, and it's an incredible experience. Out under the stars, this amphitheater offers plenty of room, excellent views of the stage from any seat, and good acoustics. Concerts are presented during summer months. In recent years the facility has attracted such big-name acts as Joan Armatrading, the Grateful Dead, B. B. King, Kenny Loggins, Anne Murray, Suzanne Vega, Ziggy Marley, Lyle Lovett, Dave Matthews, Alan Parsons Project, the Reggae Sunsplash, and, my favorite, Big Head Todd and the Monsters. For information on scheduled performers while you're in Santa Fe, contact Big River Corporation, P.O. Box 8036, Albuquerque, NM 87198 (☎ **505/256-1777**). Be sure to take a blanket to sit on, as the bench-type seats are made of poured concrete.

Plan B Evolving Arts. 1050 Old Pecos Trail. ☎ **505/982-1338.** Tickets for films $6.

Plan B Evolving Arts presents the work of internationally, nationally, and regionally known contemporary artists in art exhibitions, dance, new music concerts, poetry readings, performance-art events, theater, and video screenings. The Cinématique screens films from around the world nightly, with special series presented regularly. Plan B also runs the Warehouse/Teen Project a unique program designed to encourage creativity, individuality, and free expression by giving teens a safe, free place to create programs and events, including workshops, art exhibitions, a radio show and publication, theater ensemble, cafe (with open mike opportunities), and concerts featuring local teen bands. Plan B's galleries are open daily noon to 7pm.

✪ **St. Francis Auditorium.** In the Museum of Fine Arts, Lincoln and Palace aves. ☎ **505/ 827-4455.** Ticket prices vary; see above for specific performing-arts companies.

This atmospheric music hall, patterned after the interiors of traditional Hispanic mission churches, is noted for its excellent acoustics. The hall hosts a wide variety of musical events, including the Santa Fe Chamber Music Festival in July and August. The Santa Fe Symphony Festival Series, the Santa Fe Concert Association, the Santa Fe Women's Ensemble, and various other programs are also held here.

Sweeney Convention Center. 201 W. Marcy St. ☎ **800/777-2489** or 505/984-6760. Tickets $10–$30, depending on seating and performances. Tickets are never sold at Sweeney Convention Center; event sponsors handle ticket sales.

Santa Fe's largest indoor arena hosts a wide variety of trade expositions and other events during the year. It's also the home of the Santa Fe Symphony Orchestra and the New Mexico Symphony Orchestra's annual Santa Fe Series.

THE CLUB & MUSIC SCENE
In addition to the clubs and bars listed below, there are a number of hotels whose bars and lounges feature some type of entertainment. (See "Where to Stay," above.)

COUNTRY, JAZZ & FOLK
Cowgirl Hall of Fame. 319 S Guadalupe St. ☎ **505/982-2565.** No cover for music in the main restaurant, except on Tues when it's $2. Other performances $2–$8.

It's difficult to categorize what goes on in this bar and restaurant, but there's live entertainment nightly. Some nights there's blues guitar, others there's comedy, and others there's flamenco music and dance. You might also find something called cowboy poetry or an acoustic open microphone night. In the summer this is a great place to sit under the stars and listen to music or see some fun entertainment inside.

✪ **El Farol.** 808 Canyon Rd. ☎ **505/983-9912.** Cover $4–$10.

The original neighborhood bar of the Canyon Road artists' quarter (its name means "the lantern") is the place to head for local ambience. Its low ceilings and dark brown walls are home to Santa Fe's largest and most unusual selection of *tapas* (bar snacks and appetizers). Jazz, folk, and ethnic musicians, some of national note, perform most nights.

Fiesta Lounge. In La Fonda Hotel, 110 E. San Francisco St. ☎ **505/982-5511.** No cover.

This lively lobby bar offers cocktails and live entertainment nightly.

Rodeo Nites. 2911 Cerrillos Rd. ☎ **505/473-4138.** No cover Mon–Wed, $2.50 Thurs, $3 Fri–Sat. Closed Sun.

There's live country dance music nightly at this popular club.

ROCK & DISCO
Catamount Bar and Grille. 125 E. Water St. ☎ **505/988-7222.**

The postcollege crowd hangs out at this bar where there's live rock and blues music on weekends and some weeknights.

OneTwoFive. 125 N. Guadalupe St. ☎ **505/988-4374.** Friday and Saturday nights from 9pm–2am. Cover varies but is generally $5.

This place is doing its best to present Santa Fe with a club scene. The music is electronica and hip-hop, played to a crowd that varies greatly. Mostly this is a gay and lesbian club.

The Paramount. 331 Sandoval. ☎ **505/982-8999.** Nightly from 4pm–2am. Cover varies, but is generally $5.

Here you'll find a variety of music and dancing from country and western to salsa to disco. It's a brand-new club, so the jury's still out as to how interesting the scene is.

THE BAR SCENE
Evangelo's. 200 W. San Francisco St. ☎ **505/982-9014.** No cover.

A popular downtown hang-out, this bar can get raucous at times. It's an interesting place, with tropical decor and a mahogany bar. More than 250 varieties of imported beer are available, and pool tables are an added attraction. On Friday and Saturday night starting at 9pm, live bands play; some nights there's jazz, others rock, and others reggae. Evangelo's is extremely popular with the local crowd. You'll find your share of businesspeople, artists, and even bikers here. Open daily from noon until 1 or 2am.

Dana's After Dark. 222 N. Guadalupe. ☎ **505/982-5225.** No cover.

This after-hours club caters to late-night lesbian and gay crowds, but it's such a cool place I'd recommend it for anyone. Opened in spring 1997, it's in an old adobe house that has been painted inside with wild colors like summer squash orange and lime green. Open nightly from 6:30pm to "late," which could mean anywhere from 1am to 4am (in summer, usually until 4am), it's the place for late-night food, fine coffee, and carefully prepared desserts. You can listen to a variety of types of music from ultralounge music to cha-cha and mambo. Or you can go into the music room and play piano or conga drums, or into the game room and play board games from the '60s. No alcoholic beverages are served.

Vanessie of Santa Fe. 434 W. San Francisco St. ☎ **505/982-9966.** No cover.

This is unquestionably Santa Fe's most popular piano bar. The talented Doug Montgomery and Charles Tichenor have a loyal local following. Their repertoire ranges from Bach to Billy Joel, Gershwin to Barry Manilow. They play nightly from 8pm until closing, which could be from midnight to 2am. There's an extra microphone, so if you're daring, you can stand up and accompany the piano and vocals (though this is *not* a Karaoke scene). National celebrities have even joined in, including Harry Connick Jr. Vanessie's offers a great bar menu.

10 Touring the Pueblos Around Santa Fe

Of the eight northern pueblos, Tesuque, Pojoaque, Nambe, San Ildefonso, San Juan, and Santa Clara are within about 30 miles of Santa Fe. Picuris (San Lorenzo) is on the High Road to Taos (see "Taking the High Road to Taos," below), and Taos Pueblo is just outside the town of Taos.

The six pueblos described in this section can easily be visited in a single day's round-trip from Santa Fe, though I suggest visiting just those few that really give a feel of the ancient lifestyle. Plan to focus most of your attention on San Juan, Santa Clara, and San Ildefonso, including San Juan's arts cooperative, Santa Clara's Puye cliff dwellings, and San Ildefonso's broad plaza. If you're in the area at a time when you can catch certain rituals, that's when to see some of the others.

Remember that certain **rules of etiquette** should be observed in visiting the pueblos. These are personal dwellings and/or important historic sites, and must be respected as such. Don't climb on the buildings or peek into doors or windows. Don't enter sacred grounds, such as cemeteries and kivas. If you attend a dance or ceremony, remain silent while it is taking place and refrain from applause when it's over. Many pueblos prohibit photography or sketches; others require you to pay a fee for a permit. If you don't respect the privacy of the Native Americans who live at the pueblo, you'll be asked to leave.

TESUQUE PUEBLO

Tesuque (Te-*soo*-keh) Pueblo is located about 9 miles north of Santa Fe on U.S. 84/285. You will know that you are approaching the pueblo when you see a carpet outlet store. If you're driving north and you get to the unusual Camel Rock and a large roadside casino, you've missed the entrance. The 400 pueblo dwellers at Tesuque are faithful to their traditional religion, rituals, and ceremonies. Excavations confirm that a pueblo has existed here at least since A.D. 1200; accordingly, this pueblo is now on the National Register of Historic Places. When you come to the welcome sign at the pueblo, turn right, go a block, and park on the right. You'll see the Plaza off to the left. There's not a lot to see; to the south are some very old homes with exposed adobe walls. There's a big open area where dances are held and the church, which is simple sculpted adobe with a small bell and wooden cross on top. Visitors are asked to remain in this area.

Some Tesuque women are skilled potters; Ignacia Duran's black-and-white and red micaceous pottery and Teresa Tapia's miniatures and pots with animal figures are especially noteworthy. The **San Diego Feast Day,** which may feature buffalo, deer, flag, or Comanche dances, is November 12.

The Tesuque Pueblo address is Route 5, Box 360-T, Santa Fe, NM 87501 (☎ **505/ 983-2667**). Admission to the pueblo is free; however, there is a $20 charge for still cameras; special permission is required for movie cameras, sketching, and painting. The pueblo is open daily from 9am to 5pm. Camel Rock Casino (☎ **505/984-8414**) is open daily 7am to 4am and has a snack bar on the premises.

POJOAQUE PUEBLO

About 6 miles farther north on U.S. 84/285, at the junction of NM 502, is Pojoaque (Po-*hwa*-keh). Though small (population 200) and without a definable village (more modern dwellings exist now), Pojoaque is important as a center for traveler services; in fact, *Pojoaque,* in its Tewa form, means "water-drinking place." The historical accounts of the Pojoaque people are sketchy, but we do know that in 1890 smallpox took its toll on the Pojoaque population, forcing most of the pueblo residents to abandon their village. Since the 1930s the population has gradually increased, and in 1990 a war chief and two war captains were appointed. Today visitors won't find much to look at, but the Poeh Center, operated by the pueblo, features a museum and crafts store. Indigenous pottery, embroidery, silver work, and beadwork are available for sale at the Pojoaque Pueblo Tourist Center.

You'll want to leave U.S. 84/285 and travel on the frontage road back to where the pueblo actually was. There you'll encounter lovely orchards and alfalfa fields backed by desert and mountains. A modern community center is located near the site of the old pueblo and church. On December 12, the annual feast day of **Our Lady of Guadalupe** features a bow-and-arrow or buffalo dance. Continue on this frontage road until you come to a fork, where the road turns to dirt. This little hidden route crosses the Nambe River, then meanders by orchards and through the village of Nambe. You'll want to get to the church at Nambe, which is where this road meets NM 503.

The Pueblo's address is Route 11, Box 71, Santa Fe, NM 87501 (☎ **505/455-2278**). Admission is free. Call for information about sketching and camera fees. The Pueblo is open every day during daylight hours.

NAMBE PUEBLO

If you're still on U.S. 84/285, continue north from Pojoaque about 3 miles until you come to NM 503; turn right and travel until you see the Bureau of Reclamation sign for Nambe Falls; turn right on NP 101. Approximately 2 miles farther is Nambe ("mound of earth in the corner"), a 700-year-old Tewa-speaking pueblo (population 450), with a solar-powered tribal headquarters, at the foot of the Sangre de Cristo Range. Only a few original pueblo buildings remain, including a large round kiva, used today in ceremonies. Pueblo artisans make woven belts, beadwork, and brown micaceous pottery. One of my favorite reasons for visiting this pueblo is to see the herd of 36 bison that roam on 179 acres set aside for them.

Nambe Falls make a stunning three-tier drop through a cleft in a rock face about 4 miles beyond the pueblo, tumbling into Nambe Reservoir. A recreational site at the reservoir offers fishing, boating (nonmotor boats only), hiking, camping, and picnicking. The **Waterfall Dances** on July 4 and the **Saint Francis of Assisi Feast Day** on October 4, which has an elk dance ceremony, are observed at the sacred falls.

The address is Route 1, Box 117-BB, Santa Fe, NM 87501 (☎ **505/455-2036,** or 505/455-2304 for the Ranger Station). Admission to the pueblo is free, but there is a $7 charge for still cameras, $10 for movie cameras, and $15 for sketching. At the recreational site, the charge for fishing is $10 per day for adults, $6 per day for children; for camping it is $10 per night. The pueblo is open daily from 8am to 5pm. The recreational site is open March, September, and October from 7am to 7pm, April and May from 7am to 8pm, and June through August from 6am to 8pm.

SAN ILDEFONSO PUEBLO

Pox Oge, as this pueblo is called in its own Tewa language, means "place where the water cuts down through," possibly named for the way the Rio Grande cuts through the mountains nearby. Turn left on NM 502 at Pojoaque, and drive about 6 miles to the turnoff. This pueblo has a broad, dusty plaza, with a kiva on one side, ancient dwellings on the other, and a church at the far end. It's nationally famous for its matte-finish black-on-black pottery, developed by tribeswoman María Martinez in the 1920s. One of the most-visited pueblos in northern New Mexico, San Ildefonso attracts more than 20,000 visitors a year.

The San Ildefonsos could best be described as rebellious, since they were one of the last pueblos to succumb to the reconquest spearheaded by Don Diego de Vargas in 1692. Within view of the pueblo is the volcanic Black Mesa, a symbol of their strength. Through the years each time San Ildefonso felt itself threatened by enemy forces the residents, along with members of other pueblos, would hide out up on the butte, returning to the valley only when starvation set in. Today a visit to the pueblo is valuable mainly in order to see or buy rich black pottery. A few shops surround the plaza, and there's the **San Ildefonso Pueblo Museum** tucked away in the governor's office beyond the plaza. I especially recommend visiting during ceremonial days. **San Ildefonso Feast Day** is January 23, and features the buffalo and Comanche dances in alternate years. **Corn Dances,** held in early September, commemorate a basic element in pueblo life, the importance of fertility in all creatures—humans as well as animals—and plants.

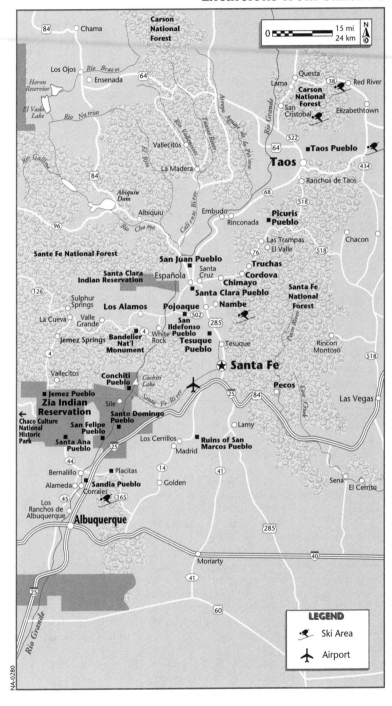

0 | 15 mi
24 km

N

LEGEND
Ski Area
✈ Airport

The pueblo has a 4½-acre fishing lake that is surrounded by bosk, open April through October. Picnicking is encouraged, though you may want to look at the sites before you decide to stay; some are nicer than others. Camping is not allowed.

The pueblo's address is Route 5, Box 315A, Santa Fe, NM 87501 (☎ 505/455-3549). The admission charge is $3 for a noncommercial vehicle and $10 for a commercial vehicle, plus 50¢ per passenger. The charge for using a still camera is $5; $15 for a video camera or sketching. If you plan to fish, the charge is $7 for adults, $3 for seniors and children under 12 years of age. The pueblo is open in the summer, daily from 8am to 5pm; call for weekend hours. In the winter, it is open Monday through Friday from 8am to 4:30pm. It is closed for major holidays and tribal events.

SAN JUAN PUEBLO

If you continue north on U.S. 84/285, you will reach the pueblo via NM 74, a mile off NM 68, about 4 miles north of Española.

The largest (population 1,950) and northernmost of the Tewa-speaking pueblos and headquarters of the Eight Northern Indian Pueblos Council, San Juan is located on the east side of the Rio Grande—opposite the 1598 site of San Gabriel, the first Spanish settlement west of the Mississippi River and the first capital of New Spain. In 1598, the Spanish, impressed with the openness and helpfulness of the people of San Juan, decided to establish a capital there (it was moved to Santa Fe 10 years later)—making San Juan Pueblo the first to be subjected to Spanish colonization. The Indians were generous, providing food, clothing, shelter, and fuel—they even helped sustain the settlement when its leader Conquistador Juan de Oñate became preoccupied with his search for gold and neglected the needs of his people. Unfortunately, the Spanish subjugation of the Indians left them virtual slaves, forced to provide the Spanish with corn, venison, cloth, and labor. They were compelled to participate in Spanish religious ceremonies and to abandon their own religious practices. Under no circumstances were Indian ceremonies allowed; those caught participating in them were punished. In 1676 several Indians were accused of sorcery and jailed in Santa Fe. Later they were led to the Plaza, where they were flogged or hanged. This despicable incident became a turning point in Indian-Spanish relations, generating an overwhelming feeling of rage in the Indian community. One of the accused, a San Juan Pueblo Indian named Po'Pay, became a leader in the Great Pueblo Revolt, which led to freedom from Spanish rule for 12 years.

The past and present cohabit here. Though Roman Catholics, members of the San Juan tribe still practice traditional religious rituals. Thus, two rectangular kivas flank the church in the main plaza, and *caciques* (pueblo priests) share power with civil authorities. The annual **San Juan Fiesta** is held June 23 and 24, and features buffalo and Comanche dances. Another annual ceremony is the **turtle dance** on December 26. The **matachine dance,** performed here Christmas day, vividly depicts the subjugation of the Native Americans by the Catholic Spaniards.

The address of the Pueblo is P.O. Box 1099, San Juan Pueblo, NM 87566 (☎ 505/852-4400). Admission is free. Photography or sketching may be allowed with prior permission from the governor's office. Call the pueblo number above to reach the governor's office. The charge for fishing is $8 for adults and $5 for children and seniors.

The **Eight Northern Indian Pueblos Council** (☎ 505/852-4265) is a sort of chamber of commerce and social-service agency.

A crafts shop, **Oke Oweenge Arts and Crafts Cooperative** (☎ 505/852-2372), specializes in local wares. This is a fine place to seek out San Juan's distinctive red pottery, a lustrous ceramic incised with traditional geometric symbols. Also displayed for sale are seed, turquoise, and silver jewelry; wood and stone carvings; indigenous clothing and weavings; embroidery; and paintings. Artisans often work on the premises and visitors can watch. The co-op is open Monday through Saturday from 9am to 5pm (but is closed San Juan Feast Day). **Sunrise Crafts,** another crafts shop, is located to the right of the co-op. There you'll find one-of-a-kind handcrafted pipes, beadwork, and burned and painted gourds.

Right on the main road that goes through the pueblo is the **Tewa Indian Restaurant,** serving traditional Pueblo chile stews, breads, blue-corn dishes, posole, teas, and desserts. It's open Monday through Friday from 9am to 2:30pm; closed holidays and feast days.

Fishing and picnicking are encouraged at the San Juan Tribal Lakes, open year-round. **Ohkay Casino** (☎ **505/747-0700**) offers tables games and slot machines, as well as live music every Friday night. It's open Monday through Thursday 6am to 2am and Friday through Sunday 24 hours.

SANTA CLARA PUEBLO

Close to Española (on NM 5), Santa Clara, with a population of about 1,600, is one of the largest pueblos, and one most special to me. I've spent a good bit of time here to write about the Santa Clara people. You'll see the village sprawling across the river basin near the beautiful Black Mesa, rows of tract homes surrounding an adobe central area. An incredible setting, the pueblo itself is not much to see; however a trip through it will give a real feel for the contemporary lives of these people. Though stories vary, the Santa Clarans teach their children that their ancestors once lived at Puye and migrated down to the river bottom.

At one time I wrote a story about a language program at Santa Clara. Artisan/elders were working with children to teach them their native Tewa language, on the brink of extinction because so many now speak English. These elder artists helped the children paint a mural depicting the Santa Clarans' migration from Puye in the 13th century. I've also written about noted potter Nancy Youngblood, who comes from a long line of famous potters, and now does alluring contemporary work.

One stunning sight here is the cemetery. Stop on the west side of the church and look over a 4-foot wall. It's a primitive site, with plain wooden crosses, as well as others adorned with plastic flowers. Within the village there are lots of little pottery and craft shops. If you write to the pueblo (address below) well in advance, you may be able to take one of the driving and walking tours offered Monday through Friday, including visits to the pueblo's historic church and artists' studios. Visitors can enter specified studios to watch artists making baskets and highly polished red-and-black pottery. Follow up your letter with a phone call.

There are corn and harvest dances on **Santa Clara Feast Day** (August 12); other special days include buffalo and deer dances (early February) and children's dances (December 28).

The famed **Puye Cliff Dwellings** (see below) are on the Santa Clara reservation.

The pueblo's address is P.O. Box 580, Española, NM 87532 (☎ **505/753-7326**). Admission is free. The charge for still cameras is $5; for movie cameras and sketching, the charge is $15. The pueblo is open every day during daylight hours; the visitor center is open Monday through Friday from 8am to 4:30pm.

PUYE CLIFF DWELLINGS

Well worth visiting, the Puye Cliff Dwellings offer a view of centuries of culture so well preserved you can almost hear ancient life clamoring around you. First you encounter dwellings believed to have been built around 1450. Above on a 200-foot tuft cliff face are dwellings dating from 1200. By 1540 this dwelling's population was at its height and Puye was the center for a number of villages of the Pajarito Plateau. Today, this settlement, which typifies Pajaritan culture in the placement of its houses and its symbolic decorations, is a series of rooms and caves reached by sturdy ladders and steps which visitors can climb up and down, clambering in and out of the homes. Petroglyphs are evident in many of the rocky cliff walls. Make your way to the 7,000-foot mesa top and you'll find on the cliff's edge ceremonial kivas as well as a labyrinth of dwellings representing four huge terraced community houses built around a court.

About 6 miles farther west is the **Santa Clara Canyon Recreational Area,** a sylvan setting for camping that is open year-round for picnicking, hiking, and fishing in ponds and Santa Clara Creek.

If you would like to visit the cliff dwellings, call the Santa Clara tribal offices at ☎ 505/753-7326. The admission is $5 for adults, $4 for children and seniors. The dwellings are open daily in the summer from 8am to 8pm; daily in the winter from 8am to 4:30pm.

11 A Side Trip to Pecos National Monument

About 15 miles east of Santa Fe, I-25 meanders through **Glorieta Pass,** site of an important Civil War skirmish. In March 1862, volunteers from Colorado and New Mexico, along with Fort Union regulars, defeated a Confederate force marching on Santa Fe, thereby turning the tide of Southern encroachment in the West.

Take NM 50 east to **Pecos,** a distance of about 7 miles. This quaint town, well off the beaten track since the interstate was constructed, is the site of a noted **Benedictine monastery.** About 26 miles north of here on NM 63 is the village of **Cowles,** gateway to the natural wonderland of the Pecos Wilderness. There are many camping, picnicking, and fishing locales en route.

Pecos National Historical Park (☎ 505/757-6414), about 2 miles south of the town of Pecos off NM 63, contains the ruins of a 15th-century pueblo and 17th- and 18th-century missions. Coronado mentioned Pecos Pueblo in 1540: "It is feared through the land," he wrote. With a population of about 2,000, the Native Americans farmed in irrigated fields and hunted wild game. Their pueblo had 660 rooms and many kivas. By 1620 Franciscan monks had established a church and convent. Military and natural disasters took their toll on the pueblo, and in 1838 the 20 surviving Pecos went to live with relatives at the Jemez Pueblo.

The **E. E. Fogelson Visitor Center** tells the history of the Pecos people in a well-done, chronologically organized exhibit, complete with dioramas. A 1½-mile loop trail begins at the center and continues through Pecos Pueblo and the **Misión de Nuestra Señora de Los Angeles de Porciuncula** (as the church was formerly called). This excavated structure—170 feet long and 90 feet wide at the transept—was once the most magnificent church north of Mexico City.

Pecos National Historical Park is open Memorial Day to Labor Day, daily from 8am to 6pm; the rest of the year, daily from 8am to 5pm; closed January 1 and December 25. Admission is $2 per person; $4 per carload.

12 A Side Trip to Los Alamos

Sitting atop the 7,300-foot Pajarito (bird) Plateau about 35 miles north of Santa Fe is this odd community known worldwide for its secret World War II bomb making. But its history stretches far back before the Manhattan Project. Pueblo tribes lived in this rugged area of piñon and juniper forests for well over 1,000 years, and an exclusive boys' school operated atop the 7,300-foot plateau from 1918 to 1943. Then the **Los Alamos National Laboratory** was established and Project Y of the Manhattan Engineer District created the world's first atomic bomb.

Project director J. Robert Oppenheimer, later succeeded by Norris E. Bradbury, worked with a team of 30 to 100 scientists in research, development, and production of the weapons. Today, more than 10,000 people work at the Los Alamos National Laboratory, making it the largest employer in northern New Mexico. Still operated by the University of California for the federal Department of Energy, its 32 technical areas occupy 43 square miles of mesa-top land.

The laboratory is known today as one of the world's foremost scientific institutions. It's still oriented primarily toward defense research—the Trident and Minuteman strategic warheads were designed here, for example—but it has many other research programs, including international nuclear safeguards and nonproliferation, space and atmospheric studies, supercomputing, theoretical physics, biomedical and materials science, and environmental restoration.

In 1995 workers at Los Alamos began preparation to build replacement plutonium pits for weapons in the enduring U.S. nuclear weapons stockpile. Los Alamos has become the only plutonium-handling facility in the United States capable of producing these pits. The laboratory produced its first demonstration war-reserve pit in 1997 and will soon be able to produce up to 50 pits per year if needed.

ESSENTIALS

GETTING THERE   Los Alamos is located about 35 miles west of Santa Fe and about 65 miles southwest of Taos. From Santa Fe, take U.S. 84/285 north approximately 16 miles to the Pojoaque junction, then turn west on NM 502. Driving time is only about 50 minutes.

Los Alamos is a town of 18,000 spread over the colorful, fingerlike mesas of the Pajarito Plateau, between the Jemez Mountains and the Rio Grande Valley. As NM 502 enters Los Alamos from Santa Fe, it follows Trinity Drive, where accommodations, restaurants, and other services are located. Central Avenue parallels Trinity Drive and has restaurants, galleries, and shops, as well as the Los Alamos Historical Museum (free) and the Bradbury Science Museum (free).

VISITOR INFORMATION   The **Los Alamos Chamber of Commerce,** P.O. Box 460, Los Alamos, NM 87544 (☎ **505/662-8105;** fax 505/662-8399; e-mail: lacoc@unix.nets.com), runs a visitor center that is open Monday through Friday from 9am to 4pm and Saturday from 10am to 4pm.

SPECIAL EVENTS   The Los Alamos events schedule includes a **Sports Skiesta** in mid-March; **art-and-crafts fairs** in May, August, and November; a **county fair, rodeo, and arts festival** in August; and a **triathlon** in August/September.

WHAT TO SEE & DO

Aside from the sights described below, Los Alamos offers the **Pajarito Mountain ski area,** Camp May Road (P.O. Box 155), Los Alamos, NM 87544 (☎ **505/662-5725**), with five chairlifts—it's only open on Saturday, Sunday, Wednesday, and federal holidays. It's an outstanding ski area that rarely gets crowded; many trails are steep with moguls. Los Alamos also offers the **Los Alamos Golf Course,** 4250 Diamond Dr. (☎ **505/662-8139**), at the edge of town; and the **Larry R. Walkup Aquatic Center,** 2760 Canyon Rd. (☎ **505/662-8170**), the highest-altitude indoor Olympic-size swimming pool in the United States. There's even an outdoor ice-skating rink, with a snack bar and skate rentals open from Thanksgiving through late February (☎ **505/662-8174**). There are no outstanding restaurants in Los Alamos, but if you get hungry you can stop at the **Blue Window**, 800 Trinity Dr. (☎ **505-662/6305**), a country-style restaurant serving pasta, sandwiches, and salads with a view of the Sangre de Cristo Mountains. The chamber of commerce has maps for self-guided historical walking tours, and Los Alamos National Laboratory has self-guided driving tour tapes available in stores and at hotels around town.

Black Hole. 4015 Arkansas, Los Alamos. ☎ **505/662-5053.** http://members.aol. blkholela/home/index.htm. Free admission. Mon–Fri 9am–5pm, Sat 11am–5pm.

This store/museum is an engineer's dream world, a creative photographer's heaven, and a Felix Unger nightmare. Owned and run by Edward Grothus, it's an old grocery store packed to the ceiling with the remains of the nuclear age, from Geiger counters to giant Waring blenders. If you go, be sure to visit with Grothus. He'll point out an A-frame building next door that he's christened the "First Church of High Technology," where he says a "critical mass" each Sunday. In this business for 47 years, Grothus has been written about in *Wired Magazine* and has supplied props for the movies *Silkwood, Earth II,* and the *Manhattan Project.* He's so concerned about the effects of the nuclear age, he made the news when he sent a can of Organic Plutonium (really soup) to President Clinton, a gift about which he said, "the Secret Service was not amused." Bring a jacket; it's dark and a cold 40° in the hole.

✪ Bradbury Science Museum. At the Los Alamos National Laboratory, 15th St. and Central Ave. ☎ **505/667-4444.** Free admission. Tues–Fri 9am–5pm, Sat–Mon 1–5pm. Closed major holidays.

This is a great place to get acquainted with what goes on at a weapons production facility *after* nuclear proliferation. Though the museum is run by Los Alamos National Laboratory, which definitely puts a positive spin on the business of producing weapons, it's a fascinating place to explore and includes more than 35 hands-on exhibits. Begin in the History Gallery where you'll learn of the evolution of the site from the Los Alamos Ranch School days through the Manhattan Project to the present, including a 1939 letter from Albert Einstein to Pres. Franklin D. Roosevelt suggesting research into uranium as a new and important source of energy. Next, move into the Research and Technology Gallery, where you can see work that's been done on the Human Genome Project and see a computer map of human DNA. You can try out a laser and learn about the workings of a particle accelerator. Meanwhile, listen for announcement of the film *The Town that Never Was,* an 18-minute presentation on this community that grew up shrouded in secrecy (shown in the auditorium). Further exploration will take you to the Defense Gallery where you can test the heaviness of plutonium against other substances, see an actual 5-ton Little Boy nuclear bomb (like the one dropped on Hiroshima), and see first-hand how Los Alamos conducts worldwide surveillance of nuclear explosions.

Fuller Lodge Art Center. 2132 Central Ave. ☎ **505/662-9331.** Free admission. Mon–Sat 10am–4pm.

This is a public showcase for work by visual artists from northern New Mexico and the surrounding region. Two annual arts-and-crafts fairs are also held here in August and October. The gallery shop sells local crafts at good prices.

In the same building is the **Los Alamos Arts Council** (☎ **505/662-8403**), a multidisciplinary organization that sponsors two art fairs (May and November), as well as evening and noontime cultural programs.

Los Alamos Historical Museum. 2132 Central Ave. ☎ **505/662-4493.** Free admission. Summer Mon–Sat 9:30am–4:30pm, Sun 11am–5pm; winter Mon–Sat 10am–4pm, Sun 1–4pm. Closed New Years Day, Thanksgiving, and Christmas.

Fuller Lodge, a massive vertical-log building built by John Gaw Meem in 1928, is well worth the visit. The log work is intricate and artistic, and the feel of the old place is warm and majestic. It once housed the dining and recreation hall for the Los Alamos Ranch School for boys and is now a National Historic Landmark. It is accessible to people with disabilities. Its current occupants include the museum office and research archives and the Fuller Lodge Art Center (see above). The museum, located in the small log-and-stone building to the north of Fuller Lodge, depicts area history, from prehistoric cliff dwellers to the present, with exhibits ranging from Native American artifacts to school memorabilia, and an excellent new permanent Manhattan Project exhibit that offers a more realistic view of the devastation resulting from use of atomic bombs than is offered at the Bradbury Science Museum. Most interesting is a quote from physicist Philip Morrison comparing the destruction by fire bombs of cities such as Osaka, Kobe, and Nagoya with destruction by nuclear bombs of Hiroshima and Nagasaki. One wall has three panoramic photographs of Hiroshima after the bomb. The museum sponsors guest speakers and operates a tax-free bookstore. Now you can even visit the museum, albeit somewhat vicariously, on the World Wide Web at www.vla.com/lahistory or www.losalamos.com/lahistory.

THE CLIFF DWELLINGS AT BANDELIER
✪ **Bandelier National Monument.** NM 4 (HCR 1, Box 1, Ste. 15, Los Alamos, NM 87544). ☎ **505/672-3861,** ext. 517. Admission $10 per vehicle. Open daily during daylight hours. Closed Jan 1 and Dec 25.

Less than 15 miles south of Los Alamos along NM 4, this National Park Service area contains both extensive ruins of the ancient cliff-dwelling Anasazi Pueblo culture and 46 square miles of canyon-and-mesa wilderness. During busy summer months head out early, as there can be a waiting line for cars to park.

After an orientation stop at the visitor center and museum to learn about the culture that flourished here between A.D. 1100 and 1550, most visitors follow a trail along Frijoles Creek to the principal ruins. The pueblo site, including an underground kiva, has been stabilized. The biggest thrill for most folks, though, is climbing hardy ponderosa pine ladders to visit an alcove—140 feet above the canyon floor—that was once home to prehistoric people. Tours are self-guided or led by a National Park Service ranger. Be aware that dogs are not allowed on trails.

On summer nights rangers offer campfire talks about the history, culture, and geology of the area. Some summer evenings, the guided night walks reveal a different, spooky aspect of the ruins and cave houses, outlined in the two-dimensional chiaroscuro of the thin cold light from the starry sky. During the day, nature programs are sometimes offered for adults and children. The small museum at the visitor center displays artifacts found in the area.

Elsewhere in the monument area, 70 miles of maintained trails lead to more tribal ruins, waterfalls, and wildlife habitats. However, a recent fire has decimated parts of this area, so periodic closings will take place in order to allow the land to reforest.

The separate **Tsankawi** section, reached by an ancient 2-mile trail close to **White Rock,** has a large unexcavated ruin on a high mesa overlooking the Rio Grande Valley. The town of White Rock, about 10 miles southeast of Los Alamos on NM 4, offers spectacular panoramas of the river valley in the direction of Santa Fe; the White Rock Overlook is a great picnic spot.

Within Bandelier, areas have been set aside for picnicking and camping. The national monument is named after the Swiss-American archaeologist Adolph Bandelier, who explored here in the 1880s.

Past Bandelier National Monument on NM4, beginning about 15 miles from Los Alamos, is **Valle Grande,** a vast meadow 16 miles in area—all that remains of a volcanic caldera created by a collapse after eruptions nearly a million years ago. When the mountain spewed ashes and dust as far away as Kansas and Nebraska, its underground magma chambers collapsed, forming this great valley, one of the largest volcanic calderas in the world. However, lava domes that pushed up after the collapse obstruct a full view across the expanse. Valle Grande is now privately owned land, though negotiations are currently underway with the U.S. government to purchase the property, possibly to turn it into a park.

13 Taking the High Road to Taos

Unless you're in a hurry to get from Santa Fe to Taos, the **High Road**—also called the Mountain Road or the King's Road—is by far the most fascinating route. It runs through tiny ridge-top villages where Hispanic traditions and way of life continue much as they did a century ago. From Santa Fe take U.S. 285 to NM 503, which heads east. Follow that highway to NM 76. Take a short leg on NM 75 to NM 518, which puts you on the outskirts of Taos.

CHIMAYO

About 28 miles north of Santa Fe on U.S. 84/285 is the historic weaving center of Chimayo. It's approximately 16 miles past the Pojoaque junction, at the junction of NM 520 and NM 76 via NM 503. In this small village, families still maintain the tradition of crafting hand-woven textiles initiated by their ancestors seven generations ago, in the early 1800s. One such family is the Ortegas, and both **Ortega's Weaving Shop** and **Galeria Ortega** are fine places to take a close look at this ancient craft.

Today, however, many more people come to Chimayo to visit ✪ **El Santuario de Nuestro Señor de Esquipulas** (the Shrine of Our Lord of Esquipulas), better known simply as "El Santuario de Chimayo." Ascribed with miraculous powers of healing, this church has attracted thousands of pilgrims since its construction in 1814–16. Up to 30,000 people participate in the annual Good Friday pilgrimage, many of them walking from as far away as Albuquerque.

Although only the earth in the anteroom beside the altar is presumed to have the gift of healing powers, the entire shrine radiates true serenity. It's quite moving to peruse the written testimonies of rapid recovery from illness or injury on the walls of the anteroom, and equally poignant to read the as-yet-unanswered entreaties made on behalf of loved ones.

A National Historic Landmark, the church has five beautiful *reredos,* or panels of sacred paintings, one behind the main altar and two on each side of the nave. Each year during the fourth weekend in July, the military exploits of the 9th-century Spanish saint Santiago are celebrated in a weekend fiesta, including the historic play **Los Moros y Los Cristianos** (Moors and Christians).

Lovely **Santa Cruz Lake** has a dual purpose: This artificial lake provides water for Chimayo Valley farms and also offers a recreation site for trout fishing and camping at the edge of the Pecos Wilderness. To reach it, turn south 4 miles on NM 503, about 2 miles east of Chimayo.

WHERE TO DINE

✪ **Restaurante Rancho de Chimayo.** P.O. Box 11, Chimayo, NM, 87522 (CTR 98). ☎ **505/351-4444.** Reservations recommended. Lunch $7.50–$13; dinner $10–$15. AE, DC, DISC, MC, V. Daily 11:30am–9pm; Sat–Sun breakfast 8:30–11am. Closed Mon Oct–May. NEW MEXICAN.

For as long as I can remember my family and all my friends' families have scheduled trips into northern New Mexico to coincide with lunch- or dinnertime at this fun restaurant in an adobe home, built by Hermenegildo Jaramillo in the 1880s, and now run as a restaurant by his descendants. Unfortunately, over the years the restaurant has become so famous that tour buses now stop here. However, the food has suffered only a little. In the warmer months request the terraced patio. During winter, you'll be seated in one of a number of cozy rooms with thick viga ceilings. The food is native New Mexican, prepared from generations-old Jaramillo family recipes. You can't go wrong with the enchiladas, served layered, northern New Mexico style, rather than rolled. For variety you might want to try the *combinación picante* (carne adovada, tamale, enchilada, beans, and posole). Each plate comes with two sopaipillas. With a little honey, who needs dessert? Margaritas from the full bar are delicious.

CORDOVA

Just as Chimayo is famous for its weaving, the village of Cordova, about 7 miles east on NM 76, is noted for its wood-carvers. Small shops and studios along the highway display *santos* (carved saints) and various decorative items carved from aspen and cedar.

TRUCHAS

Robert Redford's 1988 movie *The Milagro Beanfield War* featured the town of Truchas (which means "trout"). A former Spanish colonial outpost built on top of an 8,000-foot mesa, 4 miles east of Cordova, it was chosen as the site for the film in part because traditional Hispanic culture is still very much in evidence. Subsistence farming is prevalent here. The scenery is spectacular: 13,101-foot Truchas Peak dominates one side of the mesa, and the broad Rio Grande Valley dominates the other.

About 6 miles east of Truchas on NM 76 is the small town of **Las Trampas,** noted for its San José Church, which some call the most beautiful of all churches built during the Spanish colonial period.

PICURIS (SAN LORENZO) PUEBLO

Near the regional education center of Peñasco, about 24 miles from Chimayo near the intersection of NM 75 and NM 76, is the Picuris (San Lorenzo) Pueblo (☎ **505/587-2519** or 505/587-2957). The 375 citizens of this 15,000-acre mountain pueblo, native Tiwa speakers, consider themselves a sovereign nation: Their forebears never made a treaty with any foreign country, including the United States. Thus, they observe a traditional form of tribal council government. A few of the original mud-and-stone houses still stand and are home to tribal elders. A striking aboveground ceremonial kiva called "the Roundhouse," built at least 700 years ago, and some historic excavated kivas and storerooms are open to visitors. The **annual feast day** at San Lorenzo Church is August 10.

Still, the people here are modern enough to have fully computerized their public showcase operations, Picuris Tribal Enterprises. Besides running the Hotel Santa Fe in the state capital, they own the **Picuris Pueblo Museum and Visitor's Center,** where weaving, beadwork, and distinctive reddish-brown clay cooking pottery are exhibited daily from 9am to 6pm. Self-guided tours through the old village ruins begin at the museum and cost $1.75; the camera fee is $5 (includes entrance fee); sketching and video camera fees are $10. There's also an information center, crafts shop, and grocery store. Fishing permits ($6 for adults and children) are available, as are permits to camp at Pu-Na and Tu-Tah Lakes, regularly stocked with trout.

About a mile east of Peñasco on NM 75 is Vadito, the former center for a conservative Catholic brotherhood, the Penitentes, earlier in this century.

DIXON & EMBUDO

Taos is about 24 miles north of Peñasco via NM 518. But day-trippers from Santa Fe can loop back to the capital by taking NM 75 west from Picuris Pueblo. Dixon, approximately 12 miles west of Picuris, and its twin village Embudo, a mile farther on NM 68 at the Rio Grande, are home to many artists and craftspeople who exhibit their works during the annual **autumn show** sponsored by the Dixon Arts Association. For a taste of the local grape, you can follow signs to **La Chiripada Winery** (☎ 505/579-4437), whose product is surprisingly good, especially to those who don't know that New Mexico has a long wine-making history. Local pottery is also sold in the tasting room. The winery is open Monday through Saturday from 10am to 5pm.

Two more small villages lie in the Rio Grande Valley at 6-mile intervals south of Embudo on NM 68. **Velarde** is a fruit-growing center; in season, the road here is lined with stands selling fresh fruit or crimson chile ristras and wreaths of native plants. **Alcalde** is the site of Los Luceros, an early 17th-century home that is to be refurbished as an arts and history center. The unique **Dance of the Matachines,** a Moorish-style ritual brought from Spain by the conquistadors, is performed here on holidays and feast days.

ESPAÑOLA

The commercial center of Española (population 7,000) no longer has the railroad that led to its establishment in the 1880s, but it may have New Mexico's greatest concentration of **low riders.** These late-model customized cars, so called because their suspension leaves them sitting quite close to the ground, are definitely their owners' objects of affection. The cars have inspired a unique auto subculture. You can't miss the cars—they cruise the main streets of town, especially on weekend evenings.

Sights of interest in Española include the **Bond House Museum,** a Victorian-era adobe home that exhibits local history and art; and the **Santa Cruz Church,** built in 1733 and renovated in 1979, which houses many fine examples of Spanish colonial religious art. The new **Convento,** built to resemble a colonial cathedral, on the Española Plaza (at the junction of NM 30 and U.S. 84), will house an office of the chamber of commerce, restaurants, and shops. Major events include the July **Fiesta de Oñate,** commemorating the valley's founding in 1596; the October **Tri-Cultural Art Festival** on the Northern New Mexico Community College campus; and the weeklong **Summer Solstice** celebration staged in June by the nearby Ram Das Puri ashram of the Sikhs (☎ 888/346-2420 or 505/753-4988).

Complete information on Española and the vicinity can be obtained from the **Española Valley Chamber of Commerce,** 417 Big Rock Center, Española, NM 87532 (☎ 505/753-2831).

If you admire the work of Georgia O'Keeffe, try to plan a short trip to **Abiquiu,** a tiny town at a bend of the Rio Chama, 14 miles south of Ghost Ranch and 22 miles north of Española on U.S. 84. Once you see the surrounding terrain, it will be clear that this was the inspiration for many of her startling landscapes. Since March 1995, ✪ **Georgia O'Keeffe's Home** (where she lived and painted) has been open for public

Georgia O'Keeffe & New Mexico: The Transformation of a Great American Artist

In June 1917, during a short visit to the Southwest, the painter Georgia O'Keeffe (born 1887) visited New Mexico for the first time. She was immediately enchanted by the stark scenery; even after her return to the energy and chaos of New York City, her mind wandered frequently to New Mexico's arid land and undulating mesas. However, not until coaxed by the arts patron and "collector of people" Mabel Dodge Luhan 12 years later did O'Keeffe return to the multihued desert of her daydreams.

O'Keeffe was reportedly ill when she arrived in Santa Fe in April 1929, both physically and emotionally. New Mexico seemed to soothe her spirit and heal her physical ailments almost magically. Two days after her arrival, Mabel Dodge Luhan persuaded O'Keeffe to move into her home in Taos. There she would be free to paint and socialize as she liked.

In Taos, O'Keeffe began painting what would become some of her best-known canvases—close-ups of desert flowers and objects such as cow and horse skulls. "The color up there is different . . . the blue-green of the sage and the mountains, the wildflowers in bloom," O'Keeffe once said of Taos. "It's a different kind of color from any I've ever seen—there's nothing like that in north Texas or even in Colorado." Taos transformed not only her art, but her personality as well. She bought a car and learned to drive. Sometimes, on warm days, she ran stark naked through the sage fields. That August, a new, rejuvenated O'Keeffe rejoined her husband, photographer Alfred Stieglitz, in New York.

The artist returned to New Mexico year after year, spending time with Mabel Dodge Luhan as well as staying at the isolated Ghost Ranch. She drove through the countryside in her snappy Ford, stopping to paint in her favorite spots along the way. Up until 1949, O'Keeffe always returned to New York in the fall. Three years after Stieglitz's death, though, she relocated permanently to New Mexico, spending each winter and spring in Abiquiu and each summer and fall at Ghost Ranch. Georgia O'Keeffe died in Santa Fe in 1986.

tours. However, a reservation must be made in advance; the charge is $20 for a 1-hour tour. A number of tours are given each week—on Tuesday, Thursday, and Friday—and a limited number of people are accepted per tour. Visitors are not permitted to take pictures. Fortunately, O'Keeffe's home remains as it was when she lived there (until 1986). Call several months in advance for reservations (☎ **505/685-4539**).

A GREAT NEARBY PLACE TO STAY & DINE

✪ **Rancho de San Juan.** (U.S. 285, en route to Ojo Caliente.) P.O. Box 4140, Fairview Station, Española, NM 87533. ☎ **505/753-6818.** 9 units. TEL. $175–$350 double. Rates include full breakfast. AE, DISC, MC, V.

This inn provides an authentic northern New Mexico desert experience, with the comfort of a luxury hotel. Opened in 1994, it's the passion of architect and chef John Johnson, responsible for the design and cuisine, and interior designer David Heath, responsible for the elegant interiors. The original part of the inn comprises four rooms around a central courtyard. Five additional casitas have been added in the outlying hills. The original rooms are a bit small but very elegant, with

European antiques and spectacular views of desertscapes and distant, snow-capped peaks. All units have fireplaces, private portals, makeup mirrors, hair dryers, Italian robes and sheets, and Caswell Massey soaps in the bathroom. My favorite room in the main part is the Black Mesa, though all are consistently nice. Of the casitas, all quite roomy, my favorite is the Anasazi. It has lots of light, a raised sleeping area, and a jet tub with a view. The Kiva suite has a round bedroom and a skylight just above the bed, perfect for star-gazing.

Each morning John serves an elaborate full breakfast. In the evenings a fixed-price dinner is served, and includes four courses, the meal ranging in price from $45 to $95, depending on the wine. The food is eclectic French/Italian/American; such specialties as breast of African pheasant and sautéed Alaskan halibut are served in the cozy dining room with a sunset view.

A few minutes' hike from the inn is the **Grand Chamber,** an impressive shrine that the innkeepers commissioned to be carved into a sandstone outcropping, where weddings and other festivities are held.

Many locals like to rejuvenate at **Ojo Caliente Mineral Springs,** Ojo Caliente, NM 87549 (☎ **800/222-9162** or 505/583-2233). It's on U.S. 285, 50 miles (a 1-hour drive) northwest of Santa Fe and 50 miles southwest of Taos. This National Historic Site was considered sacred by prehistoric tribes. When Spanish explorer Cabeza de Vaca discovered and named the springs in the 16th century, he called them "the greatest treasure that I found these strange people to possess." No other hot spring in the world has Ojo Caliente's combination of iron, soda, lithium, sodium, and arsenic. The dressing rooms are fairly new and in good shape; however, the whole place could use sprucing up. If you're a fastidious type you won't be comfortable here. The resort offers herbal wraps, massages, lodging, and meals. It's open daily from 8am to 8pm (9pm Friday and Saturday).

Taos 8

I find that people either really like Taos or they really dislike it. Those who expect it to be neat and sophisticated like Santa Fe are generally disappointed. The best way to approach this town of 5,000 residents is as the renegade place that it is.

Its narrow streets tend to be either dusty or muddy, and are usually blocked by cars. Its residents are often funky, harking back to the hippie days, part of the town's 1960s history when communes set up camp in the hills outside the town. These are the impressions that often initially catch visitors.

But take a moment longer to look and you'll see the awe-inspiring adobe structures at Taos Pueblo, where some people still live without electricity or running water as their ancestors did 1,000 years ago. These are set against giant blue mountains rising fast from irrigated meadows. You'll encounter a thriving art colony, not glitzy like Santa Fe, but very real and down to earth, often with artists selling work straight out of their studios. You'll wander through amazing galleries, many displaying the town's rich history in a variety of art forms. And, my favorite, you'll eat some of the most inventive food in the Southwest, at very affordable prices.

Taos is located just 40 miles south of the Colorado border, about 70 miles north of Santa Fe and 135 miles from Albuquerque. In addition to its collection of artists and writers, it's famous for the pueblo and for the nearby ski area, one of the most highly regarded in the Rockies.

HISTORY 101

Taos's history is full of conflict. The Spanish first visited this area in 1540, colonizing it in 1598. In the last 2 decades of the 17th century, they put down three rebellions at the Taos Pueblo. During the 18th and 19th centuries, Taos was an important trade center: New Mexico's annual caravan to Chihuahua, Mexico, couldn't leave until after the annual midsummer Taos Fair. French trappers began attending the fair in 1739. Even though the Plains tribes often attacked the pueblos at other times, they would attend the market festival under a temporary annual truce. By the early 1800s, Taos had become a meeting place for American "mountain men," the most famous of whom, Kit Carson, made his home in Taos from 1826 to 1868.

Thoroughly Hispanic, Taos remained loyal to Mexico during the Mexican-American War of 1846. The town rebelled against its new

U.S. landlord in 1847, even killing newly appointed Gov. Charles Bent in his Taos home. Nevertheless, the town was incorporated into the Territory of New Mexico in 1850. During the Civil War, Taos fell into Confederate hands for 6 weeks; afterward, Carson and two other men raised the Union flag over Taos Plaza and guarded it day and night. Since that time, Taos has had the honor of flying the flag 24 hours a day.

Taos's population declined when the railroad bypassed it in favor of Santa Fe. In 1898, two East Coast artists—Ernest Blumenschein and Bert Phillips—discovered the dramatic, varied effects of sunlight on the natural environment of the Taos valley and depicted them on canvas. By 1912, thanks to the growing influence of the **Taos Society of Artists,** the town had gained a worldwide reputation as a cultural center. Today it is estimated that more than 15% of the population are painters, sculptors, writers, musicians, or otherwise earn their income from artistic pursuits.

A VARIETY OF LAND & PEOPLES

The town of Taos is merely the focal point of the rugged 2,200-square-mile Taos County. Two features dominate this sparsely populated region: the high desert mesa, split in two by the 650-foot-deep chasm of the Rio Grande; and the Sangre de Cristo Range, which tops out at 13,161-foot Wheeler Peak, New Mexico's highest mountain. From the forested uplands to the sage-carpeted mesa, the county is home to a large variety of wildlife. The human element includes Native Americans who are still living in ancient pueblos and Hispanic farmers who continue to irrigate their farmlands by centuries-old methods.

Taos is also inhabited by many people who have chosen to retreat from, or altogether drop out of, mainstream society. There's a laid-back attitude here, even more pronounced than the general *mañana* attitude for which New Mexico is known. Many Taoseños live here to play here—and that means outdoors. Many work at the ski area all winter (skiing whenever they can) and work for raft companies in the summer (to get on the river as much as they can). Others are into rock climbing, mountain biking, and backpacking. That's not to say that Taos is just a resort town. With the Hispanic and Native American populations' histories in the area, there's a richness and depth here that most resort towns lack.

Taos's biggest task these days is to try to stem the tide of overdevelopment that is flooding northern New Mexico. In "New Mexico Today," in chapter 2, I addressed the city's success in battling back airport expansion and some housing developments. A grassroots community program has been implemented recently that will give all neighborhoods a say in how their area is developed.

1 Orientation

ARRIVING

BY PLANE   The **Taos Airport** (☎ 505/758-4995) is about 8 miles northwest of town on U.S. 64. Call for information on local charter services. It's easiest to fly into **Albuquerque International Airport,** rent a car, and drive up to Taos from there (see "Getting There," in chapter 3, and "Orientation," in chapter 6). The drive will take you approximately 2½ hours. If you'd rather be picked up at Albuquerque International Airport, call **Pride of Taos** (☎ 505/758-8340). It offers charter bus service to Taos town and the Taos Ski Valley daily. **Faust's Transportation** (☎ 505/758-3410) offers a similar service.

BY BUS   The Taos Bus Center, Paseo del Pueblo Sur at the Chevron station (☎ 505/758-1144), is not far from the Plaza. **Greyhound/Trailways** and **TNM&O Coaches** arrive and depart from this depot several times a day (☎ 800/231-2222).

For more information on these and other local bus services to and from Albuquerque and Santa Fe, see "Getting There," in chapter 3.

BY CAR   Most visitors arrive in Taos via either NM 68 or U.S. 64. Northbound travelers should exit I-25 at Santa Fe, follow U.S. 285 as far as San Juan Pueblo, and then continue on the divided highway when it becomes NM 68. Taos is about 79 miles from the I-25 junction. Southbound travelers from Denver on I-25 should exit about 6 miles south of Raton at U.S. 64 and then follow it about 95 miles to Taos. Another major route is U.S. 64 from the west (214 miles from Farmington).

VISITOR INFORMATION

The **Taos County Chamber of Commerce,** at the junction of U.S. 64 and NM 68 (P.O. Drawer I), Taos, NM 87571 (☎ **800/732-TAOS** or 505/758-3873; e-mail: taos@taoswebb.com), is open year-round, daily from 9am to 5pm. It's closed on major holidays. **Carson National Forest** also has an information center in the same building. On the Internet you can access information about Taos at http://taoswebb.com.

CITY LAYOUT

The Plaza is a short block west of Taos's major intersection, where U.S. 64 (Kit Carson Road) from the east joins NM 68, **Paseo del Pueblo Sur** (also known as South Pueblo Road or South Santa Fe Road). U.S. 64 proceeds north from the intersection as **Paseo del Pueblo Norte** (North Pueblo Road). **Camino de la Placita** (Placitas Road) circles the west side of downtown, passing within a block of the other side of the Plaza. Many of the streets that join these thoroughfares are winding lanes lined by traditional adobe homes, many of them more than 100 years old.

Most of the art galleries are located on or near the Plaza, which was paved over with bricks several years ago, and along neighboring streets. Others are located in the **Ranchos de Taos** area a few miles south of the Plaza.

MAPS   To find your way around town, pick up a free copy of the Taos map from the **Chamber of Commerce at Taos Visitor Center,** 1139 Paseo del Pueblo Sur (☎ **505/758-3873**). Good, detailed city maps can be found at area bookstores as well (see "Books," under "Shopping," below).

2 Getting Around

BY BUS & TAXI

Taos Transit (☎ **505/737-2606**) provides local bus service Monday through Saturday from 7am to 9pm. The route runs from Kachina Lodge on Paseo del Pueblo Norte and ends at the Ranchos Post Office on the south side of town, with buses reaching each stop about every 45 minutes. They also go to Taos Pueblo. Bus fares are 50¢ one way, $1 all day, and $5 for a 7-day pass.

In addition, Taos has two private bus companies. **Faust's Transportation** (☎ **505/758-3410**) has a shuttle bus service linking town hotels and Taos Ski Valley; they run three times a day for $10 round-trip.

Faust's Transportation also offers town taxi service daily from 7am to 9pm, with fares of about $7 anywhere within the city limits for up to two people ($2 per additional person), $40 to Albuquerque International Airport, and $35 to Taos Ski Valley from Taos town.

BY CAR

With offices at the Taos airport, **Dollar** (☎ **800/369-4226** or 505/758-9501) is reliable and efficient. Other car-rental agencies are available out of Albuquerque (see "Getting Around," in chapter 3).

PARKING   Parking can be difficult during the summer rush, when the stream of tourists' cars moving north and south through town never ceases. If you can't find parking on the street or in the Plaza, check out some of the nearby roads (Kit Carson Road, for instance) because there are plenty of metered and unmetered lots in Taos town.

WARNING FOR DRIVERS   Reliable paved roads lead to starting points for side trips up poorer forest roads to many recreation sites. Once you get off the main roads, you won't find gas stations or cafes. Four-wheel-drive vehicles are recommended on snow and much of the otherwise unpaved terrain of the region. If you're doing some off-road adventuring, it's wise to go with a full gas tank, extra food and water, and warm clothing—just in case. At the higher-than-10,000-foot elevations of northern New Mexico, sudden summer snowstorms are not unheard of.

ROAD CONDITIONS   Information on road conditions in the Taos area can be obtained free from the **State Police** (☎ **505/758-8878** within New Mexico). Also, for highway conditions throughout the state, call the **State Highway Department** (☎ **800/432-4269**).

BY BICYCLE & ON FOOT

Bicycle rentals are available from **Gearing Up Bicycle Shop,** 129 Paseo del Pueblo Sur (☎ 505/751-0365); daily rentals run $20 for a mountain bike with front suspension. **Hot Tracks Cyclery & Ski Touring Service,** 214 Paseo del Pueblo Sur (☎ 505/ 751-0949), rents front-suspension mountain bikes and full-suspension bikes for $9 per hour, $15 per half day, and $20 per full day. **Native Sons Adventures,** 1033 Paseo del Pueblo Sur (☎ 800/753-7559 or 505/758-9342), rents unsuspended bikes for $15 for a half day and $20 for a full day; front-suspension bikes for $25 per half day and $35 per full day; and full-suspension bikes for $35 per half day and $45 per full day; they also rent car racks for $5. Each shop supplies helmets and water bottles with rentals.

Most of Taos's attractions can easily be reached by foot since they are within a few blocks of the Plaza.

FAST FACTS: Taos

Airport   See "Orientation," above.

Business Hours   Most businesses are open Monday through Friday from 10am to 5pm, though some may open an hour earlier and close an hour later. Many tourist-oriented shops are also open on Saturday morning, and some art galleries are open all day Saturday and Sunday, especially during peak tourist seasons. Banks are generally open Monday through Thursday from 9am to 3pm and often for longer hours on Friday. Call establishments for specific hours.

Car Rentals   See "Getting Around," above.

Climate   Taos's climate is similar to that of Santa Fe. Summer days are dry and sunny, except for frequent afternoon thunderstorms. Winter days are often bracing, with snowfalls common but rarely lasting too long. Average summer temperatures range from 50°F to 87°F. Winter temperatures vary between 9°F and 40°F. Annual rainfall is 12 inches; annual snowfall is 35 inches in town and 300 inches at Taos Ski Valley, where the elevation is 9,207 feet. (A foot of snow is equal to an inch of rain.)

Currency Exchange   Foreign currency can be exchanged at the Centinel Bank of Taos, 512 Paseo del Pueblo Sur (☎ **505/758-6700**).

Dentists   If you need dental work, try Dr. Walter Jakiela, 536 Paseo del Pueblo Norte (☎ **505/758-8654**); Dr. Michael Rivera, 107 Plaza Garcia, Ste. E (☎ **505/758-0531**); or Dr. Tom Simms, 923-B Paseo del Pueblo Sur (☎ **505/758-8303**).

Doctors   Members of the Taos Medical Group, on Weimer Road (☎ **505/758-2224**), are highly respected. Also recommended are Family Practice Associates of Taos, at 630 Paseo del Pueblo Sur, Suite 150 (☎ **505/758-3005**).

Driving Rules   See "Getting Around," in chapter 3.

Drugstores   See "Pharmacies," below.

Embassies/Consulates   See "Fast Facts: For the Foreign Traveler" in chapter 4.

Emergencies   Dial ☎ **911** for police, fire, and ambulance.

Eyeglasses   Taos Eyewear, in Cruz Alta Plaza (☎ **505/758-8758**), handles most needs Monday through Friday between 8:30am and 5pm. It also has emergency service.

Hospital   Holy Cross Hospital, 1397 Weimer Rd., off Paseo del Canyon (☎ **505/758-8883**), has 24-hour emergency service. Serious cases are transferred to Santa Fe or Albuquerque.

Hot Lines   The crisis hot line (☎ **505/758-9888**) is available for emergency counseling, specifically for victims of crime.

Information   See "Visitor Information," above.

Library   The Taos Public Library, at 402 Camino de la Placita (☎ **505/758-3063**), has a general collection for Taos residents, a children's library, and special collections on the Southwest and Taos art.

Liquor Laws   See "Fast Facts: New Mexico," in chapter 3.

Lost Property   Check with the city police (☎ **505/758-2216**).

Newspapers & Magazines   *The Taos News* (☎ **505/758-2241**) and the *Sangre de Cristo Chronicle* (☎ **505/377-2358**) are published every Thursday. *Taos Magazine* is also a good source of local information. The *Albuquerque Journal* and the *New Mexican* from Santa Fe are easily obtained at the Fernandez de Taos Bookstore on the Plaza.

Pharmacies   There are several full-service pharmacies in Taos. Furr's Pharmacy (☎ **505/758-1203**), Smith's Pharmacy (☎ **505/758-4824**), and Wal-Mart Pharmacy (☎ **505/758-2743**) are all located on Pueblo Sur and are easily seen from the road.

Photographic Needs   Check Plaza Photo, Taos Main Plaza (☎ **505/758-3420**). Minor camera repairs can be done the same day, but major repairs must be sent to Santa Fe and usually require several days. Plaza Photo offers a full line of photo accessories and 1-hour processing. April's 1-Hour Photos, at 613E N. Pueblo Rd. (☎ **505/758-0515**), is another good choice.

Police   In case of emergency, dial ☎ **911.** All other inquiries should be directed to Taos Police, Civic Plaza Drive (☎ **505/758-2216**). The Taos County Sheriff, with jurisdiction outside the city limits, is located in the county courthouse on Paseo del Pueblo Sur (☎ **505/758-3361**).

Post Offices   The main Taos Post Office is at 318 Paseo del Pueblo Norte, Taos, NM 87571 (☎ **505/758-2081**), a few blocks north of the Plaza traffic light. There are smaller offices in Ranchos de Taos (☎ **505/758-3944**) and at El Prado (☎ **505/758-4810**). The ZIP code for Taos is 87571.

Radio & Television   Local stations are KTAO-FM (101.7), which broadcasts an entertainment calendar daily (☎ **505/758-1017**); the National Public Radio Stations—KUNM-FM (98.5) from Albuquerque and KRZA-FM (88.7) from Alamosa—for news, sports, and weather; and KAFR-FM (99.1) from Angel Fire. Channel 2, the local access television station, is available in most hostelries. For a few hours a day there is local programming. Cable networks carry Santa Fe and Albuquerque stations.

Taxes   Gross receipts tax for Taos town is 6.8125%, and for Taos County it's 6.3125%. There is an additional local bed tax of 3.5% in Taos town and 3% on hotel rooms in Taos County.

Telephone Numbers   For information on road conditions in the Taos area, call ☎ **800/432-4269** (within New Mexico) for the state highway department, or 505/758-8878 for the state police. Taos County offices are at ☎ **505/758-8834.**

Time   See "Fast Facts: New Mexico," in chapter 3.

3 Where to Stay

A small town with a big tourist market, Taos has some 2,200 rooms in 88 hotels, motels, condominiums, and bed-and-breakfasts. Many new properties have recently opened, turning this into a buyer's market. In the slower season, you may even want to try bargaining your room rate down, because competition for travelers is steep. Most of the hotels and motels are located on Paseo del Pueblo Sur and Norte, with a few scattered just east of the town center along Kit Carson Road. The condos and bed-and-breakfasts are generally scattered throughout Taos's back streets.

Unlike in Santa Fe, there are two high seasons in Taos: winter (the Christmas-to-Easter ski season, except for January, which is surprisingly slow for a ski resort) and summer. Spring and fall are shoulder seasons, often with lower rates. The period between Easter and Memorial Day is a slow time for the tourist industry here, and many restaurants and other businesses take their annual vacations at this time. Book well ahead for ski holiday periods (especially Christmas) and for the annual arts festivals (late May to mid-June and late September to early October).

During peak winter and summer seasons, visitors without reservations may have difficulty finding a vacant room. **Taos Central Reservations,** P.O. Box 1713, Taos, NM 87571 (☎ **800/821-2437** or 505/758-9767), might be able to help.

Fifteen hundred or so of Taos County's beds are in condominiums and lodges at or near the Taos Ski Valley. The **Taos Valley Resort Association,** P.O. Box 85, Taos Ski Valley, NM 87525 (☎ **800/776-1111** or 505/776-2233; fax 505/776-8842), can book these as well as rooms in Taos and all of northern New Mexico, and can broker private home rentals. The World Wide Web address for Taos Valley Resort Association is http://taoswebb.com/nmresv. If you'd rather e-mail for a reservation, the address is res@taoswebb.com.

Some three dozen bed-and-breakfasts are listed with the Taos Chamber of Commerce. The **Taos Bed and Breakfast Association** (☎ **800/876-7857** or 505/758-4747) and the **Traditional Taos Inns Bed and Breakfast Association**

Central Taos Accommodations

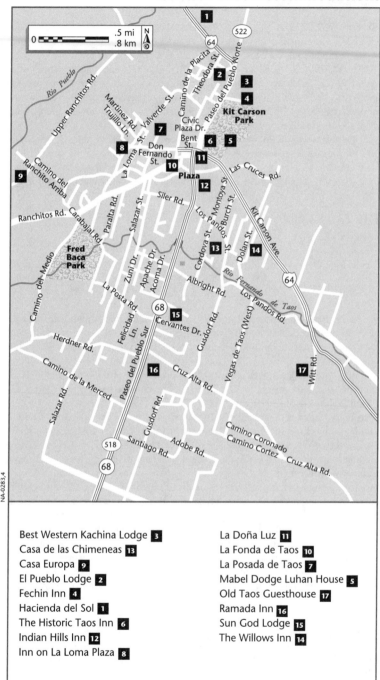

Best Western Kachina Lodge **3**
Casa de las Chimeneas **13**
Casa Europa **9**
El Pueblo Lodge **2**
Fechin Inn **4**
Hacienda del Sol **1**
The Historic Taos Inn **6**
Indian Hills Inn **12**
Inn on La Loma Plaza **8**

La Doña Luz **11**
La Fonda de Taos **10**
La Posada de Taos **7**
Mabel Dodge Luhan House **5**
Old Taos Guesthouse **17**
Ramada Inn **16**
Sun God Lodge **15**
The Willows Inn **14**

(☎ **800/ 939-2215** or 505/776-8840), both with strict guidelines for membership, will provide information and make reservations for member inns.

Accommodations and Tours of Taos, 1033-A Paseo del Pueblo Sur, Taos, NM 87571 (☎ **800/290-5384** or 505/751-1292), will help you find accommodations from bed-and-breakfasts to home rentals, hotels, and cabins throughout Taos and northern New Mexico. They'll also help you arrange rental cars and package prices for outdoor activities such as white-water rafting, horseback riding, snowmobiling, fishing trips, and ski packages.

In these listings, the following categories have been used to describe peak-season prices for a double: **expensive** applies to accommodations that charge over $100 per night; **moderate** refers to $75 to $100; and **inexpensive** indicates $75 and under. A tax of **11.38%** in Taos town and **11.1325%** in Taos County will be added to every hotel bill.

THE TAOS AREA
EXPENSIVE
Hotels/Motels
Fechin Inn. 227 Paseo del Pueblo Norte, Taos, NM 87571. ☎ **800/811-2933** or 505/751-1000. Fax 505/751-7338. www.fechin-inn.com. 99 units. A/C TV TEL. $109–$179 double; $199–$319 suite. Rates vary according to season. AE, CB, DC, DISC, MC, V. Free parking. Pets are welcome.

When this luxury hotel opened in summer 1996, word quickly spread that it hadn't lived up to expectations, and it's no wonder. People who hoped it would replicate the house built next door by Russian artist Nicolai Fechin in 1927 (see "Fechin Institute," under "What to See & Do," below) were living in the wrong century. The new hotel certainly doesn't have the refined warmth of the Inn of the Anasazi in Santa Fe. It's closer in style to the Eldorado, and considering that it's a large hotel, I would call it a qualified success.

Its main feature is the carved wood by Jeremy Morelli of Santa Fe. In line with the carving in the Fechin House, much of it is beveled and then waxed, giving it the fine texture of skin. The two-story lobby is airy, with a bank of windows and French doors looking south to a portal where chile ristras hang and diners can eat breakfast in the warmer months. The rooms are spacious and have a Southwestern motif decor with nice touches such as hickory furniture and flagstone-topped tables, all rooms with balconies or patios, guest robes, hair dryers, and minirefrigerators. All the suites have kiva fireplaces. What's notable here is the quiet. Surrounded on three sides by rural land, mostly you'll hear birds, though Kit Carson Park next door does send some sounds your way if you're on the south side of the hotel. The bathrooms are delightful, with gray Saltillo tile and warm, adjustable lighting. There's a library where you can play chess or backgammon. For an additional cost you can eat an elaborate continental breakfast. In the evening drinks are served, often to the sound of live entertainment.

Amenities: Concierge, limited room service, dry cleaning and laundry service. There's also a medium-sized health club, Jacuzzi, conference rooms, and Laundromat.

✪ **Historic Taos Inn.** 125 Paseo del Pueblo Norte, Taos, NM 87571. ☎ **800/TAOS-INN** or 505/758-2233. Fax 505/758-5776. 36 units. A/C TV TEL. $75–$225 double, depending on the type of room and season (Memorial Day to mid-October, and Christmas and spring break are high season). Rates include discounted breakfast. AE, DC, MC, V.

It's rare to see a hotel that has withstood the years with grace. The Historic Taos Inn has. Never do you forget that you're within the thick walls of a number of 19th-century Southwestern homes, and yet surrounded by 20th-century luxury. Dr. Thomas Paul Martin, the town's first (and for many years only) physician, purchased the complex in 1895. In 1936, a year after the doctor's death, his widow, Helen, enclosed the plaza—now the inn's darling two-story lobby—and turned it into a hotel. In 1981–82 the inn was restored; it's now listed on both the State and National Register of Historic Places.

The lobby doubles as the **Adobe Bar,** a real local gathering place, with adobe *bancos* (adobe benches) and a sunken fireplace, all surrounding a wishing well that was once the old town well. A number of rooms open onto a balcony that overlooks this area. If you like community and don't mind the sound of jazz and flamenco drifting up toward your room, these rooms are for you. However, if you appreciate solitude and silence, request one of the courtyard rooms downstairs. All the rooms are unique and comfortable, decorated with Spanish colonial art, Taos-style furniture, and interesting touches such as hand-woven Oaxacan bedspreads and little *nichos* often decorated with Mexican pottery, many with fireplaces; all have hair dryers, irons, and ironing boards.

Dining/Diversions: Doc Martin's, with good nouveau Southwestern cuisine and a hint of Asia, is one of Taos's leading dining establishments (see "Where to Dine," below). The **Adobe Bar,** popular among Taos artists and other locals, offers live entertainment on certain weeknights as well as a full bar menu for a light lunch or dinner, snacks, margaritas, and an espresso-dessert menu.

Amenities: Room service, baby-sitting can be arranged, free coffee or refreshments in lobby, VCRs on request, seasonal outdoor swimming pool, year-round Jacuzzi in a greenhouse.

Bed & Breakfasts

✪ **Adobe and Pines Inn.** NM 68 (Box 837), Ranchos de Taos, NM 87557. ☎ **800/ 723-8267** or 505/751-0947. Fax 505/758-8423. www.toasnet.com/adobepines/. 5 units, 3 casitas. TV. $95–$185 double. Rates include breakfast. AE, DC, DISC, MC, V.

With this inn, owners Chuck and Charil Fulkerson wanted to create a magical escape. They succeeded. Much of it is located in a 150-year-old adobe directly off NM 68, less than half a mile south of St. Francis Plaza.

The inn is set around a courtyard marked by an 80-foot-long grand portal. It's surrounded by pine and fruit trees on what's believed to be sacred land. Each room has a private entrance, fireplace (three even have a fireplace in the bathroom), and each is uniquely decorated. The theme here is the use of colors, which are richly displayed on the walls and in the furnishings. There's Puerta Azul, a cozy blue room; Puerta Verde, done in deep greens; and Puerta Turquese, a separate turquoise-painted guest cottage with a full kitchen. The two newest rooms, completed in 1996, have bold maroon and copper-yellow themes. The walls have hand prints and petroglyph motifs, and each room is furnished with rich and comfortable couches. Both have large jet tubs supplied with bubble bath and candles.

Morning brings a delicious full gourmet breakfast in front of the fire (in winter) in the glassed-in breakfast room. You can expect such delights as bansoufflé pancakes or apple caramel bread pudding, or their specialty, migas, a mixture of eggs, tortillas chips, chile, and cheese, served with salsa, turkey sausage, and a citrus fruit compote. Chuck and Charil are most gracious hosts; they will help you plan activities and make dinner reservations.

Adobe and Stars Bed and Breakfast Inn. At the corner of Hwy. 150 and Valdez Rim Rd. (P.O. Box 2285), Taos, NM 87571. ☎ **800/211-7076** or 505/776-2776. 8 units. TEL. $95–$180 double. Rates include full breakfast and hors d'oeuvres. AE, DISC, MC, V. Free parking.

On first appearance, this brand-new inn looks stark, sitting on the mesa between Taos town and Taos Ski Valley. However, once inside, it's apparent that innkeeper Judy Salathiel has an eye for detail. The breakfast area and common room are sunny, with large windows facing the mountains. A few rooms are upstairs, such as La Luna, my favorite, with views in every direction and a heart-shaped Jacuzzi tub for two. All rooms have kiva fireplaces and private decks or patios. Most of the downstairs rooms open onto a portal. All are decorated with handcrafted Southwestern-style furniture, and many have Jacuzzi tubs. The full breakfast may vary from New Mexican dishes (such as breakfast burritos served with green chile stew) to baked goods (apple and strawberry turnovers). In the afternoons, New Mexico wines are served with the inn's special salsa and blue-corn chips, as are sweets such as chocolate cake and piñon lemon bars.

✪ **Alma del Monte—Spirit of the Mountain.** 372 Hondo Seco Rd., P.O. Box 1434, Taos, NM 87571. ☎ **800/273-7203,** 505/776-2721, or 505/776-8888. 5 units. $125–$150 double; prices vary with seasons and holidays. Rates include full breakfast. AE, MC, V.

For a real Taos experience I highly recommend this bed-and-breakfast recently built on sage-covered lands bordered by fast-rising mountains and on the way to the ski area. The house is a new horseshoe-shaped, Pueblo-style adobe; each room opens onto the courtyard outfitted with a fountain and hammocks hanging in the warm months. Proprietor Suzanne Head has designed and decorated the place impeccably; the living/dining room provides excellent sunrise and sunset views, and the house has Saltillo tile floors and traditional antiques, as well as elegant Ralph Lauren bedding. Each room has a jet tub and kiva-style fireplace. Many have picture window views and skylights while others have private gardens. Above all, the rooms are quiet, since no roads border the property. Breakfasts are equally unique: Specialties such as a deep-dish baked apple pancake or French toast stuffed with fruit and cream cheese are served on china with real silverware.

✪ **Casa de las Chimeneas.** 405 Cordoba Lane at Los Pandos Rd. (Box 5303), Taos, NM 87571. ☎ **505/758-4777.** Fax 505/758-3976. www.taoswebb.com/hotel/chimneyhouse. E-mail: casa@newmex.com. 7 units. A/C TV TEL. $130–$160 double; $160 suite (for 2). Rates include breakfast and hors d'oeuvres. AE, MC, V.

This 80-year-old adobe home has, since its opening in 1988, been a model of Southwestern elegance. Now, with a new addition, it has become a full service luxury inn as well. The addition includes a spa with a small fitness room and sauna, as well as complete massage and facial treatments given by Mountain Massage and Spa Treatments, for an additional charge. If I had a choice to stay in any room New Mexico, my first would be the Rio Grande Room here and the second would be the Territorial Room. Both of these new rooms have heated Saltillo tile floors, gas kiva fireplaces, and jetted tubs. If you prefer a more antique-feeling room, the older section is delightful. Each room in the inn is decorated with original works of art and has elegant bedding, a private entrance, and minirefrigerators stocked with complimentary soft drinks, juices, and mineral water. You'll also find bathrobes, ironing boards, irons, and hair dryers, as well as a self-service Laundromat on the premises. All rooms have kiva fireplaces and most look out on flower and herb gardens. My favorite in the older section is the blue room, with handmade quilts and Saltillo tile decorated with grapes. Breakfasts are complete and delicious. Specialties include an artichoke heart and mushroom baked omelette or ricotta cream cheese blintz, as well as innkeeper Susan Vernon's special fruit frappé. In the evenings, hors d'oeuvres are elaborate. In one evening I had canapés with avocado, cheese, and tomato, a spicy broccoli soup, and moonshine cake. End the day in the large hot tub in the courtyard. Smoking is not permitted.

Inn on La Loma Plaza. 315 Ranchitos Rd. (Box 4159), Taos, NM 87571. ☎ **800/ 530-3040** or 505/758-1717. Fax 505/751-0155. 7 units. TV TEL. $95–$150 standard double;

ℹ️ Family-Friendly Hotels

Best Western Kachina Lodge & Meeting Center *(see below)*   An outdoor swimming pool and snack machines in the summer make a great late-afternoon diversion for hot, tired, and cranky kids.

El Pueblo Lodge *(see page 227)*   A slide, year-round swimming pool, and hot tub set on 3½ acres of land will please the kids; a barbecue, some minikitchens with microwave ovens, laundry facilities, and the rates will please their parents.

$170–$195 artist's studio; $320–$330 suite. Extra person $20. Children 12 and under $10 in parents' room. Discounts available. Rates include breakfast. AE, MC, V.

You may just pass by the most wonderful thing about this place if you don't look for it. The inn (formerly the Hacienda Inn) is located on a historic neighborhood plaza, complete with dirt streets and a tiny central park. It doesn't look like much, but it's a chance to glimpse a neighborhood stronghold—adobe homes built around a square, with thick outer walls to fend off marauders. The inn is made from a 200-year-old home, complete with aged vigas and maple floors, decorated tastefully with comfortable furniture and Middle Eastern rugs. Each room is unique, most with sponge-painted walls, willow shutters, and talavera tile in the bathrooms to provide an eclectic ambience. All have fireplaces, and most have balconies or terraces with views. Some have special touches, such as the Happy Trails Room, with knotty pine paneling, a brass bed, old chaps, and decorative hanging spurs. Some rooms have kitchenettes. This two-story building, a 10-minute walk from the Plaza, has a large front lawn lined with bulbs and perennials blooming in the warmer months, as well as a brick patio and Jacuzzi. Breakfast burritos and other delicacies are served in a sunroom filled with plants or on the patio.

MODERATE
Hotels

⭘ **Best Western Kachina Lodge & Meeting Center.** 413 Paseo del Pueblo Norte (P.O. Box NN), Taos, NM 87571. ☎ **800/522-4462** or 505/758-2275. Fax 505/758-9207. www.kachinalodge.com. E-mail: sales@kachinalodge.com. 118 units. A/C TV TEL. $49–$150 double, depending on the season (Memorial Day to mid-October, and Christmas and spring break are high season) and total hotel occupancy. Extra person $10. Children under 12 stay free in parents' room. AE, DC, DISC, MC, V. No pets are allowed.

This lodge on the north end of town is an ideal spot for families and travelers. Built in the early 1960s, it has a lot of charm despite the fact that it's really a motor hotel. Rooms are placed around a grassy courtyard studded with huge blue spruce trees. In the center is a stage where a family from Taos Pueblo builds a bonfire and dances nightly in the summer and explains the significance of the dances—a real treat for anyone baffled by the Pueblo rituals.

Remodeling is ongoing in the Southwest-style rooms—some have couches and most have little Taos-style *trasteros* (armoires) that hold the televisions. The rooms are solidly built and quiet, and there's plenty of outdoor space for the kids to run, as well as a Jacuzzi and a large pool area that management assures me will get needed new tile by our publication date (but they assured me of that last year too, so. . .). A few rooms have kitchenettes. A Laundromat, beauty salon, and shopping arcade are also on the premises, and a courtesy limo is available.

The lodge has a number of eating and entertainment options: The **Hopi Dining Room** offers a family style menu; the **Kiva Coffee Shop** is kiva shaped (round), making it a unique Southwestern diner; and the **Zuni Lounge** is open nightly.

Comfort Suites. 1500 Paseo del Pueblo Sur (P.O. Box 1268), Taos, NM 87571. ☎ **888/ 751-1555** or 505/751-1555. http://taoswebb.com/taoshotels/comfortsuites/. E-mail: comfort@taos.newmex.com. 62 units. A/C TV TEL. $69–$129 double. Rates include continental breakfast. AE, CB, DC, DISC, MC, V. Free parking.

New, clean, predictable. That's what you'll get in this recent addition to the Taos accommodation scene. Each room has a small living/dining area, with a sleeper/sofa, microwave, minirefrigerator and coffeemaker, and a bedroom with handcrafted wood furniture and a comfortable king and queen bed. If you have kids you might want a ground-floor poolside room. Though the pool isn't landscaped, it's roomy and is accompanied by a hot tub.

La Fonda de Taos. South Plaza (P.O. Box 1447), Taos, NM 87571. ☎ **800/833-2211** or 505/758-2211. Fax 505/758-8508. 27 units. TEL. $65 double; $110 suite. AE, MC, V.

If this hotel can make it through a difficult transition time, it could be worth the stay. Recently its flamboyant owner Saki Karavas died, and the hotel came under new ownership; the owners had big plans to remodel, but are being held up in litigation with Karavas' estate. Though the lobby is charming, with antique hand-carved pine furniture and bright Mexican-painted trim, all under a high ceiling with skylights, the hotel needs work. The only lodging on the Plaza, La Fonda once hosted many of Taos's most glamorous guests in the '40s, '50s, and '60s. Through the years it has been known for its art collection, much of which remained with the previous owner's family. However, the strange, erotic oil paintings by D. H. Lawrence are still on view—pictures he brought to Taos in 1929 when they, along with his novel *Lady Chatterley's Lover*, were banned in England. Currently, the rooms have rather downtrodden furniture and decor.

Ramada Inn. 615 Paseo del Pueblo Sur, Taos, NM 87571. ☎ **800/659-TAOS** or 505/ 758-2900. Fax 505/758-1662. 124 units. A/C TV TEL. $69–$120 double. Rollaway $15 extra. Children under 18 stay free in parents' room. Rates include extended continental breakfast. AE, CB, DC, DISC, MC, V. Free parking.

This recently remodeled adobe-style hotel, a 10-minute walk from the Plaza, gives you what you'd expect from a chain hotel and that's why its very popular for travelers as well as tour groups. Built in 1995, it came under new ownership in 1996 and underwent a remodeling that gives it a warm, Southwestern feel. The rooms have new mattresses, box springs, TVs, carpet, drapes, and floral bedspreads. Though a little dark, the units are well constructed and quiet.

The hotel offers dry cleaning and laundry service (Monday through Friday), an indoor swimming pool, Jacuzzi, and sundeck.

Sagebrush Inn. Paseo del Pueblo Sur (P.O. Box 557), Taos, NM 87571. ☎ **800/428-3626** or 505/758-2254. Fax 505/758-5077. 100 units. A/C TV TEL. $70–$95 standard double; $90–$110 deluxe double; $95–$115 minisuite; $105–$140 executive suite. Extra person $10. Children under 12 stay free in parents' room. Rates include breakfast. AE, CB, DC, DISC, MC, V. Free parking.

Three miles south of Taos, surrounded by acres of sage, this inn is a strong example of the life of an adobe building, added onto decade after decade, creating an interesting mix of accommodations. The edifice was built in 1929 as a stagecoach stop. The original structure had 3 floors and 12 rooms hand-sculpted from adobe; the roof was held in place with hand-hewn vigas. This part still remains, and the rooms are small and cozy and have the feel of old Taos—in fact, Georgia O'Keeffe lived and worked here for 10 months in the late 1930s. But for those more accustomed to refined style, it might feel dated.

The treasure of this place is the large grass courtyard dotted with elm trees, where visitors sit and read in the warm months. Beware that some of the rooms added in the '50s through '70s have a tackiness not overcome by the vigas and tile work. More recent additions (to the west) are more skillful; these suites away from the hotel proper are spacious and full of amenities, but have noisy plumbing. All rooms have coffeemakers and minirefrigerators.

The lobby-cum-cantina has an Old West feel that livens at night with country-western dancing. Traditionally this has been a family hotel, but with a new convention center and an addition of a Comfort Suites hotel on the property, they're working to appeal to convention guests as well. With this addition there are now two outdoor pools, three Jacuzzis, tennis courts, and a business center.

The **Los Vaqueros Room** is open for dinner daily. A complimentary full breakfast is served to guests daily in the **Sagebrush Dining Room.** The lobby bar is one of Taos's most active nightspots for live music and dancing (see "The Club & Music Scene," below).

The hotel provides valet laundry and a courtesy van.

Bed & Breakfasts

Casa Europa. 840 Upper Ranchitos Rd. (HC 68, Box 3F), Taos, NM 87571. ☎ **800/ 758-9798** or 505/758-9798. 6 units. TEL. $70–$165 double. Extra person $20. Rates include full breakfast and evening hors d'oeuvres or European pastries. MC, V.

This cream-colored Territorial-style adobe (just 1¾ miles west of the Plaza) under giant cottonwoods is surrounded by open pastures dotted with grazing horses and offers lovely views of the mountains in the distance. Some rooms here date from the 1700s; however, a 1983 renovation made this a contemporary two-story luxury inn. Elegant rooms, all with fireplaces, sitting areas, and full bathrooms (two have two-person hot tubs), are furnished with interesting antiques. The regional artwork in the rooms can be purchased. There's a sitting area with a television upstairs and a common sitting room for reading and/or conversation downstairs, where coffee and pastries are offered each day between 3 and 4pm; during ski season hors d'oeuvres are served from 5 to 6pm. A full gourmet breakfast (specialties include cheese blintzes with a warm strawberry sauce and vegetarian eggs Benedict) is served each morning in the formal dining room. There's also an outdoor hot tub as well as a Swedish dry sauna. In-room massages are available at an extra charge. Smoking is not permitted.

Cottonwood Inn. 2 State Rd. 230 (HCR 74, Box 24609), El Prado–Taos, NM 87529. ☎ **800/324-7120** or 505/776-5826. Fax 505/776-1141. 7 units. $85–$165 double. Rates include full breakfast and afternoon snack. MC, V.

This inn provides cozy comfort in a rural setting. Built in 1947 by a flamboyant artist, it has high ceilings with vigas and almost every room has a kiva fireplace. Renovated in 1996, the inn has new owners, Kit and Bill Owen. They have made the place luxurious, using thick carpeting in many of the rooms and Saltillo tile in the bathrooms, as well as adding Jacuzzi tubs and steam baths to some rooms. The rooms have down pillows and comforters on the beds and are decorated in a subtle, South-western style. The inn's location halfway between Taos and the ski area lends a pastoral quality to your stay, with a herd of sheep wandering in a meadow to the west. My favorite rooms are the ones that open into the main part of the house, but if you prefer a private entrance, you have that option too. Rooms for nonsmokers and people with disabilities are available.

Hacienda del Sol. 109 Mabel Dodge Lane (P.O. Box 177), Taos, NM 87571. ☎ **505/ 758-0287.** Fax 505/758-5895. 10 units. $78–$145 double. Rates include full breakfast. MC, V. Children welcome.

What's most unique about this bed-and-breakfast is its completely unobstructed view of Taos Mountain. The 1.2-acre property borders the Taos Pueblo; the land is pristine, and the inn has a rich history. It was once owned by arts patron Mabel Dodge Luhan, and it was here that author Frank Waters wrote *The People of the Valley*. Innkeeper Marcine Landon considers herself somewhat of a gypsy in her use of bold splashes of color throughout the place, from the gardens, where in summer tulips, pansies, and flax grow, to the rooms themselves, where bold woven bedspreads and original art lend a Mexican feel. The main house is 190 years old, so it has the wonderful curves of adobe as well as thick vigas and deep windowsills. Some guest rooms are in this section. Others are 2 to 8 years old. These are finely constructed and I almost recommend them over the others since they're a little more private and the bathrooms more refined. All rooms have robes and books on New Mexico. Some have mini-refrigerators and cassette players. Breakfast includes specialties such as blue-corn pancakes with blueberry sauce and eggs del sol, a crustless quiche with corn and salsa, as well as wild plum piñon nut bread baked at Taos Pueblo. The Jacuzzi has a mountain view and is available for private guest use in half-hour segments.

La Doña Luz. 114 Kit Carson Rd., Taos, NM 87571. ☎ **800/758-9187** or 505/758-4874. Fax 505/758-4541. 16 units. TV. $59–$125 double. Rates include extended continental breakfast. AE, DISC, MC, V.

There's a real artisan quality to this inn (formerly El Rincón Inn) just off the Plaza. The innkeepers, Nina Meyers and her son Paul "Paco" Castillo, have made it that way: Nina painted murals on doors and walls and Paco carved wood and set tile. The 200-year-old structure was once home to 19th-century cultural leader La Doña Luz Lucero de Martinez, who was most known for her hospitality. These innkeepers carry on her legacy. The inn comprises two dwellings separated by a flower-filled courtyard, where breakfast is served in warm weather. Fine art and hand-carved furnishings representing the three cultures of Taos (Indian, Spanish, and Anglo) are scattered through both houses, some of which are heirloom quality, reminiscent of the museum in the inn's adjacent store, **El Rincón** (see "Shopping," below).

Renovation is ongoing throughout the place. For now, I recommend rooms in the main three-story house rather than the adjacent property connected to the store. The main-house rooms are up-to-date, all with VCRs, some with stereos and hot tubs, and two with full kitchens with amenities including a stove, microwave, dishwasher (only one has this), as well as a blender and slow cooker and a full-sized washer and dryer.

La Posada de Taos. 309 Juanita Lane (P.O. Box 1118), Taos, NM 87571. ☎ **800/645-4803** or 505/758-8164. www.taosnet.com/laposada/. E-mail: laposada@taos.newmex.com. 5 units, 1 cottage. $85–$120 double. Winter discounts available except during holidays. Extra person $15. Rates include full breakfast. No credit cards. Children 13 and over welcome. No pets.

Martha Stewart would be very comfortable at this B&B situated in the historic La Loma Historic District just 2½ blocks from the Plaza, and though I have little in common with her, I was too. Full of Americana (and European antiques) collected by proprietor Nancy Brooks-Swan, it rests within thick and cozy adobe walls; the combination of Mexican tile and New England quilts is elegant. It's difficult to select a favorite room here, though I'd say the three off the common area are the coziest. All the rooms except one have fireplaces and private patios. El Solecito and the Beutler room have Jacuzzi tubs. Most delightful of all is that Nancy and Bill Swan sit down with guests for breakfast, and they'll keep you laughing while regaling you with tales of the inn and their adventures in Taos. The food is excellent. We had a fluffy egg pie with salsa and to-die-for home-baked pecan rolls. The inn provides a free pass to Taos Spa.

✪ **Little Tree Bed & Breakfast.** P.O. Drawer II, Taos, NM 87571. ☎ **505/776-8467.**
4 units. $80–$105 double. Rates include breakfast and afternoon snack. AE, DISC, MC, V.

Little Tree is one of my favorite Taos bed-and-breakfasts, partly because it's located in a beautiful, secluded setting, and partly because it's constructed with real adobe that's been left in its raw state, lending the place an authentic hacienda feel. Located 2 miles down a country road about midway between Taos and the ski area, it's surrounded by sage and piñon.

The rooms are charming and very cozy. They all have adobe floors, which are warm in the winter because radiant heat has been installed here. All rooms feature queen-size beds, private bathrooms, and access to the portal and courtyard garden, at the center of which is the little tree for which the inn is named. The Piñon (my favorite) and Juniper rooms are equipped with fireplaces and private entrances. The Piñon and Aspen rooms offer sunset views. The Spruce Room, Western in feeling, is decorated with beautiful quilts. All but one have a TV and VCR.

In the main building, the living room has a traditional viga-and-latilla ceiling and tierra blanca adobe (adobe that's naturally white; if you look closely at it you can see little pieces of mica and straw). Two cats entertain, and the visiting hummingbirds enchant guests as they enjoy a healthful breakfast on the portal during warmer months. On arrival, guests are treated to refreshments.

Mabel Dodge Luhan House. 240 Morada Lane (P.O. Box 558), Taos, NM 87571. ☎ **800/ 84-MABEL** or 505/751-9686. 18 units (13 with bathroom). $75–$150 double. Extra person $17.50. Rates include full breakfast. MC, V.

This inn is also called "Las Palomas de Taos" because of the throngs of doves (palomas; actually, they looked like pigeons to me) that live in enchanting weathered birdhouses on the property. Like so many other free spirits, they were attracted by the flamboyant Mabel Dodge (1879–1962), who came to Taos in 1916. A familiar name in these parts, she and her fourth husband, a full-blooded Pueblo named Tony Luhan, enlarged this 200-year-old home to its present size of 22 rooms in the 1920s. If you like history, and don't mind the curves and undulations it brings to a building, this is a good choice. The place has a mansion feel, evoking images of the glitterati of the 1920s—writers, artists, adventurers—sitting on the terrace under the cottonwoods drinking margaritas. The entrance is marked by a Spanish colonial–style portal.

Recently under new ownership, badly needed repairs are being made. All main rooms have thick vigas, arched Pueblo-style doorways, hand-carved doors, kiva fireplaces, and dark hardwood floors. Guest rooms in the main building feature antique furnishings. Six have fireplaces; bathrooms are either private or shared. Eight more guest rooms were recently added with the completion of a second building. All new accommodations are equipped with fireplaces. Many educational workshops are held here throughout the year; the rooms are often reserved for participants. The Mabel Dodge Luhan House is now a National Historic Landmark.

Old Taos Guesthouse. 1028 Witt Rd. (Box 6552), Taos, NM 87571. ☎ **800/758-5448** or 505/758-5448. www.taoswebb.com/hotel/oldtaoshouse/. 9 units. $70–$125 double. MC, V. Children are welcome.

Less than 2 miles from the Plaza, this 150-year-old adobe hacienda sits on 7.5 acres and provides a cozy northern New Mexico rural experience. Once a farmer's home and later an artist's estate, it's recently been restored by owners Tim and Leslie Reeves, who have carefully maintained the country charm: Mexican tile in the bathrooms, vigas on the ceilings, and kiva-style fireplaces in most of the rooms. Each room enters from the outside, some off the broad portal that shades the front of the hacienda, some from a grassy lawn in the back, with a view toward the mountains. Some rooms are more utilitarian, some more quaint, so make a request depending on your needs. One of my favorites is the Taos Suite, with a king bed, a big picture window, and a full kitchen that includes an oven, stove, minirefrigerator, and microwave. I also like the charming room (no name) that opens out toward the back; it's cozy with a low ceiling and vigas, though the bathroom is small. There's a grass-surrounded hot tub (scheduled on the half hour) with an amazing view. If you're lucky like I was, you might get to soak while big snow flakes fall. Also in back is a nature and history path, recently completed, where guests can read brief quips about chamisa bushes and acequia systems (ditch systems), and see some too. The Reeves pride themselves on their healthful breakfasts. They serve a pot of hot organic oatmeal, homemade granola (Leslie's grandmother's recipe), and baked breads and muffins, all worth lingering over in the big common room where the sun shines through wide windows. If you're lucky, Tim will pull out some of his wild skiing videos. Smoking is allowed outside only.

Salsa del Salto. P.O. Box 1468, El Prado, NM 87529. ☎ **800/530-3097** or 505/776-2422. Fax 505/776-5734. 10 units. $85–$160 double. Extra person $20. MC, V.

Situated between Taos town and the Taos Ski Valley, Salsa del Salto is a good choice for those seeking a secluded retreat equipped like a country club. The main house was built in 1971 and has the openness of that era's architecture. The rooms here are tastefully decorated with pastel shades in a Southwestern motif and the beds are covered with cozy down comforters. Each room offers views of the mountains or mesas of Taos, and the private bathrooms are modern and spacious, each with a hair dryer. Two new rooms (my favorites) are well designed, decorated in a whimsical Southwestern style, and each includes two queen beds, a minirefrigerator, fireplace, TV, VCR, and jet tub.

The focus here is on relaxation and outdoor activities. Salsa del Salto is the only bed-and-breakfast in Taos with a pool, hot tub, and private tennis courts. Innkeeper Mary Hockett, a native New Mexican and avid sportswoman, is eager to share information about her favorite activities with her guests. Mary's husband, Dadou Mayer, who was born and raised in Nice, France, is an accomplished chef (and the author of *Cuisine à Taos,* a French cookbook). Dadou has also been a member of the French National Ski Team, and was named "The Fastest Chef in the United States" when he won the Grand Marnier Ski Race. During the winter, you'll get the added bonus of an early morning briefing about ski conditions.

Willows Inn. 412 Kit Carson Rd. (at Dolan St.) (Box 6560 NDCBU), Taos, NM 87571. ☎ **800/525-8267** or 505/758-2558. Fax 505/758-5445. E-mail: willows@taos.newmex.com. 5 units. $95–$130 double. Rates include full breakfast and hors d'oeuvres. AE, MC, V.

What sets this inn apart from the rest is that it sits on the estate of E. Marin Hennings (one of the Taos Society artists). Built in the 1920s, the inn has thick adobe walls and kiva fireplaces in each guest room. It lies just a half mile from the Plaza, but within a tall adobe wall so it's very secluded. The grassy yard is decorated with fountains, and, most impressively, shaded by gargantuan weeping willow trees that may be more than 300 years old.

The common area is cozy and comes equipped with a TV, VCR, and CD player with access to innkeepers Janet and Doug Camp's extensive music collection— more than 450 classical and jazz CDs. The guest rooms are also cozy and have rich personality. Built around a courtyard, they have old latch doors, oak floors, tin light fixtures, and kiva fireplaces. I recommend the Santa Fe Room, which has a nice sitting area in front of the fireplace and looks out toward the garden. Hennings's spacious studio still has paint splattered on the floor. It has a Jacuzzi tub in the bathroom.

Breakfast specialties include apricot-stuffed French toast served with bacon, and chile-cheese egg soufflé served with applesauce muffins and sausage. The inn offers guided fly-fishing trips for novices to experts. Smoking is permitted outdoors only.

INEXPENSIVE

Abominable Snowmansion Skiers' Hostel. Taos Ski Valley Rd., Arroyo Seco (P.O. Box 3271), Taos, NM 87571. ☎ **505/776-8298.** Fax 505/776-2107. http://taoswebb.com/hotel/snowmansion. E-mail: snowman@newmex.com. 60 beds. $13–$22 for bed; $38–$60 private room, double, depending on size of accommodation and season; cabins and teepees $12, camping $10. Rates include full breakfast in winter. DISC, MC, V.

Since I was a kid, I've traveled past this hostel; it was a treat for me to finally experience the inside. Set in the quaint village of Arroyo Seco about 8 miles north of Taos and 10 miles from the Taos Ski Valley, it offers clean beds for reasonable prices, and a nice community experience. The common room has a pool table, piano, and circular fireplace. The dorm rooms (two men's and two women's) have 8 to 10 beds, and sheets, towels, and blankets are provided free in winter or for a small fee in summer. Each dorm room has its own shower and bathroom. The private rooms are spacious, though the decor is only passable. Best of all are the teepees that sit out around a grassy yard. They sleep two to four people and have an outdoor kitchen, showers, and toilets nearby.

El Pueblo Lodge. 412 Paseo del Pueblo Norte, Taos, NM 87571. ☎ **800/433-9612** or 505/758-8700. Fax 505/758-7321. http://taoswebb.com/hotel/elpueblo/. E-mail: elpueblo@newmex.com. 65 units. TV TEL. $68–$82 double; $105–$215 suite. Call for Christmas rates. Extra person $7–$10. Rates include continental breakfast. AE, DISC, MC, V. Pets are permitted for an extra $10.

Considering its location and setting, this hotel is a bargain, especially for families, although you'll want to reserve carefully. It's set on 3½ grassy, cottonwood-shaded acres on the north end of town, a reasonable walk from the Plaza. Three buildings form a U shape, each with its own high and low points. The oldest part to the south was once a 1950s court motel, and it maintains that cozy charm, with heavy vigas and tiny kitchenettes. This section could use some updating, but it's worth the price. To the north is a two-story building, constructed in 1972, that seems frail and lacks charm, but provides lots of space. The newest section (to the west) is one of Taos's best bargains, with nicely constructed suites and double rooms decorated in blonde pine with kiva fireplaces and doors that open onto the center yard or, if you're on the second floor, onto a balcony. There are also fully equipped condominium units (with 1970s construction) that are good for large families. An outdoor swimming pool and hot tub are on the premises, and there's free use of laundry facilities.

Indian Hills Inn. 233 Paseo del Pueblo Sur (P.O. Box 1229), Taos, NM 87571. ☎ **800/444-2346** or 505/758-4293. www.taosnet.com/indianhillsinn. E-mail: indianhills@taosnet.com. 55 units. A/C TV TEL. $49–$99 double; group and package rates available. Rates include continental breakfast. AE, DC, DISC, MC, V.

With its close location to the Plaza (3 blocks), this is a good choice if you're looking for a decent, functional night's stay. There are two sections to the hotel: one built in the 1950s, the other completed in 1996. The older section has just received a major face-lift: carpet, doors, artwork, drapes, bedspreads, sinks, and vanities. However, for a few more dollars you can stay in the newer section, where the rooms are larger, the bathrooms fresher. The buildings are set around a broad lawn studded with big blue spruce trees. There are picnic tables, barbecue grills, and a pool. The hotel offers golf, ski, and rafting packages at reduced rates.

☉ Sun God Lodge. 919 Paseo del Pueblo Sur (5513 NDCBU), Taos, NM 87571. ☎ **800/ 821-2437** or 505/758-3162. Fax 505/758-1716. 55 units. TV TEL. $45–$99 double; $100–$150 casita. AE, MC, DISC, V. Pets are allowed with $50 deposit.

For a comfortable, economical stay with a northern New Mexico ambience, this is my choice. This hotel, a 5-minute drive from the Plaza, has three distinct parts spread across 1½ acres of landscaped grounds. The oldest was solidly built in 1958 and has some court motel charm with a low ceiling and large windows. To update the rooms, owners added talavera tile sinks, Taos-style furniture, and new carpeting. To the south is a recently remodeled section, built in 1988. The rooms are small but have little touches that make them feel cozy, such as pink accent walls, little *nichos,* and hand-carved furnishings. In back to the east are the newest buildings built in 1994. These are two-story with portal-style porches and balconies. Some rooms have kitchenettes, which include microwaves, refrigerators, and stoves (all rooms have coffeemakers), while others have kiva fireplaces. The two rooms on the northeast corner of the property are the quietest and have the best views. There is a Jacuzzi.

TAOS SKI VALLEY
EXPENSIVE
Hotels

Alpine Village Suites. P.O. Box 98, Taos Ski Valley, NM 87525. ☎ **800/576-2666** or 505/ 776-8540. Fax 505/776-8542. 24 units. TV TEL. Summer $60–$85 double (includes continental breakfast); winter $140–$200 double, $240–$260 suite that sleeps up to 6. AE, DISC, MC, V. Covered valet parking $10.

Alpine Village is a small village within the ski valley a few steps from the lift. Owned by John and Barbara Cottam, the complex also houses a ski shop and bar/restaurant. The Cottams began with seven rooms, still nice rentals, above their ski shop. Each has a sleeping loft for the agile who care to climb a ladder, as well as sunny windows. The newer section has nicely decorated rooms, with attractive touches such as Mexican furniture and inventive tile work done by locals. As with most accommodations at Taos Ski Valley, the rooms are not especially soundproof. Fortunately, most skiers go to bed early. All rooms have VCRs and small kitchenettes equipped with stoves, microwaves, and minirefrigerators. In the newer building, rooms have fireplaces and private balconies. Request a south-facing room for a view of the slopes. The hot tub has a fireplace and a view of the slopes. There's a sauna on premises as well as massage facilities with a massage therapist.

Chalet Montesano. P.O. Box 77, Taos Ski Valley, NM 87525. ☎ **800/723-9104** or 505/776-8226. Fax 505/776-8760. http://taoswebb.com/chaletmontesano. E-mail: chalet@ taosnm.com. 7 units. TV TEL. Winter $118–$188 double; $163–$276 suite; summer $85–$90 double; $110–$165 suite. Weekly rates range from $750–$2,307, depending on type of room and number of people. AE, DISC, MC, V. Children 14 and older are accepted.

This chalet constructed from a turn-of-the-century miner's cabin is a nice romantic ski vacation retreat. A 5-minute walk from restaurants and the lift, you wouldn't expect to find such a woodsy, secluded place, but that's what innkeepers Victor and Karin Frohlich, who have been in Taos Ski Valley since the 1960s, have successfully created. All rooms have a Bavarian feel, with nice touches such as CD players, VCRs, coffeemakers, and minirefrigerators, and all but the standard rooms have fireplaces. In the studios you'll find Murphy beds that fold into hand-crafted chests to leave plenty of room for daytime living. These and the one-bedroom apartments have full kitchens, with stove, oven, microwave, and dishwasher. On the west side of the building is a picturesque lap pool, health club, and hot tub banked by windows with views of the runs and forest. No smoking is allowed here.

Hotel Edelweiss. P.O. Box 83, Taos Ski Valley, NM 87525. ☎ **800/I-LUV-SKI** or 505/776-2301. Fax 505/776-2533. www.taosnet.com/edelweiss. E-mail: edelweiss@taos.newmex.com. 10 units. TEL. May–Oct $65 double. Winter $170 double; summer "Gourmet" B&B package $49 per person. Ski season packages also available. Rates include full breakfast. AE, MC, V.

The big drawing card for this A-frame hotel built in 1973 and remodeled in 1996 is its location. Set between the beginner's hill and the main lift, it's a good place for families. You can look forward to a full breakfast (included in room packages) as well as Asian noodle lunches served in the sunny cafe. For dinner, guests get to dine at the famed and exclusive St. Bernard, well worth a visit. Families are very welcome here, and the most desirable rooms can accommodate them well. Baby-sitting can be arranged. I recommend rooms on the second and third floors, because the ground floor tends to be noisy. The upper rooms are separated from each other by stairs, so they're more quiet. All rooms have full-length robes, minirefrigerators, humidifiers, and hair dryers. There's a Jacuzzi with a view of the beginner's hill.

There is also a ski locker room with boot dryers and a full-service ski shop on the premises. Most important, with its proximity to the lifts, you can ski to and from your room. The owners, as well as others in the area, are promoting summer visits to Taos.

✪ **Inn at Snakedance.** 110 Sutton Place (P.O. Box 89), Taos Ski Valley, NM 87525. ☎ **800/ 322-9815** or 505/776-2277. Fax 505/776-1410. 60 units. TV TEL. May 22–Oct 3, $75 double; Oct 4–Nov 24, closed; Nov 25–Dec 18, $125 double; Dec 19–Dec 25, $175 double, $195 fireplace double; Dec 26–Jan 1 $250 double, $270 fireplace double; Jan 2–Feb 5 $175 double, $195 fireplace double; Feb 6–Mar 26, $195 double, $215 fireplace double; Mar 27–Apr 10, $125 double; April 11–May 20, closed. AE, MC, V. Free parking at Taos Ski Valley parking lot. Children over 6 are welcome.

This is my choice for on-slope accommodations. With all the luxuries of a full-service hotel, the Snakedance can please most family members, and it's just steps from the lift. The original structure that stood on this site (part of which has been restored for use today) was known as the Hondo Lodge. Before there was a Taos Ski Valley, Hondo Lodge served as a refuge for fishermen, hunters, and artists. Constructed from enormous pine timbers that had been cut for a copper mining operation in the 1890s, it was literally nothing more than a place for the men to bed down for the night. The Inn at Snakedance today offers comfortable guest rooms—the quietest in the valley— many of which feature wood-burning fireplaces. All of the furnishings are modern, the decor stylish, and the windows (many of which offer views) open to let in the mountain air. All rooms provide coffeemakers, hair dryers, minirefrigerators, wet bars (not stocked), humidifiers, and Spectravision movie channels. Some rooms adjoin, connecting a standard hotel room with a fireplace room—perfect for families. Smoking is prohibited in the guest rooms and most public areas.

Dining/Diversions: The **Hondo Restaurant and Bar** offers dining and entertainment daily during the ski season (schedules vary off-season) and also sponsors wine tastings and wine dinners. Grilled items, salads, and snacks are available on an outdoor deck. The slope-side bar provides great views.

Amenities: Shuttle service to nearby hotels, shops, and restaurants, video rentals, small health club (with hot tub, sauna, exercise equipment, and massage facilities), massage therapist on site, conference rooms, sundeck, in-house ski storage and boot dryers, convenience store (with food, sundries, video rental, and alcoholic beverages).

Powderhorn Suites and Condominiums. P.O. Box 69, Taos Ski Valley, NM 87525. ☎ **800/776-2346** or 505/776-2341. Fax 505/776-2341, ext. 103. http://taoswebb.com/ hotel/powderhorn/. E-mail: powder@newmex.com. 17 units. TV TEL. Winter $99–$150 double; $125–$190 suite; $190–$375 condo. Summer $59–$129 from 2–6-person occupancy. MC, V. Free parking near the inn.

For some time, the ski valley has needed this newer, moderately priced lodging just a 2-minute walk from the lift. Completely remodeled from a gutted structure in 1989, two years ago it came under new and very enthusiastic ownership. You'll find consistency here, not quite the quality of the Snakedance, nor the rustic nature of the Thunderbird and Edelweiss. There are a variety of types of units, all fairly roomy with spotless bathrooms and comfortable beds. Each also has a microwave, coffeemaker, and minirefrigerator. The larger suites have stoves, balconies, and fireplaces. Decorated in pastels that don't especially appeal to me, the rooms do have a sunny feel. All have views. There's a Jacuzzi on the fourth floor. If you're elderly or out of shape, request a room on the lower floors, as the only conveyance is stairs. Smoking is not allowed.

Condominiums

Kandahar Condominiums. P.O. Box 72, Taos Ski Valley, NM 87525. ☎ **800/756-2226** or 505/776-2226. Fax 505/776-2481. E-mail: kandahar@laplaza.org. 27 units. A/C TV TEL. Winter $250–$375; May–Oct $100–$125. Rates based on 4–6 people per unit. AE, MC, V.

These condos have almost the highest location on the slopes—and with it, ski-in/ski-out access; you actually ski down to the lift from here. Built in the 1960s, the condos have been maintained well and are sturdy and functional. Two stories and private bedrooms allow for more privacy than most condos offer. Each unit is privately owned, so decor varies, although a committee makes suggestions to owners for upgrading. Facilities include a very small health club, a Jacuzzi, Laundromat, steam room, professional massage therapist, and small conference/party facility. Situated just above the children's center, it offers good access for families with young children.

Sierra del Sol Condominiums. P.O. Box 84, Taos Ski Valley, NM 87525. ☎ **800/523-3954** or 505/776-2981. Fax 505/776-2347. http://taoswebb.com/hotel/sierradelsol. E-mail: sol@newmex.com. 32 units. TV TEL. Prices range from $65 for a studio in summer to $370 for a 2-bedroom condo in high season. AE, DISC, MC, V. Free parking.

I have wonderful memories of these condominiums, which are just a 2-minute walk from the lift; family friends used to invite me to stay with them when I was about 10. I was happy to see that the units, built in the 1960s with additions through the years, have been well maintained. Though they're privately owned, and therefore decorated at the whim of the owners, management does inspect them every year and make suggestions. They're smartly built and come in a few sizes, which they term studio, one bedroom, and two bedroom. The one- and two-bedroom units have big living rooms with fireplaces and porches that look out on the ski runs. The bedroom is spacious and has a sleeping loft. There's a full kitchen with a dishwasher, stove, oven, and refrigerator. Most rooms also have microwaves and humidifiers, and all have VCRs. There are indoor hot tubs and saunas. Two-bedroom units sleep up to six. There's also a business center, conference rooms, and a Laundromat. It's open in summer.

MODERATE
Lodges & Condominiums

Austing Haus Hotel. Taos Ski Valley Rd. (P.O. Box 8), Taos Ski Valley, NM 87525. ☎ **800/748-2932** or 505/776-2649. Fax 505/776-8751. 45 units. TV TEL. $49–$170 double. Rates include continental breakfast. AE, DISC, MC, V.

About 1½ miles from the ski resort, the Austing Haus is a beautiful example of a timber-frame building. It was hand-built by owner Paul Austing, who will gladly give you details of the process. Though an interesting structure, at times it feels a bit fragile. The guest rooms have a Victorian feel; they're comfortable if a little cutesy. Each room has its own ski locker, and there's a nice hot tub. Tasty continental cuisine is served in a sunny dining room. *Beware:* Water runs very hot from the taps—don't burn yourself.

Taos Mountain Lodge. Taos Ski Valley Rd. (P.O. Box 698), Taos Ski Valley, NM 87525. ☎ **800/530-8098** or 505/776-2229. Fax 505/776-8791. 10 units. A/C TV TEL. Winter $168–$275 suite; May–Oct $79.50–$122 suite. AE, MC, V.

About 1 mile west of the ski valley on the road from Taos, these loft suites (which can accommodate up to six) provide airy, comfortable lodging for a good price. Under new ownership, this lodge, built in 1990, is undergoing some renovation. I wouldn't expect a lot of privacy in these condominiums, but they're good for a romping ski vacation. Each unit has a small bedroom downstairs and a loft-bedroom upstairs, as well as a fold-out or futon couch in the living room. All rooms have microwaves and coffeemakers. Regular rooms have kitchenettes, with minirefrigerators and stoves, and deluxe rooms have more full kitchens, with full refrigerators, stoves, and ovens. There's daily maid service.

Thunderbird Lodge. P.O. Box 87, Taos Ski Valley, NM 87525. ☎ **800/776-2279** or 505/776-2280. Fax 505/776-2238. 32 units. $99–$142 double. Seven-day Ski Week Package $1,080–$1,350 per adult, double occupancy (7 days room, 21 meals, 6 lift tickets), depending on season and type of accommodation (if lift rates go up, these rates may change a little). AE, MC, V. Free valet parking.

Owners Elisabeth and Tom Brownell's goal at this Bavarian-style lodge is to bring people together, and they accomplish it, sometimes a little too well. The lodge sits on the sunny side of the ski area. The lobby has a stone fireplace, raw pine pillars, and tables accented with copper lamps. There's a sunny room ideal for breakfast and lunch, with a bank of windows looking out toward the notorious Al's Run and the rest of the ski village. Adjoining is a large bar/lounge with booths, a grand piano, and fireplace, where live entertainment plays during the evenings through the winter. The rooms are small, some tiny, and noise travels up and down the halls, giving these three stories a dormitory atmosphere. I suggest when making reservations that you request their widest room; otherwise you may feel as though you're stuck in a train car.

Across the road, the lodge also has a chalet with larger rooms and a brilliant sunporch. Food is the big draw here. Included in your stay, you get three gourmet meals—some of the best food available in the region. For breakfast we had blueberry pancakes and bacon, with our choice from a table of continental breakfast accompaniments, and for dinner we had four courses highlighted by rack of lamb Provençale. You can eat at your own table or join the larger communal one and get to know the guests, some of whom have been returning for as many as 28 years. You'll find saunas, a Jacuzzi, and a small conference/living area on the ground floor.

RV PARKS & CAMPGROUNDS
Carson National Forest. No. 208 Cruz Alta Rd., Taos, NM 87571. ☎ **505/758-6200.**

There are nine national forest campsites within 20 miles of Taos, all open from April or May until September or October, depending on snow conditions. For information on other public sites, contact the **Bureau of Land Management,** 226 Cruz Alta Rd., Taos, NM 87571 (☎ **505/758-8851**).

Enchanted Moon Campground. No. 7 Valle Escondido Rd. (on U.S. 64 E.), Valle Escondido, NM 87571. ☎ **505/758-3338.** 69 sites. Full RV hookup, $17 per day. Closed Nov–Apr.

At an elevation of 8,400 feet, this campground is surrounded by pine-covered mountains and sits up against Carson National Forest. There's a reasonably priced restaurant on-site.

Questa Lodge. Junction of NM 522 and NM 38 (P.O. Box 155), Questa, NM 87556. ☎ **505/586-0300.** 24 sites. Full RV hookup, $15 per day, $175 per month. Four cabins for rent in summer. AE, DISC, MC, V. Closed Nov–Apr.

On the banks of the Red River, this RV camp is just outside the small village of Questa. It's a nice pastoral setting. The cabins aren't in the best condition, but the RV and camping accommodations are pleasant—all with beautiful mountain views.

Taos RV Park. Paseo del Pueblo Sur (P.O. Box 729), Ranchos de Taos, NM 87557. ☎ **800/ 323-6009** or 505/758-1667. Fax 505/758-1989. 33 spaces. $12 without RV hookup, $19.50 with RV hookup. DISC, MC, V.

This RV park, located on the edge of town, offers a convenient location, but a city atmosphere. It has very clean, nice bathrooms and showers. Two teepees rent for $25 each, but beware, they're right on the main drag and may be noisy. It's located on a local bus line. Senior discounts are available.

✪ **Taos Valley RV Park and Campground.** 120 Estes Rd. off NM 68 (7204 NDCBU), Taos, NM 87571. ☎ **800/999-7571** or 505/758-4469. Fax 505/758-4469. www.camptaos. com/rv/. 92 spaces. $15–$17 without RV hookup, $21–$26 with RV hookup. MC, V. Limited services Nov 1–Mar 1.

Just 1½ miles south of the Plaza, this campground is surrounded by sage, with views of the surrounding mountains. Each site has a picnic table and grill. There's a small store, laundry room, playground and tent shelters, as well as a dump station and very clean restrooms.

4 Where to Dine

Taos is one of my favorite places to eat. Informality reigns; at a number of restaurants you can dine on world-class food while wearing jeans or even ski pants. Nowhere is a jacket and tie mandatory. This informality doesn't extend to reservations, however; especially during the peak season, it is important to make reservations well in advance and keep them or else cancel.

In the listings below, **expensive** refers to restaurants where most main courses are $15 or higher; **moderate** includes those where main courses generally range from $10 to $15; and **inexpensive** indicates that most main courses are $10 or less.

EXPENSIVE

Doc Martin's. In the Historic Taos Inn, 125 Paseo del Pueblo Norte. ☎ **505/758-1977.** Reservations recommended. Breakfast $3.95–$6.50; lunch $5.50–$10.50; dinner $13.50–$28; fixed-price menu $14.95–$16.95 Sun–Thurs. AE, DC, MC, V. Daily 7:30–11am, 11:30am–2:30pm and 5:30–9pm. NEW AMERICAN.

Doc Martin's restaurant (not to be confused with those urban-warrior boots *Doc Martens*) comprises Dr. Thomas Paul Martin's former home, office, and delivery room. In 1912, painters Bert Philips (Doc's brother-in-law) and Ernest Blumenschein hatched the concept of the Taos Society of Artists in the Martin dining room. Art still predominates here, in both the paintings that adorn the walls and the cuisine offered. The food is widely acclaimed, and the wine list has received numerous "Awards of Excellence" from *Wine Spectator* magazine.

The atmosphere is rich, with bins of yellow squash, eggplants, and red peppers set near the kiva fireplace. Recently redecorated, it follows a Southwestern decor. Breakfast might include local favorites: huevos rancheros (fried eggs on a blue-corn tortilla smothered with chile and Jack cheese) or "The Kit Carson" (eggs Benedict with a Southwestern flair). Lunch might include a portobello mushroom salad with bacon vinaigrette, or a shrimp burrito. For a dinner appetizer, I recommend one of the specials, such as black-bean cakes (on red chile sauce, with guacamole and goat cheese cream) or chile rellenos. This might be followed by seared salmon with brioche-lime dressing or the Southwest lacquered duck (poached, roasted, and grilled duck breast

Central Taos Dining

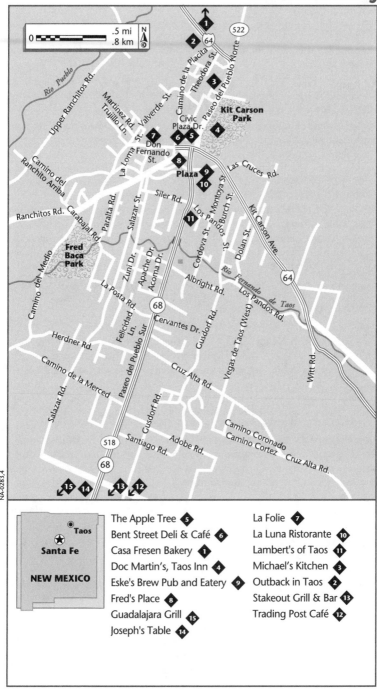

The Apple Tree ◆5	La Folie ◆7
Bent Street Deli & Café ◆6	La Luna Ristorante ◆10
Casa Fresen Bakery ◆1	Lambert's of Taos ◆11
Doc Martin's, Taos Inn ◆4	Michael's Kitchen ◆3
Eske's Brew Pub and Eatery ◆9	Outback in Taos ◆2
Fred's Place ◆8	Stakeout Grill & Bar ◆13
Guadalajara Grill ◆15	Trading Post Café ◆12
Joseph's Table ◆14	

NA-0283,4

233

served over julienne duck-leg meat and red chile broth with posole and mango relish). If you still have room, there's always a nice selection of desserts—try the citrus cheesecake, a lemon-, lime-, and orange-flavored cheesecake served with an orange-tarragon sauce.

✪ Joseph's Table. 4167 Hwy. 68, Ranchos de Taos. ☎ **505/751-4512.** Reservations recommended. Main courses $14–$20. AE, DC, DISC, MC, V. Tues–Thurs and Sun 5–10pm, Fri–Sat 5–11pm. NEW AMERICAN/MEDITERRANEAN.

Taos funk meets European flair at this intimate restaurant in Ranchos de Taos, about a 10-minute drive from the Plaza. In the original dining room, birdcages hang from the ceiling and medieval candles adorn the walls, while in a new room opera plays while diners are surrounded by a whimsical El Greco motif. Between faux-painted walls, chef/owners Joseph and Gina Wrede serve up such dishes as steak au poivre and grilled Chilean sea bass. What's interesting is the way these dishes are served. The steak sits atop a layer of smooth mashed potatoes and is crowned with an exotic mushroom salad, while the sea bass rests on potatoes, as well as a layer of mashed squash, and is surrounded by a tomato puree. For dessert try such delicacies as bread pudding or the dark- and white-chocolate marquis, which Joseph describes as "creamy like the inside of a truffle." An eclectic selection of beer and wine by the bottle and glass is available.

Lambert's of Taos. 309 Paseo del Pueblo Sur. ☎ **505/758-1009.** Reservations recommended. Main courses $8–$18.50. AE, DC, MC, V. Daily 5:50–closing, usually 9pm or so. CONTEMPORARY AMERICAN.

Zeke Lambert, a former San Francisco restaurateur who was head chef at Doc Martin's for 4 years, opened this fine dining establishment in late 1989 in the historic Randall Home near Los Pandos Road. It's a sparsely decorated place with contemporary art on the walls—a nice spot for a romantic evening. Though I've heard wonderful comments about the food here, I was not overly impressed. The service was friendly and efficient, and the meal always begins with a complimentary aperitif. I found the house salad nicely prepared with butter lettuce and radicchio. Appetizers include a Mediterranean olive plate and chile-dusted rock shrimp. I ordered the restaurant's signature dish, the pepper-crusted lamb. If you like strong flavors, this is your dish— very peppery, served with a red wine demiglace and linguine. I also tasted the shepherd's pie, lamb stew served with mashed potatoes, and wasn't overly impressed with the sauce. Others I've spoken to have enjoyed the grilled salmon with a tomato-sage sauce (at $16.50, a fair bargain). For dessert the white-chocolate ice cream and Zeke's chocolate mousse with raspberry sauce are quite delicious. Espresso coffee, beer, and wine are served.

Stakeout Grill & Bar. 101 Stakeout Dr., just off NM 68 (P.O. Box 453), Ranchos de Taos, 87557. ☎ **505/758-2042.** www.stakeoutrestaurant.com. Reservations recommended. Main courses $11.95–$25.95. AE, CB, DC, DISC, MC, V. Daily 5–9:30pm. CONTINENTAL.

Drive about a mile up a dirt road toward the base of the Sangre de Cristo Mountains, and dine looking down upon the Taos gorge while the sun sets over the Jemez Range. That's the experience at the Stakeout, south of Taos. You're enveloped in the warmth of rustic decor (which is a great contrast to the almost-white exterior). There are paneled walls, creaking hardwood floors, and a crackling fireplace in the winter. The fare, which focuses on steak and seafood, is fresh, thoughtfully prepared, and conscientiously served. You can start with baked Brie served with sliced almonds and apples or escargots baked with walnuts, herbs, white wine, and garlic. Move on to a filet mignon, served with béarnaise sauce and cooked to your liking. Or for something more exotic, try the duck Cumberland (half a duck roasted with apples and prunes and served with an orange-currant sauce). Among the seafood offerings are salmon,

---

ⓘ Family-Friendly Restaurants

Michael's Kitchen *(see page 238)*   With a broad menu, comfy booths, and a very casual, diner-type atmosphere, both kids and their parents will feel at home here.

Outback in Taos *(see page 236)*   The pizza will please both parents and kids, and so will all the odd decorations, such as the chain with foot-long links hanging over the front counter.

Alaskan king crab legs (steamed and served with drawn butter), scallops, and shrimp. Finish your meal with a fresh pastry and a cappuccino. Try to time your reservation so you can see the sunset. A full bar, extensive wine list, and cigars are available.

MODERATE

Apple Tree. 123 Bent St. ☎ **505/758-1900.** http://taoswebb.com/menu/appletree/html. E-mail: appletree@newmex.com. Reservations recommended. Lunch $5.25–$9.95; dinner $10.95–$18.95. AE, CB, DC, DISC, MC, V. Mon–Sat 11:30am–3pm; light meals and snacks daily 3–5:30pm; daily 5:30–9pm. Brunch Sun 10am–3pm. INTERNATIONAL.

Eclectic music pervades the four adobe rooms of this restaurant, a block north of the Plaza. Original paintings by Taos masters watch over the candlelit service indoors. Outside, diners sit at wooden tables on a graveled courtyard beneath a spreading apple tree.

This restaurant is popular among locals and travelers, but it doesn't appeal much to me. The recipes try too hard. I suggest ordering what looks simplest, either from the menu or from the daily specials. The Apple Tree salad (greens sprinkled with dried cranberries, walnuts, and blue cheese served with a vinaigrette) is very good, as is the posole (hominy with chile). A very popular dish, though too sweet for me, is mango chicken enchiladas (chicken simmered with onions and spices, layered between blue corn tortillas with mango chutney, sour cream, and salsa fresca and smothered with green chile). I prefer the Thai red curry (either vegetarian or with shrimp). The best thing here is the chile-jalapeño bread, served with the meal. The Apple Tree has an award-winning wine list, and the desserts are prepared fresh daily.

Bent Street Deli & Cafe. 120 Bent St. ☎ **505/758-5787.** Reservations accepted. Breakfast $1.25–$6; lunch $2.50–$8; dinner $10–$16. MC, V. Mon–Sat 8am–9pm. DELI/INTERNATIONAL.

This popular cafe a short block north of the Plaza has inventive, reliable food in a country-home atmosphere. Outside, a flower box surrounds the sidewalk cafe–style seating that is heated in winter. Inside, baskets and bottles of homemade jam accent wooden tables. The menu features breakfast burritos and homemade granola in the morning; for lunch you can choose from 18 deli sandwiches, plus a "create-your-own" column. At dinner, the menu becomes a bit more sophisticated, with dishes such as beef tenderloin medallions served over fettuccine with a chipotle-Fontina cream sauce, or roja shrimp (black tiger shrimp, red chile, and jicama, cilantro, and corn relish). All dinner entrees are served with a salad and freshly baked bread. If you'd like to grab a picnic to go, the deli offers carry-out service.

La Luna Ristorante. 223 Paseo del Pueblo Sur. ☎ **505/751-0023.** Reservations recommended. Main courses $7.95–$19.95. AE, DISC, MC, V. Daily 5pm–closing (around 10pm). ITALIAN.

This bright, airy restaurant is reminiscent of a cafe in Italy. Persimmon walls accent one area with tables nicely placed, some on a raised level. Another area has yellow walls and more intimate booths. In the warmer months there are tables outside, though, since it's a refurbished shopping center, the setting is a bit on the tarmac side. The restaurant surrounds a ceramic pizza/bread oven, which lends warmth throughout. Service is friendly and efficient. The restaurant came under new ownership in August 1997, and locals seem to think its good, though not stellar, reputation is holding. Appetizers are pretty basic, with various salads, including a Caesar. For an entree, I like the salmon, which is seared and served with rice and a honey-roasted shallot cream sauce. My friend's vegetarian pizza was crispy-crusted, with eggplant, mushrooms, artichoke hearts, and bell peppers—very tasty. I won't, however, recommend the *pollo alla Parmesan*, which was dry. There are also meat dishes and a variety of pastas. My favorite: *orechiette con salsiccia,* ear-shaped pasta with spicy Italian sausage and tomato sauce. Beer and wine are available by the glass or bottle.

✪ Outback in Taos. 712 Paseo del Pueblo Norte (just north of Allsup's). ☎ **505/ 758-3112.** Reservations recommended on holidays. Pizzas $11.25–$23.95; pastas and calzones $6.50–$9.25. MC, V. Winter Sun–Thurs 11am–9pm; Fri–Sat 11am–10pm; Summer daily 11am–10pm. PASTA AND GOURMET PIZZA.

My kayaking buddies always go here after a day on the river. That will give you an idea of the level of informality (very) as well as the quality of the food and beer (great) and the size of the portions (large). It's a raucous old hippie-decorated adobe restaurant, with friendly and eager wait staff. There are three rooms: an enclosed porch; the main room (my favorite), decorated with such works as an old gas pump topped by a lampshade; and the back (through the kitchen), where most of the tables are booths. What to order? I have one big word here. *Pizza.* Sure the spicy Greek pasta is good, as is the Veggie Zone (a calzone filled with stir-fried veggies and two cheeses)—but, why? The pizzas are incredible. All come with a delicious thin crust (no sogginess here) that's folded over on the edges and sprinkled with sesame seeds. The sauce is unthinkably tasty, and the variations are broad. There's Thai chicken pizza (pineapple, peanuts, and a spicy sauce); The Killer, with sun-dried tomatoes, Gorgonzola, green chile, and black olives; and my favorite, pizza Florentine (spinach, basil, sun-dried tomatoes, chicken breast, mushrooms, capers, and garlic sautéed in white wine). Of course, you can get the Carnivore Special if you like pepperoni and sausage. Don't leave without a Dalai Lama bar in hand (coconut, chocolate, and caramel) or without sharing the Devil Down Under (a "mongo" chocolate chip cookie with ice cream, whipped cream, and chocolate sauce). Check out the small selection of wine and large selection of microbrews.

✪ Trading Post Café. 4179 Paseo del Pueblo Sur, Ranchos de Taos. ☎ **505/758-5089.** No reservations except for parties of five or more. Menu items $6–$25. DC, CB, DISC, MC, V. Mon–Sat 11:30am–9:30pm. NORTHERN ITALIAN/INTERNATIONAL.

One of my tastiest writing assignments was when I did a profile of this restaurant for the *New York Times.* Chef/owner René Mettler spent 3 hours serving us course after course of dishes prepared especially for us. If you think this gastronomical orgy might color my opinion, just ask anyone in town where they most like to eat. Even notables such as R. C. Gorman, Dennis Hopper, and Gene Hackman will likely name the Trading Post. What draws them is a gallery atmosphere, where rough plastered walls washed with an orange hue are set off by sculptures, paintings, and photographs from the Lumina Gallery. The meals are also artistically served. "You eat with your eyes," says Mettler.

When you go, be prepared to wait for a table, and don't expect quiet romance here, unless you come on an off hour. The place bustles. A bar encloses an open-exhibition kitchen. If you're dining alone or just don't feel like waiting for a table, the bar is a fun place to sit. The menu lists a nice variety of items without distinguishing between appetizers and main courses. This small detail speaks volumes about the restaurant. Although the focus is on the fine food, diners can feel comfortable here, even if trying three appetizers and skipping the main course. The Caesar salad is traditional with an interesting twist—garlic chips. You've probably never had a Caesar salad this good. If you like pasta, you'll find a good variety on the menu. The angel-hair pasta with chicken, wild mushrooms, and Gorgonzola cream is surprisingly light and flavorful. There's also a fresh fish of the day and usually stews and soups at very reasonable prices. A new addition is the creole pepper shrimp, with saffron rice and fried leeks. For dessert try the tarts.

INEXPENSIVE

Casa Fresen Bakery. 482 Hwy. 150 (Ski Valley Rd.), Arroyo Seco, NM 87514. ☎ **505/776-2969.** All menu items under $10. Wed–Mon 7:30am–5pm. AE, DISC, MC, V. EUROPEAN CAFE.

Hardly a person passes through the quaint village of Arroyo Seco without stopping here for gourmet coffee and killer brownies or the indomitable *schneken* (pecan rolls). Many now also make it a destination in order to sit out under an apricot tree, or inside at oddly matched tables and eat delicacies ordered at the counter: a smoked turkey sandwich with brie and honey-cup mustard, apple wood–smoked trout sandwich with basil pesto, or soups such as carrot-cilantro. If you're heading into the outdoors they'll pack you an unforgettable lunch.

Eske's Brew Pub and Eatery. 106 Des Georges Lane. ☎ **505/758-1517.** All menu items under $9. MC, V. Mar–Sept and during peak times such as winter and spring break, daily 11:30am–10pm; winter Sat–Sun 11:30am–10pm. SOUTHWESTERN PUB FARE.

I have a fondness for this place that one might have for an oasis in the desert. The first time I ate here, I'd been on assignment ice climbing and spent 8 hours out in the shadow of a canyon hacking my way up an 80-foot frozen waterfall. I sat down at one of the high tables in the main room, dipped into a big bowl of Wanda's green chile turkey stew, and felt the blood return to my extremities. My climbing buddies ordered The Fatty, a whole wheat tortilla filled with beans, mashed potatoes, onions, feta, and cheddar cheese, smothered in green chile turkey stew. But we all considered bangers and mash (bratwurst cooked in beer with homemade mashed potatoes and warm apple sauce). We also enjoyed some tasty brew—a black and tan, a mixture of barley wine and stout, the heavier beer sinking to the bottom, and a Mesa pale ale. When I asked the owner, Steve "Eske" Eskeback, which was his favorite beer, he replied "the one in my hand," meaning he recommends all the beers, which are his own recipes. The service is friendly and informal. The crowd is local, a few people sitting at the bar where they can visit and watch the beer pouring and food preparation. At times it can be a rowdy place, but mostly it's just fun, lots of ski patrollers and mountain guides showing up to swap stories. In summer you can eat on picnic tables outside.

✪ **Fred's Place.** 332 Paseo del Pueblo Sur. ☎ **505/758-0514.** Main courses $5–$12. MC, V. Mon–Sat 5–9:30pm. NEW MEXICAN.

I was warned by a number of locals not to put Fred's Place in this guide. This is *our* place, they pleaded. But alas, the guide wouldn't be complete without mention of Fred's. God and the devil are at odds at this New Mexican food restaurant, and judging by the food, God has won out. The atmosphere is rich, though for some it may be a bit unnerving. Walls are hung with crucifixes and a vivid ceiling mural depicts a very hungry devil that appears to swoop down toward the dining tables.

Fred's offers New Mexican food, but it's not of the greasy spoon variety. It's very refined, the flavors carefully calculated. You have to try Dee Dee's squash stew (squash, corn, beans, and vegetarian green chile, topped with cheese and fresh oregano). For me, Fred's chicken enchilada is heaven; however, you can't go wrong with a burrito either. Daily specials include grilled trout and carne asada served with a watercress salad. For dessert try the warm apple crisp with ice cream.

Guadalajara Grill. 1384 Paseo del Pueblo Sur. ☎ **505/751-0063.** All items under $10. MC, V. Mon–Sat 10:30am–9pm, Sun 11am–9pm. MEXICAN.

My organic lettuce farmer friend Joe introduced me to this authentic Mexican restaurant; then he disappeared into Mexico, only communicating occasionally by e-mail. Did the incredible food drive him south? I wonder. The restaurant is in an odd location. On the south end of town, it shares a building with a car wash. Don't be deceived, however; the food here is excellent (and very clean!). It's Mexican rather than New Mexican, a refreshing treat. I recommend the tacos, particularly pork or chicken, served in soft homemade corn tortillas, the meat artfully seasoned and grilled. The burritos are large and smothered in chile. Plates are served with rice and beans and half orders are available for smaller appetites. Recently, the chef added seafood to the menu. Try the *mojo de ajo* (shrimp cooked with garlic), served with rice, beans, and guacamole. Beer and wine are now available.

La Folie. 122 Dona Luz. ☎ **505/758-8800.** www.silverhawk.com/taos/lafolie.html. Main courses $6.95–$12.75. AE, DC, DISC, MC, V. Tues–Sat 11am–2:30pm, 5:30–9:30pm; Sun 9am–3pm. ECLECTIC FRENCH/ASIAN.

This new restaurant opened by Mark and Lisa Felix promises delicate and rich flavors in a festive environment. Inside you're surrounded by walls faux-painted with images of pillars and birds, and outside tables are set around a charming courtyard with a fountain. For lunch try the Thai peanut chicken salad, with julienned vegetables. For dinner the mussels marinière has a fresh taste, served over fettuccine. The beef bourguignonne is also nice. For dessert the piña colada mousse is surprisingly light. Due to the restaurant's proximity to a church, no alcoholic beverages are served.

Michael's Kitchen. 304 C Paseo del Pueblo Norte. ☎ **505/758-4178.** No reservations. Breakfast $1.55–$7.95; lunch $3.25–$9.50; dinner $5–$13.95. AE, DISC, MC, V. Daily 7am–8:30pm (except major holidays). NEW MEXICAN/AMERICAN.

A couple of blocks north of the Plaza, this eatery is a throwback to earlier days, when big plates full of hearty food was the norm. Between its hardwood floor and viga ceiling are various knickknacks on posts, walls, and windows: a deer head here, a Tiffany lamp there, and several scattered antique woodstoves. Seating is at booths and tables. Breakfast dishes, including a large selection of pancakes and egg preparations (with names like the "Moofy," "Omelette Extra-ordinaire," and "Pancake Sandwich"), are served all day (because they're so good), as are lunch sandwiches (including Philly cheese steak, tuna melt, chile burger, and a veggie sandwich). One of my favorite lunch dishes is generically (and facetiously) called "Health Food," a double order of fries with red or green chile and cheese. Dinners range from veal cordon bleu to plantation-fried chicken to enchiladas rancheros. Now on Saturday evening you can get prime rib. Michael's has its own excellent full-service bakery.

5 What to See & Do

Taos has something to offer almost everybody. And no wonder, with a history shaped by pre-Colombian civilization, Spanish colonialism, and the Wild West; outdoor activities that range from ballooning to world-class skiing; and a clustering of artists, writers, and musicians. Its pueblo is the most accessible in New Mexico, and its museums, including the new Van Vechten Lineberry Taos Art Museum, represent a world-class display of regional history and culture.

SUGGESTED ITINERARIES

If You Have Only 1 Day

Spend at least 2 hours at the Taos Pueblo. You'll also have time to see the Millicent Rogers Museum and to browse in some of the town's fine art galleries. Try to make it to Ranchos de Taos to see the San Francisco de Asis Church and to shop on the Plaza there.

If You Have 2 Days

On the second day, explore the Kit Carson Historic Museums—the Martinez Hacienda, the Kit Carson Home, and the Ernest L. Blumenschein Home. Then head out of town to enjoy the view from the Rio Grande Gorge Bridge.

If You Have 3 Days or More

On your third day, drive the "Enchanted Circle" through Red River, Eagle Nest, and Angel Fire or head to the Van Vechten Lineberry Taos Art Museum. You may want to allow a full day for shopping or perhaps drive up to the Taos Ski Valley for a chairlift ride or a short hike. Of course, if you're here in the winter with skis, the mountain is your first priority.

If You're an Outdoorsperson

Start with the first-day recommendation, just to get a feel for the culture of Taos. Then, if it's spring or early summer, plan a raft trip down the Taos Box Canyon (a full-day event). It it's spring, summer, or fall, contact one of the bicycle-rental or -touring companies and have them show you the way or take you to some of the mountain rides in the area or the West Rim of the Taos Box Canyon.

The next day head up to Wheeler Peak (13,161 feet), the highest point in New Mexico (a good full-day hike up and back), where you'll have a 360° view of northern New Mexico. Or, you may want to spend the day hiking and visiting ruins around Bandelier National Monument near Los Alamos. If it's winter, plan at least a day of skiing at the world-acclaimed Taos Ski Valley; however, you also might want to take cross-country skis up into the mountains. You can also snowshoe or backcountry ski in the area. For rock climbing, there's a great site just to the west of Taos.

THE TOP ATTRACTIONS

If you would like to visit all seven museums that comprise the Museum Association of Taos—Blumenschein Home, Fechin Institute, Hacienda Martinez, Harwood Museum, Kit Carson Home and Museum, Millicent Rogers Museum, and Van Vechten Lineberry Taos Art Museum—it might be worthwhile to purchase a combination ticket for $20.

Taos Pueblo. P.O. Box 1846, Taos Pueblo, NM 87571. ☎ **505/758-1028.** Cost is $6 for parking and $4 per person for admission; $1 for children. If you would like to use a still camera, the charge is $10; for a video camera $20; if you would like to sketch or paint, written permission is required. Other charges apply for commercial use of imagery. Photography is not permitted on feast days. Winter daily 8:30am–4:30pm; summer daily 8am–5pm, with a few exceptions. Closed for 1 month every year in late winter or early spring (call to find out if it will be open at the time you expect to be in Taos). Also, since this is a living community, you can expect periodic closures.

It's amazing that in our frenetic world, 200 Taos Pueblo residents still live much as their ancestors did 1,000 years ago. When you enter the pueblo you'll see where they dwell in two large buildings, each with rooms piled on top of each other, forming structures that echo the shape of Taos Mountain (which sits to the northeast). Here, a portion of Taos residents live without electricity and running water. The remaining 2,000 residents of Taos Pueblo live in conventional homes on the pueblo's 95,000 acres.

The main buildings' distinctive flowing lines of shaped mud, with a straw-and-mud exterior plaster, are typical of Pueblo architecture throughout the Southwest. It's architecture that blends in with the surrounding land—which makes sense, given that it is itself made of earth. Bright blue doors are the same shade as the sky that frames the brown buildings.

The northernmost of New Mexico's 19 pueblos, Taos has been home to the Tiwa tribes for more than 900 years. Many residents here still practice ancestral rituals. The center of their world is still nature, many still bake bread in hornos, and most still drink water that flows down from the sacred Blue Lake. Meanwhile, arts and crafts and other tourism-related businesses support the economy, along with government services, ranching, and farming.

The village looks much the same today as it did when a regiment from Coronado's expedition first came upon it in 1540. Though the Tiwa were essentially a peaceful agrarian people, they are perhaps best remembered for spearheading the only successful revolt by Native Americans in history. Launched by Pope ("Pó pay") in 1680, the uprising drove the Spanish from Santa Fe until 1692 and from Taos until 1698.

As you explore the pueblo, you can visit the residents' studios, munch on homemade bread, look into the new **San Geronimo Chapel,** and wander past the fascinating ruins of the old church and cemetery. You're expected to ask permission from individuals before taking their photos; some will ask for a small payment, but that's for you to negotiate. Kivas and other ceremonial underground areas are restricted.

San Geronimo is the patron saint of the Taos Pueblo, and his feast day (September 30) combines Catholic and pre-Hispanic traditions. The **Old Taos Trade Fair** on that day is a joyous occasion, with foot races, pole climbs, and crafts booths. Dances are performed the evening of September 29. Other annual events include a **turtle dance on New Year's Day, deer or buffalo dances on Three Kings Day** (January 6), and **corn dances on Santa Cruz Day** (May 3), **San Antonio Day** (June 13), **San Juan Day** (June 24), **Santiago Day** (July 23), and **Santa Ana Day** (July 24). The **Taos Pueblo Powwow,** a dance competition and parade that brings together tribes from throughout North America, is held the weekend after July 4 on reservation land off NM 522. **Christmas Eve bonfires** mark the start of the children's **corn dance,** the **Christmas Day deer dance,** and the 3-day-long **Matachines dance.**

During your visit to the pueblo you will have the opportunity to purchase traditional fried and oven-baked bread as well as a variety of arts and crafts. If you would like to try traditional feast-day meals, **Tiwa Kitchen,** near the entrance to the pueblo, is a good place to stop. Close to Tiwa Kitchen is the **Oo-oonah Children's Art Center,** where you can see the creative works of Pueblo children.

As with many of the other pueblos in New Mexico, Taos Pueblo has opened a casino, featuring slot machines, blackjack, and poker. Free local transportation is available. Call ☎ **505/758-4460** for details.

✪ **Millicent Rogers Museum of Northern New Mexico.** Off NM 522, 4 miles north of Taos. ☎ **505/758-2462.** Admission $6 adults, $5 students, $1 children 6–16. Daily

Taos Attractions

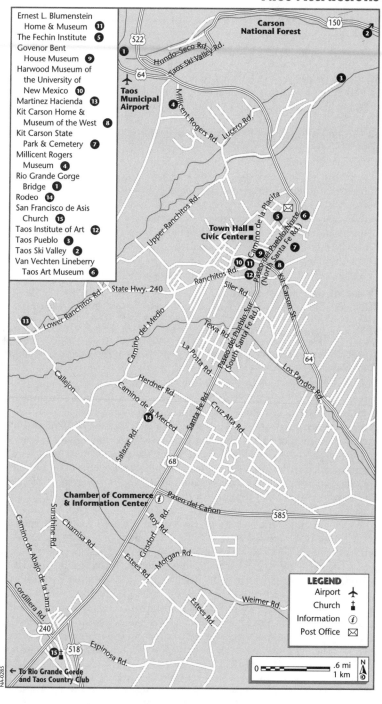

Ernest L. Blumenstein
 Home & Museum **11**
The Fechin Institute **5**
Govenor Bent
 House Museum **9**
Harwood Museum of
 the University of
 New Mexico **10**
Martinez Hacienda **13**
Kit Carson Home &
 Museum of the West **8**
Kit Carson State
 Park & Cemetery **7**
Millicent Rogers
 Museum **4**
Rio Grande Gorge
 Bridge **1**
Rodeo **14**
San Francisco de Asis
 Church **15**
Taos Institute of Art **12**
Taos Pueblo **3**
Taos Ski Valley **2**
Van Vechten Lineberry
 Taos Art Museum **6**

Carson
National Forest

Taos
Municipal
Airport

Town Hall
Civic Center

Chamber of Commerce
& Information Center

← To Rio Grande Gorge
and Taos Country Club

NA-0285

LEGEND
Airport ✈
Church ⛪
Information ⓘ
Post Office ✉

0   .6 mi
   1 km

N

10am–5pm. Closed Mon in Nov–Mar, Easter, San Geronimo Day (Sept 30), Thanksgiving, Dec 25, and Jan 1.

This museum is small enough to give a glimpse of some of the finest Southwestern arts and crafts you'll see without being overwhelming. It was founded in 1953 by family members after the death of Millicent Rogers. Rogers was a wealthy Taos émigré who in 1947 began acquiring a magnificent collection of beautiful Native American arts and crafts. Included are Navajo and Pueblo jewelry, Navajo textiles, Pueblo pottery, Hopi and Zuni kachina dolls, paintings from the Rio Grande Pueblo people, and basketry from a wide variety of Southwestern tribes. The collection continues to grow through gifts and museum acquisitions. The museum also presents changing exhibitions of Southwestern art, crafts, and design.

Since the 1970s, the scope of the museum's permanent collection has been expanded to include Anglo arts and crafts and Hispanic religious and secular arts and crafts, from Spanish and Mexican colonial to contemporary times. Included are *santos* (religious images), furniture, weavings, colcha embroideries, and decorative tinwork. Agricultural implements, domestic utensils, and craftspeople's tools dating from the 17th and 18th centuries are also displayed.

The museum gift shop has a fine collection of superior regional art. Classes and workshops, lectures, and field trips are held throughout the year.

✪ **Kit Carson Historic Museums.** P.O. Drawer CCC, Taos, NM 87571. ☎ **505/ 758-0505.** Three museums $10 adults (ages 16 and over), $5 children 6–15; family rate, $20. Two museums $7.50 adults, $4 children; family rate, $15. One museum $5 adults, $2.50 children; family rate, $10. All museums free for children under 6. Summer: Kit Carson Home daily 8am–6pm; Martinez Hacienda daily 9am–5pm; Blumenschein Home daily 9am–5pm. Winter: Kit Carson Home daily 9am–5pm; Martinez Hacienda daily 10am–4pm; Blumenschein Home daily 11am–4pm.

Three historical homes are operated as museums, affording visitors a glimpse of early Taos lifestyles. The Martinez Hacienda, Kit Carson Home, and Ernest Blumenschein home each have unique appeal.

The **Martinez Hacienda,** Lower Ranchitos Road, Hwy. 240 (☎ **505/758-1000**), is the only Spanish colonial hacienda in the United States that's open to the public year-round. This was the home of the merchant and trader Don Antonio Severino Martinez, who bought it in 1804 and lived here until his death in 1827. Located on the west bank of the Rio Pueblo de Taos about 2 miles southwest of the Plaza, the museum is remarkably beautiful, with thick, raw adobe walls and no exterior windows, to protect against raids by Plains tribes.

Twenty-one rooms were built around two *placitas,* or interior courtyards. They give you a glimpse of the austerity of frontier lives, with only a few pieces of modest period furniture in each. You'll see bedrooms, servants' quarters, stables, a kitchen, and even a large fiesta room. Exhibits in one newly renovated room tell the story of the Martinez family and life in Spanish Taos between 1598 and 1821, when Mexico gained control.

Don Antonio Martinez, who for a time was *alcalde* (mayor) of Taos, owned several caravans that he used in trade on the Chihuahua Trail to Mexico. This business was carried on by his youngest son, Don Juan Pascual, who later owned the hacienda. His eldest son was Padre Antonio José Martinez, northern New Mexico's controversial spiritual leader from 1826 to 1867.

Kit Carson Historic Museums has developed the hacienda into a living museum with weavers, blacksmiths, and wood carvers. Demonstrations are scheduled daily, and even more often during the **Taos Trade Fair** (the last weekend in September), when they run virtually nonstop. The Trade Fair commemorates the era when

Native Americans, Spanish settlers, and mountain men met here to trade with each other. The Martinez Hacienda is currently home to a new santos exhibit.

The **Kit Carson Home and Museum of the West,** East Kit Carson Road (☎ 505/ 758-4741), located a short block east of the Plaza intersection, is the town's only general museum of Taos history. The 12-room adobe home, with walls 2½ feet thick, was built in 1825 and purchased in 1843 by Carson, the famous mountain man, Indian agent, and scout, as a wedding gift for his young bride, Josefa Jaramillo. It remained their home for 25 years, until both died (exactly a month apart) in 1868.

A living room, bedroom, and kitchen are furnished as they might have been when occupied by the Carsons. The Indian Room contains artifacts crafted and used by the original inhabitants of Taos Valley; the Early American Room has a variety of pioneer items, including many antique firearms and trappers' implements; and the Carson Interpretive Room presents memorabilia from Carson's unusual life. In the kitchen is a Spanish plaque that reads: *Nadie sabe lo que tiene la olla mas que la cuchara que la menea* (Nobody better knows what the pot holds than the spoon that stirs it). New permanent exhibits in the Carson home include Native American prehistory and history as well as "Kit Carson: Life and Times."

The museum bookshop, with perhaps the town's most comprehensive inventory of New Mexico historical books, is adjacent to the entry.

The **Ernest L. Blumenschein Home & Museum,** 222 Ledoux St. (☎ 505/ 758-0505), 1½ blocks southwest of the Plaza, recreates the lifestyle of one of the founders of the Taos Society of Artists (founded 1915). An adobe home with garden walls and a courtyard, parts of which date from the 1790s, it became the home and studio of Blumenschein (1874–1960) and his family in 1919. Period furnishings include European antiques and handmade Taos furniture in Spanish colonial style.

Blumenschein was born and raised in Pittsburgh. In 1898 he arrived in Taos somewhat by accident. After training in New York and Paris, he and fellow painter Bert Phillips were on assignment for *Harper's* and *McClure's* magazines of New York when a wheel of their wagon broke while they were traversing a mountain 30 miles north of Taos. Blumenschein drew the short straw and thus was obliged to bring the wheel by horseback to Taos for repair. He later recounted his initial reaction to the valley he entered: "No artist had ever recorded the New Mexico I was now seeing. No writer had ever written down the smell of this air or the feel of that morning sky. I was receiving . . . the first great unforgettable inspiration of my life. My destiny was being decided."

That spark later led to the foundation of Taos as an art colony. An extensive collection of works by early 20th-century Taos artists is on display in several rooms of the home, including some by Blumenschein's daughter, Helen.

MORE ATTRACTIONS

D. H. Lawrence Ranch. San Cristobal. ☎ 505/776-2245.

The shrine dedicated to this controversial early 20th-century author is a pilgrimage site for literary devotees. A short uphill walk from the ranch home, it's a bit of a forgotten place, with a broken gate, peeling paint, and an eagle on an altar, where people have left a few mementos such as juniper berries and sticks of gum. Most interesting is the guest book. Reading it you really get a sense that this *is* a pilgrimage spot. One couple had tried for 24 years to get here from England.

Lawrence lived in Taos on and off between 1922 and 1925. The ranch was a gift to his wife, Frieda, from the art patron Mabel Dodge Luhan. Lawrence repaid Luhan the favor by giving her the manuscript of *Sons and Lovers*. When Lawrence died in southern France in 1930 of tuberculosis, his ashes were returned here for burial. The grave of Frieda, who died in 1956, is outside the shrine.

The shrine is the only public building at the ranch, which is operated today by the University of New Mexico as an educational and recreational retreat. To reach the site, head north from Taos about 15 miles on NM 522, then another 6 miles east into the forested Sangre de Cristo Range via a well-marked dirt road. The views getting there and upon arrival are spectacular.

✪ **Fechin Institute.** 227 Paseo del Pueblo Norte (P.O. Box 832), Taos, NM 87571. ☎ **505/ 758-1710.** Admission $4. Oct–May, Wed–Sun 10am–2pm; May–Oct, Wed–Sun 10am–5pm.

The home of Russian artist Nicolai Fechin (*Feh*-shin) from 1927 until 1933, this historic building commemorates the career of a 20th-century Renaissance man. Born in Russia in 1881, Fechin came to the United States in 1923, already acclaimed as a master of painting, drawing, sculpture, architecture, and woodwork. In Taos, he renovated a large adobe home and embellished it with hand-carved doors, windows, gates, posts, fireplaces, and other features of a Russian country home. The house and adjacent studio are now used for Fechin Institute educational activities, as well as concerts, lectures, and other programs. Fechin died in 1955.

Governor Bent House Museum. 117 Bent St. ☎ **505/758-2376.** Admission $1 adults, 50¢ children. Summer daily 9am–5pm; winter daily 10am–4pm.

Located a short block north of the Plaza, this was the residence of Charles Bent, New Mexico Territory's first American governor. Bent, a former trader who established Fort Bent, Colorado, was murdered during the 1847 Native American and Hispanic rebellion, while his wife and children escaped by digging through an adobe wall into the house next door. The hole is still visible. Period art and artifacts are on display.

Harwood Museum of the University of New Mexico. 238 Ledoux St. ☎ **505/ 758-9826.** Admission $4. Tues–Sat 10am–5pm, Sun noon–5pm.

With its high ceilings and broad wood floors, this recently restored museum has become a lovely place to wander among New Mexico–inspired images, old and new. A cultural and community center since 1923, the museum displays paintings, drawings, prints, sculpture, and photographs by Taos-area artists from 1800 to the present. Featured are paintings from the early days of the art colony by members of the Taos Society of Artists, including Oscar Berninghaus, Ernest Blumenschein, Herbert Dunton, Victor Higgins, Bert Phillips, and Walter Ufer. Also included are works by Emil Bisttram, Andrew Dasburg, Leon Gaspard, Louis Ribak, Bea Mandelman, Agnes Martin (seven new paintings in 1997), Larry Bell, and Thomas Benrimo.

Upstairs are 19th-century pounded tin pieces and *retablos,* religious paintings of saints that have traditionally been used for decoration and inspiration in the homes and churches of New Mexico. The permanent collection includes sculptures by Patrociño Barela, one of the leading Hispanic artists of 20th-century New Mexico— well worth seeing, especially his 3-foot-tall "Death Cart" a rendition of Doña Sebastiána, the bringer of death.

The museum also schedules five or six changing exhibitions a year, many of which feature works by celebrated artists currently living in Taos.

Kit Carson Park and Cemetery. Paseo del Pueblo Norte.

Major community events are held in the park in summer. The cemetery, established in 1847, contains the graves of Carson and his wife, Gov. Charles Bent, the Don Antonio Martinez family, Mabel Dodge Luhan, and many other noted historical figures and artists. Their lives are described briefly on plaques.

✪ **Rio Grande Gorge Bridge.** U.S. 64, 10 miles west of Taos.

This impressive bridge, west of the Taos airport, spans the Southwest's greatest river. At 650 feet above the canyon floor, it's one of America's highest bridges. If you can withstand the vertigo, it's interesting to come more than once, at different times of day, to observe how the changing light plays tricks with the colors of the cliff walls. A curious aside is that the wedding scene in the controversial movie *Natural Born Killers* was filmed here.

✪ **San Francisco de Asis Church.** P.O. Box 72, Ranchos de Taos NM, 87557. ☎ **505/ 758-2754.** Donations appreciated, $2 minimum. Mon–Sat 9am–noon and 1–4pm. Visitors may attend mass Sat at 6pm (mass rotates from this church to the three mission chapels) and Sun at 7 (Spanish), 9, and 11:30am. Closed to the public the first 2 weeks in June, when repairs are done; however services still take place.

From NM 68, about 4 miles south of Taos, this famous church appears as a modern adobe sculpture with no doors or windows. This is the image that has often been photographed (by Ansel Adams, among others) and painted (for example, by Georgia O'Keeffe). Visitors must walk through the garden on the east side of this remarkable two-story church to enter and get a full perspective of its massive walls, authentic adobe plaster, and beauty.

The church office and gift shop are just across the driveway north of the church. A video presentation is given here every hour on the half hour. Also, displayed on the wall is an unusual painting, *The Shadow of the Cross* by Henri Ault (1896). Under ordinary light it portrays a barefoot Christ at the Sea of Galilee; in darkness, however, the portrait becomes luminescent, and the perfect shadow of a cross forms over the left shoulder of Jesus' silhouette. The artist reportedly was as shocked as everyone else to see this. The reason for the illusion remains a mystery. Several nice galleries and crafts shops surround the square.

✪ **Van Vechten Lineberry Taos Art Museum.** 501 Paseo del Pueblo Norte (P.O. Box 1848). ☎ **505/758-2690.** Admission $5 adults, $3 students. Tues–Fri 11am–4pm, Sat–Sun 1:30–4pm.

Taos's newest museum, the Van Vechten Lineberry Taos Art Museum, offers visitors works of the Taos Society of Artists, which give a sense of what Taos was like in the late 19th and early 20th centuries. The museum was the brainchild of Ed Lineberry, who lives in the spectacular home adjacent to the museum; he conceived of it as a memorial to his late wife, Duane Van Vechten. An artist herself, Duane spent much time working in her studio, which now serves as the entryway to the 20,000-square-foot main gallery of the museum. The works of the Taos Society of Artists are rich and varied, capturing panoramas as well as the personalities of the Native American and Hispanic villagers.

Lineberry traveled throughout Europe studying techniques for preservation and storage, as well as the display space, climate control, and lighting of fine museums. As a result, the museum is state-of-the-art. There are works by Van Vechten, as well as some less accomplished local work. Among other things, the entryway features John Dunn's roulette wheel. The museum is also actively acquiring new works. Besides the main gallery space, there are smaller areas available for traveling exhibitions and a wonderful library that will be open by appointment to researchers.

ART CLASSES

Perhaps you're visiting Taos because of its renown as an arts community, but galleries and studio visits may not satisfy your own urge to create. If you'd like to pursue an artistic adventure of your own here, check out the weeklong classes in such media as writing, sculpture, painting, jewelry making, photography, clay working, and textiles that are available at the **Taos Institute of Arts,** 108-B Civic Plaza Dr., Taos, NM 87571 (☎ **800/822-7183** or 505/758-2793; www.taosnet.com/tia/; e-mail: tia@taosnet.com). Class sizes are limited, so if you're thinking about giving these workshops a try, call for information well in advance. The fees vary from class to class but are generally quite reasonable; however, they usually don't include the cost of materials.

ORGANIZED TOURS

Damaso Martinez's **Pride of Taos Tours,** P.O. Box 5271, Taos, NM 87571 (☎ **800/ 273-8340** or 505/758-8340), offers two tours a day, April through October, of the historical streets in Taos, Taos Pueblo, and Ranchos de Taos Church ($25 adults, $5 children 12 and under). The tour takes about 3 hours, and the cost includes admission to the sites.

An excellent opportunity to explore the historic downtown area is offered by **Taos Historic Walking Tours** (☎ **505/758-4020**). Tours cost $10 and take 1½ to 2 hours. Call for schedule.

If you'd really like a taste of Taos history and drama call **Enchantment Dreams Walking Tours** (☎ **505/776-2562**). Roberta Courtney Meyers, a theater artist, dramatist, and composer will tour you through Taos's history while performing a number of characters such as Georgia O'Keeffe and Kit Carson. I've seen her do a spicy performance piece of D. H. Lawrence's three women companions in life: Frieda Lawrence, Lady Dorothy Brett, and Mabel Dodge Luhan.

6 Skiing Taos

DOWNHILL

Five alpine resorts are within an hour's drive of Taos; all offer complete facilities, including equipment rentals. Although exact opening and closing dates vary according to snow conditions, the season usually begins around Thanksgiving and continues into early April.

Ski clothing can be purchased, and ski equipment rented or bought, from several Taos outlets. Among them are **Cottam's Ski & Outdoor Shops,** with four locations (call ☎ **800/322-8267** or 505/758-2822 for the one nearest you); **Taos Ski Valley Sportswear, Ski & Boot Co.,** in Taos Ski Valley (☎ **505/776-2291**); and **Stay Tuned,** also in the ski valley (☎ **505/776-8839**).

TAOS SKI VALLEY

✪ **Taos Ski Valley.** (P.O. Box 90), Taos Ski Valley, NM 87525 (☎ **505/776-2291;** http://taoswebb.com/nmusa/), is the preeminent ski resort in the southern Rocky Mountains. It was founded in 1955 by a Swiss-German immigrant, Ernie Blake. According to local legend, Blake searched for 2 years in a small plane for the perfect location for a ski resort comparable to what he was accustomed to in the Alps. He found it at the abandoned mining site of Twining, high above Taos. Today, under the management of two younger generations of Blakes, the resort has become internationally renowned for its light, dry powder (320 inches annually), its superb ski school, and its personal, friendly service.

Taos Ski Valley, however, can best be appreciated by the more experienced skier. It offers steep, high-alpine, high-adventure skiing. The mountain is more intricate than it might seem at first glance, and it holds many surprises and challenges—even for the expert. The *London Times* called the valley "without any argument the best ski resort in the world. Small, intimate, and endlessly challenging, Taos simply has no equal." And, if you're sick of dealing with yahoos on snowboards, you will be pleased to know

Shredders Unite!

As you drive around the area you may see graffiti proclaiming "Free Taos" on the sides of buildings or roadside signs. With recent developments in Montana and Texas, you might think that these are the marks of a local separatist militia. On the contrary, they are part of a campaign by mostly young people (with many of the area's lodge owners behind it as well) to open the ski area up to snowboarders. Traditional downhill skiers don't look kindly on sharing the mountain with the shredders, who they claim make the sport more dangerous. Currently, Taos Ski Valley is one of only a handful of ski resorts in the West that bans boarders completely from its slopes. However, many of the area's lodge owners feel they are losing out on significant business from families and young adults who are into snowboarding. In spring 1997, the "Free Taos" message appeared in 100-foot-high letters emblazoned in the snow across an open slope above the ski area.

that they're not permitted on the slopes of Taos Ski Valley (the only ski area in New Mexico that forbids them). The quality of the snow here (light and dry) is believed to be due to the dry southwestern air and abundant sunshine.

Between the 11,819-foot summit and the 9,207-foot base, there are 72 trails and bowls, more than half of them designated for expert and advanced skiers. Most of the remaining trails are suitable for advanced intermediates; there is little flat terrain for novices to gain experience and mileage. However, many beginning skiers find that after spending time in lessons they can enjoy the **Kachina Bowl,** which offers spectacular views as well as wide-open slopes.

The area has an uphill capacity of 15,000 skiers per hour on its five double chairs, one triple, four quads, and one surface tow. Tickets for all lifts, depending on the season, cost $29 to $42 for adults for a full day, $26 half day; $18 to $26 for children 12 or younger for a full day, $16 half day; teen ticket for 13- to 17-year-olds $24 to $34 for a full day, $21 half day; $27 seniors ages 65 to 69 for a full day, $22 half day; free for seniors over 70. Novice lift tickets cost $20 for all ages. Full rental packages are $12 for adults and $6 for children. Taos Ski Valley is open daily from 9am to 4pm from Thanksgiving to the second week of April. It should be noted that Taos Ski Valley has one of the best ski schools in the country. This school specializes in teaching people how to negotiate steep and challenging runs.

With its children's ski school, Taos Ski Valley has always been an excellent location for skiing families, but with the 1994 addition of an 18,000-square-foot children's center (Kinderkäfig Center), skiing with your children in Taos is even better. Kinderkäfig offers every service imaginable, from equipment rental for children to baby-sitting services. Call ahead for more information.

Taos Ski Valley has many lodges and condominiums with nearly 1,500 beds. (See "Taos Ski Valley," under "Where to Stay," above, for details on accommodations.) All offer ski-week packages; four of them have restaurants. There are two more restaurants on the mountain in addition to the many facilities of Village Center at the base. For reservations, call the **Taos Valley Resort Association** (☎ **800/776-1111** or 505/776-2233).

RED RIVER SKI AREA

Not far from Taos Ski Valley is **Red River Ski Area** (P.O. Box 900), Red River, NM 87558 (☎ **800/331-7669** for reservations, or 505/754-2223 for information). One of the bonuses of this ski area is the fact that lodgers at Red River can walk out their doors and be on the slopes. Two other factors make this 37-year-old, family oriented area special. First, most of its 57 trails are geared toward the intermediate skier, though beginners and experts also have some trails; and second, good snow is guaranteed early and late in the year by snowmaking equipment that can work on 75% of the runs, more than any other in New Mexico. However, be aware that this human-made snow tends to be icy, and the mountain is full of inexperienced skiers, so you really have to watch your back. Locals in the area refer to this as "Little Texas" because it's so popular with Texans and other Southerners. A very friendly atmosphere, with a touch of red-neck attitude, prevails.

There's a 1,600-foot vertical drop here to a base elevation of 8,750 feet. Lifts include four double chairs, two triple chairs, and a surface tow, with a skier capacity of 7,920 skiers per hour. The cost of a lift ticket for all lifts is $39 for adults for a full day, $29 for a half day; $34 for teens 13 to 19 for a full day, $24 for a half day; $25 for children 12 and under and seniors (60 and over) for a full day, $18 for a half day. Full rental packages start at $14 for adults, $9 for children. Lifts run daily from 9am to 4pm from Thanksgiving to about March 28.

ANGEL FIRE RESORT

Also quite close to Taos is **Angel Fire Resort** (P.O. Drawer B), Angel Fire, NM 87710 (☎ **800/633-7463** or 505/377-6401). If you don't feel up to skiing steeper Taos mountain (or your kids don't), Angel Fire is a good choice. The 62 trails are heavily oriented to beginner and intermediate skiers and snowboarders, with a few runs for more advanced skiers and snowboarders. I hadn't skied in Angel Fire since college until recently and was pleasantly surprised. Under new ownership, the mountain has received more than $7 million in improvements in the past 2 years. This is not an old village like you'll find at Taos and Red River. Instead it's a Vail-style resort, built in 1960, with a variety of activities other than skiing (see "A Scenic Drive Around the Enchanted Circle," below). The snowmaking capabilities here are excellent, and the ski school is good, though I hear so crowded it's difficult to get in during spring break. With its new high-speed quad lift (the only one in New Mexico), you can get to the top fast and have a long ski to the bottom. There are also four double lifts and one surface lift. There's a large snowboard park as well as some new hike-access advanced runs, however the hike is substantial. All-day lift tickets cost $39 for adults, $31 for teens (13 to 17 years old) and $23 for children (7 to 12 years old). Kids 6 and under and seniors 65 and over ski free. Open from approximately Thanksgiving to March 29 (depending on the weather) daily from 9am to 4:30pm.

SIPAPU SKI AREA

The oldest ski area in the Taos region, founded in 1952, **Sipapu Ski Area** (P.O. Box 29), Vadito, NM 87579 (☎ **505/587-2240**), is 25 miles southeast, on NM 518 in Tres Ritos canyon. It prides itself on being a small local area, especially popular with schoolchildren. It has just one triple chair and two surface lifts, with a vertical drop of 865 feet to the 8,200-foot base elevation. There are 18 trails, half classified as intermediate. Unfortunately beginners are limited to only a few runs here, as are advanced skiers. Still, it's a nice little area, tucked way back in the mountains, with excellent lodging rates. Be aware that since the elevation is fairly low, runs get very icy. Lift tickets are $29 for adults for a full day, $21 half day; $22 for children under 12 for a full day, $17 half day; $20 for seniors (65 and over) for a full day; and free for seniors age 70 and over, as well as children 5 and under. A package including lift tickets, equipment rental, and a lesson costs $45 for adults and $38 for children. Sipapu is open from about December 18 to the end of March, and lifts run daily from 9am to 4pm.

SKI RIO

Just south of the Colorado border is **Ski Rio** (P.O. Box 159), Costilla, NM 87524 (☎ **800/2-ASK-RIO** or 505/758-7707), a broad (and often cold and windy) ski area that can't quite get over its financial problems. In fact, you'll want to call before driving up there, as the resort may not make it into the next season. It's a pity, because there's a lot on this mountain. Half of its 83 named trails are for the intermediate skier, 30% for beginners, and 20% for advanced skiers. There are also snowboard and snow skate parks, as well as 13 miles of cross-country trails. Annual snowfall here is about 260 inches, and there are three chairlifts (two triple, one double) and three tows. At the ski base you can rent skis, snowboards, snowshoes, and snow skates, as well as find lodgings, restaurants, and a sports shop. Sleigh rides, dogsled tours, and snowmobile tours are also available. The ski school offers private and group clinics (for adults and children) in cross-country and downhill skiing, snow skating, and snowboarding. Lift tickets are in the mid-$30 range for adults and mid-$20 range for juniors. Ski Rio is open on a limited basis, generally weekends and only a few weekdays, from 9am to 4pm from November through April. Call to be sure it's open at all and for details. For information via the World Wide Web, try http://laplaza.com/tp/skirio/.

CROSS-COUNTRY SKIING

Numerous popular Nordic trails exist in Carson National Forest. If you call or write ahead, they'll send you a booklet titled *Where to Go in the Snow,* which gives cross-country skiers details about the maintained trails. One of the more popular trails is **Amole Canyon,** off NM 518 near the Sipapu Ski Area, where the Taos Nordic Ski Club maintains set tracks and signs along a 3-mile loop. It's closed to snowmobiles, a comfort to lovers of serenity. Several trails are open only to cross-country skiers.

Just east of Red River, with 22 miles of groomed trails in 600 acres of forest lands atop Bobcat Pass, is the **Enchanted Forest Cross Country Ski Area** (☎ **505/754-2374**). Full-day trail passes, good from 9am to 4:30pm, are $10 for adults, $7 for children, and free for seniors age 70 and over. Equipment rentals and lessons can be arranged at **Miller's Crossing** ski shop on Main Street in Red River (☎ **505/754-2374**). Nordic skiers can get instruction in skating, mountaineering, and telemarking.

Taos Mountain Outfitters, 114 South Plaza (☎ **505/758-9292**), offers telemark and cross-country sales, rentals, and guide service, as does **Los Rios Whitewater Ski Shop** (☎ **505/776-8854**).

Southwest Nordic Center (☎ **505/758-4761**) offers rental of four yurts (Mongolian-style huts) in the Rio Grande National Forest near Chama. These are insulated and fully equipped accommodations, each with a stove, pots, pans, dishes, silverware, mattresses, pillows, a table and benches, and wood-stove heating. Skiers trek into the huts, carrying their clothing and food in backpacks. Guide service is provided, or people can go in on their own, following directions on a map. The yurts are rented by the night and range from $65 to $90 per group. Call for reservations as much in advance as possible as they do book up. The season is mid-November through April, depending on snow conditions.

7 Other Outdoor Pursuits

Taos County's 2,200 square miles embrace a great diversity of scenic beauty, from New Mexico's highest mountain, 13,161-foot Wheeler Peak, to the 650-foot-deep chasm of the Rio Grande Gorge. Carson National Forest, which extends to the eastern city limits of Taos and cloaks a large part of the county, contains several major ski facilities as well as hundreds of miles of hiking trails through the Sangre de Cristo Range.

Recreation areas are mainly in the national forest, where pine and aspen provide refuge for abundant wildlife. Forty-eight areas are accessible by road, including 38 with campsites. There are also areas on the high desert mesa, carpeted by sagebrush, cactus, and frequently wildflowers. Two beautiful areas within a short drive of Taos are the Valle Vidal Recreation Area, north of Red River, and the Wild Rivers Recreation Area, near Questa. For complete information, contact **Carson National Forest,** 208 Cruz Alta Rd., Taos, NM 87571 (☎ 505/758-6200), or the **Bureau of Land Management,** 226 Cruz Alta Rd., Taos, NM 87571 (☎ 505/758-8851).

BALLOONING   As in many other towns throughout New Mexico, hot-air ballooning is a top attraction. Recreational trips over the Taos Valley and Rio Grande Gorge are offered by **Paradise Hot Air Balloon Adventure** (☎ 505/751-6098).

The **Taos Mountain Balloon Rally,** P.O. Box 3096, Taos, NM 87571 (☎ 800/732-8267), is held each year the last full weekend of October. (See " New Mexico Calendar of Events," in chapter 3, for details.)

BIKING   Even if you're not an avid cyclist, it won't take long for you to realize that getting around Taos by bike is preferable to driving. You won't have the usual parking problems, and you won't have to sit in the line of traffic as it snakes through the center of town. If you feel like exploring the surrounding area, Carson National Forest rangers recommend several biking trails in the greater Taos area, including those in Garcia Park and Rio Chiquito for beginner to intermediate mountain bikers, and Gallegos and Picuris peaks for experts.

Inquire at the U.S. Forest Service office next to the chamber of commerce for excellent materials that map out trails; tell you how to get to the trailhead; specify length, difficulty, and elevation; and inform you about safety tips. You can also purchase the *Taos Trails* map (created jointly by the Carson National Forest, Native Sons Adventures, and *Trail Illustrated*). It's readily available at area bookstores and is designed to withstand water damage. Once you're out riding in Carson National Forest, you'll find trails marked in green (easy), blue (moderate), or gray (expert).

Bicycle rentals are available from the **Gearing Up Bicycle Shop,** 129 Paseo del Pueblo Sur (☎ 505/751-0365); daily rentals run $20 for a mountain bike with front suspension, $40 for one with full suspension. **Hot Tracks Cyclery,** 214 Paseo del Pueblo Sur (☎ 505/751-0949), rents front-suspension mountain bikes and full-suspension bikes for $18 per half day and $25 per full day. The knowledgeable staff will supply you with a map and directions to bike trails; and **Native Sons Adventures,** 1033-A Paseo del Pueblo Sur (☎ 800/753-7559 or 505/758-9342), rents regular (unsuspended) bikes for $15 per half day and $20 per full day, front-suspension bikes for $20 per half day and $35 per full day, and full-suspension bikes for $30 per half day and $45 per full day; they also rent car racks for $5. All of these prices include use of helmets and water bottles.

Annual touring events include Red River's **Enchanted Circle Century Bike Tour** (☎ 505/754-2366) on the weekend following Labor Day.

FISHING   The fishing season in the high lakes and streams opens April 1 and continues through December, though spring and fall tend to be the best times. Naturally, the Rio Grande is a favorite fishing spot, but there is also excellent fishing in the streams around Taos. Taoseños favor the Rio Hondo, Rio Pueblo (near Tres Ritos), Rio Fernando (in Taos Canyon), Pot Creek, and Rio Chiquito. Rainbow, cutthroat, German brown trout, and kokanee (a freshwater salmon) are commonly stocked and caught. Pike and catfish have been caught in the Rio Grande as well. Jiggs, spinners, or woolly worms are recommended as lure, or worms, corn, or salmon eggs as bait; many experienced anglers prefer fly-fishing.

Licenses are required, of course and are sold, along with tackle, at several Taos sporting-goods shops. For backcountry guides, try **Deep Creek Wilderness Outfitters and Guides,** P.O. Box 721, El Prado, NM 87529 (☎ **505/776-8423**), or **Taylor Streit Flyfishing Service,** P.O. Box 2759 (☎ **505/751-1312**), in Taos.

FITNESS FACILITIES   The **Taos Spa and Court Club,** 111 Dona Ana Dr. (☎ **505/758-1980**), is a fully equipped fitness center that rivals any you'd find in a big city. There are treadmills, step machines, climbing machines, rowing machines, exercise bikes, NordicTrack, weight-training machines, saunas, indoor and outdoor hot tubs, a steam room, and indoor and outdoor pools. Thirty-five aerobic step classes a week are also offered, as well as stretch aerobics, aqua aerobics, and classes specifically designed for senior citizens. In addition, there are five tennis and two racquetball courts. Therapeutic massage is available daily by appointment. Children's programs include tennis and swimming camp, and baby-sitting programs are available in the morning and evening. The spa is open Monday through Friday from 5:30am to 9pm; Saturday and Sunday from 7am to 8pm. Monthly, weekly, and daily memberships are available for individuals and families. For visitors there's a daily rate of $10.

The **Northside Health and Fitness Center,** at 1307 Paseo del Pueblo Norte, in Taos (☎ **505/751-1242**), is also a full-service facility, featuring top-of-the-line Cybex equipment, free weights, and cardiovascular equipment. Aerobics and Jazzercise classes are scheduled daily, and there are indoor/outdoor pools and four tennis courts, as well as children's and senior citizens' programs.

GOLF   The 18-hole golf course at the **Taos Country Club,** Ranchos de Taos (☎ **800/758-7375** or 505/758-7300), is open to the public. Located on NM 570 west, just 4 miles south of the Plaza, it's a first-rate championship golf course designed for all levels of play—in fact, it is ranked as the third-best course in New Mexico. It has open fairways and no hidden greens. The club also features a driving range, practice putting and chipping green, and instruction by PGA professionals. Greens fees in 1998 were $32 during the week, $40 weekends (includes Friday) and holidays for 18 holes. Twilight fee is $23. Cart and club rentals are also available. It's always advisable to call ahead for tee times one week in advance, but it's not unusual for people to show up unannounced and still manage to find a time to tee off.

The par-72, 18-hole course at the **Angel Fire Resort Golf Course** (☎ **800/633-7463** or 505/377-3055) is PGA-endorsed. Surrounded by stands of ponderosa pine, spruce, and aspen, at 8,500 feet, it's one of the highest regulation golf courses in the world. It also has a driving range and putting green. Carts and clubs can be rented at the course, and the club pro provides instruction.

For nine-hole play, stop at the golf course at **Valle Escondido** residential village (☎ **505/758-3475**) just off U.S. 64. It's a par-36 course with mountain and valley views. Clubs and pull-carts are available for rental, and the clubhouse serves refreshments.

Another golf course is under construction in Red River. At press time nine holes were open. Call **Red Eagle Golf Course** (☎ **505/754-6569**).

HIKING   There are hundreds of miles of hiking trails in Taos County's mountain and high-mesa country. They're especially well traveled in the summer and fall, although nights turn chilly and mountain weather may be fickle by September.

Maps (for a nominal fee) and free materials and advice on all **Carson National Forest** trails and recreation areas can be obtained from the **Forest Service Building,** 208 Cruz Alta Rd. (☎ **505/758-6200**), and from the office adjacent to the chamber of commerce on Paseo del Pueblo Sur. Both are open Monday through Friday from

8am to 4:30pm. Detailed USGS topographical maps of backcountry areas can be purchased from **Taos Mountain Outfitters** on the Plaza (☎ **505/758-9292**). This is also the place to rent camping gear, if you came without your own. Tent rentals are $15 and sleeping bags are $10 each per day. Backpacks can be rented for $15 a day. Ask about special deals on weekend packages. They also have a weekly rock climbing class.

Two wilderness areas close to Taos offer outstanding hiking possibilities. The 19,663-acre **Wheeler Peak Wilderness** is a wonderland of Alpine tundra encompassing New Mexico's highest peak (13,161 feet). The 20,000-acre **Latir Peak Wilderness,** north of Red River, is noted for its high lake country. Both are under the jurisdiction of the **Questa Ranger District,** P.O. Box 110, Questa, NM 87556 (☎ **505/586-0520**).

HORSEBACK RIDING　The **Taos Indian Horse Ranch,** on Pueblo land off Ski Valley Road, just before Arroyo Seco (☎ **505/758-3212**), offers a variety of guided rides. Open by appointment, the ranch provides horses for all types of riders (English, Western, Australian, and bareback) and ability levels. Call ahead to reserve. Rates start at $32 and go up to $65 to $95 for a 2-hour trail ride. Horse-drawn hay wagon rides are also offered in summer. From late November to March, the ranch provides afternoon and evening sleigh rides to a bonfire and marshmallow roast at $25 to $37.50 per person; ask for prices for a steak cookout. Also ask about the "Paddle and Saddle Club" designed for the adrenaline junkie, 8-hour or overnight programs, which include riding, a raft trip, and pack trip for $185 to $495.

Horseback riding is also offered by the **Shadow Mountain Guest Ranch,** 6 miles east of Taos on U.S. 64 (☎ **800/405-7732** or 505/758-7732); **Rio Grande Stables** (P.O. Box 2122), El Prado (☎ **505/776-5913**); and **Llano Bonito Ranch** (P.O. Box 99), Peñasco, about 40 minutes from Taos (☎ **505/587-2636;** fax 505/587-2636). Rates at Llano Bonito Ranch are $22.50 for a 1-hour trail ride, $70 per person for a half-day ride ($95 for breakfast ride), and $125 per person for a full-day ride. In addition to trail rides, Llano Bonito Ranch offers 3-day pack trips for $595 per person (minimum of four people). On the 3-day trip you'll spend 2 nights in the high-country wilderness, and during the day you'll ride to an altitude of 12,500 feet. Meals are included on the pack trip. They also have wagon rides for $25 per person.

Most riding outfitters offer lunch trips and overnight trips. Call for further details.

HUNTING　Hunters in Carson National Forest bag deer, turkey, grouse, band-tailed pigeons, and elk by special permit. On private land, where hunters must be accompanied by qualified guides, there are also black bear and mountain lions. Hunting seasons vary year to year, so it's important to inquire ahead with the **New Mexico Game and Fish Department in Santa Fe** (☎ **505/827-7882**).

Several Taos sporting-goods shops sell hunting licenses, including **Cottam's Ski and Outdoor Shop** (☎ **505/758-2822**) 207-A Paseo del Pueblo Norte and in Taos Ski Valley, and **Wal-Mart** (☎ **505/758-3116**), 925 Paseo del Pueblo Sur. Backcountry guides include **Moreno Valley Outfitters** (☎ **505/377-3512**) in Angel Fire and **Rio Costilla Park** (☎ **505/586-0542**) in Costilla.

ICE-SKATING　For ice-skating, **Kit Carson Park Ice Rink** (☎ **505/758-8234**), located in Kit Carson Park, is open from Thanksgiving through February. Skate rentals are available for adults and children.

JOGGING　You can jog anywhere (except on private property) in and around Taos. I would especially recommend stopping by the Carson National Forest office in the chamber of commerce building to find out what trails they might recommend.

LLAMA TREKKING　For a taste of the unusual, **El Paseo Llama Expeditions** (☎ **800/455-2627** or 505/758-3111; www.elpaseollama.com) uses U.S. Forest

Service–maintained trails that wind through canyons and over mountain ridges. The llamas will carry your gear and food, allowing you to walk and explore, free of any heavy burdens. They're friendly, gentle animals that have a keen sense of sight and smell. Often, other animals, such as elk, deer, and mountain sheep, are attracted to the scent of the llamas and will venture closer to hikers if the llamas are present. Llama expeditions are scheduled from May to mid-October; and day hikes are scheduled year-round. Gourmet meals are provided. Half-day hikes cost $49, day hikes $70, and 2- to 8-day hikes run up to $850. **Wild Earth Adventures** (☎ **800/758-LAMA** or 505/586-0174; http://members.aol.com/llamatrek; e-mail: llamatrek@aol.com) offers a "Take a llama to llunch hike"—a day hike into the Sangre de Cristo Mountains, and a gourmet lunch for $75, with discounts for children under 12. Wild Earth owner Stuart Rosenberg also offers a variety of custom multiday guided pack trips tailored to travelers' needs and fitness levels. A 2-day overnight is $210; 3 days and longer, $120 per day per person. Camping gear and food are provided. On the trips, Rosenberg provides information on edible and medicinal plants, animal tracking, history, and geology.

RIVER RAFTING   Half- or full-day white-water rafting trips down the Rio Grande and Rio Chama originate in Taos and can be booked through a variety of outfitters in the area. The wild **Taos Box,** a steep-sided canyon south of the Wild Rivers Recreation Area, offers a series of Class IV rapids that rarely lets up for some 17 miles. The water drops up to 90 feet per mile, providing one of the most exciting 1-day white-water tours in the West. May and June, when the water is rising, is a good time to go. Experience is not required, but you will be required to wear a life jacket (provided), and you should be willing to get wet.

One convenient rafting service is **Rio Grande Rapid Transit,** Box A, Pilar, NM 87531 (☎ **800/222-RAFT** or 505/758-9700). In addition to Taos Box ($69 to $89 per person), Rapid Transit also runs the **Pilar Racecourse** ($30 to $35 per person) on a daily basis. A full-day Pilar trip takes a more leisurely route before getting to the Racecourse and includes lunch ($69). The new evening dinner floats—great for older people, little kids, or people with disabilities—have no white water, but plenty of scenery ($30). It lets out at Embudo Station, where rafters can dine and drink micro-brewed beer. Rapid Transit's headquarters is at the entrance to the BLM-administered **Orilla Verde Recreation Area,** 16 miles south of Taos, where most excursions through the Taos Box end. Several other serene but thrilling floats through the Pilar Racecourse start at this point.

Other rafting outfitters in the Taos area include **Los Rios River Runners,** P.O. Box 2734 (☎ **800/544-1181** or 505/776-8854); **Native Sons Adventures,** 1033-A Paseo del Pueblo Sur (☎ **800/753-7559** or 505/758-9342); and **Far Flung Adventures,** P.O Box 707, El Prado, NM 87529 (☎ **800/359-2627** or 505/758-2628).

Safety warning: Taos is not the place to experiment if you are not an experienced rafter. Do yourself a favor and check with the **Bureau of Land Management** (☎ **505/758-8851**) to make sure that you're fully equipped to go white-water rafting without a guide. Have them check your gear to make sure that it's sturdy enough—this is serious rafting!

ROCK CLIMBING   **Mountain Skills** (☎ **800/584-6863** or 505/758-9589) offers rock climbing instruction for all skill levels, from basic beginners to more advanced climbers who would like to fine-tune their skills or just find out the best area climbs.

SPAS   **Mountain Massage & Spa Treatments** (at Casa de las Chimeneas B&B), 405 Cordoba Rd. (☎ **505/758-9156**), though a small place, has large treatments. I tried the herbal steam tent, aromatherapy facial, and salt glow body scrub and felt like I'd found heaven. Massages are also excellent, and there is a sauna and hot tub.

SWIMMING The **Don Fernando Pool** (☎ **505/737-2622**), on Civic Plaza Drive at Camino de la Placita, opposite the new Convention Center, admits swimmers over age 8 without adult supervision.

SNOWMOBILING **Native Sons Adventures,** 1033-A Paseo del Pueblo Sur (☎ **800/753-7559** or 505/758-9342), runs fully guided tours in the Sangre de Cristo Mountains. Rates range from $60 to $135. Advanced reservation required.

TENNIS **Quail Ridge Inn,** Ski Valley Rd. (P.O. Box 707) (☎ **800/624-4448** or 505/776-2211), has six outdoor and two indoor tennis courts. **Taos Spa and Tennis Club** (see "Fitness Facilities," above) has five courts, and the **Northside Health and Fitness Center** (see above) in El Prado has three tennis courts. In addition, there are four free public courts in Taos, two at **Kit Carson Park,** on Paseo del Pueblo Norte, and two at **Fred Baca Memorial Park,** on Camino del Medio south of Ranchitos Road.

8 Shopping

Given the town's historical associations with the arts, it isn't surprising that many visitors come to Taos to buy fine art. Some 50-odd galleries are located within easy walking distance of the Plaza, and a couple of dozen more are just a short drive from downtown. Galleries are generally open 7 days a week, especially in the high seasons. Some artists show their work by appointment only.

The best-known artist in modern Taos is R. C. Gorman, a Navajo from Arizona who has made his home in Taos for more than 2 decades. Now in his 50s, Gorman is internationally acclaimed for his bright, somewhat surrealistic depictions of Navajo women. His **Navajo Gallery,** at 210 Ledoux St. (☎ **505/758-3250**), is a showcase for his widely varied work: acrylics, lithographs, silk screens, bronzes, tapestries, hand-cast ceramic vases, etched glass, and more.

A good place to begin exploring galleries is the **Stables Fine Art Gallery,** operated by the Taos Art Association at 133 Paseo del Pueblo Norte (☎ **505/758-2036**). A rotating group of fine arts exhibits features many of Taos's emerging and established artists. All types of work are exhibited, including painting, sculpture, printmaking, photography, and ceramics. Admission is free; it's open year-round daily from 10am to 5pm.

My favorite place to shop in Taos is in the **St. Francis Plaza** in Rancho de Taos, just a few miles south of the Plaza. This is what shopping in northern New Mexico once was. Forget T-shirt shops and fast food. Here you'll find small shops, where the owner often presides. There's even a little cafe, and of course you'll want to visit the San Francisco de Assisi church (see "What to See & Do," earlier in this chapter).

Here are a few shopping recommendations, listed according to their specialties:

ART

Act I Gallery. 226D Paseo del Pueblo Norte. ☎ **800/666-2933** or 505/758-7831.

This gallery has a broad range of works in a variety of media; you'll find watercolors, retablos, furniture, paintings, Hispanic folk art, pottery, jewelry, and sculpture.

Desurmont Art Gallery. 118 Camino de la Placita. ☎ **505/758-3299.**

Here you'll find abstract and impressionist oils and watercolors, sculpture, ceramics, and jewelry.

Fenix Gallery. 228B N. Pueblo Rd. ☎ **505/758-9120.**

The Fenix Gallery focuses on Taos artists with national and/or international collections and reputations who live and work in Taos. The work is primarily non-objective and very contemporary. Some "historic" artists are represented as well. Recent expansion has doubled the gallery space.

Franzetti Metalworks. 120-G Bent St. ☎ **505/758-7872.**

This work appeals to some more than others. The designs are surprisingly whimsical for metalwork. Much of the work is functional; you'll find laughing horse switch plates and "froggie" earthquake detectors.

Gallery A. 105–107 Kit Carson Rd. ☎ **505/758-2343.**

The oldest gallery in town, Gallery A has contemporary and traditional paintings, sculpture, and graphics, including Gene Kloss oils, watercolors, and etchings.

Hirsch Fine Art. 146 Kit Carson Rd. ☎ **505/758-2478.**

If you can find this gallery open, it's well worth the visit. Unfortunately, the hours posted are not always maintained. Spread through a beautiful old home are watercolors, etchings and lithographs, and drawings by early Southwestern artists, including the original Taos founders.

✪ **Lumina of New Mexico.** 239 Morada Rd. (P.O. Box LL). ☎ **505/758-7282.**

Located in the historic Victor Higgins home, next to the Mabel Dodge Luhan estate, Lumina is one of the loveliest galleries in New Mexico. You'll find a large variety of fine art, including paintings, sculpture, and photography. This place is as much a tourist attraction as any of the museums and historic homes in town.

Look for wonderful Picasso-esque paintings of the New Mexico village life by Andrés Martinez, and take a stroll through the new 3-acre outdoor sculpture garden with a pond and waterfall, where you'll find large outdoor pieces from all over the United States.

✪ **New Directions Gallery.** 107B North Plaza. ☎ **800/658-6903** or 505/758-2771.

Here you'll find a variety of contemporary abstract works such as Larry Bell's unique mixed-media "Mirage paintings." My favorites, though, are the impressionistic works depicting northern New Mexico villages by Tom Noble.

✪ **Philip Bareiss Contemporary Exhibitions.** 15 Ski Valley Rd. ☎ **505/776-2284.**

The works of some 30 leading Taos artists, including sculptor Gray Mercer and watercolorist Patricia Sanford, are exhibited here. In 1995 Philip Bareiss opened "Circles and Passageways," a sculptural installation by Gray Mercer, on the 2,500-acre Romero Range located just west of Taos. This is true land art; a four-wheel-drive vehicle is recommended in order to get there.

Quast Galleries–Taos. 229 and 133 E. Kit Carson Rd. ☎ **505/758-7160** or 505/758-7779.

You won't want to miss this gallery, where you'll find representational landscapes and figurative paintings and distinguished sculpture. Rotating national and international exhibits are shown here.

R. B. Ravens. No. 70 St. Francis Church Plaza (P.O. Box 850), Ranchos de Taos. ☎ **505/758-7322.**

A trader for many years, including 15 on the Ranchos Plaza, R. B. Ravens is skilled at finding exceptional period artwork. Here you'll see (and have the chance to buy) a late 19th-century Plains elk-tooth woman's dress, as well as moccasins, Navajo rugs, and pottery, all in the setting of an old home, with raw pine floors and hand-sculpted adobe walls.

Shriver Gallery. 401 Paseo del Pueblo Norte. ☎ **505/758-4994.**

Traditional paintings, drawings, etchings, and bronze sculpture.

Taos Gallery. 403 Paseo del Pueblo Norte. ☎ **505/758-2475.**

Here you'll find Southwestern impressionism, traditional Western art, contemporary fine art, and bronze sculpture.

BOOKS
Brodsky Bookshop. 218 Paseo del Pueblo Norte. ☎ **505/758-9468.**

Exceptional inventory of fiction, nonfiction, Southwestern and Native American studies, children's books, topographical and travel maps, cards, tapes, and CDs.

Kit Carson Home. E. Kit Carson Rd. ☎ **505/758-4741.**

Fine collection of books about regional history.

✪ **Moby Dickens Bookshop.** 124A Bent St. ☎ **888/442-9980** or 505/758-3050.

This is one of Taos's best bookstores. You'll find children's and adults' collections of Southwest, Native American, and out-of-print books. A renovation has added 600 square feet, much of it upstairs, where there's a comfortable place to sit and read.

Taos Book Shop. 122D Kit Carson Rd. ☎ **505/758-3733.**

Founded in 1947, this is the oldest general bookstore in New Mexico. Taos Book Shop specializes in out-of-print and Southwestern titles.

CRAFTS
Clay & Fiber Gallery. 126 W. Plaza Dr. ☎ **505/758-8093.**

Clay & Fiber represents more than 150 artists from around the country; merchandise changes frequently, but you should expect to see a variety of ceramics, fiber arts, jewelry, and wearables.

Southwest Moccasin & Drum. 803 Paseo del Pueblo Norte. ☎ **800/447-3630** or 505/758-9332.

Home of the All One Tribe Drum, this favorite local shop carries a large variety of drums in all sizes and styles, handmade by master Native American drum makers from Taos Pueblo. Southwest Moccasin & Drum also has the country's second-largest selection of moccasins, as well as an impressive inventory of indigenous world instruments and tapes, sculpture, weavings, rattles, fans, fetishes, bags, decor, and many handmade one-of-a-kind items. A percentage of the store's profits goes to support Native American causes.

✪ **Taos Artisans Cooperative Gallery.** 109 Bent St. ☎ **505/758-1558.**

This eight-member cooperative gallery, owned and operated by local artists, sells local handmade jewelry, wearables, clay work, glass, drums, baskets, leather work, garden sculpture, and woven Spirit Women. You'll always find an artist in the shop.

Taos Blue. 101A Bent St. ☎ **505/758-3561.**

This gallery has fine Native American and contemporary handcrafts; it specializes in clay and fiber work.

Twining Weavers and Contemporary Crafts. 135 Paseo del Pueblo Norte. ☎ **505/758-9000.**

Here you'll find an interesting mix of handwoven wool rugs and pillows by owner Sally Bachman, as well as creations by other gallery artists in fiber, basketry, and clay.

Weaving Southwest. 216 Paseo del Pueblo Norte. ☎ **505/758-0433.**

Contemporary tapestries by New Mexico artists, as well as one-of-a-kind rugs, blankets, and pillows, are the woven specialties found here.

FASHIONS
Mariposa Boutique. 120-F Bent St. ☎ **505/758-9028.**

What first caught my eye in this little shop were bright chile-pepper print overalls for kids. Closer scrutiny brought me to plenty of finds for myself such as suede and rayon broomstick skirts, and Mexican-style dresses, perfect for showing off turquoise jewelry.

Overland Sheepskin Company. NM 522 (a few miles north of town). ☎ **505/758-8822.**

You can't miss the romantically weathered barn sitting on a meadow north of town. Inside you'll find anything you can imagine in leather: gloves, hats, slippers, and coats. The coats here are exquisite, from oversized ranch styles to tailored blazers in a variety of leathers from sheepskin to buffalo hide.

FOOD
Amigos Co-op Natural Grocery. 136 Paseo del Pueblo Sur. ☎ **505/758-8493.**

If you've had your fill of rich food, this is the place to find healthful treats. In the front of the store are organic fruits and vegetables. And in the back, there's a small cafe, where you can eat or take out sandwiches, healthy green chile stew, or my favorite, a huge plate of stir-fried veggies over brown rice. You'll also find baked goods such as muffins and brownies.

The Cookie Gallery. 127 Bent St. ☎ **505/758-5867.**

Ready for a midmorning or midafternoon snack? Here you'll find Chinese sesame cookies, pumpkin cookies that must be kin to cupcakes, and melt-in-your-mouth Mexican wedding cookies. For a more substantial snack try the veggie empanadas. During warm months you can sit outside at tree-shaded tables.

FURNITURE
Country Furnishings of Taos. 534 Paseo del Pueblo Norte. ☎ **505/758-4633.**

Here you'll find unique hand-painted folk-art furniture that has become popular all over the country. The pieces are as individual as the styles of the local folk artists who make them. There are also home accessories, unusual gifts, clothing, and jewelry.

Greg Flores Furniture of Taos. 120 Bent St. ☎ **800/880-1090** or 505/758-8010.

This is a great little find. Greg Flores, native of Taos, fashions Southwestern furniture out of native ponderosa pine; he uses wood joinery and hand rubs each piece with an oil finish. You'll also find charming paintings by his wife, Johanna Flores.

Lo Fino. 201 Paseo del Pueblo Sur. ☎ **505/758-0298.**

With a name meaning "the refined," you know that this expansive showroom is worth taking time to wander through. You'll find a variety of home furnishings, from driftwood lamps and exotic masks made of dried flowers, to wagon-wheel furniture and finely painted *trasteros* (armoires), as well as handcrafted traditional and contemporary Southwestern furniture. Lo Fino specializes in building furniture to the specifications of its customers.

The Taos Company. 124K John Dunn Plaza, Bent St. ☎ **800/548-1141** or 505/758-1141.

This interior design showroom specializes in unique Southwestern antique furniture and decorative accessories. Especially look for wrought-iron lamps and iron-and-wood furniture.

GIFTS & SOUVENIRS

Big Sun. No. 2 St. Francis Church Plaza, Ranchos de Taos. ☎ **505/758-3100.**

This folk-art gallery and curio emporium is packed with beautiful objects, from rugs made by the Tarahumara Indians in Mexico to local tinwork made in Dixon and authentic Navajo throw rugs, made by beginning weavers, that cost around $70.

El Rincón. 114 Kit Carson Rd. (adjacent to La Doña Luz B&B). ☎ **505/758-9188.**

This shop has a real trading post feel. It's a wonderful place to find turquoise jewelry, whether you're looking for contemporary or antique. In the back of the store is a museum full of Native American and Western artifacts.

JEWELRY

Artwares Contemporary Jewelry. Taos Plaza (P.O. Box 2825). ☎ **800/527-8850** or 505/758-8850.

The gallery owners here call their contemporary jewelry "a departure from the traditional." Indeed, each piece here offers a new twist on traditional Southwestern and Native American design.

Leo Weaver Gallery. 62 St. Francis Plaza (P.O. Box 1596), Ranchos de Taos. ☎ **505/751-1003.**

This shop carries the work of more than 50 local silversmiths. There's an expansive collection of concho belts and some very fresh work, using a variety of stones from turquoise to charolite to lapis.

Taos Gems & Minerals. 637 Paseo del Pueblo Sur. ☎ **888/510-1664** or 505/758-3910.

This is a great place to explore; you can buy items like fetishes at prices much more reasonable than most galleries. Now in its 30th year of business, Taos Gems & Minerals is a fine lapidary showroom. You can also buy jewelry, carvings, and antique pieces at reasonable prices.

MUSICAL INSTRUMENTS

Taos Drum Company. 5 miles south of Taos Plaza, off NM 68. ☎ **505/758-3796.**

Drum making is an age-old tradition that local artisans give continued life to in Taos. The drums are made of hollowed-out logs stretched with rawhide, and they come in all different shapes, sizes, and styles. Taos Drums has the largest selection of Native American log and hand drums in the world. In addition to drums, the showroom displays Southwestern and wrought-iron furniture, cowboy art, and more than 60 styles of rawhide lampshades, as well as a constantly changing selection of primitive folk art, ethnic crafts, Native American music tapes, books, and other information on drumming. To find Taos Drum Company, look for the teepees and drums off NM 68. Ask about the tour that demonstrates the drum-making process.

POTTERY & TILES

Stephen Kilborn Pottery. 136D Paseo del Pueblo Norte. ☎ **800/758-0136,** 505/758-5760, or 505/758-0135 (studio).

Visiting this shop in town is a treat, but for a real adventure go 17 miles south of Taos toward Santa Fe to Stephen Kilborn's studio in Pilar, open daily 10am to 5pm, and noon to 5pm on Sunday. There you'll see him throw, decorate, and fire pottery that's fun, fantastical, and functional.

Vargas Tile Co. P.O. Box 1755, (south end of town on NM 68). ☎ **505/758-5986.**

Vargas Tile has a great little collection of hand-painted Mexican tiles at good prices. You'll find beautiful pots with sunflowers on them and colorful cabinet doorknobs, as well as inventive sinks.

9 Taos After Dark

For a small town, Taos has its share of top entertainment. Performers are attracted to Taos because of the resort atmosphere and the arts community, and the city enjoys annual programs in music and literary arts. State troupes, such as the New Mexico Repertory Theater and New Mexico Symphony Orchestra, make regular visits.

Many events are scheduled by the **Taos Art Association,** 133 Paseo del Pueblo Norte, Taos, NM 87571 (☎ **505/758-2052**), at the **Taos Community Auditorium** (☎ **505/758-4677**). The TAA imports local, regional, and national performers in theater, dance, and concerts (Roy Hargrove, the Lula Washington Dance Theater, Theater Grottesco have performed here, and the American String Quartet still performs each year). Also look for a weekly film series offered year-round.

You can obtain information on current events in the *Taos News,* published every Thursday. The **Taos County Chamber of Commerce** (☎ **800/732-TAOS** or 505/758-3873) publishes semiannual listings of "Taos County Events," as well as an annual *Taos Country Vacation Guide* that also lists events and happenings around town.

THE PERFORMING ARTS
MAJOR ANNUAL PROGRAMS

Fort Burgwin Research Center. 6580 NM 518, Ranchos de Taos, NM 87557. ☎ **505/ 758-8322.**

This historic site (of the 1,000-year-old Pot Creek Pueblo), located about 10 miles south of Taos, is a summer campus of Dallas's Southern Methodist University. From mid-May through mid-August, the SMU-In-Taos curriculum (such as studio arts, humanities, and sciences) includes courses in music and theater. There are regularly scheduled orchestral concerts, guitar, and harpsichord recitals, and theater performances available to the community, without charge, throughout the summer.

Music from Angel Fire. P.O. Box 502, Angel Fire, NM 87710. ☎ **505/377-3233** or 505/989-4772.

This acclaimed program of chamber music begins in mid-August with weekend concerts and continues up to Labor Day. Based in the small resort community of Angel Fire (located about 21 miles east of U.S. 64), it also presents numerous concerts in Taos, Las Vegas, and Raton.

Taos Poetry Circus. Office mailing address: 5275 NDCBU, Taos, NM 87571. ☎ **505/ 758-1800.** Events take place at various venues around town.

Aficionados of the literary arts appreciate this annual event, held during 8 days in mid-June. Billed as "a literary gathering and poetry showdown among nationally known writers," it includes readings, seminars, performances, public workshops, and a poetry video festival. The main event is the **World Heavyweight Championship Poetry Bout,** 10 rounds of hard-hitting readings—with the last round extemporaneous.

Taos School of Music. P.O. Box 1879, Taos, NM 87571. ☎ **505/776-2388.** Tickets for chamber music concerts $15 adults, $12 for children under 16.

Sponsored by the Taos Art Association, the Taos School of Music was founded in 1963. It is located at the Hotel St. Bernard in Taos Ski Valley. From mid-June to mid-August there is an intensive 8-week study and performance program for advanced students of violin, viola, cello, and piano. Students receive daily coaching by the American String Quartet and pianist Robert McDonald.

The 8-week **Chamber Music Festival,** an important adjunct of the school, offers 16 concerts and seminars for the public; performances are given by pianist Robert McDonald, guest musicians, and the international young student artists. In 1998, guests included the American String Quartet and violist Michael Tree (1998) of the Guarneri Quartet. Performances are held at the Taos Community Auditorium and the Hotel St. Bernard.

✪ **Taos Talking Picture Festival.** 1337 Gusdorf Rd. Ste. F. (7217 NDCBU, Taos, NM 87571). ☎ **505/751-0637.** Fax 505/751-7385; www.taosnet.com/ttpix/; e-mail: ttpix@taosnet.com. Individual screenings $7. Fast pass $300–$350.

For 1999, the festival is scheduled April 15 to 18; screenings run 9am to 11pm. Filmmakers and film enthusiasts from the Southwest and as far away as Finland gather—8,000 strong in 1988—to view a variety of films, from serious documentaries to lighthearted comedies. The festival also offers lectures about the culture of films and filmmaking, a media conference, workshops, preshowing discussions, and parties. You'll see locally made films as well as films involving Hollywood big-hitters. Each year 5 acres of land is given as a prize to encourage filmmakers to take a fresh approach to storytelling. In 1998, the festival's Land Grant Award went to Native American filmmaker Chris Eyre. His film *Smoke Signals,* shown opening night, is the first Native-written and -directed film to be introduced into national distribution. The festival's 1998 Cineaste Award went to Latino filmmaker Moctesuma Esparza, whose work includes *Selena, The Disappearance of Garcia Lorca,* and *The Milagro Beanfield War.*

THE CLUB & MUSIC SCENE

Adobe Bar. In the Historic Taos Inn, 125 Paseo del Pueblo Norte. ☎ **505/758-2233.** No cover. Noon–10:30pm.

A favorite gathering place for locals and visitors, the Adobe Bar is known for its live music series (nights vary) devoted to the eclectic talents of Taos musicians. The schedule offers a little of everything—classical, jazz, folk, Hispanic, and acoustic. The Adobe Bar features a wide selection of international beers, wines by the glass, light New Mexican dining, desserts, and an espresso menu.

Alley Cantina. 121 Teresina Lane. ☎ **505/758-2121.** Cover for live music only.

This new bar has become the hot late-night spot in Taos. The focus is on interaction—so there's no television. Instead, patrons play shuffleboard and pool, as well as chess and backgammon in this building, which is said to be the oldest house in Taos. Pastas, sandwiches, and other dishes are served until past midnight.

Hideaway Lounge. At the Holiday Inn, 1005 Paseo del Pueblo Sur. ☎ **505/758-4444.** No cover.

This hotel lounge, built around a large adobe fireplace, offers live entertainment and an extensive hors d'oeuvre buffet. Call for schedule.

Sagebrush Inn. Paseo del Pueblo Sur. ☎ **505/758-2254.** No cover.

This is a real hot spot for locals. The atmosphere is Old West, with a rustic wooden dance floor and plenty of smoke. Dancers generally two-step to country performers nightly, year-round, from 9pm.

Thunderbird Lodge. Taos Ski Valley. ☎ **505/776-2280.** No cover, except occasionally on holidays; then the cost varies widely.

Throughout the winter, the Thunderbird offers a variety of nightly entertainment at the foot of the ski slopes. You'll also find wine tastings and two-step dance lessons here.

10 A Scenic Drive Around the Enchanted Circle

If you're in the mood to explore, take this 90-mile loop north of Taos through the old Hispanic villages of Arroyo Hondo and Questa, into a pass the Apaches, Kiowas, and Comanches once used to cross through the mountains to trade with the Taos Indians. You'll come to the Wild West mining town of Red River, pass through the expansive Moreno Valley, and along the base of some of New Mexico's tallest peaks. Then you'll skim the shores of a high mountain lake at Eagle Nest, pass through the resort village of Angel Fire, and head back to Taos along the meandering Rio Fernando de Taos. Although one can drive the entire loop in 2 hours from Taos, most folks prefer to take a full day, and many take several days.

ARROYO HONDO   Traveling north from Taos via NM 522, it's a 9-mile drive to this village, the remains of an 1815 land grant along the Rio Hondo. Along the dirt roads that lead off NM 522, you may find a windowless Morada or two, marked by plain crosses in front, places of worship for the still-active Penitentes, a religious order known for self-flagellation. This is also the turnoff point for trips to the Rio Grande Box, an awesome 1-day, 17-mile white-water run for which you can book trips in Santa Fe, Taos, Red River, and Angel Fire. Arroyo Hondo was also the site of the New Buffalo commune in the 1960s. Hippies flocked here looking to escape the mores of modern society. Over the years the commune members have dispersed throughout northern New Mexico, bringing an interesting creative element to the food, architecture, and philosophy of the state. En route north, the highway passes near **San Cristobal,** where a side road turns off to the D. H. Lawrence Ranch (see "What to See & Do," above) and **Lama,** site of an isolated spiritual retreat.

QUESTA   Next Hwy. 522 passes through Questa, most of whose residents are employed at a molybdenum mine about 5 miles east of town. Mining molybdenum (an ingredient in lightbulbs, television tubes, and missile systems) in the area has not been without controversy. The process has raked across hillsides along the Red River, and though Molycorp, the mine's owner, treats the water they use before returning it to the river, studies show it has adversely affected the fish life. Still, the mine is a major employer in the area, and locals are grateful for the income it generates.

If you turn west off NM 522 onto NM 378 about 3 miles north of Questa, you'll descend 11 miles on a gravel road into the gorge of the Rio Grande at the Bureau of Land Management–administered **Wild Rivers Recreation Area** (☎ 505/770-1600). Here, where the Red River enters the gorge, is the most accessible starting point for river-rafting trips through the infamous Taos Box. Some 48 miles of the Rio Grande, south from the Colorado border, are protected under the national Wild and Scenic River Act of 1968. Information on geology and wildlife, as well as hikers' trail maps, can be obtained at the visitor center here. Ask for directions to the impressive petroglyphs in the gorge. River-rafting trips can be booked in Taos, Santa Fe, Red River, and other communities. (See the "Ballooning, Biking & Outdoor Pursuits" sections in chapter 7 and above for booking agents in Santa Fe and Taos, respectively.)

The village of **Costilla,** near the Colorado border, is 20 miles north of Questa. This is the turnoff point for four-wheel-drive jaunts and hiking trips into **Valle Vidal,** a huge U.S. Forest Service–administered reserve with 42 miles of roads and many hiking trails. A day hike in this area can bring you sightings of hundreds of elk.

RED RIVER   However, to continue on the Enchanted Circle loop, turn east at Questa onto NM 38 for a 12-mile climb to Red River, a rough-and-ready 1890s gold-mining town that has parlayed its Wild West ambience into a pleasant resort village that's especially popular with families from Texas and Oklahoma.

This community, at 8,750 feet, is a center for skiing and snowmobiling, fishing and hiking, off-road driving and horseback riding, mountain biking, river rafting, and other outdoor pursuits. Frontier-style celebrations, honky-tonk entertainment, and even staged shoot-outs on Main Street are held throughout the year.

Though it can be a charming and fun town, Questa's food and accommodations are mediocre at best. Its patrons are down-home folks, happy with a bed and a diner-style meal. If you decide to stay, try **The Lodge at Red River,** P.O. Box 189, Red River, NM 87558 (☎ 800/91-LODGE or 505/754-6280; www.redrivernm.com/lodgeatrr/), in the center of town. It offers hotel rooms beginning at $42, though I'd spend a bit more ($68 to $78), for a room with a window opening to the outside. With knotty pine throughout, the accommodations are clean and comfortable. Downstairs the restaurant serves standard breakfasts and family style dinners: fried chicken, steaks, trout, and pork chops.

If you're passing through and want a quick meal, the **Past Times Deli,** 316 E. Main St. (☎ 505/754-3400), has brought some excellent flavors to the little village. You'll find tasty house-baked muffins and stuffed baked potatoes, soups, and sub sandwiches under $8. Don't leave without trying a macadamia nut white chocolate chip cookie.

The **Red River Chamber of Commerce,** P.O. Box 870, Red River, NM 87558 (☎ 800/348-6444 or 505/754-2366), lists more than 40 accommodations, including lodges and condominiums. Some are open winters or summers only.

EAGLE NEST   About 16 miles east of Red River, on the other side of 9,850-foot Bobcat Pass, is the village of Eagle Nest, resting on the shore of Eagle Nest Lake in the Moreno Valley. Gold was mined in this area as early as 1866, starting in what is now the ghost town of **Elizabethtown** about 5 miles north; Eagle Nest itself (population 200) wasn't incorporated until 1976. The 4-square-mile lake is considered one of the top trout producers in the United States and attracts ice fishers in winter as well as summer anglers. Sailboats and Windsurfers also use the lake, although swimming, waterskiing, and camping are not permitted.

If you're heading to Cimarron or Denver, proceed east on U.S. 64 from Eagle Nest. But if you're circling back to Taos, continue southwest on U.S. 38 and U.S. 64 to Agua Fría and Angel Fire.

Shortly before the Agua Fría junction, you'll see the **DAV Vietnam Veterans Memorial.** It's a stunning structure with curved white walls soaring high against the backdrop of the Sangre de Cristo Range. Consisting of a chapel and underground visitor center, it was built by Dr. Victor Westphall in memory of his son, David, a marine lieutenant killed in Vietnam in 1968. The chapel has a changing gallery of photographs of Vietnam veterans who lost their lives in the Southeast Asian war,

Taos Area (Including Enchanted Circle)

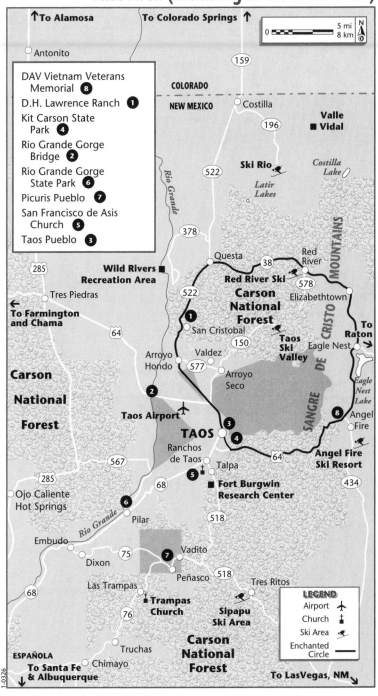

↑ To Alamosa

To Colorado Springs ↑

0 5 mi 8 km N

Antonito

DAV Vietnam Veterans Memorial **8**

D.H. Lawrence Ranch **1**

Kit Carson State Park **4**

Rio Grande Gorge Bridge **2**

Rio Grande Gorge State Park **6**

Picuris Pueblo **7**

San Francisco de Asis Church **5**

Taos Pueblo **3**

159

COLORADO

NEW MEXICO

Costilla

196

Valle
■ **Vidal**

Ski Rio

522

Costilla Lake

Latir Lakes

Rio Grande

378

Questa

38

Red River

Red River Ski

578

Carson National Forest

Elizabethtown

285

Wild Rivers Recreation Area ■

522

SANGRE DE CRISTO MOUNTAINS

Tres Piedras

1

San Cristobal

150

Taos Ski Valley

Eagle Nest

To Raton →

← **To Farmington and Chama**

64

Arroyo Hondo

577

Valdez

Arroyo Seco

Eagle Nest Lake

Carson National Forest

2

Taos Airport ✈

3

TAOS

4

8

Angel Fire

Ranchos de Taos

Talpa

64

Angel Fire Ski Resort

567

5

✝

■ **Fort Burgwin Research Center**

434

285

68

6

518

Ojo Caliente Hot Springs

Pilar

Rio Grande

Embudo

75

7

Vadito

Dixon

Peñasco

518

Tres Ritos

LEGEND

Airport ✈
Church ✝
Ski Area �skier
Enchanted Circle ──

68

Las Trampas

76

■ **Trampas Church**

Sipapu Ski Area

Truchas

Carson National Forest

ESPAÑOLA

Chimayo

To Santa Fe & Albuquerque ↓

To Las Vegas, NM ↘

1-0326

but no photo is as poignant as this inscription written by young Davis Westphall, a promising poet:

> *Greed plowed cities desolate.*
> *Lusts ran snorting through the streets.*
> *Pride reared up to desecrate Shrines,*
> *and there were no retreats.*
> *So man learned to shed the tears*
> *With which he measures out his years.*

ANGEL FIRE   If you like the clean efficiency of a resort complex, you may want to plan a night or two here, any time of year. Angel Fire is approximately 150 miles north of Albuquerque, 21 miles east of Taos. Opened in the late 1960s, this resort offers a hotel with spacious, comfortable rooms, as well as condominiums and cabins. Winter is the biggest season. This medium-sized beginner and intermediate mountain is an excellent place for families to roam about (see "Skiing Taos," above). A new high-speed quad lift zips skiers to the top quickly while allowing them a long ski down. The views of the Moreno Valley are awe-inspiring. Recently a Nordic trail has been added, running around the snow-covered golf course, and visitors can also snowmobile and take sleigh rides, including one out to a sheepherder's tent with a plank floor and a wood stove and eat dinner cooked over an open fire. Contact **Roadrunner Tours** (☎ **800/377-6416,** 505/377-6416, or 505/377-2811).

During spring, summer, and fall the resort offers golf, tennis, hiking, mountain biking (you can take your bike up on the quad lift), fly-fishing, river rafting, and horseback riding.

There are other fun family activities such as the Human Maze, 5,200 square feet of wooden passageway within which to get lost and find your way (basically seek your lower ratlike self). There's an indoor climbing wall, video arcade, miniature golf course, theater performances, and, throughout the year, a variety of festivals including a hot-air balloon festival, Winterfest, and concerts of both classical and popular music.

The unofficial community center is the **Angel Fire Resort,** North Angel Fire Road (P.O. Drawer B), Angel Fire, NM 87710 (☎ **800/633-7463** or 505/377-6401; www.angelfireresort.com), a 150-unit hotel with spacious, comfortable rooms. Rates start at $70 in the summer, $145 during holidays.

Even if you're just driving through, plan to dine at **Aldo's Cantina,** located at the base of the ski mountain and owned by the Angel Fire Resort in Angel Fire (☎ **505-377-6401**). This little nouveau Mexican restaurant is a grateful respite from the mediocre food you'll find around the rest of the Enchanted Circle. In the warm months you can enjoy tables on a wooden deck. Inside, amid persimmon walls, you can begin with a strawberry margarita. This is *not* New Mexican food, nor is it typical Mexican. It is elegant fare that people all over northern New Mexico are raving about. Aldo's is open daily from 11am to 2pm (après-ski during winter from 2 to 5pm) and for dinner from 5 to 9pm. During summer the restaurant may close on Monday, so call first. Lunches cost $5.95 to $11.95; dinner, from $12.95 to $21.95.

For more information on the Moreno Valley, including full accommodations listings, contact the **Angel Fire Chamber of Commerce,** P.O. Box 547, Angel Fire, NM 87710 (☎ **800/446-8117** or 505/377-6353; fax 505/377-3034).

A fascinating adventure you may want to try here is a 1-hour, 1-day, or overnight horseback trip with **Roadrunner Tours and Elkhorn Lodge Ltd.,** Box 274 Angel Fire, NM 87710 (☎ **800/377-6416,** 505/377-6416, or 505/377-2811). From Angel Fire, Nancy and Bill Burch guide adventurers on horseback trips through private ranchland to taste the life of the lonesome cowboy. The cattle drive trip is no bland trail ride. The first day you'll travel 15 miles through ponderosa forests, across meadows of asters and sunflowers, with bald peaks in the distance. Once at camp, riders bed down in an authentic mountain cowboy cabin. The second day, you'll move as many as 300 cows through the Moreno Valley. One-hour rides are $20; day rides $95; cattle drives $184 (includes overnight stay in a cow camp). Cattle drives take place in July and August; book early, because space is limited.

9 Northeastern New Mexico

Much of my growing up took place on the oft-dusty, oft-lush plains of northeastern New Mexico, the region north of I-40 and east of the Sangre de Cristo Mountains, where dinosaurs and buffalo once roamed. My family has a ranch here along the Cimarron cutoff of the Santa Fe trail. I grew up with the ghost of Samuel Watrous, who once had a store on that historic trade route. On the National Register of Historic places, it is now my family's home. For a time, I slept in the room where Watrous was said to have committed suicide, though he was found with not one but two bullet holes in his head. For many years I searched one corner of our property for his grave, which was said to be where the Mora and Sapello rivers meet. One day I did find a heavy chiseled stone among the bosk there. Whether you believe in ghosts or not, historical characters are present throughout this part of the state, and that's part of the eerie fun of coming here.

This is still the land of cowboys. My family raises cattle, and I long ago learned that ranchers tend to be stoic and only use words where necessary. They're comfortable with long silences in conversation, which for me defines the nature of this part of the state. There are many things to see here, but there are long, seemingly barren silences in between.

The long miles through the mountains from Las Vegas to Cimarron, or from Raton to Clayton, are worth it. The history is everywhere, from evidence of Coronado's passage during his 16th-century search of Cíbola, to the Santa Fe Trail ruts on the prairie made some 300 years later. In Cimarron you'll see evidence of the holdings of cattle baron Lucien Maxwell, who controlled most of these prairies as his private empire in the latter half of the 19th century. During his era, this was truly the Wild West. Cimarron attracted nearly every gunslinger of the era, from Butch Cassidy to Clay Allison, Black Jack Ketchum to Jesse James. Bullets still decorate the ceiling of the St. James Hotel.

Established long before its Nevada namesake, Las Vegas was the largest city in New Mexico at the turn of the 20th century, with a fast-growing cosmopolitan population. Doc Holliday, Bat Masterson, and Wyatt Earp walked its wild streets in the 1880s. A decade later, it was the headquarters of Teddy Roosevelt's Rough Riders, and early in the 20th century, it was a silent film capital (Tom Mix made movies here) and the site of a world heavyweight boxing match. Today, with a population of 17,500, it is the region's largest city, and the proud

Northeastern New Mexico

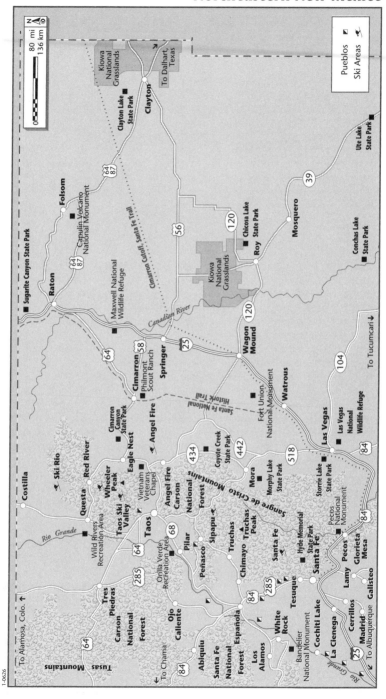

home of 900 historic properties. Raton (pop. 7,500), on I-25 in the Sangre de Cristo foothills, is the gateway to New Mexico from the north. Clayton (pop. 2,500), Tucumcari (pop. 6,831), and Santa Rosa (pop. 2,500) are all transportation hubs and ranching centers.

Two national monuments are particular points of interest. Fort Union, 24 miles north of Las Vegas, was the largest military installation in the Southwest in the 1860s and 1870s. Capulin Volcano, 33 miles east of Raton, last erupted 60,000 years ago; visitors can now walk inside the crater. Kiowa National Grasslands preserves 136,000 acres of pure prairie.

Drained by the Pecos and Canadian Rivers, northeastern New Mexico is otherwise notable for the number of small lakes that afford opportunities for fishing, hunting, boating, camping—even scuba diving. There are 11 state parks and about a half dozen designated wildlife areas within the region. Philmont Scout Ranch, south of Cimarron, is known by Boy Scouts throughout the world.

EXPLORING THE REGION BY CAR

Begin exploration of this region in **Las Vegas,** just over an hour's drive east of Santa Fe. Start by taking the walking tour, outlined later in this chapter, through Las Vegas and visit some of the historic buildings. Next head out to **Las Vegas National Wildlife Refuge,** where you'll be able to see more than 200 different species of birds and animals. If you're interested in pursuing some water sports, drive to **Storrie Lake State Park** (4 miles north via NM 518).

Stay overnight in Las Vegas, and in the morning, head north a short distance via I-25 and NM 161 to **Fort Union National Monument,** where you can visit the 19th-century ruins of what was once the largest military installation in the Southwest. When you've had your fill there, backtrack a bit on NM 161 up to NM 518, which begins the drive up the Mora River Valley. Turn north on NM 434, and you'll find yourself in **Mora,** a tiny Hispanic town founded in the early 1800s. While it's only 34 miles to the modern resort towns of Angel Fire and Eagle Nest (see chapter 8), Mora is a place where time seems to stand still. Tall cottonwoods and ponderosa pines follow the river and surrounding ditches.

As you continue north on NM 434, in the direction of Angel Fire, you'll come to **Guadalupita,** a small town that once thrived on farming, ranching, and logging, but now struggles to survive. Nearby Coyote Creek State Park, a good place to stop for a breather, offers camping, picnicking, and fishing.

Next follow NM 434 north to U.S. 64; where U.S. 64 turns east off the Enchanted Circle, follow it to **Cimarron,** where you should plan to spend the night. You'll need the rest of the day to absorb this frontier village that once played host to Kit Carson, Wyatt Earp, and Jesse James, among others.

The following day, take U.S. 64, which traces the Santa Fe Trail, northeast to **Raton.** Explore the town's historic district, then take U.S. 64/87 east to **Capulin Volcano National Monument.** If you'd rather take a more scenic route to Capulin from Raton, follow NM 72 to Folsom, and then take NM 325 south to **Capulin.** It's only a 45-mile drive from Raton to Capulin, but following this route will take quite some time, so leave early. Those driving RVs should stick to the major highways, because the state highways are narrow and difficult to negotiate in larger vehicles— good news for motorists tired of fighting RVs for space on the road. After visiting the Capulin Volcano National Monument and taking the 1-mile loop hike around the crater rim and the .2-mile hike down into the crater, continue east to the ranching center of **Clayton.**

From Clayton, take NM 370 north a short way to **Clayton Lake State Park** to check out the more than 500 dinosaur footprints. When you finish there, backtrack to Clayton and then if you really want to do the full tour of the region head south on NM 402 and southwest on U.S. 54 to **Tucumcari.** This city and Santa Rosa, an hour west on I-40, are oases in the arid east, though there's really little to see and do there, unless you want to go motorboating or fishing at one of the lakes. If you'd like to return to Las Vegas at this point, you can do so via U.S. 84, or else you can take I-40 west to Albuquerque. An alternative is to take U.S. 56/412 to I-25 south through Springer and Wagon Mound and back to Las Vegas for the night.

1 The Great Outdoors in Northeastern New Mexico

Northeastern New Mexico encompasses a variety of Southwest landscapes. The undulating grasslands of the eastern portion of the region eventually give way to the cliffs, canyons, and forests of the mighty Sangre de Cristo Mountains, which offer some of the best hiking and camping in the state. The area is drained by the Pecos and Canadian Rivers and is otherwise notable for the number of small streams and lakes, including Ute Lake, the second-largest in the state, that afford opportunities for fishing, including some great fly-fishing, boating, and other recreational pursuits (even scuba diving) in this seemingly arid region. There are 11 state parks and about a half dozen designated wildlife areas within the region.

BIKING   Favorite places to take the mountain bike in the northeastern section of New Mexico are in the areas that border Red River (particularly near Valle Vidal, discussed in chapter 8) and the areas just to the east of Santa Fe and Taos. It's best to purchase a book that describes and maps the trails for you. It's probably easiest in this region to rent your equipment in Albuquerque at **Old Town Bicycles,** 2209 Central Ave. NW (☎ 505/247-4926) or **Rio Mountain Sport,** 1210 Rio Grande Blvd. NW (☎ **505/766-9970**). There are also rental shops in Santa Fe and Taos (see individual city chapters for more information).

BIRD WATCHING   The **Las Vegas National Wildlife Refuge,** just a few miles outside of Las Vegas center, is a great place for bird watching. Species spotted year-round include prairie falcons and hawks, whereas during late fall and early winter migratory birds such as sandhill cranes, snow geese, Canada geese, and bald and golden eagles frequent the refuge. In all, more than 240 species can be sighted in the area. The **Maxwell National Wildlife Refuge,** near Raton, also boasts a rich population of resident and migratory birds, including raptors and bald eagles.

BOATING   There are opportunities for boating, windsurfing, and swimming throughout this region. Two of the most popular boating areas are **Storrie Lake State Park,** 6 miles north of Las Vegas, and **Conchas Lake State Park,** near Tucumcari. Storrie Lake is especially popular among **windsurfers,** who favor its consistent winds.

FISHING   Isolated and primitive **Morphy Lake State Park** is a favorite destination for serious anglers. The lake is regularly stocked with rainbow trout. **Cimarron Canyon State Park** is also popular with fishers. Lake Alice in **Sugarite Canyon State Park,** just north of Raton at the Colorado border, is a good spot for fly-fishing. For more information on the best fishing opportunities in the area, see the chapters for Santa Fe and Taos (chapters 7 and 8).

GOLF   Duffers can get in a few holes in or near virtually every town covered in this section. Courses I'd recommend are: **Conchas Dam Golf Course** (P.O. Box 946, Conchas Dam, NM 88416; ☎ **505/868-2988**); **New Mexico Highlands University Golf Course** (2118 8th St., Las Vegas, NM 87701; ☎ **505/425-7711**);

Raton Municipal Golf Course (P.O. Box 83, Raton, NM 87740; ☎ 505/445-8113); **Tucumcari Municipal Golf Course** (P.O. Box 1188, Tucumcari, NM 88401; ☎ 505/461-1849); and **Clayton Golf Course** (P.O. Box 4, Clayton, NM 88415; ☎ 505/374-9957).

HIKING   Northeastern New Mexico abounds in great places to hike, including the trails at Capulin Volcano; however, the best places are in the mountains to the north of Las Vegas and west of Santa Fe and Taos. **Clayton Lake, Coyote Creek, Morphy Lake, Santa Rosa Lake, Sugarite Canyon,** and **Villanueva** state parks all have hiking trails, which range from fairly informal to clearly marked. Another great hike takes you to the top of Hermit's Peak, which is only about 20 miles northwest of Las Vegas. Again, it's probably best to acquire equipment and supplies in Albuquerque before you set out. Try **REI-Albuquerque,** 1905 Mountain Rd. NW (☎ 505/247-1191).

HOT SPRINGS   In this region look for **Montezuma Hot Springs,** located on the Armand Hammer United World College of the American West Campus, near Las Vegas (see "Exploring Las Vegas," below).

SCUBA DIVING   There couldn't possibly be scuba diving in this dry, arid, land-locked state, could there? Yes, there is, with the best at Santa Rosa, where you'll find the **Blue Hole,** an 81-foot-deep artesian well that's a favorite of divers from around the world. The best place to rent equipment is at the **Santa Rosa Dive Center** on Blue Hole Road (☎ 505/472-3370).

SWIMMING   Swimming is best (although chilly) at **Clayton, Conchas, Morphy, Storrie,** and **Ute** lakes. See below for directions and specifics.

2 Las Vegas & Environs

Once known as the "gateway to New Mexico," this pleasant town in the foothills of the Sangre de Cristo Mountains was founded by a land grant from the Mexican government in 1835. A group of 29 Spanish colonists planted crops in the area and built a central plaza, which started out as a meeting place and a defense against Indian attack but soon became a main trading center on the Santa Fe Trail. Las Vegas boomed with the advent of the Atchison, Topeka, and Santa Fe Railway in 1879; almost overnight the town became the most important trading center and gathering place in the state and one of the largest towns in the Rocky Mountain West, rivaling Denver, Tucson, and El Paso in size.

Town settlers who arrived by train in the late 19th century shunned the indigenous adobe architecture, favoring instead building styles more typical of the Midwest or New England. They put up scores of fancy Queen Anne and Victorian-style houses and hotels, and the town is noted to this day for its dazzling diversity of architectural styles. Some 900 buildings in Las Vegas, both Victorian as well as earlier adobe structures, are on the National Register of Historic Buildings.

ESSENTIALS
GETTING THERE   From Santa Fe, take I-25 north (1¼ hours); from Raton, take I-25 south (1¾ hours); from Taos, follow NM 518 southeast 78 miles through Mora (2 hours); from Tucumcari, follow NM 104 west (2 hours). **Las Vegas Municipal Airport** handles private flights and charters. There is no regularly scheduled commercial service.

VISITOR INFORMATION   The **Las Vegas/San Miguel Chamber of Commerce** is at 727 Grand Ave. (P.O. Box 128), Las Vegas, NM 87701 (☎ 800/832-5947 or 505/425-8631).

EXPLORING LAS VEGAS
THE RAILROAD DISTRICT

When you first enter Las Vegas, you may want to take a brief driving tour through the railroad district and "east Las Vegas," to get a sense of how the railroad's arrival in 1870s shaped that side of the city. Turn east on Douglas Avenue and that will take you to Railroad Avenue. In this district are turn-of-the-century brick buildings housing such businesses as Moonlite Welding and Blue Dart Upholstery Shop. The center of the railroad district is the old Fred Harvey, **Castañeda Hotel** at 510 Railroad. Built in 1898, it is one of the early Harvey Houses to be built in the Mission Revival style. It no longer operates as a hotel; however, you'll want to stop and take a peek into the lobby where you'll see it's still elegant, with a molded tin ceiling and arched windows. A bar still runs in the building (when I was in high school we used to hang out here; illegally underage, of course). Now it has torn booths and a pool table; if you like to visit dive bars, stop in for a beer. Then walk along the porch and look out across the quiet tracks to the bustling interstate that practically replaced the railroad life this building represents. On the west end you'll get a view of the courtyard.

Across the street you'll see the **Rawlins Building** at 531 Railroad. Built in 1899, its pressed metal front is one of a handful in the state. The upper story boasts a row of engaged ionic columns and swag panels. The Harvey girls who staffed La Castañeda's dining room across the street lived here for many years. Turn west on East Lincoln, cross Grand Avenue, and head up 6th Street. At the corner of 6th and Douglas, you'll see the **Crockett Block** with a sign that reads Murphey's Drug Store, 600 Douglas. If you're hungry, this is a good place to stop for a sandwich. Inside you'll see it's much the way it was a century ago, with a suspended neoclassical mezzanine.

Head west on Douglas Avenue. On the corner you'll see, at 622 Douglas, the **Bank of Las Vegas.** Built in 1921, the neoclassical architecture is evident in the fluted columns and Doric capitals. Across the street is the **J. S. Johnsen Building** at 621 Douglas. Erected in 1883, it had a facelift in 1914, which featured classical details such as the banded brick pilasters on the corners. Continue down Douglas until it ends at 12th Street and follow it to National. Turn west and progress to the Plaza, where you'll find the **Plaza Hotel,** a good place to begin the walking tour.

A WALKING TOUR OF THE HISTORIC DISTRICT

The chamber of commerce on Grand Avenue (see "Essentials," above) has maps of self-guided historic-district walking tours.

Next door is the ✪ **Rough Riders Memorial and City Museum** (727 Grand Ave.; ☎ 505/454-1401). The largest contingent of the First U.S. Volunteer Cavalry, also known as the Rough Riders, was recruited from New Mexico to fight in the 1898 Spanish-American War. This museum chronicles their contribution to U.S. history and also contains artifacts relating to the history of the city. Admission is free; the museum is open Monday through Friday 9am to 12pm and 1 to 4pm and Saturday 10am to 3pm, except holidays.

What's most notable in this tour is the town's early Spanish history, adobe buildings going back to the first Spanish visits in the 16th century, still standing alongside the ornate structures of the late 1800s. In addition, you'll rarely see such a well-preserved collection of Territorial-style buildings.

Most of the interesting structures can be found in the Plaza–Bridge Street historic district. Begin at the northwest corner of the plaza at the **Veeder Buildings.** The building to the right, built in 1880, is an example of Italianate architecture. The left building, built in 1895 by the Veeder Brothers, was built with a Romanesque style, giving it a Moorish look.

Heading east, the **Plaza Hotel,** 230 Old Town Plaza, was the finest hotel in the New Mexico Territory back in 1881. Its three-story facade topped with a fancy broken pediment decoration was the town's pride and joy, and it has been happily restored. (See "Where to Stay in Las Vegas," below.) Next door, the **Charles Ilfeld Building,** at 224 Old Town Plaza, began as a one-story adobe store in 1867, grew to two stories in 1882, and finally reached three stories with an Italianate facade in 1890.

Nearby, the **Louis Ilfeld Building** shows the classic architecture coming into favor at the turn of the century in a storefront now serving as a bookstore. Though the low adobe building known as the **Dice Apartments,** 210 Old Town Plaza, is unimpressive, its history is. It is the sole building on the plaza which predates the Mexican-American War of 1846. In this year, Gen. Stephen Kearney, commander of the Army of the West, stood on a one-story building on the north side of the plaza (probably this one) to address the town's population, claiming New Mexico for the United States.

Turning south on the Plaza, you'll see **Our Lady of Sorrows,** one of the last remaining adobe buildings on the plaza. Its curving parapet on the facade dates from the 1930s. On the corner, the **Romero Building** is now Plaza Drugs, where you may want to stop for a lemonade and some ice cream. The building was erected in 1919 by Secundino Romero, a wealthy political leader.

Heading east on Bridge street, you'll come to the **Rough Rider Trading Company** at 158 Bridge (☎ **505/425-0246**), a good place to browse. You'll find Southwestern furniture and old saddle bags here. Next, on the same side of the street, you'll come to the 1884 **Anicito Baca Building,** now Estella's Cafe, a good place for some authentic New Mexican food. The building's Italianate commercial style is exemplified in the fancy arched windows modeled after Italian palazzos.

Continue down the street to the 1879 **Stern and Nahm Building,** at 114 Bridge St., where you'll note cast-iron columns and pressed and folded sheet-metal ornaments above. Next you'll come to the bridge crossing the Gallinas River with a plaque that notes that Francisco Vasquez de Coronado crossed the river here in 1541. A lush riverside park has some shade—a good place for a breather.

Crossing the street to the south side you'll note the **Kiva Theater,** an old stone structure that now runs first-run movies. Next door is a candy shop with good fudge. Soon you'll come upon the decorative brickwork adorning the 1895 **Winternitz Block,** a good example of local decorative brick work. It now houses the El Rialto, with some of the best chile in New Mexico (see "Where to Dine," below). Heading back to the Plaza, you'll come to the **E. Romero Hose and Fire Company,** put up in brick in 1909. It has banded piers capped by pressed-metal capitals with dentils in a strange neoclassical architecture.

The 1882 Italianate-style **Hedgcock Building,** at 157 Bridge St., has arched window hoods like those of the Baca building, and has served both as police station and jail as well as shoe factory, saloon, and store. On the corner, is the **First National Bank.** Built around the 1880s, it features a contrasting combination of Italianate architecture and local sandstone block work. Finally, the **Courtroom Building** at 213 Old Town Plaza was erected in 1882 and served as a courtroom for 3 years. Continue on around the Plaza and you'll come to **Plaza Antiques** (☎ **505/ 454-9447**), a fun place to browse for antique clothing and kitchen tables.

OTHER ATTRACTIONS NEAR TOWN

Las Vegas has two colleges. **New Mexico Highlands University** (☎ **505/454-3593**), a 4-year liberal arts school of almost 3,000 students, was established in 1893. In 1971, it hired the nation's first Hispanic college president. Located on University Avenue, just west of U.S. 85, it is especially strong in its minority education curriculum, and fields outstanding small-college athletic teams.

The Armand Hammer United World College, 5 miles west of Las Vegas via NM 65 (☎ **505/454-4200**), is an international school with students from more than 70 countries. It is housed in the former **Montezuma Hotel,** a luxury resort built by the Santa Fe Railroad in the 1880s and now a historic landmark. Three U.S. presidents, Germany's Kaiser Wilhelm II, and Japan's Meiji Emperor Mutsuhito stayed in the multistoried, turreted, 270-room "Montezuma Castle," as it came to be known. It was abandoned during the Depression and purchased in 1981 by Armand Hammer, philanthropist and past chair of the Occidental Petroleum Corporation.

Also on the campus are the **Montezuma Hot Springs.** The springs, which are free and open to the public, have attracted health-seekers for more than 1,000 years; there are legends that ancient Aztecs, including chief Montezuma II, journeyed here from Mexico in the early 16th century, long before the arrival of the Spanish.

EXPLORING THE AREA

Mora, a small village 31 miles north via NM 518, is the main center between Las Vegas and Taos, and the seat of sparsely populated Mora County. The 15-mile long Mora Valley is one of New Mexico's prettiest but most economically depressed regions, where families have for centuries lived by subsistence farming, and are only recently having to adapt to other means of earning an income.

Cleveland Roller Mill. P.O. Box 287, Cleveland, NM 87715. NM 518, about 2 miles west of Mora. ☎ **505/387-2645.** Admission $2 adults, $1 children 6–17, under 6 free. Memorial Day–Oct 31 10am–5pm and by appointment.

One vestige of a more prosperous past is this two-story adobe mill, which ground out 50 barrels of wheat flour a day, virtually every day from 1901 to 1947. It was the last flour mill to be built in New Mexico, the last to stop running, and is the only roller mill in the state to have its original milling works intact. Today, it's been converted into a museum with exhibits on regional history and culture. The Annual Millfest, on Labor Day weekend, features the mill in operation, dances, arts and crafts, music, and more. It's advisable to call ahead because the mill is closed from time to time.

La Cueva National Historic Site and Salman Ranch. P.O. Box 1307 (NM 518 en route 6 miles east of Mora), Las Vegas, NM 87701. ☎ **505/387-2900.** Admission free. Summer Mon–Sat 9am–5pm, Sun 10am–5pm; winter hours limited; call first.

Each fall I make a bit of a pilgrimage to this spot in a lush valley along the Mora River. Its history is rich, dating from the early 1800s when a man named Vicente Romero began farming and raising sheep here. He completed an elegant two-story northern New Mexico home that still stands, and a mill that ground flour and supplied electricity for the area (the real draw). Just north of these historic sites is the San Rafael Mission Church, with exquisite French Gothic windows. Recently restored by local people, it's now painted blue and white. The trip through these sites is worth the time during any season, but in the fall, the raspberries ripen and turn this into a must-do trip. The ranch's current owner David Salman planted 20 acres of the delectable fruit and now sells it by the basket or crate, as well as in jams and over soft vanilla ice cream. Delicious.

Victory Ranch. P.O. Box 680 (1 mile north of Mora on S.R. 434), Mora, NM 87732. ☎ **505/387-2254.** Admission free. Thurs–Mon 10am–4pm, with tours at 10:30am, and 1:30 and 3:30pm.

Few things surprise me in this strange part of the state, where images of Jesus are known to appear upon stucco walls and ghosts are said to inhabit the old haciendas, but I must say that my head turned when I saw alpacas grazing in a meadow here. I stopped immediately and stepped out of my car just in time for a tour. With a small cup of feed I purchased for 25¢, I followed a young boy out to some lush pens where the odd South American Andean creatures greeted us with a harmonica-like hum. Very friendly, they ate from our hands while the babies roamed about, heads held high, marble-clear-blue eyes looking quizzical. Also on site is a store that sells sweaters and shawls made from alpaca wool, as well as a loom where visitors can try weaving.

GETTING OUTSIDE: OFF-THE-BEATEN-PATH STATE PARKS & OTHER SCENIC HIGHLIGHTS

A short drive north of the Montezuma Hot Springs takes you to a pond on the Gallinas River that provides winter skating and summer fishing.

Other nearby parklands include **Las Vegas National Wildlife Refuge** (☎ 505/ 425-3581), 5 miles southeast via NM 104 and NM 281, open Monday through Friday from 8am to 4:30pm, boasting 220 species of birds and animals on 8,750 acres of wetland; and **Storrie Lake State Park** (☎ 505/425-7278), 6 miles north via NM 518, which offers fishing, swimming, windsurfing, waterskiing, camping, and a visitor center with historic exhibits.

Villanueva State Park (☎ 505/421-2957), 31 miles southwest via I-25 and NM 3, offers excellent hiking, camping, and picnicking between red sandstone bluffs in the Pecos River Valley. Nearby are the Spanish colonial villages of **Villanueva** and **San Miguel del Vado;** the latter is a national historic district built around an impressive 1805 church.

Beautiful and isolated **Morphy Lake State Park** (☎ 505/387-2328) is reached via NM 518 to Mora and NM 94 south for 4 miles. Located on the edge of the Pecos Wilderness, the pretty lake is set in a basin of pine forest; it offers primitive camping, swimming, and trout fishing, and is a good starting point for hikes into the wilderness. Check on driving conditions before going; the road to the park is rough and best suited for four-wheel-drive vehicles, although usually passable by cars. Fourteen miles north of Mora via NM 434 is another out-of-the-way beauty, **Coyote Creek State Park** (☎ 505/387-2328), with campsites beside a stream dotted with beaver ponds. The fishing is good, and a few well-marked hiking trails head into the mountains.

If you prefer your nature a little less primitive, head for the **Pendaries Lodge and Country Club,** P.O. Box 820, Rociada, NM 87742 (☎ 505/425-3561), located 13 miles south of Mora and 27 miles northwest of Las Vegas, on NM 105 off NM 94. This lovely foothills lodge boasts the region's finest 18-hole golf course, tennis courts, and fishing. It also has overnight accommodations and a restaurant/lounge.

FORT UNION NATIONAL MONUMENT

Established in 1851 to defend the Santa Fe Trail against attacks from Plains Indians, Fort Union was expanded in 1861 in anticipation of a Confederate invasion, subsequently thwarted at Glorieta Pass, 20 miles southeast of Santa Fe. Its location on the Santa Fe Trail made it a welcome way station for travelers, but when the railroad replaced the trail in 1879, the fort was on its way out. It was abandoned in 1891. Today Fort Union, the largest military installation in the 19th-century Southwest, is in ruins. There's little to see but adobe walls and chimneys, but the very scope of the fort is impressive. Santa Fe Trail wagon ruts can still be seen nearby. Follow the 1.6-mile self-guided interpretive trail that wanders through the ruins and imagine yourself a weary 19th-century wagon traveler stopping for rest and supplies.

The national monument has a small visitor center and museum with exhibits and booklets on fort's history. Visitors should allow 2 hours to tour the ruins.

JUST THE FACTS   To reach the site from Las Vegas, drive 18 miles north on I-25 to the Watrous exit, then another 8 miles northwest on NM 161. Admission is $4 per car or $2 per person for persons aged 18 to 62. Fort Union National Monument is open Memorial Day through Labor Day from daily 8am to 6pm; during the rest of the year it is open daily from 8am to 5pm. Closed Christmas and New Year's Day.

There is a gift shop that carries a wide selection of books on New Mexico history, women's history, and frontier military books. Camping is not available at the monument, but there are facilities in nearby Las Vegas.

For more information on the monument, write to Fort Union National Monument, P.O. Box 127, Watrous, NM 87753 (☎ 505/425-8025).

WHERE TO STAY IN LAS VEGAS

Most motels are on U.S. 85 (Grand Avenue), the main north-south highway through downtown Las Vegas. (An exception is the Plaza Hotel, below.)

Inn on the Santa Fe Trail. 1133 Grand Ave., Las Vegas, NM 87701. ☎ **888/448-8438** or 505/425-6791. 42 units. A/C TV TEL. $44–$64 double; $65–$90 suite. Rates include continental breakfast. Extra person $5. AE, DC, DISC, MC, V. Pets are permitted at an extra charge of $5.

Built in the 1920s as a court motel, this inn has been remodeled in a hacienda style with all rooms looking out onto the central courtyard, creating a quiet, intimate, and sophisticated retreat just off the busy Grand Avenue. Though not as historical as the Plaza Hotel (see below), the rooms are a bit more up-to-date and functional, and you can park your car right outside. Rooms are medium-sized with nice accents, such as hand-crafted iron light fixtures and towel racks, and hand-carved pine furniture— even *trasteros* (armoires)—to conceal the television. The beds are comfortably firm, and each room has a table with two chairs and a desk. The bathrooms are small but very clean. Suites have a sleeper sofa and minirefrigerator. Be sure to read about the motel's restaurant, Blackjack's Grill, in "Where to Dine," below. The heated outdoor pool, open seasonally, is lovely. Be sure to ask about the regional cultural events that the inn helps organize.

✪ **Plaza Hotel.** 230 Old Town Plaza, Las Vegas, NM 87701. ☎ **800/328-1882** or 505/ 425-3591. Fax 505/425-9659. www.worldplaces.com/plaza/. Email: plazanewmex@nmhu. campus.mci.net. 41 units. A/C TV TEL. $68–$98 double; $115–$130 suite. AE, DC, DISC, MC, V.

A stay in this hotel offers a romantic peek into the past with a view of the plaza. The windows look out on the spot where, in 1846, a ceremony led by Gen. Stephen Kearny marked the takeover of New Mexico by the United States. The inn was built in Italianate bracketed style in 1882, in the days when Western towns, newly connected with the East by train, vied with one another in constructing fancy "railroad hotels," as they were known. Considered the finest hotel in the New Mexico Territory when it was built, it underwent a $2 million renovation exactly 100 years later. Stately walnut staircases frame the lobby and conservatory (with its piano); throughout the hotel, the architecture is true to its era.

As with most renovations in northern New Mexico, don't expect to see the elegance of the Ritz. Instead, expect a more frontier style, with antiques a bit worn, and old rugs a bit torn. Rooms are a variety of sizes, but most are average size, with elegantly high ceilings, and furnished with antiques, with comfortably firm beds, and armoires concealing the televisions. All have coffeemakers. The bathrooms also range in size; most are small, with lots of original tile, but with up-to-date fixtures. The rooms are built around a central air duct, leaving those on the outside with views and those on the inside with more quiet, so reserve accordingly. The rooms all open onto spacious hallways with casual seating areas.

The hotel offers limited room service from its Landmark Grill, which has good food, especially the New Mexican dishes, in a period setting. Notice the walls of the Landmark. The original 19th-century stenciling has been restored. The restaurant is open for breakfast, lunch, and dinner. There's often live music in the evenings at Byron T's 19th-century saloon.

✪ **Star Hill Inn.** P.O. Box 1-A, Sapello, NM, 87745. ☎ **505/425-5605.** www.starhillinn.com. E-mail: starhillinn@nmhu.campus.mci.net. 7 cottages. $80–$120 double. $10 each additional guest over 12 years old. Minimum 2-night stay. Credit cards are not accepted.

Located "in the Orion Spiral Arm of the Milky Way Galaxy," this inn 12 miles northwest of Las Vegas is a haven for astronomers, stargazers, and anyone else in search of a peaceful mountain retreat. Owner Phil Mahon picked the site in the late 1980s for its nighttime darkness and frequently clear skies. On 195 pine-covered acres at the base of the Sangre de Cristo Mountains, this large property has seven cottages with plenty of space between them. Each unit is furnished with a fully equipped kitchen (including a range/oven, refrigerator, coffeemaker, and toaster), a covered porch, and small fireplace. Meal service is not provided, but there are grocery stores and restaurants 20 minutes away in Las Vegas.

Beds are comfortable and the bathrooms are clean and functional. The cottages are decorated with photos, taken on site, of the Hale Bopp Comet.

Star Hill rents a variety of astronomical observing equipment, from an 8-inch Celestron telescope ($20 per night) to the massive 24-inch R-C Cassegrain ($90 per night) which is housed inside its own protective dome. Telescopes can be rented by the night or the week, and camera mounts and tripods are also available. One-hour "sky tours" are available for $20 to demonstrate the telescopes and introduce visitors to the intricacies of the night sky. During the days, guests can hike the trails to nearby ridges, browse through star atlases in the library, or just enjoy the tranquility. Four-day workshops are offered occasionally through the year on topics such as astrophotography and birding.

CAMPING

There's plenty of camping available in and around Las Vegas. I recommend the **KOA Las Vegas** (☎ **505/454-0180**), which has 60 sites, 15 with full hookups, 26 with water and electricity. Laundry, grocery, ice, and recreational (including a pool) facilities are available, as well as a large gift shop. From I-25 (Exit 339) go 1 block southeast on U.S. 84, then ½ mile southwest on Frontage Road (also called County Road A25A).

Also in Las Vegas is **Vegas RV Park** (☎ **505/425-5640**), which offers 40 sites, 33 with full hookups, and cable TV availability. It's located at 504 Harris Rd. in Las Vegas.

If you'd rather camp at a state park, try **Storrie Lake State Park** (☎ **505/ 425-7278**), which offers 20 sites with electricity, 23 sites without it, and primitive camping in an open area close to the lake. Developed sites have water, picnic tables, and grills, and there's a visitor center nearby.

Camping is also allowed in the secluded **Morphy Lake State Park** as well as in **Coyote Creek State Park.** Each of these parks offers sites with picnic tables, fire rings, and pit toilets as well as primitive camping. In addition, Coyote Creek has 17 sites with hookups, some with shelters, and a bathhouse with showers. There's no drinking water available in Morphy Lake's campground. For more information about either park, call ☎ **505/387-2328.**

WHERE TO DINE IN LAS VEGAS

✪ **Blackjack's Grill.** In the Inn on the Santa Fe Trail, 1133 Grand Ave. ☎ **888/448-8438** or 505/425-6791. Reservations recommended. Main courses lunch $5–$8; dinner $10–$19. AE, DC, MC, V. Wed–Sat 11:30am–2pm; 5:30–9pm. Sun 10am–2pm and 5:30–9pm. NEW AMERICAN.

Las Vegas has long needed a sophisticated restaurant, and now has one here. Though at press time Blackjack's was only serving during the summer months, the owner hopes to be open year-round by the time you arrive. The main dining room is small and cozy, done in brilliant colors with moody lighting. In the warmer months diners can sit out on the patio under white cloth umbrellas. As befits the area, it's a fairly informal restaurant that does fill up, so try to make reservations. The service is formal but friendly, and there's plenty of room to spread out on the patio. Each night the chef serves some special dishes. My meal began with an excellent tortilla soup crowned by red, yellow, and blue corn tortilla crisps confetti. Then came a good-sized portion of raspberry sorbet to cleanse my palate. My main course was one of the specials— halibut with a sesame seed crust. The meal was very structural, with risotto as the first layer and the halibut on top making a tower. On the plate were crisply cooked zucchini and carrots spreading out like rays. The portions are large. Lunches are a little simpler, with dishes such as lamb tacos (soft corn tortillas stuffed with roasted lamb, avocado, and cheese with a tomatillo sauce) and a penne vegetali (artichokes, mushrooms, spinach and tomatoes tossed with sun-dried tomato pesto and penne pasta). Be aware that though prices may seem high, each meal comes with bread, a choice of salad or soup, and a vegetable. A variety of dessert specials are available. Beer and wine are served.

✪ **El Rialto Restaurant & Lounge.** 141 Bridge St. ☎ **505/454-0037.** Reservations recommended. Main courses $5–$23. AE, DC, DISC, MC, V. Mon–Sat 10:30am–9pm. NEW MEXICAN.

Since I was a young girl, this has been one of my favorite restaurants. In fact, my mother still has owner Ralph Garcia cater any big parties she has. The food is simply, excellent. It's a locals place, full of families, old Hispanic farmers, and students from the United World College. The decor is cheesy pastels, but can be overlooked for the comfort, especially of the booths. The lounge still retains the original red upholstery, which was much more to my liking. Service is friendly and efficient. The chile, especially the green, is outstanding here (order anything smothered with it). My favorite is the chicken enchilada plate. The beef is good, too, and the rellenos are quite tasty. There are a variety of stuffed sopaipillas, and steaks too, as well as sandwiches and a kids' menu. For dessert, I usually smother my sopaipilla with honey, though you can order pie or flan. There's a full bar here.

Hillcrest Restaurant. 1106 Grand Ave. ☎ **505/425-7211.** Reservations accepted. Main courses $7–$13. AE, DISC, MC, V. Daily 6am–8:45pm. AMERICAN.

My high school held its reunion here recently, and I got to sample their steaks and baked potatoes. My conclusion, even after all these years, is that this restaurant still has good, reliable food. It's diner style, with everything from chicken-fried steaks to corn-fried catfish. There's also a good selection of New Mexican food. The breakfasts are big and tasty. The dining room is open for lunch and dinner only; the coffee shop is busy all day. The adjoining Trading Post Saloon offers full bar service.

3 Cimarron & Raton: Historic Towns on the Santa Fe Trail

CIMARRON

Few towns in the American West have as much lore or legend attached to them as Cimarron, 41 miles southwest of Raton via U.S. 64. Nestled against the eastern slope of the Sangre de Cristo mountain range, the town (its name is Spanish for "wild" or "untamed") achieved its greatest fame as a "wild and woolly" outpost on the Santa Fe Trail between the 1850s and 1880s and a gathering place for area ranchers, traders, gamblers, gunslingers, and other characters.

ESSENTIALS

GETTING THERE   From Fort Union National Monument, head north on I-25, then west on U.S. 58 to Cimarron.

VISITOR INFORMATION   The **Cimarron Chamber of Commerce,** P.O. Box 604, Cimarron, NM 87714 (☎ **800/700-4298** or 505/376-2417), has complete information on the region.

EXPLORING THE WILD WEST TOWN

Frontier personalities including Kit Carson and Wyatt Earp, Buffalo Bill Cody and Annie Oakley, Bat Masterson and Doc Holliday, Butch Cassidy and Jesse James, painter Frederic Remington and novelist Zane Grey, all passed through and stayed in Cimarron—most of them at the **St. James Hotel** (see "Where to Stay & Dine in Cimarron," below). Even if you're not planning an overnight stay here, it's a fun place to visit for an hour or two.

Land baron Lucien Maxwell founded the town in 1848 as base of operations for his 1.7 million-acre empire. In 1857, he built a mansion at his **Maxwell Ranch,** furnishing it opulently with heavy draperies, gold-framed paintings, and two grand pianos. In the gaming room the tables saw high stakes, as guests bet silver Mexican pesos or pokes of yellow gold dust. Gold was struck in 1867 on Maxwell's land, near Baldy Mountain, and the rush of prospectors that followed caused him to sell out 3 years later.

The ranch isn't open for inspection today, but Maxwell's 1864 stone grist mill, built to supply flour to Fort Union, is. The **Old Mill Museum,** a grand, three-story stone structure, well worth visiting, houses an interesting collection of early photos and lots of memorabilia, from a saddle that belonged to Kit Carson to dresses worn by Virginia Maxwell. It's open May to October, Monday through Wednesday and Friday and Saturday from 9am to 5pm and Sunday from 1 to 5pm. Admission is $2 adults, $1 seniors and children.

Cimarron has numerous other buildings of historic note, and a walking tour to see them only takes about a half hour. A walking tour map is included in the Old Mill Museum brochure, which you can pick up at the museum.

NEARBY ATTRACTIONS

Cimarron is also the gateway to the ✪ **Philmont Scout Ranch** (☎ **505/376-2281**), a 137,000-acre property donated to the Boy Scouts of America by Texas oilman Waite Phillips, beginning in 1938. Scouts from all over the world use the ranch for back-country camping and leadership training from June through August and for conferences the remainder of the year. On my recent visit, after touring the incredible Villa (worth seeing even if you have no interest in scouting), I got a flat tire. If you're going to get a flat tire anywhere in the West, this is probably the place to do it. Two young scouts, an Eagle Scout, and two girls who were working at the camp for the summer came to my rescue, and I was back on the road in a half hour.

There are three museums on the ranch, all open to the public. **Villa Philmonte,** Phillips's lavish Mediterranean-style summer home, was built in 1927 and remains furnished with the family's European antiques. Located 4 miles south of Cimarron, it's open for guided tours from 8am to 4:30pm daily in summer (early June through late August); its hours are limited the rest of the year, and it's closed on weekends in winter. Admission is $4. The **Philmont Museum and Seton Memorial Library** commemorates the art and taxidermy of Ernest Thompson Seton, the naturalist and author who founded the Boy Scouts of America, and has exhibits on the varied history of the Cimarron area. It's open from 8am to 6pm daily from early June to late August; winter hours are more limited. Admission is free.

The **Kit Carson Museum,** 7 miles south of Philmont headquarters in Rayado, is a period hacienda furnished in 1850s style. Staff members in historic costumes lead tours daily from early June through late August. It's open from 8am to 5pm, and admission is free.

GETTING OUTSIDE: CIMARRON CANYON STATE PARK

U.S. 64 from Cimarron leads west 24 miles to Eagle Nest, passing en route to the popular, and often crowded **Cimarron Canyon State Park** (☎ 505/377-6271). A 32,000-acre designated state wildlife area, it sits at the foot of crenelated granite cliffs, 800 feet high in some areas, known as the Palisades. Rock climbing is allowed throughout the park except in the Palisades area. The river and the two park lakes attract anglers; for the best fishing, move away from the heavily populated campgrounds.

Just east of Cimarron, County Road 204 offers access to the Carson National Forest's **Valle Vidal** recreation area (see chapter 8), an incredible place to hike and backpack and see hundreds of elk.

WHERE TO STAY & DINE IN CIMARRON

Casa de Gavilan. P.O. Box 518 Cimarron, NM, 87114. ☎ **800/GAVILAN** or 505/ 376-2246. Fax 505/376-2247. 4 units. $70–$125, double. AE, DISC, MC, V.

This sprawling adobe villa, built in 1910 on a broad hill overlooking Philmont and the mountains beyond, provides a quiet Southwest ranch-style experience. The common areas have high ceilings with thick vigas and wooden floors, and the hallways are painted bright Southwestern blue and green. The rooms lie around a central court-yard, a nice place to sit and relax in the cool evenings. The rooms are spacious, with comfortably firm beds and plenty of antiques. The bathrooms are medium-sized and maintain an old-style charm, with touches such as tiny white tile on the floors but with new fixtures. The two-bedroom suite, which is housed in what's called the Guest House is good for families, though lower ceilings give it a slightly newer feel. There isn't a television on the premises, but there is a hiking trail just off the courtyard. Breakfast is served in a big, sunny dining room; you'll find such specialties as baked French toast with ham and fruit salad and a baked apple pancake served with sausage.

✪ **St. James Hotel.** Rte. 1, Box 2, Cimarron, NM 87714. ☎ **800/748-2694** or 505/ 376-2664. Fax 505/376-2623. 27 units. Hotel $80 double, $100 suite; motel $53 double. AE, DISC, MC, V.

This landmark hotel offers travelers a romantically historic stay in this Old West town. It looks much the same today as it did in 1873, when it was built by Henri Lambert, previously a chef for Napoléon, Abraham Lincoln, and Gen. Ulysses S. Grant. In its early years, as a rare luxury hotel on the Santa Fe Trail, it had a dining room, a saloon, gambling rooms, and lavish guest rooms outfitted with Victorian furniture. Today, you will find lace and cherry wood in the bedrooms, though, like the Plaza in Las Vegas, the feel is frontier elegance rather than lavishness. Rooms don't have televisions or phones—the better to evoke the days when famous guests such as Zane Grey, who wrote *Fighting Caravans* at the hotel, were residents. Annie Oakley's bed is here, and a glass case holds a register with the signatures of Buffalo Bill Cody and the notorious Jesse James. The beds are comfortably soft, and the bathrooms are small and basic. One room just off the lobby is left open so those not staying the night can have a peek.

The St. James also was a place of some lawlessness: 26 men were said to have been killed within the 2-foot-thick adobe walls, and owner Perry Champion can point out bullet holes in the pressed-tin ceiling of the dining room. The ghosts of some are believed to inhabit the hotel still.

Next door are 12 more rooms in a motel, which I don't recommend. These rooms are narrow and cheaply made, though they do provide TV and telephone for those who prefer the late 20th century.

Lambert's at the St. James serves good food in an atmosphere that doesn't quite bridge the century gap. The molded tin ceiling and textured wallpaper are lovely, but the tables and chairs are contemporary. The menu is short, but good, with dishes such as pasta primavera and filet mignon priced from $14 to $25. A separate coffee shop serves three meals daily, purveying large portions of tasty New Mexican food. The hotel also offers a tour desk, an outdoor patio with bar and grill, gift shop, and package store.

RATON

Raton was founded in 1879 at the site of Willow Springs, a watering stop on the Santa Fe Trail. Mountain man "Uncle Dick" Wooton, a closet entrepreneur, had blasted a pass through the Rocky Mountains just north of the spring, and began charging toll. When the railroad bought Wooton's road, Raton developed as the railroad, mining, and ranching center for this part of the New Mexico Territory. Today it has a well-preserved historic district and the finest shooting facility in the United States.

East of Raton is Capulin Mountain, home to Capulin Volcano National Monument. The volcanic crater of the majestic 8,182-foot peak, inactive for 10,000 years, is open to visitors. See section 4 below for more about Capulin Volcano National Monument.

ESSENTIALS

GETTING THERE   From Santa Fe, take I-25 north; from Taos, take U.S. 64 east.

VISITOR INFORMATION   The tourist information center is in the **Raton Chamber and Economic Development Council,** 100 Clayton Rd., at the corner of Second Street (P.O. Box 1211), Raton, NM 87740 (☎ **800/638-6161** or 505/ 445-3689).

A WALKING TOUR OF HISTORIC RATON

Five blocks of Raton's original town site are listed on the National Register of Historic Places, with some 70 significant buildings. It's best to explore the historic district by foot. Allow 1 to 2 hours.

Start at the **Raton Museum,** 216 S. First St. (☎ 505/445-8979), where you can pick up a walking tour map. The museum, open Tuesday through Saturday from 9am to 5pm, displays a wide variety of mining, railroad, and ranching items from the early days of the town. It's housed in the **Coors Building** (1906), previously a Coors Brewing Company warehouse. Next door is the **Haven Hotel** (1913), built of ivory brick with green brick trim, and adorned with a pair of pineapples and three lion heads. At the corner of First and Cook is the **Palace Hotel** (1896), the first three-story building in Colfax County.

The **Santa Fe Depot,** First and Cook, was built in 1903 in Spanish mission-revival style. It is still used by Amtrak passengers today. Next door is the **Wells Fargo Express Company,** built in 1910.

Opposite the station, as you head north on First, is the **Roth Building** (1893), whose ornate metal facade boasts Corinthian pilasters and a bracketed cornice. Next you'll come to the **Abourezk Building** (1906) at 132 First St., with two female figureheads on the upper storefront; the **Marchiondo Building** (1882), a former dry-goods store painted bright yellow with green trim, is still a store, selling antique bottles and clothing, a bizarre place with mannequins missing body parts; and the **Joseph Building** (1890s), worth peeking in through the windows to see the cupids near the ceiling when it was the Gem Saloon. Continue north on First Street to **The Home Ranch Saloon** at 132 First. Built in 1884, it has a brick facade and is topped by a pedimented metal cornice. Next door is the **Investment Block** (1896) office of Swastika Coal, once the largest coal producer in the region. Across Clark Street you can see some stone buildings, now storage sheds. The **Labadie House,** built in 1882, is one of the oldest dwellings in town.

Walk west 1 block to Second Street and proceed south. At 131 N. Second St. is the **Shuler Theater** (☎ 505/445-5528). Built in 1915, it housed the opera company, fire station, and city offices. The interior of the theater, designed in European rococo style, has superb acoustics. The lobby is decorated with murals recalling local history. It's still in active use year-round. Directly across the street, you'll find the **Cooke Hotel** (1901), adorned with a pair of cresting topped bay windows on its second story. Right next door in the 1905 **Odd Fellows Building,** you'll find **Eva's Bakery,** a great place for a pastry and coffee, or a big breakfast (see "Where to Dine," below). Or, if this Italianate architecture is whetting your palate, go down two more doors to **The Grapevine** for delicious pizza (see "Where to Dine," below).

Farther south, on the southeast intersection of Second and Park, you'll come to a must-see: **Solano's Boot and Western Wear,** 101 S. Second (☎ 505/445-2632). Occupying the 1905 **Roth Block,** it now houses a cowboy hat "cemetery" unparalleled in (as far as I know) the universe. Some 250 mangled and sweat-soaked hats are on display. This is a great place to shop for hats, hat bands, flashy belt buckles, and fancy beaded leather skirt outfits.

Farther south at Second and Cook you'll find the **Raton Realty Building** (1928), characterized by a red tile roof and terra-cotta trimmed windows, and the **Di Lisio Building** (1918), a former bank with three Doric columns at its entrance and stained glass topping the lower windows. At Third and Cook, the neoclassical U.S. Post Office (1917) is now the **Arthur Johnson Memorial Library,** with a fine collection on Southwestern art. The south side of Cook between Second and Third is dominated by the **Swastika Hotel** (1929), now the International State Bank, a seven-story brick building decorated at the roofline with the swastika, a Native American symbol of good luck. The hotel's name was changed to the Yucca Hotel when the Nazis adopted the swastika as their symbol.

NEARBY ATTRACTIONS

The **NRA Whittington Center** (☎ 505/445-3615), off U.S. 64 about 10 miles south of Raton, is considered the most complete nonmilitary shooting and training facility in the world. Operated by the National Rifle Association, it spans 50 square miles of rolling hills. It has 14 instructional and competitive ranges, a handful of condominium units, and hookups for campers. Classes in pistol, rifle, and shotgun shooting, firearm safety, and conservation are offered. National championship events are held annually. The center is open daily to the public for tours.

In the little town of **Springer** (pop. 1,300), 39 miles south of Raton via I-25, the **Santa Fe Trail Museum** (☎ 505/483-5554) is housed in the old three-story 1881 Colfax County Courthouse. It contains pioneer artifacts and memorabilia from travelers along the Santa Fe Trail and early residents of the area, as well as a livery stable and New Mexico's only electric chair, which was used to execute seven convicted murderers between 1933 and 1956. Hours are Monday through Saturday from 9am to 4pm, Memorial Day through Labor Day. Admission is $2 for adults, $1.50 for seniors, and $1 for children 12 to 18; children under 12 are free. The **Colfax County Fair** takes place in Springer annually in mid-August, with a rodeo and 4-H fair. Call ☎ **505/445-8071** for more information.

About 30 miles east of Springer, via U.S. 56 and 12 miles on a dirt road, is the **Dorsey Mansion,** a two-story log-and-stone home built in the 1880s by U.S. senator and cattleman Stephen Dorsey. With 36 rooms, hardwood floors, Italian marble fireplaces, hand-carved cherry staircase, and dining-room table that sat 60, it was quite a masterpiece! Public tours are offered by appointment (☎ **505/375-2222**) Monday through Saturday from 10am to 4pm, Sunday 1 to 5pm, and may be arranged during other hours. Admission costs $3 for adults (with a $5 minimum per tour) and $1 for children under 6. The mansion served briefly as a bed-and-breakfast in the late 1980s but no longer offers accommodations.

GETTING OUTSIDE

Sugarite Canyon State Park (☎ 505/445-5607), 10 miles northeast of Raton via NM 72 and NM 526, offers historic exhibits, camping, boating, and excellent fishing at three trout-stocked lakes. Lake Alice is the best place in the park for fly-fishing. Numerous hiking trails meander through the park, and a museum at the visitors' center traces the canyon's mining history.

Heading down I-25, **Maxwell National Wildlife Refuge** (☎ 505/375-2331), on the Canadian River 24 miles southwest of Raton, has a rich resident and migratory bird population and numerous native mammals. More than 200 species have been recorded in the refuge, which offers some of the best bird watching in this part of the state.

South of U.S. 56 via NM 39 is the western of the two parcels that comprise **Kiowa National Grasslands.** The 263,954-acre area is a project to reclaim once-barren prairie land, the result of overfarming in the late 19th and early 20th centuries and the Great Plains Dustbowl of the 1930s. Today the plains are irrigated and green, and the area provides food, cover, and water for a wide variety of wildlife, such as antelope, bear, Barbary sheep, mountain lion, wild turkey, pheasant, and quail. Another portion of the grasslands is located east of here, along U.S. 56/412, near the town of Clayton just west of the Oklahoma border.

WHERE TO STAY IN RATON

✪ **Best Western Sands.** 300 Clayton Hwy., Raton, NM 87740. ☎ **800/518-2581,** 800/528-1234, or 505/445-2737. Fax 505/445-4053. 50 units. A/C TV TEL. $44–$89 double. Extra person $3. AE, CB, DC, DISC, MC, V.

Rooms in this hotel, equidistant between downtown and the interstate, are so clean and roomy that reservations are a must during summer months. Built in 1959, the hotel underwent a $250,000 renovation in 1993, and continues to update. All rooms are decorated with Southwest prints with nice touches such as ceramic lamps and finely made oak furniture. In the luxury wing, rooms have minirefrigerators, recliners, hair dryers, and Neutrogena soaps. All have comfortably firm beds, down pillows,

HBO, coffeemakers, and hair dryers. The standard rooms are more than adequate and provide plenty of space and parking right outside your door. There is a hot tub, playground, gift shop, family style eatery, and seasonal outdoor heated swimming pool. There's also a "lenders library" and a selection of family games. The hotel also offers an assistive telephone kit for hearing-impaired.

✪ **Melody Lane Motel.** 136 Canyon Dr., Raton, NM 87740. ☎ **800/421-5210** or 505/445-3655. Fax 505/445-3461. 27 units. A/C TV TEL. Mid-May to Labor Day $49 double. Labor Day to mid-May $41 double. Rates include continental breakfast. Weekly rates are available. AE, CB, DC, DISC, MC, V. Small pets are permitted.

Though not much on the outside, this cinder-block hotel provides large, very well cared for rooms close to downtown at a decent price. Wood paneling darkens the rooms a bit, but they are very clean, most with a hair dryer, and many with a steam shower (be sure to request one of these enclosed bathtubs that fills with steam; there's no extra charge). Rooms are especially quiet, with medium-firm beds and good reading lights. Bathrooms are small but have a changing room and sink/vanity. Courtesy transportation is available from Amtrak and the bus station.

Camping

There are quite a few campgrounds in the Raton area, including **KOA Raton,** in town at 1330 S. 2nd St. (☎ 800/562-9033 or 505/445-3488), with 54 sites, grocery and laundry facilities, as well as picnic tables and grills.

　　Summerland RV Park, at 1900 S. Cedar/I-25 and U.S. 87 (☎ **505/445-9536**), which is convenient to the interstate, has 42 sites (plus 16 monthly sites), laundry and grocery facilities, and picnic tables.

WHERE TO DINE IN RATON

Eva's Bakery. 134 N. 2nd St. ☎ **505/445-3781.** All menu items under $5. No credit cards. Mon–Sat 5am–2pm. BAKERY/NEW MEXICAN/AMERICAN.

When political candidates are campaigning in the area, they come here to shake hands and kiss babies. That's because Eva's is the local's hangout, with good reason. Located in the 1905 Odd Fellows Building, it has simple decor, with faux wood tables, a linoleum floor, and luminescent lighting. There are two glass pastry counters, with such delicious traditional treats as apple fritters and donuts. Everything here is made from scratch, Eva stresses. Her biggest seller? The smothered breakfast burrito. She also serves omelettes, burgers, and a few salads.

The Grapevine. 120 N. 2nd St. ☎ **505/445-0969.** Main courses lunch $5–$8; dinner $7–$18. Pizzas $6.95–$15. AE, DC, DISC, MC, V. ITALIAN/NEW YORK–STYLE PIZZA.

This is *the* place to eat pizza in northeastern New Mexico. Amy and Christopher Eissler have created a quaint cafe, with red checked table cloths, microbrew beers, and a decent wine selection. I created my own "personal pizza," with eggplant, mushrooms, and spinach; you can do the same selecting from 17 ingredients including such traditionals as pepperoni and olives. Or you can choose from a variety of "specialty pizzas" such as the rustica (with pesto and ricotta) or the Southwest chicken and green chile. There also are pasta dishes both traditional (pasta and meatballs) and elaborate (seafood ravioli with a vodka cream sauce). Service is efficient and friendly, though the pizzas take time to make.

Pappas' Sweet Shop Restaurant. 1201 S. 2nd St. ☎ **505/445-9811.** Reservations suggested at dinner in summer. Lunch $5–$10; dinner $8–$30. AE, DC, MC, V. Daily 9am–2pm and 5–9pm. Closed Sun in winter. AMERICAN/TEX-MEX.

Founded more than 75 years ago, this restaurant still seems to draw praise from most locals. It's an interesting place, with counters full of fudge up front, and a big dining room painted a sky/turquoise blue from ceiling to floor. It has a tea room feel, with only one window. Though the food isn't sophisticated, it is carefully prepared and tasty. Best known are the beef dishes, with prime rib a big seller here. I had a steak that was perfectly prepared, served with nicely cooked vegetables. The meal also came with homemade bread with sunflower seeds in it, a salad, and choice of potato dish or pasta. The broiled breast of chicken is also popular. Across-the-border dishes include Tex-Mex steak, fajitas, and enchiladas. A full-service lounge adjoins the restaurant. Save room for a piece of cheesecake fudge.

4 Capulin Volcano National Monument

Capulin Volcano National Monument offers visitors the rare opportunity to walk inside a volcanic crater. A 2-mile road spirals up from the visitor center more than 600 feet to the crater of the 8,182-foot peak, where two self-guiding trails leave from the parking area: an energetic and spectacular 1-mile hike around the crater rim and a 100-foot descent into the crater to the ancient volcanic vent. One of its most interesting features here is the symmetry of the main cinder cone. The volcano was last active about 60,000 years ago, when it sent out the last of four lava flows. Scientists consider it dormant, with a potential for future activity, rather than extinct. As far back as 1891 public settlement on Capulin Mountain was prohibited by Congress. In 1916 it was protected by presidential proclamation as Capulin Mountain National Monument for its scientific and geologic interest. The final name change came in 1987.

Because of the elevation, wear light jackets in the summer and layers during the rest of the year. Be aware that the road up to the crater rim is frequently closed due to weather conditions. Plan on spending 1 to 3 hours at the volcano; a more in-depth exploration could take several days, but camping is not permitted.

A short nature trail behind the center introduces plant and animal life of the area and is great for kids and accessible to people with disabilities. There's also a longer hike from park headquarters up to the parking lot at the crater rim. The crater rim offers magnificent panoramic views of the surrounding landscape, the Sangre de Cristo Mountains, and, on clear days, portions of four contiguous states: Kansas, Texas, Colorado, and Oklahoma. During the summer, the volcano attracts swarms of ladybird beetles (ladybugs).

ESSENTIALS

GETTING THERE The monument is located 30 miles east of Raton via U.S. 64/87 and north 3 miles on NM 325.

VISITOR INFORMATION The visitor center, located at the base of the northern side of the volcano, is open Memorial Day through Labor Day daily from 7:30am to 6:30pm Sunday through Thursday, and 7:30am to 8:30pm Friday and Saturday; the rest of the year it's open 8m to 4pm. An audiovisual program discusses volcanism and park personnel will answer questions. Admission is $4 per car or $2 per person. For more information, contact Capulin Volcano National Monument, P.O. Box 40 Capulin, NM 88414 (☎ 505/278-2201; www.nps.gov/cavo/).

CAMPING

Camping is not permitted inside the monument; however, camping facilities are available only 3 miles away in Capulin town (try the **Capulin RV Park** at ☎ 505/278-2921), as well as in the neighboring towns of Raton and Clayton.

5 Along the Clayton Highway: Dinosaurs, Outlaws & Folsom Man

FOLSOM

This is a wide open area (no radio stations out here). En route to Folsom from Capulin, I saw locals selling such items as a .357 Magnum, Chihuahua puppies, and alfalfa bails. Suddenly zipping across the highway in front of me, taking up one lane of the road, was a pink snake. Later at the Folsom Museum, the guides told me it was a red racer, common to the area, as are the blue variety, both known to chase people from their outhouses (though neither is poisonous). To get to Folsom, take NM 325 off the Clayton Highway (U.S. 64/87, running 83 miles east-southeast from Raton to Clayton), 7 miles.

Near here, cowboy George McJunkin discovered the 10,000-year-old remains of "Folsom Man." The find, excavated by the Denver Museum of Natural History in 1926, represented the first association of the artifacts of prehistoric people (spear points) with the fossil bones of extinct animals (a species of bison). The site is on private property and is closed to the public, but some artifacts (prehistoric as well as from the 19th century) are displayed at the **Folsom Museum,** Main Street, Folsom (☎ **505/278-2122** in summer; 505/278-3616 in winter). It does not, however, contain any authentic Folsom points, only copies. The museum has limited exhibits on prehistoric and historic Native Americans of the area, as well as Folsom's settlement by whites. Hours are 10am to 5pm daily from Memorial Day through Labor Day, winter by appointment. Admission is $1 for adults, 50¢ for children 6 to 12, and free for children under 6.

To get to Folsom, take NM 325 off the Clayton Highway (U.S. 64/87, running 83 miles east-southeast from Raton to Clayton), 7 miles.

CLAYTON

Clayton (pop. 2,454) is a ranching center just 9 miles west of the Texas and Oklahoma panhandle borders. Rich prairie grasses, typical of nearby **Kiowa National Grasslands** (☎ **505/374-9652**), led to its founding in 1887 at the site of a longtime cowboy resting spot and watering hole. In the early 19th century, the Cimarron Cutoff of the Santa Fe Trail, along which numerous bloody battles between Plains Indians and Anglo settlers and traders were waged, passed through this area. Clayton is also known as the town where the notorious train robber Thomas "Black Jack" Ketchum was inadvertently decapitated while being hanged in 1901 (a doctor carefully reunited head and body before Ketchum was buried here).

Tracks from 8 species of dinosaurs can be clearly seen in **Clayton Lake State Park,** 12 miles north of town off NM 370, near the distinctive Rabbit Ears Mountains (☎ **505/374-8808**). The lake is crystalline blue, strange to come upon after driving across these pale prairies. It offers fishing, swimming, boating, hiking, and camping. A half-mile trail on the southeast side of the lake leads across the dam to an exhibit describing the types of dinosaurs that roamed this area. From there, you can wander along a boardwalk to the amazingly intact dinosaur tracks. Another trail starts on the north side of the lake and is 1.5 miles long; if hikers wish they can follow it farther to the dinosaur tracks, making for a 3.5-mile hike.

VISITOR INFORMATION   For information on other area attractions, as well as lodging and dining, contact the **Clayton-Union County Chamber of Commerce,** 1103 S. First St. (P.O. Box 476) Clayton, NM 88415 (☎ **505/374-9253**).

6 The I-40 Corridor

The 216 freeway miles on I-40 from Albuquerque to the Texas border cross straight, featureless prairie and very few towns. But the valleys of the Pecos River (site of Santa Rosa) and the Canadian River (Tucumcari is on its banks) have several attractions, including natural lakes. There's not a lot to explore here unless you're a bird watcher or a fisher, but both towns can make a day's stopover worthwhile.

ESSENTIALS

GETTING THERE   Travel time from Albuquerque to Tucumcari via I-40 is 2 hours, 40 minutes; to Santa Rosa, 1 hour, 45 minutes. There's no regularly scheduled commercial service into either Tucumcari or Santa Rosa. Private planes can land at **Tucumcari Municipal Airport** (☎ 505/461-3229).

VISITOR INFORMATION   Contact the **Tucumcari–Quay County Chamber of Commerce,** 404 W. Tucumcari Blvd. (P.O. Drawer E), Tucumcari, NM 88401 (☎ 505/461-1694) or the **Santa Rosa Chamber of Commerce,** 486 Parker Ave., Santa Rosa, NM 88435 (☎ 505/472-3763).

SEEING THE SIGHTS

The **Tucumcari Historical Museum,** 416 S. Adams (☎ 505/461-4201), 1 block east of First Street, is open from 9am to 6pm Monday through Saturday and from 1 to 6pm Sunday in summer, and Tuesday through Saturday from 9am to 5pm and from 1 to 5pm Sunday in winter. Admission costs $2 for adults and 50¢ for children ages 6 to 15; kids under 6 are free. Here you'll find an old sheriff's office, an authentic Western schoolroom, and other set exhibits, as well as oddities such as a late 1800s slot machine called "The Owl" (it's elaborately carved and painted with owls), a tightly woven Mexican vaquero hat, and a finely tooled sidesaddle that looks terribly uncomfortable.

The moonlike **Mesa Redondo,** a round mesa rising 11 miles south of town via NM 209, was once train robber Black Jack Ketchum's hideout—he was eventually captured and executed in Clayton in 1901.

To the northwest, 34 miles distant over NM 104, is **Conchas Lake State Park** (☎ 505/868-2270), with a reservoir 25 miles long. I spent a lot of my growing up years waterskiing and diving off cliffs at this lake. Though the water is a beautiful aqua, it sits within a desert environment, with lots of sand and little shade. A marina on the northern side provides facilities for boating, fishing, and waterskiing, while nearby are a store, cafe, RV park with hookups, and trailers available to rent. The south side of the lake, which is managed by a private concessionaire (☎ 505/868-2988), contains a lodge, campgrounds, a nine-hole golf course, and a marina with boat-launch facilities.

Ute Lake State Park is 22 miles northeast on U.S. 54, near the town of Logan. It has a full-service marina, docking facilities, picnic tables, campsites, and rental boats.

Quay County around Tucumcari is noted for its blue-quail hunting, said to be the best anywhere in the United States.

Santa Rosa calls itself "the city of natural lakes." Those bodies of water include **Blue Hole,** a crystal-clear, 81-foot-deep artesian well just east of downtown. Fed by a subterranean river that flows 3,000 gallons per minute at a constant 61°, it's a favorite of scuba divers (equipment can be rented at a nearby shop), and deep enough to merit open water certification. Divers must be certified, or with a certified instructor, and purchase a permit from the Santa Rosa Police Department. In fact, I got my certification here. For those accustomed to diving in the ocean, it doesn't provide much room for exploration. The experience reminds me of swimming in a fish bowl, often with a number of other fish (divers) swimming about. No permit is required for swimming or snorkeling, however, and there's a bathhouse on site. **Park Lake** (☎ **505/ 472-3763**), in the middle of town, serves as the town's municipal pool. It's a lovely spot to take the kids. They can swim with the geese while you cool off under the elm trees. The lake offers free swimming, picnicking, and fishing, and contains a softball field and playground. **Santa Rosa Lake State Park,** P.O. Box 384, Santa Rosa, NM 88435 (☎ **505/472-3110**), on a dammed portion of the Pecos River, has camping, hiking, and excellent fishing. Ten miles south of town via NM 91, the village of **Puerto de Luna** is a 19th-century county seat with a mid-1800s courthouse and church, Nuestra Señora del Refugio. Francisco Vásquez de Coronado was believed to have camped here as he traveled en route to Kansas. For insight into village life here, read Rudolfo Anaya's *Bless Me, Ultima,* a tale of growing up on the *llano* (plains) of the area.

WHERE TO STAY

Major chain hotels are at I-40 interchanges in both Tucumcari and Santa Rosa. Smaller "Ma and Pa" motels can be found along the main streets through town that were once segments of legendary Route 66—Tucumcari Boulevard in Tucumcari and Will Rogers Drive in Santa Rosa. All told, there are about 2,000 rooms in Tucumcari and Santa Rosa.

IN TUCUMCARI

✪ **Best Western Discovery Inn.** 200 E. Estrella Ave. at Exit 332, Tucumcari, NM 88401. ☎ **800/528-1234** or 505/461-4884. 107 units. A/C TV TEL. May–Oct $65–$70 double; Nov–Apr $50–$60 double. AE, CB, DC, DISC, MC, V. Pets accepted for $5 fee.

This pink mission-style motel has large quiet rooms and provides an oasis stop in the somewhat barren eastern part of the state. It's located off the strip, but near I-40; take Exit 332. Opened in 1985, remodeling is ongoing. Rooms are decorated in earth tones, with comfortably firm beds. Bathrooms are small but have an outer sink/vanity and dressing room. Everything is very clean. There's a large outdoor pool and indoor hot tub surrounded by lots of greenery. The hotel also has guest Laundromat and gift shop. Complimentary morning coffee is an added touch. K-Bob's restaurant is right next door.

Best Western Pow Wow Inn. 801 W. Tucumcari Blvd. (P.O. Box 1306), Tucumcari, NM 88401. ☎ **800/527-6996**, 800/528-1234, or 505/461-0500. Fax 505/461-0135. 106 units. A/C TV TEL. $45–$55 double; $65–$90 suite. AE, CB, DC, DISC, MC, V. Pets are accepted, but must not be left unattended.

Located downtown on the "strip," this is where most New Mexican ranchers stay while in Tucumcari. A single-story hotel, built around a central courtyard, it provides a more sophisticated stay than the Discovery Inn, but with the rooms built in the 1960s it has a less "new" feel. A major remodel took place in 1997, however, adding whimsical touches such as sage and paprika colored walls and faux-painted furniture in the rooms, which are medium-sized, with nice medium-firm beds and small, clean bathrooms. The outdoor pool (open seasonally) is surrounded by gardens. Some units have kitchens (utensils not provided). Other facilities include a children's playground, a coin-op Laundromat, and a gift shop. Guests get complimentary greens fees at the local golf club. The Pow Wow Restaurant is open for three meals daily.

CAMPING NEAR TUCUMCARI   There are four good campgrounds around Tucumcari. **KOA Tucumcari** (☎ 505/461-1841) has 111 sites, laundry and grocery facilities, RV supplies, picnic tables, and grills. It also offers a recreation hall with video games, a heated swimming pool, basketball hoop, playground, horseshoes, and

Route 66 Revisited: Rediscovering New Mexico's Stretch of the Mother Road

Everyone's heard of Route 66. The highway that once stretched from Chicago to California was hailed as the road to freedom. During the Great Depression, it was the way west for farmers escaping Dust Bowl poverty out on the plains. If you found yourself in a rut in the late 1940s and '50s, all you had to do was hop in the car and head west on Route 66.

Of course, the road existed long before it gained such widespread fascination. Built in the late 1920s and paved in 1937, it was the lifeblood of communities in 8 states. Nowadays, however, U.S. 66 is as elusive as the fantasies that once carried hundreds of thousands west in search of a better life. Replaced by other roads, covered up by interstates (mostly I-40), and just plain out of use, Route 66 still exists in New Mexico, but you'll have to do a little searching and take some extra time to find it.

Motorists driving west from Texas can take a spin (make that a slow spin) on a 20-mile gravel stretch of the original highway running from Glenrio (Texas) to San Jon. From San Jon to Tucumcari, you can get your kicks on nearly 24 continuous paved miles of vintage 66. In Tucumcari, the historic route sliced through the center of town along what is today Tucumcari Boulevard. Santa Rosa's Will Rogers Drive is that city's 4-mile claim to the Mother Road. In Albuquerque, U.S. 66 follows Central Avenue for 18 miles, from the 1936 State Fairgrounds, past original 1930s motels and the historic Nob Hill district, on west through downtown.

One of the best spots to pretend you are a 1950s road warrior crossing the desert, whizzing past rattlesnakes, teepees, and tumbleweeds, is along NM 124, which winds 25 miles from Mesita to Acoma in northwestern New Mexico. You can next pick up old Route 66 in Grants, along the 6-mile Santa Fe Avenue. In Gallup, a 9-mile segment of U.S. 66 is lined with restaurants and hotels reminiscent of the city's days as a Western film capital from 1929 through 1964. Just outside Gallup, the historic route continues west to the Arizona border as NM 118.

For more information about Route 66, contact the Grants/Cíbola County Chamber of Commerce (☎ 800/748-2142) or the New Mexico Department of Tourism (☎ 800/545-2040).

shuffleboard, along with lots of elm trees for shade. To get there from I-40, get off the interstate at Exit 335, and then go ¼ mile east on South Frontage Road.

Mt. Road RV Park (☎ 505/461-9628) has 60 sites with full hookups, tenting, laundry facilities, and picnic tables. From I-40 take Exit 333 to Mountain Road; the park isn't far from the U.S. 54 bypass.

The campground in **Conchas Lake State Park** (☎ 505/868-2270) has 104 sites, 40 full hookups, lake swimming, boating, and fishing.

IN SANTA ROSA

Best Western Adobe Inn. E. Business Loop 40 at I-40 (P.O. Box 410), Santa Rosa, NM 88435. ☎ 800/528-1234 or 505/472-3446. 58 units. A/C TV TEL. May–Oct $54–$65 double; Nov–Apr $44–$58 double. AE, CB, DC, DISC, MC, V. Small pets allowed.

This two-story adobe-colored stone building with turquoise trim provides spacious, very clean and quiet rooms. The beds are medium firm and the furniture is good and solid, though the style a bit dated. Bathrooms are medium-size and clean, with an outer vanity, a dressing area, and two sinks. There's a nice pool, open seasonally, a gift shop, a courtesy car, and a restaurant next door.

Motel 6. 3400 Will Rogers Dr., Santa Rosa, NM 88435. ☎ **505/472-3045.** 90 units. A/C TV TEL. $33 double. Under 18 free with parent. AE, CB, DC, DISC, MC, V.

This motel on the east end of town off Exit 277 is made of white stucco with green doors and had a total renovation in 1998. Like most Motel 6s, it provides small, clean, efficient rooms. Bathrooms are medium-sized, spotless, with a shower. Ask for a room in the front part of the building to avoid sound from I-40. There's a nice pool, open seasonally.

Camping Near Santa Rosa

The **Santa Rosa KOA** (☎ 505/472-3126) offers 94 sites, 33 full hookups, laundry and grocery facilities, fire rings, grills, a heated swimming pool, and a playground for the kids. Situated in a piñon and juniper forest near town, the campground has a few small elm trees on the grounds. Coming from the east on I-40, take exit 277 and go 1 mile west on Business Loop; coming from the west on I-40, take exit 275 and go ¼ mile east on Business Loop.

Also in the area is **Santa Rosa Lake State Park** (☎ 505/472-3110), with year-round camping. There are 75 sites (about a third with electric hookups) as well as grills, boating, fishing, and hiking trails. Swimming in the lake is permitted but not encouraged because of its uneven bottom and lack of beaches; children would be safer swimming in Park Lake in Santa Rosa.

TWO GOOD PLACES TO EAT IN THE AREA

Del's Family Restaurant. 1202 E. Tucumcari Blvd., Tucumcari. ☎ **505/461-1740.** $3.95–$14.99. DISC, MC, V. Mon–Sat 6am–9pm. AMERICAN/MEXICAN.

The big cow atop Del's neon sign is not only a Route 66 landmark—it also points to the fine steaks inside. The restaurant has big windows along most every wall letting in plenty of daylight or neon light at night. It's a casual, diner-style eatery with lots of plants. Roast beef is a big seller here, served with a scoop of mashed potatoes, and a trip to the salad bar. You can also order a grilled chicken breast. The New Mexican food is good but not great. Del's is not licensed for alcoholic beverages.

✪ Joseph's Restaurant & Cantina. 865 Will Rogers Dr., Santa Rosa. ☎ **505/472-3361.** Main courses $4–$12. Daily summer 6am–10pm; winter 6am–9pm. AE, DISC, MC, V. AMERICAN/NEW MEXICAN.

You might want to plan your drive so you can eat a meal at "Joe's." In business since 1956, it's a real Route 66 diner, with linoleum tables, comfortable window-side booths and plenty of memorabilia, from license plates to vintage RC Cola posters. The locals all eat here: You'll see Hispanic grandmothers, skinny cowboys in straw hats, and dusty farm hands just in from the fields. The varied menu offers excellent fare. After many days on the road I needed something healthful so I ordered a salad topped with juicy grilled chicken (*beware:* the chef was determined to cover it with cheese, even after I asked him not to). The New Mexican dishes are large and chile-smothered, and the burgers are juicy with a variety of toppings, from the Rio Pecos topped with green chile to the Acapulco, with guacamole. Steaks are a big seller also, at a good price. For dessert, try a piece of pie or a shake.

10 Northwestern New Mexico

I'm always amazed when adventures in my home state rival ones in "exotic" places I've traveled, such as Borneo or Bolivia. Out here in New Mexico's "Indian Country," they do.

At Acoma, I peeked through a hole in the wall of an ancient cemetery on a mesa hundreds of feet above the ground. It had been left there so the spirits of some children who were taken from the pueblo could return. In Grants (population 8,900), a former uranium-mining boomtown, I traveled deep into a mine. In Gallup (pop. 20,000), self-proclaimed "Indian capital of the world" and a mecca for silver jewelry shoppers, I jogged along Route 66 and up on top of a pink mesa overlooking the city. In Farmington (pop. 36,000), center of the fertile San Juan valley and gateway to the Four Corners region, I slept in a cave. And in Chama (pop. 1,000), I rode on the Cumbres and Toltec Railroad—the longest and highest narrow-gauge steam railroad in the country—while it blew steam into an azure sky.

Each was an adventure in its own right, but what really made them special for me was the people I encountered along the way. My Zuni friend Jim met me for dinner in Gallup, and talked of his efforts to conserve the traditions of the tribe into which he was born. In Farmington, I stumbled upon a couple of old childhood friends, and in Chama the owner of the bed-and-breakfast where I stayed acted as a de facto tour guide.

The biggest presence here is the Native American culture, old and new. Each time I travel to this area I'm pleasantly surprised by the number of Pueblo, Navajo, and Apache who inhabit it. Truly, they are the majority, and they set the pace and tone of the place. The Zuni, Acoma, and Laguna Pueblos are each located within a short distance of I-40. Acoma's "Sky City" has been continually occupied for more than 9 centuries. A huge chunk of the northwest is taken up by a part of the Navajo Reservation, the largest in America; and the Jicarilla Apache Reservation stretches 65 miles south from the Colorado border. All share their arts and crafts as well as their distinctive cultures with visitors, but ask that their personal privacy and religious traditions be respected.

The past lives here, too. The pueblo people believe their ancestors' spirits still inhabit the ruins. Chaco Culture National Historical Park, with 12 major ruins and hundreds of smaller ones, represents the development of Anasazi civilization, which reached its peak in the 11th century. Aztec Ruins National Monument and the nearby

Northwestern New Mexico

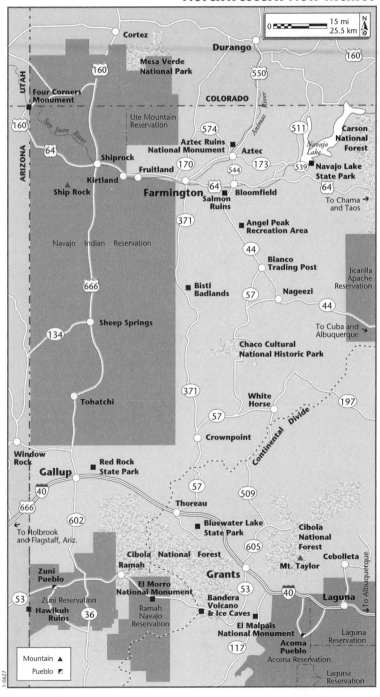

0 ___ 15 mi
___ 25.5 km

N

Cortez

Durango

160

Mesa Verde
National Park

550

COLORADO

UTAH

Four Corners
Monument

Ute Mountain
Reservation

574

511

Carson
National
Forest

160

San Juan River

64

Shiprock

Aztec Ruins
National Monument

Aztec

Navajo
Lake

ARIZONA

Fruitland

170

544

173

539

Navajo Lake
State Park

Kirtland

Farmington

64

Bloomfield

64

Ship Rock

Salmon
Ruins

To Chama
and Taos

371

Angel Peak
Recreation Area

Navajo   Indian   Reservation

44

Blanco
Trading Post

Animas River

666

Bisti
Badlands

57

Nageezi

44

Jicarilla
Apache
Reservation

Sheep Springs

To Cuba and
Albuquerque

134

Chaco Cultural
National Historic Park

Tohatchi

371

White
Horse

197

57

Continental Divide

Window
Rock

Crownpoint

Gallup

Red Rock
State Park

40

666

602

57

509

To Holbrook
and Flagstaff, Ariz.

Thoreau

Bluewater Lake
State Park

605

Cibola
National
Forest

Cebolleta

Cibola   National   Forest

Ramah

Mt. Taylor

To Albuquerque

Zuni
Pueblo

El Morro
National Monument

Grants

53

53

Hawikuh
Ruins

36

Zuni Reservation

Ramah
Navajo
Reservation

Bandera
Volcano
& Ice Caves

40

Laguna

Laguna
Reservation

El Malpais
National Monument

Acoma
Pueblo

117

Acoma Reservation

Laguna
Reservation

Mountain ▲
Pueblo ◪

1-0627

291

Salmon Ruins are similarly spectacular Pueblo preservations. The most interesting thing I learned while traveling here is that the contemporary Puebloan tribes no longer want to use the word *Anasazi* to refer to the people who once inhabited the ruins of Chaco, Salmon, Aztec, Mesa Verde, and others. Anasazi is a Navajo word meaning "ancient ones," or possibly "ancient enemies." The Pueblo tribes, believed to be the ancestors of the "Anasazi," prefer the term *Ancestral Puebloan People.*

This is at the core of changes that are taking place in the region. With the passing of the Native American Graves and Repatriation Act in 1990, tribes all over the country began claiming rights to ancient religious and burial artifacts. You may note these changes in museums throughout the region, where pottery has been claimed by tribes or simply removed from exhibits. During my visit to the Aztec Ruins, one large space stood empty. A warrior's remains had been exhibited there, and now a sign tells visitors that to the native people such a display of the dead was offensive. Though I would have liked to have seen the warrior, in some ways his absence spoke even more eloquently to me, and I hope it will to others, about the nature of these people and their struggle to maintain their beliefs amid the overpowering culture surrounding them.

Two other national monuments in northwestern New Mexico also speak of the region's history. El Morro is a sandstone monolith known as "Inscription Rock," where travelers and explorers documented their journeys for centuries; El Malpais is a volcanic badland with spectacular cinder cones, ice caves, and lava tubes.

EXPLORING THE REGION BY CAR

Beginning in Albuquerque, head west on I-40 via Laguna to Acoma Pueblo to tour the amazing **Acoma Pueblo,** the fabled "Sky City." Running alongside this section of I-40, though you'd barely know it today, is what was once part of historic Route 66 (see the box in chapter 9). If you're in no real hurry to get to Acoma Pueblo, I'd recommend driving this section of the old road. If you do, look for today's NM 6 and follow it to Mesita, where Route 66 picks up on NM 124. That will take you right through Laguna, where you might want to make a stop at Laguna Pueblo before continuing on to Acoma. During this portion of your trip, you'll be on Indian Reservation land, which accounts for the lack of major development in the area.

After taking the tour at Acoma, which is the only way you can see the pueblo, proceed west on I-40 in the direction of Grants. Make a detour on NM 117 to see **El Malpais National Monument,** where you may want to do some hiking. From there head to Grants where you can spend the night. The next morning in **Grants,** visit the New Mexico Museum of Mining, where you'll travel down into a replica mine and experience what mining life was like in New Mexico.

Later in the day, head south and west from Grants on NM 53 to **Bandera Volcano and Ice Caves, El Morro National Monument,** and the **Zuni Pueblo.** Then proceed north on NM 602 to **Gallup,** where you'll want to browse in trading posts for Native American jewelry and crafts and possibly follow the walking tour outlined below. If you've still got some time and energy left after touring Gallup and the area attractions, head out to **Red Rock State Park** and check out the displays on prehistoric Anasazi culture. It's a good little preview to what you're going to find in Chaco Canyon National Historical Park later in your journey. Next, return to Gallup where you will probably want to spend the night.

The next morning when you leave Gallup, make sure you have a full tank of gas and then head out on I-40 east to **Thoreau.** From Thoreau, take NM 371 north to

Crownpoint, and then NM 57 east and then north to **Chaco Canyon National Historical Park,** the crown jewel of ancient Anasazi culture in North America. You'll want to spend at least 1 full day at the park, so plan accordingly. Also give yourself some time to get from the canyon to a campsite or motel. It can take awhile to get out of Chaco Canyon. Please note that if the weather is bad or the roads are particularly muddy, it's best not to even try to get to the canyon unless you have a four-wheel-drive vehicle. You can camp in the canyon, but prepare accordingly—there are absolutely no opportunities to gather provisions once you enter the park.

To get to **Farmington,** our next stop, from Chaco Canyon, take NM 57 north to NM 44 and NM 44 north to Bloomfield and then go west on U.S. 64. If you're camping, the towns of **Bloomfield** and **Aztec** (which leave you slightly closer to your first stop in the morning) both have campsites; otherwise, Farmington is your best bet for finding a decent motel room.

Points of interest in the Farmington/Aztec area are **Aztec Ruins National Monument** and the **Salmon Ruins.** The average visit to Aztec Ruins National Monument and Salmon Ruins combined lasts about 2 hours, so you'll have plenty of time to explore **Navajo Lake State Park** (off U.S. 64 east), where you can take a cool dip or fish for trout, salmon, bass, or crappie before continuing on to **Dulce,** in the Jicarilla Apache Indian Reservation, and another half hour to **Chama,** where you'll probably want to spend the night. Plan for some outdoor adventure in Chama, where there are hiking, biking, and skiing trails, as well as good fishing, hunting, and snowmobiling. You'll also want to plan a trip on the **Cumbres and Toltec Scenic Railroad** in the morning. This is one of New Mexico's premier attractions.

When you've waved the train good-bye, follow U.S. 84 south to Santa Fe, leaving time for midway stops at the **Ghost Ranch Living Museum** north of Abiquiu and **Georgia O'Keeffe's former home** in Abiquiu. Return to Albuquerque via I-25.

1 The Great Outdoors in Northwestern New Mexico

As with the rest of New Mexico, the northwest region offers much to do in the way of outdoor recreation. If you're an outdoor enthusiast you could spend months here hiking, biking, and exploring.

BIKING   Mountain biking is permitted in parts of **Cíbola National Forest** (☎ 505/346-2650), which, in this region, is located on both sides of I-40 in the Grants to Gallup area. The national forest has six districts; call the number above for a referral to the one where you want to go. Some of the best biking is in Farmington. This is where the "Durangatangs" come during the winter to train and ride (Durango is a mountain-bike mecca). *Best Mountain Biking Trails in Farmington* is your guide for the area; it's available at the visitor's bureau or at the following bike shops, which also rent bikes: **Cottonwood Cycles,** 3030 East Main, T-2 (☎ 505/326-0429) or **Bicycle Express,** 103 North Main Ave. (☎ 505/334-4354) in Farmington. Be sure to check out the **Lions Wilderness Park** and the **Road Apple Trail,** both on the north end of town. Additionally, bikers are also welcome at the **Bureau of Land Management Conservation Area** just off NM 117 near **El Malpais National Monument** (see section 2 on Grants, below). For equipment rental in that area, try calling **Scoreboard Sporting Goods,** 107 West Coal Ave. (☎ 505/722-6077) in Gallup; or you might opt to rent something before you leave Albuquerque at **Rio Mountain Sport,** 1210 Rio Grande NW (☎ 505/766-9970). At Chaco Canyon, check out the Wijiji Ruin trail, nice and easy but through beautiful country leading to an Anasazi ruin.

BOATING   If you're towing a boat, good places to stop are **Bluewater Lake State Park** (☎ 505/876-2391), a reservoir located between Gallup and Grants, and **Navajo Lake State Park** (☎ 505/632-2278), located about 25 miles east of Bloomfield. Both Bluewater and Navajo Lake state parks have boat ramps, and Navajo Lake has several marinas (from which visitors can rent boats), picnic areas, a visitor center, and groceries for those who plan to make a day of it. **Zuni Lakes,** six bodies of water operated by the Zuni tribe, also offer opportunities for boating, although you're not allowed to use gasoline motors and you must receive a permit from tribal headquarters (☎ 505/782-5851) before setting out.

FISHING   **Bluewater Lake State Park** (mentioned above for boating) is one of the best places to fish in the area. In fact, some people believe it has the highest catch rate of all New Mexico lakes. Look to catch trout here. **Ramah Lake** (no phone) was created in the late 1800s by Mormons for the purpose of irrigation, and was privately owned until 1987 when it became available for public use. There's nothing here but the lake and the fish (bass, trout, and bluegills). Fishing is also allowed by permit at **Zuni Lakes** (see "Boating," above). **Navajo Lake State Park** (see "Boating," above) features about 150 miles of shoreline where fishers go to catch trout, bass, catfish, and pike. Navajo Lake is one of the largest in New Mexico, and the park is very heavily trafficked, so if crowds aren't your thing, look for another fishing hole. Just 4 miles south of Kirtland is **Morgan Lake,** a quiet spot for largemouth bass and catfish. If you need fishing gear while in the area, contact **Duranglers on the San Juan,** 1003 Hwy. 511, Navajo Dam (☎ 505/632-5952), or the nearby **Abe's Motel and Fly Shop,** 1791 U.S. 173, Navajo Dam (☎ 505/632-2194). In Farmington, contact **Dad's Bait, Boats, and Upholstery,** 210 E. Piñon St. (☎ 505/326-1870), or **Zia Sporting Goods,** 500 E. Main (☎ 505/327-6004). In Chama contact **Tom Capelli's High Country Fishing,** HCR 75, Box 1197, Rutheron, NM 87551 (☎ 505/588-7674).

GOLF   In its November 1995 edition, *Golf Digest* rated **Pinon Hills Golf Course,** 2101 Sunrise Pkwy. in Farmington (☎ 505/326-6066), the "best public golf course" in the United States. Also in Farmington is the **Civitan Golf Course,** 2200 North Dustin (☎ 505/599-1194). If you're going to be in or near Aztec, try **Hidden Valley Country Club,** County Rd. 3025, no. 29 (☎ 505/334-3248). In Kirtland your opportunities are limited to **Riverview Golf Course,** located on County Road 6500, no. 89 (☎ 505/598-0140).

HIKING   This part of the state has some great hiking trails. You'll get to see ancient archaeological ruins in places like Aztec Ruins and Chaco Canyon. In **Cíbola National Forest** (☎ 505/287-8833), the hike to the summit of Mount Taylor is excellent. In cooler months, but not winter, try hiking around **El Malpais National Monument** (☎ 505/285-4641). Two good hikes to try in El Malpais are the Zuni-Acoma Trail (this one is extremely taxing, so if you're not in shape, don't expect to make the 15-mile round-trip hike) and the Big Lava Tubes Trail (1 mile round-trip). For quiet hiking in state parks, head to **Bluewater Lake State Park** (☎ 505/876-2391), **Red Rock State Park** (☎ 505/722-3839), or **Angel Peak Recreation Area** (☎ 505/599-8900).

Sporting goods stores where you can get hiking gear include **REI-Albuquerque** at 1905 W. Mountain Rd. in Albuquerque (☎ 505/247-1191), **Frontier Sports** at 4601 E. Main in Farmington (☎ 505/327-0800), and **Zia Sporting Goods** at 500 E. Main, also in Farmington (☎ 505/327-6004).

HORSEBACK RIDING   You'll find lots of riding opportunities around Chama. A good bet is **5M Outfitters,** who charge $40 for a half-day ride and $80 for a full day.

Rides with a chuck wagon dinner are also available, as are overnight pack trips. Contact Bruce Maker at P.O. Box 361, Chama 87520 (☎ **505/588-7003**).

RAFTING & KAYAKING   The Chama River Canyon Wilderness begins just below El Vado Dam and runs past the Christ in the Desert Monastery, usually an overnight trip, though some last up to 3 nights. The river snakes through one of the most spectacular canyons I've ever seen, at one point rising 1,500 feet above your head. Rapids are mostly Class II (on a scale from I to V), but there are some big waves. Water is released on most weekends throughout the summer, so you can count on enough to make the trip exciting. Contact **Far Flung Adventures** at ☎ **800/359-2627** or 505/359-2627.

SKIING   If you're tired of fighting for space on the cross-country ski trails in other parts of the state, try skiing the old logging roads of Mount Taylor in **Cíbola National Forest** near Grants. Contact the Ranger Station in Grants at ☎ **505/287-8833** for more information. If you need to rent ski equipment I'd recommend doing so in Albuquerque before you head north. See chapter 6 for details.

SNOWMOBILING   Chama is an excellent place to ride those mean machines. Contact **Mountain Mike's Recreation** at P.O. Box 746, Chama, NM 87520 (☎ **800/645-3242** or 505/756-9154).

SWIMMING   Good swimming is available at **Navajo Lake State Park** (☎ **505/ 632-2278**). Before diving in at other lakes in state parks, make sure swimming is permitted.

2 Acoma & Laguna Pueblos

Your best base for exploring Acoma and Laguna Pueblos, as well as the El Malpais and El Morro National Monuments (see section 3, below), is the town of Grants, 1¼ hours west of Albuquerque on I-40 west. Where to stay and dine in Grants, as well as details on the interesting New Mexico Museum of Mining in Grants, are discussed later in this section.

ACOMA PUEBLO

The spectacular Acoma Sky City, a walled adobe village perched high atop a sheer rock mesa 367 feet above the 6,600-foot valley floor, is said to have been inhabited at least since the 11th century—it's the longest continuously occupied community in the United States. Native history says it has been inhabited since before the time of Christ. Both the pueblo and its mission church of San Esteban del Rey are National Historic Landmarks. When Coronado visited in 1540, he suggested that Acoma was "the greatest stronghold in the world"; those who attempt to follow the cliff-side footpath down after their guided tour, rather than take the bus back down, might agree.

About 50 to 75 Keresan-speaking Acoma (pronounced *Ack*-oo-mah) reside year-round on the 70-acre mesa top. Many others maintain ancestral homes and occupy them during ceremonial periods. The terraced three-story buildings face south for maximum exposure to the winter sun. Most of Sky City's permanent residents make their living off the throngs of tourists who flock here to see the magnificent church, built in 1639 and containing numerous masterpieces of Spanish colonial art, and to purchase the thin-walled white pottery, with brown-and-black designs, for which the pueblo is famous.

Many Acomas work in Grants, 15 miles west of the pueblo, in Albuquerque, or for one of Acoma's business enterprises such as Sky City Casino; others are cattle ranchers and farm individual family gardens.

ESSENTIALS

GETTING THERE   To reach Acoma from Grants, drive east 15 miles on I-40 to McCartys, then south 13 miles on paved tribal roads to the visitor center. From Albuquerque, drive west 52 miles to the Acoma-Sky City exit, then 12 miles southwest.

VISITOR INFORMATION   For additional information before you leave home, contact the pueblo at P.O. Box 309, Acoma, NM 87034 (☎ **800/747-0181** or 505/470-4966).

ADMISSION FEES & HOURS   The admission charge is $8 for adults, $7 for seniors (60 and over), $6 for children 6 through 17, and free for children under 6. Group discounts apply to parties of 15 or more, and there's also a discount for Native American visitors. The charge to take still photographs is $10; no videotaping, sketching, or painting is allowed except by special permission. The pueblo is open daily in the summer from 8am to 7pm and daily the rest of the year from 8am to 4:30pm.

SEEING THE HIGHLIGHTS

You absolutely cannot wander freely around Acoma Pueblo, but you can start your tour of Acoma at the visitor center at the base of the mesa. One-hour tours begin every 30 minutes, depending on the demand; the last tour is scheduled 1 hour before closing. The pueblo is closed to visitors on Easter weekend (some years), June 24 and 29, July 9 through 12 or 10 through 13, and the first or second weekend in October.

While waiting, peruse the excellent little museum of Acoma history and crafts, or dine on Native American (fast) food in an adjoining cafe. Then board the tour bus, which climbs through a rock garden of 50-foot sandstone monoliths and past precipitously dangling outhouses to the mesa's summit. There's no running water or electricity in this medieval-looking village; a small reservoir collects rainwater for most uses, and drinking water is transported up from below. Wood-hole ladders and mica windows are prevalent among the 300-odd adobe structures. As you tour the village there will be many opportunities to buy pottery and other pueblo treasures. Pottery is expensive here, but you're not going to find it any cheaper anywhere else, and you'll be guaranteed that it's authentic if you buy it directly from the craftsperson. Along the way, be sure to sample some Indian fry bread topped with honey.

DANCES & CEREMONIES

The annual San Esteban del Rey feast day is September 2, when the pueblo's patron saint is honored with a midmorning mass, a procession, an afternoon corn dance, and an arts-and-crafts fair. A Governor's Feast is held annually in February; and 4 days of Christmas festivals run from December 25 to 28. Cameras are not allowed and guided tours do not operate on the mesa during feast days.

Other celebrations are held in low-lying pueblo villages at Easter (in Acomita), the first weekend in May (Santa Maria feast at McCartys), and August 10 (San Lorenzo Day in Acomita).

LAGUNA PUEBLO

This major Keresan-speaking pueblo consists of a central settlement and five smaller villages not far from Acoma Pueblo and just over a half hour from Grants. In fact, Lagunas are closely related to the Acomas who live just 14 miles away. Founded after the 1680 revolt by refugees from the Rio Grande Valley, Laguna is the youngest of New Mexico's pueblos and has about 7,000 residents. Today many Lagunas are engaged in agriculture or private business, including a tribal-operated commercial

---

Pueblo Pottery: A Glossary of Terms

Burnishing   Potters rub a smooth stone on the surface of a pot or bowl after slip (see below) has been applied in order to create a shiny surface on the finished product.

Coiling   Pieces of clay are rolled into long, snakelike pieces and then are "coiled" in order to build up the walls of a pot. After the desired size and shape have been created, the pot walls are thinned, scraped, and finally smoothed. This is the method most frequently used by Pueblo potters.

Firing   Today, most potters fire (bake in order to harden) their work in an electric or gas-fired kiln, but Pueblo potters fire their work in outdoor ovens using a variety of fuels, including animal dung.

Incising   The cutting of designs into the surface of a pot before the firing process.

Matte   The opposite of burnished, a matte finish is dull. Many Pueblo Indians, including Acoma, Picuris, and Zia, use matte finishes.

Micaceous   The clay of micaceous pots contains small particles of mica, which sparkle when held up to the light. Taos and Picuris Pueblo clays contain quite a bit of mica.

Polychrome   If a potter uses three or more colors on a pot, it is referred to as polychrome.

Sgraffito   The scratching of a pot surface to create designs after it has been fired.

Slip   Put simply, slip is very watery clay. It is applied to a piece of pottery just before firing in order to fill in air holes and create a uniform color.

---

center. Federal funds brought modern housing facilities and scholarship programs, one of which helped start the career of famous Laguna author Leslie Marmon Silko. The employment rate here is high, and this is widely considered one of New Mexico's wealthiest pueblos.

ESSENTIALS

GETTING THERE   From Grants, take I-40 east for 32 miles. The pueblo is 50 miles west of Albuquerque along I-40.

VISITOR INFORMATION   For information about Laguna before you leave home, contact the tribal governor's office at P.O. Box 194, Laguna Pueblo, NM 87026, or call ☎ 505/552-6654.

ADMISSION FEES & HOURS   No admission is charged, and there is no photo fee, but some restrictions apply from village to village. Visitors are welcome during daylight hours year-round.

SEEING THE HIGHLIGHTS

New to the Pueblo and surrounding area are organized tours; call ☎ 505/552-9771 for the latest information. You can also wander around (respecting the fact that this is home to thousands of people) on your own at your leisure. The outlying villages of Mesita, Paguate, Paraje, Encinal, and Seama are interesting in their own rights, but the best place to visit is the old pueblo where you can see the massive stone church, San Jose de Laguna, built in 1699, and famous for its interior. It was restored in the 1930s.

DANCES & CEREMONIES

Pueblo and Navajo people from throughout the region attend St. Joseph's Feast Day (September 19) at Old Laguna Village. The fair begins in the morning with a mass and procession, followed by a harvest dance, sports events, and a carnival. New Year's Day (January 1) and Three Kings Day (January 6) are also celebrated at the pueblo with processions and dances. Each smaller village has its own feast day between July 26 and October 17; call the pueblo office for details.

AN ATTRACTION NEAR LAGUNA

Seboyeta, the oldest Hispanic community in western New Mexico, is 3½ miles north of Paguate, outside Laguna Pueblo. It still shows ruins of adobe fortress walls built in the 1830s to protect the village from Navajo attack. The Mission of Our Lady of Sorrows was built in the 1830s, as was the nearby Shrine of Los Portales, built in a cave north of town.

AN ATTRACTION IN NEARBY GRANTS

✪ **The New Mexico Museum of Mining.** 100 N. Iron St. at Santa Fe Ave. ☎ **800/ 748-2142** or 505/287-4802. Admission $3 adults, $2 seniors over 60 and kids 7–18; free for children 6 and under. Admission includes guided tour or self-guiding "sound stick." May 1–Sept 30 Mon–Sat 9am–4pm, Sun 9am–3pm; Oct 1–Apr 30 Mon–Sat 9am–4pm.

This enormously interesting little museum primes you for the underground adventure of traveling into a re-creation of a mine shaft by showing you, on ground level, some geology such as a fossilized dinosaur leg bone and a piece of Malpais lava. The world's only uranium-mining museum also gives you a sense of the context within which uranium was mined, through photos of the uranium mining pioneers. "Word went out that uranium was in demand before people even knew why" reads one quote, which further explains that only scientists and physicists knew about its use as an explosive and fuel. Thus sets the stage for your walk into a mineshaft-like doorway adorned with rusty metal hats.

An elevator takes you down into a spooky, low-lit place with stone walls. You begin in the station where uranium was loaded and unloaded and travel back into the earth through places defined on wall plaques with such interesting names as "track drift" (where ore comes up in cars from the mine) and "stope" (a room stripped of all ore and off-limits in an actual mine) and you learn the functions of equipment such as a "mucker" (a machine that digs the tunnel for tracks) and a "loaded round" (which blasts holes in rock). Most of all you get to sense the dark and dirty work that mining can be, and when the elevator pauses a moment before taking you to the surface, you may hold your breath fearful that you won't get to return from this strange underworld. If you call in advance, the museum will arrange for a tour guide from the local college.

WHERE TO STAY IN NEARBY GRANTS

If you've ever wondered what a "boom and bust town" looks like, come to Grants and find out. Grants first boomed with the coming of the railroad in the late 19th century when 4,000 workers descended on the tiny farm town. When the railroad was completed, the workers left and the town was bust. Next Grants saw high times in the 1940s growing carrots and sending them to the east coast, but when packaging became more advanced, it lost its foothold in the market and busted again. Then came the 1950s, when a Navajo sheep rancher named Paddy Martinez discovered some strange yellow rocks near Haystack Mountain, northwest of town. The United States was in need of uranium and his find led to the biggest boom in the area.

(Martinez rented land for the mining, and took his profits to the shores of Bluewater Lake, where he continued to raise sheep.) By the early 1980s demand for uranium had dropped and so went the big wages and big spenders that the ore's popularity had produced. Today, the city is little more than a segment of Route 66 with some interesting old buildings marking its banks.

Look closely and you'll see dilapidated court motels and store signs. Note the Uranium Cafe, with a sign in the window that reads "Our food will blow your mine."

The city is the seat of expansive Cíbola County, which stretches from the Arizona border nearly to the Albuquerque area. For more information, contact the **Grants/ Cíbola Country Chamber of Commerce** at 100 N. Iron Ave. (P.O. Box 297), Grants, NM 87020 (☎ **800/748-2142** or 505/287-4802). It's located in the same building as the Mining Museum.

Grants hotels are all on or near Route 66, with major properties near I-40 interchanges, and smaller or older motels nearer downtown. Lodger's tax is 5%, which is added to the gross receipts tax of 6.8125% for a total room tax of just under 12%. Parking is usually free.

Best Western Inn & Suites. 1501 E. Santa Fe Ave, I-40 Exit 85 (P.O. Drawer T), Grants, NM 87020. ☎ **800/528-1234,** 800/600-5221, or 505/287-7901. Fax 505/285-5751. 125 units. A/C TV TEL. $66–$97 double. AE, CB, DC, DISC, MC, V. Pets are welcome.

Built in 1976 and remodeled in 1996, this is one of four New Mexico hotels owned by Southwest Innkeepers that provides spacious rooms and good amenities, though you have to like to walk. Rooms are built around a huge quadrangle with an indoor pool in a sunny, plant-filled courtyard at the center. Request a room at one of the four corner entrances and you'll avoid trudging down the long hallways. Also request a room facing outside rather than in toward the courtyard, where noise from the pool carries. Though not quite as efficient as the Holiday Inn Express (see below), more amenities are provided here. Rooms are bright, done in with floral prints, with textured wallpaper with Aztec trim. Beds are firm and the water pressure is good. All rooms have coffeemakers, and the suites have a microwave, wet bar, minirefrigerator, a phone at a working desk, an oversize dresser, and a sleeper sofa in a sitting area. An elaborate buffet breakfast comes with the price of the room and is served in the sky-lit courtyard.

Services and facilities include room service limited to dinner hours, valet laundry, 24-hour desk, an indoor swimming pool, men's and women's saunas, hot tub, guest Laundromat, video games area, and gift shop.

Holiday Inn Express. 1496 E. Santa Fe Ave., Grants, NM 87020. ☎ **800-HOLIDAY** or 505/ 285-4676. Fax 505/285-6998. 58 units. A/C TV TEL. $54–$70 double. Rates include continental breakfast. AE, DC, DISC, MC, V.

Located just off the interstate, this two-story, 1994 vintage motel provides large, well-conceived rooms with a comfortable atmosphere. In fact, I was surprised at how nice the rooms were, and with the way the ground-level ones open both off an inner corridor and from an outside door where your car is parked. Rooms are spacious with high ceilings and large bathrooms. Each has a hair dryer, iron and ironing board, and large TV. There's a hot tub and a small indoor pool.

✪ Sands Motel. 112 McArthur St. (P.O. Box 1437), Grants, NM 87020. ☎ **800/424-7679** or 505/287-2996. Fax 500/287-2996. 24 units. A/C TV TEL. $43 double. Continental breakfast included. AE, CB, DC, DISC, MC, V. Pets welcome for a $5 fee.

On first glance you wonder why anyone would want to stay at this older hotel rather than the newer chain hotels near the interstate, and yet the Sands draws crowds.

Mostly, the price is good, and the rooms are clean and spacious, though the furnishings and carpet aren't as new as at those more recent competitors. Located a block from Route 66 in the center of town, it gives travelers a break from the noise of the interstate. Rooms are spacious with a table, chairs, and refrigerator; the beds are comfortable; and the bathrooms are clean. The parking area is enclosed by a wall and you can park right in front of your room to keep an eye on your stuff.

CAMPING   There are three decent campgrounds in Grants with both tent and RV facilities. All range in price from $7.50 to $14 for tent camping and $10 to $18 for full hookups. **Blue Spruce RV Park** (☎ 505/287-2560) has 28 sites and 19 full hookups and is open year-round. It has enough trees to block the wind. There's some grass and the roads and parking spaces are gravel, so dust is minimized. Cable television hookups are available, as are laundry facilities and a recreation room. To reach the park, take I-40 to Exit 81 and then go ¼ mile south on NM 53.

Cíbola Sands RV Park (☎ 505/287-4376), also open year-round, offers 54 sites, 38 full hookups. The site is a bit desolate, with cinder roads and only a few ash trees, though it is quite well kept with very clean bathrooms. There's free cable TV hookup, laundry, and limited grocery facilities, a recreation room, and a playground. From the junction of I-40 and NM 53 (westbound Exit 81, eastbound Exit 81A) go ¼ mile south on NM 53, then 1 block east on Frontage Road.

Lavaland RV Park (☎ 505/287-8665), the closest site to Grants, has 58 sites and 39 full hookups. Located near a lava outcropping, the site is clean, though a little desolate and dusty, with a few pine trees to block the wind. There are some free cable and telephone hookups. Air-conditioning and heating hookups are available at an extra charge. In addition, there are cabins, laundry, and limited grocery facilities, picnic tables and grills, and recreation facilities. Lavaland is open year-round. From I-40, get off at Exit 85 and go 100 yards south on Access Road.

WHERE TO DINE IN NEARBY GRANTS

In general, you won't find places to eat at pueblos or national monuments, so you're best off looking for a restaurant in Grants.

✪ **El Jardin Palacios.** 319 W. Santa Fe Ave. ☎ **505/285-5231.** $2.50–$7.95. AE, MC, V. Mon–Fri 11am–2:30pm, Mon–Sat 5–9pm. NEW MEXICAN.

This friendly restaurant, owned and operated by the Palacio family, serves authentic New Mexican food in the only intentionally decorated atmosphere I was able to find in Grants. Plants hang in the windows, and original oils adorn the walls, giving the place a homey feeling. The stucco building with Mexican furniture inside is located on Route 66.

The food is of high quality. Beef is shredded and sautéed for tacos, not ground and fried. The specialty is chimichangas—meat, chicken, or machaca (seasoned shredded beef). There is also trout, shrimp, and scampi; shrimp, beef, and chicken fajitas; and chicken enchiladas. If you have room, try the florencita, a dessert special with fruit filling. Beer and wine are served.

La Ventana. 110½ Geis St., Hillcrest Center. ☎ **505/287-9393.** Reservations recommended. Main courses $4–$11 lunch, $13–$24 dinner. AE, CB, DC, DISC, MC, V. Mon–Sat 11am–11pm. STEAKS.

This is where the Grants locals go for a big dinner or lunch out. One large room seating about 50 people, the restaurant is done in a cheesy Southwestern decor, with a two-horse sculpture on one wall and some dancing kachinas in nichos. The place is dark with few windows, so if you can catch Grants on a nonwindy day, opt for the patio. Service is friendly, if slow. You can't go wrong with one of the salads such as the chicken Caesar, or with the prime rib. You'll also find pasta dishes such as a garden fettuccine and sandwiches such as a turkey avocado served on seven grain bread. There's a full bar where you can sit if you want to tell your problems to the bartender.

✪ **Monte Carlo Restaurant and Lounge.** 721 W. Santa Fe Ave. ☎ **505/287-9250.** Breakfast and lunch menu items under $5; dinner main courses $5.50–$14. AE, DISC, MC, V. Daily 7am–10pm. NEW MEXICAN/STEAKS.

From the outside this two-story restaurant, in business for more than 40 years, appears dark and foreboding, but once inside it has a casual, friendly, open atmosphere and very good food. A number of small dining rooms have wooden tables and comfortable chairs. Arched windows let in plenty of light to the front rooms where you'll want to sit. As with most of these small-town all-purpose eateries, the food ranges broadly from omelettes to sandwiches to steaks and seafood. I recommend the New Mexican dishes. The Navajo taco (fry bread topped with beans, chile, cheese, lettuce, and tomato) makes for a nice lunch. Or you might try the huevos rancheros (one egg on a corn tortilla, topped with chile and cheese). Locals love the "mix and match" in which you can choose any two items ranging from an enchilada to a relleno. For dessert, there are pies, cheesecake, and natillas (frothy custard). There's occasional live music as well as a full bar in the Cíbola Room. A children's menu is available.

3 El Malpais & El Morro National Monuments

Northwestern New Mexico has two national monuments that are must-sees for anyone touring this region: El Malpais and El Morro.

EL MALPAIS: EXPLORING THE BADLANDS

Designated a national monument in 1987, El Malpais (Spanish for "badlands") is considered one of the outstanding examples of volcanic landscapes in the United States. El Malpais contains 115,000 acres of cinder cones, vast lava flows, hundreds of lava tubes, ice caves, sandstone cliffs, natural bridges and arches, Anasazi ruins, ancient Native American trails, and Spanish and Anglo homesteads.

ESSENTIALS

GETTING THERE   There are two approaches to El Malpais, via NM 117 and NM 53. Route 117 exits I-40, 7 miles east of Grants.

VISITOR INFORMATION   Admission to El Malpais is free (unless you're visiting the privately owned Ice Caves), and it's open to visitors year-round. The visitor center, located off route 53 between mile markers 63 and 64, is open daily from 8:30am to 4:30pm. Here you can pick up maps of the park, leaflets on specific trails, and other details about exploring the monument. For more information, write **El Malpais National Monument,** NPS, P.O. Box 939, Grants, NM 87020 (☎ **505/285-4641**).

SEEING THE HIGHLIGHTS

From **Sandstone Bluffs Overlook** (10 miles south of I-40 off NM 117) many craters are visible in the lava flow, which extends for miles along the eastern flank of the Continental Divide. The most recent flows are only 1,000 years old; Native American legends tell of rivers of "fire rock." Seventeen miles south of I-40 is **La Ventana Natural Arch,** the largest accessible natural arch in New Mexico.

From NM 53, which exits I-40 just west of Grants, visitors have access to the **Zuni-Acoma Trail,** an ancient Pueblo trade route that crosses four major lava flows in a 7½-mile (one-way) hike. A printed trail guide is available. **El Calderon,** a forested area 20 miles south of I-40, is a trailhead for exploring a cinder cone, lava tubes, and a bat cave. (*Warning:* Hikers should not enter the bat cave or otherwise disturb the bats.)

The largest of all Malpais cinder cones, **Bandera Crater** is on private property 25 miles south of I-40. The National Park Service has laid plans to absorb this commercial operation, known as **Ice Caves Resort** (☎ **888/ICE-CAVE** or 505/ 783-4303; www.icecaves.com). For a fee of $7 for adults and $3.50 for children ages 5 through 12, visitors hike up the crater or walk to the edge of an ice cave. It's open daily 8am to 1 hour before sunset; that means hikers can start out no later than 7pm in summertime or 4:30pm in midwinter.

Perhaps the most fascinating phenomenon of El Malpais is the lava tubes, formed when the outer surface of a lava flow cooled and solidified. When the lava river drained, tunnel-like caves were left. Ice caves within some of the tubes have delicate ice-crystal ceilings, ice stalactites, and floors like ice rinks.

HIKING & CAMPING

Several hiking trails can be found throughout El Malpais, including the above-mentioned Zuni-Acoma Trail. Most are marked with rock cairns; some are dirt trails. The best times to hike this area are spring and fall, when it's not too hot. You are pretty much on your own when exploring this area, so prepare accordingly. Be sure to carry plenty of water with you; do not drink surface water. Carrying first-aid gear is always a good idea; the lava rocks can be extremely sharp and inflict nasty cuts. Hikers should wear sturdy boots, long pants, and leather gloves when exploring the lava and caves. In addition, never go into a cave alone. The park service advises wearing hard hats, boots, protective clothing, and gloves and carrying three sources of light when entering lava tubes. The weather can change suddenly, so be prepared; if lightning is around, move off the lava as soon as possible

Primitive camping is allowed in the park, but you must first obtain a free back-country permit from the visitor center.

EL MORRO NATIONAL MONUMENT

Travelers who like to look history straight in the eye are fascinated by "Inscription Rock," 43 miles west of Grants along NM 53. Looming up out of the sand and sagebrush is a bluff 200 feet high, holding some of the most captivating messages in North America. Its sandstone face displays a written record of the many who inhabited and traveled through this land, beginning with the Anasazi who lived atop the formation around 1200. Carved with steel points are the signatures and comments of almost every explorer, conquistador, missionary, army officer, surveyor, and pioneer emigrant who passed this way between 1605, when Gov. Don Juan de Oñate carved the first inscription, and 1906, when it was preserved by the National Park Service. Oñate's inscription, dated April 16, 1605, was perhaps the first graffiti left by any European in America.

A paved walkway makes it easy to walk to the writings, and there is a stone stairway leading up to other treasures. One reads: "Year of 1716 on the 26th of August passed by here Don Feliz Martinez, Governor and Captain General of this realm to the reduction and conquest of the Moqui." Confident of success as he was, Martinez actually got nowhere with any "conquest of the Moqui," or Hopi, peoples. After a 2-month battle, they chased him back to Santa Fe.

Another special group to pass by this way was the U.S. Camel Corps, trekking past on their way from Texas to California in 1857. The camels worked out fine in mountains and deserts, outlasting horses and mules 10 to 1, but the Civil War ended the experiment. When Peachy Breckinridge, fresh out of the Virginia Military Academy, came by with 25 camels, he noted the fact on the stone here.

El Morro was at one time as famous as the Blarney Stone of Ireland: Everybody had to stop by and make a mark. But when the Santa Fe Railroad was laid 25 miles to the north, El Morro was no longer on the main route to California, and from the 1870s, the tradition began to die out.

Atop Inscription Rock via a short, steep trail are ruins of an Anasazi pueblo occupying an area 200 by 300 feet. Its name, Atsinna, suggests that carving one's name here is a very old custom indeed: The word, in Zuni, means "writing on rock."

ESSENTIALS

GETTING THERE   El Morro is located 43 miles west of Grants along NM 53.

VISITOR INFORMATION   For information, contact **El Morro National Monument,** Route 2, Box 43, Ramah, NM 87321-9603 (☎ **505/783-4226**). Self-guided trail booklets are available at the visitor center (turn off Highway 53 at El Morro sign, and travel approximately ½ mile), open from 9am to 7pm in summer; 9am to 5pm in winter. Trails are open in the summer from 9am to 6pm, and 9am to 4pm in winter. The park is closed on December 25 and January 1. A museum at the visitor center features exhibits on the 700 years of human activity at El Morro. A 15-minute video gives visitors a good introduction to the park. Also within the visitor center is a bookstore where you can pick up souvenirs or educational and informational books.

ADMISSION FEES & HOURS   Admission to El Morro is $4 per car or $2 per person. The visitor center is open in the summer from 9am to 7pm, and from 9am to 5pm in the winter. It will take you between 2 and 4 hours to visit the museum and hike a couple of trails.

CAMPING

Though it isn't necessary to camp here in order to see most of the park, a nine-site campground at El Morro is open from approximately Memorial Day to Labor Day, and costs $5 per night. There are no supplies available within the park, so if you're planning on spending a night or two, be sure to arrive well equipped.

One nearby private enterprise, **El Morro RV Park,** Route 2, Box 44, El Morro, NM 87321 (☎ **505/783-4612**), has cabins, RV and tent camping, and a cafe.

EXPLORING THE AREA: CÍBOLA NATIONAL FOREST

If you do a lot of hiking and national forest/park exploration, you'll know that there's a big difference between a national park and a national forest. Usually national parks are 100% protected parcels of land (in some places pets aren't even allowed), whereas national forests are federally owned pieces of land on which certain activities are permitted: logging, hunting, camping, hiking, and sometimes there are even maintained trails for motorcycles. **Cíbola National Forest** is actually a combination of parcels of land throughout the state that total more than 1.6 million acres. Elevation varies from 5,000 to 11,301 feet, and the forest includes the Datil, Gallinas, Bear, Manzano, Sandia, San Mateo, and Zuni Mountains.

Two major pieces of the forest flank I-40 on either side of Grants, near the pueblos and monuments described above. To the northeast of Grants, NM 547 leads some 20 miles into the San Mateo Mountains. The range's high point, and the highest point in the forest, 11,301-foot Mount Taylor, is home of the annual Mount Taylor Winter Quadrathlon in February. The route passes two campgrounds: Lobo Canyon and Coal

Mine Canyon. Hiking, enjoying magnificent scenery, and elk hunting are popular in summer, cross-country skiing in winter.

To the west of Grants run the Zuni Mountains, a heavily forested range topped by 9,253-foot Mount Sedgewick. Ask at the **Grants/Cíbola County Chamber of Commerce,** 100 N Iron Ave. (☎ **800/748-2142** or 505/287-4802), or the Mount Taylor Ranger District (see address and phone below) in Grants, for the *Zuni Mountain Historic Auto Tour* brochure. This describes a 61-mile loop (about a half-day trip) that winds through Zuni Canyon into Agua Fria Valley, to the historic town of Sawyer, and loops back to Grants by way of Bluewater Lake. The route includes more than 45 miles of unpaved road with no gas or water en route. It gives unusual insight into the region's early 20th-century logging and mining activities. It's also a good mountain-bike route.

On the northern slope of the Zuni Mountains, but outside of the national forest, is **Bluewater Lake State Park** (☎ 505/876-2391). At 7,400 feet, this forested recreational site offers fishing for rainbow trout and catfish, boating, hiking, picnicking, and camping, and ice fishing is popular in winter. To reach the park, 18 miles west of Grants, leave I-40 at Exit 63 and continue south for 7 miles.

JUST THE FACTS   For more information about this section of Cíbola National Forest, contact **Mount Taylor Ranger District,** 1800 Lobo Canyon Rd., Grants, NM 87020 (☎ 505/287-8833). For general information about all six districts of the National Forest, contact **Cíbola National Forest,** 2113 Osuna Rd. NE, Suite A, Albuquerque, NM 87113-1001 (☎ 505/346-2650).

A modern road stop on I-40 heading west, 17 miles before Gallup, is the **Giant Travel Center** (☎ 505/722-6655). This is my idea of what a space station would be like. Not only can you get gas here but there's a Pizza Hut, Taco Bell, and A&W Root Beer stand, plus a full restaurant with a salad and hot food bar. There are plenty of pay phones, clean bathrooms, a post office, and a video arcade.

4 Gallup: Gateway to Indian Country

For me, Gallup has always been a mysterious place, home to so many Native Americans, with dust left from its Wild West days, and with an unmistakable Route 66 architectural presence; it just doesn't seem to exist in this era. The best way to get a sense of the place is through walking around downtown, wandering through the trading posts and pawn shops and by the historic buildings. In doing so you'll probably encounter many locals, and get a real feel for this "Heart of Indian Country."

Gallup started when the railroad from Arizona reached this spot in 1881. At that time the town consisted of a stagecoach stop and a saloon, the Blue Goose. Within 2 years coal mining had made the town boom, and some 22 saloons (including the Bucket of Blood) and an opera house filled the town, most of which was inhabited by immigrants from mining areas in eastern Europe, England, Wales, Germany, and Italy.

When the popularity of the railroads declined, Gallup turned briefly to the movie business as its boom ticket. The area's red-rock canyons and lonely deserts were perfect for Westerns of the era such as *Big Carnival,* with Kirk Douglas; *Four Faces West* with Joel McCrea; and *The Bad Man,* starring Wallace Beery, Lionel Barrymore, and Ronald Reagan. These stars and many others stayed in a very Route 66 hotel built by R. E. Griffith in 1937. Today, the El Rancho Hotel and Motel is one of Gallup's most notable landmarks and worth strolling through (see "Where to Stay," below). Gallup's next income generator was trade and tourism. Its central location within the Navajo Reservation and the Zuni lands, as well as its proximity to the ancient ruins at Chaco, make it a crossroads for trade and travel.

Gallup's most notable special event is the **Inter-Tribal Indian Ceremonial** every August. Native Americans converge on the town for a parade, dances, and an all-Indian rodeo east of town at Red Rock State Park. It's a busy time in Gallup and reservations must be made way in advance. If you're not in town for the Ceremonial, try hitting Gallup on a Saturday. This is the day many Native Americans come to town to trade, and the place gets busy. Best of all on this day is the **Flea Market,** located north of town just off U.S. 666. Here you can sample fry bread, Zuni bread, and Acoma bread, eat real mutton stew, and shop for anything from jewelry to underwear. After the Flea, most Gallup area residents native and nonnative alike go to Earl's (see "Where to Dine," below) to eat and then to Wal-Mart to shop.

ESSENTIALS

GETTING THERE   From Albuquerque, take I-40 west (2½ hours). From Farmington, take U.S. 64 west to Shiprock, then U.S. 666 south (2½ hours). From Flagstaff, Arizona, take I-40 east (3 hours). **Gallup Municipal Airport,** West Highway 66 (☎ **505/722-4896**), is served several times daily by **America West Express** (☎ **800/235-9292** or 505/722-5404). There are regular connections to and from Farmington and Phoenix, Arizona.

VISITOR INFORMATION   The **Gallup Convention and Visitors Bureau,** 701 Montoya Blvd. (P.O. Box 600), Gallup, NM 87305 (☎ **800/242-4282** or 505/863-3841; www.gallupnm.org), is conveniently located in Miyamura Park, just north of the main I-40 interchange for downtown Gallup. Or contact the **Gallup–McKinley County Chamber of Commerce,** 103 W. Historic 66, Gallup, NM 87301 (☎ **505/722-2228**).

WHAT TO SEE & DO
A WALKING TOUR OF GALLUP

Gallup has 20 buildings that are either listed on, or have been nominated to, the National Register of Historic Places. Some hold trading posts worth visiting. Start at the **Santa Fe Railroad Depot,** East 66 Avenue and Strong Street. Built in 1923 in modified mission style with heavy Spanish-Pueblo revival–style massing, it has recently been renovated into a community transportation and cultural center, with a small museum worth visiting. Across the highway, the **Drake Hotel** (later the Turquoise Club but now abandoned; renovation plans are in the works), built of blond brick in 1919, had the Prohibition-era reputation of being controlled by bootleggers, with wine running in the faucets in place of water.

From there walk west and stop in **First American Traders,** 120 E. Highway 66 (☎ **505/722-6601**). Here you'll find a warehouse-type place packed with kachinas and pottery. The front has an old trading post feel, even a Sky Chief gas pump. Continue west to **Shi Wi Trading Co.,** 100 E. Highway 66 (☎ **505/722-5555**), where you'll find some finely carved fetishes and lovely jewelry. A jewelry maker works on-site while you watch. Two blocks west, the 1928 **White Cafe,** 100 W. 66 Ave., is an elaborate decorative brick structure that catered to the early auto tourist traffic. Now it's the **All Tribes Indian Center** (☎ **505/722-6272**) with some interesting stone carvings as well as innovative use of stones such as charolite and lapis, and some big fetishes.

Continue west, past a bank built in 1904, to **Indian Gallery,** 212 W. Highway 66 (☎ **505/722-7771**). Here you'll find a bold and lethal collection of knives with elaborate lapis, jet, and turquoise inlay handles, as well as beautiful fetishes and Navajo alabaster carvings. You'll recognize the place by the stuffed deer wearing sunglasses in the window.

Farther west, the **Kitchen's Opera House,** 218 W. 66 Ave., which dates from 1895, has a second-floor stage for all kinds of functions and performances and a first-floor funky **Eagle Cafe** (☎ 505/722-3220) with a long bar and red-upholstered booths and a giant Route 66 sign. This is a good place to stop for a Coke and a burger. Next door is **Richardson's Trading Company,** 222 W. Highway 66 (☎ 505/722-4762), the place to buy and look at saddles, blankets, and rugs. They have two shops, the second down the street at 236 W. 66 Ave. in a brownstone building. A block farther, the **Rex Hotel,** 300 W. 66 Ave., was constructed of locally quarried sandstone; once known for its "ladies of the night," it's now the **Gallup Historical Museum,** open Monday through Saturday 8am to 4pm, worth perusing.

A block north of the museum, at 101 N. Third St., is the **C. N. Cotton Warehouse** (now Associated Grocers). Built about 1897 in the New Mexico vernacular style, with a sandstone foundation and adobe-block walls, it has a statue in front that is a city landmark: **Manuelito,** the last Navajo chief to surrender to U.S. soldiers. Mr. Cotton, a trader who admired the Navajo's bravery, commissioned the statue.

Reverse course, and head back south 2 blocks on Third Street to Coal Avenue. To the west is **Dominics Downtown Cafe,** 303 W Coal Ave. (☎ 505/722-0117), a good place to stop for a bite. Turn west on coal and go a half block to the **Grand Hotel,** 306 W. Coal Ave., built about 1925 as the depot for transcontinental buses on Route 66, as well as a travelers' hotel; it's now unoccupied.

Turn east and backtrack across Third to the **Chief Theater,** 228 W. Coal Ave. This structure was built in 1920; in 1936 it was completely redesigned in Pueblo-deco style, with zigzag relief and geometric form, by R. E. "Griff" Griffith (also built El Rancho Hotel), brother of Hollywood producer D. W. Griffith. Now this is **City Electric Shoe Shop.** This is where the Native Americans go to buy feathers, leather, and other goods to make ceremonial clothing. Known to locals simply as "City Electric," it's name arose because it was the first shop in town to have an automated shoe repair machine.

Just down the street, the 1928 **El Morro Theater** is of Spanish colonial revival style with Spanish Baroque plaster carving and bright polychromatic painting; it's where locals come to see movies and dance performances. Across the street is the **Chili Pepper Cafe,** a good place to stop for a meal (see "Where to Dine," below), or head across the street to the **Ruiz Optical Building,** which has been decorated with Native American kachinas between the second-floor windows. It now houses **The Coffee House,** 203 W. Coal Ave., worth trying (see "Where to Dine," below).

South 2 blocks, the **McKinley County Court House,** 201 W. Hill Ave., was built in 1938 in Spanish Pueblo revival style. The bell tower and upper stories display stylized projecting vigas, while wood beams and corbels define the entry. Indian-motif reliefs, tiles, and paintings are found throughout. Back at the corner of First and Coal, the **Old Post Office** (now TCI Cablevision) is an eclectic mix of Mediterranean, decorative brick commercial, and Spanish Pueblo revival styles. Large carved eagles are used as corbels, and the beams have brightly painted rope molding lines.

GETTING OUTSIDE: A NEARBY STATE PARK

Six miles east of downtown Gallup, **Red Rock State Park,** NM 566 (P.O. Box 328), Church Rock, NM 87311 (☎ 505/722-3839), with its natural amphitheater, is set against elegantly shaped red sandstone buttes. It includes an auditorium/ convention center, historical museum, post office, trading post, stables, and modern campgrounds.

The 8,000-seat arena is the site of numerous annual events, including the Intertribal Indian Ceremonial in mid-August. Red Rock Convention Center accommodates 600 for trade shows or concert performances.

A nature trail leads up into these stone monuments, and makes for a nice break after hours on the road. See "Where to Stay," below for camping information. There's also a playground, horse riding trails, and a sports field.

The **Red Rock Museum** has displays on prehistoric Anasazi and modern Zuni, Hopi, and Navajo cultures, including an interesting collection of very intricate kachinas. There's a gallery that features changing exhibits. In my most recent visit, there was a display of prayer and dancing fans, bold art made with blue and gold macaw feathers. From June through September, corn, beans, and squash are grown outside in a traditional Pueblo "waffle garden." The museum is open Monday through Friday from 8:30am to 4:30pm, with extended hours in summer. Admission is $1 for adults, 50¢ for children.

Also at this site, in early December is the **Red Rock Balloon Rally,** a high point on the sporting balloonist's calendar. For information, call the Gallup–McKinley County Chamber of Commerce (see "Visitor Information," above).

SHOPPING: BEST BUYS ON JEWELRY & CRAFTS

Nowhere are the jewelry and crafts of Navajo, Zuni, and Hopi tribes less expensive than in Gallup. The most intriguing places to shop are the trading posts and pawn-shops, which provide a surprising range of services for their largely Native American clientele and have little in common with the pawnshops of large American cities.

Navajoland ✪ **pawnbrokers** in essence are bankers, at least from the Navajo and Zuni viewpoint. In fact, they're an integral part of the economic structure of the Gallup area. Security systems in Navajo hogans and Zuni pueblos are nonexistent, and banks won't take jewelry or guns as loan collateral, so pawnshops provide such services as the safekeeping of valuable personal goods and making small-collateral loans. Native Americans hock their turquoise and silver jewelry, ceremonial baskets, hand-tanned hides, saddles, and guns for safekeeping. The trader will hold onto the items for months or even years before deeming it "dead" and putting it up for sale. Less than 5% of items ever go unredeemed. For their part, the Native Americans may accept a payment far less than the value of the goods, because the smaller the amount of the loan, the easier it is to redeem the items when they are needed.

If you're shopping for jewelry, look for silver concho belts, worn with jeans and Southwestern skirts, cuff bracelets, and necklaces, from traditional squash blossoms to silver beads and *heishi,* to very fine beads worn in several strands. Earrings may be only in silver, or they may be decorated with varying stones.

Also be on the lookout for bolo ties and belt buckles of silver and/or turquoise. Silver concho hatbands go great on Stetson hats. A silver or gold handcrafted earring, sometimes decorated with turquoise, is a big seller.

Handwoven Native American rugs may be draped on couches, hung on walls, or used on floors. Also look for pottery, kachinas, and sculpture.

Most shops are open Monday through Saturday from 9am to 5pm. Some shops and pawnbrokers in town include those listed above on the walking tour.

For a look at everything from pawn jewelry to Pendleton robes and shawls to enamel and cast-iron kitchenware, visit **Ellis Tanner Trading Company,** Highway 602 Bypass (head south from I-40 on Highway 602 about 2 miles; it's at the corner of Nizhoni Boulevard) (☎ **505/863-4434**); and **Tobe Turpen's Indian Trading Company,** 1710 S. Second St. (☎ **505/722-3806**), farther out on Second Street, a big freestanding brick building full of jewelry, rugs, kachinas, and pottery.

INDIAN DANCES

Nightly Native American dance performances take place at the corner of 66 Avenue and First Street in Gallup, each evening at 7pm from Memorial Day through Labor Day.

WHERE TO STAY

Virtually every accommodation in Gallup is somewhere along Route 66, either near the I-40 interchanges or on the highway through downtown.

MODERATE

Best Western Inn & Suites. 3009 W. Hwy. 66, Gallup, NM 87301. ☎ **800/600-5221,** 800/528-1234, or 505/722-2221. Fax 505/722-7442. 145 units. A/C TV TEL. $64–$98 double; $68–$106 suite. AE, CB, DC, DISC, MC, V. Pets allowed.

Like the Best Western in Grants and owned by the same company, this hotel provides spacious and comfortable rooms, with a bit of a walk to get to some. It's located a few miles west of town, so if you're looking for more convenience, you may want to try one of the others, such as the Best Western Red Rock Inn (see below). The trademark of this property is its huge central atrium courtyard that contains a sitting area at one end, a swimming pool at the other, and skylit trees and plants in between.

Request a room at one of the four corner entrances and you'll avoid trudging down the long hallways. Also request a room facing outside rather than in toward the courtyard, where noise from the pool carries. Though not quite as nice as the other Best Western, more amenities are offered here. Rooms are bright, done with floral prints. Beds are firm, and all rooms have shower massagers. All rooms also have coffeemakers, and the suites have a microwave, wet bar, minirefrigerator, a phone at a working desk, an oversize dresser, and a sleeper sofa in a sitting area.

A restaurant serves breakfast and dinner daily. There is a lounge and the hotel has limited room service, dry cleaning, valet laundry service, a 24-hour desk, an indoor swimming pool, hot tub, saunas, weight/exercise room, video games, guest laundry, and gift shop.

Best Western Red Rock Inn. 3010 E. Hwy. 66, Gallup, NM 87301. ☎ **888/639-7600** or 505/722-7600. 77 units. A/C TV TEL. $54–$99 double; $85–$125 suite. Children under 12 stay free in parents' room. AE, CB, DC, DISC, MC, V. Some pets accepted.

Built in 1990, with remodeling ongoing, this pink stucco hotel offers lovely rooms on the east end of town. The accommodations are average sized, with English-style print bedspreads and dark wood furniture. The beds are firm and each room opens off a corridor and has a sliding glass door for easy access to your car. All rooms have coffeemakers and some have hair dryers and balconies. Each suite has a minirefrigerator, microwave, and fold-out couch; some have jetted tubs. The indoor pool could use some updating, but it does have a sunny skylight and a hot tub and some exercise equipment close by.

Days Inn—East. 1603 W. Hwy. 66, Gallup, NM 87301 (I-40 Exit 20). ☎ **800/DAYS-INN** or 505/863-3891. 78 units. A/C TV TEL. Summer high season $47–$58 double; low season $33–$44. Rates include continental breakfast. AE, DISC, MC, V.

Of the two Days Inns in Gallup, this one is a little closer to town. Built 20 years ago, it received a full remodeling in 1998. The outside has a country barn appearance—two stories, with a pitched roof. Rooms are sunny, decorated in subtle earth tones and light wooden furniture. All rooms are average-sized, have firm beds, coffeemakers, and small, clean bathrooms. The hotel has a nice outdoor heated pool, guest laundry, and large-vehicle parking.

Built in 1990, **Days Inn—West,** 3201 W. Hwy. 66 (☎ **505/863-6889**), is newer but offers similar prices, rooms, and amenities, except the pool is indoors and there is a hot tub.

✪ **El Rancho Hotel and Motel.** 1000 E. 66 Ave., Gallup, NM 87301. ☎ **800/543-6351** or 505/863-9311. Fax 505/722-5917. 100 units. A/C TV TEL. $47–$65 double; $76 suite. AE, CB, DISC, MC, V.

This historic hotel owes as much to Hollywood as to Gallup. Built in 1937 by R. E. "Griff" Griffith, brother of movie mogul D. W. Griffith, it became the place for film companies to set up headquarters when filming here. Between the 1940s and 1960s, a who's who of Hollywood stayed here. Their autographed photos line the walls of the hotel's cafe. Spencer Tracy and Katharine Hepburn stayed here during production of *The Sea of Grass;* Burt Lancaster and Lee Remick were guests when they made *The Hallelujah Trail.* The list goes on and on: Gene Autry, Lucille Ball, Jack Benny, Humphrey Bogart, James Cagney, Rhonda Flemming, Errol Flynn, Henry Fonda, John Forsythe, Paulette Goddard, Susan Hayward, William Holden, the Marx Brothers, Fred MacMurray, Robert Mitchum, Gregory Peck, Tyrone Power, Ronald Reagan, Rosalind Russell, James Stewart, Robert Taylor, Gene Tierney, John Wayne, and Mae West all stayed here.

In 1986, Gallup businessman Armand Ortega, a longtime jewelry merchant, bought the then run-down El Rancho and restored it to its earlier elegance. The lobby staircase rises to the mezzanine on either side of an enormous stone fireplace, while heavy ceiling beams and railings made of tree limbs give the room a hunting-lodge ambience. The hotel is on the National Register of Historic Places.

Rooms in El Rancho differ one to the next, and are named for the stars who stayed in them. Most are long and medium-sized, with wagon wheel headboards and good heavy pine furniture stained dark. Bathrooms are small, some with showers, others with shower/bathtub combos. All have lovely small white hexagonal tiles. Many rooms have balconies.

El Rancho has a lounge, a full-service restaurant, and gift shop. Services and facilities include a 24-hour desk, courtesy car (by request), a seasonal outdoor pool, and guest Laundromat.

INEXPENSIVE

✪ **Blue Spruce Lodge.** 1119 E. 66 Ave., Gallup, NM 87301. ☎ **505/863-5211.** Fax 505/863-6104. 20 units. A/C TV TEL. $26–$32 double. AE, CB, DC, DISC, MC, V. Pets allowed with $10 refundable deposit.

A Route 66 court motel, this place isn't flashy and sterile like some of the newer chains, but the rooms are comfortable and quite clean. It's located at the center of town and has RV and trailer parking. Rooms are medium-sized with nice dark furniture, floral prints bedspreads, and decently firm beds. Bathrooms are medium-sized and clean, with tile showers. The rooms come in a variety of configurations, some with an extra bedroom—good for those traveling with kids. Free coffee and refreshments are available in the lobby.

CAMPING

As in the rest of the state, there are plenty of places in the Gallup area to pitch a tent or hook up your RV. **KOA Gallup** (☎ **800/562-3915** or 505/863-5021) has 145 sites, 50 full hookups (cable TV will cost extra), and cabins. There are grocery and laundry facilities. Recreation facilities include coin games, a seasonal heated swimming pool, and a playground. An outdoor breakfast and dinner are served at an extra cost, and there's live entertainment such as country singing in the summer. Sites cost from $20 for tents to $26 for a full hookup. To reach the campground, take I-40 to the U.S. 66/Business I-40 junction (exit 16); go 1 mile east on U.S. 66/Business I-40.

Red Rock State Park campground (☎ **505/722-1329**) has 106 sites—50 with no hookups and 56 with water and electricity. Tent sites are available. The campground offers dry camping for $8 and with water and electrical hookups for $12. The sites are right against the buttes, though in the spring they will surely be dusty since there's little protection from the wind. Also accessible are a convenience store, picnic tables, and grills. Red Rock State Park, open year-round, also has a playground, horse riding trails, a sports field, and hiking trails.

WHERE TO DINE

Chili Pepper Cafe. 206 W. Coal Ave., Gallup. ☎ **505/726-1401.** Reservations accepted. Main courses $5.50–$11. AE, DISC, MC, V. Mon–Sat 11am–9pm. NEW MEXICAN/ITALIAN.

My Zuni friend Jim took me to this new restaurant right in the center of town. For Gallup, he said, the food was really good. I agreed. It has a casual New Mexican decor with pink and green neons adding a hip feel. There are comfortable booths and big family style tables. The food ranges broadly. I enjoyed the stuffed sopaipilla (with beans, beef, lettuce, tomato, cheese, guacamole, and chile), but was even more impressed with Jim's chicken pasta with roasted piñon-bacon Alfredo sauce. There are also burgers and salads. The kid's menu is very economical, and they offer a "bottomless cup of coffee."

The Coffee House. 203 W. Coal Ave., Gallup. ☎ **505/726-0291.** All menu items under $8. No credit cards. Mon–Thurs 7am–9:30pm; Fri 7am–11pm; Sat 8am–11pm. BAKED GOODS AND SANDWICHES.

This cafe in a historic building in the center of town offers a little big-city flair. Sparse decor with wood tables, under an old tin ceiling is accented by local art shows. The espresso and cappuccino are delicious, as are the scones and muffins. For lunch or dinner, try the turkey and Swiss sandwich or the Waldorf chicken salad.

✪ **Earl's.** 1400 E. 66 Ave., Gallup. ☎ **505/863-4201.** Reservations accepted except Fri–Sat. All menu items under $10. AE, DC, MC, V. Mon–Sat 6am–9:30pm; Sun 7am–9pm. NEW MEXICAN and AMERICAN.

This is where the locals come to eat, particularly on weekends en route to and from trading in Gallup. The place fills up with a variety of clientele, from college students to Navajo grandmothers. A Denny's-style diner, with comfortable booths and chairs, the restaurant allows Native Americans to shop their wares to you while you eat; you, however, have the option of putting up a sign asking not to be disturbed. Often on weekends vendors set up tables out front, so the whole place takes on a bustling bazaar atmosphere. And the food is good. I recommend the New Mexican dishes such as the huevos rancheros, enchilada plate, or smothered grande burrito. There's a kid's menu and Earl's half-portion items for smaller appetites, as well as some salads and a "baked potato meal." Open since 1947, Earl's continues to please.

5 Zuni Pueblo & the Navajo Reservation

ZUNI PUEBLO

Because of its remoteness and its fierce clinging to its roots, Zuni is one of the most interesting pueblos in New Mexico. When the Spanish first arrived, there were approximately 3,000 Zunis living in six different villages, and they had occupied the region for more than 300 years.

One of the main villages amid the high pink and gold sandstone formations of the area was **Hawikuh.** It was the first Southwestern village to encounter Europeans. In

1539 Fray Marcos de Niza, guided by the Moor Esteban (who had accompanied Cabeza de Baca in his earlier roaming of the area), came to New Mexico in search of the Seven Cities of Cíbola, cities Baca had said were made of gold, silver, and precious stones. Esteban antagonized the inhabitants and was killed. De Niza was forced to retreat without really seeing the pueblo, although he described it in exaggerated terms on his return to Mexico, and the legend of the golden city was fueled.

The following year Coronado arrived at the village. Though the Zunis took up arms against him, he conquered the village easily and the Zuni fled to *Towayalane* (Corn Mountain), a noble mile-long sandstone mesa near the present-day pueblo, as they would later do during the 1680 Pueblo Revolt.

At the time the Zunis had a sophisticated civilization, with a relationship to the land and to each other that had sustained them for thousands of years. Today, the tribe continues efforts to preserve its cultural heritage. They've recovered valuable seed strains once used for dryland farming, they're teaching the Zuni language in schools, and they're taking measures to preserve the wildlife in the area that's critical to their faith.

The Zunis didn't fully accept the Christianity thrust upon them. Occasionally they burned mission churches and killed priests. Though the Catholic mission, dedicated to Our Lady of Guadalupe, sits in the center of their village, clearly their primary religion is their own ancient one, and it's practiced most notably during the days of Shalako, an elaborate ceremony that takes place in late November or early December, which is a reenactment of the creation and migration of the Zuni people to Heptina, or the "Middle Place," which was destined to be their home.

ESSENTIALS

GETTING THERE   Zuni Pueblo is located about 38 miles south of Gallup via state roads 602 and 53.

VISITOR INFORMATION   For advance information, write to the Tribal Office, P.O. Box 339, Zuni, NM 87327 or call ☎ 505/782-4481, ext. 401. As at all Indian reservations, visitors are asked to respect tribal customs and individuals' privacy. No sketching or painting is allowed, but still photography is permitted for a $5 fee, and videotaping for $10. Although there is no time when the pueblo is completely closed to outside visitors, certain areas may be off limits during ceremonies, and photography may be prohibited at times.

ADMISSION FEES & HOURS   Admission is free and visitors are welcome daily from dawn to dusk.

SEEING THE HIGHLIGHTS

Most of the pueblo consists of modern housing, so there isn't really that much to see; nevertheless, you'll get a feeling for time gone by if you take a walk through the old pueblo. Make a stop at the Catholic mission, dedicated to Our Lady of Guadalupe. Within you'll find a series of murals that depict events in the Zuni ceremonial calendar. In addition, there are some Native American archaeological ruins on Zuni land that date from the early 1200s, but you must obtain permission from the Tribal Office well in advance of your visit in order to see them.

Today, Zuni tribal members are widely acclaimed for their jewelry, made from turquoise, shell, and jet, set in silver in intricate patterns called "needlepoint." The tribe also does fine beadwork, carving in shell and stone (look for fetishes), and some pottery. Jewelry and other crafts are sold at the tribally owned **Pueblo of Zuni Arts and Crafts** (☎ 505/782-5531).

If you're planning your visit for late August, call ahead and see if you're going to be around during the pueblo's annual fair and rodeo.

NAVAJO INDIAN RESERVATION

Navajos comprise the largest Native American tribe in the United States, with more than 200,000 members. Their reservation, known to them as Navajoland, spreads across 24,000 square miles of Arizona, Utah, and New Mexico. The New Mexico portion, extending in a band 45 miles wide from just north of Gallup to the Colorado border, comprises only about 15% of the total area.

Until the 1920s, the Navajo Nation governed itself with a complex clan system. When oil was discovered on reservation land, the Navajos established a tribal government to handle the complexities of the 20th century. Today, the Navajo Tribal Council has 88 council delegates representing 110 regional chapters, some two dozen of which are in New Mexico. They meet at least four times a year as a full body in **Window Rock,** Arizona, capital of the Navajo nation, near the New Mexico border 24 miles northwest of Gallup.

Natural resources and tourism are the mainstays of the Navajo economy. Coal, oil, gas, and uranium earn much of the Navajo's money, as does tourism, especially on the Arizona side of the border, which contains or abuts Grand Canyon and Petrified Forest National Parks, Canyon de Chelly, Wupatki, and Navajo National Monuments, and Monument Valley Navajo Tribal Park; and in Utah, Glen Canyon National Recreation Area, Rainbow Bridge and Hovenweep National Monuments, and Four Corners Monument.

The Navajos, like their linguistic cousins the Apaches, belong to the large family of Athapaskan Indians found across Alaska and northwestern Canada and in parts of the Northern California coast. They are believed to have migrated to the Southwest about the 14th century. In 1864, after nearly two decades of conflict with the U.S. Army, the entire tribe was rounded up and forced into internment at an agricultural colony near Fort Sumner, New Mexico—an event still recalled as "The Long March." Four years of near-starvation later, the experiment was declared a failure, and the now-contrite Navajos returned to their homeland.

During the Second World War, 320 Navajo young men served in the U.S. Marine Corps as communications specialists in the Pacific. The code they created, 437 terms based on the extremely complex Navajo language, was never broken by the Japanese. Among those heroes was artist Carl Gorman, coordinator of the Navajo Medicine Man Organization and father of internationally famed painter R. C. Gorman.

While Navajos express themselves artistically in all media, they are best known for their work in silversmithing, sand painting, basketry, and weaving. Distinctive styles of handwoven rugs from Two Grey Hills, Ganado, and Crystal are known worldwide.

ESSENTIALS

GETTING THERE   From Gallup, U.S. Route 666 goes directly through the Navajo Indian Reservation up to Shiprock. From there you can head over to Farmington (see section 7, below) on U.S. 64. *Warning:* U.S. 666 between Gallup and Shiprock has been labeled America's "most dangerous highway" by *USA Today.* Drive carefully!

VISITOR INFORMATION   For information before your trip, contact the **Navajo Tourism Department,** P.O. Box 663, Window Rock, AZ 86515 (☎ **520/871-6436** or 520/871-6659).

WHAT TO SEE & DO

Attractions in Window Rock, Arizona, include the **Navajo Nation Council Chambers,** the **Navajo Nation Arts** and **Crafts Enterprise,** the huge new **Navajo Museum,**

Library, and Visitor's Center, and Window Rock Tribal Park, containing the natural red-rock arch after which the community is named.

Nearby attractions include Hubbell Trading Post National Historic Site at Ganado, 30 miles west of Window Rock, and Canyon de Chelly National Monument, 39 miles north of Ganado.

In early September, the annual 5-day Navajo Nation Fair (☎ 520/871-6478) attracts more than 100,000 people to Window Rock for a huge rodeo, parade, carnival, Miss Navajo Nation contest, arts-and-crafts shows, intertribal powwow, concerts, country dancing, and agricultural exhibits. It's the country's largest Native American fair. A smaller, but older and more traditional, annual tribal fair is the early October Northern Navajo Nation Fair (☎ 520/871-6436), held 90 miles north of Gallup in the town of Shiprock.

The Crownpoint Rug Weavers Association has 12 public auctions a year, normally on Friday evening, about 5 weeks apart. For more information, call ☎ 505/786-5302.

WHERE TO STAY & DINE

The place to stay on the reservation is the Navajo Nation Inn, 48 W. Highway 264 (P.O. Box 2340), Window Rock, AZ 86515 (☎ 800/662-6189 or 520/871-4108). The modern guest rooms are comfortable and moderately priced, and the restaurant offers Navajo specialties.

6 Chaco Culture National Historical Park & Aztec Ruins National Monument

These two important historical sights provide insight into the culture of the Anasazi, an advanced Indian civilization that thrived in the Four Corners region between A.D. 750 and 1300.

CHACO CULTURE NATIONAL HISTORICAL PARK

A combination of a stunning setting and well-preserved ruins makes the dusty drive to Chaco Canyon worth the trip. Whether you come from the north or south, you drive in on a graded (and sometimes muddy) dirt road that seems to add to the authenticity and adventure of this remote New Mexico experience.

When you finally arrive, you walk through stark desert country that seems perhaps ill-suited as a center of culture. However, the ancient Anasazi people successfully farmed the lowlands and built great masonry towns, which connected with other towns over a wide-ranging network of roads crossing this desolate place.

What's most interesting here is how changes in architecture chart the area's cultural progress. These changes began in the mid-800s, when the Anasazi started building on a larger scale than they had previously. They used the same masonry techniques that tribes had used in smaller villages in the region, walls one stone thick with generous use of mud mortar, but they built stone villages of multiple stories with rooms several times larger than in the previous stage of their culture. Within a century, six large pueblos were underway. This pattern of a single large pueblo with oversized rooms, surrounded by conventional villages, caught on throughout the region. New communities built along these lines sprang up. Old villages built similarly large pueblos. Eventually there were more than 75 such towns, most of them closely tied to Chaco by an extensive system of roads.

This progress led to Chaco becoming the economic center of the San Juan Basin by A.D. 1000. As many as 5,000 people may have lived in some 400 settlements in and around Chaco. As masonry techniques advanced through the years, walls rose more than four stories in height. Some of these are still visible today.

Chaco's decline after 1½ centuries of success coincided with a drought in the San Juan Basin between A.D. 1130 and 1180. Scientists still argue vehemently over why the site was abandoned and where the Chacoans went. Many believe that an influx of outsiders may have brought new rituals to the region, causing a schism among tribal members. Most agree, however, that the people drifted away to more hospitable places in the region and that their descendants live among the Pueblo people today.

This is an isolated area, and there are **no services** available within or close to the park—no food, gas, auto repairs, firewood, lodging (besides the campground) or drinking water (other than at the visitor center) are available. Overnight camping is permitted year-round. Or, a nice stop on the way back is the **Riverdancer Inn** off State Highway 44, 16 miles on Highway 4 in Jemez Springs (☎ **800/809-3262** or 505/829-3262).

ESSENTIALS

GETTING THERE   There are two entrances, one on NM 57 and the other on San Juan County Road 7900. To get to Chaco from Santa Fe, take I-25 south to Bernalillo, then NM 44 northwest through Cuba to Nageezi. Turn left onto a dirt road that runs almost 30 miles south to the park's boundary. The trip takes about 3½ to 4 hours. Farmington is the nearest population center, and it's still a 75-mile, 2-hour drive to these ruins. NM 44 takes you as far as the Nageezi Trading Post (the last stop for food, gas, or lodging), but the final 26 miles are graded dirt—fine in dry weather but dangerous when it rains, and often flooded where arroyos cross it. (A turnoff at Blanco Trading Post, 8 miles before Nageezi, cuts 5 miles off the trip, but the road is more subject to hazardous conditions.) The park can also be reached from Grants via I-40 west to NM 371, then north on NM 57 (with the final 19 miles graded dirt).

Whichever way you come, call ahead to inquire about **road conditions** (☎ **505/786-7014**) before leaving the paved highways. The dirt roads can get extremely muddy after rain or snow, and afternoon thunderstorms are common in late summer. There's also a 24-hour emergency assistance line at ☎ **505/786-7060,** which connects directly to the homes of law-enforcement rangers in the park.

VISITOR INFORMATION   Ranger-guided walks and campfire talks are available in the summer at the visitor center (where you can get self-guiding trail brochures and permits for the overnight campground (which has nonpotable water, tables, and fire grates; bring your own wood or charcoal). If you want information before you leave home, write to the Superintendent, Chaco Culture National Historical Park, Star NM 4 (P.O. Box 6500), Bloomfield, NM 87413 (☎ **505/786-7014**).

ADMISSION FEES & HOURS   Admission is $8 per car, campsite extra. The visitor center, with a bookstore and a museum showing films on Anasazi culture, is open Memorial Day through Labor Day, daily from 8am to 6pm; the rest of the year it's open daily from 8am to 5pm. Trails are open from sunrise to sunset.

SEEING THE HIGHLIGHTS

Exploring the ruins and hiking are the most popular activities here. A series of pueblo ruins stand within 5 or 6 miles of each other on the broad, flat, treeless canyon floor. Plan to spend at least 3 or 4 hours here driving to and exploring the different pueblos. A one-way road from the visitor center loops up one side of the canyon and down the other. Parking lots are scattered along the road near the various pueblos; from most it's only a short walk to the ruins.

You may want to focus your energy on seeing **Pueblo Bonito,** the largest pre-historic Southwest Native American dwelling ever excavated. It contains giant kivas and 800 rooms covering more than 3 acres. Also, the **Pueblo Alto Trail** is a nice hike that takes you up on the canyon rim so you can see the ruins from above—in the afternoon, with thunderheads building, the views are spectacular. If you're a cycler, there's a special map with ridable trails outlined, an excellent way to traverse the vast expanse while experiencing the quiet of these ancient dwellings.

Other ruins accessible directly from the auto road or via short walks are Chetro Ketl, Pueblo del Arroyo, Kin Kletso, Casa Chiquita, Casa Rinconada, Hungo Pavi, and Una Vida. Backcountry hikes (from 2 to 5 hours) are required to reach some ruins; they include Penasco Blanco, Tsin Kletsin, and Wijiji.

Most ruins are on the north side of the canyon. **Chetro Ketl** had some 500 rooms, 16 kivas, and an impressive enclosed plaza. **Pueblo del Arroyo** was a four-story, D-shaped structure, with about 280 rooms and 20 kivas; **Kin Kletso** had three stories, 100 rooms, and 5 kivas. **Una Vida,** a short walk from the visitor center, was one of the first pueblos built and has been left only partially excavated; it had 150 rooms and five kivas. **Casa Rinconada,** on the south side of the canyon, is the largest "great kiva" in the park, and is astronomically aligned to the cardinal directions and the summer solstice. It may have been a center for the community at large, used for major spiritual observances.

Aerial photos show hundreds of miles of roads connecting these towns with the Chaco pueblos, one of the longest running 42 miles straight north to Salmon Ruin and the Aztec Ruins (see below). Settlements were spaced along the road at travel intervals of 1 day. They were not simple trails worn into the stone by foot travel, but engineered roadways 30 feet wide with a berm of rock to contain the fill. Where the road went over flat rock, walls were built along the sides of it. It is this road network that leads some scholars to believe Chaco was the center of a unified Anasazi society.

The Chacoans' trade network, as suggested by artifacts found here, stretched from California to Texas and south into Mexico. Seashell necklaces, copper bells, and the remains of macaws or parrots were found among Chaco artifacts. Some of these items are displayed in the museum at the visitor center.

CAMPING

Gallo Campground, located within the park, is quite popular with hikers. It's located about 1 mile east of the visitor center; fees are $10 per night. The campground has 64 sites (group sites are also available), with fire grates (bring your own wood or charcoal), central toilets, and nonpotable water. Drinking water is available only at the visitor center. The campground cannot accommodate trailers over 30 feet.

As I said above, there's no place to stock up on supplies once you start the arduous drive to the canyon, so if you're camping, make sure to be well supplied, especially with water, before you leave home base.

AZTEC RUINS NATIONAL MONUMENT

What's most striking about these ruins is the central kiva, which visitors can enter and sit within, sensing the site's ancient history. The ruins of this 450-room Native American pueblo, left by the Anasazi 7 centuries ago, are located 14 miles northeast of Farmington in the town of Aztec on the Animas River. Early Anglo settlers, convinced that the ruins were of Aztec origin, misnamed the site. Despite the fact that this pueblo was built long before the Aztecs of central Mexico lived, the name persisted.

The influence of the Chaco culture is strong at Aztec, as evidenced in the pre-planned architecture, the open plaza, and the fine stone masonry in the old walls. But a later occupation shows signs of Mesa Verde (flourished 1200 to 1275) influence. This second group of settlers remodeled the old pueblo and built others nearby, using techniques less elaborate and decorative than the Chacoans.

Aztec is best known for its Great Kiva, the only completely reconstructed Anasazi great kiva in existence. About 50 feet in diameter, with a main floor sunken 8 feet below the surface of the surrounding ground, this circular ceremonial room rivets the imagination. It's hard not to feel spiritually overwhelmed, and perhaps to feel the presence of people who walked here nearly 1,000 years ago. (Though, be aware that doubt has been cast on the reconstruction job performed by archaeologist Earl H. Morris in 1934; some believe the structure is much taller than the original.)

Visiting Aztec Ruins National Monument will take you approximately 1 hour, even if you take the ¼-mile self-guided trail and spend some time in the visitor center, which displays some outstanding examples of Anasazi ceramics and basketry, as well as such finds as an intact Pueblo ladder, turkey feather woven cloth bound with yucca cordage, and most importantly, an empty case where a warrior's remains had been, but were removed because the Pueblo people felt the display was offensive. Add another half hour if you plan to watch the video imaginatively documenting the history of native cultures in the area.

ESSENTIALS

GETTING THERE   Aztec Ruins is approximately ½ mile north of U.S. 550 on Ruins Road (County Road 2900) on the north edge of the city of Aztec. Ruins Road is the first street immediately west of the Animas River bridge on Highway 550 in Aztec.

VISITOR INFORMATION   For more information, write to the Superintendent, Aztec Ruins National Monument, P.O. Box 640, Aztec, NM 87410-0640 or call ☎ **505/334-6174,** ext. 30.

ADMISSION FEES & HOURS   Admission is $4 per person and children under 17 are admitted free. The monument is open daily in summer (Memorial Day to Labor Day) from 8am to 6pm and in winter from 8am to 5pm; closed Thanksgiving, Christmas, and New Year's Day.

CAMPING

Camping is not permitted at the monument. Nearby, **KOA Bloomfield** (☎ **505/ 632-8339**), on Blanco Boulevard, offers 83 sites, 73 full hookups, tenting, cabins, laundry and grocery facilities, picnic tables, grills, and firewood. The recreation room/area has coin games, a heated swimming pool, basketball hoop, playground, horseshoes, and volleyball.

Camping is also available at **Navajo Lake State Park** (☎ **505/632-2278**).

7 Farmington: Gateway to the Four Corners Region

Farmington has historic and outdoor finds that can keep you occupied for at least a day or two. A town of 36,500 residents, it sits at the junction of the San Juan, The Animas, and the La Plata Rivers. Adorned with arced globe willow trees, it's a lush place by New Mexico standards. A system of five parks along the San Juan River and its tributaries is its pride and joy. What's most notable for me, however, is the quaint downtown area, where century-old buildings still house thriving businesses, and some trading posts with great prices. It's also an industrial center (coal, oil, natural gas, and hydroelectricity), and a shopping center for people within a 100-mile radius.

For visitors, Farmington is a takeoff point for explorations of the Navajo Reservation and Chaco Culture National Historical Park. For outdoor lovers, it's the spot to head to the Bisti/De-Na-Zin Wilderness, world-class fly-fishing on the San Juan River, hiking through the Angel Peak Recreational Area, and even a trip up to Durango to raft, kayak, ski, and mountain bike. Nearby towns of Aztec and Bloomfield offer a variety of attractions as well.

ESSENTIALS

GETTING THERE   By Car   From Albuquerque, take NM 44 (through Cuba) from the I-25 Bernalillo exit, then turn left (west) on U.S. 64 at Bloomfield (45 minutes). From Gallup, take U.S. 666 north to Shiprock, then turn right (east) on U.S. 64 (2¼ hours). From Taos, follow U.S. 64 all the way (4½ hours). From Durango, Colorado, take U.S. 500 south (1 hour).

All commercial flights arrive at busy **Four Corners Regional Airport** on West Navajo Drive (☎ **505/599-1395**). The principal carriers are **Mountain West Airlines** (☎ **800/637-2247** or 505/326-3338), with flights from Albuquerque and major New Mexico cities; **United Express** (☎ **800/241-6522** or 505/326-4495), with flights from Denver and other Colorado cities; and **America West Express** (☎ **800/ 235-9292** or 505/326-4494), with flights from Phoenix and other Arizona cities.

Car-rental agencies at Four Corners airport include **Avis** (☎ **800/331-1212** or 505/327-9864), **Budget** (☎ **800/748-2540** or 505/327-7304), **Hertz** (☎ **800/ 654-3131** or 505/327-6093), and **National** (☎ **800/CAR-RENT** or 505/327-0215).

VISITOR INFORMATION   The **Farmington Convention and Visitors Bureau,** 3041 E Main St. (☎ **800/448-1240** or 505/326-7602), is the clearinghouse for tourist information. It shares an address with the **Farmington Chamber of Commerce** (☎ **505/325-0279**).

SEEING THE SIGHTS IN THE AREA
IN FARMINGTON

Farmington Museum. 3041 E. Main St. ☎ **505/599-1174.** Free admission. Tues–Fri noon–5pm, Sat 10am–5pm.

Small town museums can be completely precious, and this one, along with its neighbor in Aztec (see below), typify why I like roaming through them. They can be celebrations of some tiny part of the world, and yet the truths they reveal span continents. Here, you get to see the everyday struggle of a people to support themselves within a fairly inhospitable part of the world, spanning boom and bust years of agriculture, oil and gas production, and tourism. You'll start in a 1930s trading post, a strong replica, with an old enameled scale, cloth bolts, and even a vintage box of Cracker Jacks. Next you'll get a look at the oil and gas history of the area, including a photo of the lethally named Rattlesnake Refinery, a desolate place in operation in 1925. A blacksmith shop, a dress and millinery shop, and a bit of history on important pioneer businesswomen of the area lead you toward the back room where you'll find geologic displays on such land features as the Hogback near Shiprock, the Bisti Badlands, and Shiprock itself. If all goes as planned, at the new site there will be a nature center and agricultural barn.

Note: The museum's curator assured me that they would be in their new location by our publication date (they have been at 302 N. Orchard St.), but you may want to call before setting out to be sure.

IN NEARBY AZTEC

Founder's Day, held the second Saturday of September, turns the village of Aztec into a living museum with demonstrations, Wild West shoot-outs, and a melodrama. Gunfights are staged at various times, and during Christmastime the village is decorated with farolitos and little lights. There's a parade with carolers.

Aztec Museum and Pioneer Village. 125 N. Main St., Aztec. ☎ **505/334-9829.** Donations accepted. Summer Mon–Sat 9am–5pm; winter Mon–Sat 10am–4pm.

A real treat for kids, this museum and village transport visitors back a full century to a place populated by strangely ubiquitous mannequins. The museum is crammed with memorabilia, but the outer exhibit of replicas and real buildings, with all the trimmings, is what will hold interest. You'll walk through the actual 1912 Aztec jail—nowhere you'd want to live—into the sheriff's office where a stuffed Andy of Mayberry look-alike is strangely lethargic. The blacksmith shop has an anvil and lots of dusty, uncomfortable saddles, even some oddly shaped burro shoes. The Citizens Bank has a lovely oak cage and counter, and it's run by attentive mannequin women. You'll see an authentic 1906 church and a schoolhouse where mannequins Dick and Jane lead a possibly heated discussion.

IN NEARBY BLOOMFIELD

✪ **Salmon Ruin and San Juan County Archaeological Research Center.** 6131 U.S. Hwy. 64, Farmington (P.O. Box 125, Bloomfield, NM 87413). ☎ **505/632-2013.** Fax 505/632-1707. Admission $3 adults, $1 children 6–16, $2 seniors. Summer daily 9am–5pm; winter Mon–Sat 9am–5pm; Sun noon–5pm.

What really marks the 150 rooms of these ruins 11 miles west of Farmington near Bloomfield is their setting on a hillside surrounded by lush San Juan River bosk.

You'll begin in the museum, though, where a number of informative displays range from one showing the variety of types of Anasazi vessels, from pitchers to canteens, to wild plants the Anasazi harvested. Like the ruins at Aztec, here there are two strong architectural influences visible. First the Chacoan; they built the village around the 11th century, walls with an intricate rubble filled core with sandstone veneer. The more simple Mesa Verde masonry was added in the 13th century. A trail guide will lead you to each site. There's a marvelous elevated ceremonial chamber or "tower kiva" and a Great Kiva, now a low-lying ruin, but with some engaging remains such as the central fire pit and an antechamber possibly used by leaders for storage of ceremonial goods.

One of the most recently excavated ruins in the West, the site today is only 30% excavated, by design. It's being saved for future generations of archaeologists, who, it's assumed, will be able to apply advanced research techniques. For now, the archaeological research center studies regional sites earmarked for natural-resource exploitation.

Built in 1990, **Heritage Park** on an adjoining plot of land comprises a series of reconstructed ancient and historic dwellings representing the area's cultures, from a paleoarchaic sand-dune site to an Anasazi pit house, from Apache wickiups and teepees to Navajo hogans, and an original pioneer homestead. Visitors are encouraged to enter the re-creations.

In the visitor center you'll find a gift shop and a scholarly research library.

SHOPPING

Downtown Farmington shops are generally open 10am to 6pm Monday through Saturday. Native American arts and crafts are best purchased at trading posts, either downtown on Main or Broadway streets, or west of Farmington on U.S. 64/550 toward Shiprock. You might want to check out the following stores.

Blanco Trading Post, NM 44, 25 miles south of Bloomfield (☎ **505/632-1597**), is worth checking out en route to or from Chaco.

Foutz Indian Room, 301 W. Main St. (☎ **505/325-9413**). Here you'll find some affordable jewelry, as well as whimsical Navajo folk art such as painted carvings of pickups carrying sheep and chickens. The store also sells wool and leather to artisans.

Hogback Trading Company, 3221 U.S. 64, Waterflow, 17 miles west of Farmington (☎ **505/598-5154**), has large displays of jewelry, rugs, and folk art.

Navajo Trading Company, 126 E. Main St. (☎ **505/325-1685**), is a real pawn-shop with lots of exquisite old jewelry, including the most incredible concho belt I've ever seen, priced at $2,500; you can peruse bracelets and necklaces while listening to clerks speaking Navajo.

GETTING OUTSIDE: NEARBY PARKS & RECREATION AREAS

If you're not quite sure where to explore in this part of the state, call **Suzanne Ninos** (☎ **505/326-2226**), who runs a personalized tour guide service. She has the inside scoop on area petroglyphs, hiking, fishing, golfing, and history. Fees range from $40 per hour to $150 per day, with multiday tours available.

SHIPROCK PEAK

This distinctive landmark, located on the Navajo Indian Reservation southwest of Shiprock, 29 miles west of Farmington via U.S. 64, is known to the Navajo as *Tse bidá hi,* "Rock with wings." Composed of igneous rock flanked by long upright walls of solidified lava, it rises 1,700 feet off the desert floor to an elevation of 7,178 feet. There are viewpoints off U.S. 666, 6 to 7 miles south of the town of Shiprock. You can get closer by taking the tribal road to the community of Red Rock, but you must have permission to get any nearer this sacred Navajo rock. Climbing is not permitted.

The town named after the rock is a gateway to the Navajo reservation and the Four Corners region. There's a tribal visitor center here.

From Shiprock, you might want to make the 32-mile drive west on U.S. 64 to Teec Nos Pos, Arizona, then north on U.S. 160, to the **Four Corners Monument.** A marker here sits astride the only point in the United States where four states meet: New Mexico, Colorado, Utah, and Arizona. Kids especially like the idea of standing at the center and occupying four states at once. There are no facilities.

NAVAJO LAKE STATE PARK

The **San Juan River, Pine River, and Sims Mesa recreation sites,** all with camping, fishing, and boating, make this the most popular water-sports destination for residents of northwestern New Mexico. Trout, northern pike, largemouth bass, and catfish are caught in lake and river waters, and the surrounding hills attract hunters seeking deer and elk. A visitor center at Pine River Recreation Area has interpretive displays on natural history and on the construction and purposes of the dam.

Navajo Lake, with an area of 15,000 acres, extends from the confluence of the San Juan and Los Pinos Rivers 25 miles north into Colorado. Navajo Dam, an earthen embankment, is ¾ mile long and 400 feet high. It provides Farmington-area cities, industries, and farms with their principal water supply. It's also the main storage reservoir for the Navajo Indian Irrigation Project, designed to irrigate 110,000 acres.

Anglers come from all over the world to fish the San Juan below the dam, a pastoral spot bordered by green hills, where golden light reflects off the water. Much of the water is designated "catch and release" and is teeming with rainbow, brown, and cutthroat trout. When I tried casting here, the huge fish swam around my ankles while

I waited for them to swallow my fly. Some of these fish have been caught so many times, they're attuned to the best tricks, which is why expert fishers find this place such a challenge. For more information, see section 1, "The Great Outdoors in Northwestern New Mexico," above.

The park is located 40 miles east of Farmington on NM 511. For more information, call ☎ 505/632-2278.

ANGEL PEAK RECREATION AREA

The distinctive pinnacle of 6,991-foot Angel Peak can often be spotted from the hillsides around Farmington. The area offers a short nature trail and a variety of unusual, colorful geological formations and canyons to explore on foot. The Bureau of Land Management has developed a small campground and provided picnic tables in a few spots, but there is no drinking water available here. The park is located about 35 miles south of Farmington on NM 44; the last 6 miles of access, after turning off Highway 44, are over a graded dirt road. For more information on the park, call ☎ 505/599-8900.

BISTI/DE-NA-ZIN WILDERNESS

Often referred to as Bisti Badlands (pronounced Bist-*eye*), this barren region may merit that name today, but it was once very different. Around 70 million years ago, large dinosaurs lived near what was then a coastal swamp, bordering a retreating inland sea. Today, their bones, and those of fish, turtles, lizards, and small mammals, are eroding slowly from the low shale hills.

Kirtland Shale, containing several bands of color, dominates the eastern part of the Wilderness and caps the mushroom-shaped formations found there. Along with the spires and fanciful shapes of rock, hikers may find petrified wood sprinkled in small chips throughout the area, or even an occasional log. Removing petrified wood, fossils, or anything else from the Wilderness is prohibited.

Hiking in the Bisti is fairly easy; from the small parking lot, follow an arroyo east 2 or 3 miles into the heart of the formations. The De-Na-Zin Wilderness to the east requires more climbing and navigational skills. There are no designated trails here, and bikes and motorized vehicles are prohibited. There is also no water or significant shade; the hour just after sunset or, especially, just before sunrise is a pleasant and quite magical time to see this starkly beautiful landscape. Primitive camping is allowed, but bring plenty of water and other supplies.

The Wilderness is located just off NM 371, 37 miles south of Farmington. For more information, call the Bureau of Land Management at ☎ 505/599-8900.

WHERE TO STAY IN FARMINGTON & AZTEC
MODERATE

Best Western Inn and Suites. 700 Scott Ave., Farmington, NM 87401. ☎ **800/ 528-1234,** 800/600-5221, or 505/327-5221. Fax 505/327-1565. 194 units. A/C TV TEL. $70–$99 double. AE, CB, DC, DISC, MC, V. Small pets accepted.

This is where my brother stays when he's doing business in Farmington. Built in 1976 and remodeled in 1996, it provides spacious rooms and good amenities, though you have to like to walk, since the rooms are built around a huge quadrangle with an indoor pool in a sunny, plant-filled courtyard at the center. Request a room at one of the four corner entrances and you'll avoid trudging down the long hallways. Also request a room facing outside rather than in toward the courtyard, where noise from the pool carries. Though not quite as nice as the Holiday Inn (see below), this is a good choice for wintertime, when you can enjoy the courtyard. Rooms are bright, done in with floral prints, with textured wallpaper with Aztec trim. Beds are firm, and all rooms have coffeemakers and minirefrigerators, and the suites have a microwave, wet bar, an extra phone at a desk, an iron and ironing board, and a sleeper sofa in a sitting area. Best of all, the hotel is steps away from the Riverwalk, a great place to get your morning or evening exercise.

The hotel's restaurant, the Riverwalk Patio and Grille, offers a wide selection of New Mexican and Southwest Italian cuisine. Rookie's Sports Bar, which features pool tables and televised sporting events and specials, always offers a drink special. Other amenities include room service during restaurant hours, valet laundry, 24-hour guest services, heated indoor pool, Jacuzzi, saunas, complimentary in-room movies, fitness facility, video arcade, and guest laundry.

Holiday Inn of Farmington. 600 E. Broadway at Scott Ave., Farmington, NM 87401. ☎ **800/HOLIDAY,** 888/327-9812, or 505/327-9811. Fax 505/325-2288. 155 units. A/C TV TEL. $63–$75 double; $75–$99 suite. AE, CB, DC, DISC, JCB, MC, V. Pets are accepted.

Your best bet is to choose this hotel for the summer when you can take advantage of the lovely outdoor heated pool, and stay at the Best Western (see above) in winter where the indoor pool and atrium will transport you to the tropics.

Built in 1972 and remodeled in 1997–98, it has a similar quadrangle style as the Best Western, with long walks to your room, unless you request to stay near one of the entrances. The rooms here are a little narrower than the Best Western, but they do have more amenities. As well as a coffeemaker, each has a hair dryer, iron, and ironing board. Many rooms have a sliding glass door leading out to a walkway bordered by grass. My mother's room was burgled here once, so be sure to check the latch well when you leave your room. Suites have a sleeper sofa, stereo, and a big TV.

The Brass Apple Restaurant is open daily for breakfast, lunch, and dinner and offers Southwestern and continental cuisine. The Sportz Club Lounge, also open daily, has many TV monitors, two of them big screens. The hotel provides room service during restaurant hours, valet laundry, 24-hour desk, an outdoor swimming pool, sauna, hot tub, and fitness center.

INEXPENSIVE

✪ **Anasazi Inn.** 903 W. Main St., Farmington, NM 87401. ☎ **505/325-4564.** 74 units. A/C TV TEL. $40 single or double; $48–$55 suite. AE, CB, DC, DISC, MC, V.

Don't be misled by the outside of this aging two-story stucco hotel on the west end of town. Inside, the medium-size rooms are clean and well kept. Though there's been no remodeling within the past few years, the furnishings are holding up well, with only the carpet showing age. The rooms have oak-style furniture and fairly soft beds. The bathrooms are also average-sized with 1950s tile in excellent condition. Be aware that main thoroughfares on both sides of the motel contribute noise to the rooms, though the area does quiet down some at night.

The dining room serves a Mexican buffet that's draws locals. There's a courtesy car and a gift shop. Laundry service available and there's free coffee in lobby.

✪ **Enchantment Lodge.** 1800 W. Aztec Blvd., Aztec, NM 87410. ☎ **800/847-2194** for reservations only, or 505/334-6143. Fax 505/334-6144. 20 units. A/C TV TEL. $44–$52 double. Rates include continental breakfast. AE, DC, DISC, MC, V.

Lots of fishers, including my mother and me when we go angling on the San Juan, enjoy this pleasant and very reasonable small roadside motel, marked by pink neon lights, reminiscent of the late 1950s when it was built. With remodeling ongoing, the rooms are medium-sized and simple, with floral print bedspreads and 1950s tile in the bathrooms. A small pool has recently been refurbished. All rooms have minirefrigerators, and a guest laundry is available. Request a room to the back to avoid highway noise.

Motel 6 Farmington. 1600 Bloomfield Hwy. at Cedar St., Farmington, NM 87401. ☎ **505/326-4501.** 134 units. A/C TV TEL. $35 double; kids 17 and under stay free in parents' room. AE, DC, DISC, MC, V. One small pet allowed free.

If you like to sleep and go and don't mind cold efficiency, this is your place. Rooms here are small and basic, with two double beds, or one queen, a desk, and TV. Bathrooms are also small, with a corner shower, but quite clean. In the back a nice-sized pool (open seasonally) is surrounded by grass. Ask for a north-facing room for more quiet. There's a guest laundry. The motel is located just east of downtown Farmington on U.S. Highway 64.

BED & BREAKFASTS

Casa Blanca. 505 E. LaPlata St., Farmington, NM 87401. ☎ **505/327-6503.** Fax 505/326-5680. 4 units. A/C TV TEL. $75–$135 double. AE, DISC, MC, V.

Located within a residential neighborhood just a few blocks from the shops and restaurants of Main Street, this inn provides a touch of elegance that you wouldn't expect to find in Farmington. Run by professional innkeepers Mary and Jim Fabian, the inn combines old-world elegance with contemporary amenities. It was built in the 1940s by a wealthy family that traded with the Navajos.

Now, each of the spacious rooms has its own bent, from one with a four-poster pencil-post bed (the Aztec) to another with an elaborate hand-carved headboard and French doors leading out to a lushly landscaped yard (the Caballero). All have very comfortable beds and nice bathrooms, each with a tub, except for the Aztec, which has a shower. Breakfasts include such delicacies as peach melba waffles and eggs Benedict. Mine started with a fruit plate that included mango, blueberries, strawberries, and yogurt.

✪ Kokopelli's Cave. 206 W. 38th St., Farmington, NM 87401. ☎ **505/325-7855.** Fax 505/325-9671. www.bbonline.com/nm/kokopelli. 1 unit. TV TEL. $175, double; $210 for 3–4 people. Closed Dec–Feb. AE, MC, V.

After a long day of sightseeing, I lay on a queen bed under 200 feet of sandstone, listening to Beethoven, with a sliding glass door open to a view hundreds of feet down to a river snaking across a valley. It began to rain, slow big drops that made the air smell like wet sage. It suddenly struck me: I was staying in a cave. I can't quite stress how cool an experience it was.

Here's the story: Retired geologist Bruce Black wanted to build an office in a cave, so he gave some laid-off Grants miners $20,000 to bore as deeply as they could into the side of a cliff face. This luxury apartment was the result. Through time it worked better as a living space than a work space, and that is what it remains. Built in a semi-circle, both the entry hall and the bedroom have wide sliding glass doors leading to little balconies beyond which the cliff face drops hundreds of feet below. This really is a cliff dwelling, one that you must hike a bit down to, though there are good guardrails to guide you.

The apartment is laid out around a broad central pillar, and the ceilings and walls are thick, undulating stone. There's a stove, refrigerator, coffeemaker, microwave, and washer/dryer. The dining area has a table and six chairs set on flagstone next to a mock kiva, used for storage. The living room has a TV, VCR, and futon couch. This and the bedroom are on a carpet-covered platform that provides an elegant feel. Best of all is the bathroom. Water pours off rocks above, creating a waterfall, and if that's not enough, there are Jacuzzi jets in the flagstone tub. Golden eagles nest in the area, and ring-tail cats tend to wander onto the balcony. There's a grill outside, as well as chairs where you can relax in the mornings and evenings. Fruit, juice, coffee, and pastries make up a self-serve breakfast.

Miss Gail's Inn. 300 S. Main, Aztec, NM 87410. ☎ **888/534-3452** or 505/334-3452. Fax 505/334-9664. TV. $60–$70 double. Rates include full or continental breakfast. AE, DISC, MC, V.

This turn-of-the-century brick inn at the center of Aztec provides a reasonably priced B&B stay in comfy charm. Owned and run by Gail Aspromonte, it has a Victorian Old West feel with smallish rooms, each with bright furnishings and plenty of light. The bathrooms are mostly small and not modernized with an eye for history, but they are functional. A few have kitchenettes with various combinations of amenities such as microwaves, minirefrigerators, and stoves. This is an especially reasonable and comfortable option if you're planning to tour the area for a few days and want a home base. Durango is less than an hour away and accommodations there are *much* more expensive. Best of all is the restaurant which is reviewed below.

CAMPING

Downs RV Park (☎ **800/582-6427**) has 35 sites, 31 of them with full hookups. Phone hookups and tenting space are also available. The park has a playground, arcade and game room, and laundry facilities. It's located 5 miles west of Farmington on U.S. 64. **Mom and Pop RV Park** (☎ **800/748-2807**) has 42 sites, 32 full hookups, tenting, a recreation room/area, and a toy soldier shop. The sites are a bit desolate around an asphalt central area, but there is a little grassy spot at the office with an incredible electric train set that Pop runs at certain times during the day. Mom and Pop RV park is located at 901 Illinois Ave. in Farmington (just off U.S. 64).

WHERE TO DINE IN FARMINGTON & AZTEC

✪ **3 Rivers Eatery & Brewhouse.** 101 E. Main St., Farmington. ☎ **505/324-2187.** Main courses $5–$17. AE, MC, V. Mon–Sat 10am–10pm; Sun 10am–8pm. AMERICAN.

After a long day of traveling, I went to this brew pub on an elegant corner in the center of downtown. One sip of their Badlands Pale Ale, and I was ready to recommend the place. It's set in a big two-story brick building that once housed the Farmington Drug Store and the Farmington *Times-Hustler* newspaper. Wood floors and framed vintage advertisements for Philip Morris cigarettes and American Motorcycles add to the charm. I'd most recommend the burgers that come in a variety of flavors, from grilled onion and Swiss to jack and green chile. The garden burger was excellent. You'll also find barbecue pork ribs, steaks, and seafood. The grilled swordfish is good but needed more lemon. The waiter brought me another beer flavor to sample, Arroyo Amber Ale, which I liked as well as the pale ale. For dessert, try the brewmaster's root beer float.

Giovanni's. In Miss Gail's Inn, 300 S. Main St., Aztec. ☎ **505/334-3452.** Main courses under $7. AE, DISC, MC, V. Mon–Fri 11am–2pm, with plans to open for dinner Fri–Sat. STEAKS/SEAFOOD.

After perusing the Aztec ruins, I found myself tired and hungry. I asked a few people if there was anyplace to eat, and each seemed to withhold a broad smile while saying Giovanni's. Located at Miss Gail's Inn, the restaurant is the cherished spot of Gail Aspromonte, where excellent soups and sandwiches are served for lunch during the week. The room is made of aged brick, with country tables, and some Victorian flower wreaths on the walls. My choice for the day was chicken marsala soup (broth-based with mushrooms, carrots, and big chunks of chicken cooked in wine). The alternative was a grilled ham sandwich on homemade bread with mozzarella and tomatoes. I also had a cucumber and tomato salad with raspberry vinaigrette. While eating I listened to Aztec locals at nearby tables talk about school board meetings and their gardens. For dessert, try a big slice of pie (cherry when I was there) or other delicacies such as German chocolate cake.

K. B. Dillon's. 101 W. Broadway, at Orchard Ave., Farmington. ☎ **505/325-0222.** Reservations recommended. Main courses $11–$20; lunch $4–$14. AE, MC, V. Mon–Fri 11am–10:30pm; Sat 5:30–10:30pm. STEAKS/SEAFOOD.

This is a shadowy place well suited for those who want to retreat from life to a rustic old-time atmosphere. Resin-coated pine tables are well spaced and ferns hang in the skylights. A big-screen TV and a number of smaller TVs light up whenever a game is on. There are volleyball trophies and a dartboard too. Be aware that it really is a bar, and on busy nights such as Friday it can get smoky.

The menu includes lots of sandwiches, steaks, and even lobster (at night). Chicken à la Dillon (a sautéed breast topped with fresh tomato, avocado, and melted provolone cheese) is a local favorite; as is fresh mountain trout amandine, Cajun, or Oscar. My brother and I enjoyed a light lunch here recently that included a Spanish chicken soup and an inventive salad (with kidney beans and lots of veggies). The restaurant has a full bar.

Señor Pepper's. Municipal Airport, 1400 W. Navajo, Farmington. ☎ **505/327-0436.** Main courses $6–$16. AE, DISC, MC, V. Daily 6am–10pm. MEXICAN.

Go *to* an airport to eat? I must admit I was skeptical. But then someone told me the restaurant was written up in *The Wall Street Journal.* Since I'd never considered the *Journal* an epicurean authority, my curiosity was piqued and I headed to where the jets fly. The restaurant has Mexican-style furniture and *piñatas* hanging about. Along one wall are windows so diners can enjoy watching the (mostly small) planes and jets taking off and landing. Frozen margaritas are a favorite, as is the fruity wine drink *sangría.* The chile is flavorful and not too hot. I had mine over an enchilada, though many enjoy a variety of "combinaciones" of tacos, enchiladas, tamales, and rellenos. The menu also has steaks and seafood, and some special "light" dishes such as enchiladas stuffed with crab or shrimp. On Friday and Saturday night at 9pm, you can enjoy live comedy—some acts you may have seen on HBO. So, why was the restaurant in *The Wall Street Journal?* It was listed in an article on successful airport restaurants around the United States.

✪ **Something Special Bakery and Tea Room.** 116 N. Auburn Ave., near Main St., Farmington. ☎ **505/325-8183.** Breakfast $3–$6; lunch $8; desserts $3.50. AE, DISC, MC, V. Mon–Fri 7am–2pm. GOURMET HOME COOKING AND VEGETARIAN.

Ask people in Farmington where to eat and they'll recommend this little shop. In a quaint Victorian home, it has wooden floors and tables and an open, friendly feel. Best of all is the vine-draped arbor-shaded patio in back. Breakfast is decadent pastries, such as a blueberry cream cheese or a spinach and feta croissant, all made with wholesome ingredients. Each day diners have a choice of two lunch entrees such as a vegetable quiche, or a mild Thai chicken served over veggies and rice. Every day there are 10 desserts, such delicacies as blueberry/raspberry chocolate cake or a strawberry Napoleon. I opted for an amazing white chocolate macadamia nut cookie. Believe it or not, amid all this richness are low-fat "heart smart" menu choices as well.

FARMINGTON AFTER DARK: BLACK RIVER TRADERS PAGEANT

Black River Traders, an annual outdoor historical drama, depicts 1910 trading post life in the Four Corners region. Presented in the Lions Wilderness Park Amphitheater (off College Boulevard) against a sandstone backdrop, the drama tells of the struggle for survival by both Navajos and whites as two cultures fought to understand each other. This new play using dance and mime was written by Mark R. Summer. A Southwestern-style dinner is also available. The production company also presents other musicals at the amphitheater. For information and advance ticket sales call

☎ **505/599-1145,** or you can purchase tickets at the gate. Admission to the dinner and show is $17 adults, $15 seniors 62 and over, $15 students 13 to 18, $11 children 2 to 12. The show only costs $10 adults, $8 seniors and students, $5 children. Shows are Wednesday through Saturday from late June to mid-August, with dinner at 6:30pm and the performance at 8pm.

8 The Jicarilla Apache Reservation

About 3,200 Apaches live on the Jicarilla Apache Indian Reservation along U.S. 64 and NM 537. Its 768,000 acres stretch from the Colorado border south 65 miles to NM 44 near Cuba, New Mexico.

The word *jicarilla* (pronounced hick-ah-*ree*-ah) means "little basket," so it's no surprise that tribal craftspeople are noted for their basket weaving and beadwork. See their work, both contemporary and museum quality, at the **Jicarilla Apache Arts and Crafts Shop and Museum,** a green building along U.S. 64 west of the central village on the reservation (☎ 505/759-3242, ext. 274). In the back rooms here I found women listening to '50s rock while they wove baskets and strung beads. Two isolated pueblo ruins, open to the public, are found on the reservation: **Cordova Canyon** ruins on tribal Road 13 and **Honolulu** ruin on Road 63.

Though the area is lovely, there's not much reason to come here, unless you're interested in hunting and fishing. Tribe members guide fishers and trophy hunters, most of whom seek elk, mule deer, or bear, into the reservation's rugged wilderness backcountry. Fishing permits for seven reservation lakes and the Navajo River run $10 per day for adults, $5 for seniors and children under 12. Rainbow, cutthroat, and brown trout are regularly stocked.

Just south of Chama on Jicarilla's northeastern flank is **Horse Lake Mesa Game Park,** P.O. Box 313, Dulce, NM 87528 (☎ 505/759-3442), a 20,000-acre reserve surrounded by a predator-proof fence. At an altitude of around 8,500 feet, this is the home of Rocky Mountain elk, mule deer, bobcats, bears, and coyotes.

Highlights of the Jicarilla calendar are the Little Beaver Celebration (mid-July), which features a rodeo, a 5-mile run, draft-horse pull, and a powwow. The Stone Lake Fiesta (September 14 to 15 annually) includes a rodeo, ceremonial dances, and a footrace. For more information, call ☎ 505/759-3242, ext. 275 or 277.

Admission to Jicarilla Apache Reservation is free and visitors are welcome year-round. For more **information,** contact the tribal Game and Fish office at P.O. Box 313, Dulce, NM 87528 (☎ 505/759-3255), or the Tribal Office at P.O. Box 507 (☎ 505/759-3242).

The **Best Western Jicarilla Inn** on U.S. 64 (P.O. Box 233), Dulce, NM 87528 (☎ 800/742-1938, 800/528-1234, or 505/759-3663), offers decent rooms, though there are better accommodations in Chama (see below).

9 Chama: Home of the Cumbres & Toltec Scenic Railroad

Some of my best outdoor adventuring has taken place in the area surrounding this pioneer village of 1,250 people at the base of the 10,000-foot Cumbres Pass. With backpack on, I cross-country skied high into the mountains and stayed the night in a yurt (Mongolian hut), the next day waking to hundreds of acres of snowy fields to explore. Another time, on rafts and in kayaks we headed down the Chama River, an official Wild and Scenic River, following the course that Navajos, Utes, and

Comanches once traveled to raid the Pueblo Indians down river. The campsites along the way were pristine, with mule deer threading through the trees beyond our tents. In my most recent visit to the village, it was summertime, and I'd just come from Durango, which was packed with tourists, there to hike, raft, and ride the train. Chama was still quiet, and I realized Chama is New Mexico's undiscovered Durango, without the masses.

Bordered by three wilderness areas, the Carson, Rio Grande, and Santa Fe national forests, the area is indeed prime for hunting, fishing, cross-country skiing, snowmobiling, snowshoeing, and hiking.

Another highlight here is America's longest and highest narrow-gauge coal-fired steam line, the Cumbres and Toltec Scenic Railroad, which winds through valleys and mountain meadows 64 miles between Chama and Antonito, Colorado. The village of Chama boomed when the railroad arrived in 1881. A rough-and-ready frontier town, the place still maintains that flavor, with lumber and ranching making up a big part of the economy. Some locals are leery of their town's newfound attention as an outdoor recreation destination. I received a very mixed reception, from a few cold shoulders to some open arms; if your experience is similar, don't take it personally.

Landmarks to watch for are the Brazos Cliffs and waterfall and Heron and El Vado Lakes. Tierra Amarilla, the Rio Arriba County seat, is 14 miles south, and is at the center, along with Los Ojos and Los Brazos, of a wool-raising and weaving tradition where local craftspeople still weave masterpieces; Dulce, governmental seat of the Jicarilla Apache Indian Reservation, is 27 miles west.

ESSENTIALS

GETTING THERE   From Santa Fe, take U.S. 84 north (2 hours). From Taos, take U.S. 64 west (2½ hours). From Farmington, take U.S. 64 east (2¼ hours).

VISITOR INFORMATION   The **Chama Welcome Center,** P.O. Box 306-RB, Chama, NM 87520 (☎ **800/477-0149** or 505/756-2235), is at the south end of town, at the "Y" junction of U.S. 64/84 and NM 17. It's open daily from 8am to 6pm in the summer, 8am to 5pm in the winter. For complete local information, contact the **Chama Valley Chamber of Commerce,** Cumbres Mall, 499 Main St. (P.O. Box 306), Chama, NM 87520 (☎ **800/477-0149** or 505/756-2306).

ALL ABOARD THE HISTORIC C&T RAILROAD

✪ **Cumbres and Toltec Scenic Railroad.** P.O. Box 789, Chama, NM 87520. ☎ **505/ 756-2151.** Fax 505/756-2694. Round-trip to Osier and return, adults $34, children 11 and under $27. Through trip to Antonito, return by van (or to Antonito by van, return by train), adults $52, children $29. Reservations highly recommended. MC, V. Memorial Day to mid-Oct trains leave Chama daily at 10:30am; vans depart for Antonito at 8pm.

If you have a passion for the past and for incredible scenery, climb aboard America's longest and highest narrow-gauge steam railroad, the historic C&T. It operates on a 64-mile track between Chama and Antonito, Colorado. Built in 1880 as an extension of the Denver and Rio Grande line to serve the mining camps of the San Juan Mountains, it is perhaps the finest surviving example of what once was a vast network of remote Rocky Mountain railways.

The C&T passes through forests of pine and aspen, past striking rock formations, and over the magnificent Toltec Gorge of the Rio de los Pinos. It crests at the 10,015-foot Cumbres Pass, the highest in the United States used by scheduled passenger trains.

Halfway through the route, at Osier, Colorado, the *New Mexico Express* from Chama meets the *Colorado Limited* from Antonito. They stop to exchange greetings, engines, and through passengers. Round-trip day passengers return to their starting point after enjoying a picnic or catered lunch beside the old water tank and stock pens in Osier. Through passengers continue on to Antonito and return by van. Be aware that both trips are nearly full-day events. For me, they are a little long to just be a passenger, and not be out in the scenic beauty hiking or skiing.

A walking tour brochure, describing 23 points of interest in the Chama railroad yards, can be picked up at the 1899 depot in Chama. A registered National Historic Site, the C&T is owned by the states of Colorado and New Mexico. Special cars with lifts for people with disabilities are available with a 7-day advance reservation.

WHERE TO STAY IN CHAMA

Virtually all accommodations in this area are found on NM 17 or south of the U.S. 64/84 junction, known as the "Y."

✪ **Chama Trails Inn.** 2362 Hwy. 17 (P.O. Box 975), Chama, NM 87520. ☎ **800/289-1421** or 505/756-2156. 16 units. TV TEL. $50–$85 double, depending on the season. AE, DC, DISC, MC, V.

This white stucco building adorned with chile ristras (decorative strung chiles) incorporates the work of a different artist into the decor of each room. The place is impeccably kept, all rooms with queen-size beds and custom-made pine furnishings. Some units have ceiling fans, gas fireplaces, and/or Mexican-tiled bathroom floors. A redwood sauna is available for guest use.

Elkhorn Lodge. On Hwy. 84, Chama, NM 87520. ☎ **800/532-8874** or 505/756-2105. 33 units. TV TEL. $63 double; cabins $64–$101 double. Extra person $6. Open on a limited basis in winter. DISC, MC, V. Small pets accepted.

This lodge just outside the center of Chama has simple pine cabins that will fulfill your mountain-wilderness-living fantasies. Fairly rustic, the cabins have pine walls and very simple furnishings. Beds are soft and bathrooms are large and quite clean. Plenty of windows let in sunlight and allow views of the bosk bordering the nearby Chama River. Outside the door of each room, on the motel-style porch, are chairs and grills. For the most quiet, request a cabin to the back of the property. There are also some more modern motel-style rooms that are less desirable but functional. The newer units have fake, dark-wood paneling and are medium-sized with clean bathrooms. There is a small cafe and a hiking trail available to guests.

✪ **The Timbers at Chama.** HC 75, Box 136 (off NM 512 to the Brazos), Chama, NM 87520. ☎ **505/588-7950.** E-mail: timbers@cvn.com. 5 units. $100–$150 double. Rates include full breakfast. MC, V.

Quick, make your reservations here before the prices go up. And they certainly will once word gets out about this newly opened luxury lodge set on 400 acres of meadow, with only streams, birds, and elk to disturb your sleep. Designed as a hunting and fishing lodge, the first floor is an elegant great room with vaulted ceilings, a giant stone fireplace, and big-screen TV. Outside is a broad deck with a hot tub and outdoor fireplace overlooking a little pond. The rooms, all decorated in an elegant Montana ranch style, are medium-sized (the suite is large) with heavy pine furniture, views, and medium-sized bathrooms. The beds are comfortably firm and have fine linens. All have coffeemakers, jet tubs, robes, safes, and are decorated with original art. The Bonanza suite has a TV with Primestar, gas fireplace, private balcony, and an extra-large jet tub. The only thing that could impress me more than these amenities is the 10,000 acres of land containing five lakes and three streams for which the Timbers holds a recreational lease. Hunting and fishing guides are available, as are horses for guests to ride, all for an additional charge.

BED & BREAKFASTS

Gandy Dancer. 299 Maple Ave. (P.O. Box 810), Chama, NM 87520. ☎ **800/424-6702** or 505/756-2191. 7 units. A/C TV. Winter $65–$85 double; summer $95–$115 double. Rates include full breakfast. AE, CB, DC, DISC, MC, V.

Located in a 1912 two-story Victorian from the early railroad era, this B&B offers an old-world feel with up-to-date amenities. Anita Dismuke is a gracious host, while her husband, Darryl, is responsible for the renovation and upkeep. His renovation included new fixtures in the bathrooms, which are medium-sized, well equipped, and quite functional. In some ways the Dismukes have gone all out in the renovation, such as putting in solid-core doors to make the rooms quiet. In other ways the place loses charm to functionality; for example, the carpet has an industrial feel. Still, attractive antique beds and bureaus make each room, all named with railroad lingo, unique. My favorite is the Parlour Car. Though small, it has a cozy feel and a view out the second-story window. Larger rooms upstairs (where I recommend staying because the rooms are in the original house) are the Double Header and the Caboose. An outdoor Jacuzzi is surrounded by plants. With such specialties as a fresh veggie omelette with a French pancake and fruit on the side, the large breakfast will hold you until dinner.

The Refuge. P.O. Box 819 (at the west end of 7th St.), Chama, NM 87520. ☎ **800/566-4799** or 505/756-2136. 5 units. $90–$120 double. Rates include full breakfast. MC, V. Kennel provided for dogs.

This newly constructed inn opened in 1996 has the intimacy of a B&B, with the consistency of a hotel. Rooms are medium-sized and range in amenities from the Cattlebaron, with Western decor, vaulted ceilings, and a jet tub in the bathroom, to the Starry Night, with a pine sleigh bed. The whole place has an early American Ranch feel. My favorite is the Cumbres & Toltec, which has an electric train on a loft above the bedroom. All beds are comfortably firm with good linens, bathrooms are roomy, and one room accommodates travelers with disabilities. Breakfasts are served family style in a sunny room, and include such delicacies as frittatas with homemade sausage or sour cream and lemon crepes. The inn will meet special dietary needs and also serves dinner with advance notice. Best of all, the inn's backed by 20,000 acres of wildlife refuge, with fishing, hiking, and cross-country trails right out the door.

Winter's Junction. 241 Maple Ave. (P.O. Box 619), Chama, NM 87520. ☎ **505/756-2794.** 3 units. TV. Winter $69–$79 double; summer $75–$95 double. Extra person $15. Rates include full breakfast. DISC, MC, V. Children welcome.

Grass lawns and gardens of roses surround this 1902 two-story Victorian house, now a small, antique-filled B&B. The feel is cozy with lots of floral prints and lacy curtains. The rooms are standard-sized, with comfortably firm beds, and medium-sized bathrooms. My favorite is the upstairs room, which is sunny with a view. Nice for families is the back room, with a private entrance and an extra bed. A full gourmet breakfast is served, with such specialties as Southwest eggs Benedict with corn casserole and sausage.

CAMPING

At an altitude of 8,100 feet, **L&L Ranch Resort** (☎ **505/588-7173**) is a lovely campground in a scenic mountain setting. There are 42 sites, 12 full hookups, and tenting is available for individuals and groups. Group RV sites can also be requested. Limited grocery facilities, ice, picnic tables, and firewood are provided. Recreation possibilities here include pond and stream fishing, basketball, horseshoes, hiking, volleyball, cross-country skiing, and snowmobiling. L&L is open all year and is 10 miles east of the U.S. 84/64 junction on U.S. 64.

At ✪ **Rio Chama RV Campground** (☎ 505/756-2303), you're within easy walking distance of the Cumbres and Toltec Scenic Railroad depot. This shady campground with 60 sites along the Rio Chama is ideal for RVers and tenters who plan train rides. The campground also offers great photo opportunities of the old steam trains leaving the depot. There are hot showers, a dump station, and complete hookups available. It's open mid-May through mid-October only. The campground is located 2¼ miles north of the U.S. 84/64 junction on NM 17.

Twin Rivers Trailer Park (☎ 505/756-2218) has 85 sites and 50 full hookups; phone hookups are offered. Tenting is available, and there are laundry facilities, as well as ice and picnic tables. River swimming and fishing are popular activities; other sports facilities include basketball, volleyball, badminton, and horseshoes. Twin Rivers is open from April 15 to November 15 and is located 100 yards west of the junction of NM 17 and U.S. 84/64.

WHERE TO DINE

✪ **Cafe Los Ojos.** At the end of the village (P.O. Box 265), Los Ojos 87551. ☎ **505/ 588-7054.** Menu items under $5. No credit cards. Tues–Fri 11am–4pm. SANDWICHES, SOUPS, AND SALADS.

A B&B owner told me to stop here, that the food was incredible. Knowing the village of Los Ojos—darling, with a few century-old buildings, some cows and coyotes— I was skeptical, until I stepped inside. Immediately I detected signs of great civilization: good, dark coffee brewing and an elegant apple pie out on a counter. The cafe sits within the cozy front room of chef Jackie Magaña's adobe house, and on the sunny back patio, which you access through the kitchen. The menu revealed more sophistication: a variety of sandwiches served on bread Jackie imports from Santa Fe's notable Sage Bakehouse. I had a feta cheese sandwich on olive sourdough, with pesto, fresh spinach, and roasted red peppers, grilled. Also on the menu was a mesquite smoked turkey breast with jack cheese on sourdough, and a pastrami and Swiss. Sandwiches come with a choice of chips, salad, or soup. No alcohol is served. If you don't quite hit Los Ojos at mealtime, stop in and get a box lunch.

✪ **High Country Restaurant and Lounge.** Main St. (0.1 mile north of "Y"). ☎ **505/ 756-2384.** Main courses $6–$17; breakfast $3–$8, with a buffet Sat–Sun for $7. AE, DISC, MC, V. Daily 7am–11pm. Closed Thanksgiving and Christmas. STEAKS/SEAFOOD/ NEW MEXICAN.

This is definitely a country place with functional furniture, orange vinyl chairs, brown carpet, and a big stone fireplace. But, it's *the* place innkeepers recommend, and one traveling couple I spoke to had eaten lunch and dinner here every day of their week-long stay. Big sellers here are the St. Louis–style pork ribs sold with the tantalizing moniker of "full slab" or "half slab." The half chicken is rubbed with spices and herbs and smoked with mesquite. Both are served with potato salad and barbecue beans. More sophisticated appetites might like the *trucha con piñon,* dusted in flour and cooked with pine nuts, garlic, and shallots. The New Mexican food is also good. The attached saloon has a full bar and bustles with people eating peanuts and throwing the shells on the floor.

✪ **Viva Vera's Mexican Kitchen.** 2202 Hwy. 17, Chama. ☎ **505/756-2557.** Main courses $4–$12; breakfast $3–$7. AE, MC, V. Daily winter 8am—8pm; summer 8am–9pm. NEW MEXICAN/AMERICAN.

A friend of mine who lives in nearby Abiquiu told me a story of years ago stumbling upon a little diner in Chama run by a woman named Vera. He said she served some of the best New Mexican food he'd eaten. Then one day he went back and Vera's had moved into a fancy new building and the food wasn't quite so good. That's the fate of many good New Mexican restaurants. Fortunately, Vera's had room to decline—a little. The food is still good, tasty sauces over the rich enchiladas and burritos, followed by fluffy sopaipillas soaked with honey. Some complain the chile is too hot, but for me, I say bring it on. The setting is pastoral with fields of gazing horses stretching to the river. There's a porch—*the* place to sit on warmer days. Inside, the restaurant has a vaulted ceiling and typical Mexican memorabilia hangs on the walls, even sequined sombreros. The tables are well spaced and there's a TV in the corner. Beer and wine are served, but the favorite seems to be wine margaritas, frothy and frozen, served in big glasses.

ON THE ROAD: WHAT TO SEE & DO ON U.S. 84 SOUTH

Note: For a map of this area, see "Touring the Pueblos Around Santa Fe," in chapter 7.

Distinctive yellow earth provided a name for the town of **Tierra Amarilla,** 14 miles south of Chama at the junction of U.S. 84/64. Throughout New Mexico, this name is synonymous with a continuing controversy over the land-grant rights of the descendants of the original Hispanic settlers. But the economy of this community of 1,000 is dyed in the wool, literally.

The organization Ganados del Valle (Livestock Growers of the Valley) is at work to save the longhaired Spanish churro sheep from extinction through breeding, to introduce other unusual wool breeds to the valley, and to perpetuate a 200-year-old tradition of shepherding, spinning, weaving, and dyeing. Many of the craftspeople work in conjunction with **Tierra Wools,** P.O. Box 229, Los Ojos, NM 87551 (☎ 505/588-7231), which has a showroom and workshop in a century-old mercantile building just north of Tierra Amarilla. One-of-a-kind blankets and men's and women's apparel are among the products displayed and sold.

Two state parks are a short drive west from Tierra Amarilla. **El Vado Lake State Park,** 14 miles southwest on NM 112 (☎ 505/588-7247), offers boating and waterskiing, fishing, and camping in summer; cross-country skiing and ice fishing in winter. **Heron Lake State Park,** 11 miles west on U.S. 64 and NM 95 (☎ 505/588-7470), has a no-wake speed limit for motor vessels, adding to its appeal for fishing, sailing, windsurfing, canoeing, and swimming. The park has an interpretive center, plus camping, picnic sites, hiking trails, and cross-country skiing in the winter. The scenic 5½-mile Rio Chama trail connects the two lakes.

East of Tierra Amarilla, the Rio Brazos cuts a canyon through the Tusas Mountains and around 11,403-foot Brazos Peak. Just north of Los Ojos, NM 512 heads east 7½ miles up the **Brazos Box Canyon.** High cliffs that rise straight from the valley floor give it a Yosemite-like appearance—which is even more apparent from an overlook on U.S. 64, 18 miles east of Tierra Amarilla en route to Taos. **El Chorro,** an impressive waterfall at the mouth of the canyon, usually flows only from early May to mid-June, but this is a tremendous hiking area any time of year. There are several resort lodges in the area.

About 37 miles south of Tierra Amarilla on U.S. 84, and 3 miles north of Ghost Ranch, is **Echo Canyon Amphitheater** (☎ 505/684-2486), a U.S. Forest Service campground and picnic area. The natural "theater," hollowed out of sandstone by thousands of years of erosion, is a natural artwork with layers of stone ranging from pearl-color to blood red. The walls send back eerie echoes and even clips of conversations. It's just a 10-minute walk from the parking area. The Little Echo trail winds into a smaller canyon where the erosion is industriously working to form a new amphitheater. Some 13 miles west of here, via a dirt road into the

Chama River Canyon Wilderness, is the isolated **Christ-in-the-Desert Monastery,** built in 1964 by Benedictine monks. The chapel is a graceful structure set against bold cliffs, worth visiting if you like to taste solemnity. The brothers produce crafts, sold at a small gift shop, and operate a guest house.

The **Ghost Ranch Living Museum** (☎ 505/685-4312) is a U.S. Forest Service–operated exhibit of regional plant and animal life, geology, paleontology, and ecology. A miniature national forest, complete with a fire lookout tower, illustrates conservation techniques. It's inhabited by 27 species of native New Mexican animals, most of them brought here injured or orphaned. A trail through a severely eroded arroyo affords an opportunity to study soil ecology and range management. The new **Gateway to the Past** museum interprets the cultures of the Chama Valley. It's open from 9am to 4pm year-round, except for federal holidays and a 1-month period in the winter (approximately mid-December to mid-January). Admission costs $3 for adults, $2 for students ages 6 to 18, and it's free for kids under 6; national park passes are honored.

A 2-mile drive from there is **Ghost Ranch,** a collection of adobe buildings making up an adult study center maintained by the United Presbyterian Church. A number of hauntingly memorable hikes originate from this place which gets its name from the *brujas,* or witches, said to inhabit the canyons. World-renowned painter Georgia O'Keeffe spent time at the ranch painting these canyons and other land formations. Eventually she bought a portion of the ranch and lived in a humble adobe house there. The Ranch now offers seminars on a variety of topics open to all.

The **Florence Hawley Ellis Museum of Anthropology** there has interpretative exhibits of a Spanish ranch house and Native American anthropology, and the **Ruth Hall Museum of Paleontology** (both museums ☎ 505/685-4333) displays fossils of the early dinosaur named coelophysis found on the ranch. A lightly built creature, it was very fast when chasing food. It roamed the area 250 million years ago, making it the oldest dinosaur found in New Mexico.

Celebrated artist Georgia O'Keeffe spent most of her adult life in **Abiquiu,** a tiny town in a bend of the Rio Chama 14 miles south of the Ghost Ranch, and 22 miles north of Española, on U.S. 84. The inspiration for O'Keeffe's startling landscapes (many of which can now be seen in the new Georgia O'Keeffe Museum; see chapter 7) is clear in the surrounding terrain. **O'Keeffe's adobe home** (where she lived and painted until her death in 1986) is open for public tours, but reservations are required (call ☎ 505/685-4539 months in advance). The charge is $20 for a 1-hour tour. A number of tours are given each week—on Tuesday, Thursday, and Friday—and a limited number of people are accepted per tour. Visitors are not permitted to take pictures. Fortunately, O'Keeffe's home remains as it was when she lived there (until 1986).

Many dinosaur skeletons have been found in rocks along the base of cliffs near **Abiquiu Reservoir** (☎ 505/685-4371), a popular boating and fishing spot formed by the Abiquiu Dam.

A good place to stay in the area is the **Abiquiu Inn,** a small country inn, restaurant, art gallery, and gift shop, ½ mile north of the village of Abiquiu (☎ 505/685-4378). Especially nice are the casitas in back. Rates are $60 to $130.

Heading south from Abiquiu, watch for **Dar al-Islam** (☎ 505/685-4515), a spiritual center with a circular Middle Eastern–style mosque made of adobe; the small community of **Mendanales,** where you'll find the shop of renowned weaver Cordelia Coronado; and **Hernandez,** the village immortalized in Ansel Adams's famous 1941 photograph *Moonrise, Hernandez, New Mexico.*

A GREAT NEARBY PLACE TO STAY & DINE

✪ **Rancho de San Juan.** U.S. Hwy. 285, en route to Ojo Caliente (P.O. Box 4140), Fairview Station, Española, NM 87533. ☎ **505/753-6818.** 9 units. TEL. $175–$350 double. Rates include full breakfast. AE, DISC. MC, V.

This inn provides an authentic northern New Mexico desert experience, with the comfort of a luxury hotel. Opened in 1994, it's the passion of architect and chef John Johnson, responsible for the design and cuisine, and interior designer, David Heath, responsible for the elegant interiors.

The original part of the inn comprises four rooms around a central courtyard. Five additional casitas have been added in the outlying hills. The original rooms are a bit small but very elegant, with European antiques and spectacular views of desertscapes and distant, snow-capped peaks. All units have fireplaces, private portals, makeup mirrors, hair dryers, Italian robes and sheets, and Caswell Massey soaps in the bathroom. My favorite room in the main part is the Black Mesa, though all are consistently nice. Of the casitas, all quite roomy, my favorite is the Anasazi. It has lots of light, a raised sleeping area, and a jet tub with a view. The Kiva suite has a round bedroom and a skylight just above the bed, perfect for star-gazing.

Each morning, John serves an elaborate full breakfast. In the evenings, a fixed-price dinner is served, and includes four courses; the price ranges from $45 to $95, depending on the wine. The food is eclectic French/Italian/American; such specialties as breast of African pheasant and or sautéed Alaskan halibut are served in the cozy dining room with a sunset view.

A few minutes' hike from the inn is the **Grand Chamber,** an impressive shrine that the innkeepers commissioned to be carved into a sandstone outcropping, where weddings and other festivities are held.

Southwestern New Mexico

The lonely drive from Grants down through Quemado and Reserve to Silver City takes you along excellent but winding roads through the 3.3 million-acre Gila National Forest, which contains one of the nation's largest and most spectacular wilderness areas. For me, ruggedness and remoteness define this part of the state—and make it an undiscovered wonder.

It was and still is a good place to hide out. Billy the Kid lived here; so did Geronimo. You'll stumble upon relics of their past at many junctures. You'll see thousands of snow geese taking flight at the Bosque Del Apache Wildlife Refuge. You can even contemplate the vastness of space at the Very Large Array (VLA), the world's most powerful radio telescope.

Though there are no large cities within the area, the most settled part is down the center of the state where the Rio Grande marks a distinct bosk-rich line. Throughout history this river has nourished the Native American, Hispanic, and Anglo settlers who have built their homes beside its banks. The river land was especially fertile around modern Las Cruces; the settlement of La Mesilla was southern New Mexico's major center for 3 centuries.

West of the river, the Black Range and Mogollon Mountains rise in the area now cloaked by Gila National Forest. This was the homeland of the Mogollon Indians 1,000 years ago. Gila Cliff Dwellings National Monument preserves one of their great legacies. It was also the homeland of the fiercely independent Chiricahua Apaches in the 19th century. Considered the last North American Indians to succumb to the whites, they counted Cochise and Geronimo among their leaders.

Mining and outdoor recreation, centered in historic Silver City (pop. 11,508), are now the economic stanchions of the region. But dozens of mining towns have boomed and busted in the past 140 years, as a smattering of ghost towns throughout the region attest.

Las Cruces, at the foot of the Organ Mountains, is New Mexico's second largest city, with 73,600 people. It's a busy agricultural and education center. North up the valley are Truth or Consequences (pop. 7,500), a spa town named for the 1950s radio and TV game show, and Socorro (pop. 9,000), a historic city with Spanish roots. West, on the I-10 corridor to Arizona, are the ranching centers of Deming (pop. 14,500) and Lordsburg (pop. 3,010).

EXPLORING THE REGION BY CAR

From Albuquerque, follow I-25 south to **Socorro,** which won't take too long, so if you start early you'll have a full day of sightseeing ahead of you. You might notice **Sevilleta National Wildlife Refuge** during this part of the drive between La Joya and Chamizal. It's a long-term ecological research site under the direction of the National Science Foundation, open only to researchers by appointment. When you arrive in Socorro, you might want to spend an hour or so looking around, but the real points of interest are in the surrounding area.

Just south of Socorro on I-25 is **Bosque del Apache National Wildlife Refuge,** where you can see hundreds of species of birds, amphibians, reptiles, and mammals. If you're here in winter, you're in for a real treat. Also nearby is the **Very Large Array National Radio Astronomy Observatory,** which makes for an interesting visit. After seeing the sights in this area, either spend the night in Socorro or head down to Truth or Consequences, our next stop (although your opportunities for food and lodging are better in Socorro).

The main attraction in **Truth or Consequences** is the hot springs; however, other opportunities for sightseeing await you as well. For one thing, this area is excellent for fishing and camping. From Truth or Consequences, take NM 152, which connects with U.S. 180 for a short distance, on to **Silver City.** I suggest using Silver City as a base for exploring the attractions in this area: the downtown historic district and the **Gila Cliff Dwellings National Monument.** You'll probably want to spend a couple of nights in Silver City or at nearby campgrounds. The best way to see this area is either to leave Truth or Consequences very early and head straight over to Gila Cliff Dwellings, or to have a leisurely morning in Truth or Consequences and then explore the sights of Silver City, saving the Cliff Dwellings for the following day.

After seeing the sights in the Silver City area, it's time to head south. If you're a ghost town fan, take NM 90 to **Lordsburg.** It's only 40 miles to Lordsburg, so take your time getting there. You may even want to pass right by town and head over to **Stein's Ghost Town** first before going back to visit **Shakespeare Ghost Town.** However, if you're more into interesting land formations, you might want to skip Lordsburg and head south on U.S. 180, taking some time to explore the **City of Rocks State Park.**

If you've gone to Lordsburg, next drive east on I-10 to **Deming,** about 60 miles. If you've gone to City of Rocks, you'll continue south to Deming. From there, if rockhounding is your thing, head over to **Rock Hound State Park.**

Plan to spend the night in Deming if you're going to spend the entire day poking around Lordsburg, Deming, and the surrounding areas. Otherwise, continue east to Las Cruces via I-10.

In Las Cruces, you'll want to spend time at Old Mesilla Plaza, especially if you appreciate the feel of 16th-century plaza or you're a Wild West fanatic. There's also plenty to do in the way of sports and recreation, so plan on spending a couple of nights here.

From Las Cruces, you can head north via I-25 to Albuquerque, or continue over to Alamogordo (see chapter 12) via U.S. 70.

1 The Great Outdoors in Southwestern New Mexico

Rugged, remote, forested, and fascinating all describe southwestern New Mexico, where few tourists venture—lucky for you if you're looking for backcountry adventure.

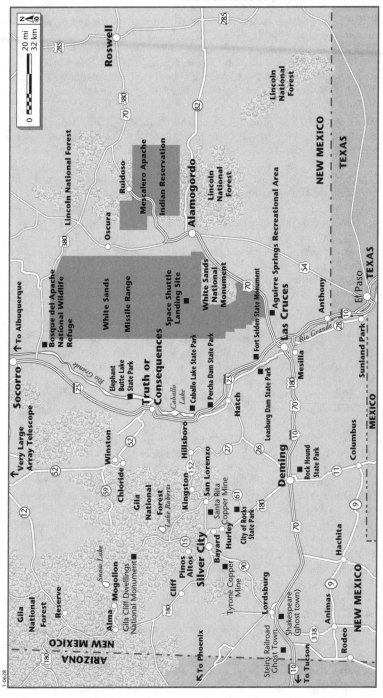

Southwestern New Mexico

N

20 mi
32 km
0

Roswell

285

285

70 380

Lincoln National Forest

82

Ruidoso

Lincoln National Forest

Mescalero Apache Indian Reservation

Oscura

Alamogordo

380

Bosque del Apache National Wildlife Refuge

↑ To Albuquerque

White Sands Missile Range

Space Shuttle Landing Site

White Sands National Monument

Aguirre Springs Recreational Area

54

NEW MEXICO

TEXAS

El Paso

TEXAS

Socorro

70

Fort Selden State Park

Las Cruces

Anthony

10

↑ Very Large Array Telescope

25

Rio Grande

Truth or Consequences

Elephant Butte Lake State Park

Caballo Lake

Caballo Lake State Park

Percha Dam State Park

Mesilla

28

Rio Grande

Sunland Park

Leasburg Dam State Park

MEXICO

Winston

52

Hatch

25

180 70 70

Chloride

59

Hillsboro

152

27

26

Deming

10

Rock Hound State Park

11

Columbus

9

52

12

Gila National Forest

Lake Roberts

Kingston

San Lorenzo

Santa Rita Copper Mine

61

180

70

Snow Lake

Mogollon

Gila Cliff Dwellings National Monument

15

Pinos Altos

Bayard

Hurley

City of Rocks State Park

90

Hachita

NEW MEXICO

Reserve

Cliff

Silver City

Tyrone Copper Mine

Lordsburg

180

ARIZONA
NEW MEXICO

← To Phoenix

Steins Railroad Ghost Town

Shakespeare (ghost town)

338

10

↓ To Tucson

Animas

9

Rodeo

Gila National Forest

180

1-0628

335

BIKING   A popular cycling area is located in the Socorro area at **Bosque del Apache National Wildlife Refuge** (☎ 505/835-1828), where cyclists enjoy the 15-mile loop tour. Bikes are not allowed in the Gila Wilderness, but they are permitted in other parts of **Gila National Forest** (☎ 505/388-8201). Refer to section 9 below for some specific ride suggestions and contact **Gila Hike and Bike** (☎ 505/388-3222) in Silver City for rentals and guidebooks to riding in the Gila National Forest.

BIRD WATCHING   **Bosque del Apache National Wildlife Refuge** (☎ 505/835-1828) is a refuge for migratory waterfowl such as snow geese and cranes. It's located 16 miles south of Socorro. **North Monticello Point** (☎ 505/744-5421), located off Elephant Butte Lake, is a great place to see pelicans, bald eagles, and a variety of waterfowl, while **Water Canyon** (☎ 505/854-2281), 13 miles west of Socorro in the **Cíbola National Forest,** is home to golden eagles.

BOATING   In the Gila National Forest, **Lake Roberts** (☎ 505/536-2250), about 40 miles north of Silver City on NM 15, and **Snow Lake** (☎ 505/533-6231), north on U.S. 180 from Silver City and then east on NM 159, both allow boating. Lake Roberts features motorboat rentals, whereas Snow Lake only permits canoes, rowboats, and other boats without gas motors.

   Elephant Butte Lake State Park (☎ 505/744-5421), the largest body of water in New Mexico, is 43 miles long and popular with boating enthusiasts. Five ramps provide boating access to the lake, and there are also launching areas for smaller vessels.

FISHING   **Caballo Lake State Park** (☎ 505/743-3942), located about 18 miles south of Truth or Consequences, offers great bass, crappie, catfish, and walleye fishing in its 11,500-acre lake. **Elephant Butte Lake State Park** (☎ 505/744-5421), also near Truth or Consequences, is another great fishing location. Look to catch white bass, black bass, catfish, walleye, crappie, and stripers here. **Lake Roberts** (☎ 505/524-6090), located about 40 miles north of Silver City in the Gila National Forest, is prime trout fishing waters.

HIKING   It goes without saying that there's great hiking available in the **Gila National Forest** (☎ 505/388-8201), which has more than 1,400 miles of trails ranging in length and difficulty. Your best bet for hiking in the area is to purchase a guidebook devoted entirely to hiking the Gila Forest, but popular areas include the Crest Trail, West Fork Trail, and the Aldo Leopold Wilderness. One favorite day hike in the forest is The Catwalk, a moderately strenuous hike along a series of steel bridges and walkways suspended over Whitewater Canyon. See section 9 below for more hiking suggestions. Whenever and wherever you go hiking, be sure to carry plenty of water.

HORSEBACK RIDING   If you want to go horseback riding in this area, contact **Circle S Stables** (☎ 505/382-7708) near Las Cruces, open from November to May, **or Gila Wilderness Lodge** (☎ 505/722-5772) in Winston.

HOT SPRINGS   This is hot springs country. For locations in Truth or Consequences, call ☎ 800/831-9487 or 505/894-3536 or see section 4 for my choices of bathhouses. Near City of Rocks State Park is **Faywood Hotsprings** (☎ 505/536-9663), where you can soak in outdoor pools (clothing is required, and massage and camping are available). **Lightfeather Hot Spring** is a clothing-optional spring near the Gila Cliff Dwellings National Monument visitor center (☎ 505/536-2250).

SWIMMING   Swimming is permitted at **Elephant Butte Lake State Park** (☎ 505/744-5421) and **Caballo Lake State Park** (☎ 505/743-3942), but not at some others. Be sure to ask first.

2 Socorro: Gateway to Bosque del Apache & the VLA

This quiet, pleasant town of about 9,000 is an unusual mix of the 19th and 20th centuries. Established as a mining settlement and ranching center, its downtown area is dominated by numerous mid-1800s buildings and the 17th-century San Miguel Mission. The New Mexico Institute of Mining and Technology (New Mexico Tech) is a major research center. Socorro is also the gateway to a vast and varied two-county region that includes the Bosque del Apache National Wildlife Refuge, the Very Large Array National Radio Astronomy Observatory (VLA), and three national forests.

ESSENTIALS

GETTING THERE   From Albuquerque, take I-25 south (1¼ hours). From Las Cruces, take I-25 north (2¾ hours).

VISITOR INFORMATION   The **Socorro County Chamber of Commerce,** which is also the visitor information headquarters, is just off North California Street (Highway 85) at 103 Francisco de Avondo (P.O. Box 743), Socorro, NM 87801 (☎ **505/835-0424**).

EXPLORING THE TOWN
A WALKING TOUR OF HISTORIC SOCORRO

The best introduction to Socorro is a walking tour of the historic district. Start from the parklike **Plaza,** 1 block west of California Street on Manzanares Street. A brochure published by the chamber of commerce includes a map and points out several historical buildings, many on the National Register of Historic Places. Don't bother to take the whole tour, which will eat up a good three hours. Instead, head straight east on Bernard Road, taking note of the **Zingerie House** to the north and other late 19th-century haciendas. Of special interest along the route on the south side of the street is an old home with an amazing display of porcelain flower beds. Vintage sinks, bathtubs, washing machines, and, of course, toilets have been carefully planted with native wildflowers and even tomato plants.

When you reach the **San Miguel Church,** turn around and head back to the Plaza. This is a good time to poke your head into the **Doug West Gallery** (☎ 505/ 835-4445). Renowned across the Southwest for his serigraph landscapes, Doug West also carries in the gallery pottery and jewelry by regional artists. Directly to the west of the gallery is a decent break spot for lunch, a snack or just a cup of coffee: **Martha's Black Dog Coffeehouse** (☎ 505/838-0311).

Heading from the Plaza down Manzanares Avenue you'll pass a few Territorial-style buildings from the mid-1800s, including the **J. N. Garcia Opera House** (take a short jog east on California Street). This will take you by more 19th-century neighborhoods with their rambling haciendas and Victorian homes to the old **Val Verde Hotel.** Though the hotel is no longer in operation, **The Dana Book Store** (☎ 800/ 524-3434 within New Mexico, or 505/835-3434) on the premises has a fine selection of Southwestern books. If it's dinner time, the **Valverde Steak House** (see "Where to Dine in the Socorro Area," below) is a good place to stop.

OTHER ATTRACTIONS IN TOWN

Old San Miguel Mission. 403 El Camino Real NW, 2 blocks north of the Plaza. ☎ **505/ 835-1620.** Free admission. Daily 8am–6pm.

Built during the period from 1615 to 1626 but abandoned during the Pueblo Revolt of 1680, this church was subsequently restored, and a new wing built in 1853. It boasts thick adobe walls, large carved vigas (rafters), and supporting corbel arches. English-language masses are Saturday at 5:30pm and Sunday at 10am and noon.

New Mexico Institute of Mining and Technology. College St. at Leroy St. ☎ **505/835-5011.**

Founded in 1889, New Mexico Tech is a highly regarded institution of approximately 1,500 students, whose course work focuses on science and engineering. Its internationally acclaimed research facilities include centers for petroleum recovery, explosives technology, and atmospheric research. Golfers also visit to play the 18-hole university course, considered one of the best in the state. **Macey Center** has a 600-seat auditorium for performing arts and a gallery of rotating art.

Mineral Museum. Campus Rd., New Mexico Tech campus. ☎ **505/835-5420.** Free admission. Mon–Fri 8am–5pm, Sat–Sun 10am–3pm.

Run by the New Mexico Bureau of Mines and Mineral Resources, this museum has the largest geological collection in the state. Its more than 10,000 specimens include mineral samples from all over the world, fossils, mining artifacts, and photographs.

SEEING THE SIGHTS NEARBY

SOUTH OF SOCORRO   The village of **San Antonio,** the boyhood home of Conrad Hilton, is 10 miles from Socorro via I-25. During the panic of 1907, his merchant father, Augustus Hilton, converted part of his store into a rooming house. This gave Conrad his first exposure to the hospitality industry, and he went on to worldwide fame as a hotelier. Only ruins of the store/boardinghouse remain.

WEST OF SOCORRO   U.S. 60, running west to Arizona, is the avenue to several points of interest. **Magdalena,** 27 miles from Socorro, is a mining and ranching town that preserves an 1880s Old West spirit. In mid-November this little town holds its Fall Festival, which includes a variety of studio tours, artist demonstrations, and a silent auction. If you want to stay in Magdalena I recommend the **Western Motel** (☎ **505/243-0747**). Owned by the mayor and his wife, it's rustic and quaint, with pine walls decorating most rooms. While there, ask the owners about the Murder Mystery Theater staged at various times throughout the year.

Three miles south, the ghost town of **Kelly** produced more than $40 million worth of lead, zinc, copper, silver, and gold in the late 19th and early 20th centuries. Today, the ghost town is a fun site for a hike.

Thirty-two miles north of Magdalena on a dead-end road is the home of the **Alamo Navajo Nation.** On special occasions, the public may be allowed to visit the band of 1,400 Navajo who live on this reservation: Inquire with the Alamo Chapter Office (☎ **505/854-2686**).

Southeast of Magdalena, atop 10,783-foot South Baldy Mountain, the **Langmuir Research Laboratory** studies thunderstorms and atmospheric electricity from June through August. There is a visitor center with exhibits. The research center can be reached by high-clearance and four-wheel-drive vehicles only; visitors should call ☎ 505/835-5423 in advance to check on road conditions.

Fifty-four miles west of Socorro via U.S. 60 is the ✪ **Very Large Array National Radio Astronomy Observatory (VLA)** (Socorro office at 1003 Lopezville Rd. NW; ☎ **505/835-7000**), where 27 dish-shaped antennae, each 82 feet in diameter, are spread across the plains of San Agustin, forming a single gigantic radio telescope. Photographs taken are similar to the largest optical telescopes, except that radio telescopes are sensitive to low-frequency radio waves. All types of celestial objects are photographed, including the sun and its planets, stars, quasars, galaxies, and even the faint remains of the "big bang" that scientists say occurred some 10 billion years ago. You'll begin in the visitor center, viewing a film describing the reason for the VLA, how it came about, why it's where it is, and what it does. In the museum you'll also see how radio waves can be transformed into space pictures and why this is such an effective method of exploration. On the outdoors, self-guided walking tour, you'll have a chance to get a closer look at the massive antennas, which resemble giant TV satellite dishes. Don't miss the whispering display, where you can sample firsthand how a dish collects and transmits sound. Admission is free, and visitors are welcomed daily from 8:30am to sunset.

WHERE TO STAY IN THE SOCORRO AREA

Most accommodations are along California Street, the main highway through town, or the adjacent I-25 frontage road. Most lodgings provide free parking.

Casa Blanca. P.O. Box 31, San Antonio, NM 87832. ☎ **505/835-3027.** 3 units. $50–$70 double. Rates include continental breakfast. No credit cards. Closed June–July. Children and pets welcome.

The ideal situation in this part of the world is to be just a few minutes away from the Bosque del Apache. That way, you only have to get out of bed a half hour or so before sunup in order to get to the Bosque del Apache and see the morning flight. This is the place to stay for this reason. It's a cozy Victorian farmhouse and home to proprietor Phoebe Wood, who, however, doesn't seem thrilled to run a B&B, so don't expect a great warm greeting. The place has a real home quality, though—comfortable, well maintained. The best room is the Crane, with a queen-sized bed and private bathroom. The other two share a bathroom but still offer plenty of privacy. Breakfast is simple and can be eaten early on the way out to the Bosque or upon return later. Fruit, cereals, and home-baked muffins are served in a home-style kitchen. Smoking is not permitted.

Super 8 Motel. 1121 Frontage Rd. NW, Socorro, NM 87801. ☎ **800/800-8000** or 505/835-4626. Fax 505/835-3988. 99 units. A/C TV TEL. $53 double; $100 suite. Rates include a limited continental breakfast with toast and cereal. AE, DC, DISC, MC, V.

This chain hotel just off the highway provides a clean, comfortable stay at a decent price. Built in 1989, renovations are ongoing and a new addition toward the back (worth requesting) is especially nice. All rooms have minirefrigerators and coffeemakers, and half the rooms have microwaves. Facilities include a guest laundry, an outdoor swimming pool, and hot tub. There's a 24-hour desk.

CAMPING

Casey's Socorro RV Park (☎ **505/835-2234**) offers mountain and valley views and plenty of shade. There are 100 sites and 30 full hookups. Tenting is available, as are picnic tables, grills, and ice. A playground and swimming pool are open all year. To reach Casey's, take I-25 to Exit 147, then go 1 block west on Business I-25 and then 1 block south on West Frontage Road.

WHERE TO DINE IN THE SOCORRO AREA

El Sombrero. 210 Mesquite NE. ☎ **505/835-3945.** Main courses $4–$11. AE, DC, DISC, MC, V. Daily 11am–9pm. NEW MEXICAN.

This is a real locals' place. My Socorran friends always request the garden room where tables surround a small fountain. This is some of the best New Mexican food around. I especially enjoy the chicken enchiladas, though my friend Dennis always orders the spinach ones. They come rolled, with beans, rice, and a sopaipilla. Most popular on the menu are the fajitas, beef or chicken, served with rice, beans, tortillas, and guacamole. For dessert, try the churro, a cinnamon sugared stick with vanilla ice cream. Beer and wine are served.

Owl Bar and Cafe. (P.O. Box 215) State Hwy. 1 and U.S. 380, San Antonio. ☎ **505/835-9946.** Main courses $2.25–$10.95. DISC, MC, V. Mon–Sat 8am–10pm. AMERICAN.

A low-lit tavern in a one-story adobe building, 7 miles south of Socorro, the Owl was once *the* place to stop for a green chile cheeseburger. Unfortunately, this is no longer the case. The burgers are mediocre, at best, but it's a decent refreshment stop en route.

✪ **Valverde Steak House.** In the Val Verde Hotel, 203 Manzanares Ave., Socorro. ☎ **505/835-3380.** Reservations recommended. Main courses $6.75–$32.50; lunch $4.25–$6.75. AE, CB, DC, DISC, MC, V. Mon–Thurs 11am–2pm and 5–9:30pm; Fri 11am–2pm and 5–10pm, Sat 5–10pm, Sun noon–9pm. Closed July 4. AMERICAN.

Whenever my dad is traveling south, this is where he stops to eat. The restaurant is housed in the horseshoe-shaped Val Verde Hotel, a National Historic Landmark, built in 1919 in California mission style. The hotel has been converted to apartments, but the public can still enjoy the old dining room. Lunch menu items are simple but tasty: homemade soups, salads, sandwiches, plus steaks and seafood. There's also a lunch buffet, with a different theme every day from Mexican to country-style barbecue. Dinner is more elaborate. House specials include beef Stroganoff and pepper steak Capri (in Madeira sauce). I enjoyed a chile-infused broiled pork loin, with potato, vegetable, and selections from the salad bar. Gourmet Southwestern dishes are also served. The restaurant is about 2 blocks off California Street (Highway 85), directly east of the Plaza. The nightclub is open daily until midnight, and until 2am on Thursday through Saturday, when there's live folk music.

3 Oasis in the Desert: Bosque del Apache National Wildlife Refuge

By Ian Wilker

The barren lands to either side of I-25 south of Albuquerque seem hardly fit for rattlesnakes, much less one of the Southwest's greatest concentrations of wildlife. The plants that do find purchase in the parched washes and small canyons along the road—forbiddingly named hardies such as creosote bush, tarbush, and white thorn—serve notice that you are indeed within the northernmost finger of the great Chihuahuan Desert, which covers southern New Mexico, southwestern Texas, and runs deep into Mexico.

However, to the east of the interstate is the green-margined Rio Grande. In the midst of such a blasted landscape the river stands out as an inviting beacon to wildlife, and nowhere does it shine more brightly than at Bosque del Apache's 7,000 acres of carefully managed riparian habitat, which includes marshlands, meadows, agricultural fields, arrow-weed thickets on the riverbanks, and big old-growth cottonwoods lining what were once the oxbows of the river. The refuge supports a riot of wildlife, including all the characteristic mammals and reptiles of the Southwest (mule deer, jackrabbits, and coyotes are common) and more than 300 species of birds.

The stately cottonwood, mesquite, and willow *bosque* (forest, in Spanish) lining this part of the Rio Grande used to be a familiar sight throughout the Southwest. Sadly, the last century has seen most such habitat disappear. The big trees were heavily logged, and salt cedar (tamarisk) trees, an introduced Asian species, have overpowered the native species; the spectacular bird life—flycatchers and tanagers, among other species—that favored the old bosks has in many cases gone with them. In addition, the rivers have been dammed at many points, which has impoverished the naturally occurring wetlands that migratory waterfowl depend on: The springtime floods would spread the rivers out over floodplains, and as they waned, rivers would meander through new channels each year, cutting oxbows, creating marshes, and enriching the soil.

But in the Bosque del Apache this part of the Rio Grande has enjoyed protected status since 1939, when the refuge was established. An elaborate system of canals, dikes, and water ditches was built to manage the wetlands in the absence of annual floods. In 1986, the U.S. Fish and Wildlife Service decided to make Bosque del Apache one of its flagship refuges, and in addition to refurbishing the water and implementing soil management systems began an ambitious cottonwood rehabilitation program, rooting out the salt cedars and planting thousands of cottonwoods and black willows. The refuge also began hiring local farmers to grow corn, winter wheat, and other crops to feed the wintering waterfowl and sandhill cranes.

The result has been that Bosque del Apache is a very rich, healthy environment for wildlife, particularly for wintering birds. A visit here during the peak winter season—from November through March—is one of the most consistently thrilling wildlife spectaculars you can see anywhere in the Lower 48. Bosque del Apache is, you might say, the LAX of the Central Flyway, one of four paths that migratory birds follow every year between their summer breeding grounds in the tundral north and wintering grounds in the southern United States, Mexico, even as far away as South America—and many of these birds either stop over here to recharge their batteries or settle down for the winter.

It is not enough to say that there are hundreds of species of birds on hand. The wonder is in the sheer numbers of them: In early December the refuge may harbor as many as 45,000 snow geese, 57,000 ducks of many different species, and 18,000 sandhill cranes—huge, ungainly birds that nonetheless have a special majesty in flight, pinkish in the sun at dawn or dusk. There are also plenty of raptors about—numerous red-tailed hawks and northern harriers (sometimes called marsh hawks), Cooper's hawks and kestrels, and even bald and golden eagles—as well as Bosque del Apache's many year-round avian residents: pheasants and quail, wild turkeys, and much-mythologized roadrunners (El Paisano, in Mexican folklore). The interest of experienced birders will be whetted by the presence of Mexican mallards, Chihuahuan ravens, burrowing owls, rare grebes, beautiful, long-billed American avocets, and especially whooping cranes (a very few remain from an experiment to imprint the migratory path of sandhills on whoopers). Everyone will be mesmerized by the huge societies of sandhills, ducks, and geese, going about their daily business of feeding, gabbling, quarreling, honking, and otherwise making an immense racket.

The refuge has a 15-mile auto tour loop, which you should drive very slowly; the south half of the loop travels past numerous water impoundments, where the majority of the ducks and geese hang out, and the north half has the meadows and farmland, where you'll see the roadrunners and other land birds, and where the cranes and geese feed from midmorning through the afternoon.

A few special experiences bear further explanation. Dawn is definitely the best time to be here—songbirds are far more active in the first hours of the day, and the cranes and geese will fly to the fields very early. This last is not to be missed: On my visit I was watching the geese spread across tens of acres of marsh, upwards of 30,000 birds making their characteristic hullabaloo, when as if on some mysterious cue, on the far edge of the mass, the geese began to take flight. It was as if a tsunami of wings was building toward me—it took the huge flock fully 3 minutes to get aloft, during which the sound of beating wings grew to a quite deafening roar. (Perhaps I should also add that when 30,000 birds fly over your head, don't be surprised when a foul rain starts to fall.)

Ducks, in their many species and numerous eccentric habits, are a lot of fun to watch. Try to pick out the different species: In addition to good old mallards, you'll also see green-winged teal, whose brown heads are cut by a marvelously iridescent bright-green stripe; shovelers, with an iridescent green head and comically long and broad bill; goldeneyes and buffleheads, whose round, puffy, elaborately plumaged heads defy description; wood ducks, perhaps the most beautiful of ducks, with intricately patterned and colored plumage; and diminutive ruddy ducks, which break up their placid paddle round the ponds with sudden dives for food—and come up so far away you'll think they simply disappeared.

Don't despair if you can't be at the Bosque del Apache during the prime winter months, for it's a special place any time of year. By April, the geese and ducks have flown north, and the refuge drains the water impoundments to allow the marsh plants to regenerate; the resulting mud flats are an ideal feeding ground for the migrating shorebirds that arrive in April and May. You'll see many species of sandpipers, black-necked stilts, and yellowlegs. Summer sees numerous nesting wading birds—ibises, great-blue and green herons, and snowy egrets—along with a cormorant rookery, and plenty of songbirds: great-tailed grackles, say's phoebes, and brilliantly colored common yellowthroat, wilson's warblers, and summer tanagers. During late summer and early fall, the refuge hosts a number of migratory American white pelicans—a huge bird, with a wingspan as broad as 9½ feet.

JUST THE FACTS   The Bosque del Apache is about a 1½-hour drive from Albuquerque. Follow I-25 for 9 miles south of Socorro, then take the San Antonio exit. At the main intersection of San Antonio, turn south onto State Highway 1. In 3 miles you'll be on refuge lands, and another 4 miles will bring you to the excellent visitor center, which has a small museum with interpretive displays and a large shelf of field guides, natural histories, and other books of interest for visitors to New Mexico. The visitor center is open from 7:30am to 4pm Monday through Friday, and on weekends 8am to 4:30pm. The refuge itself is open daily year-round from 1 hour before sunrise to 1 hour after sunset. Admission is $3 per vehicle. For more information, write **Bosque del Apache NWR,** P.O. Box 1246, Socorro, NM 87801 (☎ **505/835-1828**).

4 Truth or Consequences

Originally known as Hot Springs, after the therapeutic mineral springs bubbling up near the river, the town took the name Truth or Consequences—best known as "T or C"—in 1950. That was the year that Ralph Edwards, producer of the popular radio and television program *Truth or Consequences,* began his weekly broadcast with these words: "I wish that some town in the United States liked and respected our show so much that it would like to change its name to Truth or Consequences." The reward to any city willing to do so was to become the site of the 10th-anniversary broadcast of the program, which would put it on the national map in a big way. The locals voted for the name change, which has survived three protest elections over the years.

Although the TV program was canceled decades ago, Ralph Edwards, now in his 80s, continues to return for the annual **Truth or Consequences Fiesta,** the first weekend of May. Another popular annual festival is Geronimo Days, the first weekend of October. Despite its festive roots, I find T or C depressing and forlorn and wouldn't recommend a very long stay here. Its economy struggles and even many of the hot springs need serious updating.

ESSENTIALS

GETTING THERE   From Albuquerque take I-25 south (2½ hours). From Las Cruces take I-25 north (1¼ hours). For information on private flights and charters, call Enchantment Aviation at the **Truth or Consequences Municipal Airport,** Old North Highway 85 (☎ **505/894-6199**).

VISITOR INFORMATION   The **visitor information center** is at the corner of Main Street (Business Loop 25) and Foch Street in downtown Truth or Consequences. It is administered by the **Truth or Consequences/Sierra County Chamber of Commerce,** P.O. Box 31, Truth or Consequences, NM 87901 (☎ **800/831-9487** or 505/894-3536).

CITY LAYOUT   This year-round resort town and retirement community of 7,500 is spread along the Rio Grande between Elephant Butte and Caballo reservoirs, two of the three largest bodies of water in the state. Business Loop 25 branches off from I-25 to wind through the city, splitting into Main Street (one way west) and South Broadway (one way east) in the downtown area. Third Avenue connects T or C with the Elephant Butte resort community, 5 miles east.

TAKING THE WATERS AT THE HISTORIC HOT SPRINGS

Truth or Consequences' "original" attraction is its hot springs. The entire downtown area is located over a table of odorless hot mineral water, 98° to 115°F, that bubbles to the surface through wells or pools. The first bathhouse was built in the 1880s; most of the half dozen historic spas operating today date from the 1930s. Generally open from morning to early evening, these spas welcome visitors for soaks and massages. Baths of 20 minutes or longer start at $3 per person.

The chamber of commerce has information on all the local spas (see "Visitor Information," above). Among them is **Sierra Grande Lodge and Health Spa,** 501 McAdoo St. (☎ **505/894-6976**), where Geronimo himself is rumored to have taken a break. **Artesian Bath House,** 312 Marr St. (☎ **505/894-2684**), has an RV park on the premises. I highly recommend the ✪ **Hay-Yo-Kay Hot Springs,** 300 Austin St. (☎ **505/894-2228**). Recently renovated, it has natural-flow pools (versus tubs filled with spring water). The tub-rooms are private and gracefully tiled.

✪ **Geronimo Springs Museum.** 211 Main St. ☎ **505/894-6600.** Admission $2 adults, $1 students; family rates available. Mon–Sat 9am–5pm.

Outside the museum is Geronimo's Spring, where the great Apache shaman is said to have taken his warriors to bathe their battle wounds. Turtleback Mountain, looming over the Rio Grande east of the city, is believed to have been sacred to Native Americans.

Exhibits include prehistoric Mimbres pottery (A.D. 950–1250); the Spanish Heritage Room, featuring artifacts of the first families of Sierra County; and artists' work, including historical murals and sculptured bronzes. Exhibits in the other rooms feature army forts and mining towns; the construction of Elephant Butte Dam; local history, featuring photos and artifacts; Native American artifacts, both prehistoric and of more recent culture; the story of ranching and farming in the county; and the rise and fall of mining camps and cattle towns. An authentic miner's cabin has been moved here from the nearby mountains. The Ralph Edwards Wing contains the history and highlights of the annual fiestas, and celebrates the city's name change. The museum is geothermally heated.

GETTING OUTSIDE

Elephant Butte Lake State Park encompasses New Mexico's largest body of water, with 36,500 lake surface acres. It is one of the most popular state parks in New Mexico, attracting water-sports enthusiasts and fishers from throughout the south and central regions of the state. Fishing for white bass, black bass, catfish, walleye, crappie, and stripers goes on all year long. Trout are stocked in the Rio Grande below Elephant Butte Dam. The park has sandy beaches for tanning and swimming (though don't expect the white sands of the Cayman Islands here). My favorite beach is called Cow Camp. There's a small pier there good for diving off. There's also boating, sailing, waterskiing, windsurfing, jet-skiing, scuba diving, nature trails, and camping, at both primitive and developed sites. Beware of going to the lake on summer weekends and Labor Day weekend in particular, when the crowds are overwhelming. However, in the other seasons and during the week in summer it's a quiet place.

Bird watchers also enjoy the park, spotting hundreds of species, including bald eagles, great blue herons, and more than 20 species of ducks during migrations in spring and fall. The lake was named for a huge rock formation that makes an island; before the inundation that created the lake, it clearly looked like an elephant! Today, it's partially submerged.

The park is about 5 miles north of Truth or Consequences via I-25. For more information on the park, call ☎ **505/744-5421.**

About 18 miles south of Truth or Consequences via I-25 is another recreation area, **Caballo Lake State Park** (☎ **505/743-3942**), which, like Elephant Butte, has year-round water sports, fishing, swimming, and campsites. The lofty ridge of the Caballo Mountains just to the east of the lake makes a handsome backdrop. Park facilities include a full-service marina with a shop for boaters and full hookups for recreational vehicles.

Reached from the same exit off I-25 is yet another recreation area, **Percha Dam State Park** (☎ **505/743-3942**), a lovely shaded spot under great cottonwood trees, part of the ancient bosk, or woods, the Spanish found bordering the Rio Grande when they first arrived in this area in the 1530s. The dam here diverts river water for irrigation. The park offers campsites, rest rooms and showers, hiking trails, and access to fishing.

EXPLORING THE GHOST TOWNS IN THE AREA

NORTH OF TRUTH OR CONSEQUENCES   About 40 miles from Truth or Consequences you'll find the precarious remains of Winston and Chloride, two so-called ghost towns—abandoned mining centers that nevertheless do have a few residents. **Winston,** 37 miles northwest of Truth or Consequences on NM 52, was abandoned in the early 1900s when silver prices dropped and local mining became unprofitable. Some of the original structures are still standing from that era. A similar fate befell **Chloride,** 5 miles west of Winston on a side road off NM 52, where famed silver mines had such names as Nana, Wall Street, and Unknown. Chloride also figured in many battles in the turn-of-the-century war between cattle-ranching and sheep-ranching interests.

SOUTH OF TRUTH OR CONSEQUENCES   Thirty-two miles from Truth or Consequences, via I-25 south to NM 152, then west, is ✪ **Hillsboro,** another ghost town fast losing its ghosts to a small invasion of artists and craftspeople, antique shops, and galleries. This town boomed after an 1877 gold strike nearby, and during its heyday produced $6 million in silver and gold. It was the county seat from 1884 to 1938. Its Labor Day weekend Apple Festival is famous throughout the state.

The **Black Range Historical Museum** (☎ **505/895-5233** or 505/895-5685) contains exhibits and artifacts from Hillsboro's mining boom. Located in the former Ocean Grove Hotel, a turn-of-the-century brothel operated by Londoner Sadie Orchard, the museum collection includes some of the madam's effects. This volunteer-staffed museum is supposed to be open Thursday through Saturday 11am to 4pm, but isn't always. It may be open extra hours occasionally, or by appointment on other days of the week. It's closed the entire months of December and January, and most major holidays.

The **Enchanted Villa** bed-and-breakfast inn, P.O. Box 456, Hillsboro, NM 88042 (☎ **505/895-5686**), is a 1941 two-story adobe offering five large rooms with king-size beds and private bathrooms. The rate, $70 for a double, includes full hot breakfasts. Full meal service is also available.

Nine miles west of Hillsboro on NM 152, just after you've entered the Gila National Forest, is **Kingston,** born with a rich silver strike in 1880 and locally reputed to have been among the wildest mining towns in the region, with 7,000 people, 22 saloons, a notorious red-light district (conveniently located on Virtue Avenue), and an opera house. Kingston was also once the home of Albert Fall, a U.S. secretary of state who gained notoriety for his role in the Teapot Dome Scandal.

Your headquarters in Kingston should be the **Black Range Lodge,** Star Route 2, Box 119, Kingston, NM 88042 (☎ **505/895-5652**), a rustic stone lodge that dates from the 1880s, and over the years has housed miners and soldiers, as well as Pretty Sam's Casino and the Monarch Saloon. There are seven rooms—all with private bathrooms and some with private balconies—a large game room with pool table and video games, and family suites. I recommend the rooms on the north side of the building because they have windows opening to the outside rather the greenhouse. Life here is relaxed and homey. When I arrived I hadn't eaten dinner and the proprietors invited me to sit down and dine with them. You might want to bring your own food to prepare in the family style kitchen. Breakfast is provided—fresh-baked bread, cereals, and health conscious additions such as soy milk and herbal teas. Rates are $59 for a double, with multiple-night discounts; both children and pets are welcome. Besides being a great source of facts about the local area, the lodge has become a clearinghouse for information on natural building methods like straw-bale house construction, and hosts workshops occasionally.

Among historic buildings in Kingston are the brick assay office, **Victorio Hotel,** and the **Percha Bank,** now a museum open by appointment—ask at the lodge. The town bell in front of the Volunteer Fire Department was first used to warn residents of Native American attacks, until the Apaches' final surrender in 1886. Nearby, **Camp Shiloh** has a public outdoor swimming pool open in summer (again, ask at Black Range Lodge). Also ask about the mountain bike and hiking trails in the area. I biked two of them, one going north, which climbed through the pines, another that followed a creek to the west. **Emory Pass** (20 minutes on NM 152) is your driving route to a 10-mile round trip Hillsboro Peak hike.

WHERE TO STAY

Best Western Hot Springs Inn. 2270 N. Date St. at I-25 Exit 79, Truth or Consequences, NM 87901. ☎ **800/528-1234** or 505/894-6665. 40 units. A/C TV TEL. $52–$57 double. AE, CB, DC, DISC, MC, V.

This freeway-exit motel lives up to the Best Western standard with spacious, comfortable units in a quiet setting. Rooms have up-to-date furnishings and include remote-control television, clock radio, and most have refrigerators. There's an outdoor pool, open seasonally; K-Bob's steak house is adjacent.

A Winery East of Truth or Consequences

Had your fill of ghost towns? Then you might prefer to head east of town via NM 51 where you will find **Chateau Sassenage** (☎ 505/894-7244), a winery near the community of Engle producing fine wines in limited quantities. Call to make an appointment first.

✪ **Inn at the Butte.** NM 195 (P.O. Box E), Elephant Butte, NM 87935. ☎ **505/744-5431.** 48 units. A/C TV TEL. Mid-Sept to April $49–$59 double; May–early Sept $59–$69 double. AE, CB, DC, DISC, MC, V.

Now under the same ownership as Goulding's Lodge in Monument Valley, this inn has received a complete face lift. It sits above the shores of Elephant Butte Reservoir, and caters to boaters, fishers, and other relaxation lovers. Rooms are not large but comfortable, furnished with medium-firm king- or queen-size beds. Bathrooms are small but functional. All rooms come with coffeemakers. I recommend the lakeside view, which costs an extra $10 but is worth it, as there's a big grassy lawn stretching down to tennis courts. The restaurant has been revamped (see "Where to Dine," below). The inn has a swimming pool, tennis courts, and room service.

Rio Grande Motel. 720 Broadway, P.O. Box 67, Williamsburg, NM 87942. ☎ **505/894-9769.** 50 units. A/C TV TEL. $36–$44 double. DISC, MC, V.

Located in the suburb of Williamsburg near the south access to Truth or Consequences from I-25, the Rio Grande offers clean, comfortable rooms for a budget price. This is a fine place to stay for a short stop off the highway, but the furnishings are worn and dated. For more than a 1-night stay, I'd recommend the Best Western at the other end of town. There's an outdoor swimming pool, a guest Laundromat, and a restaurant next door.

River Bend Hot Springs Hostel. 100 Austin St., Truth or Consequences, NM 87901. ☎ **505/894-6183.** 16 dormitory beds, 2 apts. Dorm beds $13; apts. $35–$45 double. AE, DISC, MC, V.

This pleasant hostel is clean and comfortable with an inviting Southwest hippie atmosphere. Outdoor communal hot mineral baths on the premises overlook a swampy section of the Rio Grande. There are kitchenette units, family units, and couples can be accommodated. There is also a campground on the property ($7.50 per person). A guest laundry is available and day tours of area attractions can be arranged.

CAMPING

Elephant Butte Lake State Park (☎ 505/744-5421) welcomes backpackers and RVs alike. There are 125 sites, picnic tables, and access points for swimming, hiking, boating, and fishing. Kids love the playground.

Not far from Elephant Butte Lake is **Monticello Point RV Park** (☎ 505/894-6468), which offers 69 sites, 58 full hookups, and tenting. Laundry and grocery facilities are also on the premises. To reach Monticello Point, take I-25 to Exit 89, then go 5½ miles east on the gravel road—follow the signs.

Lakeside RV Park and Lodging (☎ 505/744-5996), also near Elephant Butte, has 54 sites, 43 full hookups, and tenting, as well as a recreation room/area and laundry facilities. If you are headed southbound on I-25, the RV park is located 4 miles southeast of the I-25 and NM 195 junction (Exit 83) on NM 195. To reach the RV park headed northbound on I-25, take I-25 to exit 79, go ½ mile east on the paved road, then 1½ miles north on NM 181, then 1½ miles east on NM 171, and finally ¼ mile south on NM 195.

Camping is also available at **Caballo Lake State Park** and **Percha Dam State Park.**
For information on either park, call ☎ **505/743-3942.**

WHERE TO DINE

Inn at the Butte. Hwy. 195 (P.O. Box E), Elephant Butte. ☎ **505/744-5431.** Reservations
accepted. Main courses $5–$17. AE, CB, DC, DISC, MC, V. Sun—Thurs 7am–9pm; Fri–Sat
7am–9:30pm. AMERICAN/NEW MEXICAN.

With a recent renovation has come a revamping of this restaurant in both its style and
its flavors. Request to sit in the patio area and you'll be surrounded by glass, which
during breakfast and lunch makes for a sunny atmosphere and a view of the lake. At
night the room is romantically lit with kerosene lanterns. This is a casual place serving
big portions. Breakfasts are standard but tasty. For lunch try a burger or sandwich. At
dinner I was impressed with a crab legs and steak special that was only $14.95. A small
filet mignon runs only $9.95, and these steaks are well seasoned and tasty. There is also
catfish and baby back ribs.

✪ **La Cocina.** 280 Date St. ☎ **505/894-6499.** Reservations recommended on weekends.
Main courses $3.95–$14.50. No credit cards. Mon–Thurs 10:30am–9pm, Fri–Sun
10:30am–10pm. NEW MEXICAN.

One evening on a trip through this area, I found myself sitting at a big booth reading
the paper and enjoying some excellent New Mexican food, when I looked up and saw
that many people in the restaurant were watching me. After checking to be sure
I didn't have food in my hair or red chile down the front of my shirt, I realized they
were merely curious. A real locals place, it's rare for a woman to be sitting here alone.
This is the real thing, with big, comfortable booths and lots of wood. The compuestas
and chile rellenos are good, but my favorite is the cheese enchiladas. The walls are
decorated with the work of local artists, and you'll be astonished by the size of
their sopaipillas. The owners plan to open a patio for dining soon.

✪ **Los Arcos Steak & Lobster.** 1400 Date St. (Hwy. 85). ☎ **505/894-6200.**
Reservations recommended. Main courses $9–$29.95. AE, CB, DC, DISC, MC, V. Sun–Thurs
5–10:30pm, Fri–Sat 5–11pm. AMERICAN.

A favorite of my father's, this spacious hacienda-style restaurant fronted by a lovely
desert garden is intimate and friendly in atmosphere, as if you're at an old friend's
home. Its steaks are regionally famous; my choice is always the filet mignon, served
with choice of potato and salad. The fish dishes are also good. You might try a fresh
local catch such as walleye pike or catfish. The restaurant also has a fine dessert list and
cordial selection. They have plans to add an outdoor patio.

5 Las Cruces

Picture a valley full of weathered wooden crosses marking graves of settlers brutally
murdered by Apaches, behind them mountains with peaks so jagged they resemble
organ pipes. Such was the scene that brought people to begin calling this city Las
Cruces, meaning "the crosses." Even today the place has a mysterious presence, its rich
history haunting it still. Reminders of characters such as Billy the Kid, who was
sentenced to death here, and of Pancho Villa, who spent time here, are present
throughout the area.

Established in 1849 on El Camino Real, the "royal highway" between Santa Fe and
Mexico City, Las Cruces became a supply center for miners prospecting the Organ
Mountains and soldiers stationed at nearby Fort Selden. Today, it is New Mexico's
second-largest urban area, with 73,600 people. It is noted as an agricultural center,

especially for its cotton, pecans, and chiles; as a regional transportation hub; and as the gateway to the White Sands Missile Range and other defense installations.

Las Cruces manages to survive within a desert landscape that gets only 8 inches of moisture a year, pulling enough moisture from the Rio Grande, which runs through, to irrigate a broad swatch of valley.

ESSENTIALS

GETTING THERE   By Car   From Albuquerque, take I-25 south (4 hours). From El Paso, take I-10 north (¾ hour). From Tucson, take I-25 east (5 hours).

By Plane   Las Cruces International Airport (☎ 505/524-2762), 8 miles west, has service several times daily to and from Albuquerque on **Mesa Airlines** (☎ 800/ MESA-AIR or 505/526-9743). **El Paso International Airport** (☎ 915/772-4271), 47 miles south, has daily flights to Albuquerque, Phoenix, Dallas, and Houston, among other cities. The **Las Cruces Shuttle Service,** P.O. Box 3172, Las Cruces, NM 88003 (☎ 800/288-1784 or 505/525-1784), provides service between the El Paso airport and Las Cruces. It leaves Las Cruces 13 times daily between 4:30am and 11:45pm for a charge of $23 ($38 round-trip) per person, with large discounts for additional passengers traveling together. There's a $6 charge for pickup or drop-off at places other than its regular stops at major hotels. Connections can also be made three times a day from Las Cruces to Deming and Silver City.

VISITOR INFORMATION   The **Las Cruces Convention and Visitors Bureau** is at 211 N. Water St., Las Cruces, NM 88001 (☎ 800/FIESTAS or 505/541-2444). The **Las Cruces Chamber of Commerce** can be reached by writing P.O. Drawer 519, Las Cruces, NM 88004, or calling ☎ 505/524-1968.

WHAT TO SEE & DO IN TOWN

On a hot day when the church bells are ringing and you're wandering the brick streets of ✪ **Mesilla,** you may for a moment slip back into the late 16th century, or certainly feel as though you have. This village on Las Cruces's southwestern flank was established in the late 1500s by Mexican colonists. It became the crossroads of El Camino Real and the Butterfield Overland Stagecoach route. The Gadsden Purchase, which annexed Mesilla to the United States and fixed the current inter-national boundaries of New Mexico and Arizona, was signed here in 1854.

Mesilla's most notorious resident, William Bonney, otherwise known as Billy the Kid, was sentenced to death at the county courthouse here. He was sent back to Lincoln, New Mexico, to be hanged, but escaped before the sentence was carried out. Legendary hero Pat Garrett eventually tracked down and killed The Kid at Fort Sumner; later, Garrett was mysteriously murdered in an arroyo just outside Las Cruces. He is buried in the local Masonic cemetery.

Thick-walled adobe buildings, which once protected residents against Apache attacks, now house art galleries, restaurants, museums, and gift shops. Throughout Mesilla, colorful red-chile ristras decorate homes and businesses. On Sunday during the summer locals sell crafts and baked goods, and mariachi bands play.

A WALKING TOUR OF MESILLA

Begin at the **San Albino Church** (see "Other Attractions," below). From here you can get a view of the plaza and even peek down the side streets leading away, where some of the old adobe houses have been restored and painted bold pinks and greens. Head east on Calle de Santiago until you come to **Silver Assets** (☎ 505/523-8747). Located in the old Valles Gallegos building (1880s), it was once a carpentry shop.

Turn south on Avenida de Mesilla and go to Boutz street, east on which you'll come to the **Gadsden Museum,** a grand old house full of memorabilia (see "Attractions," below). In the back of the museum parking lot is a replica of the old Mesilla jail, a dismal storage shed with original jail doors that once helped to incarcerate Billy the Kid.

Travel back west along Boutz Street and you'll see a sign for **Country Living Antiques** (☎ 505/526-9593) at the corner of Avenida de Mesilla and Calle de Parian. This 1860s building housed the customs house for the area. Country Living Antiques and the other three antique shops in the complex are great for browsing.

Continuing west on Calle de Parian, and you'll come to the **William Bonney Gallery** (☎ 505/526-8275). Here you'll find some nice local paintings as well as some less desirable curios. Across the street is **La Posta de Mesilla Restaurant,** a decent place to stop for a meal (see "Where to Dine," below) though not the best in the area. The building dates from the mid–18th century, and is the only surviving stagecoach station of the Butterfield, Overland Mail route from Missouri to San Francisco. Kit Carson, Pancho Villa, and Billy the Kid all were here.

Then continue west around the plaza to the **Nambé** (☎ 505/527-4623), a shop displaying handcrafted tableware by Nambé Mills in Santa Fe. It's a great place to shop for gifts. On the southwest corner of the plaza is the oldest documented brick building in New Mexico built by Augustin Maurin in 1860. It has a sad history of its proprietors being murdered by robbers.

Continue north along the plaza and be sure to stop at the **Mesilla Book Center** (☎ 505/536-6220). Housed in a historic mercantile building (ca. 1856), the building has tall ceilings with elaborate vigas and latillas. The bookstore has a strong selection of Southwestern books and children's titles. A few doors down is **El Platero** (☎ 505/523-5561), a store selling mostly tourists trinkets, but also large snow cones, perfect to cool you off after a walking tour.

A DRIVING OR WALKING TOUR OF HISTORIC LAS CRUCES

Though it has a much less romantic atmosphere than Mesilla, downtown Las Cruces has a few historical buildings, which make a walking tour worthwhile if you're up for a few miles of exercise. Otherwise, you may want to drive much of the tour.

Begin at the **Bicentennial Log Cabin,** Main Street and Lucero Avenue, Downtown Mall (☎ 505/541-2155). It is a circa-1850 structure moved to Las Cruces from the Black Range Mountains, containing authentic furnishings and artifacts. This municipal museum is open year-round by appointment. Nearby, you can park at the **Branigan Cultural Center,** 500 N. Water St. (☎ 505/541-2155). This museum features traveling and local exhibits of art and local history, and presents performing arts, educational programs, and special events. Next door on the Mall is the **Museum of Fine Arts and Culture,** 490 N. Water St. (☎ 505/541-2155), which, at this writing, was just being built. Plans are to have galleries, theaters, and art studios. The rest of the Mall doesn't offer much except on Saturday in summer, when there's one of the best grower's markets in the area, well worth browsing through. Otherwise this is a good place to get back in your car, or simply continue walking. In either case you'll want to head due south on Water Street until you reach the **Amador Hotel,** Amador Avenue and Water Street. A noble three-story structure built in 1850, it once hosted Benito Juarez, Pat Garrett, and Billy the Kid; restored, it's now the county courthouse.

Now head across the courthouse parking lot to Lohman Avenue and head east. Almost across the street you'll see the **Our Lady at the Foot of the Cross Shrine,** near Water Street and Lohman Avenue. It's a reproduction of Michelangelo's *Pietà,* dedicated to the Sisters of Loretto. Heading south across the parking lot you'll see

El Molino, a grinding wheel from an 1853 flour mill that commemorates the work and hardships of early pioneers. Farther east on Lohman you'll come to the **Old Armijo House,** just east of Lohman Avenue and Main Street. It's an 1860s home that has elegant Territorial touches such as a New Orleans–style balcony. It was at one time restored with original furnishings and second-floor display rooms. At this writing, the building was vacant. If you'd like to get a feel for a Las Cruces neighborhood, continue east on Lohman until you come to San Pedro, and turn north. You'll pass through old adobe neighborhoods with houses painted turquoise and pink, by a small plaza, and past a mission church. When you reach Picacho you can head west and you'll soon see the log cabin where you began.

OTHER ATTRACTIONS

San Albino Church. North side of Old Mesilla Plaza. ☎ **505/526-9349.** Free admission; donations appreciated. Mon–Sat 1–3pm; English-language masses Sat 5:30pm and Sun 11am, Spanish mass Sun 8am; weekdays 7am.

This is one of the oldest churches in the Mesilla valley. The present structure was built in 1906 on the foundation of the original church, constructed in 1851. It was named for St. Albin, medieval English bishop of North Africa, on whose day an important irrigation ditch from the Rio Grande was completed. The church bells date from the early 1870s; the pews were made in Taos of Philippine mahogany.

Gadsden Museum. Hwy. 28 and Barker Rd. ☎ **505/526-6293.** Admission $2 adults, $1 children 6–12. Mon–Sat 9–11am and daily 1–5pm.

A famous painting of the signing of the Gadsden Purchase is a highlight of this collection, from the Albert Jennings Fountain family. The museum, 3 blocks east of the Old Mesilla Plaza in the 1875 Fountain family home, also houses Indian and Civil War relics and Old West artifacts. All visitors go on the museum's guided tour.

New Mexico Farm and Ranch Heritage Museum. P.O. Drawer 1898 (follow University Ave. east beyond the edge of town). ☎ **505/522-4100.** Memorial Day to Labor Day 9am–6pm; rest of the year 9am–5pm. Admission $2; 16 and under free.

Having grown up on a New Mexico ranch, I was anxious to see how the Western lifestyle would be presented in this new museum. It's housed within a huge structure well designed to look like a hacienda-style barn, with a U-shaped courtyard in back and exhibits surrounding it on expansive grounds. A young girl took me through the dairy barn, where I saw a milking demonstration (offered twice daily; call for times). I saw memorabilia and was able to bottle-feed a calf outside. The museum lacked a really exciting draw, but for someone like my brother who loves farm and ranch equipment, it would appear like Disneyland, with such relics as a 1937 John Deere tractor and a number of examples of how ranchers "make do," ingeniously combining tools such as a tractor seat with a milk barrel to come up with a chair. Most interesting for me were the art exhibits, in particular pencil drawings by Robert Shufelt and photographs documenting homesteading (95% of homesteaders went broke, I learned). You may want to plan your visit around a meal at the **Purple Sage** restaurant here, with upscale versions of Mexican dishes and burgers served in an elegant new Southwest atmosphere—very Santa Fe, if I do say so.

New Mexico State University. University Ave. and Locust St. ☎ **505/646-0111.**

Established in 1888, this institution of 24,000 students is especially noted for its schools of engineering and agriculture. Its facilities include the Solar Energy Institute and the Water Resources Institute of New Mexico.

    University Museum in Kent Hall (☎ **505/646-3739**) has exhibits of historic and prehistoric Native American culture and art; it's open Tuesday through Friday from

10am to 4pm and Sunday from 1 to 4pm, with free admission. The **University Art Gallery** (☎ 505/646-2545) features monthly exhibits of contemporary and historical art, and a permanent collection of prints, photographs, and folk art. **Corbett Center Gallery,** in the student center (☎ 505/646-3200), has various exhibits throughout the year; a 12-foot copper-alloy triangle outside has a notch that symbolizes the transition from youth to adulthood. **Clyde Tombaugh Observatory,** named for the discoverer of the planet Pluto (who is a current resident of Las Cruces), has a high-powered telescope open for public viewing one evening a month.

ESPECIALLY FOR KIDS

Las Cruces Museum of Natural History. Mesilla Valley Mall, 700 S. Telshor. ☎ 505/522-3120. Free admission. Mon–Thurs noon–5pm, Fri noon–9pm, Sat 10am–6pm, Sun noon–6pm.

This small city-funded museum offers a variety of exhibits, changing quarterly, that emphasize science and natural history. The museum features live animals of the Chihuahuan Desert, hands-on science activities, and a small native plant garden. The Cenozoic Shop offers scientific toys and books about the region. Exhibits such as "Insects and Bugs" change every few months.

SPECTATOR SPORTS

New Mexico State University football, basketball, baseball, and other teams play inter-collegiate schedules in the Big West Conference, against schools from California, Nevada, and Utah. The "Aggies" play their home games on the NMSU campus, south of University Avenue on Locust Street. Football is played in the Chili Bowl, basketball in Pan Am Center arena. For information, call the **Athletic Department** (☎ 505/646-1420).

Fans of motor sports will find sprint and stock car racing at **The Speedway,** at Southern New Mexico State Fairgrounds, 11 miles west of Las Cruces via I-10 (☎ 505/524-7913), open weekends from April through November.

New Mexico's longest racing season takes place 45 miles south of Las Cruces at **Sunland Park Racetrack and Casino** (☎ 505/589-1131). Live races run Friday, Saturday, and Sunday (and also Monday, beginning in early 1999), December through the first week of May. Construction of the casino is underway and should be completed by spring 1999.

SHOPPING

Shoppers should be aware that in Las Cruces, Monday is a notoriously quiet day. Some stores close for the day, so it's best to call ahead before traveling to a specific store.

For **art,** visit **Lundeen's Inn of the Arts,** 618 S. Alameda Blvd. (☎ 505/526-3326); **Rising Sky Artworks,** 415 E. Foster (☎ 505/525-8454), which features works in clay by local and Western artists; and the **William Bonney Gallery,** 2060 Calle de Parian, just off the southeast corner of Old Mesilla Plaza (☎ 505/526-8275).

For **books,** try **Mesilla Book Center,** in an 1856 mercantile building on the west side of Old Mesilla Plaza (☎ 505/526-6220).

For native **crafts and jewelry,** check out **Silver Assets,** 1948 Calle de Santiago (☎ 505/523-8747), 1½ blocks east of San Albino Church in Mesilla.

Got a sweet tooth? **J. Eric Chocolatier,** featuring elegant hand-dipped and molded chocolates, is on the east side of Old Mesilla Plaza (☎ 505/526-2744).

Mesilla Valley Mall is a full-service shopping center at 700 S. Telshor Blvd., just off the I-25 interchange with Lohman Avenue (☎ 505/522-1001), with well over 100 stores. The mall is open Monday through Saturday from 10am to 9pm, and Sunday from noon to 6pm.

There are two **wineries** in the Las Cruces area. **Blue Teal Vineyards** (☎ 505/524-0390) has a tasting room in the historic Fountain Theater, Calle de Guadalupe, south of Old Mesilla Plaza. The tasting room at **La Viña Winery** (☎ 505/882-7632), south of Las Cruces off NM 28, is open Saturday and Sunday from noon to 5pm, and by appointment.

LAS CRUCES AFTER DARK

National recording artists frequently perform at NMSU's **Pan Am Center** (☎ 505/646-4413). The NMSU Music Department (☎ 505/646-2421) offers free jazz, classical, and pop concerts, and the **Las Cruces Symphony** (☎ 505/646-3709) often performs here as well.

Hershel Zohn Theater (☎ 505/646-4515), at NMSU, presents plays of the professional/student **American Southwest Theatre Company:** dramas, comedies, musicals, and original works September through May.

The **Las Cruces Community Theatre** (☎ 505/523-1200) mounts six productions a year at its own facility on the Downtown Mall.

A popular country-music and dancing club is **Cowboys,** 2205 S. Main St. (☎ 505/525-9050), with no cover Tuesday or Wednesday, $3 Thursday through Saturday. There are free hamburgers on Thursday, and free french fries on Friday. Live bands are featured Tuesday through Saturday. Cowboys is closed Sunday and Monday.

EXPLORING THE AREA

NORTH OF LAS CRUCES   The town of **Hatch,** 39 miles via I-25 or 34 miles via NM 185, calls itself the "chile capital of the world." It is the center of a 22,000-acre agricultural belt that grows and processes more chile than anywhere else in the world. The annual Hatch Chile Festival over the Labor Day weekend celebrates the harvest. For information, call the **Hatch Chamber of Commerce** (☎ 505/267-5050).

✪ **Fort Selden State Monument** is located 15 miles north of Las Cruces between 1-25 (Exit 19) and NM 185. Founded in 1865, Fort Selden housed the famous Black Cavalry, the "Buffalo Soldiers" who protected settlers from marauding natives. It was subsequently the boyhood home of Gen. Douglas MacArthur, whose father, Arthur, was in charge of troops patrolling the U.S.-Mexican border in the 1880s. There are only eroding ruins remaining today. Displays in the visitor center tell Fort Selden's story, including photos of young Douglas and his family. The fort closed permanently in 1891. The monument is open daily from 8:30am to 5pm; admission is $2 for adults and free for children 16 and under. For more information, call ☎ 505/526-8911.

Adjacent to the state monument, **Leasburg Dam State Park** (☎ 505/524-4068) offers picnicking, camping, canoeing, and fishing.

SOUTH OF LAS CRUCES   **Stahmann Farms,** 10 miles south of La Mesilla on NM 28, is one of the world's largest single producers of pecans. Several million pounds are harvested, mostly during November, from orchards in the bed of an ancient lake. **Stahmann's Country Store** (☎ 505/526-8974) sells pecans and pecan candy, other specialty foods, and has a small cafe. It's open weekdays from 9am to 5:30pm, weekends from 10am to 5pm.

✪ **War Eagles Air Museum** (☎ 505/589-2000), at the Santa Teresa Airport, about 35 miles south of Las Cruces via I-10 (call for directions), has an extensive collection of historic aircraft from World War II and the Korean conflict, plus automobiles and a tank. The aircraft include a beautifully restored P-38 Lightning, P-51 Mustang, F-86 Sabre, and several Russian MIG-15s. Most of the museum's 28 planes are in flying condition, and are kept inside a well-lighted, 64,000-square-foot hangar. The museum is open Tuesday through Sunday from 10am to 4pm;

admission is $5 for adults, $4 for senior citizens age 65 and over, and children under 12 are admitted free.

EAST OF LAS CRUCES   The **Organ Mountains,** so-called because they resemble the pipes of a church organ, draw inevitable comparisons to Wyoming's Grand Tetons. Organ Peak, at 9,119 feet, is the highest point in Doña Ana County.

The **Aguirre Springs Recreation Area** (☎ **505/525-4300**), off U.S. 70 on the western slope of the Organ Mountains, is operated by the Bureau of Land Management. Visitors to the area can hike, camp, picnic, or ride horseback (no horse rentals on site).

WHERE TO STAY

✪ **Best Western Mission Inn.** 1765 S. Main St., Las Cruces, NM 88005. ☎ **800/390-1440,** 800/528-1234, or 505/524-8591. Fax 505/523-4740. 70 units. A/C TV TEL. $58 double; $82 suite. Rates include full breakfast. AE, CB, DC, DISC, MC, V.

There are few more welcoming places on a hot day than this two-story mission-style motel, an 8-minute drive from Mesilla. The rooms are large, decorated in an Aztec/floral style with comfortable sitting chairs. A recessed headboard with a tile counter, and hand-painted Mexican flowers on the wall above add even more style to these rooms built sturdily in 1948 and remodeled thoroughly in 1996. Beds are perfectly firm. The bathrooms are large, and have a large dressing area with a sink/vanity all accented in Mexican tile. The pool sits within the courtyard; it's medium-sized and partially shaded by globe willows. There's a shuffle board and play area. For those who like to get some exercise, there's an *acequia* (irrigation ditch) behind the hotel that runs for miles toward the east, perfect for running or walking. Breakfast offers a number of choices, from pancakes to huevos rancheros. The restaurant is open for three meals daily and the lounge has entertainment. The inn has a 24-hour desk, same-day laundry, and offers access to a nearby health club.

✪ **Hampton Inn.** 755 Avenida de Mesilla (I-10 Exit 140), Las Cruces, NM 88005. ☎ **800/426-7866** or 505/526-8311. Fax 505/527-2015. 118 units. A/C TV TEL. $57–$63 double. Rates include continental breakfast. AE, CB, DC, DISC, MC, V.

This is a real find for those who want a convenient, economical stay. Built in 1985, it had a major remodel in 1998. It's only 5 minutes from Mesilla and very near I-10. Rooms are medium-sized, decorated in Southwest-floral prints. Each has a big window, large TV, coffeemaker, and iron and ironing board. The beds are firm. Bathrooms are small with an outer sink/vanity, and very clean. Breakfast is served in a spacious garden room overlooking the pool. For the most quiet, request a room facing the courtyard and the medium-sized and very inviting bean-shaped pool.

✪ **Las Cruces Hilton.** 705 S. Telshor Blvd., Las Cruces, NM 88001. ☎ **800/284-0616** or 505/522-4300. Fax 505/521-4707. 210 units. A/C TV TEL. $87–$97 double; $104–$300 suite. Weekend packages from $77 for a family, including breakfast. AE, CB, DC, DISC, MC, V.

South-of-the-border romance and elegance defines this seven-story hotel on the east side of town about a 15-minute drive from Mesilla, with an incredible view of the city and the Organ Mountains. The hotel was built in 1986, with remodeling ongoing. The lobby has a fountain, lots of colorful Mexican tile, and plenty of ferns. Rooms are spacious, with the same south-of-the border feel, done in sturdy pine furniture. Each has a coffeemaker, hair dryer, iron and ironing board, and medium firm beds. Baths are medium-sized and very clean. A nice-sized triangular pool has palm trees and a little cabana on its banks. Some rooms flank this area and have little patios.

The Ventana Terrace serves breakfast, lunch, and dinner. The hotel also offers limited room service, a 24-hour desk, courtesy van, valet laundry, a whirlpool, gift shop, car rental, and a small exercise facility.

BED & BREAKFASTS

Lundeen's Inn of the Arts. 618 S. Alameda Blvd., Las Cruces, NM 88005. ☎ **888/ 526-3326** or 505/526-3326. Fax 505/647-1334. www.lundeen@innofthearts.com. 24 units. A/C TV TEL. $72 double; $78–$130 suite. Rates include breakfast. AE, CB, DC, DISC, MC, V.

This inn offers a bit of a villa feel in a late 1890s adobe home built in Territorial style. It's a complex composite of rooms stretching across 14,000 square feet of floor space, that at some moments seems completely orderly and at others a bit unkempt. There's a wide range of rooms, each named for an artist. My favorites are in the main part of the house, set around a two-story garden room, with elegant antiques and arched windows. Most rooms are medium-sized with comfortably firm beds dressed in fine linens. Bathrooms are generally small and simple but clean and come with Caswell Massey soap, shampoo, and lotion. My favorite rooms are the Maria Martinez (the only room without a TV), which has wood floors, a working fireplace, and gets lots of sun. The Frederic Remington has a more masculine feel and includes a kitchenette with a microwave, minirefrigerator, stove, and coffeemaker. Other rooms have similarly equipped kitchenettes. At press time, innkeepers Linda and Gerald Lundeen had embarked on an addition to the inn. The inn is also an art gallery, displaying the works of about 30 Southwest painters, sculptors, and potters.

Breakfast includes fresh fruit and such specialties as pumpkin waffles and huevos rancheros. Guests get reduced rates at a local health club, and Gerry Lundeen will take them on architectural walking tours of nearby Old Mesilla.

The inn is surrounded by a 10-foot stone privacy wall with iron gates. Services include laundry service, baby-sitting, and secretarial services. The **Las Cruces Shuttle Service** (☎ **800/288-1784**) stops at the inn.

Mesón de Mesilla. 1803 Avenida de Mesilla, Mesilla, NM 88046. ☎ **800/732-6025** or 505/525-2380. Fax 505/527-4196. 13 units. A/C TV TEL. $58–$92 double. Rates include breakfast. AE, CB, DC, DISC, MC, V.

The closest lodging to Old Mesilla, this inn provides decent rooms that have a motel feel. Built in the early 1980s, with remodeling ongoing, the rooms could use a little more care, but they do range greatly in size and price, giving the place broad appeal. What's most notable here is the lovely outdoor swimming pool with a view of the Organ Mountains. The rooms are medium-sized, decorated in Southwestern earth tones, with medium-firm beds and basic bathrooms. Most rooms have brass headboards, antique furniture, and ceiling fans. A full breakfast is served in the garden atrium of the restaurant (see "Where to Dine," below).

T.R.H. Smith Mansion. 909 N. Alameda Blvd., Las Cruces, NM, 88005. ☎ **800/526-1914** or 505/525-2525. Fax 505/5248227. www.weblifepro.com/smithmansion. E-mail: SmithMansion@zianet.com. 4 units. A/C TEL. $60–$109 double. Rates include full breakfast. AE, DISC, MC, V. Children over 10 welcome.

Built in 1914, this mansion at the center of the historic Alameda Depot District and walking distance from downtown is suspected to have buried treasure somewhere within its walls and was for a time a brothel. In 1995, Marlene and Jay Tebo began welcoming guests here in accommodations that border on elegance. For the price, I would still select the Best Western Mission Inn listed above, but if you like the feel of an old Queen Anne–style mansion, you'll enjoy your stay here. Your best bet, however, is fall, spring, or winter, as only the individual rooms are air-conditioned, leaving the common areas hot in summer. The European and the Americas rooms are large and elegantly decorated with rosy florals and sizeable bathrooms. All rooms have hardwood floors. The beds are comfortable, as are the other furnishings, and each room comes equipped with a small radio/tape player. The other two rooms share a bathroom, and neither is as bright as the larger rooms, though of the two I'd recommend the Southwest room. Breakfasts are large and delicious, often with a German touch, drawing from the Tebo's ancestry. Mine began with fruit and delicious homemade breads, and moved onto an egg puff (much like a soufflé) covered with strawberries. Another specialty is French toast made with French flute bread. In the basement of the mansion is a pool table, large TV, VCR, and library.

CAMPING

There are quite a few campgrounds located within or near Las Cruces. All of the ones listed here include full hookups for RVs, tenting areas, and recreation areas. **Best View RV Park** (☎ 505/526-6555) also offers cabins and laundry and grocery facilities. From the junction of I-10 and U.S. 70 (Exit 135), go 1½ miles east on U.S. 70, then ½ block south on Weinrich Road.

Another option is **Dalmont's RV Park** (☎ 505/523-2992). If you're coming from the west, when you reach the junction of I-25 and I-10, go 2½ miles northwest on I-10 to the Main Street exit, then go 2 blocks west on Valley Drive. If you're coming from the east, at the junction of I-10 and Main Street, go ¼ mile north on Main Street and then 1 block west on Valley Drive. To reach **Siesta RV Park** (☎ 505/523-6816), at the junction of I-10 and NM 28 take Exit 140 and go ½ mile south on NM 28. **Leasburg Dam State Park** (☎ 505/524-4068) is a smaller park that also offers RV and tent camping, but there are no laundry or grocery facilities. Hiking and fishing are available.

WHERE TO DINE
EXPENSIVE

✪ **Double Eagle.** 308 Calle Guadalupe, on the east side of Old Mesilla Plaza. ☎ 505/523-6700. Reservations recommended. Main courses $10.95–$24.95; lunch $5.25–$11.50. AE, CB, DC, DISC, MC, V. Mon–Sat 11am–10pm, Sun 11am–9pm. CONTINENTAL.

When I was a kid, whenever we went to Las Cruces we always made a special trip to this elegant restaurant imbued with Old West high style. I'm pleased to say that it's still a quality place to dine. This 150-year-old Territorial-style hacienda is on the National Register of Historic Places. Built around a central courtyard, it has a number of rooms, one that is said to be frequented by a woman's ghost. In another, there's a 30-foot-long bar with Corinthian columns in gold leaf, and there are Gay Nineties oil paintings and 18-armed brass chandeliers hung with Baccarat crystals. The menu is quite varied and includes pasta, chicken, fish, and steak dishes. My favorite is the filet mignon bordelaise, served on a French rusk with a rich red-wine sauce. The Columbia River salmon, served with a triple citrus-chipotle chile sauce is also delicious. All entrees come with salad, vegetable, and choice of potato or pasta. There's a full bar, and for dessert you can end it all with the Death by Chocolate Cake.

Mesón de Mesilla. 1803 Avenida de Mesilla, Mesilla. ☎ 505/525-2380. Reservations required. Main courses lunch $7–$17; dinner $17–$31; Sun brunch $16.95. AE, CB, DC, DISC, MC, V. Mon–Fri 11:30am–2pm; daily 5:30–9pm; champagne brunch Sun 11am–1:45pm. CONTINENTAL.

Located in a bed-and-breakfast at the northeast gateway to La Mesilla (see "Where to Stay," above), this restaurant serves good food in a Spanish colonial ambience. The dining room has carved wooden pillars, stained-glass windows, wrought-iron chairs, though they don't quite disguise the early 1980s construction with its square corners. Two years ago the whole place came under new ownership, but has continued to maintain a good reputation. The entrees are elaborate; you may want to try the bourbon pecan chicken (a breast with a creamy pecan bourbon sauce) or the oven-roasted quail. There's also chateâubriand for two. Meals are served with a choice of potato, polenta, rice, or linguine. Lunches feature salads, sandwiches, and quiches. There's an extensive wine and beer list.

MODERATE

Peppers. 306 Calle Guadalupe, on the east side of Old Mesilla Plaza. ☎ **505/523-4999.** Reservations for large parties only. Tapas $1.35–$4.95; lunch $4.95–$8.25; dinner $7.95–$13.95. AE, CB, DC, DISC, MC, V. Mon–Sat 11am–10pm, Sun noon–9pm. NEW MEXICAN.

This restaurant shares a building and the same ownership with the Double Eagle, but the resemblance ends there. The Eagle has age and grace; Peppers has youthful exuberance. Hispanic folk art, including traditional masks and *santos,* greets guests in the entryway, and diners can sit within a lush atrium central courtyard (a great place to sit and drink margaritas) around which the Double Eagle dining rooms reside.

The cuisine is Santa Fe–style New Mexican, the chef adding interesting touches to traditional dishes. For starters try the green chile and cheese wontons, a house specialty. Unfortunately in my most recent visit here, the service was very slow and the chef sent the wrong sauce with this dish. I was halfway through and little impressed when I remembered the promised sauce; it made the dish delectable, so I'm cautioning you to be on your toes here. The chicken, beef, or shark fajitas are also delicious, served with Mennonite cheese, guacamole, black beans, and flour tortillas. For dessert, the banana enchiladas sound weird, but are actually delicious crepes with ice cream and Mesilla Valley Pecan sauce.

✪ **Tatsu.** 930 El Paseo Rd. ☎ **505/526-7144.** Reservations recommended. Main courses $9–$19; lunch $7–$12. AE, DC, MC, V. Mon–Thurs 11am–9pm, Fri 11am–10pm, Sat 5–10pm, Sun (brunch) 11am–2pm and 5–9pm. JAPANESE/NEW ORIENTAL.

After days of eating steaks and sandwiches, I practically melted into the sophisticated flavors at this oddly set restaurant. Elegant contemporary furniture and round rice paper lamps succeed in transforming what once was a Denny's-type building into a hip Asian ambience. I especially like to sit in one of the booths up front, though the dining room in back is cooler in summer. The food is elegant as well. Each entree comes with a choice of egg drop or miso soup and a graduated tray of simple appetizers. I enjoyed the Pacific Rim grilled chicken salad. It was simply elaborate, meaning it had a variety of vegetables—radicchio, endive, peas, but all were light and critical to the flavor, served artistically and enhanced with a sesame dressing. Another delicious dish is the sesame tempura-seared rare tuna, flash fried and served with garlic chile sauce. This and other regular entrees come with soup and salad. There's an elaborate selection of wine, beer, and desserts. There's a children's menu as well.

INEXPENSIVE

La Posta de Mesilla. Southeast corner of Old Mesilla Plaza. ☎ **505/524-3524.** Reservations recommended. Main courses $2.50–$12.50. AE, CB, DC, DISC, MC, V. Sun, Tues–Thurs 11am–9pm, Fri–Sat 11am–9:30pm. NEW MEXICAN/STEAKS.

If you're on the Old Mesilla Plaza and want to eat New Mexican food for not much money, walk in here. The restaurant occupies a mid–18th-century adobe building, that is the only surviving stagecoach station of the Butterfield, Overland Mail Route from Tipton, Missouri, to San Francisco. Kit Carson, Pancho Villa, and Billy the Kid were all here at one time. The entrance leads through a jungle of tall plants beneath a Plexiglas roof, past a tank of piranhas and a noisy aviary of macaws, cocktails, and Amazon parrots, to nine dining rooms with bright, festive decor. You may want to request the atrium where you can dine under ficus trees. The tables are basic, however, with vinyl and metal chairs, giving it a cheap air. Such is an indication of the food. If you want really good New Mexican food, go to Nellie's (see below). If you come here, try the enchiladas, which come with a nice chile sauce. Avoid the dry rellenos and the soggy tacos. The tostadas (tortilla cups filled with beans and topped with chile and cheese) are a house specialty. There's a full-service bar.

✪ **Nellie's.** 1226 West Hadley. ☎ **505/524-9982** or 505/526-6816. Main courses $3–$8. No credit cards. Mon–Wed 8am–4pm; Thurs–Sat 8am–8pm. NEW MEXICAN.

A good indication of the quality of food of this restaurant that serves "chile with an attitude" is that at 10:45am on a Monday morning the place was full. I told three young guys wearing baseball caps at the next table where I was from and one said, "This is the best damn New Mexican food in the world—too bad Santa Fe doesn't have a place this good." If I weren't so fond of my hometown, I'd have agreed. It's a small cafe with two rooms, totally unassuming, with big windows up front that let in lots of light. There's a jukebox and, on the walls, R. C. Gorman prints. Order anything on the menu and you'll be pleased. The sopaipilla compuesta (sopaipilla topped with beans, meat, lettuce, tomatoes, and cheese) is amazing. The combination plate gives you a sampling of a number of delicacies. As should be the case with any true New Mexican restaurant, you can also have menudo, what they call the "breakfast of champions" (beef tripe and hominy in red chile), and though I didn't dare, I heard it, too, is tasty. No alcoholic beverages are served.

✪ **Way Out West Restaurant and Brewing Company.** 1720 Avenida de Mesilla. ☎ **505/541-1969.** Reservations accepted. Main courses lunch $4–$7; dinner $7.50–$13. AE, DC, DISC, MC, V. Sun–Thurs 11am–10pm; Fri–Sat 11am–11pm. TAPAS/NEW AMERICAN.

In a large new building with a long portal, this restaurant is a fun place to go for a beer and some delicious food. The decor is new Southwest in muted turquoise, with tile tables and metal desert scene sculptures on the walls. Big windows offer a fantastic view of the Organ Mountains. The broad veranda is an excellent place to sit in the spring and fall, and occasional live music plays there. Inside the place has high ceilings and long windows and can be noisy. I began with the Santa Fe Swill, a medium-dark beer with moderate hoppiness. Every day there's a special "catch of the day." The halibut was served with a raita of cucumbers, curry, raisins, pecans, and coconut milk, and came with rice and veggies—excellent. There are less elaborate dishes such as fajitas and burgers on the menu as well, but they're cooked with no less care. A well thought out tapas menu offers great beer-side snacks. There's also a good selection of wines, a product of this brewery as well.

6 Deming & Lordsburg

New Mexico's least populated corner is this one, which includes the "boot heel" of the Gadsden Purchase that pokes 40 miles down into Mexico (a great place for back-packing). These two railroad towns, an hour apart on I-10, see a lot of traffic; but whereas Deming (pop. 14,500) is thriving as a ranching and retirement center, Lordsburg has had a steady population of about 3,000 for years. This is a popular area for rock hounds, aficionados of ghost towns, and history buffs: Columbus, 32 miles south of Deming, was the site of the last foreign incursion on continental American soil, by the Mexican bandit-revolutionary Pancho Villa in 1916.

ESSENTIALS

GETTING THERE   By Car   From Las Cruces, take I-10 west (1 hour to Deming, 2 hours to Lordsburg). From Tucson, take I-10 east (3 hours to Lordsburg, 4 hours to Deming). The **Grant County Airport** (☎ **505/546-8848**), 15 miles south of Silver

City, is served by **Mesa Airlines** (☎ **800/MESA-AIR** or 505/388-4115), with daily flights to Albuquerque. The **Las Cruces Shuttle Service,** P.O. Box 3172, Las Cruces, NM 88003 (☎ **800/288-1784** or 505/525-1784), runs several times daily between Deming and the El Paso airport by way of Las Cruces.

VISITOR INFORMATION The **Deming–Luna County Chamber of Commerce** is located at 800 E. Pine St., Deming (☎ **800/848-4955** or 505/ 546-2674). You can write to them at P.O. Box 8, Deming, NM 88031. The **Lordsburg Hidalgo County Chamber of Commerce** is located at 208 Motel Dr., Lordsburg, NM 88045 (☎ **505/542-9864**).

WHAT TO SEE & DO NEAR DEMING

✪ **Deming Luna Mimbres Museum.** 301 S. Silver Ave., Deming. ☎ **505/546-2382.** Admission by donation. Mon–Sat 9am–4pm, Sun 1:30–4pm.

Deming was the meeting place of the second east-west railroad to connect the Pacific and Atlantic coasts, and that heritage is recalled in this museum, run by the Luna County Historical Society. It shows some pioneer-era quilts and laces; a military room containing exhibits from the Indian Wars, Pancho Villa's raid, both world wars, and the Korean and Vietnam wars; a room featuring the John and Mary Alice King Collection of Mimbres pottery; and a doll room with more than 800 dolls. There's a gem and mineral room; a display of ladies' fashions from the Gay Nineties to the Roaring Twenties; a variety of pioneer silver, china, and crystal; and a new Transportation Annex with a chuck wagon, a "traveling kitchen."

The museum also houses a collection of 2,200 bells from all over the world, as well as about 1,800 liquor decanters. Across the street in the Custom House, a turn-of-the-century adobe home that has been turned into a walk-though exhibit, you can see a period bedroom, kitchen, and living room, inhabited by mannequins. Most interesting here are the customs books from that era, showing what goods were brought up from Mexico.

GETTING OUTSIDE

At **Rock Hound State Park,** 14 miles southeast of Deming via NM 11, visitors are encouraged to pick and take home with them as much as 15 pounds of minerals— jasper, agate, quartz crystal, flow-banded rhyolite, and others. Located at the base of the Little Florida Mountains, the park is a lovely, arid, cactus-covered land with paths leading down into dry gullies and canyons. (You may have to walk a bit, as the more accessible minerals have been largely picked out.)

The campground ($7 to $11 per night), which has shelters, rest rooms, and showers, gives a distant view of mountain ranges all the way to the Mexican border. The park also has one marked hiking trail and a playground. Admission is $3 per vehicle, and the park is open year-round from dawn to dusk. For more information, call ☎ **505/546-6182.**

Some 35 miles south of Deming is the tiny border town of **Columbus,** looking across at Mexico. The **Pancho Villa State Park** here marks the last foreign invasion of American soil. A temporary fort, where a tiny garrison was housed in tents, was attacked in 1916 by 600 Mexican revolutionaries, who cut through the boundary fence at Columbus. Eighteen Americans were killed, 12 wounded; an estimated 200 Mexicans died. The Mexicans immediately retreated across their border. An American punitive expedition, headed by Gen. John J. Pershing, was launched into Mexico, but got nowhere. Villa restricted his banditry to Mexico after that, until his assassination in 1923.

The state park includes ruins of the old fort and a visitor center with exhibits and a film. The park also has a strikingly beautiful desert botanical garden, worth the trip alone, plus campsites ($7 to $11), rest rooms, showers, an RV dump station, and a playground. There's a $3 per vehicle entrance fee; the park is staffed from 8am to 5pm daily. For more information, call ☎ **505/531-2711.**

Across the street from the state park is the old Southern Pacific Railroad Depot, which has been restored by the Columbus Historical Society and now houses the **Columbus Historical Museum** (☎ 505/531-2620), containing railroad memorabilia and exhibits on local history. Call for hours, as they vary.

Three miles south across the border in Mexico is **Las Palomas, Chihuahua** (pop. 1,500). The port of entry is open 24 hours. A few desirable restaurants and tourist-oriented businesses are located in Las Palomas. Mostly, though, it's a drug-trafficking town. Beware of bar hopping in Palomas at night, as it can be dangerous. **Casa de Pancho Villa Restaurant & Bar** (☎ 011-52-166-60106), better known as **The Pink Store,** because of the excellent gift shop attached, offers one notable dish: the General Zapata—marinated beef in a taco, with avocado, onions, pico de gallo, and beans. The restaurant accepts American dollars and is open daily from 10am to 8pm.

WHAT TO SEE & DO NEAR LORDSBURG

Visitors to Lordsburg can go ✪ **rockhounding** in an area rich in minerals of many kinds. Desert roses can be found near Summit, and agate is known to exist in many abandoned mines locally. Mine dumps, southwest of Hachita, contain lead, zinc, and gold. There is manganese in the Animas mountains. Volcanic glass can be picked up in Coronado National Forest, and there is panning for gold in Gold Gulch.

Rodeo, 30 miles southwest via I-10 and NM 80, is the home of the **Chiricahua Gallery** (☎ 505/557-2225), open Monday through Saturday from 10am to 4pm. Regional artists have joined in a nonprofit, cooperative venture to exhibit works and offer classes in a variety of media. Many choose to live on the high-desert slopes of the Chiricahua Range. The gallery is on State Highway 80 en route to Douglas, Arizona.

Shakespeare Ghost Town. P.O. Box 253, Lordsburg, NM 88045. ☎ **505/542-9034.** Admission $3 adults, $2 children 6–12; for shoot-outs and special events $4 adults, $3 children. Open 10am and 2pm second and fourth weekends of every month except Dec. Special tours by appointment.

A national historic site, Shakespeare was once the home of 3,000 miners, promoters, and dealers of various kinds. Under the name *Ralston,* it enjoyed a silver boom in 1870. This was followed by a notorious diamond fraud in 1872 in which a mine was salted with diamonds in order to raise prices on mining stock; many notables were sucked in, particularly William Ralston, founder of the Bank of California. It enjoyed a mining revival in 1879 under its new name, Shakespeare. It was a town with no church, no newspaper, and no local law. Some serious fights resulted in hangings from the roof timbers in the Stage Station.

Since 1935, it's been privately owned by the Hill family, which has kept it uncommercialized with no souvenir hype or gift shops. Six original buildings and two reconstructed buildings survive in various stages of repair. Two-hour guided tours are offered on a limited basis, and reenactments and special events are staged on the fourth weekends of April, June, August, and October *if* performers are available. Phone to confirm the performances.

To reach Shakespeare, drive 1.3 miles south from I-10 on Main Street. Just before the town cemetery, turn right, proceed .6 mile and turn right again. Follow the dirt road .4 mile into Shakespeare.

Stein's Railroad Ghost Town. Exit 3, I-10 (P.O. Box 2185, Road Forks, NM 88045). ☎ **505/542-9791.** Admission $2.50 over 12 years; under 12, free. Daily 9am–dusk.

This settlement 19 miles west of Lordsburg started as a Butterfield Stage stop, then was a railroad town of about 1,000 residents from 1880 to 1955. It was so isolated that water, hauled from Doubtful Canyon, brought $1 a barrel!

Today there remain 12 buildings, with 16 rooms filled with artifacts and furnishings from the 19th and early 20th century. There is also a petting zoo for kids and the Steins Mercantile shop. Recently the owners began offering horseback and stagecoach rides Wednesday through Sunday; they hope to continue offering them. They also have plans to build a hotel.

WHERE TO STAY
IN DEMING

Grand Hotel. U.S. 70/180 east of downtown (P.O. Box 309), Deming, NM 88031. ☎ **505/546-2631.** Fax 505/546-4446. 60 units. A/C TV TEL. About $50 double. AE, CB, DC, DISC, MC, V.

Looking like a redbrick Colonial Williamsburg manor and situated close to town, the Grand isn't quite as refined as the Holiday Inn (see below), but its construction is older (1967) and more substantial. It's built around a central lawn and shrubbery garden with a large pool for adults and a small one for children. At the time of my visit the rooms were receiving a needed major renovation. Request one of the rooms that is complete, as it appears this renovation may take some time. Rooms are medium-sized with antique-style furnishings. Mattresses are firm and the rooms are quiet. Bathrooms are medium-sized with an outer vanity and dressing area. A restaurant is open for three meals daily. A courtesy car provides service to and from the airport and train station.

✪ **Holiday Inn.** Off I-10 (P.O. Box 1138), Deming NM 88031. ☎ **800/HOLIDAY** or 505/546-2661. Fax 505/546-6308. 117 units. A/C TV TEL. $58–$68 double. AE, CB, DC, DISC, MC, V. Pets are welcome.

This hotel just off I-10 brings a bit of style to dusty Deming. Though from the outside the 1974 two-story white brick structure appears basic, the rooms—completely renovated in 1996—tell another story. Each is medium-sized with light pine furniture and is decorated in Aztec prints with bold expressionistic paintings on the walls. All rooms have nicely firm beds, coffeemakers, irons and ironing boards, and big TVs. Bathrooms are small but also have a vanity and dressing area. The large pool is surrounded by lush grass; request a poolside room and you'll have a bit of a resort feel. There is a coin-operated laundry as well as valet laundry, and coffee is available in the lobby 24 hours a day. Room service is available during restaurant hours.

The hotel's restaurant is open for breakfast, lunch, and dinner and serves New Mexican and American cuisine.

✪ **Wagon Wheel Motel.** 1109 W. Pine St., Deming, NM 88030. ☎ **505/546-2681.** 19 units. A/C TV TEL. $29–$33 double. DISC, MC, V. Pets are accepted.

You'll find clean, comfortable, and inexpensive lodging in this mom-and-pop motel, which is within walking distance of several restaurants. Built in 1958, the motel has now been completely renovated. Rooms are medium-sized with basic furnishings, beds on the soft side. There is a heated swimming pool open in summer, 30-channel cable television, and guest laundry.

IN LORDSBURG

Best Western American Motor Inn. 944 E. Motel Dr. (Alt. I-10), Lordsburg, NM 88045. ☎ **800/528-1234** or 505/542-3591. 60 units. A/C TV TEL. $49–$70 double. AE, CB, DC, DISC, MC, V.

Located well off I-10 on the old highway through town, the American caters to families by offering an outdoor swimming pool, a small playground with swings, and a handful of family units. Rooms are medium-sized, have lightly colored oak furnishings and R. C. Gorman prints on the walls. Beds are firm but springy. The bathrooms are small with an outer vanity and dressing area. The restaurant, under separate management, serves three reasonably priced meals daily, and offers a kids' menu. There's also a hot tub. The motel is reachable by Greyhound and Amtrak. In-room massage and video rentals are available.

✪ **Best Western, Western Skies Inn.** 1303 S. Main St. at I-10 (Exit 22), Lordsburg, NM 88045. ☎ **800/528-1234** or 505/542-8807. 40 units. A/C TV TEL. $58 double. AE, CB, DC, DISC, MC, V.

This redbrick motel built in 1990 at the I-10 interchange offers comfortable and quiet rooms on well-landscaped grounds. Remodeling is ongoing and well done. The large rooms have oak furnishings and medium-firm beds. Bathrooms are medium-sized and have an outer vanity with a sink. All have a minirefrigerator. Complimentary coffee is offered 24-hours a day in the lobby. There's a small outdoor pool and Kranberry's Family Restaurant (see "Where to Dine," below) is next door.

Martha's Bed & Breakfast. Main and Lima sts., Columbus, NM 88029. ☎ **505/ 531-2467.** Fax 505/531-2479. 5 units. A/C TV TEL. $55 double. Breakfast included. MC, V. Children and pets are welcome.

If you'd like to add a little Mexico adventure to your southern New Mexico stay, head south of Deming 30 miles and stay with Martha. She has a two-story stucco Pueblo-style adobe painted cream and green, with Victorian touches inside. Built in 1991, it's just 3 miles from the Mexican border town of Las Palomas. The place is furnished with some nice antiques as well as furniture made in their family's *maquilladora* (manufacturing plant) across the border. The medium-sized rooms have comfortably firm beds and good bedding. Each has French doors and a balcony. Bathrooms are medium-sized and basic with showers, and very clean. This is not a luxury B&B, nor is great care taken in making your stay perfect, but Martha is a complete character and enjoys being a host, which is worth a lot. She'll fill you with stories of border town life, and tell you exactly when and how to see what. Breakfasts are simple and full. I had fruit, egg-toast, and Canadian bacon. If you're lucky you'll arrive on one of the two weeks of the year when the Tumbleweed Theater has a melodrama performance, held in back of the inn, with Martha presiding.

Camping in & around Deming & Lordsburg

City of Rocks State Park, in Deming (☎ 505/536-2800), has 62 campsites, 10 with electric hookups; tenting is available, and there are picnic tables and a hiking trail nearby. **Dreamcatcher RV Park** (☎ 505/544-4004), also in Deming (take Exit 85, Motel Drive, off I-10 and go 1 block south on Business I-10) has 92 sites, all with full hookups. It also offers free access to a nearby swimming pool, and on-site laundry facilities. **Little Vineyard RV Park** (☎ 505/546-3560) near Deming (from I-10 take Exit 85 and go 1 mile southwest on Business I-10 toward Deming) is larger than those already mentioned. It offers the same facilities as Dreamcatcher RV Park, with the addition of limited groceries, an indoor pool and hot tub, grills, cable TV hookups, and a small RV parts store. The campground at **Rockhound State Park** (☎ 505/ 546-6182) is picturesque and great for rock hounds who can't get enough of their hobby. RV sites with hookups and tenting are both available, and there are shelters, rest rooms, and showers.

If you'd rather camp near Lordsburg, try **KOA Lordsburg** (☎ 505/542-8003). It's in a desert setting, but there are shade trees and tenting is permitted. Grocery and laundry facilities are available in addition to a recreation room/area, swimming pool, playground, and horseshoes. To reach the campground, take I-10 to Exit 22 and then go 1 block south; next, go right at the Chevron station and follow the signs to the campground.

WHERE TO DINE

Kranberry's Family Restaurant. 1405 S. Main St., Lordsburg. ☎ **505/542-9400.** Lunch and dinner main courses $2.80–$14.50. AE, CB, DC, DISC, MC, V. Daily 6am–9:30pm. AMERICAN/MEXICAN.

A friendly, casual family restaurant decorated with Southwest art, Kranberry's offers home-style American favorites including burgers, chicken, beef, and salads, as well as Mexican selections. Baked goods are made on the premises daily, and there's a children's menu.

✪ **Veranda Deli.** 110 S. Silver Ave., Deming. ☎ **505/546-8585.** All menu items under $6. Open Mon, Tues, and Thurs–Sat winter 9am–6pm; summer 11am–7pm. AE, DC, DISC, MC, V. GOURMET BAKERY AND SANDWICH SHOP.

Located in a historic 1902 power plant building, this cafe lends a bit of sophistication to very provincial Deming. After I'd eaten here and checked the place out, I met with owner Esta Guy, a strong and vocal woman, who brought me back into the kitchen and had me try the roast beef, just so I could see that these were not store-purchased lunch meats on her sandwiches but home-roasted meats, and she was right. The decor is simple, with nonmatching wood tables and a variety of chairs. The patio, which is graced with 2-century-old fig trees and has a mist-cooler, is especially nice in the early evenings. I had a veggie wrap (black beans, veggies, and three kinds of sprouts) served with delicious potato salad. There are always soups of the day such as beef noodle and chicken/rice, rich and delectable concoctions made by Esta. For breakfast try an applesauce oat bran or blueberry muffin and a good espresso or cappuccino. If you like dessert, a number of rich delicacies are displayed at the front counter.

7 Silver City: Gateway to the Gila Cliff Dwellings

Silver City (pop. 11,508) is an old mining town, located in the foothills of the Pinos Altos Range of the Mogollon Mountains, and gateway to the Gila Wilderness and the Gila Cliff Dwellings. Early Native Americans mined turquoise from these hills, and by 1804 Spanish settlers were digging for copper. In 1870, a group of prospectors discovered silver, and the rush was on. In 10 short months, the newly christened Silver City grew from a single cabin to more than 80 buildings. Early visitors included Billy the Kid, Judge Roy Bean, and William Randolph Hearst.

This comparatively isolated community kept pace with every modern convenience: telephones in 1883, electric lights in 1884 (only 2 years after New York City installed its lighting), and a water system in 1887. Typically, the town should have busted with the crash of silver prices in 1893. But unlike many Western towns, Silver City did not become a picturesque memory. It capitalized on its high dry climate to become today's county seat and trade center. Copper mining and processing are still the major industry. But Silver City also can boast a famous son: the late Harrison (Jack) Schmitt, the first civilian geologist to visit the moon, and later a U.S. senator, was born and raised in nearby Santa Rita.

ESSENTIALS

GETTING THERE   From Albuquerque take I-25 south, 15 miles past Truth or Consequences; then west on NM 152 and U.S. 180 (5 hours). From Las Cruces take I-10 west to Deming, then north on U.S. 180 (2 hours).

Mesa Airlines (☎ 800/ MESA-AIR or 505/388-4115) flies daily from Albuquerque to Grant County Airport, 15 miles south of Silver City near Hurley. Pick up a car there from **Grimes Aviation and Car Rental** (☎ 505/538-2142). **Silver Stage Lines** (☎ 800/522-0162) offers daily shuttle service to the El Paso airport, and charter service to Tucson. The **Las Cruces Shuttle Service** (☎ 800/288-1784) runs several times daily from Silver City to the El Paso airport, by way of Las Cruces.

VISITOR INFORMATION The **Silver City-Grant County Chamber of Commerce,** at 201 N. Hudson St., Silver City, NM 88061 (☎ 800/548-9378 or 505/538-3785), maintains a visitor information headquarters on NM 90, a few blocks south of U.S. 180. The chamber produces extremely useful tourist publications.

WHAT TO SEE & DO IN TOWN

Silver City's downtown ✪ **Historic District,** the first such district to receive National Register recognition, is a must for visitors. The downtown core is marked by the extensive use of brick in construction: Brick clay was discovered in the area soon after the town's founding in 1870, and an 1880 ordinance prohibited frame construction within the town limits. Mansard-roofed Victorian houses, Queen Anne and Italianate residences, and commercial buildings show off the cast-iron architecture of the period. Some are still undergoing restoration.

An 1895 flood washed out Main Street and turned it into a gaping chasm, which was eventually bridged over; finally, the **Big Ditch,** as it's called, was made into a green park in the center of town. Facing downtown, in the 500 block of North Hudson Street, was a famous red-light district from the turn of the century until the late 1960s.

Billy the Kid lived in Silver City as a youth. You can see his cabin site a block north of the Broadway bridge, on the east side of the Big Ditch. The Kid (William Bonney) waited tables at the Star Hotel, Hudson Street and Broadway. He was jailed (at 304 N. Hudson St.) in 1875 at the age of 15, after being convicted of stealing from a Chinese laundry, but he escaped—a first for The Kid. The grave of Bonney's mother, Catherine McCarty, is in Silver City Cemetery, east of town on Memory Lane, off U.S. 180. She died of tuberculosis about a year after the family moved here in 1873.

✪ **Silver City Museum.** 312 W. Broadway. ☎ **505/538-5921.** Fax 505/538-5921. E-mail: SCMuseum@zianet.com. Free admission. Tues–Fri 9am–4:30pm, Sat–Sun 10am–4pm. Closed Mon except Memorial Day and Labor Day.

This very well presented museum of city and regional history contains collections relating to southwest New Mexico history, mining displays, Native American pottery, and early photographs. Exhibits include a southwest New Mexico history time line; a parlor displaying Victorian decorative arts; and a chronicle of commerce in early Silver City. A local history research library is available to visitors also. The main gallery features changing exhibits.

The museum is lodged in the newly restored 1881 H. B. Ailman House, a former city hall and fire station remarkable for its cupola and Victorian mansard roof. Ailman came to Silver City penniless in 1871, made a fortune in mining, and went on to start the Meredith and Ailman Bank. Guided historic district walking tours are offered on Memorial Day and Labor Day. There is also a museum store.

Western New Mexico University Museum. 1000 W. College, Fleming Hall, WNMU. ☎ **505/538-6386.** Admission by donation. Mon–Fri 9am–4:30pm, Sat–Sun 10am–4pm.

Spread across 80 acres on the west side of Silver City, WNMU celebrated its centennial in 1993. The university boasts a 2,500-student enrollment and 24 major buildings. Among them is historic Fleming Hall, which houses this interesting museum.

The WNMU museum has the largest permanent exhibit of prehistoric Mimbres pottery in the United States. Also displayed are Casas Grandes Indian pottery, stone tools, ancient jewelry, historical photographs, and mining and military artifacts. Displays change regularly, so there is always something new to see, such as vanishing Americana, riparian fossils, Nigerian folk art, or a collection of 18th- to 20th-century timepieces. There is a gift shop here.

EXPLORING THE AREA

NORTH OF SILVER CITY   The virtual ghost town of ✪ **Pinos Altos,** straddling the Continental Divide, is 6 miles north of Silver City on NM 15. Dubbed "Tall Pines" when it was founded in the gold- and silver-rush era, Apache attacks and mine failures have taken their toll.

The adobe **Methodist-Episcopal Church** was built with William Randolph Hearst's money in 1898 and now houses the Grant County Art Guild. The **Pinos Altos Museum** displays a ¾-scale reproduction of the Santa Rita del Cobre Fort and Trading Post, built at Santa Rita copper mine in 1804 to protect the area from Apaches. (It was renamed Fort Webster in 1851.) It's still possible to pan for gold in Pinos Altos. The town also has the **Log Cabin Curio Shop and Museum** located in an 1866 cabin (☎ **505/388-1882**), and the Buckhorn Saloon and Opera House (see "Where to Dine," below).

SOUTH OF SILVER CITY   South 12 miles on NM 90 is the **Phelps Dodge Open Pit Copper Mine** (☎ **505/538-5331**). Some 80 million tons of rock are taken out every year.

Phelps Dodge consolidated its Tyrone holdings in 1909 and hired famous architect Bertram Goodhue to design a "Mediterranean-style" company town. **Tyrone,** later referred to as the Million Dollar Ghost Town, was constructed between 1914 and 1918. A large bank and shop building, administration office, mercantile store, and passenger depot were grouped around a central plaza. Eighty-three single and multiple-unit dwellings, accommodating 235 families, were built on the nearby hillsides; and a school, chapel, garage, restaurant, justice court, hospital, morgue, and recreation building were added. A drop in copper prices caused it to be abandoned virtually overnight.

After a pre–World War II incarnation as a luxurious dude ranch, Tyrone lay dormant for years until the late 1960s, when the town made way for the present-day open pit mine and mill. A new town site was created 7 miles north. Most of the original homes and major buildings were removed between 1967 and 1969; today, the only remaining structures are Union Chapel, the justice court, and the pump house. The copper mine supplies copper concentrates to the modern Hidalgo Smelter near Playas, southeast of Lordsburg.

EAST OF SILVER CITY   The oldest active mine in the Southwest, and among the largest in America, is the **Chino Mines Co. Open Pit Copper Mine** (☎ **505/ 537-3381**) at Santa Rita, 15 miles east of Silver City via U.S. 180 and NM 152. The multicolored open pit is a mile wide and 1,000 feet deep, and can be viewed from an observation point. Guided tours, lasting 3½ hours, are offered weekday mornings at 8, 8:30, and 9am.

Apaches once scratched the surface for metallic copper. By 1800, the Spanish, under Col. Jose Manuel Carrasco, were working "Santa Rita del Cobre." Convict labor from New Spain mined the shafts, with mule trains full of ore sent down the Janos Trail to Chihuahua, Mexico. An impressive adobe fort was built near the mine, along with smelters and numerous buildings, but Apache raids finally forced the mine's abandonment. In the late 19th century, the mine was reopened, and the town of Santa Rita was reborn. The huge open pit, started around 1910, soon consumed Santa Rita. Giant-sized machines scoop the ore from the earth and huge 175-ton ore trucks transport it to the reduction mill to the southwest of the pit.

✪ **City of Rocks State Park** (☎ **505/536-2800**), 30 miles from Silver City via U.S. 180 and NM 61, is an area of fantastically shaped volcanic rock formations, formed in ancient times from thick blankets of ash that hardened into tuff. This soft stone, eroded by wind and rain, was shaped into monolithic blocks reminiscent of Stonehenge. For some, the park resembles a medieval village; for others, it is a collection of misshapen, albeit benign giants. Complete with a desert garden, the park offers excellent camping and picnic sites. Day use is allowed from 7am to 9pm for $3 per vehicle; a campsite costs $7 to $11. The visitor center is typically open from 10am to 4pm, but its hours vary depending on the size of its volunteer staff.

WEST OF SILVER CITY   U.S. 180, heading northwest from Silver City, is the gateway to Catron County and most of the Gila National Forest, including the villages of Glenwood, Reserve, and Quemado. For details on this area, see section 9, below.

WHERE TO STAY

Standard motels are strung along U.S. 180 east of NM 90. Some of the more interesting accommodations, however, are not! Most lodgings provide free parking.

Copper Manor Motel. 710 Silver Heights Blvd. (U.S. 180) (P.O. Box 1405), Silver City, NM 88061. ☎ **800/853-2916** or 505/538-5392. 67 units. A/C TV TEL. $48–$54 double. AE, CB, DC, MC, V.

This centrally located motel built in the early 1970s and well remodeled in 1998 has very comfortable rooms that feel brand new. The medium sized rooms have floral print decor, white wood furniture, and springy but comfortable beds. Bathrooms are small, simple, and clean with an outer sink/vanity. Rooms are fairly quiet; to be sure, request one toward the back of the property, away from the street. The Red Barn Steak House is next door. Facilities include an indoor pool and whirlpool; guests can also use the Drifter's outdoor pool.

Holiday Motor Hotel. 3420 U.S. 180 E., Silver City, NM 88061. ☎ **800/828-8291** or 505/538-3711. Fax 505/538-3711. 80 units. A/C TV TEL. $55–$65 double. AE, DC, DISC, MC, V. Pets allowed.

Located about 3 miles east of downtown near the junction of U.S. 180 and NM 15, this motel is a step above the ordinary with its landscaped grounds, attractive outdoor heated swimming pool, playground, all-night security guard, and guest Laundromat. Rooms are medium-sized with Aztec print decor and basic oak furnishings. The medium-sized bathroom has an outer vanity and is very clean. Beds are medium firm. Ask for a west-facing room and you'll have a view of the lawn and pool. The restaurant serves three meals daily with a menu superior to the typical hotel coffee shop. There's free coffee and refreshments in the lobby, dry-cleaning service, and access to a nearby health club.

SMALLER INNS

✪ **Bear Mountain Guest Ranch.** Cottage San Rd., Silver City, NM 88061. ☎ **800/ 880-2538** or 505/538-2538. www.BearMtGuestRanch.com. E-mail: innkeeper@ BearMtGuestRanch.com. 13 units, 1 cottage. $105–$125 for 2 people. Rates include 3 meals daily. Cottage with kitchenette (meals not included) $65–$90 for 1 to 4 persons. No credit cards. To reach the ranch, turn north off U.S. 180 on Alabama St. (½ mile west of NM 90 intersection). Proceed 2.8 miles (Alabama becomes Cottage San Rd.) to dirt road turnoff to left; the ranch is another 0.6 miles.

Rustic and austere, this is my kind of guest ranch, but it's not for those who expect perfection. Spread across 160 acres just 3½ miles northwest of downtown Silver City, Myra McCormick's ranch has been a New Mexico institution since 1959. This is a nature-lover's delight—McCormick hosts birding, wild plant, and archaeological workshops throughout the year, and a "Lodge and Learn" series (for adults of all ages) is a feature every month. Rooms are large with maple floors, high ceilings, and French windows. They have good but basic furnishings; mine had no bedside tables, and I've heard that some beds bow toward the middle, though mine was comfortably soft. What's best here is you can count on complete quiet. The rooms in the two-story ranch house have higher ceilings and more charm than those in the adjacent cottage. Meals are served family style and always begin with a very structured introduction session that works well at getting the guests talking. The food is basic ranch fare, well prepared and tasty. There is public transportation to the door by Silver Stage Line.

✪ **The Palace Hotel.** 106 W. Broadway (P.O. Box 5093), Silver City, NM 88061. ☎ **505/ 388-1811.** 20 units. TV TEL. $30–$41 double; $43–$55 suite. Rates include continental breakfast. AE, CB, DC, DISC, MC, V.

Old-West elegance and Victorian decor are earmarks of this property, first established 1882 and reopened in July 1990 as a historic small European-style hotel. It sits at the center of the downtown historic district. Each of the rooms on the second floor are shaped and decorated differently. All are decorated with antiques, have quilts as bed coverings, ceiling fans, and new carpet. Beds are soft and springy. The medium-sized bathrooms are very clean with old fixtures, but new toilets. A few rooms don't have windows to the outside, and you may want to avoid these. It appears that the rooms closest to the upstairs sitting room and breakfast area are the nicest. Suites have minirefrigerators. Two share bathrooms; all others have bathtubs and showers. That's a sight better than in 1882! The owners provide fresh fruit, bread, juice, fruit, coffee, and tea for breakfast, which is served in the upstairs skylit garden room. The hotel is reachable from El Paso by the Las Cruces Shuttle and Silver Stage Shuttle.

CAMPING

KOA Silver City (☎ 800/KOA-7623) has 82 sites and 42 full hookups, and offers groceries, laundry facilities, a restaurant, and pool. The campground is 5 miles east of the NM 90/U.S. 180 junction on U.S. 180. **Silver City RV Park** (☎ 505/538-2239) has 48 sites, 45 full hookups, laundry facilities, and picnic tables. It's located downtown on Bennett Street, behind Furr's supermarket. Camping is also available at the Gila Cliff Dwellings (see section 8 below).

WHERE TO DINE

✪ **Buckhorn Saloon and Opera House.** 32 Main St., Pinos Altos. ☎ **505/538-9911.** Reservations strongly recommended. Main courses $12.95–$28.95. MC, V. Mon–Sat 6–10pm. CONTINENTAL/STEAKS.

Seven miles north of Silver City in Pinos Altos, the Buckhorn offers elegant dining in 1860s decor. It's noted for its Western-style steaks, seafood, homemade desserts, and excellent wine list. If you've got a big appetite, try the New York strip with green chile and cheese. I liked the big fried shrimp. Entrees are served with a salad or soup and choice of potatoes or rice. There's live entertainment nightly, except Tuesday; the saloon opens at 3pm during the week. Many come to this saloon to have excellent burgers.

Jalisco's. 103 S. Bullard, Silver City. ☎ **505/388-2060.** Reservations accepted. Main courses $3–$8. No credit cards. Mon–Sat 11am–8:30pm, Fri 11am–9pm. NEW MEXICAN.

Set within an enchanting brick building in the historic district, this festive restaurant serves decent food. Three dining rooms fill the old structure, which has been Latinized with arched doorways and bold Mexican street-scene calendars on the walls. The combination plates are large and popular, as are the enchiladas. There are also burgers and a children's menu. Whatever you do, be sure to order a sopaipilla for dessert. They're delicious and huge. No alcoholic beverages are served.

Vickie's Downtown Deli. 107 W. Yankie, Silver City. ☎ **505/388-5430.** All menu items under $7. Mon 11am–4pm, Tues–Thurs 11am–7:30pm, Fri–Sat 11am–8:30pm. AE, MC, DISC, V. GOURMET SOUPS AND SANDWICHES.

It's worthwhile to spend some time wandering around historical Silver City, particularly making your way down the street where this deli is located. Many galleries surround it, and the food is sophisticated and tasty. Set in a historic building, the dining rooms are a little dark but have an artsy, city cafe feel. Along the side there is a tree-shaded patio. Each day there are specials worth checking out. Otherwise, I suggest the Rueben sandwich made with Emmentaler Swiss cheese and served with chips and salsa or German potato salad. The Mediterranean salad plate is also tasty and comes with feta, kalamata olives, hummus, and pita bread.

8 Gila Cliff Dwellings National Monument

It takes at least 1½ to 2 hours to reach the Gila Cliff Dwellings from Silver City, but it's definitely worth the trip. First-time visitors are inevitably awed by the sight. At this stone-within-stone-on-stone relic of a long-gone civilization, reality is somehow exaggerated in the dazzling sunlight and contrasting shadow, making the dwellings look, from a distance, as two-dimensional as a stage set. The solid masonry walls are well preserved, even though they've been abandoned for 7 centuries.

The cliff dwellings were discovered by Anglo settlers in the early 1870s, near where the three forks of the Gila River rise. Seven natural caves occur in the southeast-facing cliff of a side canyon; six of them contain the ruins of dwellings, which had about 42 rooms. Probably not more than 8 or 10 Mogollon families (40 to 50 people) lived in these dwellings at any one time. Tree-ring dating indicates their residence didn't last longer than 30 to 40 years at the end of the 13th century.

ESSENTIALS

GETTING THERE   From Silver City take NM 15 up 44 miles to the Gila Cliff Dwellings. Travel time from Silver City is approximately 2 hours. Keep in mind that there are no gas stations available between Silver City and Gila Cliff Dwellings, so plan accordingly. Once you get to the monument, you should know that vehicles are permitted on paved roads only.

VISITOR INFORMATION   For more information contact **Gila Cliff Dwellings National Monument,** Route 11, Box 100, Silver City, NM 88061 (☎ **505/536-9461**).

ADMISSION FEES & HOURS   Admission to the monument is $3 per person, with children ages 8 and under admitted free. The visitor center, where you can pick up detailed brochures, is open from 8am to 5pm Memorial Day to Labor Day, and from 8am to 4:30pm the rest of the year. The cliff dwellings are open from 8am to 6pm in the summer, and from 9am to 4pm the rest of the year.

SEEING THE HIGHLIGHTS

Today, the dwellings allow a rare glimpse inside the homes and lives of prehistoric Native Americans. About 75% of what is seen is original, although the walls have been capped and the foundations strengthened to prevent further deterioration. It took a great deal of effort to build these homes: The stones were held in place by mortar, and all of the clay and water for the mortar had to be carried up from the stream, as the Mogollon did not have any pack animals. The vigas for the roof were cut and shaped with stone axes or fire.

The people who lived here were farmers, as shown by the remains of beans, squash, and corn in their homes. The fields were along the valley of the west fork of the Gila River and on the mesa across the canyon. No signs of irrigation have been found.

A 1-mile loop trail, rising 175 feet from the canyon floor, provides access to the dwellings.

Near the visitor center, about a mile away, the remains of an earlier (A.D. 100–400) pit house, built below ground level, and later pit houses (up to A.D. 1000), above-ground structures of adobe or wattle, have been found.

CAMPING

Camping and picnicking are encouraged in the national monument, and there are four developed campgrounds. Overnight lodging can be found in Silver City and in the nearby town of Gila Hot Springs, which also has a grocery store, horse rentals, and guided pack trips.

9 Other Adventures in Gila National Forest

Gila National Forest, which offers some of the most spectacular mountain scenery in the Southwest, comprises 3.3 million acres in four counties. Nearly one-fourth of that acreage (790,000 acres) comprises the **Gila, Aldo Leopold,** and **Blue Range Wildernesses.** Its highest peak is Whitewater Baldy, 10,892 feet. Within the forest six out of seven life zones can be found, so the range of plant and wildlife is broad. You may see mule deer, elk, antelope, black bear, mountain lion, and bighorn sheep. Nearly 400 miles of streams and a few small lakes sustain healthy populations of trout as well as bass, bluegill, and catfish. Anglers can head to Lake Roberts, Snow Lake, and Quemado Lake.

JUST THE FACTS   For more information on the national forest, contact **U.S. Forest Service,** Forest Supervisor's Office, 3005 East Camino del Bosque, Silver City, NM 88061 (☎ 505/388-8201).

Eighteen campgrounds can be found in the national forest, seven with drinking water and toilets. Car and backpack camping are also permitted throughout the forest.

HIKING & OTHER ACTIVITIES

Within the forest are 1,490 miles of trails for hiking and horseback riding, and in winter, cross-country skiing. Outside of the wilderness areas, trail bikes and off-road vehicles are also permitted. Hiking trails in the Gila Wilderness, especially the 41-mile Middle Fork Trail, with its east end near Gila Cliff Dwellings, are among the most popular in the state, and can sometimes be crowded. If you are more interested in communing with nature than with fellow hikers, however, you will find plenty of trails to suit you, both in and out of the officially designated wilderness areas.

Most of the trails are maintained and easy to follow. Trails along river bottoms, however, have many stream crossings (so be prepared for hiking with wet feet) and may be washed out by summer flash floods. It's best to inquire about trail conditions before you set out. More than 50 trailheads provide roadside parking.

Some of the best hikes in the area are the Frisco Box, Pueblo Creek, Whitewater Baldy, The Catwalk and Beyond, Middle Fork/Little Bear Loop, and the Black Range Crest Trail. The Gila National Forest contains several wilderness areas that are off-limits to mountain bikes, including the Gila, Aldo Leopold, and the Blue Range Primitive Area. However cyclers can access quite a few trails. Some to look for are the Cleveland Mine trail, Silver City Loop, Continental Divide, Signal Peak, Pinos Altos Loop, Fort Bayard Historical Trails, and Forest Trail 100.

The ✪ **Catwalk National Recreation Trail** (☎ **505/539-2481**), 68 miles north of Silver City on U.S. 180, then 5 miles east of Glenwood via NM 174, is a great break after a long drive. Kids are especially thrilled with this hike reached by foot from a parking area. It follows the route of a pipeline built in 1897 to carry water to the now-defunct town of Graham and its electric generator. About ¼ mile above the parking area is the beginning of a striking 250-foot metal causeway clinging to the sides of the boulder-choked Whitewater Canyon, which in spots is 20 feet wide and 250 feet deep. Along the way you'll find water pouring through caves formed from boulders and waterfalls spitting off the cliff side. Farther up the canyon, a suspension bridge spans the chasm. Picnic facilities are located near the parking area.

OTHER HIGHLIGHTS

The scenic ghost town of **Mogollon** is 3½ miles north of Glenwood on U.S. 180, then 9 miles east on NM 159, a narrow mountain road that takes a good 25 minutes to negotiate. The village bears witness to silver and gold mining booms beginning in the late 19th century, and to the disastrous effects of floods and fire in later years. Remains of its last operating mine, the Little Fanny (which ceased operation in the 1950s), are still visible, along with dozens of other old buildings, miner's shacks, and mining paraphernalia. An art gallery and museum are found along Mogollon's main street. The movie *My Name Is Nobody,* starring Henry Fonda, was shot here.

Reserve (pop. 300), Catron County seat, is noted as the place where, in 1882, Deputy Sheriff Elfego Baca made an epic stand in a 33-hour gun battle with 80 cowboys. Cochise, Geronimo, and other Apache war chiefs held forth in these mountains in the late 19th century.

Southeastern New Mexico

I'd been to Carlsbad Caverns and to White Sands National Monument while I was growing up in New Mexico, but I'd seen them then through the eyes of a child. When I returned to these places as an adult, their immensity overwhelmed me and their intricate beauty stirred my soul.

Running east of the Rio Grande (the I-25 corridor) and south of I-40, Southeastern New Mexico has other wonderful sites as well. Along with the natural wonders, this is the home of the fierce Mescalero Apaches and of the world's richest horse race. Billy the Kid lived and died in southeastern New Mexico in the 19th century, and the world's first atomic bomb was exploded here in the 20th. From west to east, barren desert gives way to high, forested peaks, snow-covered in winter; to the fertile valley of the Pecos River; and to high plains beloved by ranchers along the Texas border.

The main population center in this section of the state is Roswell (pop. 50,000), famous as the purported landing place of an unidentified flying object (UFO). Carlsbad (pop. 27,800), 76 miles south of Roswell, and Alamogordo (pop. 31,000), 117 miles west of Roswell, are of more immediate interest to tourists. Other sizable towns are Clovis (pop. 38,100) and Hobbs (pop.32,000), both on the Texas border, and Artesia (pop. 11,958), between Roswell and Carlsbad. Ruidoso (pop. 8,500), in the mountains between Alamogordo and Roswell, is a booming resort town.

EXPLORING THE REGION BY CAR

From Albuquerque, head south on I-25 to San Antonio, just beyond Socorro, then turn east on U.S. 380 through Carrizozo. This route will take you first to the Ruidoso area, whose major attractions can be defined by a triangle formed by U.S. 380, U.S. 70, and NM 48. **Ruidoso** is the home of the world's richest horse race, and nearby **Lincoln National Forest** attracts outdoor enthusiasts. This is also Billy the Kid country, and the historic village of **Lincoln** recounts those Wild West days.

Next, drive south on U.S. 70 to explore **Alamogordo** and **White Sands National Monument.** Spend the night in Alamogordo. I recommend camping out so you can watch the sunrise over the white sands. The next day, follow U.S. 82 east through the charming mountain village of **Cloudcroft** and down the valley of

Southeastern New Mexico

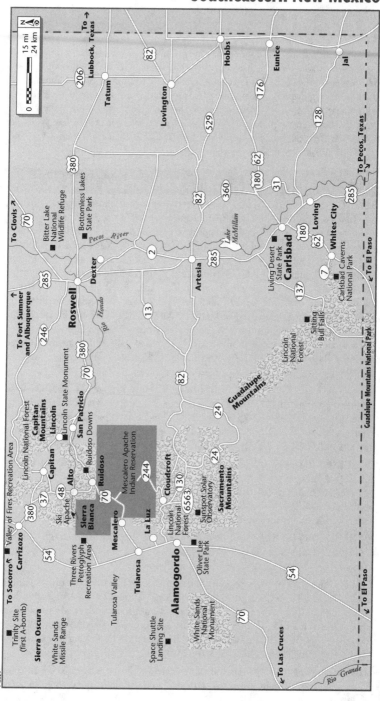

1-0629

the Rio Penasco with its fruit orchards. At Artesia, turn south on U.S. 285 to **Carlsbad,** where you can explore the town and the famous **Carlsbad Caverns.**

From Carlsbad, you can follow two routes. You can reverse course back up U.S. 285 to **Roswell,** where you can check out the International UFO Museum or the Roswell Art Center and (via NM 20) **Fort Sumner,** site of Fort Sumner State Monument and Billy the Kid's grave. Or you can meander through the Llano Estacado along the Texas border, taking U.S. 62/180 east to Hobbs, then turning north on NM 206 to Clovis. From the latter city, Fort Sumner is an hour's drive west on U.S. 60/84. Next, head north from Fort Sumner on U.S. 84 to I-40 at Santa Rosa; from there it's a 2-hour drive west to Albuquerque.

1 The Great Outdoors in Southeastern New Mexico

BIKING   Several unpaved roads in this region are favorites with mountain bikers. In the Ruidoso area, near Cloudcroft, the **Rim Trail,** a 17-mile intermediate trail that offers views of the White Sands, is considered one of the top 10 trails in the nation. To reach the trail, take NM 130 from Cloudcroft and look for the Rim Trail signs. The Cloudcroft area offers three other good trails, the La Luz Canyon, Silver Springs Loop, and Pumphouse Canyon. For directions, contact the Cloudcroft Ranger Station (☎ **505/683-2551**). For beginners, the Bonito Lake Road offers a scenic but easy 20-mile (round-trip) ride through the forest and around the lake. To reach the trail, take NM 48 from Ruidoso and turn off at NM 37. The road from Ski Apache Road up to Monjeau Campground as well as several other roads in the Bonito Lake area near Ruidoso are also well-traveled bike routes. The paved road up to **Carlsbad Caverns National Park** is scenic and the auto traffic drives slowly, but it's very hot in the summer.

BIRD WATCHING   **Bitter Lake National Wildlife Refuge** (☎ **505/622-6755**), northeast of Roswell, is particularly good for watching migratory waterfowl, and **Bluff Springs** (☎ **505/682-2551**), south of Cloudcroft, is popular with turkeys and hummingbirds. If you find turkey vultures particularly fascinating, **Rattlesnake Springs** (☎ **505/785-2232**), located south of Carlsbad, is the place to go.

BOATING   Boating, waterskiing, jet-skiing, and sailing are permitted at **Carlsbad Municipal Park,** which runs through town for just over a mile along the west bank of Lake Carlsbad. The lake also has a beach that's open to swimmers. **Brantley Lake State Park** (☎ **505/457-2384**), 15 miles north of Carlsbad, is popular with windsurfers who favor its consistent desert winds.

FISHING   **Bonito Lake** and **Rio Ruidoso** are popular destinations for trout fishing, and **Oasis State Park** (☎ **505/356-5331**) just north of Portales also offers fishing.

GOLF   There are plenty of opportunities in this region. **Cree Meadows Country Club,** Country Club Drive off Sudderth Drive (☎ **505/257-5815**), is an 18-hole public course. Also public are the 18-hole courses at the **Inn of the Mountain Gods,** Carrizo Canyon Road (☎ **505/257-5141**); **The Links at Sierra Blanca,** 105 Sierra Blanca Dr. (☎ **505/258-5330**); and the **Alto Lakes Golf and Country Club,** High Mesa Drive, Alto Village (☎ **505/336-4231**), is an 18-hole private course.

HIKING   More than 225 miles of trails weave a web through Smokey Bear Ranger District of the **Lincoln National Forest.** From Ruidoso, a favorite destination of hikers is the White Mountain Wilderness, with nine trailheads, and the Capitan Mountains Wilderness, with 11 trails. Smokey Bear Ranger District office,

901 Mechem Dr., Ruidoso, has excellent and inexpensive maps of each wilderness area. Monjeau Lookout is a popular destination off Ski Run Road (NM 532). **Carlsbad Caverns National Park** has an extensive trail system as well (outside of the caves, of course), and cars are not permitted. From the **Ski Apache** area, there's also a 5-mile trail that leads to the top of Sierra Blanca, the area's highest mountain.

HORSEBACK RIDING   Horseback riding is easily found in Ruidoso. Try the **Inn of the Mountain Gods** (☎ **505/257-5141**), **Buddy's Stable** (☎ **505/258-4027**), and **Cowboy Stables** (☎ **505/378-8217**).

SKIING   Southern New Mexico's premier ski resort is **Ski Apache** (☎ **505/ 257-9001** for snow report, or 505/336-4356 for information), only 20 miles northwest of Ruidoso in the Mescalero Apache Reservation. Situated on an 11,500-foot ridge of the 12,003-foot Sierra Blanca, the resort boasts a gondola, two quad chairs, five triple chairs, one double chair, a day lodge, sport shop, rental shop, ski school, first-aid center, four snack bars, and a lounge. Ski Apache has 55 trails and slopes (20% beginner, 35% intermediate, and 45% advanced), with a vertical drop of 1,900 feet and a total skier capacity of 16,500 an hour. Though its location seems remote, a lot of skiers fill this mountain during weekends and holidays. Your best bet is to ski during the week, particularly in January. What's especially unique about the mountain is that, since it is owned and run by the Apaches, you can experience another culture while skiing. All-day lift tickets for adults cost $40 to $43, and $25 to $28 for children (12 and under). The mountain is open Thanksgiving to Easter daily from 8:45am to 4pm. Lift-and-lodging packages can be booked through the **Inn of the Mountain Gods** (☎ **800/545-9011**). **Ski Cloudcroft** (☎ **505/682-2333**) is a small ski area that is open only some winters. The mountain has 21 runs and a 700-foot vertical, served by one double chair and two surface lifts. It appeals primarily to beginning skiers. When there's snow (usually December through March), it's open from 9am to 4pm daily. Snowboarding is permitted. Lift rates are $25 for adults; $16 for children 12 and under; $12 for night skiing.

2 Alamogordo

Famous for its leading role in America's space research and military technology industries, Alamogordo (pop. 31,000) first achieved worldwide fame on July 16, 1945, when the first atomic bomb was exploded at nearby Trinity Site. Today, it is home of the Space Center and International Space Hall of Fame, White Sands National Monument, and Holloman Air Force Base. While traveling in this area, I came to call it Alamageddin, mostly because the town itself is fairly desolate without many amenities. Twenty miles east and twice as high, the resort village of Cloudcroft (elevation 8,650 feet) attracts vacationers to the forested heights of the Sacramento Mountains.

ESSENTIALS

GETTING THERE   From Albuquerque take I-25 south 87 miles to San Antonio; turn east on U.S. 380, 66 miles to Carrizozo; then south on U.S. 54 for 58 miles (4 hours). From Las Cruces, take U.S. 70 northeast (1½ hours). (Note, however, that U.S. 70 may be closed for up to 2 hours during tests on White Sands Missile Range.) From El Paso, take U.S. 54 north (1½ hours). The nearest major airport is **El Paso International.** The local airport, **Alamogordo–White Sands Regional Airport,** is served by **Mesa Airlines** (☎ **800/MESA-AIR** or 505/437-9111), which has flights from Albuquerque several times daily. **Avis** (☎ **800/831-2847** or 505/437-3140) rents cars at the municipal airport.

VISITOR INFORMATION The **Alamogordo Chamber of Commerce** and visitor center is at 1301 N. White Sands Blvd. Write to P.O. Box 2828, Alamogordo, NM 88311 (☎ 800/826-0294 or 505/437-6120).

CITY LAYOUT Alamogordo is on the eastern edge of the Tularosa Valley, at the foot of the Sacramento Mountains. U.S. 54 (White Sands Boulevard) is the main street, extending several miles north and south. The downtown district is actually 3 blocks east of White Sands Boulevard, off 10th Street.

WHAT TO SEE & DO

In addition to the attractions in Alamogordo itself, also enjoyable is the small, historic village of **La Luz,** just 3 miles north of Alamogordo. It has attracted a number of resident artists and craftspeople who live, work, and display some of their products for sale. Worth seeing are the old adobe corral and the small Our Lady of Light Church.

✪ **Space Center.** Scenic Dr. and Indian Wells Rd. ☎ **800/545-4021** outside New Mexico, or 505/437-2840. Admission to Space Hall $2.50 adults and seniors (60 and older), $2 teens (13–17) and youths (6–18); free for children 5 and under. Theater $5.50 adults, $5 seniors, $4.50 teens, $3 youths; additional for double feature; free for children 5 and under. Prices subject to change without notice. Daily 9am–6pm summer; 9am–5pm winter.

The Space Center comes in two parts: the **International Space Hall of Fame** and the **Clyde W. Tombaugh IMAX Dome Theater.** Both are located on the lower slopes of the Sacramento Mountains, 2 miles east of U.S. 54, and just above New Mexico State University's Alamogordo branch campus.

The Space Hall of Fame occupies the "Golden Cube," a five-story building with walls of golden glass. Visitors are encouraged to start on the top floor and work their way down. En route, they recall the accomplishments of the first astronauts and cosmonauts, including America's Mercury, Gemini, and Apollo programs, and the early Soviet orbital flights. Spacecraft and a lunar exploration module are exhibited. There's a space-station plan, a hands-on cutaway of crew module "Space Station 2001," and explanations of life in space aboard Skylab and Salyut. Other displays tell the history and purposes of rocketry, missiles, and satellites; provide an orientation to astronomy and exploration of other planets; and tell about New Mexico's role in space exploration history, from ancient Indians to rocketry pioneer Robert Goddard to astronauts.

On adjacent grounds is the "Sonic Wind No. 1" sled, which tested human endurance to speeds exceeding 600 m.p.h. in preparation for future space flights; the "Little Joe II" rocket, which tested Apollo launch escape systems; and other historic artifacts of space travel.

Each year, on the third Saturday of October, new members of the Space Hall of Fame are inducted in a special ceremony here.

At the Tombaugh Theater, IMAX projection and Spitz 512 Planetarium Systems create earthly and cosmic experiences on a 2,700-square-foot dome screen. Twenty special-effects projectors can show 2,354 stars, the Milky Way, all the visible planets, the sun, and the moon, and can duplicate the night sky anywhere on earth, anytime of the year. Special programs allow visitors to take part in a laser-concert symphony of sight and sound, learn about the cosmos, and share a variety of IMAX experiences.

Toy Train Depot. 1991 N. White Sands Blvd. ☎ **505/437-2855.** Admission $2 adults, $1.50 children; train rides $2 adults, $1.50 children. Wed–Mon noon–5pm.

The brainchild of John Koval (whom you're likely to meet at the door), this is an interesting attraction for train fanatics and laypeople. Koval started the nonprofit museum housed in a genuine 1898 railroad depot 10 years ago as a means to celebrate the railroad's important presence in the area. The museum meanders back through three rooms, each filled with tracks laid along colorful miniature city- and countryscapes, 1,200 feet of track altogether. The highlight is the last room, a re-creation of Alamogordo, Carrizoso and Cloudcroft where six trains swirl over bridges, through tunnels and along flats, while train whistles blow and switch lights blink. The trains date from the 1800s, as well as numerous examples from the 1930s through the 1950s. Rides through the grounds on 12-inch and 16-inch gauge trains are also offered. There's also a railroad hobby shop.

SOMETHING UNUSUAL

✪ **Eagle Ranch Pistachio Groves.** 7288 U.S. 54/70, Alamogordo, 88310. ☎ **800/ 432-0999** or 505/434-0035. www.eagleranchpistacios.com. Admission free. Gift shop and gallery daily 9am–6pm.

My father is an apple farmer, so he's totally into the tree-tours here. But even without his bias, I recommend this stop. New Mexico's first and largest pistachio groves, Eagle Ranch offers 45-minute tours each weekday at 1:30pm, with a 10am tour added during the summer. The tour offers a brief history of the pistachio grove, a tour of their shipping and receiving facility, salting and roasting department, and out through the groves. There's also a visitors' center with an art gallery displaying the work of local artists, and a gift shop where you can buy pistachio nuts and a variety of other items.

TRINITY SITE

The world's first atomic bomb was exploded in this desert never-never land on July 16, 1945. It is strictly off-limits to civilians—except twice a year, on the first Saturday of April and October. A small lava monument commemorates the explosion, which left a crater a quarter mile across, 8 feet deep, and transformed the desert sand into a jade green glaze called "Trinitite" that remains today. The McDonald House, where the bomb's plutonium core was assembled 2 miles from Ground Zero, has been restored to its 1945 condition. The site is on the west slope of Sierra Oscura, 90 air miles northwest of Alamogordo. For more information, call the public affairs office of **White Sands Missile Range** (☎ **505/678-1134**).

GETTING OUTSIDE

Fifteen miles southeast of Alamogordo via U.S. 54 and Dog Canyon Road you'll find **Oliver Lee Memorial State Park.** Nestled at the mouth of Dog Canyon, a stunning break in the steep escarpment of the Sacramento Mountains, the site has drawn human visitors for thousands of years. Springs and seeps support a variety of rare and endangered plant species, as well as a rich wildlife. Hiking trails into the foothills are well marked; the park also offers a visitor's center with excellent exhibits on local history, and picnic and camping grounds, with showers, electricity, and a dump station.

Dog Canyon was one of the last strongholds of the Mescalero Apache, and was the site of battles between Native Americans and the U.S. Cavalry in the 19th century. Around the turn of the 20th century, rancher Oliver Lee built a home near here and raised cattle; guided tours from the visitor center to his restored house give a taste of early ranch life in southern New Mexico.

The park is open daily from 7am to sunset, and admission is $3 per car. The visitor center is open daily from 9am to 4pm. Guided tours are offered Saturday and Sunday at 3pm, weather permitting. For more information, call ☎ **505/437-8284.**

EXPLORING THE SURROUNDING AREA

✪ **Cloudcroft** is a picturesque mountain village of 750 people high in the Sacramento Mountains, surrounded by Lincoln National Forest. Though only about 20 miles east of Alamogordo via U.S. 82, it is twice as high, overlooking the Tularosa Valley from a dizzying elevation of about 9,000 feet. It was founded in 1899 when railroad surveyors reached the mountain summit and built a lodge for Southern Pacific Railroad workers. Today, the Lodge is Cloudcroft's biggest attraction and biggest employer (see "A Great Nearby Place to Stay and Dine," below). There are also other accommodations in town, and lots of recreational opportunities and community festivals. For information, contact the **Cloudcroft Chamber of Commerce,** P.O. Box 1290, Cloudcroft, NM 88317 (☎ 505/682-2733). It's located in a log cabin in the center of town, on the south side of U.S. 82.

The **Sacramento Mountains Historical Museum and Pioneer Village,** U.S. 82 east of downtown Cloudcroft (☎ **505/682-2932**), recalls the community's early days with several pioneer buildings, historic photos, and exhibits of turn-of-the-century railroad memorabilia, clothing, and other artifacts. Call for hours. Nearby, **Lincoln National Forest** (☎ **505/682-2551**) maintains the unique **La Pasada Encantada Nature Trail,** a short foot path from Sleepygrass Campground, off NM 130 south of town, with signs in Braille inviting walkers to touch the various plants, leaves, and trees. A new trail is a several-mile moderate hike to the historic **Mexican Canyon Railroad Trestle.** The trailhead is in a U.S. Forest Service picnic area west of the junction of U.S. 82 and NM 130, where you'll also find a short walk to an observation point offering spectacular views across White Sands Missile Range and the Tularosa Basin. This picnic area also has tables, grills, drinking water, and rest rooms.

National Solar Observatory—Sacramento Peak (☎ **505/434-7000**), 18 miles south of Cloudcroft via NM 6563, a National Scenic Byway, attracts astronomers from around the world to study the sun and its effects on planet Earth. There are actually three observatories here, with two open to the public for self-guided tours (allow at least 1 hour), open daily from 8am to 6pm. Free guided tours are offered Saturday at 2pm from May through October.

Ski Cloudcroft, 2 miles east of Cloudcroft on U.S. 82 (☎ **505/682-2333**), has 21 runs and a 700-foot vertical, served by one double chair and two surface lifts. It appeals primarily to beginning skiers. When there's snow (usually December through March), it's open from 9am to 4pm daily. Snowboarding is permitted. Lift rates are $25 for adults; $16 for children 12 and under; $12 for night skiing.

WHERE TO STAY IN ALAMOGORDO

All accommodations in Alamogordo are along White Sands Boulevard, the north-south highway through town.

Best Western Desert Aire. 1021 S. White Sands Blvd., Alamogordo, NM 88310. ☎ **800/ 528-1234** or 505/437-2110. Fax 505/437-1898. 109 units. A/C TV TEL. $58–$64 double; $65–$79 suite. Rates include continental breakfast. AE, CB, DC, DISC, MC, V.

This brick and stucco hotel is the place to stay in Alamogordo. The medium-sized rooms are cozy, and come with contemporary furnishings and minirefrigerators. You'll find firm beds and average-sized, functional bathrooms. Kitchenettes, also available, contain a stove, oven, and microwave. The suites are inexpensive and have 3-foot-deep Jacuzzi tubs. Near the lobby is a guest game room with a big-screen TV and pool table, a very nice outdoor swimming pool heated year-round, hot tub, and sauna.

Days Inn Alamogordo. 907 S. White Sands Blvd., Alamogordo, NM 88310. ☎ **800/ DAYS-INN** or 505/437-5090. 40 units. A/C TV TEL. $52–$60 single or double. AE, CB, DC, DISC, MC, V.

Clean, comfortable rooms with standard furnishings are what you'll find at this two-story motel built in 1987. Remodeling is ongoing, though some rooms seemed to need more of it. Each unit is medium-sized with decent beds and a small bathroom, and has a microwave and minirefrigerator. There is a guest laundry, and an outdoor unheated swimming pool is wedged in at the back of the parking lot.

CAMPING

I strongly recommend camping at **White Sands National Monument,** especially if you want to see the sunrise over the dunes or catch them under a full moon (see "Camping," in section 3, below). Only tents are allowed, however, and the monument has no formal campground or facilities.

If you'd rather have amenities, try **KOA-Alamogordo/White Sands** (☎ **800/ 562-3992** for KOA central reservations, or 505/437-3003). It has laundry and grocery facilities as well as a recreation room/area, swimming pool, playground, shuffleboard, and planned group activities in winter. The campground is located on 24th Street in Alamogordo, just east of the U.S. 54/70/82 junction. If you're looking for something in between, **Oliver Lee State Park** (☎ **505/437-8284**) is a good choice. There are 44 sites, 10 full hookups, picnic tables, grills, tenting availability, a playground, and hiking trails.

WHERE TO DINE IN ALAMOGORDO

Keg's Brewery and Fine Dining. 817 Scenic Dr. ☎ **505/437-9564.** Main courses $4.25–$12. MC, V. Mon–Sat 11am–10pm. Sun noon–8pm. Closed Christmas. AMERICAN.

This restaurant is definitely going for a pub atmosphere, with lots of ceiling fans and dim lights except for beer neons. It's the kind of place you come when your main focus is drinking rather than eating. The restaurant does serve decent bar food. The chicken strips had a tasty crust and came with good french fries. They also serve enchiladas, burgers, and sandwiches, as well as steaks and seafood. The sports bar section (open until 2am) has televisions, pool tables, a jukebox, and Karaoke. There's no cover charge. As the restaurant's name suggests, there is a microbrewery on the premises. Located 1.3 miles south of the Space Center near 10th Street.

✪ **Ramona's Restaurant.** 2913 N. White Sands Blvd. ☎ **505/437-7616.** Main courses $4.75–$9.50; lunch $2.50–$6.50; breakfast $2.50–$6.95. AE, MC, V. Daily 6am–10pm. MEXICAN/AMERICAN.

This is *the* place to eat in Alamogordo, although as the local coffee shop and hang out, the air can be a little smoky. And don't expect a lot of atmosphere: It's a cinder-block building still holding onto its 1970s decor, with a few Spanish touches and murals on the walls. The food is excellent, however, with rich chile sauces smothering a variety of dishes. A sure bet is a huge plateful of huevos rancheros with beans on the side. Ramona's special is also good: a chicken enchilada, chile relleno, and chicken chimichanga (deep-fried burrito), topped with guacamole and sour cream, served with beans and rice. American dishes include chicken-fried steak and Rocky Mountain trout. Beer and wine are served.

A GREAT NEARBY PLACE TO STAY & DINE

✪ **The Lodge at Cloudcroft.** One Corona Place (P.O. Box 497), Cloudcroft, NM 88317. ☎ **800/395-6343** in New Mexico, or 505/682-2566. Fax 505/682-2715. 66 units. TV TEL. $79–$125 double; $129–$215 suite. AE, CB, DC, DISC, MC, V.

The only establishment in New Mexico listed in the "Top 100 Hotels in the United States," the Lodge is an antique jewel, a well-preserved survivor of another era. From the grand fireplace in the lobby to the homey Victorian decor in the guest rooms, this mansion exudes gentility and class. Its nine-hole golf course, one of the nation's highest, challenges golfers across rolling hills between 8,600 and 9,200 feet elevation and is the site of numerous regional tournaments.

All rooms in the Lodge have views and are filled with antiques, from sideboards and lamps to mirrors and steam radiators. Each unit is medium-sized and has a hair dryer and coffeemaker. Some suites have jet tubs. Guests are greeted by a stuffed bear sitting on their bed with a sampler of homemade fudge from the Lodge Mercantile. In 1991, more rooms were added in the form of the Pavilion and the Retreat, which were built adjacent to the Lodge. These are most often rented out in blocks and are less desirable than those in the main hotel.

Rebecca's (☎ 505/682-2566), the lodge's restaurant, is named for the its resident ghost, believed to have been a chambermaid in the 1930s who was killed by her lumberjack lover. Three meals, plus a midday snack menu, are served daily. Service is friendly and very efficient and the atmosphere is elegant, with nice sun during the day and romantic lighting at night. I recommend the marlin with a crab bérnaise sauce, served with a twice-baked potato. For dessert, try the chocolate mousse pie with Oreo crust.

Amenities include room service, laundry, baby-sitting, newspaper delivery, in-room massage, and free coffee in the lobby. There's a heated outdoor pool, Jacuzzi, sauna, massage, sundeck, tennis courts, bicycle rental, cross-country ski rental, nine-hole golf course, nature trails, fax and photocopying services, and boutiques.

3 White Sands National Monument

Arguably the most memorable natural area in this part of the Southwest, White Sands National Monument preserves the best part of the world's largest gypsum dune field, an area of 275 square miles of pure white gypsum sand reaching out over the floor of the Tularosa Basin in wavelike dunes. Plants and animals have evolved in special ways to adapt to the bright white environment here. Some creatures have a bleached coloration to match the whiteness all around them, whereas some plants have evolved means for surviving against the smothering pressures of the blowing sands.

The surrounding mountains—the Sacramentos to the east, with their forested slopes, and the serene San Andres to the west—are composed of sandstone, limestone, sedimentary rocks, and pockets of gypsum. Over millions of years, rains and melting snows dissolved the gypsum and carried it down into Lake Lucero. Here the hot sun and dry winds evaporate the water, leaving the pure white gypsum to crystallize. Then the persistent winds blow these crystals, in the form of minuscule bits of sand, in a northeastern direction, adding them to growing dunes. As each dune grows and moves farther from the lake, new ones form, rank after rank, in what seems an endless procession.

The dunes are especially enchanting at sunrise and under the light of a full moon, but you'll have to camp here to experience this extraordinary sight (see "Camping," below). If you're not camping, you'll probably want to spend only a couple of hours here. Refreshments and snacks can be purchased at the visitor center, along with books, maps, posters, and other souvenirs; however, there are no dining or grocery facilities available here.

ESSENTIALS

GETTING THERE   The visitor center is 15 miles southwest of Alamogordo on U.S. 70/82 (*but note:* due to missile testing on the adjacent White Sands Missile Range, this road is sometimes closed for up to 2 hours at a time). The nearest major airport is **El Paso International,** 90 miles away. You can drive from there or from take a commuter flight from Albuquerque to **Alamogordo–White Sands Regional Airport** (see "Getting There," in section 2, above).

VISITOR INFORMATION   For more information, contact **White Sands National Monument,** P.O. Box 1086, Holloman, AFB, NM 88330-1086 (☎ **505/ 479-6124**). When driving near or in the monument, tune a radio to 1610 AM for information on what's doing.

ADMISSION FEES & HOURS   Admission is $3 for adults 17 and over. From Memorial Day to Labor Day the visitor center is open from 8am to 7pm and Dunes Drive is open from 7am to 9pm. Ranger talks and sunset strolls are given nightly at 7 and 8:30pm during summer. During the rest of the year, the visitor center is open from 8am to 4:30pm and Dunes Drive is open from 7am to sunset.

SEEING THE HIGHLIGHTS

A 16-mile **Dunes Drive** loops through the "heart of sands" from the visitor center. Information available at the center will tell you what to look for on your drive. Sometimes the winds blow the dunes over the road, which must then be rerouted. The dunes are in fact all moving slowly to the northeast, pushed by prevailing southwest winds, some at the rate of as much as 20 feet a year.

In the center of the monument, the road itself is made of hard-packed gypsum (it can be especially slick after an afternoon thunderstorm, so drive cautiously!). Visitors are invited to get out of their cars at established parking areas and explore a bit; some like to climb a dune for a better view of the endless sea of sand. If you'd rather taste the park by hiking rather on the long drive, a good trail right near the entrance is the Big Dune Trail. It will take you on a 45-minute loop along the edges of the dunes and then into their whiteness, ending atop a 60-foot-tall one.

Safety tips: The National Park Service emphasizes that (1) tunneling in this sand can be dangerous, for it collapses easily and could suffocate a person; (2) sand-surfing down the dune slopes, although permitted, can also be hazardous, so it should be undertaken with care, and never near an auto road; and (3) hikers can get lost in a sudden sandstorm should they stray from marked trails or areas.

In summer, there are nature walks and evening programs in the dunes. Ranger-guided activities include orientation talks and nature walks.

CAMPING

I strongly recommend camping here, especially to see the dunes at sunrise or under a full moon. The park closes at dusk, and you'll have to leave if you're not camping. It doesn't reopen until after dawn so there's no way you'll see the sunrise unless you camp. There are no campgrounds and no facilities, however, so this is strictly a backcountry adventure. Only tent camping is allowed, and you must register and get clearance from monument headquarters before you pitch yours. Call ☎ **505/ 479-6124** for information.

If backcountry camping isn't your speed, there are other campgrounds in nearby Alamogordo and Las Cruces (see the "Where to Stay" sections under Alamogordo, in section 2 above, and Las Cruces in chapter 11).

4 Ruidoso & the Mescalero Apache Indian Reservation

Ruidoso (most New Mexicans pronounce it Ree-uh-*do*-so) is situated at 6,900 feet in the timbered Sacramento Mountains, the southernmost finger of the Rockies. It is a mountain resort town named for its site on a noisy stream and is most famous for the nearby Ruidoso Downs Racetrack, where the world's richest race is run for a $2.5 million purse. Outdoor lovers, hikers, horseback riders, fishers, and hunters are drawn to the surrounding Lincoln National Forest. Southern New Mexico's most important ski resort, Ski Apache, is just out of town. The nearby Mescalero Apache Indian Reservation includes the Inn of the Mountain Gods resort hotel. Not far away, the historic village of Lincoln recalls the Wild West days of Billy the Kid.

ESSENTIALS

GETTING THERE From Albuquerque, take I-25 south 87 miles to San Antonio; turn east on U.S. 380, 74 miles; then south on NM 37/48 (4 hours). From Alamogordo, take U.S. 70 northeast via Tularosa (1 hour). From Roswell, take U.S. 70 west (1½ hours). There is no commercial service to **Sierra Blanca Regional Airport** (☎ 505/336-8111), 17 miles north near Fort Stanton.

VISITOR INFORMATION The **Ruidoso Valley Chamber of Commerce** and visitor center is at 720 Sudderth Dr. For more information, contact P.O. Box 698, Ruidoso, NM 88345 (☎ 800/253-2255 or 505/257-7395; www.ruidoso.net).

EXPLORING RUIDOSO
GALLERY HOPPING

Many noted artists—among them Peter Hurd, Henriette Wyeth, and Gordon Snidow—have made their homes in Ruidoso and the surrounding Lincoln County. Dozens of other art-world hopefuls have followed them here, resulting in a proliferation of galleries in town. Most are open daily from 10am to 6pm, except where noted. Among my favorites are: **Casa Bonita,** 2330 Sudderth Dr. (☎ 505/257-5024); **Crucis Art Bronze Foundry and Gallery,** 524 Sudderth Dr. (☎ 505/257-7186); **Fenton's Gallery,** 2629 Sudderth Dr. (☎ 505/257-9738); **Stampede Leather,** 2615 W. Sudderth Dr. (☎ 505/257-4559); **McGary Studios,** a bronze foundry at 819 Gavilan Canyon Rd. (☎ 505/257-1000); **Buckhorn Gallery,** Glencoe, open by appointment (☎ 505/378-4126); and **Hurd-La Rinconada,** in San Patricio, 20 miles east of Ruidoso on U.S. 70 (see "A Scenic Drive Around the Lincoln Loop," below) (☎ 505/653-4331), open Monday to Saturday from 10am to 5pm.

RUIDOSO DOWNS

The famous **Ruidoso Downs Racetrack** (☎ 505/378-4431), 2 miles east on U.S. 70, is home to the ✪ **Museum of the Horse** (☎ 505/378-4142), which contains a collection of more than 10,000 horse-related items, including saddles from all over the world, a Russian sleigh, a horse-drawn "fire engine," and an 1860 stagecoach. Several great American artists including Frederic Remington, Charles M. Russell, Frank Tenney Johnson, and Henry Alkins, are represented here as well. The Anne C. Stradling Collection, also housed here, is composed of family memorabilia that spans six generations. There is a gift shop with some interesting books and curios. Admission is $5 for adults, $4 for seniors, and $3 for children 5 to 17 (under 5 free). It's open May through Labor Day 9am to 5:30pm and Labor Day through April 10am to 5pm.

The world's richest quarter horse race, the $2.5 million All-American Futurity, is run each year on Labor Day at the racetrack. Many other days of quarter horse and thoroughbred racing lead up to the big one, beginning in May and running through Labor Day. Post time is 1pm Friday through Sunday. Grandstand admission is free. Call for reserved seating ($2.50 and up, plus box seating for four to six persons).

RUIDOSO AFTER DARK: SPENCER THEATER FOR THE PERFORMING ARTS

The dream of Alto, New Mexico residents Jackie and Dr. A. N. Spencer, the 514-seat Spencer Theater (on Sierra Blanca Airport Highway 220, 4½ miles east of Highway

48) (☎ **888/818-7872** or 505/336-4800) is a model performance space that cost more than $20 million to construct. Opened in 1997, the theater has drawn such talents as the Paul Taylor Dance Company and Marvin Hamlisch. Slated for the 1999 season is pianist Navah Perlman, the House of Blues, and the Russian National Ballet. Performances take place on Saturday night. The season runs year-round and tickets cost from $12 to $35.

MESCALERO APACHE INDIAN RESERVATION

Immediately south and west of Ruidoso, the Mescalero Apache Indian Reservation covers over 460,000 acres (719 square miles) and is home to about 2,800 members of the Mescalero, Chiricahua, and Lipan bands of Apaches. Established by order of Pres. Ulysses S. Grant in 1873, it sustains a profitable cattle-ranching industry and the Apache-run logging firm of Mescalero Forest Products.

SEEING THE HIGHLIGHTS

Even if you're not staying or dining here, don't fail to visit the **Inn of the Mountain Gods,** a luxury year-round resort owned and operated by the tribe (see "Where to Stay Around Ruidoso," below); it's the crowning achievement of Wendell Chino, president of the Mescalero Apache tribe for all but 4 years since 1952.

Also on the reservation, on U.S. 70 about 17 miles southwest of Ruidoso, is the ✪ **Mescalero Cultural Center,** open from 8am to 4:30pm Monday through Friday. Photos, artifacts, clothing, crafts, and other exhibits demonstrate the history and culture of the tribe.

St. Joseph's Church, just off U.S. 70 in Mescalero, on a hill overlooking the reservation, is a Gothic-style structure with walls 4 feet thick, built between the two world wars. The interior has the symbols of Apache mountain gods along with Roman Catholic saints in paintings and carvings (see "A Scenic Drive Around the Lincoln Loop," in section 5 below).

DANCES & CEREMONIES

Throughout the year, the center hosts powwows of colorful dancing and traditional drumming, open to the public and unrestricted photography. The most accessible to visitors are dances and a rodeo on July 4th.

Restrictions do apply, however, to the annual **Coming of Age Ceremony,** held over 4 days in early July. A traditional rite reenacted in the tribal community of Mescalero, it includes an Apache maidens' puberty rites ceremony at dawn and a mountain spirits dance at night. Check ahead to learn what you can and can't see, and what you can and can't photograph.

For more information on the reservation before you visit, write to the Tribal Office at P.O. Box 227, Mescalero, NM 88340 or call ☎ **505/671-4494.**

LINCOLN STATE MONUMENT:
A WALK IN THE FOOTSTEPS OF BILLY THE KID

One of the last historic yet uncommercialized 19th-century towns remaining in the American West, this tiny community lies 37 miles northeast of Ruidoso on U.S. 380, in the valley of the Rio Bonito. Only 70 people live here today, but it was once the seat of the largest county in the United States, and the focal point of the notorious Lincoln County War of 1878–79. The entire town is now a New Mexico State Monument and a National Historic Landmark.

The bloody Lincoln County War was fought between various ranching and merchant factions over the issue of beef contracts for nearby Fort Stanton. A sharpshooting teenager named William Bonney—soon to be known as "Billy the Kid"—took sides in this issue with "the good guys," escaping from the burning McSween House after his employer and colleague were shot and killed. Three years later, after shooting down a sheriff, he was captured in Lincoln and sentenced to be hanged. But he shot his way out of his cell in the **Old Courthouse,** now a state museum that still has a hole made by a bullet from The Kid's gun. Today's visitors can hear a talk on this famous jail escape, by request, at the Old Courthouse.

Many of the original structures from that era have been preserved and restored under the aegis of the Museum of New Mexico, the Lincoln County Historical Society, or the Lincoln County Heritage Trust (☎ **505/653-4025**).

JUST THE FACTS   Typically the monument is open year-round 8:30am to 5pm; however, at press time there was talk of closing for the winter, so call first. Admission is $3.

At the trust's **Historical Center,** exhibits explain the role in Lincoln's history of Apaches, Hispanics, Anglo cowboys, and the black Buffalo Soldiers, and detail the Lincoln County War. A brief slide show on Lincoln history is presented in an old-fashioned theater. Start your visit here and either join a tour, included in the admission cost, or pick up a brochure describing the trust's self-guided walking tour ($1). Across the courtyard is the **Luna Museum Store.**

An annual **folk pageant,** *The Last Escape of Billy the Kid,* has been presented outdoors since 1949 as a highly romanticized version of the Lincoln County War. It's staged Friday and Saturday night and Sunday afternoon during the first full weekend in August as part of the **Old Lincoln Days** celebration. The festival also includes living-history demonstrations of traditional crafts, musical programs, and food booths throughout the village.

ESSENTIALS   The monument is open year-round 8:30am to 5pm. Admission is $3 adults (includes entry to five buildings); winter prices are usually less; children 16 and under are free. For more information, write P.O. Box 36, Lincoln, NM 88338, or call ☎ **505/653-4372.**

WHERE TO STAY AROUND RUIDOSO
IN TOWN

Best Western Swiss Chalet Inn. 1451 Mechem Dr. (P.O. Box 759), Ruidoso, NM 88345. ☎ **800/477-9477,** 800/528-1234, or 505/258-3333. Fax 505/258-5325. 83 units. A/C TV TEL. $60–$104 double; $99–$139 suite. AE, CB, DC, DISC, MC, V.

This blue-and-white chalet-style motel, with Swiss flags hanging outside its entry, provides spacious rooms in a mountain environment. Decorated in soft colors, the rooms have comfortably firm beds and medium-sized, very clean bathrooms. The building's construction seems a bit light and sounds do carry. Each room has a coffeemaker.

In Ahna-Michelle's Restaurant, Swiss and American food, including Wiener schnitzel, wursts, Luzern cordon bleu, and davos platz (peppered beef tips), is served in an alpine atmosphere of Swiss bells and other souvenirs. The restaurant is open for breakfast and dinner daily. The inn has room service, connecting and nonsmoking rooms, a small indoor swimming pool, Jacuzzi, and guest Laundromat. VCRs and videos are available at the front desk.

Enchantment Inn. 307 U.S. 70 (P.O. Box 8060), Ruidoso, NM 88355. ☎ **800/435-0280** or 505/378-4051. Fax 505/378-5427. 79 units. A/C TV TEL. $75–$85 double and econo-suite; $90–$195 suite. AE, DC, DISC, MC, V.

A big remodel in fall 1997 turned this hotel into a comfortable and attractive place to stay. The construction is more solid here than at the Carrizo Condos or the Swiss

Chalet; however, the location here is less attractive than either of those more rural settings. The standard rooms are spacious and have new bedspreads and televisions. There are a variety of types of suites, some with two rooms, others with Jacuzzi tubs, so be specific about your desires. All have kitchenettes, with stove, minirefrigerator, microwave, and coffeemaker. The econo-suites have the same kitchen amenities. These rooms are small but nicely decorated with attractive red wood furniture. Guests have use of an outdoor patio with barbecue grills, video game room, guest laundry, and indoor pool and whirlpool. The Screaming Eagle Restaurant and Lounge serves three meals daily, with most main courses priced under $10. There's also a gift shop on the premises.

✪ **Pines Motel on the River.** 620 Sudderth Dr., Ruidoso, NM 88345. ☎ **800/ 257-4834** or 505/257-4334. 11 units. TV TEL. $40–$85 double. AE, DISC, MC, V.

This is my choice of motels in Ruidoso. It's centrally located and well maintained, with plenty of old-fashioned roadside motel charm. Since it's family owned and operated, you're likely to be well looked after. There are seven older but completely refurbished rooms, plus four new, more luxurious units overlooking the Rio Ruidoso. The older rooms are my favorites and received a 1997 renovation that reduced noise and made the bathrooms larger. All rooms have ceiling fans and minirefrigerators. The units in back by the river are newer and more spacious but not quite as charming. Guests can fish for trout in the river at the back of the property, and play horseshoes in a shady area along the river.

In Upper Canyon

Dan Dee Cabins Resort. 310 Main Rd., Upper Canyon (P.O. Box 844), Ruidoso, NM 88355. ☎ **800/345-4848** or 505/257-2165. 12 cabins. TV. June 15 to Labor Day $85 one-bedroom cabin, $108 two-bedroom cabin, $127 three-bedroom cabin; Dec 15–Easter $79 one-bedroom, $98 two-bedroom, $121 three-bedroom; rest of year $68 one-bedroom, $87 two-bedroom, $103 three-bedroom. DISC, MC, V.

If you're looking for a rustic, woodsy experience, this is the place to stay. This 5-acre cottage resort started in the 1940s has separate cabins that are cozy, though a bit dark. Built beside a stream, the cabins all have sitting porches, fireplaces, and kitchens, with stove, oven, refrigerator, and coffee pot. The only phone is in the office. The rooms are very clean, though the furnishings and carpet could use some updating, which I hear is happening, though hadn't yet upon my visit. There's a gazebo with Ping-Pong and barbecue grill, as well as woods in which to explore.

Shadow Mountain Lodge. 107 Main Rd., Ruidoso, NM 88345. ☎ **800/441-4331** or 505/257-4886. Fax 505/257-2000. 19 units. A/C TV TEL. Memorial Day to Oct 20 and holidays $79–$94 single or double; Oct 21 to Memorial Day $64–$79 single or double. Ski packages available. AE, CB, DC, DISC, MC, V.

Advertising "luxury lodging for couples," this is a good spot for a romantic getaway, though I wouldn't exactly use the term *luxury*. This property doesn't accept pets and though children are welcome, it's not exactly the place for them. Built in 1984, it came under new ownership in 1994 and the new owners are constantly updating the decor, such as installing ceramic tile in the bathrooms and kitchens. Each unit has a comfortable king-size bed, a fireplace, and a coffeemaker. Ten rooms have full kitchens, with stove, oven, and refrigerator; the other nine have a wet bar and microwave. All rooms have hair dryers. I recommend the rooms that open out to the north, which have windows facing south and receive the most sunlight. The grounds are attractive and well kept, and include a barbecue area, hot tub, and self-serve Laundromat.

NEARBY PLACES TO STAY
Two Historic B&Bs in Lincoln

✪ **Casa de Patrón Bed and Breakfast.** On U.S. 380 (P.O. Box 27), Lincoln, NM 88338. ☎ **800/524-5202** or 505/653-4676. Fax 505/653-4671. www.casapatron.com. E-mail: patron@pvtnetworks.net. 5 units, 2 casitas. $79–$107 double; $97 casita. Rates include breakfast. MC, V.

The main building of Casa de Patrón, an adobe, was built around 1860 and housed Juan Patrón's old store (the home is on the National Register of Historic Places). In addition, Billy the Kid used part of the house as a hideout at some point during his time in the Lincoln area. Jeremy and Cleis Jordan have capitalized on the presence of that notorious punk by collecting portraits and photographs and hanging them throughout the cozy sitting and dining areas of the inn.

Rooms in the old part of the house are friendly, with a homey feel created by quilts and a major collection of washboards adorning the walls. More sophisticated are the Old Trail House rooms, one with a Jacuzzi tub, the other for people with disabilities, both with fireplaces, wet bars, and minirefrigerators. A short walk from there are the casitas, ideal and reasonably priced places for families to stay. The Casita Bonita has a vaulted ceiling, loft bedroom, and a kitchen with stove, oven, microwave and refrigerator, while the Casita de Paz is funkier, a 1960s New Mexico house added onto over the years and with a minirefrigerator. If you choose to stay in a casita, a continental-plus breakfast is delivered to your door. If you stay in the main house or the recently added Old Trail House, Cleis and Jeremy will prepare you a full breakfast. Specialties include Dutch babies (a soufflé) served with apple compote and sausage, or stuffed French toast with piñon nuts.

✪ **Ellis Store and Co. Country Inn.** U.S. 380 (P.O. Box 15), Lincoln, NM 88338. ☎ **800/653-6460** or 505/653-4609. 7 units (4 with bathroom). $79–$109 double. Rates include breakfast. DC, DISC, MC, V. Pets are not permitted inside, but kennels are available, and those with horses are invited to use the property's stables.

With part of this house dating from 1850, this is believed to be the oldest existing residence in Lincoln County, and as a B&B it gives visitors a real taste of 19th century living but with most of today's luxuries. The house has plenty of history. Billy the Kid spent several weeks here, although somewhat unwillingly, according to court records that show payment of $64 for 2 weeks' food and lodging for The Kid and a companion held under house arrest. Today, guests of innkeepers Virginia and David Vigil can come and go as they please, wandering over the inn's 6 quiet acres, or using the inn as a base while exploring Lincoln and nearby attractions.

Three rooms in the main house are a step back into the 1800s, with wood-burning fireplaces or stoves providing heat, antique furnishings, and handmade quilts. I recommend the Dr. James Room at the end of the house. Often used as a honeymoon suite, it has a wedding picture of Danny Vigil's grandfather and grandmother and access to the front portal. The separate Mill House, built of adobe and hand-hewn lumber in the 1880s, isn't quite as cozy as the main house, but definitely holds an Old West feel. It has one room with a private bathroom and three that share a bathroom. The Mill House also has a large sitting room loft area available for guest use. Rooms have no televisions or telephones, but a phone is available for guest use and the Vigils are happy to take messages.

People are talking about the gourmet meals served at Ellis. Lunch and dinner are by reservation only, a six-course meal with such specialties as exotic game (African antelope or venison) or the more familiar dishes such as chateâubriand. Meals cost from around $40 per person. Gourmet breakfasts are cooked to order from an extensive menu. Nonguests are also welcome for meals, by reservation.

ADOBE GUEST HOMES

Hurd Ranch Guest Homes. P.O. Box 100 (mile marker 281) San Patricio, NM 88348. ☎ 800/658-6912 or 505/653-4331. Fax 505/653-4218. 4 casitas. TV TEL. $100–$300 per casita (2-night minimum). AE, DISC, MC, V.

Located about 20 miles east of Ruidoso on 2,500-acre Sentinel Ranch, these attractive casitas are part of the Hurd–La Rinconada Gallery, which displays the work of well-known artists Peter and Michael Hurd, Henriette Wyeth Hurd, N. C. Wyeth, and Andrew Wyeth. The grounds also include the San Patricio Polo Fields, where matches take place from Memorial Day to Labor Day.

There are two older one-bedroom casitas, built in the early part of the century, and two new and much larger units. Of the smaller, the Orchard house is my favorite, sitting on the edge of an apple orchard, furnished in weathered Southwestern antiques (though some noise from the highway travels through its walls). Both of the larger units are elegant, especially the newer La Helenita, a pitched roofed adobe house large enough for two families. All have completely equipped kitchens, with stove, oven, refrigerator, microwave, and dishwasher. They also have fireplaces and comfortable living areas, and are decorated with antiques, primitives, and art by the Hurd-Wyeth family. A stay here wins you access to fine fly-fishing along the Rio Ruidoso. If you want the feel of real southern New Mexico country living this is the place to be. Note that a 2-day minimum stay is required.

A LUXURY RESORT

Inn of the Mountain Gods. Carrizo Canyon Rd. (P.O. Box 269), Mescalero, NM 88340. ☎ 800/545-9011 or 505/257-5141. Fax 505/257-6173. 263 units. A/C TV TEL. June to Labor Day $130 double, $140 suite; Apr–May and Labor Day to Oct $105 double, $115 suite; Nov–Mar $95 double, $105 suite. Golf, tennis, and ski packages available. AE, CB, DC, DISC, MC, V.

What's most impressive about this resort is its location, set on a grassy slope above a mountain lake on the Mescalero Apache Reservation, 3½ miles southwest of Ruidoso. It is the successful dream of the tribal president, Wendell Chino, who wanted to help his people get into the recreation and tourism business.

Nine interconnected brown-shake buildings comprise the hotel and an associated convention center, all built in 1975 with renovations ongoing. Guests cross a covered wooden bridge over a cascading stream to reach the three-story lobby, dominated by a huge, cone-shaped, copper fireplace. Modern tribal art and trophies of wild animals bagged on the reservation are on display. The property includes an 18-hole golf course designed by Ted Robinson, whose work includes the famed course at the Princess in Acapulco. In winter, buses shuttle skiers to the Ski Apache resort, also owned by the tribe.

The guest rooms are spacious and comfortable, though I wouldn't use the term *luxurious,* which the inn bandies about. They do have high ceilings, tasteful furnishings, and patios or balconies. Beds are comfortable and bathrooms are very clean and functional. Lithographs on the walls depict typical 19th-century tribal scenes.

Dining/Diversions: The Dan Li Ka Room, a huge dining room with a view of the lake and mountain beyond, features steak, poultry, seafood, and pasta, and the Apache Tee Restaurant by the golf course offers casual dining. The Ina Da Lounge has ample seating and a big floor for dancing and drinks, and there's a piano bar off the lobby. Casino Apache is a smoky building filled with slot machines. There are also card rooms.

Amenities: Room service (7am to 10pm), valet laundry. There's also a pool, hot tub, sauna, sundeck, outdoor tennis courts, volleyball, basketball, badminton, golf course, video arcade, boutique, fishing lake stocked with rainbow trout, boating (rowboats, pedal boats, and aqua cycles can be rented), and a base for hunting trips.

CAMPING

Lincoln National Forest has more than a dozen campgrounds in the region; four of them are within the immediate area. Maps (at $2) and details can be obtained from all campground offices, including the **Smokey Bear Ranger Station,** 901 Mechem Dr., Ruidoso (☎ **505/257-4095**), open from Memorial Day to Labor Day, 7:30am to 4:30pm, Monday through Saturday and the same hours Monday through Friday the rest of the year.

WHERE TO DINE
EXPENSIVE

✪ **Victoria's Romantic Hideaway.** 2117 Sudderth Dr. ☎ **800/959-1328** or 505/257-5440. Reservations required (1 day in advance suggested). $75 per person fixed-price (including tax and gratuity). AE, DISC, MC, V. Daily 6pm–closing (with reservation). SICILIAN/MEDITERRANEAN.

To say one goes to Victoria's Romantic Hideaway for dinner would be a gross understatement. You go to Victoria's for a wonderful 2- to 3-hour dining experience, perhaps a romantic evening by soft candlelight to celebrate a special occasion. Don Baker has created a unique restaurant where guests are outrageously pampered during a relaxed eight-course meal. Although the restaurant will seat up to 16, no more than four couples are usually served on any given evening, each couple in a private, elegantly decorated section of the restaurant.

One basic meal is served each night; however, dishes are customized for each particular diner. Those dining at the same table receive different meals according to the chef's choice, allowing the kitchen to show off its classic Sicilian style of cooking. Don serves the dishes right from the pan to the table, using an array of ingredients. The meal may start with his homemade foccacia, which you dip in olive oil with garlic and sheep cheese in it. This is also the olive and peppers time when you can taste a variety of the luscious fruit or even feed your companion. Entrees vary broadly, from sautéed meat dishes such as chicken or homemade Italian sausage to pasta dishes such as angel hair in butter with Greek cheese. Wine tasting is also part of the evening; Don serves small portions of different wines (many from Sicily) to complement the various courses. Dress is casual, except shorts are not permitted, and smoking is allowed only on an outdoor porch. Due to the abundance of Victorian antiques and the length of the evening, children would be out of place here.

MODERATE

Cattle Baron Steak House. 657 Sudderth Dr. ☎ **505/257-9355.** Reservations recommended. Main courses $7.95–$18.25; lunch $4.95–$8.95. AE, DISC, MC, V. Sun–Thurs 11am–9:30pm, Fri–Sat 11am–10:30pm. STEAK/SEAFOOD.

This is the place to go if you really have an appetite. It's a casually elegant restaurant, part of a chain with six locations around the Southwest, that serves not the best steaks and seafood you've tasted, but good quality food. It's a casual restaurant decorated in an opulent Western style with lots of maroon upholstery and brass. Often the place is busy and festive, so it's not ideal for a romantic getaway. Service is efficient and friendly. For lunch, try the turkey and avocado sandwich or the teriyaki kabob. For dinner, I usually order the filet mignon, wrapped with bacon, or the shrimp scampi sautéed in garlic butter. There are also steak and seafood combinations. A large salad bar dominates the main dining room, and a comfortable lounge sits near the entryway.

✪ **La Lorraine.** 2523 Sudderth Dr. ☎ **505/257-2954.** Reservations recommended. Main courses $12.95–$24.95; lunch $5.95–$8.95. AE, MC, V. Tues–Sat 11:30am–2pm; Mon–Thurs 5:30–9pm, Fri–Sat 5:30–9:30pm. FRENCH.

This piece of Paris is a bit hard to imagine in a New Mexico mountain town, but here it is, in an adobe building on the main street no less. Inside, there's French provincial decor, with lace curtains and candlelight. The restaurant came under new ownership a few years ago, and although its popularity has waned some, I still found the food to be excellent: pâtés, bisques, salads, and dishes like canard (duck) à l'orange, apples and almonds in the sauce, with rich mashed potatoes and green beans on the side. The grilled rack of lamb is another favorite, served with polenta.

INEXPENSIVE

✪ **Cafe Rio.** 2547 Sudderth Dr. ☎ **505/257-7746.** Reservations not accepted. Main courses $4.25–$9.95. No credit cards. Daily 11:30am–8pm. Closed Dec 1–21 and for 1 month after Easter. INTERNATIONAL/PIZZA.

The first time I ate at this unpretentious pizzeria-style restaurant I was determined to write about it. That was years ago and finally I have my chance. This unpretentious pizzeria-style restaurant is quite out of place in Ruidoso, offering deep-dish pizza like some you'd find in Chicago. My favorite is the Hawaiian combo, with Canadian bacon and pineapple. Some people rave about the calzones which come with three cheeses and any of four fillings. There are also Greek, Portuguese, and Cajun dishes. You can sample from an extensive selection of domestic and imported beers, including seasonal beers. Finish with the double layer chocolate cake with chocolate espresso frosting, unless you care about sleeping.

Hummingbird Tearoom. 2306 Sudderth Dr., Village Plaza. ☎ **505/257-5100.** $2.55–$5.95. MC, V. Mon–Sat 11am–2:30pm (afternoon tea and desserts served until 5pm in summer). AMERICAN.

If you're looking for a light, white-bread kind of lunch, go to this little room pinched into a corner of a small strip mall in the center of town. The owners David and Jerry Sailor are ever present, seeing to each patron's comfort. Though you won't find anything extravagant on the menu, everything is well prepared and tasty. I had a tuna salad sandwich made the way my mother does with sweet pickles. You can also order roast beef or ham sandwiches. The tomato soup is broth-based and very tasty. For something heartier, try the cream of broccoli. Jerry does all the baking and usually manages by early afternoon to sell out of her peach cobbler and cheesecake with fresh strawberries.

NEARBY PLACES TO DINE

✪ **Chango's.** (P.O. Box 639) Smokey Bear Blvd., Capitan. ☎ **505/354-4213.** Reservations strongly recommended. $16.50–$22. DISC, MC, V. Tues–Sat 5pm–closing. INTERNATIONAL.

Owner Jerrold Donti Flores left San Francisco in the late 1970s to return to the land of his birth, and found his calling in this small (24-seat) and highly rated restaurant in a turn-of-the-century adobe building. Flores, an accomplished avant-garde sculptor and painter, also displays his art, works by other artists, plus international primitives, in changing exhibits at the restaurant. A choice of four to six gourmet dinners changes every other week, with selections such as fillet of beef tenderloin layered with smoked gouda ravioli, roasted portobello mushrooms, and Cabernet Sauvignon shallot sauce, or skewered prawns encrusted with fresh herb *mole* (*mol*-ay—a spicy, unsweetened chocolate sauce) and sautéed, served with red curry coconut rice and pineapple black bean salsa. An excellent wine list includes 20 ports, plus Italian, Spanish, French, Australian, German, and domestic wines.

✪ **Flying J Ranch.** Hwy. 48, 1 mile north of Alto (Box 2505), Ruidoso, NM 88355. ☎ **505/ 336-4330.** Reservations highly recommended. $14 for 12 and up; $7.50 ages 4 through 11; 3 and under free. DISC, MC, V. May–Labor Day, Mon–Sat 7:30pm. CHUCK WAGON.

A treat for the whole family, this ranch is like a Western village, complete with staged gunfights and pony rides for the kids. Gates open at 6pm; a chuck-wagon dinner of barbecue beef or chicken, baked potato, beans, biscuits, applesauce cake, and coffee or lemonade is served promptly at 7:30. Then, at 8:15pm, the Flying J Wranglers present a fast-paced stage show with Western music, a world champion fiddle player, and a world champion yodeler.

5 A Scenic Drive Around the Lincoln Loop

An enjoyable way to see many of the sights of the area while staying in Ruidoso is on a 1- or 2-day 162-mile loop tour.

Heading east from Ruidoso on U.S. 70, about 18 miles past Ruidoso Downs, is the small community of **San Patricio,** where you'll find (watch for signs) the **Hurd-La Rinconada Gallery** (☎ 505/653-4331). Late artist Peter Hurd, a Roswell native, flunked out of West Point before studying with artist N. C. Wyeth and marrying Wyeth's daughter, Henriette, and eventually returning with her to New Mexico. This gallery shows and sells works by Peter Hurd, Henriette Wyeth, their son Michael Hurd, Andrew Wyeth, and N. C. Wyeth. Many of the works capture the ambience of the landscape in the San Patricio area. In addition to original works, signed reproductions are available. The gallery is open Monday through Saturday from 9am to 5pm, and Sunday from 10am to 4pm. Several rooms and guest houses are also available by the night or for longer periods (see "Nearby Places to Stay," in the Ruidoso section 4 above).

From San Patricio, continue east on U.S. 70 for 4 miles to the community of Hondo, at the confluence of the Rio Hondo and Rio Bonito, and turn west onto U.S. 380. From here it's about 10 miles to **Lincoln,** a fascinating little town that is also a National Historic Landmark (see "Lincoln State Monument," in section 4 above). From Lincoln, continue west on U.S. 380 about a dozen miles to **Capitan** and **Smokey Bear Historical State Park,** 118 First St. (☎ 505/354-2748), open daily 9am to 5pm. Smokey, the national symbol of forest fire prevention, was born near here and found as an orphaned cub by firefighters in the early 1950s. This state park (admission 25¢) has exhibits on Smokey's rescue and life at the National Zoo in Washington, D.C., as well as fire prevention from World War II to the present. Visitors can also stop at Smokey's grave, and explore a nature path that represents six vegetation zones of the area.

Heading west from Capitan about 20 miles takes you to **Carrizozo,** the Lincoln County seat since 1912. For a quick sandwich or burger, stop at **Barb's East Coast Subs,** Twelfth Street and South U.S. 54 (☎ 505/648-2155), though you'll want to carry food out as the restaurant can be smoky. If you're craving New Mexican food, check to see if Paul's Coffee Cup, 1108 Avenue E (just off S. U.S. 54) (☎ 505/ 648-2832), is open. Hours are erratic, but the food is excellent, served in a little diner with red vinyl booths. Or if you're in the mood for coffee or a milkshake, stop at **Roy's Gift Gallery & Flowers,** Twelfth Street and S. U.S. 54 (1200 Avenue E) (☎ 505/ 648-2921), "where everyone in town clutches coffee," as Roy says.

Continue west on U.S. 380 for 4 miles to **Valley of Fires Recreation Area** (☎ 505/648-2241), where you'll find what is considered one of the youngest and best-preserved lava fields in the United States. Among the black lava formations, there's a ¾-mile self-guided nature trail, which is well worth the walk. Part of it is handicapped accessible. You'll discover a strange new landscape that at first glance appears inhospitable, but really is rich with plant and wildlife. Be sure to walk far enough to see the 400-year-old juniper wringing itself from the black stone. A small visitors' center and bookstore is in the park campground. Admission is $3 per person or $5 per car for day use, and camping costs $7 to $11. The park is open year-round.

To continue the loop tour, return 4 miles to Carrizozo, turn south onto U.S. 54, and go about 28 miles to the turnoff to **Three Rivers Petroglyph National Recreation Area** (☎ **505/525-4300**), about 5 miles east on a paved road. There are some 20,000 individual rock art images here, carved by Mogollon peoples who lived in the area centuries ago. A trail about .8 mile long links many of the more interesting petroglyphs, while the view surrounding the area, with mountains to the east and White Sands to the southwest, is outstanding. Be sure to go far enough to see site 7, a vividly depicted bighorn sheep pierced with three arrows. The park also includes the partially excavated ruins of an ancient Native American village, including a multiroom adobe building, pit house, and masonry house that have been partially reconstructed. Administered by the U.S. Bureau of Land Management, the park has facilities for picnicking and camping. Day use or camping fee is $3 per vehicle. The U.S. Forest Service also has a campground in the area, about 5 miles east via a gravel road.

From the recreation area, return 5 miles to U.S. 54 and continue south about 15 miles to **Tularosa Vineyards** (☎ **505/585-2260**), which offers tours and tastings daily from noon until 5pm. Using all New Mexico grapes, the winery is especially known for its award-winning reds. Wines can be purchased by the bottle, with prices ranging from $5 to $18.

Continuing south from the winery, drive about 2 miles to Tularosa and turn east onto U.S. 70, which you take for about 16 miles to the village of **Mescalero** on the Mescalero Indian Reservation. From U.S. 70, turn south onto Eagle Drive to get to the imposing **St. Joseph's Church,** standing over 100 feet tall to the tip of the cross, with stone walls up to 4 feet thick. Built between 1920 and 1939, the mission church also contains an icon of the Apache Christ, with Christ depicted as a Mescalero holy man. Local arts and crafts and religious items are for sale at the parish office. Mass is celebrated Sunday at 10:30am. From the church go south to Apache Boulevard and then east to Trout Loop, site of the **Mescalero National Fish Hatchery** (☎ **505/671-4401**), which has displays on the life cycle of trout and a self-guided walking tour through the tank house and raceway. The hatchery, which raises and distributes almost half a million trout annually, is open Monday through Friday from 8am to 4pm. Call for weekend hours (usually the same as weekday hours because "somebody has to come in and feed the fish") and to arrange guided tours. Admission is free.

Returning to U.S. 70, it's about 19 miles back to Ruidoso.

6 Roswell

Best known as a destination for UFO enthusiasts and conspiracy theorists, Roswell has become a household name in the last few years thanks to Mulder, Scully, and their friends. And even if you're not glued to your set for *The X-Files* every week, you might remember Roswell as the setting for major scenes from the 1996 blockbuster *Independence Day.* Government coverups, alien autopsies, and cigarette-smoking feds . . . come along as we venture into the UFO capital of the world.

The Incident at Roswell

In July of 1947, something "happened" in Roswell. What was it? Debate still rages. On July 8, 1947, a local rancher named MacBrazel found unusual debris scattered across his property. The U.S. military first released a statement saying the debris was wreckage from a spaceship crash. Four hours later, however, the military retracted the statement, claiming what fell from the sky that summer night was "only a weather balloon." Most of the community didn't believe the weather balloon story, although some did suspect that the military was somehow involved—Robert Goddard had been working on rockets in this area since the 1930s, and the Roswell Air Base was located along the city limits to the south. Eyewitnesses to the account, however, maintain the debris "was not of this world."

Theorists believe that the crash actually involved two spacecraft. One disintegrated, hence the debris across the MacBrazel ranch, and the other crash-landed, hence the four alien bodies that were also claimed to have been discovered.

UFO believers have remained dissatisfied with the U.S. Air Force's claim that the debris was from a weather balloon and have insisted on an explanation of the "alien bodies." The most recent comment from the Air Force came in 1997, 2 weeks before the 50th anniversary of the "crash." The Air Force said the most likely explanation for the unverified alien reports might be that people were simply remembering and misplacing in time a number of life-sized dummies dropped from the sky during a series of experiments in the 1950s.

The main place to go in Roswell to learn more about the incident is the **International UFO Museum and Research Center** (☎ 505/625-9495), located in the old Plains Theater on Main Street. Staffers will be more than happy to discuss the crash and the alleged military cover-up. Especially interesting is Dennis Balthaser, operations manager and certified UFO investigator. He tells of a recent bizarre *X-Files* encounter he had with an alleged witness of the crash. Apparently this search has set the government against him, he fears, and has caused him to lose 30 pounds. Such encounters are what make Roswell an interesting place to visit, and make this museum a must-see. As well as an hour-by-hour time line of the "incident," the museum has photographs of bizarre and elaborate "crop circles," and a videotape in which an alleged witness tells his account. The museum is open daily in winter from 10am to 5pm, in summer from 9am to 5pm; admission is free.

If you want to see one of the two possible crash sites, call the museum and ask for the tour office or call ☎ 505/623-8104. Tours are offered daily and start at $30; combination tours are available, including packages that include other area attractions such as Carlsbad Caverns and White Sands. Call ahead for times and reservations.

Roswell hosts a **UFO Festival** every year during the first week in July. Some of the special events include guest speakers, the Crash and Burn Expo Race, concerts, out-of-this-world food, a laser light show, and an alien invasion at the Bottomless Lakes recreation area. In 1997, during the 50th anniversary of the crash, Roswell made the cover of *Time*. For details on the event, contact the festival coordinator at ☎ 888-ROSWELL.

By Su Hudson

ESSENTIALS

GETTING THERE   From Albuquerque take I-40 east 59 miles to Clines Corners; turn south on U.S. 285, 140 miles to Roswell (4 hours). From Las Cruces, take U.S. 70 east (4 hours). From Carlsbad, take U.S. 285 north (1½ hours).

   Roswell Airport, at Roswell Industrial Air Center on South Main Street (☎ **505/ 347-5703**), is served commercially by **Mesa Airlines** (☎ **800/MESA-AIR** or 505/347-5501), which flies to Albuquerque almost hourly throughout the day and direct to Dallas, Texas, twice daily.

VISITOR INFORMATION   The **Roswell Chamber of Commerce** is at 131 W. Second St. (P.O. Box 70), Roswell, NM 88202 (☎ **505/623-5695**). The Roswell Convention and Visitors Bureau is at 912 N. Main (☎ **505/624-7860**).

SEEING THE SIGHTS

✪ **Roswell Museum and Art Center.** 100 W. 11th St., Roswell, NM 88201. ☎ **505/ 624-6744.** Free admission. Mon–Sat 9am–5pm, Sun and holidays 1–5pm.

This highly acclaimed small museum is a good place to stop in order to get a sense of this area before heading out to explore. Established in the 1930s through the efforts of city government, local archaeological and historical societies, and the WPA, the museum proclaims this city's role as a center for the arts and a cradle of America's space industry.

   The art center contains the world's finest collection of works by Peter Hurd and his wife, Henriette Wyeth, many works depicting gentry-ranching lifestyle in this area. There are also works by Georgia O'Keeffe, Ernest Blumenschein, Joseph Sharp, and others famed from the early 20th-century Taos and Santa Fe art colonies. The permanent and temporary exhibits of late 20th-century works are refreshing, and the Native American and Hispanic art exhibits interesting as well.

   It has an early historical section, but its pride and joy is the **Robert Goddard Collection,** which presents actual engines, rocket assemblies, and specialized parts developed by Goddard in the 1930s, when he lived and worked in Roswell. Goddard's workshop has been re-created for the exhibit. A special display commemorates the Apollo 17, which undertook the last manned lunar landing in 1972; it includes the space suit worn on the moon by New Mexican Harrison Schmitt. The Goddard Planetarium is used as a science classroom for local students and for special programs. Ask about "the Roswell Incident," an alleged UFO crash near here in 1947 (see box, above).

✪ **Historical Center for Southeast New Mexico.** 200 N. Lea Ave. at W. 2nd St., Roswell, NM 88201. ☎ **505/622-8333.** Free admission. Daily 1–4pm.

The handsome mansion that houses this historical collection is as much a part of the museum as the collection itself. A three-story yellow-brick structure, it was built between 1910 and 1912 by rancher J. P. White. Its gently sweeping rooflines and large porches reflect the prairie style of architecture made popular by Frank Lloyd Wright. The White family lived here until 1972; today this home, on the National Register of Historic Places, is a monument to turn-of-the-century lifestyles.

   First- and second-floor rooms, including the parlor, bedrooms, dining room, and kitchen, have been restored and furnished with early 20th-century antiques. The second floor has a gallery of changing historic exhibits, from fashions to children's toys. The third floor, once White's private library, now houses the Pecos Valley Collection and the archives of the Historical Center for Southeast New Mexico.

New Mexico Military Institute. 101 W. College Blvd. at N. Main St., Roswell, NM 88201. ☎ **505/622-6250** or 505/624-8100. Free admission. Museum hours: Tues–Fri 8:30–11:30am and 1–3pm.

Considered one of the most distinguished military schools in the United States, the "West Point of the West" celebrated its centennial in 1991. It's the alma mater of luminaries as disparate as former Dallas Cowboys football star Roger Staubach and television newsman Sam Donaldson.

On campus is the **General Douglas L. McBride Military Museum** (101 W. College Blvd.; ☎ **505/624-8220**), with a unique collection artifacts documenting New Mexico's role in America's wars. Among the memorabilia are a machine-gun–equipped Harley Davidson used in 1916 in General Pershing's attack on Pancho Villa and items from the Bataan Death March. Tours of the campus are offered by appointment.

Spring River Park and Zoo. 1306 E. College Blvd. (at Atkinson Ave.) Roswell, NM 88201. ☎ **505/624-6760.** Free admission. Summer daily 10am–8pm; winter 10am–6:30pm; 10am–5:30pm during daylight saving time.

This lovely park, covering 48 acres on either side of a stream a mile east of New Mexico Military Institute, incorporates a miniature train, antique carousel, large prairie-dog town, children's fishing pond, picnic ground, and playgrounds. There's also a children's zoo and Texas longhorns.

GETTING OUTSIDE IN THE AREA

Fifteen miles northeast of Roswell, on the Pecos River, is the ✪ **Bitter Lake National Wildlife Refuge,** where a great variety of waterfowl—including cormorants, herons, pelicans, sandhill cranes, and snow geese—find a winter home. The refuge, reached via U.S. 380 and NM 265 from Roswell, comprises 24,000 acres of river bottomland, marsh, stands of salt cedar, and open range. Seven gypsum sinkhole lakes, covering an area of 700 acres, are of a peculiar beauty. If you're here between December and February, don't miss seeing the sky actually darken with birds. Once threatened with extinction, the sandhill crane now appears, along with puddle and diving ducks every winter. Snow geese were unknown here 20 years back, but now turn up to the tune of some 40,000 every winter. All told, over 300 species of birds have been sighted. You can get information at the headquarters building at the entrance, or call ☎ **505/622-6755.**

Bottomless Lakes State Park is a chain of seven lakes surrounded by rock bluffs located 16 miles east of Roswell via NM 409 off of U.S. 380. It got its name from early cowboys, who tried to fathom the lakes' depth by plumbing them with lariats. No matter how many ropes they tied together and lowered into the limpid water, they never touched bottom. In truth, though, none of the lakes are deeper than 100 feet. The largest, Lea Lake, is so clear that scuba divers frequent it. Another, aptly called Devil's Inkwell, is so shaded by surrounding bluffs that the sun rarely reaches it. Mirror, Cottonwood, Pasture, and Figure 8 lakes got their monikers with similar logic; No Name Lake, which apparently didn't have anything to distinguish it, has been renamed Lazy Lagoon.

This park is a popular recreation site for Roswell residents. There's fishing for rainbow trout, swimming and windsurfing, campsites for trailers or tents, and shelters, showers, a dump station, and a concession area with vending machines and paddle-boat rentals (open 9am to 6pm Memorial Day to Labor Day). The park is open year-round from 6am to 9pm daily, and admission is $3 per vehicle. For more information, call ☎ **505/624-6058.**

Originally built to raise bass and catfish, the ✪ **Dexter National Fish Hatchery,** located 1½ miles east of Dexter on NM 190, about 16 miles southeast of Roswell via NM 2, is now a center for the study and raising of 15 threatened and endangered fish species, such as the razorback sucker, Colorado squawfish, and Chihuahuan chub. Year-round, visitors can take self-guided tours among the hatchery's ponds; and from late March through October the visitors' center is open, with exhibits and an aquarium containing endangered fish. A short film is also shown. The hatchery (☎ 505/734-5910) is open daily from 7am to 4pm, and admission is free.

WHERE TO STAY

Best Western Inn & Suites. 2000 N. Main St., Roswell, NM 88201. ☎ **800/600-5221,** 800/528-1234, or 505/622-6430. Fax 505/623-7631. 124 units. A/C TV TEL. $75–$110 double. AE, CB, DC, DISC, MC, V. Pets accepted.

Built in 1976 and remodeled in 1996, this hotel provides spacious rooms and good amenities, though you have to like to walk. The hotel is at the center of town, adjacent to New Mexico Military Institute. Rooms are built around a huge quadrangle with an indoor pool in a sunny, plant-filled courtyard at the center. Request a room at one of the four corner entrances and you'll avoid trudging down the long hallways. Also request a room facing outside rather than in toward the courtyard, where you'll get noise from the pool. This is your best bet for Roswell lodging. The bright rooms, decorated in floral prints, have textured wallpaper with Aztec trim. Beds are firm. All rooms have coffeemakers, and the suites have a microwave, wet bar, minirefrigerator, a phone at a working desk, an oversize dresser, and a sleeper sofa in a sitting area.

Services and facilities include room service at dinner hours, valet laundry, 24-hour desk, an indoor swimming pool, men's and women's saunas, hot tub, guest Laundromat, video games area, and gift shop. An 18-hole golf course is right behind the hotel.

Days Inn. 1310 N. Main St., Roswell, NM 88201. ☎ **505/623-4021.** Fax 505/623-0079. 62 units. A/C TV TEL. $52–$62 double. Rates include continental breakfast. AE, DC, DISC, MC, V. Pets are allowed.

The clean lines of the outside of this two-story motel are indicative of what you'll find here: good, functional rooms at a reasonable price. Situated at the center of town, it was built in 1962, remodeled in 1991, and receives constant upgrading. The standard rooms are medium-sized with comfortable beds and functional bathrooms with an outer vanity. Rooms have dark oak furniture and Southwest decor. "Business Place" rooms also have hair dryers, coffeemakers, irons and ironing boards, and microwave/minirefrigerator combinations. Some standard rooms have these micro/fridges too, so you may want to request one. The large pool has brickwork and a gazebo and hot tub nearby. There's also an oddly placed sauna in the guest laundry room. There is a full-service restaurant and lounge on the premises, which offers limited room service.

Frontier Motel. 3010 N. Main St., Roswell, NM 88201. ☎ **800/678-1401** or 505/ 622-1400. Fax 505/622-1405. 38 units. A/C TV TEL. $38–$47 double; $50 suite. Rates include continental breakfast. AE, CB, DC, DISC, MC, V. Pets accepted.

This comfortable motel just north of the center of town offers clean and attractive rooms in a variety of sizes and decors. Part of the motel was built in the 1960s, and the other part in the early 1980s. All units are medium-sized with basic, dated furniture, and new carpeting and bedspreads. Beds are on the soft side but comfortable. Bathrooms are clean, some with 1950s tile, others with more modern tile, all with an outer sink/vanity. Refrigerators are available and there is an outdoor, unheated pool.

CAMPING

Trailer Village Campgrounds (☎ 505/623-6040) in Roswell is your best bet. Situated on the outskirts of town there's some grass and big cottonwood and elm tree for shade. The campground has 53 sites and 53 full hookups. Cable TV and phone hookups are available, and air-conditioning and heating are provided at an extra charge. Tenting is available and so are group tent sites. Bathrooms are newly remodeled. Laundry and limited grocery facilities are also available. The campgrounds are located 1⅓ miles east of the U.S. 285 and U.S. 70/380 junction on U.S. 380.

WHERE TO DINE IN ROSWELL

Cattle Baron. 1113 N. Main St. ☎ 505/622-2465. Main courses lunch $5–$10; dinner $6–$17. Mon–Thurs 11am–9:30pm; Fri–Sat 11am–10pm; Sun 11am–9pm. AE, DISC, MC, V. STEAK AND SEAFOOD.

This must be Roswell's most popular restaurant, for it's always busy during mealtimes. You usually can get a table, however, and they are nicely spaced so the noise level is minimal. It's an informal place with a wealthy ranch feel—lots of maroon and brass. Service is fast and friendly. Many come here just to feast at the salad bar, which is one of the best I've seen; not only does it have lots of good veggies, it has many potato and pasta dishes as well as a choice of two soups. Everything is made fresh here—the bread baked in house, the beef even hand cut by the manager. You can't go wrong with the steaks such as the quite tender filet mignon wrapped in bacon. You can also get dishes like shrimp scampi sautéed in garlic butter at a price that will make you glad for Roswell's provincialism. The lounge is a comfortable place to come for evening drinks and there's a full bar here.

The Grinder Coffee Shoppe. 104 W. Fourth St. ☎ 505/623-2997. All menu items under $5. Mon–Fri 8:30am–4pm; Sat 8:30am–2pm (may stay open into evening). DISC, MC, V. BAKERY, SOUPS, AND SANDWICHES.

Cecile Tydings, owner of this hip little cafe with a 1950s decor highlighting luminaries such as Marilyn Monroe and Elvis, initially had a tough time educating the local populace on the finer points of coffee and bagels, but she's developing a following (she has another shop called **Alien Caffeine** at the International UFO Museum). You'll find a variety of 60 drinks at the Grinder, some Cecile's own creations such as her cappuccino fizz, for which she wouldn't reveal the recipe because she says other shops are quickly copying her ideas. She also serves a mean espresso milkshake, and a good mocha. All her muffins and cookies are home baked. Sandwiches can come on good bread or bagels, such combinations as olives and pecans with cream cheese, or smoked turkey and cream cheese with green chile. All her ingredients are low fat and all meals come with chips and pickles. The place is very casual, the food served on plastic plates.

Mario's. 200 E. 2nd St. ☎ 505/623-1740. Main courses $4.95–$13.95; lunch $3.70–$4.95. AE, MC, V. Mon–Sat 11am–9pm. AMERICAN.

Mario Reid, the owner and namesake of this casual restaurant at the center of town, is ever present, accounting for its quality food and strong local following. The restaurant has a pub decor with lots of ceiling fan lights and comfortable booths. Most enjoyable for me here was starting my meal with a bottle of Alien Amber Ale, a beer brewed especially for Mario by a Carrizoso brewery. It's hoppy and flavorful, and has a very sincere-looking green alien on the label—the best souvenir I got in Roswell. All meals come with a trip to the salad bar. This is an elaborate place with lots of condiments, and desserts as well. For an entree I had the Cajun catfish, grilled. It was juicy and spicy, served with a choice of potato, broccoli, or rice. Shrimp, chicken, or beef fajitas, served in a sizzling pan are also tasty dishes. Mario travels all over the state tasting and bringing back New Mexico wines, so be sure to sample from his list. An adjoining lounge has complimentary hors d'oeuvres and a big-screen TV. In fine weather, you can dine on the patio.

7 Also Worth a Look: Fort Sumner & Environs

This little town of 1,300 people, located 84 miles north of Roswell via U.S. 285 and NM 20, is important in New Mexico history because it's the site of Fort Sumner State Monument and is the burial place of the notorious Billy the Kid. Neither is really worth going far out of your way to see, but definitely stop if you're in the vicinity and have some time to spare.

Fort Sumner State Monument (☎ 505/355-2573) recalls a tragic U.S. Army experiment (1864–68) to create a self-sustaining agricultural colony for captive Navajos and Mesclero Apaches. Many still recall the "Long March," during which some Navajos walked a distance of more than 400 miles. By fall 1864, some 9,000 people were held captive here, site of the Bosque Redondo Reservation. Disaster followed: disease, blighted crops, alkaline water, Comanche raids, and a devastating alienation from their homelands. Some 3,000 Native Americans died here. Part of the fort where the military lived and worked has been reconstructed at the site. A short walking tour takes you to various signposts explaining what was once upon the land, illustrated with sad photographs of the dismal conditions. The visitor center (open daily from 9am to 5pm) gives you a good background before you head out to the site. It's located 7 miles southeast of the modern town, via U.S. 60/84 and NM 272.

Nearby, the **Old Fort Sumner Museum** (☎ 505/355-2942) displays artifacts, pictures, and documents, a private enterprise that may not quite be worth the $3 admission price.

Behind the museum (you don't have to go through the museum) is the **Grave of Billy the Kid,** its 6-foot tombstone engraved to "William H. Bonney, alias 'Billy the Kid,' died July 16, 1881," and to two previously slain comrades with whom he was buried. Also in the graveyard is the tomb of Lucien Maxwell, the land czar from the Cimmarron, New Mexico area, who purchased Fort Sumner after the military had abandoned it.

If you're curious about the notorious Kid, just 21 when Sheriff Pat Garrett shot him in Fort Sumner, you can learn more at the **Billy the Kid Museum** (☎ 505/ 355-2380), 1 mile east of downtown Fort Sumner on U.S. 60/84. In its 46th year, it contains more than 60,000 relics of the Old West, including some recalling the life of young Bonney himself, such as his rifle. Admission is $4 for adults, $2 for children.

The **Old Fort Days** celebration, the second week of June, is Fort Sumner's big annual event. It includes the World's Richest Tombstone Race (inspired by the actual theft of Billy's tombstone, since recovered), 2 nights of rodeo, a country music show, barbecue, and parade.

Sumner Lake State Park (☎ 505/355-2541), 16 miles northwest of Fort Sumner via U.S. 84 and NM 203, is a 1,000-acre property with a campground, with electric and water hookups. Boating, fishing, swimming, and waterskiing are popular recreations.

For more information on the town, contact the **De Baca County Chamber of Commerce,** P.O. Box 28, Fort Sumner, NM 88119 (☎ **505/355-7705**).

CLOVIS/PORTALES

Clovis, 110 miles northeast of Roswell via U.S. 70, is a major market center on the Texas border. Founded in 1906 as a railway town, it is now the focus of an active ranching and farming region, with about 38,100 population. **Cannon Air Force Base,** a part of the Tactical Air Command, is just northwest of the city. **The Lyceum Theatre,** 411 Main St. (☎ **505/763-6085**), is a magnificent restoration of a former vaudeville theater; it's now the city's center for performing arts. The **H. A. "Pappy" Thornton Homestead and Museum** in Ned Houk Park (no phone) displays antique farming equipment in a prairie farmhouse. A major rodeo on the national circuit is held the first weekend in June. "Clovis Man," who hunted mammoths in this region about 10,000 B.C., was first discovered at a site near the city. For more information contact the **Clovis/Curry County Chamber of Commerce** at ☎ **800/261-7656** or 505/763-3435.

South of Clovis 19 miles is **Portales,** a town of 12,500 people that is the home of the main campus of **Eastern New Mexico University.** On campus are the **Roosevelt County Historical Museum** (☎ **505/562-2592**) of regional ranching history and the **Natural History Museum** (☎ **505/562-2174**), with wildlife exhibits, including a bee colony. There are anthropology and paleontology exhibits at the **Blackwater Draw Archaeological Site and Museum** (☎ **505/562-2202**), 7 miles northeast of Portales on U.S. 70 toward Clovis. For more information contact the **Portales Chamber of Commerce** at ☎ **505/356-8541.**

For lodging in the Clovis/Portales area, try the **Best Western LaViata Inn,** 1516 Mabry Dr. (U.S. 60/70/84), Clovis, NM 88101 (☎ **800/528-1234** or 505/762-3808), or the **Holiday Inn,** 2700 Mabry Dr., Clovis, NM 88101 (☎ **800/HOLIDAY** or 505/762-4491). Clovis is the site of the original restaurant of the **K-Bob's Steakhouse** chain. The restaurant is at 1600 Mabry Dr. (☎ **505/763-4443**).

8 Carlsbad & Environs

Carlsbad is a city of 27,800 on the Pecos River. Founded in the late 1800s, its area was controlled by Apaches and Comanches until just a little over a century ago. Besides a good tourist business from Carlsbad Caverns, the town thrives on farming, with irrigated crops of cotton, hay, and pecans. Pecans grow so well in Carlsbad that it is said the nuts from just two trees in your yard will pay your property taxes. The area is the largest producer of potash in the United States. The town was named for the spa in Bohemia of the same name.

The caverns (see section 9, below) are the big attraction, having drawn more than 33 million visitors since opening in 1923. A satellite community, Whites City, was created 20 miles south of Carlsbad at the park entrance junction. The family of Jack White Jr. owns all of its motels, restaurants, gift shops, and other attractions.

ESSENTIALS

GETTING THERE   From Albuquerque take I-40 east 59 miles to Clines Corners; turn south on U.S. 285, 216 miles to Carlsbad via Roswell (6 hours). From El Paso, take U.S. 62/180 east (3 hours). **Mesa Airlines** (☎ **800/MESA-AIR** or 505/885-0245) provides commercial service with four flights daily between Albuquerque and **Cavern City Air Terminal** (☎ **505/887-9001**), 4 miles south of the city via National Parks Highway (U.S. 62/180). You can rent a car at the airport from **Hertz** (☎ **800/654-3131** or 505/887-1500).

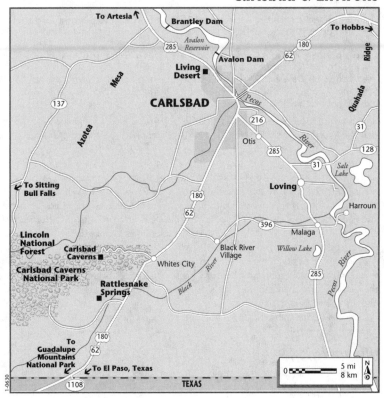

VISITOR INFORMATION The **Carlsbad Chamber of Commerce** and the **Carlsbad Convention and Visitors Bureau,** both at 302 S. Canal St. (U.S. 285) at Green Street (U.S. 62/180), P.O. Box 910, Carlsbad, NM 88220 (☎ **800/221-1224** or 505/887-6516), are open from 8am to 5pm Monday to Friday.

SEEING THE SIGHTS

Carlsbad's pride and joy is the broad Pecos River, with a 3½-mile **Riverwalk** along the tree-shaded banks, beginning near the north end of Riverside Drive. This is a lovely place for a picnic, and if you'd like to cool off there's a municipal beach at the north end with changing rooms and showers. Annual **Christmas on the Pecos** pontoon boat rides take place each evening from Thanksgiving to New Year's Eve (except Christmas Eve), past a fascinating display of Christmas lights on riverside homes and businesses. Advance reservations are required, available from the chamber of commerce. Cost is $7 per person; lap tickets are available free for children under three.

The **Carlsbad Museum and Art Center,** 418 W. Fox St., 1 block west of Canal Street (☎ 505/887-0276), contains Apache relics, pioneer artifacts such as guns and saddles, and an impressive art collection. The museum's store has a small but fine selection of jewelry at reasonable prices. The museum is open Monday through Saturday from 10am to 6pm; admission is free, although donations are welcome.

GETTING OUTSIDE

Recreational facilities in the Carlsbad area include some two dozen parks, several golf courses, numerous tennis courts and swimming pools, a municipal beach, and a shooting and archery range. Contact the **City of Carlsbad Recreation Department** (☎ **505/887-1191**).

✪ **Living Desert Zoo and Gardens State Park.** 1504 Miehls Dr. (P.O. Box 100), Carlsbad, NM 88221-0100. ☎ **505/887-5516.** Admission $3, children 7–12 $1, children 6 and under free. Group rates are available. Memorial Day weekend to Labor Day 8am–7pm; rest of year 9am–4pm. Closed Christmas. Take Miehls Dr. off U.S. 285 west of town and proceed just over a mile.

Situated within 1,200 acres of authentic Chihuahuan Desert, this park contains more than 50 species of desert mammals, birds, and reptiles, and almost 500 varieties of plants. Even for someone like me, who cringes at the thought of zoos, this was a pleasant 1 ³/₁₀-mile walk. You pass through displays with plaques pointing out vegetation such as mountain mahogany, and geologic formations such as gypsum sinkholes. You're likely to see lizards and other wild creatures, as well as the captive ones.

Rehabilitation programs provide the park's animals, which have been sick or injured and could no longer survive in the wild. You'll see golden eagles and great horned owls among the birds of prey in the aviary, and large animals such as deer and elk in outdoor pastures. An arroyo exhibit houses javelina, and you'll also see bears, bobcats, and cougars. A prairie dog town is a children's favorite, and a visitors' center houses additional exhibits and a gift shop. Best of all is the Succulents of the World exhibit near the visitor center, a greenhouse that shelters such exotics as Kranz's Ball from Bolivia and velvet leaf from Madagascar.

The view from the park, high atop the Ocotillo Hills on the northwest side of Carlsbad, is superb.

WHERE TO STAY

Most properties are along the highway south toward Carlsbad Caverns National Park (see section 9, below).

Best Western Cavern Inn. 17 Carlsbad Cavern Hwy. at NM 7 (P.O. Box 128), Whites City, NM 88268. ☎ **800/CAVERNS** or 505/785-2291. Fax 505/785-2283. 63 units. A/C TV TEL. May 15–Sept 15 $59–$75 double; Sept 16–May 14 $49–$65 double. AE, CB, DC, DISC, MC, V.

If you'd like to be close to the caverns, this is the place to stay, though you'll want to reserve carefully. The lobby is within an Old West storefront and the accommodations are across the street. The staff here seems to be overworked, so you may not get the service you would in Carlsbad. The motel has three sections. The best is the Guadalupe Inn. This section is built around a courtyard and rooms have a rich feel, with vigas on the ceilings and nice Southwest pine furniture. Bathrooms are roomy enough and the beds are comfortably firm. In back is a big pool surrounded by greenery. Next door, the two-story Cavern Inn provides 1970s rooms that are adequate, with springy beds, and small bathrooms with jetted tubs. I cannot recommend the Walnut Canyon Inn, which is used for overflow. During my visit, these rooms were in dire need of a remodel, beds soft and saggy, and small, but bathrooms were clean.

Most folks dine and drink across the highway at the Velvet Garter Saloon and Restaurant, although, as one local said, "teenagers are doing the cooking there." The Whites City arcade contains a post office, grocery store, gift shop, Million Dollar Museum of various antiques and paraphernalia, and Granny's Opera House, a theater for weekend melodramas scheduled intermittently. Between the Cavern Inn and its neighbor properties, there are two swimming pools, two hot tubs, and a court for tennis, volleyball, and basketball, Spectravision movie channels for an extra cost; and free coffee and refreshments in the lobby. Pets are not allowed.

✪ **Best Western Motel Stevens.** 1829 S. Canal St., Carlsbad, NM 88220. ☎ **800/ 730-2851,** 800/528-1234, or 505/887-2851. Fax 505/887-6338. 221 units. A/C TV TEL. $59–69 double; $69–$85 suite. AE, CB, DC, DISC, MC, V. Pets allowed.

This is a comfortable and welcoming place after the rigor of traveling in this part of the state where there are miles between stops. The grounds are carefully landscaped and there are a number of types of rooms built in different eras. I stayed in a two-story structure built in 1992. Others built in 1945 have vaulted ceilings, and at press time brand-new structures were being planned. All rooms are spacious, decorated in a Southwestern print, and have firm beds. Bathrooms are small but have an outer two-sink/vanity. Each room has a coffeemaker and hair dryer; some have microwave/refrigerator combos. The pool, open seasonally, is fairly large, well kept, and often busy. The motel offers transportation to and from the airport, a 24-hour desk, limited room service, dry cleaning, laundry service, free coffee in the lobby, VCRs, video rentals, swimming and wading pools, a playground, and self-service Laundromat.

The Flume (located within this motel) is one of the best restaurants in town (see "Where to Dine," below).

Continental Inn. 3820 National Parks Hwy., Carlsbad, NM 88220. ☎ **505/887-0341.** Fax 505/885-1186. 60 units. A/C TV TEL. $45–$50 double; from $50 suite. AE, CB, DC, DISC, MC, V.

This economical two-story redbrick motel, built in 1983 with remodeling ongoing, has all the necessities for travelers on a budget. The medium-sized rooms have oak furniture and are decorated in earth tones. Beds are fairly soft, and the rooms could use new carpets. Each room comes with a coffeemaker and minirefrigerator. Bathrooms are also medium-sized and very clean. Suites are quite large, with a large sleeper sofa, wet bar and minirefrigerator, a good place for a small family. There's an outdoor heated swimming pool that's good-sized but has no shade. Services include dry cleaning, newspaper delivery, and courtesy car.

✪ **Holiday Inn.** 601 S. Canal St. (P.O. Box 128), Carlsbad, NM 88220. ☎ **800/742-9586,** 800/HOLIDAY, or 505/885-8500. Fax 505/887-5999. 100 units. A/C TV TEL. $86–$115 double. Rates include full breakfast. AE, CB, DC, DISC, MC, V.

A handsome New Mexico Territorial–style building houses this first-rate full-service hotel in downtown Carlsbad. It was built in 1960 but received a major renovation in 1995. Rooms aren't as large as those at the Best Western Motel Stevens (see above), but they're refined, with white wooden furniture and decorated in Southwest prints. The beds are medium-firm and comfortable; bathrooms are average size, with an outer vanity. Each room gets plenty of light and has a coffeemaker. Large executive rooms have a comfortable chair and ottoman as well as a jetted tub. Amenities in these rooms include robes and nice soaps and shampoo. The pool is large, with a mist-cooled patio nearby. There's also a sauna, whirlpool, exercise room, and playground. Guests have free self-service laundry facilities. There's a complimentary shuttle from the airport, limited room service, and dry-cleaning service.

The hotel has two restaurants: Ventanas offers fine dining, serving steaks, seafood, and pastas; the Phenix Bar and Grill has sandwiches, burgers, soups, and salads.

CAMPING

Brantley Lake State Park (☎ **505/457-2384**) in Carlsbad has RV hookups as well as tent camp sites. Picnic tables, grills, and recreational facilities are available. Boating and lake fishing are popular here. **Carlsbad Campground** (☎ **505/885-6333**) is a large, full-service campground with a swimming pool and playground. In Artesia, try

Bill's RV Park (☎ 505/746-6184), a more moderately sized campground located on Hermosa Drive just south of the junction of U.S. 82/285. Laundry facilities are available.

WHERE TO DINE IN CARLSBAD

The Flume. At Best Western Motel Stevens, 1829 S. Canal St. ☎ **505/887-2851.** Reservations recommended for dinner. Main courses $7.50–$15.95; lunch $3.25–$7.95. AE, CB, DC, DISC, MC, V. Mon–Sat 6am–10pm, Sun 6am–9pm. AMERICAN.

This locals' favorite has a New England feel, with comfortable chairs and low light. Windows look out toward the main road and the tracks where you might see a train pass by. It's the kind of place that has butter and crackers waiting for you on the table and serves big portions. I had the petite filet mignon—tender and juicy—which came wrapped in bacon and was served with my choice of potato or rice pilaf. The prime rib is also popular, as is the fisherman's seafood platter (jumbo shrimp, clam strips, fish fillet, and deviled crab and oysters) served with coleslaw and a choice of potato. There are usually specials such as chicken Alfredo. Meals come with a trip to the salad bar. Drinks from a full bar are available.

Lucy's. 701 S. Canal St. ☎ **505/887-7714.** Reservations recommended on weekends. Main courses $3.75–$11.95. AE, CB, DC, DISC, MC, V. Mon–Sat 11am–10pm. MEXICAN.

When you walk in the door of this restaurant that, upon this writing, was about to move to a larger building a few doors down, Lucy is likely to wave you toward the dining room and tell you to find a seat. Since 1974, Lucy and Justo Yanez's restaurant has been dedicated to the words of a Mexican proverb printed on the menu: *El hambre es un fuego, y la comida es fresca* (Hunger is a burning, and eating is a coolness). You'll probably want to start with a margarita or Mexican beer. The food is tasty, with Lucy's personal adaptations of old favorites, often invented by requests from regulars. "Barbara's Favorite Fix" (one beef enchilada and one chile relleno) was named after a local woman who had this meal six times every week. Everything is made by hand, including the tamales. I recommend the chicken fajita burrito or the combination plate. Finish with a dessert of buñelos, sprinkled with cinnamon sugar. Children's plates are available; diners can choose mild or hot chile.

Velvet Garter Saloon and Restaurant. 26 Carlsbad Cavern Hwy., Whites City. ☎ **505/785-2291.** Reservations recommended in summer. Main courses $6.95–$12.95. AE, DC, DISC, MC, V. Daily 4–9pm. AMERICAN.

I include this place because it is the only restaurant in the Carlsbad Caverns area. The food isn't great, but it will suffice after you've worked up a hunger while touring underground. The menu includes steak, chicken, and fish. Nearby, **Fat Jack's** caters to fast-food diets with three meals daily; the saloon is unmistakable, with the longhorns mounted over the door.

EXPLORING THE ENVIRONS
A Side Trip to Texas: Guadalupe Mountains National Park

Some 250 million years ago, the Guadalupe Mountains were an immense reef poking up through a tropical ocean. Marine organisms fossilized this 400-mile-long Capitan Reef as limestone; later, as the sea evaporated, a blanket of sediments and mineral salts buried the reef. Then just 10 to 12 million years ago, a mountain-building uplift exposed a part of the fossil reef. This has given modern scientists a unique opportunity to explore earth's geologic history and outdoor lovers a playground for wilderness experience.

The steep southern end of the range makes up the park, while the northern part lies within Lincoln National Forest and Carlsbad Caverns National Park. Deer, elk, mountain lion, and bear are found in the forests, which contrast strikingly with the desert around them. In these isolated basins and protected valleys is a proliferation of vegetation rare elsewhere in the Southwest.

JUST THE FACTS   To reach the park, take U.S. 62/180, 55 miles southwest of Carlsbad. Admission to the park is free, and the visitor center is open from June to August from 8am to 6pm; September to May from 8am to 4:30pm. For more information, write to **Park Ranger,** HC-60, Box 400, Salt Flat, TX 79847 or call ☎ **915/ 828-3251.** The park has more than 80 miles of trails; most are steep, rugged, and rocky. There's no lodging, restaurants, stores, or gas within 35 miles of the park. Pets are permitted on a leash only in campground parking area.

SEEING THE HIGHLIGHTS   The visitor center offers a variety of exhibits and slide programs telling the story of the Guadalupe Mountains, as well as ranger-guided walks and lectures. Information, maps, and backcountry permits can also be obtained at McKittrick Canyon Visitor Center (10 miles northeast via U.S. 62/180 and a side road) and Dog Canyon Ranger Station (reached through Carlsbad via NM 137 and County Road 414, about 70 miles).

McKittrick Canyon, protected by its high sheer walls, with a green swatch of trees growing along the banks of its spring-fed stream, is a beautiful location. It is a great spot for bird watching and viewing other wildlife, and an especially lovely sight during fall foliage time, late October to mid-November. Most of the national park's 86,416 acres are reached only by 80 miles of foot or horse trail through desert, canyon, and high forest. Backcountry hikers require water and permits; camping must be in designated areas.

CAMPING   Pine Springs and Dog Canyon both have developed camping areas, with rest rooms and water, but no hookups or showers. Fires, including charcoal, are not permitted.

ARTESIA

The principal attraction of this quiet town of about 12,000 people, 36 miles north of Carlsbad on U.S. 285, is the **Artesia Historical Museum and Art Center,** housed in a Victorian home at 505 W. Richardson Ave., Artesia (☎ **505/748-2390**). It's worth visiting just to see the Queen Anne–style home with the outside covered with round river stones. Open Tuesday to Saturday from 8m to 5pm, it exhibits Native American and pioneer artifacts, traveling exhibits, and art shows.

If you want to stopover in Artesia, consider the **Best Western Pecos Inn,** 2209 W. Main St. (U.S. 82), Artesia, NM 88211 (☎ **505/748-3324**). Further information can be obtained from the **Artesia Chamber of Commerce,** P.O. Box 99, Artesia, NM 88211 (☎ **505/746-2744**).

HOBBS

Located 69 miles east of Carlsbad on U.S. 62/180, on the edge of the Llano Estacado tableland, Hobbs (pop. 32,000) is at the center of New Mexico's richest oil field. Many oil companies have their headquarters here.

Points of interest include the **Lea County Cowboy Hall of Fame and Western Heritage Center** at New Mexico Junior College, on the Lovington Highway (☎ **505/ 392-1275**). It honors the area's ranchers, both men and women, and rodeo performers and is open Wednesday through Saturday 1 to 5pm (closed college holidays). The **Confederate Air Force Museum** (☎ **505/397-3202**) at Lea County Airport, on

U.S. 62/180, displays World War II aircraft, and the **Soaring Society of America** (☎ 505/392-1177) has its national headquarters at the Hobbs Industrial Air Park, north of town on NM 18. Native American artifacts and pioneer mementos are displayed by appointment at the **Linam Ranch Museum** (☎ 505/393-4784), located west of town on U.S. 62/180.

Twenty-two miles northwest of Hobbs via NM 18, at the junction with U.S. 82, is the town of **Lovington** (pop. 9,500), another ranching and oil center. The **Lea County Historical Museum**, 103 S. Love St. (☎ 505/396-4805), presents memorabilia of the region's unique history in a World War I–era hotel.

If you plan to stay in Hobbs, try the **Ramada Inn,** 501 N. Marland St. (☎ 505/397-3251). **Harry McAdams State Park,** 4 miles north of Hobbs on NM 18 (☎ 505/392-5845), has campsites and a visitor center. You can get a good square meal at the **Cattle Baron Steak and Seafood Restaurant,** 1930 N. Grimes St. (☎ 505/393-2800). For more information, contact the **Hobbs Chamber of Commerce,** 400 N. Marland St. (☎ 800/658-6291 or 505/397-3202), or the **Lovington Chamber of Commerce,** 1535 Main St. (☎ 505/396-5311).

9 Carlsbad Caverns National Park

One of the largest and most spectacular cave systems in the world, Carlsbad Caverns comprise some 80 known caves that snake through the porous limestone reef of the Guadalupe Mountains. Fantastic and grotesque formations fascinate visitors, who find every shape imaginable (and unimaginable) naturally sculpted in the underground world—from frozen waterfalls to strands of pearls, from soda straws to miniature castles, from draperies to ice-cream cones.

Although Native Americans had known of the caverns for centuries, they were not discovered by whites until about a century ago, when settlers were attracted by sunset flights of bats from the cave. Jim White, a guano miner, began to explore the main cave in the early 1900s and to share its wonders with tourists. By 1923, the caverns had become a national monument, upgraded to national park in 1930.

ESSENTIALS

GETTING THERE   Take U.S. 62/180 from either Carlsbad, New Mexico (see "Getting There," in section 8, above), which is 23 miles to the northeast, or El Paso, Texas (150 miles west). The scenic entrance road to the park is 7 miles long and originates at the park gate at Whites City. Van service to Carlsbad Caverns National Park from Whites City, south of Carlsbad, is provided by **Sun Country Tours/Whites City Services** (☎ 505/785-2291).

VISITOR INFORMATION   For more information about the park, contact **Carlsbad Caverns National Park,** 3225 National Parks Hwy., Carlsbad, NM 88220 (☎ 800/967-CAVE for tour reservations, 505/785-2232, ext. 429, for information about guided tours, or 505/785-2107 for recorded information).

ADMISSION FEES & HOURS   General admission to the park is $6 for adults, $3 for children 6 to 15, and children under 6 are free. Admission is good for 3 days and includes entry to the two self-guided walking tours. Guided tours range in price from $6 to $20 depending on the type of tour, and reservations are required. The visitor center and park are open daily from Memorial Day to mid-August from 8am to 7pm; the rest of the year they're open from 8am to 5:30pm.

Carlsbad Caverns National Park

TOURING THE CAVES

Two caves, Carlsbad Cavern and Slaughter Canyon (formerly New) Cave, are open to the public. The National Park Service has provided facilities, including elevators, to make it easy for everyone to visit the cavern, and a kennel for pets is available. Visitors in wheelchairs are common.

In addition to the tours described below, inquire at the visitor center information desk about other ranger-guided tours, including climbing and crawling "wild" cave tours. Be sure to call days in advance because some tours are only offered 1 day per week. Spelunkers who seek access to the park's undeveloped caves require special permission from the park superintendent.

CARLSBAD CAVERN TOURS

You can tour the caverns in one of three ways, depending on your time, interest, and level of ability. The first, and least difficult, option is to take the elevator from the visitor center down 750 feet to the start of the self-guided tour of the Big Room. More difficult and time-consuming, but vastly more rewarding, is the 1-mile self-guided tour along the Natural Entrance route, which follows the traditional explorer's route, entering the cavern through the large historic natural entrance. The paved walkway through the natural entrance winds into the depths of the cavern and leads through a series of underground rooms; this tour takes about an hour. Parts of it are steep. At its lowest point, the trail reaches 750 feet below the surface, ending finally at an underground rest area.

Both visitors who take the elevator and those who take the Natural Entrance route begin the self-guided tour of the spectacular Big Room near the rest area. The floor of this room covers 14 acres; the tour, over a relatively level path, is 1¼ miles in length and takes about an hour.

The third option is the 1½-hour ranger-guided Kings Palace tour, which also departs from the underground rest area. This tour descends 830 feet beneath the surface of the desert to the deepest portion of the cavern open to the public. Reservations are required and an additional fee is charged.

TOUR TIPS   Wear flat shoes with rubber soles and heels because of the slippery paths. A light sweater or jacket feels good in the constant temperature of 56°, especially when it's 100° outside in the sun. The cavern is well lit, but you might want to bring along a flashlight as well. Rangers are stationed in the cave to answer questions.

SLAUGHTER CANYON CAVE TOUR

Slaughter Canyon Cave was discovered in 1937 and was mined for bat guano commercially until the 1950s. It consists of a corridor 1,140 feet long with many side passageways. The lowest point is 250 feet below the surface, and the passage traversed by the ranger-guided tours is 1¾ miles long, but more strenuous than hiking through the main cavern. There is also a strenuous 500-foot-rise hike from the parking lot to the cave mouth. The tour lasts about 2½ hours. No more than 25 people may take part in a tour, and then by reservation only. Everyone needs a flashlight, hiking boots or shoes, and a container of drinking water. Slaughter Canyon Cave is reached via U.S. 180, south 5 miles from Whites City, to a marked turnoff that leads 11 miles into a parking lot.

OTHER GUIDED TOURS

Be sure to ask about the Left Hand Tunnel, Lower Cave, Hall of the White Giant, and Spider Cave tours. These vary in degree of difficulty and adventure, from Left Hand which is an easy ½-mile lantern tour, to Spider Cave, where you can expect tight crawlways and canyonlike passages, to Hall of the White Giant, a strenuous tour in which you're required to crawl long distances, squeeze through tight crevices, and climb up slippery flow-stone–lined passages. Call in advance for times of each tour. All of these tours depart from the visitor center.

BAT FLIGHTS

Every sunset from early spring through October, a crowd gathers at the natural entrance of the cave to watch a quarter of a million bats take flight for a night of insect feasting. (The bats, like some of the people, winter in Mexico.) All day long the Mexican free-tailed bats, approximately 1 million of them, sleep in the cavern; at night they all strike out on an insect hunt. A ranger program is offered about 7:30pm (verify the time at the visitor center) at the outdoor Bat Flight Amphitheater. On the second Thursday in August (usually), the park sponsors a **Bat Flight Breakfast** from 5 to 7am, during which visitors watch the bats return to the cavern.

OTHER PARK ACTIVITIES

Aside from the caves, the national park offers a 10-mile one-way scenic loop drive through the Chihuahuan Desert to view Rattlesnake and Upper Walnut Canyons. Picnickers can head for Rattlesnake Springs Picnic Area, on County Road 418 near

Slaughter Canyon Cave, a water source for hundreds of years for the Native Americans of the area. Backcountry hikers must register at the visitor center before going out on any of the trails in the 46,766 acres of the park.

AND FINALLY: RADIOACTIVE WASTE!

If you're interested in world history in the making, you'll want to look into the **Waste Isolation Pilot Plant,** located 26 miles from Carlsbad. Our nation's first deep-geologic repository for permanent disposal of radioactive waste is embedded in a 225 million-year-old salt formation. At press time, the facility was getting ready for its first shipments of waste, so no one could assure me that tours of the site would continue. If they do, visitors will travel 2,150 feet (almost one-half mile) underground to see where the U.S. Department of Energy disposes of transuranic waste (trash from the production of nuclear materials) from more than 20 temporary storage sites nationwide. If you don't get to tour the facility, you can stop by the **WIPP Information Center** at 4021 National Parks Highway (☎ **800/336-9477;** www.wipp.carlsbad.nm.us) where you'll find a reading room. If tours are offered, visitors will need to book months in advance.

Appendix: Useful Toll-Free Numbers & Web Sites

AIRLINES

Air Canada
☎ 800/776-3000
www.aircanada.ca

Alaska Airlines
☎ 800/426-0333
www.alaskaair.com

America West Airlines
☎ 800/235-9292
www.americawest.com

American Airlines
☎ 800/433-7300
www.americanair.com

British Airways
☎ 800/247-9297
☎ 0345/222-111 in Britain
www.british-airways.com

Canadian Airlines International
☎ 800/426-7000
www.cdnair.ca

Continental Airlines
☎ 800/525-0280
www.flycontinental.com

Delta Air Lines
☎ 800/221-1212
www.delta-air.com

Kiwi International Air Lines
☎ 800/538-5494
www.jetkiwi.com

CAR RENTAL AGENCIES

Advantage
☎ 800/777-5500
www.arac.com

Midway Airlines
☎ 800/446-4392

Northwest Airlines
☎ 800/225-2525
www.nwa.com

Southwest Airlines
☎ 800/435-9792
www.iflyswa.com

Tower Air
☎ 800/34-TOWER;
800/348-6937 outside
New York; ☎ 718/553-8500
in New York;
www.towerair.com

Trans World Airlines (TWA)
☎ 800/221-2000
www.twa.com

United Airlines
☎ 800/241-6522
www.ual.com

US Airways
☎ 800/428-4322
www.usairways.com

Virgin Atlantic Airways
☎ 800/862-8621 in the
continental U.S.
☎ 0293/747-747 in Britain
www.fly.virgin.com

Alamo
☎ 800/327-9633
www.goalamo.com

Auto Europe
☎ 800/223-5555
www.autoeurope.com

Avis
☎ 800/331-1212 in the Continental U.S.
☎ 800/TRY-AVIS in Canada
www.avis.com

Budget
☎ 800/527-0700
www.budgetrentacar.com

Dollar
☎ 800/800-4000
www.dollarcar.com

Enterprise
☎ 800/325-8007
www.pickenterprise.com

Hertz
☎ 800/654-3131
www.hertz.com

Kemwel Holiday Auto
☎ 800/678-0678
www.kemwel.com

National
☎ 800/CAR-RENT
www.nationalcar.com

Payless
☎ 800/PAYLESS
www.paylesscar.com

Rent-A-Wreck
☎ 800/535-1391
rent-a-wreck.com

Thrifty
☎ 800/367-2277
www.thrifty.com

Value
☎ 800/327-2501
www.go-value.com

Index

Page numbers in italics refer to maps.

412 Index

FROMMER'S® COMPLETE TRAVEL GUIDES

Alaska
Amsterdam
Arizona
Atlanta
Australia
Austria
Bahamas
Barcelona, Madrid & Seville
Belgium, Holland & Luxembourg
Bermuda
Boston
Budapest & the Best of Hungary
California
Canada
Cancún, Cozumel & the Yucatán
Cape Cod, Nantucket & Martha's Vineyard
Caribbean
Caribbean Cruises & Ports of Call
Caribbean Ports of Call
Carolinas & Georgia
Chicago
China
Colorado
Costa Rica
Denver, Boulder & Colorado Springs
England
Europe
Florida
France
Germany
Greece
Greek Islands
Hawaii
Hong Kong
Honolulu, Waikiki & Oahu
Ireland
Israel
Italy
Jamaica & Barbados
Japan
Las Vegas
London
Los Angeles
Maryland & Delaware
Maui
Mexico
Miami & the Keys
Montana & Wyoming
Montréal & Québec City
Munich & the Bavarian Alps
Nashville & Memphis
Nepal
New England
New Mexico
New Orleans
New York City
Nova Scotia, New Brunswick & Prince Edward Island
Oregon
Paris
Philadelphia & the Amish Country
Portugal
Prague & the Best of the Czech Republic
Provence & the Riviera
Puerto Rico
Rome
San Antonio & Austin
San Diego
San Francisco
Santa Fe, Taos & Albuquerque
Scandinavia
Scotland
Seattle & Portland
Singapore & Malaysia
South Pacific
Spain
Switzerland
Thailand
Tokyo
Toronto
Tuscany & Umbria
USA
Utah
Vancouver & Victoria
Vermont, New Hampshire & Maine
Vienna & the Danube Valley
Virgin Islands
Virginia
Walt Disney World & Orlando
Washington, D.C.
Washington State

FROMMER'S® DOLLAR-A-DAY GUIDES

Australia from $50 a Day
California from $60 a Day
Caribbean from $60 a Day
England from $60 a Day
Europe from $50 a Day
Florida from $60 a Day
Greece from $50 a Day
Hawaii from $60 a Day
Ireland from $50 a Day
Israel from $45 a Day
Italy from $50 a Day
London from $75 a Day
New York from $75 a Day
New Zealand from $50 a Day
Paris from $70 a Day
San Francisco from $60 a Day
Washington, D.C., from $60 a Day

FROMMER'S® PORTABLE GUIDES

Acapulco, Ixtapa & Zihuatanejo
Alaska Cruises & Ports of Call
Bahamas
California Wine Country
Charleston & Savannah
Chicago
Dublin
Las Vegas
London
Maine Coast
New Orleans
New York City
Paris
Puerto Vallarta, Manzanillo & Guadalajara
San Francisco
Sydney
Tampa & St. Petersburg
Venice
Washington, D.C.

FROMMER'S® NATIONAL PARK GUIDES

Family Vacations in the
National Parks
Grand Canyon

National Parks of the
American West
Yellowstone & Grand Teton

Yosemite & Sequoia/
Kings Canyon
Zion & Bryce Canyon

FROMMER'S® GREAT OUTDOOR GUIDES

New England
Northern California

Southern California & Baja
Pacific Northwest

FROMMER'S® MEMORABLE WALKS

Chicago
London

New York
Paris

San Francisco
Washington D.C.

FROMMER'S® IRREVERENT GUIDES

Amsterdam
Boston
Chicago

London
Manhattan

New Orleans
Paris

San Francisco
Walt Disney World
Washington, D.C.

FROMMER'S® DRIVING TOURS

America
Britain
California

Florida
France
Germany

Ireland
Italy
New England

Scotland
Spain
Western Europe

THE COMPLETE IDIOT'S TRAVEL GUIDES

Boston
Cruise Vacations
Planning Your Trip to Europe
Hawaii

Las Vegas
London
Mexico's Beach Resorts
New Orleans

New York City
San Francisco
Walt Disney World
Washington D.C.

THE UNOFFICIAL GUIDES®

Branson, Missouri
California with Kids
Chicago
Cruises
Disney Companion

Florida with Kids
The Great Smoky &
Blue Ridge
Mountains

Las Vegas
Miami & the Keys
Mini-Mickey
New Orleans

New York City
San Francisco
Skiing in the West
Walt Disney World
Washington, D.C.

SPECIAL-INTEREST TITLES

Born to Shop: Caribbean Ports of Call
Born to Shop: France
Born to Shop: Hong Kong
Born to Shop: Italy
Born to Shop: New York
Born to Shop: Paris
Frommer's Britain's Best Bike Rides
The Civil War Trust's Official Guide
to the Civil War Discovery Trail
Frommer's Caribbean Hideaways
Frommer's Europe's Greatest Driving Tours
Frommer's Food Lover's Companion to France
Frommer's Food Lover's Companion to Italy
Frommer's Gay & Lesbian Europe

Israel Past & Present
Monks' Guide to California
Monks' Guide to New York City
New York City with Kids
New York Times Weekends
Outside Magazine's Guide
to Family Vacations
Places Rated Almanac
Retirement Places Rated
Washington, D.C., with Kids
Wonderful Weekends from Boston
Wonderful Weekends from New York City
Wonderful Weekends from San Francisco
Wonderful Weekends from Los Angeles